GEORGE W. NORRIS

The Persistence of a Progressive

1913–1933

GEORGE W. NORRIS

The Persistence of a Progressive

1913–1933

Richard Lowitt

UNIVERSITY OF ILLINOIS PRESS

Urbana   Chicago   London

For
Donald J. Lowitt and Bruce F. Carson,
brother and brother-in-law, who have aided
and comforted me more than they know

Acknowledgments

While this volume was basically written from manuscripts, the *Congressional Record,* and other primary sources, just as in the earlier volume I have had to rely on the books and articles of other scholars for an insight into and understanding of men and events. Fortunately, the Wilson years and the 1920s have already generated an abundant literature, and pertinent items are mentioned in the footnotes. In addition, several scholars have made material available to me and many more have discussed mutual problems and interests. All has been grist to my mill. Since I cannot mention their many names, I want to express my gratitude to them collectively; at appropriate places in the volume I thank individually those whose material has found its way into my text.

I have been particularly fortunate in that the Norris family continually has been helpful to me, Mr. and Mrs. John P. Robertson in particular. Mrs. Hazel Robertson is Norris's oldest daughter and his son-in-law served as his secretary from the mid-1920s to the end of Norris's senatorial service. They have answered my questions and have recounted their experiences and impressions while extending their gracious hospitality to me and my family both in Washington, D.C., and in Waupaca, Wisconsin, where they now own the cottage Norris helped build and where he loved to spend his summers.

This volume was written over a period of years during which I was a member of the faculties of Connecticut College, Florida

State University, and the University of Kentucky. The research councils at all three institutions awarded me funds, as did the American Philosophical Society and the American Council of Learned Societies. To all I owe a debt of gratitude; their grants enabled me to research the voluminous Norris collection in the Manuscript Division of the Library of Congress, whose staff, as always, has been most cordial and cooperative. A special word of thanks should be extended to the late Lloyd Dunlap, who, as a native Nebraskan and admirer of Norris, went out of his way to be of help whenever I appeared in the Manuscript Division. Thanks also to the many librarians at the above-mentioned institutions who eased my way with their suggestions and efficient cooperation. Here, too, special thanks are extended to Miss Helen Aitner at Connecticut College and Messrs. Reno Bupp and Joseph Evans at Florida State University. I would also like to thank Mrs. Bonnie Depp of the University of Illinois Press for her editorial assistance and Mrs. Jean Seaburg for preparing the index.

The various typists who somehow managed to interpret my illegible scrawl also must be mentioned: Mrs. Betty McCord in Tallahassee and Mrs. Betty L. Gunther and Mrs. Mary M. Sewell in Lexington. Several students at Connecticut College, many years ago, served as research assistants for me. Though I cannot now recall all their names, I wish to express my gratitude to them. Professors Richard L. Watson, Jr., of Duke University and Albert Bowman of the University of Tennessee, Chattanooga, must be singled out among the host of scholars who in one way or another assisted me. Professor Watson, by inviting me to teach at Duke in the summer of 1963, enabled me to discover the hidden treasures of the Harry Slattery Papers in the Duke Manuscripts Room. This collection provided valuable nuggets that added underpinnings to my manuscript. Professor Bowman, by inviting me to participate in a NDEA Institute in Chattanooga in 1965, enabled me to become acquainted with parts of the Tennessee River Valley. Traveling in the valley in several states enabled me to gain insight and understanding that would have been harder to achieve had I to rely exclusively on printed words. While I alone am responsible for the contents of this volume, it has benefited enormously from the writings of others, in and out of the academic world. Many of those in the academic world in one way or another have discussed their scholarship and mine with me to my great advantage.

Finally, I would like to express my gratitude to my wife, Suzanne, without whose help this volume would not yet be ready, and to our children, Peter and Pamela, who know all about Senator Norris.

Preface

When I completed *George W. Norris: The Making of a Progressive, 1861–1912,* I envisioned only a second and concluding volume as necessary to complete my project. However, I had to change my plans for two important reasons. One involved the mountains of manuscript material I had to master and the other pertained to my conception and understanding of Norris and his career.

The George W. Norris Papers in the Manuscript Division of the Library of Congress comprise more than 1,000 boxes of correspondence. About half the boxes pertain to the period covered in this volume, 1913–1933. But more important than the thousands upon thousands of items I had to peruse was my increasing awareness of the fact that the first twenty years of Norris's service in the U.S. Senate fitted into an overall pattern. For Norris the Wilson years and the period of Republican ascendancy were similar. He was an outsider, critical of administration policies, unsuccessful in almost all his efforts to create meaningful legislation. But in these years he did come to national attention as a prominent progressive. As the progressive impulse began to wane nationally, Norris gained prominence by championing river valley development, the cause of the farmer and the working man, and other issues that were not at the center of the progressive thrust in the period of its predominance. He also espoused more orthodox progressive reforms associated with efficiency in government service, broader democracy, and hostility to monopoly capitalism. Battling for social change within a traditional focus, Norris met increasing hostility throughout these two decades. As America became an urban nation, as the New Freedom gave way to conservatism and reaction, Norris persisted in championing the progressive cause. It was only after prosperity faltered and then collapsed during the Hoover years that Norris, as the leader of a handful of progressives, emerged as a dominant figure holding the balance of power in the Senate. Persistence paid off; he achieved two significant reforms and championed several more that expanded the efficiency of the governmental structure and broadened its democracy. Though it was clear after the election of Franklin D. Roosevelt that Norris's most significant reform, one that would add a new institution to the governmental structure, would be achieved, it did not occur until the advent of the New Deal. Norris's persistence and parliamentary acumen throughout the twenties meant that the wartime installations at Muscle Shoals soon would become part of a government-owned-and-operated system designed to promote the welfare and happiness of people in a vast underdeveloped river valley system. In the New Deal period, beyond the scope of this volume, in this and other significant ways Norris helped change the institutional apparatus of the United States.

During the twenty years examined in this volume, as the United States became an urban nation and the future of American politics shifted to the city, Norris, unaware of these developments, remained an unabashed spokesman for rural America, battling presidents, corporations, machine politicians, and others who put private gain ahead of the public interest as he saw it from his agrarian frame of reference. If virtue was located in rural America, it was not necessarily excluded from urban America. There was nothing Manichaean in Norris's conception. By the end of the 1920s he had emerged as a champion of the working man and is still highly regarded in labor circles for his espousal of the cause of the American worker in the lean years before it came of age in the United States.

As a U.S. senator, more than in his earlier career, Norris could concern himself with momentous national issues ranging from New Freedom legislation to the depression. International relations, centering about World War I and America's role, brought him national attention first as an opponent of American entrance into the war and then as a critic of the peace treaty. Local issues were not ignored, but his range of interest was broader than during his tenure in the House of Representatives. Yet his constituents, despite bitter opposition, continually re-elected him; as a result Norris's independence of all ties save that of conscience increased along with his denunciations of partisanship and its evil effects. With only the force of his conviction, the power of his logic, and persistence mingled with a little bit of luck, Norris was able to achieve some remarkable victories and be on the verge of several more at the end of these two decades, in the waning years of the Hoover administration.

Examining Norris's career during this twenty-year period has given me greater insight and understanding into both the man and the politics, the issues and the events of the Wilson era and the 1920s. My regard for George W. Norris, if anything, has increased as a result of my labors. But it is not my purpose to puff my subject. Rather, I have found that his senatorial career can serve as a cutting edge, allowing further understanding and possible re-evaluation of important themes and developments in recent American history. In a third volume I intend to complete Norris's biography, devoting much attention to his notable achievements which modified the institutional apparatus of both his state and the United States and his efforts to salvage drought- and depression-ridden Nebraska.

Those who would carry on great public schemes must be proof against the worst fatiguing delays, the most mortifying disappointments, the most shocking insults, and, worst of all, the presumptuous judgment of the ignorant upon their designs.

—Edmund Burke

Dream on, you Senator from Nebraska, for your dreams mean but one thing. Your dreams, sir, mean that humanity may benefit, people may prosper, and human beings may be a bit happier.

—Hiram Johnson,
remarks in the U.S. Senate,
December 19, 1924

The New Freedom?

1

Spring in Washington is a glorious time of year. Fruit trees in blossom, flowers in bloom, delightfully cool days, and clear, star-filled nights add zest to the daily routine and an anticipation of better things to come—a zest and anticipation that soon pall and wilt under the oppressive heat and intense humidity of the summer season. The spring of 1913 was doubly a time of zest and anticipation. The "New Freedom" expounded by the new president in his campaign speeches was made more specific in his notable inaugural address. The new Congress—the Sixty-third—was summoned into special session on April 7 to enact the legislative program called for by the president. By the time this Congress finished its business, it had been in session 567 days without an adjournment, the longest continuous session to that time. Though Congress gave the president the legislation he desired, the honeymoon period —like the Washington springtime—soon faded and the inevitable bickering and fault-finding appeared.

Yet for the Democrats, in control of Congress for the first time since Grover Cleveland's second administration, the time was auspicious. Falling heir to the presidency owing to the split in the Republican party, they would have almost twenty months to compile a record of achievements to win support in their own right. The party would stand or fall on the program and achievements of Woodrow Wilson. That the Democratic interlude would last eight years and would include complete control of Congress

3

for six of them was something that would have surprised prognosticators in the spring of 1913. That the Republican party was unable to resolve its differences was, of course, a factor in the success of their opponents. But it was only one. The achievements of Woodrow Wilson were another.

While the Democrats had won control of the House in 1910, the Senate in 1912 was theirs again after a lapse of eighteen years. Only nine senators, three of them Democrats, had served previously under a Democratic president, while twenty-three new members—George W. Norris among them—would start their senatorial service under another Democratic president. Compared to the House, where there were two Democrats for every member of the opposition (290 to 145), the balance in the Senate was precarious—fifty-one Democrats to forty-four Republicans and one Progressive. To operate effectively, the president insisted on strict party discipline. He insisted, despite the fact that he was a minority president, that he was the head of the government and the responsible leader of his party. To establish effective leadership, he revived the custom, lapsed since John Adams left the presidency, of addressing Congress in person. And he insisted on utilizing the party caucus. Democrats from both chambers would meet formally to discuss and debate impending measures. Disagreements, while fully aired, nevertheless were private; once the caucus decided on a position, the bill became a party measure which all Democrats adhered to on the floor of Congress. Amendments were few and usually were first agreed upon in caucus. "The silvern speech spent in caucus," Wilson wrote, "secures the golden silence maintained on the floor of Congress, making each party rich in concord and happy in cooperation." [1] The system worked well during the Sixty-third Congress and the administration achieved an impressive legislative record to redeem the president's pledges and to dangle before the voters in forthcoming elections.

To George W. Norris, a progressive but not a prodigal Republican starting his service in the Senate as the New Freedom unfolded, springtime quickly wilted into an oppressive, almost stifling summer atmosphere. During and after the insurgency fight against

[1] Woodrow Wilson, *Congressional Government*, 15th ed. (New York, 1913), p. 328.

the power of the Speaker, he had insisted that caucus control was as powerful as the House rules in thwarting individual initiative. It resulted only in bad government. Having helped to establish freer discussion and to improve legislation during his career in the House of Representatives, Norris found service in the Senate disagreeable and reminiscent of the dark days under Speaker Cannon early in the Taft administration.

There were differences. For one thing, Senate debate was unlimited and, at times, barbarous. A member could speak till overcome by exhaustion, whereas in the House the problem was one of gaining recognition to offer a few well-chosen remarks before one's allotted time expired. Thus service in the House was good training for a senator. It taught him to be precise and to state what he meant with a minimum of effusive oratory. The tendency in the Senate, given the lack of effective cloture, was to ramify one's views continually and to consume time. In the House it was to concentrate and to say as much as possible in a short time.

Another difference was that most of the measures Norris had to vote upon were part of a program with which he was in sympathy. Always, owing to caucus control, he had to decide whether its assets outweighed its liabilities; rarely was he given a chance to amend and improve any measure. The Democratic party, in short, was guilty of engaging in abuses for which it previously had criticized the Republicans. Norris not only sympathized with these criticisms but took part in leveling them. Responsibility, he realized, rested with the president. Though Wilson had previously denounced rank partisanship and machine politics, under his leadership the majority unhesitatingly used the "antiquated and widely condemned secret caucus" in important legislative matters.[2] Thus service in the Senate would find Norris cast in the role of a critic, albeit a constructive one. With his conscience as his guide, he found that he was able to endorse substantial portions of the New Freedom.

Getting settled in Washington was another problem that had unpleasant aspects about it. It was not a new problem; Norris

[2] *Chadron* (Nebr.) *Journal,* Oct. 9, 1914. The paper carried a concise statement by Norris on caucus control. See also his remarks in *Congressional Record,* 63rd Cong., 1st sess., Aug. 29, 1913, pp. 3863–64.

had been through it every two years as a member of the House. A six-year term as senator meant that more permanent arrangements could be made. But Norris's chief difficulty was financial. His expenses mounted; his funds were limited. Until July he lived at the YMCA and took nearly all of his meals at cheap restaurants and boarding houses. At times, instead of having dinner after leaving the Senate late at night, he would satisfy his hunger at a nearby lunch counter with a 10- or 15-cent meal. In July the family arrived on borrowed funds and he found it necessary to buy additional furniture for their apartment at the Mendota on Kalorama Road. Mrs. Norris and the girls performed all the housework to keep expenses at a minimum. By 1915 the family was satisfactorily ensconced in a house of their own in the Cleveland Park section at 3300 Ross Place.[3]

Property that Norris owned in Nebraska was proving to be an expense rather than an asset. Taxes, insurance, and improvements were costing more money than the property yielded. Then, too, once he entered the Senate, numerous friends thought they could borrow money from him without limit. At the outset an "easy touch," he loaned money or stood as security for individuals who were unable to meet their obligations.[4] Norris further found himself a victim of the once-valid belief that the Senate was a rich man's club, a belief that would be modified as members were chosen by direct election and not by state legislatures. Direct election, incidentally, helped establish the belief, already evident during the Wilson period, that the Senate was the more liberal chamber of the national legislature.

He found it to be invariably true that everyone, habitually, would overcharge a senator. In 1916, when his youngest daughter, Gertrude, suffered an attack of appendicitis, it took him almost half a year to pay the doctor's bill. A dentist enraged him by charging $122 for filling three cavities. Early in his senatorial career he purchased an overcoat and a suit with an extra pair of

---

[3] George W. Norris to M. B. Carman, Aug. 16, 1913. Norris to Munsey Trust Company, Sept. 3, 1914, provides details on the purchase of the house in Washington (George W. Norris Papers, Manuscript Division, Library of Congress). Unless otherwise noted, all manuscript citations are from this collection.

[4] Norris to Carman, Aug. 16, 1913; to Elmer Brown, Apr. 23, 1913; to W. C. Israel, Jan. 2, 1915.

trousers. Six years later he said that his wife had used one pair of trousers to patch up the other and that the vest had been cut up to patch the coat. Both suit and coat were expected to serve for several more years.[5] Financial stringency for Norris and his family would be further aggravated during the war years in Washington.

There was also the expense of educating his daughters. Hazel, the eldest, had already begun her studies at the University of Nebraska. Her parents would have preferred that she remain there and that Marian join her, but for the distance between Lincoln and Washington. After visiting the campus, Norris decided to send his daughters to Goucher College in nearby Baltimore. Goucher was not a large school and its campus, he felt, did not compare favorably with many others, but he was satisfied that its officials were determined "to keep up their reputation as being one of the very best." [6]

To supplement his senatorial salary of $7,500, Norris occasionally received rent money from his Nebraska property. But, as previously noted, this income was neither dependable nor large. Early in his senatorial service he decided, as did many other political figures, to lecture on a Chautauqua circuit. In November, 1914, Norris traveled for three weeks for $400 per week and expenses. The lectures were those presented earlier, chiefly to Nebraska audiences: "A Political Conscience," "A Dream of Peace," and "The Overthrow of Cannonism," among others. He lectured again in 1915, but by this time most Chautauqua company managers had had enough of politicians. So many canceled at the last moment that few were being booked for the 1916 season. While Norris's performances were "very satisfactory" and he had never canceled a booking, nevertheless he fell victim to this policy; a lucrative supplementary source of income was thus denied him before radio and the motion picture brought about the end of this exciting venture in popular education.[7]

[5] Norris to Grant D. Harrington, Jan. 20, 1916. See also an anonymous article, actually written by Norris, entitled "A Senator's Story," Part II, *Saturday Evening Post,* Aug. 14, 1920, p. 22.

[6] Norris to Charles W. Taylor, Mar. 27, 1914.

[7] Norris to Louis Alber, Dec. 29, 1913; O. B. Stephenson to Norris, Sept. 25, Dec. 23, 1915; J. R. McCarl to P. F. Ockerman, May 31, 1915; to Hardy W. Campbell, May 29, 1915; *Omaha Bee, Omaha News,* Apr. 12, 1915.

Many of the familiar themes from his House career, presented on the lecture circuit, were repeated on the floor of the Senate and before other audiences as well. Shortly before the Sixty-third Congress got under way on April 7, 1913, Norris addressed the Nebraska legislature. His remarks were in line with the independent and nonpartisan tone he had assumed as a member of the House of Representatives. With Democrats in the majority in both the Nebraska and national legislatures, Norris talked of the impossibility of reform as long as partisanship and patronage prevailed.[8]

Public interest should predominate over partisan politics; this was the message Norris had been preaching since the early days of the Taft administration. The evil was partisanship, not necessarily the political party. As he said in an address in December, 1913, "Under present conditions parties are perhaps necessary, and organization is not only desirable but absolutely essential. But when party or organization goes to the extent of coercion, then it has passed its usefulness, and . . . it has become a fire that instead of warming is consuming." [9]

Basically, of course, Norris now and for the rest of his career was not much of a party man. His allegiance to the Republican party, whose label he wore, was not so great that he would support it contrary to the dictates of his conscience. Individual and not party responsibility was for him the *sine qua non* of political action. This viewpoint was central to his criticism of the president and his program as it unfolded in the Sixty-third Congress. The president, by insisting that important bills become party measures, violated Norris's canons of responsible political behavior.[10]

Related to partisanship were several themes that Norris reiterated again as a senator; for example, he denounced patronage and supported in its place the merit system, particularly as it applied to the postal service. Every weakening of the merit system in favor of political appointments aroused his ire; every extension of it received his support. As he had done in the House, Norris spoke

[8] *Sioux City* (Iowa) *Tribune,* Apr. 6, 1913, "George W. Norris, Leader" (editorial).

[9] From "A Nonpartisan Party," an address before the first National Conference on Popular Government, Dec. 6, 1913 (printed as Senate Doc. 372, 63rd Cong., 2nd sess., *Senate Documents,* vol. 26).

[10] Norris to R. R. Reed, Feb. 9, 1914.

of putting the Post Office Department, including the Postmaster General, on a merit basis and running the department as a business and not as a patronage operation.[11] Since he knew it would be futile, he did not—unlike his action as a congressman—introduce a bill for this purpose.[12]

While service in the Senate gave him an opportunity to continue to expound views which earlier had helped him to national attention, and though these views were central to his criticisms of the New Freedom, the main business of the Congress was consideration of the program outlined in Wilson's inaugural address and specified in messages delivered to the entire membership assembled in joint session. The first measure the president called for was a tariff and Norris had much to say on this subject. The Senate received the bill in May, but the Democrats held it in caucus until it was clear that party discipline would prevail. It passed the Senate in September and in October the president signed the Underwood-Simmons tariff into law.

Norris opposed the measure because he felt it would operate disastrously against agriculture. It removed the tariff on everything the farmer had to sell while retaining it on nearly everything he had to buy. It was filled with inequalities for his Nebraska constituents, often providing a higher tariff on the raw material than on the finished product. Indeed, the agriculture schedule was as bad as the reciprocity arrangement presented during the Taft administration, though the reciprocity bill did get something in return for the free admission of Canadian agricultural products.[13]

By discriminating against agriculture, particularly midwestern and western farmers, the tariff would weaken "the strongest element of our Government." Norris said, "It is in the overcrowded cities where poverty prevails, where crime spreads, where misery lives, where disease is located, where anarchy is born; but in the

[11] See, for example, *Congressional Record,* 63rd Cong., 2nd sess., May 2, p. 7608, June 13, 1914, pp. 10402–3.

[12] Norris explained how the merit system could be applied to the Post Office Department in an address before the annual meeting of the National Civil Service League on Dec. 2, 1915 (printed as Senate Doc. 439, 64th Cong., 1st sess., *Senate Documents,* vol. 42).

[13] *Congressional Record,* 63rd Cong., 1st sess., Aug. 14, 1913, pp. 3372–73; *Chadron* (Nebr.) *Journal,* Oct. 9, 1914.

country, in the agricultural communities, we find a stronger and more patriotic citizenship, and in case of danger and in need it is to the farm that the Government must go for its strong arm of protection and defense." [14]

Furthermore, the tariff measure allowed him to air his views against the "International Coffee Trust" and its valorization scheme for controlling production and prices. Substitutes for coffee, he said, should be added to the free list.[15] While his concern for coffee affected consumers everywhere, his concern for a tariff on sugar affected some of his constituents. Free sugar, as called for in the bill, would drive out of existence beet-sugar factories, some of which were located in Nebraska, along with Louisiana cane-sugar producers and those in the various American dependencies. Norris argued that free sugar, by driving domestic producers of beet and cane sugar out of business, would allow the "Sugar Trust" to further manipulate the price to the detriment of consumers everywhere.[16] Caucus control led to the quick rejection of Norris's efforts to provide consumer protection.

There was one aspect of the Underwood-Simmons tariff that pleased him. But even this aspect, calling for an income tax to replace revenue lost by reduced rates, he tried to replace with an inheritance tax. And he objected to the provision that a man with two children would be entitled to a $500 exemption for each dependent while a man with three or more children would not be entitled to any further exemption.[17]

Since the income tax tried to take into account ability to pay and since its burdens fell upon the shoulders of those who could

[14] *Congressional Record,* 63rd Cong., 1st sess., Aug. 14, 1913, p. 3376. As Norris was well aware, the thesis that the tariff measure benefited the South at the expense of the West would have to exclude Louisiana cane-sugar producers who did not benefit from the free-sugar clause. Both Louisiana senators and four Louisiana congressmen—all Democrats—voted against the tariff.

[15] Norris gave a long speech describing and denouncing the "International Coffee Trust" in the Senate in May. He called for adding substitutes to the free list several months later; see *Congressional Record,* 63rd Cong., 1st sess., May 16, pp. 1583–89 (speech), Aug. 16, p. 3454, Sept. 2, p. 4085, Sept. 9, 1913, pp. 4561–62 (remarks on coffee substitutes).

[16] *Ibid.,* Aug. 19, 1913, pp. 3511–12; Norris to A. T. Lardin, Aug. 2, 1913.

[17] *Congressional Record,* 63rd Cong., 1st sess., Aug. 28, 1913, p. 3851; Norris to Ross Hammond, Feb. 12, 1914.

best afford to bear them, it was a fair tax. However, an inheritance tax was fairer and less of a burden. It could be easily and inexpensively collected, and it would take only a part of the property that state or nation had a right to confiscate, since the right to inherit property was usually not claimed as a natural right. As Norris viewed it, an inheritance tax would also break up swollen fortunes and reduce the power and privilege that enhanced inherited wealth without leaving the heirs of the wealthy destitute. As he expected, his inheritance tax amendment was overwhelmingly rejected, conservative Republicans joining caucus Democrats in voting against it.[18]

On September 9 Norris voted against the tariff measure as it passed the Senate; later in October he voted against the final version as it emerged from conference committee. Only two progressive Republicans, Robert LaFollette and Miles Poindexter, supported the Underwood-Simmons tariff, Wilson's first notable legislative victory. Norris's opposition was not along party lines; he simply thought it a poor measure, though he agreed with its general intent. And he was disturbed about the way it was framed. Only when a nonpartisan tariff commission was created could Congress obtain all the facts and data upon which a just tariff bill could be built.[19]

Some of his grievances about the act disappeared in 1916 when Congress created the Tariff Commission. Norris was concerned that members be appointed without partisan bias so that legislators could obtain necessary information and the country and Congress could have confidence in it. He had long advocated such a measure. A commission went naturally and logically with a protective tariff system. Its purpose, Norris claimed, was to measure the difference in cost of production both at home and abroad or, as Democrats desired, to ascertain competitive rates for legitimate industries.[20]

[18] *Congressional Record,* 63rd Cong., 1st sess., Sept. 8, 1913, pp. 4424–26. Norris's amendment was defeated by a 58-12 vote with twenty-five members not voting. It would have established an inheritance tax ranging from 1 to 75 percent, with the first $50,000 of any inheritance exempt.

[19] *Ibid.,* Aug. 27, 1913, p. 3810.

[20] *Ibid.,* 64th Cong., 1st sess., Sept. 5, 1916, pp. 13849, 13851, 13871. F. W. Taussig, *The Tariff History of the United States* (New York, 1931), p.

The next major item in the president's program called for banking and currency reform. In November, 1913, the Senate plunged into a discussion of the bill establishing the Federal Reserve System. Norris, functioning again as a constructive critic, supported the measure, though he criticized caucus control of it. He favored an elastic currency and governmental control of banking, at the same time insisting that politics be eliminated from it. Therefore, he opposed the Glass bill as it passed the House because it provided for two members of the cabinet plus the Comptroller of the Currency to be placed on the Federal Reserve Board and allowed the president to appoint additional members. These appointments would constitute a majority and make the seven-man board a partisan one. Members, like those of the Interstate Commerce Commission, ought to be nonpartisan and able to devote their time to managing the finances and banking of the country. The Senate heeded Norris's plea. Cabinet members were removed from the Federal Reserve Board, though the Secretary of the Treasury and the Comptroller of the Currency both retained connections with it in the final version of the law.[21]

Norris gave the bill careful study. While not serving on the Banking and Currency Committee, he attended its meetings as regularly as any member. He desired greater centralization and favored four regional banks rather than the twelve finally established. He wanted to extend the time of notes eligible for rediscount to six months rather than ninety days. And he particularly desired amendments, introduced after the system was in operation, granting national banks permission whenever possible to avail themselves of state laws guaranteeing deposits and allowing postal savings funds to be deposited in state and national banks without any discrimination between the two systems. Though all the amendments he favored were rejected, Norris enthusiastically supported the measure because it achieved an elastic currency, government control of the banking and currency system, and the

---

419, concludes that "fairly and consistently applied the principle of a competitive tariff cannot be said to differ in essentials from that of a tariff equalizing cost of production." The difference was largely a matter of semantics.

[21] Norris statement on the Federal Reserve bill as it passed the House of Representatives, n.d. (the bill passed the House on Sept. 18, 1913); *Congressional Record*, 63rd Cong., 2nd sess., Dec. 11, 1913, p. 679.

virtual elimination of political machinery from the operation of the Federal Reserve Board. Considering it the most important bill to come before Congress since the Civil War, Norris devoted most of his remarks to insisting that partisanship had no place in a banking and currency system controlled by the government.[22] While he did not play a major role in the discussion of the Federal Reserve Act, he impressed the Senate with his knowledge and understanding. In the Sixty-fourth Congress Norris was appointed to membership on the Banking and Currency Committee.

Within a month after signing the Federal Reserve bill, the president appeared before Congress requesting that government join hands with business in a common effort to eliminate practices that allowed giant corporations to crush competition and take advantage of consumers. This was a subject that greatly interested Norris. But he did not always find himself in harmony with the administration as the legislative wheels began to grind. On this matter, it is interesting to note, caucus control broke. The president was not clear in his own mind about exactly what type of legislation he desired. He endorsed the Federal Trade Commission bill, providing enforcement machinery, and criticized the antitrust measure which attempted to formulate a trust policy.

Norris, like all progressives, readily admitted that the Sherman Act needed modification. He readily agreed, too, like many progressives, that agricultural and labor organizations should be exempted from punishment under the Sherman Act and that such exemption be written into a new piece of antitrust legislation. The use of injunctions also disturbed Norris: from the time an alleged illegality began until it was finally decided by the Supreme Court, enough time elapsed for the offending corporation to profit excessively from the contested practice. Moreover, dissolution of a trust, as shown in the cases of Standard Oil and the American Tobacco Company, gave no relief to consumers and actually increased the value of its stock. Norris desired instead that some punishment of a financial nature be worked out, such as deter-

[22] *Congressional Record,* 63rd Cong., 2nd sess., Dec. 18, 1913, pp. 1136–37, Sept. 11, 1914, pp. 14489–90; 64th Cong., 1st sess., Mar. 15, 1916, p. 4115. The *New York Times,* Feb. 1, 1914, noted that on the previous day Norris introduced a bill permitting national banks to avail themselves of state law providing for the guaranteeing of deposits.

mining how much profit a corporation made and then compelling
the payment of about twice that amount to the Treasury of the
United States. If necessary the government would hold possession
of the property through a receiver until the money was paid. One
or two instances of dissolution, he believed, would be more effective than criminal prosecutions which could convict hirelings but
would not get at the powerful people responsible for the violations.[23]

Generally speaking, Norris said, the best way to resolve the
trust problem was for Congress to take steps to prevent the acquisition of different lines of activity by giant corporations so that
competitive citizens would not in effect become slaves. Legislation
preventing the piling up of immense fortunes and the ownership
of huge quantities of land and other natural resources would be a
major step in the right direction. Though aware that an overall
solution was not contemplated, Norris was pleased with the Federal Trade Commission bill which passed the Senate early in
August. It was not a caucus measure and, therefore, constructive
criticism in the form of amendments further improved it.[24]

However, he was not happy with the Clayton bill, which came
to the Senate early in June and was at once referred to the
members of the Judiciary Committee. In committee much
controversy occurred over the role Republican members played
in modifying the measure. The House bill contained twenty-
three sections and proposed many valuable amendments and
additions to existing law. Though Norris was far from satisfied with the Senate measure, he voted for it because, owing to
Wilson's indecision, caucus control again broke down. He supported numerous amendments and voted to keep in the bill some
of the House provisions that had been removed in committee. In
all, Norris thought the Senate bill had some excellent provisions;

[23] *Congressional Record,* 63rd Cong., 1st sess., May 7, 1913, pp. 1271, 1272–73; 2nd sess., July 2, 1914, p. 11533; Norris to F. A. Good, June 15, 1914.

[24] *Congressional Record,* 63rd Cong., 2nd sess., July 2, 1914, p. 11597; 3rd sess., Feb. 16, 1915, pp. 3850–53. In these 1915 remarks Norris denounced the caucus system as detrimental to good legislation. The *Omaha Daily News,* Apr. 12, 1915, reported a speech by Norris at the Commercial Club wherein he commented on the Federal Trade Commission.

if the conference committee had retained what was good in both measures, a strong law could have resulted.[25]

But what emerged from conference retained in Norris's judgment what was bad in both bills. It was a "milk and water proposition," "a fraud and a sham." If enacted, it would represent "the greatest victory of a legislative nature that had been won by the trusts and combinations within the lifetime of any man here [in the Senate]." His major criticism was that the criminal provision was deleted. The conferees simply stated that certain unfair business practices should not be indulged in; no penalty for violation was provided. Thus Congress refused to consider either of the approaches Norris thought necessary to a successful solution of the trust proposition: criminal prosecution for antitrust violations or, as suggested in the House version of the bill, make it financially unprofitable for any individual or set of men to organize a trust. Since neither of these approaches was considered in the conference committee bill, Norris voted against the measure.[26]

Moreover, by including vague, ill-defined terminology, trusts and business promoters were offered additional avenues of escape. Delays and the resort to technicalities, Norris claimed, would be inevitable because of the widespread use, for example, of the word "substantially." He correctly predicted that it would be years before any further antitrust legislation appeared. Democrats would consider the matter settled; most Republicans would not be interested in it.[27] Disappointed with the passage of the Clayton Act, which, incidentally, not a single Republican senator finally supported, Norris continued his agitation against monopoly and the Wilson administration on this matter.

In May, 1914, he introduced a resolution calling the attention of the Justice Department to the New York Central's control of three railroads: the Lake Shore, the Michigan Central, and the

[25] *Congressional Record,* 63rd Cong., 2nd sess., Oct. 2, 1914, p. 16042; Norris to Good, June 15, 1914; to O. E. Jones, July 22, 1914. There is a good brief discussion of this complex situation in Arthur S. Link, *Woodrow Wilson and the Progressive Era* (New York, 1954), pp. 68–74.

[26] *Congressional Record,* 63rd Cong., 2nd sess., Oct. 2, 1914, pp. 16042, 16050, 16051.

[27] *Ibid.,* pp. 16052–53.

Nickel Plate, all operating on parallel lines, occasionally in plain sight of one another, from Buffalo to Chicago. In addition, it owned the Western Transit Company, a boat line operating between these two terminal cities. Norris inquired whether this control constituted a violation of the Sherman Antitrust Act and whether the Attorney General contemplated action for the dissolution of the combination. Since the New York Central was then engaged in consolidating its system,[28] Norris thought that the time was ripe to dissolve the combination and to prevent further action in throttling competition. But neither the Senate nor the Attorney General did anything about his resolution.[29] Earlier in the session Norris had achieved notable success with investigatory resolutions affecting the New York, New Haven and Hartford Railroad Company.

On February 3, 1914, over the protests of the Justice Department, Norris, prodded by Louis D. Brandeis, successfully introduced a resolution requesting the Interstate Commerce Commission to reopen its investigation of the New York, New Haven and Hartford Railroad. He claimed the previous investigation, conducted at the outset of the Wilson administration, had not gone far enough in ascertaining what had become of funds invested by the company or in determining if those guilty of mismanagement could be punished. Laws remedying such conditions, Norris asserted, could only be enacted if public sentiment was aroused by full disclosure of the facts. Then on February 19 he introduced another resolution asking the Attorney General whether the recently announced plan for the reorganization of the railroad involved immunity for former officials and whether it would hinder suits for the recovery of lost funds. He introduced this resolution after a conference with one of the largest individual stockholders in the Boston and Maine Railroad, a subsidiary of the New Haven, so that minority interests might know how to proceed. By

[28] Among others, it recently acquired by itself or through a subsidiary the Western Maryland Railroad and the Pittsburgh and Lake Erie Railroad. In addition, the New York Central controlled the West Shore Railroad, whose tracks paralleled its own from Buffalo to New York City.

[29] *Congressional Record*, 63rd Cong., 2nd sess., May 29, 1914, pp. 9428, 9430; *New York Times*, May 29, 1914; Norris statement about New York Central, May 28, 1914.

asking the Attorney General for an opinion, Norris hoped to commit the administration to a strong stand against violations of the Sherman Act. This second resolution, after a lively debate in which party lines were ignored, was tabled on February 24, 1914.[30]

The Interstate Commerce Commission resumed public hearings on April 9, 1914. Norris wanted the Attorney General to institute criminal proceedings against some of the men responsible for the building of the New York, New Haven and Hartford's monopoly on transportation in New England. In May, 1914, in company with Senator John W. Kern of Indiana and Joseph W. Folk, chief counsel for the Interstate Commerce Commission, Norris called on the Attorney General to discuss the wisdom of calling before the ICC the leading figures in the New York, New Haven and Hartford Railroad and of having charges instituted against them. The conversation became so heated that James C. McReynolds ordered Folk to leave his office. Later Norris charged the Attorney General with having no intention of instituting criminal proceedings. McReynolds denied this allegation, whereupon Norris demanded he initiate prosecutions as proof that he had been misrepresented. None were immediately forthcoming.[31]

Several months after this incident, when McReynolds's name was presented to the Senate as Wilson's first nominee to the Supreme Court, Norris led the fight against his confirmation. He spoke for three days, criticizing McReynolds's handling of the New Haven case, his enforcement of the Supreme Court's mandate dissolving the Standard Oil Company, and his sympathetic atti-

[30] *Congressional Record,* 63rd Cong., 2nd sess., Feb. 6, pp. 3024, 3026–28, Feb. 7, p. 3107, Feb. 24, 1914, pp. 3824, 3826–29; *New York Times,* Feb. 4, 7, 19, and 24, 1914; Alpheus T. Mason, *Brandeis: A Free Man's Life* (New York, 1946), p. 211.

[31] *New York Times,* June 27, 1914. For a thorough and fairly recent study of the New York, New Haven and Hartford's transportation monopoly in New England, see Henry Lee Staples and Alpheus T. Mason, *The Fall of a Railroad Empire* (Syracuse, N.Y., 1947). In July Wilson ordered McReynolds to start dissolution proceedings against the New York, New Haven and Hartford Railroad Company, but in October the suit was withdrawn and a consent decree accepted. Criminal proceedings against the New Haven directors failed to result in convictions. Norris in all of his remarks made it clear that he intended no criticism of the current management of the road. The previous Morgan-dominated management led by Charles S. Mellen and Lewis Cass Ledyard was at the center of his concern.

tude to monopoly and reluctance to enforce the antitrust laws. Five senators joined him in voting against McReynolds on August 29, 1914.[32]

On the other hand, almost two years later in June, 1916, Norris was one of three progressive Republicans (Poindexter and LaFollette were the others) who endorsed Brandeis's appointment to the Supreme Court.[33] In the case of McReynolds, Norris criticized his willingness to work with corporations, helping draft codes of behavior that would meet the law; in the case of Brandeis, Norris was in basic agreement with his actions and views. He agreed with Brandeis that the most important objections to monopoly were those threats posed to individual freedom inherent in the concentration of power and in abuses that could be perpetrated on people.

Indeed, with the notable exception of Brandeis, the appointments of the president during his first term led Norris to conclude that Wilson had cast aside his allegiance to progressive principles and had surrendered to big business. His appointments to the Interstate Commerce Commission and the Federal Reserve Board were the most conspicuous examples, aside from McReynolds's appointment, of Wilson's capitulation "to Wall Street." Too many important and powerful positions, Norris said, were filled with reactionaries by a president who professed to be a progressive, a believer in the rule of the people.[34]

Norris's experiences helped reinforce his views, as they did for many of his contemporaries, about unscrupulous business practices and convinced him of the need for further reform in curbing corporations. In the realm of transportation the only effective solution was public ownership under central control. A government corporation, similar to the one utilized in constructing the Panama Canal, should manage the railroad network and provide a fair return on investment.[35] Since this sensible solution, according to Norris, received inadequate support during the years of the New

[32] *New York Times*, Aug. 28 and 30, 1914.

[33] *Congressional Record*, 64th Cong., 1st sess., June 1, 1915, p. 9032. Brandeis was confirmed by a vote of 47 to 22. Most progressive Republicans were listed as not voting.

[34] *Chadron* (Nebr.) *Journal*, Oct. 9, 1914.

[35] Norris address entitled "Keeping the Railroads out of Politics," n.d.

Freedom, he had to satisfy himself with efforts to strengthen the Interstate Commerce Commission and with getting Congress to enact more effective railroad legislation.

He desired, for example, legislation prohibiting interstate railroads from expending money, incurring liability, or acquiring property for purposes other than the effective and efficient operation of its own system. A railroad attempting to engage in other activities would have to satisfy the Interstate Commerce Commission as to their legitimacy and necessity. Further investigations of railroad practices, he believed, were no longer necessary. Yet this is what the Congress proposed to do in 1916 and Norris protested. Basic facts and conditions pertaining to financial mismanagement were easily available; investigation would serve only to stall and possibly to thwart congressional action. Failure to resolve transportation problems effectively added to Norris's discouragement with the Wilson administration.[36]

On one matter concerning transportation and the trusts Norris heartily endorsed the president. While the Panama Canal tolls dispute was regarded by the administration as a diplomatic issue, Norris saw it as a domestic one. But his conclusions agreed with those of Woodrow Wilson, who in March, 1914, appeared before Congress and announced that all American ships using the canal should be compelled to pay tolls like those of any other nation. Norris had consistently endorsed this position. He had voted as a congressman in 1912 for no exemptions for American ships passing through the Panama Canal. He made much of the circuitous route by which the president and his party reached the same conclusion, citing the 1912 Democratic platform to show that the Democratic party first favored no tolls for American ships using the canal.[37]

Norris believed, as did the administration, that the Hay-Pauncefote Treaty of 1901 with Great Britain gave the United States no right to exempt from toll charges privately owned ships engaged in the coastwise trade, as was provided by law during the

---

[36] *Congressional Record,* 64th Cong., 1st sess., Jan. 25, pp. 1488–89, 1496–97, Feb. 16, 1916, pp. 2629–30; Norris to William C. Niblack, Feb. 16, 1916 (this letter was inserted in *ibid.,* Feb. 16, 1916, p. 2622).

[37] *Congressional Record,* 64th Cong., 1st sess., May 19, 1916, p. 8294.

Taft administration. To those senators who argued that the treaty gave the United States the right to exempt American ships from tolls, Norris said that he would be willing to submit this matter to arbitration. He proposed and pleaded for an amendment to this effect. Throughout he insisted that repeal of the tolls exemption would in no way threaten American ships engaged in the coastwise trade. The real question, as he saw it, was, should the U.S. government grant to privately owned ships engaged in coastwise traffic a subsidy to the extent of permitting them free use of the Panama Canal? To Norris it was not an economically sound proposition. He opposed granting, by means of tolls exemption, a subsidy to coastwide shipping which already enjoyed a lawful monopoly with respect to foreign competition. Indeed, "subsidizing the ships engaged only in coastwise traffic would prove of advantage to the ship owners and might prove of some advantage to the coast states," but Norris doubted that "it would prove of any benefit whatever to the interior states."

In short, Norris argued, the opening of the Panama Canal was bringing benefits to the coastwise shipper and to the people in general. Tolls exemption by itself did not bring any benefits to consumers. Only ship owners would benefit, and they already stood to gain enormously from the opening of the canal. Exempting American ships from tolls would be saddling upon the taxpayer an additional burden while the profits of an industry already in possession of a monopoly would be increased. Thus Norris supported Woodrow Wilson on this facet of the New Freedom.[38]

That the New Freedom was not entirely to Norris's liking is evident from material discussed in this chapter. He had reservations and he doubted whether freedom was involved in the legislative process. His criticisms derived from his experience in the House of Representatives where he first encountered the prominent issues involved in Wilson's legislative programs. While his criticisms were usually constructive, his support was sporadic. On some issues, banking and canal tolls to cite but two, he supported the administration; on others, the tariff and aspects of the trust

[38] *Ibid.*, 63rd Cong., 2nd sess., May 1, pp. 7532–42, June 10, 1914, pp. 10168–69, 10173, 10230–31; Norris to J. L. McPheely, Apr. 2, 1914; to J. L. Welsh and H. A. Butler, June 22, 1929.

issue, he was at odds with it. Always his conscience was his guide
and rarely did all progressive Republicans see issues as he saw
them. This group formed no organized and central core of constructive criticism during the New Freedom as they did during the
later stages of the Taft administration. Each progressive Republican senator evaluated the prominent issues of the New Freedom
for himself in terms of his previous experience. In Norris's case it
was in the realm of secondary issues, particularly in the field of
natural resources, that he began to develop a point of view that
characterized his later service in the Senate. In so doing Norris
found himself more in accord with the administration's domestic
policies in the Sixty-fourth Congress.[39]

[39] James Holt in *Congressional Insurgents and the Party System: 1909–1916*
(Cambridge, Mass., 1967) makes much of caucus control and the failure of
Senate progressives to support the New Freedom. His discussion is flawed be-
cause he focuses almost exclusively on "Wilson and the Underwood Tariff"
(Chapter Six) and does not realize that caucus control broke down when other
Wilsonian legislative items were discussed.

Progressivism: New Style

2

Norris's committee assignments did not enable him to play a prominent role at the outset of the New Freedom. Membership on the Railroads Committee allowed him to gain intimate familiarity with one aspect of the trust problem, but none of his other assignments brought him into contact with immediately important issues. Service on the Public Lands Committee made him familiar with western problems and issues pertaining to natural resources, while membership on the Agriculture and Forestry Committee deepened his understanding and sympathy for the farmer and his problems.

The Wilson years provided opportunities for Norris to develop an interest in public power and multiple-purpose resource development. The initial incident that attracted his attention pertained to the use of the Hetch Hetchy Valley in Yosemite National Park as a source of San Francisco's water supply. The measure introduced by California Congressman John E. Raker in 1913 for this purpose was not important enough to be covered by caucus control; consequently, full and vigorous debate occurred on an issue which, though ostensibly a California problem, had national ramifications. Norris strongly supported the bill in the Public Lands Committee and later on the Senate floor.

The prospect of building a dam in the Hetch Hetchy Valley aroused nature lovers and conservation groups that favored preservation as something superior to the scientific management of natural resources. It also aroused conflict between a great city and large farming communities in the San Joaquin Valley about which could make the best use of the available water. In December, 1913, Norris had much to say in the Senate on the subject of Hetch Hetchy and pronounced for the first time a point of view forever after associated with his name.

He did not believe that the proposed dam in the Hetch Hetchy Valley would destroy the beauties of Yosemite National Park. It was a natural reservoir site, located in a mountainous district, inaccessible to all but the hardiest and most experienced of tourists willing to engage in a long, tedious, and even dangerous journey. As of 1913 no woman or child had ever been there and no more than a dozen people, outside of officials making investigations, visited it annually. Although it was a beautiful site, Norris noted it was similar to others that could be reached without great expense, effort, and danger.

The Hetch Hetchy was a valley of about two and a half square miles in the northern part of Yosemite National Park. The Raker bill called for a dam 300 feet high across the valley mouth, thereby impounding the spring floodwaters of the Tuolumne River that flowed through it. It also provided that the city of San Francisco build roads into the valley and around the lake created by the dam, thereby making the valley easily accessible to visitors at small expense without hardship or danger. Since there were only scrub pine trees growing on the floor of the valley, nothing of importance would be lost by the construction of the dam; Norris felt the beauty of the spot actually would be enhanced by a lake nestling between 5,000-foot mountains with a dam the color of the surrounding mountains. Conservation to Norris did not involve locking up natural resources; rather, it provided for their wisest and fullest use according to the most advanced knowledge and techniques of scientific management.

Having disposed of the nature lovers, Norris next turned to the irrigationists. San Francisco, he said, already owned in fee simple most of the land that would be covered by the water and had title under California law to all the water of the stream not used for irrigation. The rights of the irrigation farmers were fully protected in the bill for all the water they needed, the object being to impound for beneficial purposes floodwaters that brought only damage and destruction. Though other sources of water were available to San Francisco, informed opinion consistently concluded that the Hetch Hetchy project was the most practicable, the fairest, the most inexpensive, and the only one with a feasible power proposition to meet the expanding needs of bay area communities. Moreover, the entire project would be constructed at no expense to the government. The bill gave San Francisco permission to build the dam and to run the water right-of-way over government land. For this privilege the government insisted that the city build roads to make the valley accessible and pay an annual fee to the federal Treasury.[1]

Now Norris came to what he regarded as the crux of the matter, namely, that every electric utility company on the Pacific coast was opposing the Raker bill with virtually every weapon at its disposal. The power proposition, one of the chief reasons for his support of the bill, was also the reason for most of the opposition. The pattern was evident to progressives: big business in its own selfish concern was opposing the public interest.

Here was a measure that could mean pure water for a million or more people; it could provide inexpensive industrial power and household electricity and at the same time reduce streetcar fares and improve recreational facilities for the citizens of San Francisco and travelers to Yosemite National Park. The proper development of the Hetch Hetchy Valley had ramifications that would benefit large numbers of people. Since organized wealth in the form of large corporations opposed it, Norris found it necessary to battle against these interests. He did so not because of a preconceived conspiracy thesis but because in almost every fight of this nature that arose, he found ample evidence of the opposition of corporate wealth.[2] In the case of Hetch Hetchy he was later disappointed. The people of San Francisco never obtained the full and direct benefit of the power that was produced because private

[1] *Congressional Record,* 63rd Cong., 2nd sess., Dec. 5, pp. 289, 314, Dec. 6, 1913, pp. 339–52.

[2] Norris made much of the opposition of power companies in the latter portion of his lengthy remarks to the Senate on Dec. 6, 1913.

interests gained control of its distribution and sale.[3] But in December, 1913, he rejoiced when the measure was signed into law and the Secretary read to the Senate a statement by the president: "I have signed this bill because it seemed to serve the pressing public needs of the region concerned better than they could be served in any other way and yet did not impair the usefulness or materially detract from the beauty of the public domain. . . ." [4]

If Hetch Hetchy represented Norris's initial concern for public power and multiple-purpose resource development, the use of the Potomac River, particularly the Great Falls above Washington, D.C., was the second project to arouse his interest. However, by 1914 he realized that the water power question went beyond individual and specific projects. Already important, it would become one of the major issues confronting large segments of the American people, once long-distance transmission, presaging the dawn of a great electrical age, was perfected. He knew, too, that powerful men and corporations, sensing or realizing the tremendous value of hydroelectric power, were busily acquiring sites. Proper safeguards had to be placed about "the water-power proposition" to prevent it from falling into the clutches of corporate control. While Norris never claimed that the federal government owned the water, he did claim that it often owned the land through which it flowed. And it was this ownership that gave government the authority to impose conditions upon its disposition, thereby protecting sites and people against encroachment by monopoly.

Whereas in the instance of Hetch Hetchy Norris experienced

---

[3] George W. Norris to Louis Bartlett, Nov. 29, 1930; to William Kent, Nov. 2, 1925; to John Q. Sargent, Aug. 10, 1925. In his autobiography, *Fighting Liberal* (New York, 1945), is an interesting chapter entitled "Hetch Hetchy" wherein Norris recorded the later history of the project and his disappointment with it. For another version of the Hetch Hetchy controversy, see Robert Underwood Johnson, *Remembered Yesterdays* (Boston, 1923), pp. 309–13; see also the important chapter entitled "Hetch Hetchy" in Roderick Nash, *Wilderness and the American Mind* (New Haven, Conn., 1967), pp. 160–81. For a more detailed discussion of Norris and public power controversies at this time, see Richard Lowitt, "A Neglected Aspect of the Progressive Movement: George W. Norris and Public Control of Hydroelectric Power, 1913–1919," *The Historian*, 27 (1965): 350–65.

[4] *Congressional Record*, 63rd Cong., 2nd sess., Dec. 19, 1913, p. 1189.

a measure of success, in the case of Great Falls his efforts met
rebuff after rebuff. For more than twenty years after his death
the struggle for the sensible development of the Potomac River
continued. In both the Sixty-third and Sixty-fourth Congresses
he introduced bills providing for government construction of a
dam in the vicinity of Great Falls predicated on an exhaustive
study by Colonel W. C. Langfitt of the Corps of Engineers. In
1912 Congress had appropriated $20,000 to the Secretary of War
to allow the corps to investigate and make this report. The objects to be obtained from this construction were twofold: to provide electricity for government use and to provide an increased
water supply for the city of Washington. To protect the beauty
of Great Falls, the bills called for the construction of a dam nine
miles downstream, thereby creating a lake extending to the foot
of the falls.[5]

All of Norris's remarks supporting this project were based
on the comprehensive report submitted by the Secretary of War.
The only reason he could comprehend that its power possibilities
should not be developed was the opposition of the Potomac Electric Power Company, the dominant utility corporation servicing
the District of Columbia. "The bitterest opposition on earth," he
remarked, "that comes to legislation of that kind comes from the
interests that are making money out of the people—the poor
people of the city of Washington in charging them exorbitant rates
for electric light." Since the government of the United States
would be the greatest patron and user of the electricity to be
developed and the city of Washington would be the other great
patron, and since Congress was bound to legislate for the District
of Columbia, the objections against government construction and
control, Norris said, ought to be less than anywhere else in the
United States. While he criticized no man who opposed the bills,
Norris was outspoken in his denunciation of utility company opposition.[6]

  [5] *Ibid.,* May 14, 1914, pp. 8562–63; 3rd sess., Jan. 11, 1915, pp. 1355–56;
64th Cong., 1st sess., Mar. 7, 1916, pp. 3680–84; Norris to Joseph H. Baker,
Oct. 1, 1917.
  [6] *Congressional Record,* 64th Cong., 1st sess., Mar. 8, p. 3737, May 19, 1916,
p. 8296; Norris to Oliver P. Newman, Jan. 10, 1916. In this letter Norris discussed with District Commissioner Newman possible ways of getting the bill

Twice during the Wilson period the Senate, convinced by Norris's prodding, provided for the construction of the dam as described in the report of Colonel Langfitt. But on both occasions the House rejected it and the conferees refused to include the item in their conference report. After the first rejection in 1916 an Army board, "after going out and viewing the landscape through the periscope of a War Department limousine . . . decided it was not advisable to spend this money and make this development" because it would produce a great deal more electric power than the government and the district could use. Since the charge for the entire development would come from consumers of electricity, it would be an expensive proposition. Norris protested this conclusion and he was surprised that it received Newton D. Baker's approval. He asked the Secretary of War to compare electric rates in Cleveland and Washington, D.C., certain that Baker could only conclude that residents of the capital city were paying an exorbitant price. But with Baker's opposition, Norris realized there was little hope of bringing about this development until a new administration took office.[7]

With the advent of World War I, Norris was willing to let the matter rest. When he learned in 1918 that the government was developing electric power in connection with the work of government agencies and local military installations, he suggested the construction of the Great Falls project as a way of meeting this situation, but nothing came of it.[8] Then at the end of the Wilson administration, recalling wartime water and fuel shortages and noting Washington's increasing population, Norris succeeded in having the Senate include the project as an item in an appropriation bill. The House again rejected it but this time the conferees

out of the District of Columbia Committee and some of the activities of the Potomac Electric Power Company in opposing it. He also commented on these activities on the Senate floor; see, for example, *Congressional Record,* 66th Cong., 1st sess., June 18, 1919, p. 1295; 2nd sess., May 28, 1920, p. 7776. Incidentally, the commissioners of the District of Columbia favored the project as presented in the Langfitt report.

[7] *Congressional Record,* 66th Cong., 1st sess., June 18, 1919, p. 1295; 2nd sess., May 28, 1920, pp. 7775–77; Norris to Newton D. Baker, Nov. 29, 1916. Norris later claimed that Baker was first very enthusiastic but later changed his mind; see Norris to William C. Hammer, Mar. 16, 1924.

[8] Norris to William G. McAdoo, Feb. 7, 1918.

called for, and Congress approved, another survey and investigation of the proposal. In the last days of the Wilson administration Major Max C. Tyler of the Army Engineers presented another exhaustive survey recommending not only the building of a dam to furnish water power at Great Falls but the erection of storage reservoirs on the Potomac and one of its tributaries. It called for an outlay of over $44 million and reported that it would be possible, as soon as the work was completed, to cut drastically the price of electricity to consumers in the District of Columbia. By setting aside funds, the report observed, the entire works could be kept in first-class condition and completely paid for in thirty years. Here the matter rested when the change of administrations occurred.[9] In the 1920s Norris again would fight for a Great Falls project to provide ample water and cheaper power for the government and the residents of the District of Columbia. The battle during the Wilson years revealed that the Senate was more receptive to the idea of public power than either the House of Representatives or the executive branch, a fact that would be reiterated throughout the following decade.

While the Great Falls project focused on the Potomac and the needs of the federal government, Congress during these years concerned itself with the development of the nation's hydroelectric power. Two major leasing measures were introduced: one, by Representative Scott Ferris of Oklahoma, sought to protect the public interest and had conservationist and administration support; the other, sponsored by John K. Shields of Tennessee, represented the viewpoint of the private utility corporations. Norris in 1916 and again in 1917 had much to say on this subject, favoring the Ferris bill and calling for amendments to the Shields bill. In the Public Lands Committee he was in the minority, champion-

[9] *Congressional Record*, 66th Cong., 2nd sess., Jan. 13, pp. 1480–81, May 28, 1920, p. 7778; Norris, "A Brief History of the Proposed Water Power Development at Great Falls," Nov., 1923 (draft copy of an article in the Norris Papers); Norris to Hammer, May 30, 1924. The building of storage dams would help eliminate the great variation between low and high water on the Potomac and thus make available a large amount of what would ordinarily have been secondary power for conversion to primary power that would always be available. Colonel Langfitt suggested to Norris the necessity of storage dams, though he did not include such a proposition in his report; see *Congressional Record*, 66th Cong., 1st sess., June 18, 1919, p. 1294.

ing the conservationist position and demanding, among other things, a workable recapture clause allowing the government to regain control of a dam site if the utility corporation violated its lease. He announced to the Senate on February 17, 1916, that he would not vote for the Shields bill unless it was substantially modified.[10]

As with other pieces of New Freedom legislation, Norris was opposed to granting cabinet members authority over leases. He proposed a separate commission, comparable to the Interstate Commerce Commission, which could devote full time to administering the law. "The power that will be developed and the industries that will flow from that development," he said, ". . . will be perhaps second only to the great railroad systems of the country." Transportation control was placed in the hands of a nonpartisan commission whose only business was to examine interstate railroad propositions. However, Congress was willing to put electric power into the hands of cabinet members selected without reference to their knowledge of the subject and whose appointment might be predicated entirely on political purposes. Power developed on a stream in the public lands would be supervised by the Secretary of the Interior, while power developed on a navigable stream would be under the jurisdiction of the Secretary of War. Norris preferred a single agency to consider all cases. If this was not feasible, he desired a cabinet commission consisting of the Secretaries of War, Interior, and Agriculture (since they had jurisdiction over lands and dam sites) to decide jointly on each permit and its various details.[11]

He also desired that whoever granted permission to a corporation to develop hydroelectric power have the authority to charge a rental fee based upon the amount of electricity generated at the site. Norris desired a lower fee for electricity sold directly to municipalities than to corporations who transmitted the power elsewhere for sale. And he favored preference to municipalities over corporations in granting the right to dam a stream and

---

[10] *Congressional Record,* 65th Cong., 2nd sess., Dec. 14, 1917, p. 278. In his 1917 remarks Norris briefly reiterated the position he had fully developed in 1916.

[11] *Ibid.,* 64th Cong., 1st sess., Feb. 17, 1916, pp. 2700–2701.

develop power. Furthermore, the higher the rates set by the producing corporation, the higher should be the rental fee charged by
the government, the object being the widest possible development
at the lowest possible price.[12]

Realizing that hydroelectric power was a new and expanding
industry with enormous potentialities, Norris was concerned lest
by legislation power sites be given away "to corporations and
water-power trusts, without any compensation and without any
recompense." What aroused his ire was a provision in the Shields
bill requiring any person who received a water power right to pay
nothing unless he acquired some government land with it. He
would then pay only what the land itself was worth, regardless of
its location, and if he improved navigation, he could get credit
for the value of such improvement. Norris thought this provision
would result in nobody paying anything: "The power of regulation, the power of control, is absolutely gone, turned over to
private corporations, without any string tied to it, for them to
enjoy now and forever." To the argument that there were numerous utility commissions already in existence, Norris quickly responded with evidence that often they did not regulate. The existence of state utility commissions did not provide a satisfactory
reason, when the government owned the land upon which dams
were to be built and when many power companies engaged in
interstate activities, for opposition to federal regulation.[13]

Finally, some critics argued that government had no right to
impede navigable streams by granting permission to construct
dams. Norris responded by noting that the government of the
United States had the power to regulate commerce. It could, if
it desired, prevent the building of a dam because it would interfere with trade and commerce on a navigable stream. Therefore
the government, as he saw it, could allow the building of a dam
on a stream under such conditions and terms as it formulated.
And if in so doing Congress exceeded its authority, in due time
the Supreme Court would call a halt. If the federal government
did not exact any condition for damming navigable streams, then
nobody could; no one claimed that states had a right to do it.

12 *Ibid.*, Feb. 24, pp. 3057–60, Feb. 26, 1916, p. 3185.
13 *Ibid.*, Feb. 26, pp. 3171–73, Feb. 29, 1916, pp. 3304–5.

Moreover, when the government allowed under specified conditions the building of a dam on a navigable stream, it would be doing what other governments, the province of Ontario and the Norwegian and French governments—to cite those Norris mentioned—were already doing. If under the Constitution states had control of navigation, Norris readily admitted that the right to exact conditions would reside with the various states. Of course, such was not the case.[14]

In the debate over the Shields bill, which the Senate considered in March, 1916, and again in December, 1917, Norris expressed many of the concepts and utilized one of the techniques that he later impressed upon the American public. He made little impression on his colleagues, however, and most of his amendments were defeated. He was opposed to having cabinet members on boards deciding leasing problems, preferring instead separate commissions or agencies divorced from politics and devoting all their time to this problem. He desired preference for municipalities and other public bodies over private corporations in the granting of sites and the sale of power. Rental fees should be levied so that the rates in effect could give the governmental agency a chance to regulate the lessee's activities. Only federal regulation, allowing the government to terminate the lease if necessary, could be effective in the expanding hydroelectric power field. The one technique that he later utilized effectively was to compare what other governments were doing in this field. Out of these debates and discussions, the conclusion of which was delayed by the advent of World War I, came the Water Power Act of 1920, a measure which incorporated few of the concepts Norris favored. Consequently, he voted against it, though his fight for the concepts continued throughout the following decade.[15]

Early in 1917, because of his efforts in fighting for public ownership and control of natural resources, Gifford Pinchot informed Norris that he had been elected a director of the National Conservation Association. Because of his congressional commit-

[14] *Ibid.*, Mar. 1, 1916, p. 3355.

[15] *Ibid.*, 66th Cong., 2nd sess., Dec. 6, 1919, p. 246, May 28, 1922, p. 7774. For an excellent discussion of the legislative history of the Federal Water Power Act of 1920, see Jerome G. Kerwin, *Federal Water Power Legislation* (New York, 1926).

ments he declined to serve, noting, however, that Pinchot's zeal had made him "a leader in public thought in the entire civilized world on the question of conservation." [16]

The Wilson administration, while unsuccessful, as far as Norris was concerned, in most efforts to secure adequate water power legislation, was successful in securing legislation for the development and protection of Alaska's natural resources. In this matter Norris gave the administration warm support. He voted for government construction and operation of an Alaskan railroad. He favored government guarantees of equal opportunities in the development of Alaska's coal and mineral resources, though he would have preferred government operation of territorial coal mines to their leasing under strict supervision.[17]

Norris went beyond the administration program when he called for a federal steamship line, thereby challenging the monopoly control over freight and passengers enjoyed by private lines, between Alaska and the ports of the Pacific coast. By constructing ships and then leasing them to the Panama Railroad Company, a government corporation with a proven record of operating efficiency on the Isthmus of Panama, the federal government would take a long step toward developing the merchant marine. And a small fleet of federally owned vessels, by providing competition on the Alaskan sea-lanes, would insure fair and reasonable charges for all shippers.[18]

But with regard to another phase of resource development Norris was adamant in opposition to federal assistance. Though silver mines were being shut down and miners thrown out of work, while the price of silver was declining owing to the loss of war-torn European markets, still Norris did not believe the gov-

[16] Gifford Pinchot to Norris, Mar. 12, 1917 (Gifford Pinchot Papers, Manuscript Division, Library of Congress); *Congressional Record,* 64th Cong., 1st sess., Feb. 28, 1916, p. 3231. Norris to Harry Slattery, May 25, 1916 (Gifford Pinchot Papers), indicates that Norris was working closely with Pinchot and the National Conservation Association in the fight for the Ferris bill and against the Shields bill. In Norris to Pinchot, Mar. 23, 1917, he claimed that the president was "patting each side on the back and urging them into the fight" with regard to the leasing legislation.

[17] *Congressional Record,* 63rd Cong., 2nd sess., Mar. 10, p. 4582, Oct. 14, 1914, p. 16590.

[18] *Ibid.,* Jan. 21, pp. 2033–39, Jan. 24, 1914, p. 2230.

ernment should purchase silver to keep up the price and maintain employment, worthy though these objects were. If the government purchased silver to aid this depressed industry, a precedent would be created whereby any other industry facing difficulty could receive financial assistance. He saw no reason in 1914 for the government to support any segment of the economy merely because it was in difficulty. Successful in his opposition at this time, in coming years the other point of view would predominate in his thinking.[19]

While Norris's concern with resource development largely focused on the fight against monopoly control, he was also concerned lest it become pervaded with politics. This latter possibility was evident most obviously in river and harbor appropriation measures. Though not opposed to large appropriations or to river and harbor development, he was opposed to pork-barrel legislation. The way to keep politics out was to create a nonpartisan, permanent board of experts, provided with lump-sum appropriations, to develop a system the outlines of which were charted by Congress. Steps should also be taken to prevent railroads from crushing companies engaged in navigation on rivers and lakes and, of course, to prevent monopoly domination of any aspect of this traffic. Though he knew his views, which, incidentally, he had never expounded as a congressman, would win few if any converts, Norris expounded them whenever the Senate considered river and harbor appropriations because, he said, "to sin by silence when we should protest makes cowards out of men." [20]

River and harbor development was related to reclamation, a field in which he had long legislative experience and interest. Knowing that the Reclamation Act of 1902 made no provision for the reclamation fund from any source except the sale of public

---

[19] *Ibid.*, Aug. 22, 1914, pp. 14121–22. During the war Norris voted for the Pittman Act wherein the government provided Great Britain with silver to bolster the sagging Indian economy. The Secretary of the Treasury was required to purchase only American silver to supply the loss in domestic silver circulation. After the war he favored modifying the act but found little sentiment in Congress to do so; see the draft article entitled "Stabilizing the Price of Silver" Norris prepared for the Feb., 1921, issue of the *Nebraska Farmer*.

[20] *Congressional Record,* 64th Cong., 1st sess., May 19, p. 8297, May 29, 1916, p. 8842.

lands, Norris opposed efforts to turn these proceeds back to the states. But he endorsed a measure to divide the money acquired from leasing public lands between the states and the reclamation fund. During these years he developed a broader vision, viewing aspects of reclamation as part of a vast project of Mississippi River flood control.

The practical projection of this vision would benefit irrigation farmers far from the Mississippi River. These farmers incurred the entire expense of building dams while the federal Treasury spent millions of dollars to build levees to save bottom lands from damage and destruction. Since irrigation dams also kept potential floodwaters in check, Norris argued that their expense should be divided between the farmers who specifically used the water and the general public that had been spared the cost of constructing dikes and levees. The water that wrought havoc in Louisiana, if it were retained at its sources in South Dakota, Wyoming, Nebraska, and elsewhere, would not do any damage. Norris realized, too, that sharing expenses to insure irrigation, navigation, and flood control was most feasible in western regions where fertile farm lands need not be expropriated for the construction of big dams. By holding water behind these dams when the Mississippi and its main tributaries were at a high level and releasing it at a later season, the water, besides irrigating farm lands, would also insure adequate navigation throughout the entire year. Every time a dam was built in the Great Plains or the Rocky Mountains, less money would be required for levees and dikes along the lower Mississippi.[21]

In 1917, for the first time, Norris specifically called for federal funds amounting to one-half the cost of every dam constructed by the Reclamation Service for withholding floodwaters that otherwise would empty into the Mississippi River. Thus farmers in reclamation projects would be relieved of one-half the charge of the dam, thereby obviating the difficulty of making heavy payments as they were getting their irrigation systems under way. To Norris it was just as fair to let farmers in the arid regions get the

[21] *Ibid.*, Jan. 8, pp. 709–10, Feb. 21, 1916, p. 2877; Norris to John J. Halligan, Oct. 4, 1912; to J. C. Hopper, Mar. 18, 1914; to F. W. Putney, June 20, 1922.

benefit of a government appropriation to hold back floodwaters as it was to give all the benefit to people in the lower Mississippi Valley. Moreover, his proposition would cost less and achieve more. Whereas the government helped farmers construct levees in Mississippi and Louisiana by paying $2 for every $1 contributed and in California it matched the amount farmers furnished for flood control purposes, in the arid regions on the Great Plains, where man was striving to reclaim depleted lands, the government would not pay a penny.[22]

Farmers and their problems, as was to be expected, loomed large in his mind during these years. But Norris's interest in farm problems prior to World War I involved no overall approach, while his concern for natural resources was rapidly leading to a comprehensive concept of multiple-purpose development. He expounded agricultural views that he had previously expressed in the House of Representatives, this time somewhat more successfully. In 1914 and again in 1915 Norris introduced in committee an item which the Senate accepted, authorizing the Secretary of Agriculture in the first instance and the Geological Survey in the other to spend $100,000 investigating artesian and other underground water supplies in those arid regions suitable for irrigation. He said that experimentation on the part of the federal government for the general good of agriculture and the arid regions was a legitimate expense. While his arguments convinced the Senate, they did not convince the House conferees, and the item failed of final enactment.[23]

It is interesting to observe that while Norris was willing to use federal funds in various ways to aid agriculture, including, for example, the construction of weather stations and experimentation

[22] *Congressional Record,* 64th Cong., 2nd sess., Feb. 26, 1917, pp. 4295, 4299, 4304; 66th Cong., 1st sess., June 28, 1919, p. 2002. For an extensive analysis of how and why Congress refused to consider a comprehensive flood control plan but rather supported a regional approach to dealing with the problem in the lower Mississippi River region, see Arthur DeWitt Frank, *The Development of the Federal Program of Flood Control on the Mississippi River* (New York, 1930). In 1917, Norris recalled later, every southern senator voted against his amendment; see Norris to Putney, June 20, 1922.

[23] *Congressional Record,* 63rd Cong., 2nd sess., June 29, 1914, p. 11295; 3rd sess., Feb. 24, 1915, p. 4514; Norris to W. P. Snyder, July 17, 1914; to George Otis Smith, Mar. 5, 1915.

with grasses in the Nebraska sand hills, he was unwilling for government either to impose restrictions on agricultural production or to purchase surplus crops, believing that such action would cause farmers to raise more for sale to the government. Interfering with agricultural production could only produce "bad results." Though Norris later changed his mind, before World War I he could proclaim, "I believe it is economically wrong to pass a law against the curtailment of the production of one of the necessities of life." [24]

In 1916 Norris endorsed the most significant agricultural measure of the Wilson administration, the rural credits bill. Earlier, when the administration frowned upon a federal farm loan system, Norris had proposed government loans on farm mortgages, the necessary funds to be raised by issuing bonds. But with a marked shift in Wilson's point of view in favor of a federally controlled system, Norris found no difficulty in supporting the administration, though he was dissatisfied with some aspects of the 1916 law.[25]

In lengthy remarks approving the measure, Norris vividly proclaimed his agrarian bias. He further argued that adequate credit, by providing encouragement to farmers, could curb the drift to the city. It also would curtail mounting farm tenancy. By obviating weaknesses in the credit structure which forced farmers to pay the highest rate of interest of any class of citizens, actual owners might again till the soil on farms that provided support for the entire family. While the bill provided adequate rural credit, Norris feared it was "top-heavy." There were "too many middlemen to receive commissions; too much machinery to be oiled; too much overhead expense." His criticisms were made, he said, "not as an enemy but as a friend." [26]

His solution for simplifying the structure and at the same time providing money at a low rate of interest was embodied in the

[24] *Congressional Record,* 63rd Cong., 2nd sess., Oct. 17, 1914, pp. 16772–74; 64th Cong., 2nd sess., Feb. 2, 1917, p. 2484; Norris to G. H. Beers, June 6, 1914; to A. F. Stryker, May 24, 1916. Norris's remarks regarding government restrictions on production can be found in the Feb. 2, 1917, citation in *Congressional Record.*

[25] *New York Times,* Jan. 7 and 20, 1914; Norris to Elmer E. Strain, Dec. 22, 1920.

[26] *Congressional Record,* 64th Cong., 1st sess., Apr. 28, 1916, pp. 6951–52.

creation of a bureau of farm loans, which he had previously suggested in 1914. Norris made much of the fact that his measure was geared to help tenants become proprietors. It was also designed to help urban dwellers return to the land by providing ample and inexpensive long-term credit with the borrower's land as security. The difference between the interest rate charged the farmer and the rate paid by the government on the bonds sold to raise funds for this system, a .5 percent difference, Norris said, "would much more than pay all the expenses of operation and would build up in a very short time, an enormous surplus." [27]

But his measure was doomed; in May, 1916, Norris had to consider the creation of the Federal Farm Loan Board called for in the rural credits bill. He criticized what he considered its partisan nature. Representatives of both political parties were to be chosen and they would decide, without regard to civil service, upon numerous minor appointments extending throughout the United States. In Norris's judgment the system would quickly become pervaded with politics while concern for farm credit would be secondary. Therefore, he called for civil service appointments to all but the top positions in the system and announced his preference for board appointments regardless of party, with knowledge of the subject as the chief criterion.[28]

Norris was also critical of another aspect of the bill. It called for three kinds of securities: bonds issued by farm loan associations and based upon mortgages with unlimited liability, bonds issued by farm loan banks based upon mortgages with limited liability from farm loan associations, and bonds issued by joint-stock banks organized with private capital. He believed there ought to be only one type of security. Otherwise different kinds of bonds might compete with one another for the funds of the investing public. Norris could see no reason why a federal system furnishing the farmer with cheap money by a sort of mutual or-

---

[27] *Ibid.,* pp. 6952–56. Herein Norris argued fervently, albeit unconvincingly, for his measure calling for a bureau of farm loans. The Norris Papers contain a draft statement by Norris about his bill providing for a bureau of farm loans as well as an extract from an article written by him for *Farm and Fireside* on the same subject.

[28] *Congressional Record,* 64th Cong., 1st sess., May 1, 1916, pp. 7138–39, 7141–42.

ganization plan would in the same law put that system into competition with privately owned, privately managed, and profit-moti-
vated joint-stock banks. Congress, he felt, should concern itself
exclusively with a plan by which farmers could organize for the
purpose of combining their credit and getting money at as near
cost as possible. Norris would have eliminated the privately organized joint-stock companies and the unlimited liability farm loan
associations. However, he was not adamant on the latter point
because he realized that few such associations would be organized
given the limited liability alternative. Despite doubts, Norris voted
for the bill because he felt it would relieve, albeit inadequately,
the farm credit situation.[29]

Related to his agrarian bias was his attitude toward immigration. While he favored restriction, he was opposed to the literacy
test provided in the bill sponsored by Alabama Congressman
John L. Burnett. He explained, "It is grating on my conscience
to prevent an immigrant from landing on our shores simply because he can neither read nor write." He also felt that refugees
from political persecution should be granted the same exemption
from the literacy test as those fleeing religious persecution. But
despite his opposition to the test and his belief that a quota system
provided a more satisfactory method of restricting immigration,
Norris voted for the Burnett bill because he believed it would
"have the effect of keeping out undesirable people" and because
the parliamentary situation made it impossible to offer alternatives
to the literacy test.[30]

Finally, with regard to most of the remaining items of progressive domestic legislation sponsored by the Wilson administration
before World War I, Norris supported them, though he might not
have been in full accord with them. He expressed himself infrequently and most of his remarks concerned fiscal matters. When
the Senate considered the president's request in September, 1914,
to raise an additional $100 million through internal taxes to com-
pensate for loss of tariff revenue occasioned by the outbreak of

[29] *Ibid.*, May 4, 1916, pp. 7407–8, 7410–11. By including three different
kinds of securities in the measure, overwhelming support for it was assured:
critics were assuaged by inclusion of their ideas about how the system should
be financed.

[30] *Ibid.*, 63rd Cong., 3rd sess., Dec. 31, 1914, p. 802.

war in Europe, Norris disagreed, stating that the proposed taxes would fall equally on common man and millionaire alike. Instead he called for levies on beer, whiskey, and tobacco and "upon those who had incomes exceeding $250,000 per annum." A graduated inheritance tax would have made special taxation unnecessary; calling for such a tax, he voted against the revenue measure.[31]

But by 1916 the Wilson administration, plagued by increased governmental expenditure, seemingly heeded Norris's remarks, and he in turn called for unanimous approval of the revenue measure then before the Senate. It provided for an increased income tax and an inheritance tax, which Norris called, despite minor disagreements, "the best inheritance tax or estate tax . . . that has ever been enacted by Congress in any law that it has ever passed." The bill also imposed a tax on munitions makers, whose stocks, he noted, were worth $2,212,986,000 at the end of 1915, an increase of nearly a billion dollars over the previous year. And it provided for the creation of a tariff commission. Though Norris had voted against nearly all the appropriations that made additional revenue necessary, this measure contained so many features he had previously endorsed that he could not consistently vote against it. In all, he concluded, "it would be difficult to draft a bill, according to my judgment, more systematically or better adapted to properly raise revenue for the payment of the debts that we have so foolishly and so extravagantly and ruthlessly contracted." [32]

He followed his support of the revenue measure with an amendment calling upon the Secretary of the Treasury to prepare an annual estimate of income. Then if congressional appropriations exceeded the estimated income by $25 million or less, the president would issue a proclamation increasing income tax schedules by .25 percent. A further rate of tax increase was predicated upon increased expenditures. Similarly, the amendment provided for a reduction according to a sliding scale if congressional appropriations were less than the income of the government. The merits of this suggestion were that it placed a premium on economy and provided some insurance against flagrant pork-barrel legislation.

[31] *Ibid.*, 2nd sess., Oct. 17, pp. 16804–5, Oct. 22, 1914, pp. 16920–21.
[32] *Ibid.*, 64th Cong., 1st sess., Sept. 5, 1916, pp. 13871–72.

Norris also envisioned it as a step toward a much-needed budget system for the federal government.[33] Though his suggestion did not prevail, he found much to support in Wilson's revenue program.

With regard to further progressive legislation, Norris voted for both the seamen's bill in 1915 and the child labor bill in 1916 without comment. But he had something to say about labor legislation calling for an eight-hour day for railroad workers. Norris believed it did not effectively prevent, through overtime pay or other means, employers from forcing railroad workers to remain on the job for more than eight hours. Most important, he did not believe that the wages and hours of a particular industry should be set by Congress. Rather, the Interstate Commerce Commission ought to set the conditions and rates for overtime work and be responsible for settling wage disputes and other grievances as well as ascertaining if executive salaries were too high. Norris made these suggestions because both wages and salaries were involved in fixing freight and passenger rates. So serious were his reservations that he voted against the measure on September 2, 1916.[34]

Norris showed no hesitancy when it came to developing another facet of the national transportation system. He believed that the federal government should contribute toward the building of roads. But what proportion ought to be paid was a question that concerned him. While the administration suggested matching dollar for dollar, Norris thought that the larger contribution should be made by state and local authorities and that the state should be responsible for highway maintenance. The higher the federal contribution, the closer government came to making a pork-barrel proposition of the system. In his judgment a federal contribution of 33⅓ percent was very liberal, though he realized that any figure necessarily would be an arbitrary one. But in the final vote he supported the administration measure calling for matching funds on a "fifty-fifty" basis.[35]

Throughout Wilson's first administration, despite the difficulty of functioning effectively in opposition to caucus control, which,

[33] *Ibid.,* Feb. 28, 1917, pp. 4486–87.

[34] *Ibid.,* Sept. 2, 1916, pp. 13634–35, 13651.

[35] *Ibid.,* Apr. 20, pp. 6499–6501, 6503, Apr. 26, 1916, p. 6845; Norris to J. E. George, Mar. 15, 1916; to E. H. Morey, May 15, 1920.

incidentally, was more noticeable in the first two years than in the last two, Norris's record of attendance and diligence both on the floor and in committee was outstanding. As an independent progressive Republican, he judged measures on their merits and in many instances found himself able to support the New Freedom. When he voted in opposition, it was generally because he felt the measure did not go far enough in protecting the public interest. His opposition was that of a liberal critic who favored extension of governmental authority primarily in the regulatory realm. But at times, particularly in the area of water resources, he was willing for the government to promote multiple-purpose development by entering the managerial field as well. Whether he supported or opposed a bill, his reasons were usually made clear in his remarks on the Senate floor. In all, his progressivism, extending further than that of the New Freedom, was focusing on issues that were not yet in the main current of American politics. Though his colleagues recognized his emerging leadership, the public, rarely recalling his role in the insurgency revolt of 1910, did not accord him recognition among the top echelon of progressives.

Two topics at the outset of his service in the Senate barely attracted his interest. These were foreign policy and party politics: foreign policy because his committee assignments and his immediate interests did not enter this realm, and party politics because he was secure in his Senate seat until 1918. But with revolution in Mexico, war in Europe, off-year elections in 1914, a presidential election in 1916, and a preparedness movement rapidly assuming alarming dimensions, Norris could not totally ignore these issues.

The Road to War

3

George W. Norris, like Woodrow Wilson, was little concerned with foreign affairs at the outset of the New Freedom. Though he was not unaware of the outside world, having traveled as a congressman to Europe, Hawaii, and the Canal Zone, it rarely impinged upon Norris's focus on domestic, economic, and social problems. When it did impinge, it usually did so in the form of a conspiracy, as in the case of the coffee valorization scheme, designed to extort profits from American consumers. As a progressive, he saw the influence of monopoly extending its tentacles into the international scene.

Also like the president, Norris was a moralist and an idealist. But he lacked the insight and experience Wilson had gained and he had little conception of the intricacies involved in diplomacy. As an idealist, he favored open, as opposed to secret, diplomacy and considered arbitration the most sensible and realistic method of settling disputes among civilized nations. His sympathies extended to common men of all nations; his suspicions were against monarchy and militarism. Neither a pacifist nor a believer in "peace at any price," Norris wished to maintain the honor of the United States. And he understood that this stance involved an adequate military posture. But entering the arms race could only mean war or bankruptcy or both. On the other hand, Norris was willing to use force, if necessary, to subdue what his generation called "uncivilized peoples" or "barbarians," particularly in Asia or Latin America. Once they were pacified, he desired to extend to them the blessings of American democracy, eventually making them American citizens or granting them complete independence.

The point to be emphasized is that Norris was much more concerned with domestic matters than foreign policy. When he looked at the world, it was from an angle of vision that started with McCook, Nebraska, and its environs. International affairs were largely an extension of domestic policy, a much-expanded version of the ideas, attitudes, and policies of small-town America. Norris did not investigate foreign policy or seek an understanding of world problems; foreign policy and world events intruded upon the business of the Senate. As diligent members of that august body, he and his colleagues, many of whom were in the same predicament, were forced to consider them.

In the Sixty-third Congress, aside from his remarks during the Panama Canal tolls controversy which he viewed as a domestic issue, only once did Norris discuss events beyond the environs of the United States. The crisis leading to the occupation of Vera Cruz by U.S. naval units in April, 1914, provoked the comment that while war was sometimes necessary, a civilized nation was not justified in the use of force because somebody refused to salute its flag. While Norris was in accord with Wilson's refusal to recognize Victoriano Huerta as president of Mexico, he preferred to let the flag incident rest with the apologies already received rather "than to lose a single human life to preserve this ancient courtesy of barbarism existing between nations." Norris came to this conclusion despite his belief that it was the duty of the citizen to follow the president "in time of war or in dealing with foreign relations." Though he had previously supported President Wilson's Mexican policy, Norris now announced his intention of doing what he thought was right at the risk of being condemned and criticized.[1]

Against one other aspect of the administration's Latin American policy Norris also protested. He opposed the Bryan-Chamorro Treaty, ratified by the Senate in February, 1916, because it represented a noticeable shift from missionary to dollar diplomacy.

[1] *Congressional Record,* 63rd Cong., 2nd sess., Apr. 21, 1914, pp. 6999–7000; *New York Times,* Apr. 19, 1914.

The government of Nicaragua, Norris claimed, was a creation of the United States, kept in power by American Marines stationed there because "Wall Street bankers" had financial interests in the country. Not that he was opposed, per se, to American intervention. He realized that it might be necessary for the United States to establish and administer a stable government in a country wracked by revolution. If this was the proper course to pursue, Norris wished it done "openly and above-board" without financial interests profiting from the arrangement or the occupied nation surrendering sovereignty over a portion of its territory.[2]

In January and February of 1916, prior to his remarks on Nicaragua, Norris commented on another aspect of American interventionism; these remarks, together with his comments on Latin American policy, constituted the sum total of his interest in foreign policy during his early years in the Senate, aside from his slowly developing concern with war in Europe. Though the Senate accepted on March 4, 1916, the Jones bill with the so-called Clarke amendment, promising independence to the Filipinos within five years, Norris objected but voted for it on the final roll call. If the United States intended to leave the Philippine Islands, it had no need for the coaling stations and naval bases called for in the Clarke amendment. He said:

> I believe, first that the Filipino people do not want to become citizens of the United States; that they have no desire to become citizens of the United States; that they are anxious for an independent citizenship of their own; and, further, that the retention of the islands can do us no good; that it is a constant menace, and in the case of war would be a liability that would mean that we would have to spend thousands of lives and millions of dollars in defense of the islands.[3]

Not wishing to govern people without their consent, Norris wanted the United States to depart from the Philippine Islands. He was not in favor of keeping any people under American control unless they could be made citizens on an equal basis with all other

---

[2] George W. Norris to C. E. Carhart, Feb. 24, 1916. For an excellent discussion of the complex policy that aroused Norris's ire, see Arthur S. Link, *Wilson: The New Freedom* (Princeton, N.J., 1956), pp. 331–42.

[3] *Congressional Record,* 64th Cong., 1st sess., Jan. 31, 1916, p. 1793.

American citizens. The Filipino, with a history and a heritage vastly different from the American, had little desire to remain under American authority. Moreover, he could see no reason for guaranteeing their independence over a period of years, as provided in the Clarke amendment. If the United States were to be responsible for Philippine international relations, it ought to retain possession. In short, the honorable and fair solution was for the United States to grant these people complete independence without any reservations, military, commercial, or otherwise.[4]

Norris offered an amendment to strike from the measure the clauses that retained naval bases. It received only fourteen votes. But between fifteen and twenty additional senators let Norris know privately that they were in favor of turning over the islands to the Philippine people without the retention of any naval base or coaling station. After several changes were made in the Clarke amendment, including the elimination of the five-year guarantee of Philippine independence and the substitution of the word "may" for "shall," thereby allowing the president to use discretion about retaining a naval base, Norris decided to vote for the Jones bill with the Clarke amendment. The Senate did likewise, but the House never endorsed the amendment. Therefore only the Jones bill, which said nothing specific about independence though it granted the Philippine people a wider measure of self-government, was signed into law by the president.[5]

While Mexico, Nicaragua, and the Philippine Islands were isolated situations, controversy regarding neutral rights and mounting preparedness sentiment were continuing issues that crept into Norris's ken. His limited understanding and his idealistic and moral frame of reference gave some of his responses an element of naïveté. They were difficult to disregard, though one might disagree with their angle of vision, more attuned as it was to the democratic faith of nineteenth-century America than to the organized, integrated, and interdependent world of the twentieth century.

Like the president, Norris believed the United States ought to maintain strict neutrality in the European conflict. Since international law recognized the right to sell arms and munitions to

[4] *Ibid.*, pp. 1794–96.
[5] *Ibid.*, Feb. 4, 1916, pp. 2122–23.

belligerent nations, Norris was unwilling to impose an embargo upon war materials. But he believed the United States did have a right to prevent any passenger ship from leaving an American port if her hold was filled with munitions of war. And he desired legislation to this effect.

Upon the right of merchant vessels to arm for defensive purposes international law was equally clear but, in his judgment, illogical, unreasonable, and entirely wrong. Nevertheless, it had the approval of both England and Germany. Thus, if the United States remained neutral, it could not change this rule. But since Congress had the right to regulate interstate and foreign commerce, it could make certain that armed merchant vessels leaving an American port did not carry passengers. While resolutions warning people not to travel could have only a moral effect, the real remedy would be a law prohibiting such travel.[6]

At the outset Germany claimed that she had the right to sink without warning merchant vessels flying the flag of her enemies. Thus she sank the *Lusitania* and other ships. Norris never excused these acts, regarding them as "inhuman and barbarous" and contrary to international law. He supported the president's warning to Germany that unless reparations were promptly made and a promise given not to repeat such an action, the United States would break off diplomatic relations. When Germany agreed not to attack such vessels without warning, Norris believed public sentiment to be one of the potent factors that led her to change this policy. Therefore he could see no reason for neutral vessels to arm for defensive purposes. The effect of such action would be to invite U-boat attacks without warning. Arming for defensive purposes, for protection from an attack that would not take place if the vessel was unarmed, seemed to Norris an illogical and unreasonable proposition.[7]

Having expounded his views, it came as no surprise when in February, 1916, Norris allied himself with the group in the Senate that wanted to keep Americans off armed merchant ships, thereby

6 Norris to "Dear Sir," n.d.; *Congressional Record,* 64th Cong., 1st sess., Mar. 3, 1916, p. 3486.

7 Norris to "Dear Sir," n.d.; to Charles S. Scranton, May 15, 1915; *Congressional Record,* 64th Cong., 1st sess., Mar. 3, 1916, p. 3486.

challenging the president for control of the nation's foreign policy. Since Wilson did not support the Gore-McLemore resolution embodying this point of view, Norris concluded that Congress was trying to preserve peace while the president could "bring the balance of the country into imminent danger of war." Since the Constitution granted Congress the right to declare war, Norris exclaimed, "The President is leading toward war and Congress is holding back, trying to keep the country at peace. The object of warning our people to keep off armed vessels is to maintain peace. I fear the course of the President will lead our country into war, and for that reason I want Congress to warn our people to keep off armed vessels and thus avoid friction."[8] The Senate on March 3 tabled the Gore resolution and several days later the House capitulated to the president's position. Norris said surrender was achieved because the president had his party so well under control that many Democrats were afraid to oppose him.

It seemed inconsistent that while Congress had the constitutional right to declare war, the president had control over all negotiations and therefore indirectly had the power to make war. To allow Congress to perform its constitutional function adequately, Norris wanted the president to report all available facts and evidence before taking steps that might lead to war. By the spring of 1916 he was convinced that unchecked executive action, allowing the president to act without taking Congress into his confidence, plus powerful political pressures which forced many members to follow the president and put party above country, could force the nation to follow the president into war.[9]

To alter this situation, Norris suggested arbitration as the way for the United States to intercede and help end the conflict in Europe. He wished Congress to authorize the president to propose to belligerent nations "that we desire to enter with them into a treaty of peace, and that we are anxious to provide in such treaty

[8] *Congressional Record,* 64th Cong., 1st sess., Mar. 3, 1916, p. 3485; Norris to Amos Musbach, Feb. 24, 1916. The quote is found in the *Congressional Record.*

[9] Norris to S. G. Sumerholder, Mar. 7, 1916; to John H. Hindrickson, Mar. 9, 1916; to A. F. Buechler, May 1, 1916. By the spring of 1916 Norris, too, was aware that a vast majority of Nebraska citizens were opposed to any action, either presidential or congressional, that could lead to war; see Buechler to Norris, Apr. 27, 1916.

for the settlement of all future international disputes and controversies through the establishment of a permanent court of arbitration." He wanted the treaty to provide for arms reduction and
an international navy to enforce the peace. No mention was made
of any other international force.[10]

Believing that the time was ripe, that war weariness pervaded
the belligerent nations, Norris wanted the United States to take the
lead in ending the conflict and establishing a permanent court of
arbitration. Instead, he found mounting clamor for preparedness
pervading many echelons of American society. Propaganda for
preparedness made his dream of peace sound visionary. When the
president fell into line and accepted its necessity, Norris was convinced that Wilson was leading the country down the road to
war.[11]

Since the outset of the conflict in Europe voices on the American
scene demanded increased military expenditures and expansion of
the armed forces. By 1916 forebodings, prophecies, and warnings
were emanating, Norris noted, "from the rostrum, from the theatre, from moving picture films, from editorial columns of great
newspapers, from magazine articles, from fascinating books . . .
even from the pulpit, and also from ex-Presidents and from the
present occupant of the White House." Behind this outpouring he
sensed sinister corporate interests at work:

> Just how much this organized effort to create public sentiment
> in favor of military expansion has been influenced and created by
> men and corporations who have already made billions out of prof-
> its from the manufacture of war materials, and who fear that
> at the close of the present war they will find themselves, like
> Othello, without occupation, may be a question of honest dispute,
> but that material assistance has been given to this propaganda by
> these interests will not, I think, be denied.[12]

To curb these interests, Norris proposed to take the profit out of
preparedness through government ownership. He first expressed

[10] *Congressional Record,* 64th Cong., 1st sess., July 13, 1916, pp. 10931–33;
Nebraska State Journal, Sept. 24, 1916.

[11] *Congressional Record,* 64th Cong., 1st sess., July 13, 1916, pp. 10933–34;
Norris to Nicholas Norris, Jan. 27, 1916.

[12] *Congressional Record,* 64th Cong., 1st sess., July 13, 1916, p. 10934.

this view in the Senate fight of 1915 to secure passage of a ship purchase bill. The measure was designed to permit the government to buy or build and then to own and operate a merchant fleet which would guarantee shippers space in American ships, free from the uncertainties involved in using belligerent vessels. Though some Democrats broke with the president on this matter, Norris was one of the three Republicans who endorsed it.

He endorsed the bill because, besides taking profits out of preparedness, it would rebuild the merchant marine. The bill called for a government corporation to operate the vessels. This technique would free government-owned ships from bureaucratic interference and place them on an equal basis with private firms. The government corporation could sue and be sued and conduct its business in the same way as a private corporation. Norris cited the Panama Railroad Company as an example of how effective and efficient a government corporation could be.[13]

On January 29, 1915, he spoke in the Senate supporting the measure but opposing the clause which called for the eventual leasing or sale of the vessels. Norris also opposed direct subsidization of private shippers because he did not want the government to pay private parties to keep their ships on the seas and then in time of national emergency purchase the ships themselves. If the government was to go into business, then reason and justice demanded that it remain in business and give the taxpayers the opportunity to reap indirectly the profits as well. Since caucus action prevailed on this measure, Norris spoke to convince the administration of the necessity and efficacy of the changes he suggested, lest suspicions regarding the government's intentions be aroused.[14]

These remarks revealed that he was no pacifist. The ship purchase bill was a preparedness measure. In instances when he thought the United States was in the right, Norris would support all necessary measures and actions. But he was not in favor of inviting trouble or seeking a quarrel. With the bulk of the world at war, Norris believed the United States would soon have the responsibility of helping to settle the strife. Therefore it could ill

---

[13] *Ibid.,* 63rd Cong., 3rd sess., Jan. 7, 1915, p. 1103.
[14] *Ibid.,* Jan. 29, 1915, pp. 2538–48.

afford, "for the sake of making a few dollars, to run any risk of putting ourselves in disrepute before the world or endangering our country and our flag." [15]

Though the administration accepted some of his criticisms, it did not agree to his plea for a permanent corporation. The final version of the bill stated that within two years after the end of the conflict the government's merchant fleet would be turned over to the Navy for use as auxiliary vessels. Earlier, on February 2, 1915, at the White House Norris told Wilson he would support the measure only if the government corporation was made permanent. Thus, before the measure was "sent to a conference committee for a decent burial" on February 18, 1916, Norris had come out against it. [16]

Henry Cabot Lodge, one of the leaders in opposition to the ship purchase bill, regarded Norris as a "thoroughly untrustworthy man, eager only to get a little notoriety." He suggested to Theodore Roosevelt that a letter to Norris might bolster his wavering opposition to the administration in this fight. The ex-president quickly complied, excoriating Wilson and Bryan, who were threatening "the safety of the country." Roosevelt's reason for opposition was surprisingly similar to one of Norris's criticisms: foreign firms would make huge profits selling government-interned ships in American ports. In reply Norris informed Roosevelt that "in the main we are in agreement as to the Shipping Bill" and enclosed a statement reiterating the views he had expressed in the Senate. [17]

In the course of parliamentary maneuvering during this fight the Democrats started a filibuster until two absent senators could

[15] *Ibid.,* p. 2549.

[16] For a comprehensive discussion of the complicated legislative situation at the time, see Arthur S. Link, *Wilson: The Struggle for Neutrality, 1914–1915* (Princeton, N.J., 1960), pp. 153–58. The quote and the information about the conference with the president (Senators Moses E. Clapp and William S. Kenyon also attended) are from this source. See also Elting E. Morison, ed., *The Letters of Theodore Roosevelt,* 8 (Cambridge, Mass., 1954): 889, note 1.

[17] Henry Cabot Lodge to Theodore Roosevelt, Feb. 5 and 8, 1915 (Henry Cabot Lodge Papers, Massachusetts Historical Society; these items were graciously made available to me by Professor Richard W. Leopold); Roosevelt to Norris, Feb. 6, 1915; Norris to Roosevelt, Feb. 8, 1915; a Norris statement about the shipping bill is attached to the letter to Roosevelt (all of these items are in the Theodore Roosevelt Papers, Manuscript Division, Library of Congress).

return to bolster their beleaguered colleagues. This tactic illustrated to Norris "that the Senate under its rules is absolutely powerless to do business." He denounced filibustering and called for a rule that would end debate within a reasonable time. But he made it clear that he was not finding fault with any minority that resorted to the Senate rules. They had "an honorable right" to use all available methods under the rules, which imposed cloture only after a "physical-endurance test" that had nothing to do with reason and logic. "I am inclined to think," he observed with prophetic accuracy, that "it would be a good thing if some Senator would filibuster against every bill to which he is opposed in order that we may be brought, as I believe we eventually will be brought to have a cloture rule that of itself, under proper and guarded circumstances, would close debate." Two years later Norris was instrumental in bringing about the first Senate cloture rule.[18]

At this time he sought an amendment to the rules that would have prevented a senator, once the call for cloture was made, from speaking more than three hours except by unanimous consent. A cloture rule automatically would bring about a final vote; "it would end not by brute force prevailing, but [by] action coming from the application of the aggregated logic and wisdom of the entire Senate." [19]

Although the ship purchase bill went down to defeat, other preparedness measures did not meet the same fate. Norris's standard of measurement remained the same. Taking the profits out of preparedness would eliminate much propaganda in favor of a big navy and a large army by firms manufacturing materials necessary for national defense. This point of view was expressed several weeks after the demise of the ship purchase bill when Norris called for a government armor-plate factory.

The Senate had under consideration the conference report on the naval appropriation bill. Norris called attention to two amendments authorizing the Secretary of the Navy to construct and equip plants if he could not purchase projectiles and armor plate at a

[18] *Congressional Record,* 63rd Cong., 3rd sess., Feb. 3, pp. 2935–36, Feb. 8, 1915, pp. 3409–10.

[19] *Ibid.,* Feb. 8, pp. 3410–11, Feb. 19, 1915, p. 4091. In the first session of the Sixty-fourth Congress Norris introduced a slight variation of his cloture resolution; see *ibid.,* Mar. 8, 1916, p. 3736.

reasonable price. Norris thought the government ought to go further and construct armor-plate and projectile factories. Since the "armor-plate people" had only one customer and a monopoly as well, they charged exorbitant prices. It would be more economical for the government to manufacture its own munitions and armaments; by such action sentiment for increased military expenditures quickly would subside.

Government operation was further justified, despite cries of state socialism, on two grounds: first, the government had a right to make articles needed for its own use, and second, in case of emergency it could operate its own factories so as to be independent of private producers. Despite Norris's plea and the known sentiment of the Secretary of the Navy in favor of a government armor-plate factory, the conferees suggested, and the Senate finally accepted, the deletion of these amendments from the appropriation measure. But a year later, in May, 1916, Congress approved a bill establishing a government armor-plate factory without extensive encouragement on Norris's part.[20]

Especially interesting was Norris's support of a government plant to make nitrates for explosives as a valid part of the preparedness program. Realizing that some senators would vote for the measure because they envisioned the government producing inexpensive fertilizer, he emphasized that the prime reason for the measure was that it provided for the manufacture of explosives. Since nitrates could be utilized for explosives as well as fertilizer, Norris thought it both the business and the duty of the government to dispose of surplus nitrates to farmers. A government nitrates plant would serve the nation in time of war; in time of peace it could benefit people who had been dependent upon firms that controlled "the fertilizer proposition." While the proposal involved "something comparatively new in the scientific world," Norris could "see no loss anywhere" in it.[21]

[20] *Ibid.,* 63rd Cong., 3rd sess., Mar. 3, 1915, pp. 5237–38, 5242. In 1916 Norris used similar arguments in calling for a government powder factory and opposing reduced appropriations for two government arsenals; see *ibid.,* 64th Cong., 1st sess., June 27, p. 10073, July 24, 1916, pp. 11480–81; *New York Times,* July 25, 1916.

[21] *Congressional Record,* 64th Cong., 1st sess., Apr. 14, 1916, pp. 6107–8, 6112, 6119.

Similarly, with regard to another phase of preparedness Norris supported federal aid to schools and colleges for military training. He believed that military training "assists in making good citizens to the same extent that it assists in making good soldiers" and that schools and colleges were appropriate places for Army officers to give instruction in military and kindred subjects. Such training would make available in time of emergency citizens who would be almost as well prepared as regular soldiers. In time of peace it would make for healthier men "better able to cope with the business affairs of life." [22]

Opposed to a large standing army, Norris claimed that short-term enlistments and a large reserve would provide an available pool of trained soldiers. By calling for retirement of regular soldiers at a relatively early age, these men could contribute to civilian life and in time of war still be available for active service. Thus in the debate over the reorganization of the Army Norris supported the more moderate House bill, providing for a smaller standing army than the Senate measure. In May, 1916, he voted for the final measure, which also called for a government-operated nitrate plant and civilian military training.[23]

When it came to increased naval expenditures, Norris was more critical. He favored spending federal funds to improve the facilities of Navy yards and for investigations to promote maximum efficiency. But he was opposed to increasing the size of the Navy. Submarines and airplanes were revolutionizing warfare and Norris thought that lessons learned from the conflict in Europe would cause the United States to modify its military and particularly its naval program. He preferred to wait until the war was over before adopting a naval expansion program that otherwise might become obsolete.[24]

The Navy bill reflected the viewpoint of the "big navy" forces in the Senate. Norris opposed it; Wilson supported it. The more modest House proposal was overwhelmed in conference committee. In his comments on the approved bill Norris said that it appropri-

22 *Ibid.,* Apr. 18, 1916, pp. 6340–41.

23 *Ibid.,* pp. 6340, 6351, May 17, 1916, p. 8139. The conference report on May 17, 1916, was merely agreed to; no roll call was taken.

24 *Ibid.,* May 19, pp. 8307–8, July 24, p. 11480, July 15, p. 11096, July 17, 1916, pp. 1185, 1191; *New York Times,* Nov. 13, 1915.

ated more money "than was ever appropriated in the history of the world by any nation on earth in time of peace" to help provide a first line of defense "against those people who will come over here in rafts and rowboats after their navies have been, in the present war, sunk to the bottom of the ocean." He insisted that the battleships to be constructed would probably be obsolete before they were used.[25]

In the discussion of the naval appropriation bill Norris revealed his basic presumptions about American foreign policy. He did not believe there existed any danger or threat to the United States from Japan, Germany, or any other foreign country. He doubted that preparedness preserved peace, citing the arms race as a causative factor in the European war. Yet he recognized that the armed strength of the United States depended upon the military posture of other nations. But extended participation in the arms race, while enriching a few, would mean higher and higher taxes and eventually war, bankruptcy, and even revolution.[26]

These views explain why Norris became bitter against Woodrow Wilson. A man of peace, the president gradually became a man who favored a program so extreme in its military and naval aspects that it could only be considered a menace by other nations. By advocating preparedness all out of proportion to defensive needs, the president would make American participation in the European conflict inevitable. By assuming this posture in an election year, Wilson made certain that Norris would campaign against him and his policies. But he focused on the theme that organized wealth and the military spirit were proceeding at a pace that could only lead to disaster unless a halt were called and the profit taken out of preparedness.

Not needing to worry about re-election until 1918, Norris was free in 1914 and 1916 to campaign as he desired. In October,

[25] *Congressional Record,* 64th Cong., 1st sess., July 24, 1916, p. 11480; *New York Times,* July 18, 1916.

[26] Another clear statement of these views can be found in Norris to Gifford Pinchot, Jan. 3, 1916 (Gifford Pinchot Papers, Manuscript Division, Library of Congress). This letter, incidentally, covers the whole spectrum of Norris's views on preparedness as well. Entire sentences and phrases from it reappear in his Senate remarks and in his correspondence; see *Congressional Record,* 64th Cong., 1st sess., July 17, 1916, pp. 11188–89.

1914, he went to Pennsylvania and appealed to Republican voters to assist in rehabilitating the party by voting for Gifford Pinchot, the Progressive party candidate for U.S. senator. His aim was to defeat Boies Penrose, an obstacle to the enactment of legislation for other than the "selfish and unpatriotic purposes" of special interests.[27]

Earlier in the month he had spoken in Nebraska in favor of the gubernatorial aspirations of R. B. Howell. As Republican National Committeeman, Howell had been instrumental in 1912 in driving conservative elements from control of the party. He had ardently supported Norris in his senatorial campaign. In these speeches Norris denounced the New Freedom, charging that Wilson had repudiated nearly every plank in his party platform and that he was "the most partisan President that ever occupied the White House." In both Pennsylvania and Nebraska the split in the Republican party, unhealed since 1912, accounted in good measure for the failure of Norris's candidates in the November elections.[28]

Unsuccessful though his endorsement of Howell was, Norris was popular enough in Nebraska to have his name filed in December, 1915, as a candidate for the Republican presidential nomination at the primaries to be held the following April. He quickly requested that it be withdrawn. Thus he was free to campaign against Woodrow Wilson and the preparedness movement and for progressive Republican candidates. Though he took no active part in healing the breach in the Republican party, he did sound a note of warning. If the party nominated a reactionary or conservative candidate, it was sure to be defeated. As for Theodore Roosevelt, Norris was equally blunt, claiming that "if he ran with preparedness as a paramount issue, I should oppose him myself." [29]

By the end of August Norris was in Wisconsin speaking for Robert M. LaFollette as he had done in 1910. He denounced pre-

---

[27] Norris to Romain C. Hasserick, Oct. 22, 1914; *New York Times,* Oct. 20, 1914.

[28] Patricia C. Mulvey, "The Republican Party in Nebraska" (M.A. thesis, University of Nebraska, 1934), p. 176; *Chadron* (Nebr.) *Journal,* Oct. 9, 1914; *Fremont Herald,* Oct. 29, 1914; *Lincoln Star,* Oct. 31, 1914.

[29] Addison E. Sheldon, *Nebraska: The Land and the People* (Chicago, 1931), 1: 897; *New York Times,* Dec. 19 and 28, 1915, Apr. 7, 1916; *Nebraska State Journal,* Dec. 28, 1915.

paredness and insisted that "if Senator LaFollette is not returned to the United States Senate it will be the severest blow that could be dealt the progressive movement throughout the country." [30] In October Norris spoke for Charles Evans Hughes or, more precisely, against Woodrow Wilson in Ohio, Kansas, Colorado, Nebraska, and other western states. Earlier the breach in the Republican party in his home state had been worked out; the Progressive party's State Committee unanimously agreed with the National Committee on Hughes's candidacy. Norris had little to do with this process of unification which left progressive Republicans in control of the party in Nebraska.[31]

In his speeches Norris denounced the Democratic party for violating 1912 campaign pledges. He lambasted segments of its legislative record, claiming that the New Freedom had "appropriated more money and [had] been more extravagant in the management of the Government than any other administration in our history,—and this is aside and independent of any and all appropriations made on account of so-called preparedness." His bitterest barbs were reserved for the administration's fumbling foreign policy, particularly in Mexico, and its preparedness policy. But war in Europe and its impact on the American economy prevented the "evil effects" of President Wilson's policies from being everywhere manifest. Norris, of course, intended to make these

[30] *New York Times,* Aug. 26, 1916; Norris to W. A. Hayes, Sept. 14, 1916; Belle Case and Fola LaFollette, *Robert M. LaFollette,* 2 vols. (New York, 1953), 1: 579–80. Norris's remarks about a trunk line were not out of place, owing to a controversial railroad labor dispute which led to the enactment of the Adamson Act. Both Norris and LaFollette had to return to Washington to vote on this measure, Norris against it and LaFollette for it, the only Republican senator to do so. The Adamson Act, along with Wilson's strong endorsement and Hughes's criticism of it, became an important campaign issue in some sections. That Norris took more than a passing interest in Wisconsin politics is evident in the 1914 correspondence of Irvine Lenroot, who observed that Norris was an active participant in discussions with the Wisconsin delegation on Capitol Hill; see Irvine Lenroot to Herman L. Ekern, Feb. 23, 1914 (Box 2, Irvine Lenroot Papers, Manuscript Division, Library of Congress).

[31] Norris to Willis Vickery, May 19, 1932; Benjamin H. Bristow to Jonathan Bourne, Oct. 11, 1916 (Benjamin H. Bristow Papers, Kansas State Historical Society); George W. Perkins to Charles Evans Hughes, July 14, 1916 (Charles Evans Hughes Papers, Manuscript Division, Library of Congress). The Perkins letter discusses the political situation in Nebraska while the Bristow item comments on Norris's speeches.

effects manifest; at least one observer insisted that he made some of the most effective Republican speeches in the 1916 campaign. But for the very reason Norris noted, namely, mounting prosperity owing to war in Europe, there were few symptoms of a landslide in favor of Hughes, and Wilson was much stronger in the rural regions than most Republican leaders expected.[32]

With the re-election of Woodrow Wilson and the legislative triumph of his preparedness policies, the stage was set for the deterioration of American relations with Germany and the entrance of the United States into World War I. The crisis in American-German relations also brought George W. Norris, whose views were not in the mainstream of American opinion, to the most extreme crisis of his entire career.

[32] Norris 1916 campaign statement (though undated, this statement is obviously a draft of a campaign speech); Bristow to Bourne, Oct. 11, 1916 (Bristow Papers); *Congressional Record,* 65th Cong., 2nd sess., Dec. 14, 1917, p. 277. Norris herein cites an incident pertaining to some of his 1916 campaign speeches.

Congress Alone Has the Right
to Declare War

4

In January, 1917, German military leaders, deciding that an all-out submarine campaign coordinated with an all-out army offensive might end the war before America could fully mobilize, set in motion the final phase leading to the collapse of American neutrality. The president, seeking with the aid of his personal envoy Colonel E. M. House to bring an end to the conflict by means of a negotiated peace, was informed that after February 1 German submarines would sink without warning all ships in a war zone that included waters around Great Britain and France. Wilson immediately severed relations with Germany, a drastic step considered to be just short of an actual declaration of war.

In his reaction to this situation Norris presented the thesis he reiterated throughout the coming crisis. The Constitution stated that Congress alone had the power to declare war, but the president had authority to take steps that might make war inevitable: "If the President can sever at his pleasure diplomatic relations with foreign governments, then in the President lies the real power to declare war, because although the Constitution says Congress has the sole right to declare war, the President having diplomatic matters supremely in his own hands can get Congress and the Country in a position where they can not avoid war." [1]

Initially, however, Norris weighed his doubts in Wilson's favor and endorsed the severance of relations. But shortly thereafter he

---

[1] *Congressional Record,* 64th Cong., 2nd sess., Feb. 7, 1917, p. 2735.

cast aside all hesitation and was outspoken in opposition to the president and his handling of the crisis. In early February, seemingly aware of the crisis that soon would engulf him, Norris made inquiries about starting a new career as a lawyer in New York City when his Senate tenure was concluded.[2]

Once his position was made clear after Wilson severed relations with Germany, Norris remained silent. As the crisis deepened when the Zimmerman note was released to the public and the president called for an armed-ship bill, Norris made no speeches in the Senate. In the first two days of March, with the Senate in continual session prior to its scheduled adjournment at noon on March 4, coincident with the first term of Woodrow Wilson, he briefly protested the inability of members to consider seriously the appropriation and authorization bills still to be acted upon.[3] Then on the last two days of the session, when debate focused on the armed-ship bill, Norris's lengthy remarks centered on his opposition to the president's steps that could lead to war.

With war an imminent possibility and Congress scheduled to adjourn on March 4 until the following December, Republican leaders were concerned lest the president be deprived of the advice of the Senate in directing the nation throughout this grave international crisis. This possibility brought into accord both factions of the Republican party though for different reasons. The "regulars," led by Lodge, Penrose, Reed Smoot, and others, wanted "to hold up the hands of the President" and prevent him from acting without the benefit of their advice and consent. The progressives, led by LaFollette and Norris, wanted merely to restrain the Chief Executive. The possibility of unilateral executive action, besides helping to heal the breach in the Republican party, helped to unite progressive Republican senators in their determination to prevent the president from leading the American people into the European

[2] *Ibid.*; George W. Norris to "My dear Sir," Feb. 17, 1917; Norris A. Huse to Norris, Feb. 9, 1917. Norris's inquiry about a law practice in New York City soon reached Nebraska and prompted numerous letters asking if his home and property in McCook were for sale. Norris denied that he planned to leave Nebraska and branded the suggestion a rumor; see Norris to John E. Kelley, Mar. 19, 1917; to C. B. Gray, Feb. 26, 1917; Gray to Norris, Feb. 22, Mar. 5, 1917.

[3] *Congressional Record*, 64th Cong., 2nd sess., Mar. 1, p. 4582, Mar. 2, 1917, p. 4732.

conflict. Progressive Republican unity had not prevailed during
the New Freedom years. It is rather ironic that the progressives,
primarily interested in domestic issues, closed ranks and agreed
among themselves and with the partisan strategy of the regular
Republicans over a matter of foreign policy.[4]

The matter came to a head when the president, speaking before
a joint session, asked Congress for authority to protect American
rights on the high seas. The next day, February 27, 1917, Senator
William J. Stone, chairman of the Foreign Relations Committee,
introduced the armed-ship bill. Now Norris had to consider a
measure whose enactment in effect would bring the United States
into the war.

At the time Stone introduced the measure, six major appropriation bills required Senate action and adjournment was only a week
away. Immediately, the air filled with rumors of a Republican filibuster to force Wilson to call Congress into special session.[5] Tension mounted further on February 28 when the government released the text of the intercepted Zimmerman note proposing a
German alliance with Mexico "to reconquer the lost territory in
New Mexico, Texas, and Arizona." Its publication helped release
a wave of patriotic feeling that rallied the country to the president's
support and helped pressure the Congress to follow suit.[6]

On March 1, 1917, the House approved the armed-ship bill and
the next day the Senate decided to consider it after the naval appropriation bill. Thus, with the end of the Sixty-fourth Congress
less than fifty hours away and with other appropriation measures
to consider, the Senate began discussion of this controversial measure in an atmosphere permeated with partisanship. The president
made no mention of calling Congress into special session after
March 4, though it was evident he would have to do so. Republican

---

[4] *Washington Post*, Feb. 24, 1917. Norris participated in the party caucus held
on Feb. 23 wherein it was decided that Congress should remain in session.

[5] *New York Times*, Feb. 26, 1917.

[6] Several newspapers complained about the timing of the release of the Zimmerman note (dated Jan. 19, 1917), claiming it had been in the hands of the
president since he broke off diplomatic relations with Germany and implying that
it was released at this time to prod a hesitating Congress into giving him full authority to deal with Germany; see *Cincinnati Commercial Tribune*, *Des Moines
Register*, *Christian Science Register*, *Boston Daily Globe*, Mar. 1, 1917; *New
York Post*, Mar. 2, 1917.

senators, exhibiting their new unanimity of purpose, sided and consulted with Robert M. LaFollette in offering amendments, demanding roll calls, and presenting comments to slow the functioning of the Senate to insure a special session and thereby prevent Wilson from solely directing the national destiny from March to December. As the Senate adjourned late in the evening on March 2, Norris purportedly remarked to LaFollette, "We've got them beaten. We can hold out now. We've enough speakers to filibuster from tomorrow on." [7]

Throughout most of the skirmishing on the armed-ship bill Norris did little to stall the proceedings, though on March 3 he stated frankly, "I would not hesitate to kill the bill if I could." He also noted a fact often overlooked in this controversy: most of the time spent in discussing the armed-ship bill was consumed by its friends. He objected "to having the debate run for a couple of days by those who are in favor of the bill and then an effort be made to gag those who are opposed to it"—thus his refusal to agree to Senator Hitchcock's continued request on March 3 to limit speeches to fifteen minutes and to take cognizance of a manifesto signed by twenty-five senators supporting the bill. [8]

As the debate continued into the evening of March 3, it became obvious that a handful of progressive Republican senators who opposed the bill by refusing to agree to limit debate and thereby to bring the measure to a vote would become targets of national opprobrium, while their conservative colleagues by talking in its favor would avoid this stigma and yet help to achieve what all

[7] *New York Times*, Mar. 1, 1917, comments on the new unanimity among Senate Republicans and on their consulting with Senator LaFollette. R. S. Baker, *Woodrow Wilson*, 6 (New York, 1937): 480, says the statement by Norris is from a memorandum of a May, 1936, conversation between Harley A. Notter and the senator.

[8] *Congressional Record*, 64th Cong., 2nd sess., Mar. 3, 1917, pp. 4894–95; *Philadelphia North American, Washington Star*, Mar. 4, 1917. In 1939 Norris recalled for Fola LaFollette that two senators who were afraid to speak and vote against the bill agreed to help prevent its passage by speaking for it. But he refused to name the senators, though he subsequently stated that they were prominent Democrats; see Norris to Fola LaFollette, Feb. 15, 1939 (transcript of an interview between Miss LaFollette and Norris); Norris to Fola LaFollette, Mar. 13, 1939. The same recollection appears in Norris to Morris A. Bealle, July 8, 1933. See also Richard Lowitt, "The Armed-Ship Bill Controversy: A Legislative View," *Mid-America*, 46 (Jan., 1964): 38–47.

Republican senators desired: a special session of Congress. As night gave way to day, administration senators grew more and more dubious about the president's strategy. On March 4, as the debate droned on before packed galleries, including many notables some of whom were in evening dress, Wilson appeared in his room just off the Senate chamber to sign bills and to take the oath of office for a second term.[9]

On the morning of March 4, a Sunday, Norris obtained the floor, the last opposition speaker to do so. LaFollette, the leading opponent of the armed-ship bill, never spoke against it. The final hours of the session were utilized by its chief spokesman, Gilbert M. Hitchcock, who, incidentally, opposed the bill in committee. In his remarks Norris said that if it was eventually passed and if the United States entered the war, he would back the president "to bring to a successful issue such a war."

He also cited the tangle of legislative business at the time the armed-ship bill was introduced. The civil appropriation bill, the Army appropriation bill, the espionage bill, the navy appropriation bill—all had been "hurled in the face of the Senate" in the last weeks of the session; all demanded discussion and debate. Then, with the session almost over, another more controversial measure was introduced, and the president insisted upon its enactment. Though charges of filibustering were leveled against the bill's opponents, Norris noted that friends of the measure had spent most of the time discussing it, that throughout the long, weary night of debate now coming to an end there was never a point made of "no quorum," a dilatory tactic calling for a time-consuming roll call. Indeed, no time-consuming tactics, characteristic of a filibuster, had been employed by any opponents of the bill.

That an extra session was justified by the situation in the Senate seemed evident. If the president had called for one, the situation would have eased. Free and full discussion of all measures, some involving hundreds of millions of dollars, would have become possible. But in the prevailing situation unanimous consent was required if Congress was to complete its business before noon on March 4. And Norris did not intend to give his consent.

---

[9] *Washington Star,* Mar. 4, 1917; *New York Times,* Mar. 4 and 5, 1917.

Since an extra session was necessary, owing to the impossibility of considering the appropriation bills, what was the great importance of hasty action on the armed-ship bill? Norris criticized the president, who on February 26 informed the Congress, "We are moving through critical times, during which it seems to me to be my duty to keep in close touch with the Houses of Congress." If Wilson meant what he said, then an extra session was imperative. But Norris, voicing the sentiments of his Republican colleagues, asserted, "It seems the President does not want us to be in session" during this critical period.

He then stated that while opposed to the armed-ship bill, he was not opposed to arming merchant vessels provided they were prohibited from carrying munitions of war. Though he believed submarine warfare to be "illegal and wrong and inhuman," he was not ready to declare war because of it:

> I think both parties to this great war in Europe have violated international law. England has violated it over and over again, but she has never violated it to the extent that I would be willing to go to war on account of it. Up to the present time I would not vote for a proposition to declare war against Germany or England or any of the belligerent nations, and as long as I do not believe in declaring war I cannot consistently or conscientiously vote for a bill that in my judgment, while it does not directly declare war, gives a power to the President, which, if he exercises it, will make war, and there is no escape from it.

Clause by clause and section by section, he dissected and criticized the measure, stressing its vague terminology and broad grants of power to the executive: "Under this bill the President can do anything; his power is absolutely limitless. The Constitution says that Congress has the sole power to declare war. This [bill] in effect is an amendment of the Constitution, an illegal amendment. We are abdicating, we are surrendering our authority."

To embarrass his opponents, including the president, Norris next read sections of Wilson's *Congressional Government* which called for congressional control of the legislative process and denounced subservience to executive power. He also singled out his Nebraska colleague Gilbert M. Hitchcock, floor manager of the pending bill, by noting that previously he had called for an embargo on munitions of war. He observed that Commonwealth countries had laws preventing women and children from sailing into the war zone while the United States insisted that American passengers could travel "in any old boat, loaded to the brim with munitions of war." Yet boats on Alaskan rivers as well as interstate railroads could not carry passengers and explosives at the same time. It was contrary to American law. "We have no right to demand," he exclaimed, "that an American passenger shall become an insurance policy against loss of a shipload of munitions going from this country to belligerent nations." Throughout his extended remarks Norris's thrust was against the president, his blundering foreign policy, and his usurpation of power that constitutionally resided with Congress. And, finally, it was directed against the president's tactic in the last days of the session, with appropriation and other bills to be considered, of refusing to call a special session to insure adequate discussion.[10]

Norris's was the last speech in the Senate against the bill. He had spoken about an hour and a half and concluded around 9:30 A.M. Senators Robert L. Owen and Gilbert M. Hitchcock then held the floor, the former only briefly, until the end of the Sixty-fourth Congress at noon on March 4, 1917, thereby preventing Robert M. LaFollette from speaking. Norris sat beside LaFollette and tried to calm him, saying, "For God's sake don't do anything now. We've won the fight." No vote was taken on the armed-ship bill. While rain came down hard on the glass skylight of the Senate chamber, on the floor below there was irritation, ill humor, and "a snarling unfriendliness" instead of the usual spirit of amity and customary tributes to retiring members. The president, thoroughly angry, realized an extra session was now necessary. It was ironic too, since Wilson had asked for an endorsement of authority which he thought the president already possessed. Late that evening Wilson gave vent to his wrath and issued a statement in which he said that "a little group of willful men, repre-

[10] *Congressional Record*, 64th Cong., 2nd sess., Mar. 4, 1917, pp. 5004–9. Norris to Willis McBride, Mar. 11, 1917, summarizes the reason for his opposition.

senting no opinion but their own, have rendered the great Government of the United States helpless and contemptible." [11]

This was only the beginning. Norris and his colleagues in opposition were showered with criticism and denunciations from press and pulpit, from meetings and gathering places, from friend and foe alike in Nebraska and throughout the country. A resolution offered in the Nebraska Senate said, "In his opposition to said bill, Senator Norris did not voice the sentiment of Nebraska, nor reflect the patriotic judgment of its citizens." "Two men alone," wrote David Lawrence, "really stand out as unquestionably guilty of the successful attempt to kill the Armed Neutrality bill. These are Senators LaFollette, of Wisconsin, and Norris of Nebraska." [12] Norris's Senate remark that he would "kill the bill" if he could was widely quoted and he was accused of pro-German sympathies and of being an enemy of his country along with Benedict Arnold, Charles Lee, and Aaron Burr.[13] Indeed, at the time the only consolation he had was the knowledge that he remained constant in convictions he honestly held and had publicly proclaimed. On March 11 he was able to write, "After more mature deliberation I am more convinced than ever that my course was right, and that it will be justified." [14]

Before Norris could concern himself with reaching the people in Nebraska whom, he believed, he was properly representing, the

[11] Norris to Fola LaFollette, Feb. 15, 1939; *Philadelphia Public Ledger,* Mar. 5, 1917; Baker, *Woodrow Wilson,* 6: 481. Baker makes the point that Wilson was anxious to avoid an extra session.

[12] *New York Times,* Mar. 6, 1917. On Mar. 7 this resolution was tabled by a vote of 18 to 13; see *Senate Journal of the Legislature of the State of Nebraska,* 35th sess., p. 487; *New York Evening Post,* Mar. 6, 1917. Louis Lochner, who spoke at a Philadelphia meeting with Norris, said that "literally thousands had to be turned away because of lack of accommodations" at the Grand Opera House; see Lochner to Amos Pinchot, Mar. 12, 1917 (Box 30, Amos Pinchot Papers, Manuscript Division, Library of Congress).

[13] *Baltimore News,* Mar. 5, 1917. See also, for example, Theodore Roosevelt to J. C. O'Laughlin, Mar. 8, 1917 (Theodore Roosevelt Papers, Manuscript Division, Library of Congress), in which Roosevelt wrote of "the treason committed by the eleven Senators in fighting the armed neutrality bill."

[14] Norris to McBride, Mar. 11, 1917. The *Boston Evening Transcript,* Mar. 5, 1917, was one of the very few papers to note that the bill was "talked to death partly by its own friends" and to suggest the situation in the Senate at the time it was introduced.

special session that all Republican senators desired came into being. When Wilson on March 12 gave notice that all American merchant vessels sailing through the war zone would be armed, the Senate was considering the appropriation bills on the calendar when the controversy over the armed-ship bill had begun. Previously, on March 8, 1917, it had enacted for the first time in its history a cloture rule to cut off debate. Norris supported it as a technique by which the majority eventually could have its way. But he insisted that "in the President's bill which failed on March 4, there was no filibuster," citing again the absence of dilatory motions, the fact that supporters of the bill took most of the time, and that legitimate debate was never exhausted.[15]

While the president's views were widely known, the full story was not. Norris reiterated his analysis of the controversy by reviewing the legislative situation in the Senate on March 2 when the armed-ship bill was brought up for consideration. He concluded that it would have been "a physical impossibility" for the Senate to finish its business by noon on March 4 without the injection of the armed-ship bill. Norris said that he had spent more time attacking the Shields water power bill in the Sixty-fourth Congress and nobody had accused him of filibustering. Neither he nor any other senator denounced by the president was to blame for the legislative situation in the last days of the session. He then bitterly remarked, "Was it done purposely? . . . Sometimes it looks to me as though it was, that all these things were forced down on us at once when it was physically impossible in the time that remained even to read the bills, and then you say you must swallow this dose or you are a filibuster or a traitor to your country." [16]

Support of his position was soon forthcoming. Radical pacifists banded together in the Emergency Peace Federation sent him a telegram expressing "grateful recognition of the courage and devotion with which you have served the cause of peace and democracy." The *Nebraska State Journal* editorialized, "He had his own ideas and the courage to follow them. For this he is entitled to

---

[15] *Congressional Record*, 65th Cong., special sess. of the Senate, Mar. 8, 1917, p. 27.

[16] *Ibid.*, pp. 28–31 (the quote is on p. 31); see also *New York Times*, Mar. 9, 1917.

praise." In Philadelphia at a mass meeting on March 11 Norris said he wanted first "to see the Senate Appropriation bills passed, and if talking about the expenditure of over $1,600,000,000 was a filibuster, then I suppose I am guilty." [17]

Nebraska sentiment in Norris's favor had difficulty making itself felt. A peace rally in Lincoln on March 11, attended by over 500 citizens, endorsed his position and applauded the mention of his name and that of Senator LaFollette. But the meeting received scant attention in the press. A "Scotch-Irish American," a Democrat who had never voted for Norris, wrote to the *Hastings Tribune* approving his position and claimed Norris a stronger supporter of the Wilson program than his Democratic colleague Gilbert M. Hitchcock. And mail pouring into Norris's office indicated that grass-roots sentiment supported him. In answering these letters, Norris criticized Washington press reports for trying "to place all of those who opposed the bill in a false light before the country." [18]

Desirous of speaking to his constituents but unable to afford the expense involved in holding numerous meetings and presenting the facts that newspapers failed to print, Norris decided to arrange for a special primary or recall election so that voters, as final arbiters, could seal his fate or vindicate his position. He wrote the chairman of the Nebraska Republican Committee, asking him to call a primary submitting his name to the voters. Though the vote could have no legal effect, Norris said he would agree in writing to resign if a majority decided against him. When the Republican chairman refused, Norris wrote virtually the same letter to Governor Keith Neville, a Democrat, but stipulated that the election, which would require special enactment by the legislature, be held not later than May 1, 1917.[19]

Governor Neville, as Norris possibly expected, thought it "undesirable and inexpedient" to call a special election and suggested

[17] *New York Times,* Mar. 7 and 12, 1917; *Nebraska State Journal,* Mar. 7, 1917.

[18] *Hastings Daily Tribune,* Mar. 10, 1917; Norris to C. E. Scarr, Mar. 10, 1917; to A. F. Buechler, Mar. 10, 1917; to J. W. Linkhart, Mar. 11, 1917; to Origen Williams, Mar. 15, 1917. The information about the Lincoln peace meeting is from a confidential source.

[19] Norris to Fola LaFollette, Feb. 15, 1939; *New York Times,* Mar. 19, 1917. The letter to Governor Neville was published in the *New York Times.*

that time would demonstrate the validity of his position, while a special election would not repair the harm done if he were in error. But before he received this response, Norris decided to return to Nebraska "to lay his case before the voters." While the matter of the primary was pending, several senators, including LaFollette and Asle J. Gronna, came to his office and urged Norris not to carry out his intention. When they found him determined, they immediately offered to speak for him and Gronna said he had $500 to help in the campaign.[20]

By March 24 Norris had left Washington. He rented the city auditorium in Lincoln for $50 for the evening of March 26. A meeting was scheduled at Holdrege on the following day. Thereafter he planned to remain in McCook until Congress reconvened. While en route to Nebraska his Washington office released a strong statement by Senator William E. Borah professing his "sincere esteem and admiration" for Norris as an able, industrious, and conscientious public servant who acted from conviction in the belief that he was serving the best interests of the people. Borah, who did not agree with Norris's stand on the armed-ship bill, said that he was "one of the best men in the public service today." [21]

Norris arrived in Lincoln on Sunday morning, March 25, and checked into the Lindell Hotel, across the corner from the auditorium where he was scheduled to speak the following night. Though he expected reporters to deluge him with questions, none were on hand and few callers appeared at his room. Among them were R. B. Howell, the Republican National Committeeman from Nebraska who had made a special trip from Omaha, and Frank P. Corrick, the head of the Progressive party in Nebraska. Both men tried to convince him not to speak the following evening. Corrick said an attempt would be made to disrupt the meeting and suggested that he conveniently get sick, cancel the meeting, and go on to McCook. A doctor could be found who would authenticate the tale. Norris refused to abide by these suggestions and in turn asked

[20] Keith Neville to Norris, May 20, 1917; Norris to Fola LaFollette, Feb. 15, 1939; *Nebraska State Journal,* Mar. 20, 1917. Senators Cummins and Kenyon of Iowa also said they would speak for Norris, as did Senator Gronna; see Norris to Asle J. Gronna, Apr. 7, 1917.

[21] *Nebraska State Journal,* Mar. 20, 1917; *Omaha World-Herald,* Mar. 25, 1917; Norris to Fola LaFollette, Feb. 15, 1939.

Howell, who said he had to return immediately to Omaha, to act as chairman of the meeting. Other friends offered similar advice. But Norris continued with his plans, requesting the manager of the auditorium to fill the stage with chairs, arrange tables for reporters, open the doors at the appointed time, and let all enter and sit where they desired on a first come–first served basis.[22]

Late Sunday evening there was a knock on his door and a young reporter, the only newspaperman Norris had seen all day, requested an interview. The reporter, Frederic Babcock, represented the *Nebraska State Journal,* a paper unfriendly to Norris at the time. But Babcock assured Norris that whatever he told him would be fully and faithfully reported, since all his superiors had gone home and would not return to their desks until the next day, hours after the morning edition had gone to press. Babcock's sympathy was the first assurance Norris received that Sunday that not everyone in Nebraska disagreed with his point of view. Though Babcock, who wrote up the interview in the hotel room, never realized it, Norris was grateful for his visit and the story that resulted from it.[23]

The next day a young friend, George H. Thomas, spent much time with the senator. He went with him to the statehouse to pay a courtesy call on the governor and possibly attended when Norris spoke briefly before the legislature at noon. Unlike the previous day, many people saw and spoke with him that afternoon. In the evening, long before the auditorium was opened, the street in front was jammed with people. When the doors opened, the hall quickly filled; every seat, including those on the stage, was taken. Policemen then refused to let people enter until the mayor of Lincoln, Charles W. Bryan, appeared and insisted that the doors remain open, whereupon additional chairs were placed in the aisles to accommodate standees outside the hall. At least 3,000 people were present.

At about five minutes of eight Norris left his room at the Lindell Hotel and went across the street to the auditorium. It was a dramatic situation: no band, no music, no announcements, not even a

[22] Norris to Fola LaFollette, Feb. 15, Mar. 13, 1939; to O. G. Villard, Dec. 21, 1927.

[23] Norris to Villard, Dec. 21, 1927.

chairman. The air was vibrant with excitement. Norris walked from one of the wings onto the stage and was met at first with absolute silence. He had no prepared speech, no notes. His opening words were, "I have come to Nebraska to tell you the truth. You have not been able to get the truth from the newspapers." Whereupon pandemonium burst loose. People stood and yelled, "What's the matter with Senator Norris?" And the forceful echo resounded: "He's all right!" Time and again the hall rang with applause, especially when he denounced the Nebraska press for presenting only one side of the controversy. "At times during the speech," the *Nebraska State Journal* reported, "like the old-time Bryan demonstrations in Lincoln, the cheering would die down as if for lack of breath, and then would spring up again more tremendous than before." [24]

His remarks were simple, straightforward, precise, and compelling. Only once was he interrupted by an unfriendly question, and no one jeered or contradicted him. After talking for more than an hour, he gave signs of concluding. But the crowd cried, "Go on, go on," and he yielded to their request. Step by step he soberly defined his position and sought to show how neither he nor those associated with him deserved the opprobrium heaped upon them. But as the evening wore on, he got into the spirit of the occasion, and by the end of it he was standing with clenched fists, defying his enemies "to repeat their charges of treachery." [25]

In the course of his remarks he read a letter from a member of the New York Stock Exchange relating that war was preferable to the uncertainty prevailing at the time and that Japan and Canada, recently neutral, were more prosperous at war than ever before. Then, in terms that must have warmed the hearts of all ex-Populists and Bryan men in the audience, he denounced Wall Street men who "sat behind mahogany desks, coldly calculating the time until war could be declared and every drop of blood

[24] Norris to Fola LaFollette, Feb. 15, 1939; George H. Thomas to John P. Robertson, Mar. 31, 1939. Robertson, who was Norris's secretary, had requested Thomas to write his reminiscences of the meeting. The *Nebraska State Journal,* Mar. 27, 1917, published a comprehensive and fair account of the meeting, despite the fact that Norris denounced it; see also *Omaha Daily Tribune,* Mar. 27, 1917.

[25] *Omaha Daily Tribune, Nebraska State Journal,* Mar. 27, 1917.

spilled in the trench, every tear shed by mothers at home, could be converted into gold for its filthy pockets." And, possibly recalling Bryan's famous 1896 peroration, he admitted that he was proud to stand with that small group of willful men who in effect said to Wall Street: "You shall not coin into gold the life blood of our brothers." [26]

As his remarks became more emotional, Norris revealed an agrarian bias against Wall Street, banks, organized wealth, and high society that brought thunderous applause from his audience. But he always came back to his main point: in opposing the president he was honestly and conscientiously performing his duty as a U.S. senator, representing his own convictions and, judging by the reception he received in the auditorium, those of a good portion of the citizens of Nebraska.

After the meeting members of the audience proceeded to the lobby of the Lindell Hotel to congratulate the speaker. For an hour the place was bedlam. Prominent Nebraskans and old friends assured him of their approval and support of his position. This evening, Norris said, repaid him "for all the turmoil, the agony, and the suffering" that he had endured. His course of action in the last days of the Sixty-fourth Congress was vindicated.[27]

The following morning, Tuesday, March 27, he took the train for Holdrege, where he spoke that evening. A similar speech was delivered in McCook and plans were underway for him to speak in Omaha on Friday of the same week. But by that time Norris was en route to Washington for the convening of the Sixty-fifth Congress on April 2, 1917, to receive from the president "a communication concerning grave matters of national policy." [28]

At 8:30 P.M. on April 2, 1917, in the chamber of the House of Representatives Doorkeeper J. J. Sinnott announced the vice-president of the United States and the members of the U.S. Senate.

[26] *Nebraska State Journal,* Mar. 27, 1917.

[27] Norris to Fola LaFollette, Feb. 15, 1939; Thomas to Robertson, Mar. 31, 1939; Norris to Villard, Dec. 21, 1927.

[28] *Nebraska State Journal, Omaha Daily Tribune,* Mar. 27, 1917. The *Omaha Daily Tribune* was a German-language newspaper edited by Val J. Peter, who provided a translation of the Mar. 27, 1917, story to John Robertson in Apr., 1939. Wilson issued the statement convening Congress on Mar. 21, 1917, while Norris was still in Washington; see Baker, *Woodrow Wilson,* 6: 504.

The members of the House rose as their colleagues from the other end of the Capitol Building filed in. Each man was wearing or carrying a small American flag. The vice-president took the chair to the right of the Speaker and the members of the Senate took seats reserved for them. The Speaker appointed a committee to wait on the president in conjunction with a Senate committee chosen by the vice-president. Each committee contained two men who were opposed to the president's policies: Congressmen Claude Kitchin and Henry Allen Cooper and Senators William J. Stone and George W. Norris. At 8:37 P.M. the president, escorted by the committee of senators and representatives, entered the hall of the House and stood at the Clerk's desk amid prolonged applause. The Speaker presented the president, who launched into his memorable address calling for American participation in the European conflict to make the world safe for democracy. While no observer recorded Norris's reaction to the speech, it must have been similar to LaFollette's, who, amidst the "tumultuous, roaring, deafening applause," was silent, "arms folded high on his chest," "opposition etched in every grim look." [29]

On the morning of April 4 the Senate began debate on the president's request for a declaration of war. Though feeling ran high, it was not as intense as the armed-ship controversy because senators realized the result was a foregone conclusion. No minority would be able to prevent its approval. During the debate Norris later recalled two younger senators confessing their lack of courage to vote against the war resolution. He replied that that was "a little reason. Your people are no different from my people." [30]

Convinced by his trip to Nebraska that voters supported his position, Norris strenuously opposed the war resolution. Other senators, likewise convinced that the American people favored American participation, were strong in their criticism of his position. At the outset Norris made his position clear, explaining, "I am bitterly opposed to my country entering the war, but if, notwithstanding my opposition, we do enter it, all of my energy

[29] *Congressional Record,* 65th Cong., 1st sess., Apr. 2, 1918, p. 118; Baker, *Woodrow Wilson,* 6: 514–15; *New York Times,* Apr. 3, 1917. Norris was not mentioned among the exceptions, i.e., those senators not carrying a flag.

[30] Norris to Fola LaFollette, Feb. 15, 1939.

and all of my power will be behind our flag carrying it on to victory."

Surveying American neutrality, Norris claimed that the government persisted in protesting German violations while submitting to English interference with American neutral rights. He said that if ships were not permitted to sail to the war zones, "the zones would have been of short duration" and concessions then could have been wrested from England and Germany in return for American goods. True neutrality would not have led the nation to the verge of war.

Then, more soberly than in his Lincoln speech, Norris developed the theme that "the great combination of wealth," controlling most channels of communication, had "a direct financial interest" in American participation in the war. He read extracts of a customer letter by a member of the New York Stock Exchange, indicating that America's entry into the war would be a means of increasing their financial returns. This was the same letter he had read in his Lincoln speech. Years later he said he had received the letter from Senator William S. Kenyon of Iowa, who wanted it read but did not have the courage to do so. Actually, however, the letter came to his attention in March, 1917, as the result of a newspaper advertisement signed by Amos Pinchot and other opponents of war. Norris, about to depart for Nebraska to defend his stand on the armed-ship bill, wrote Pinchot and learned that the newsletter was mailed by Callahan and Company, a member of the New York Stock Exchange. It struck Norris "as one of the most cold blooded propositions" he had ever seen and, he informed Pinchot, "the American people should know about it." No longer was the president solely responsible for dragging the nation into war; "men of money and wealth, who want to make more money and wealth for themselves," also played a role.[31]

[31] Norris to Fola LaFollette, Feb. 15, Mar. 13, 1939; to Pinchot, Mar. 12 and 16, 1917 (Box 30, Amos Pinchot Papers); Pinchot to Norris, Mar. 26, 1917 (Box 30, Amos Pinchot Papers). For an interesting discussion of the role of Wall Street in favoring war, see the correspondence between John Moody and Pinchot throughout Mar., 1917, in the Amos Pinchot Papers. Moody argued that Wall Street was not more interested in plunging the country into war than any other sector of the American populace. Pinchot disagreed and cited evidence which Moody said was not indicative of the views of Wall Street leaders. One of the

The consequences of "going into the war upon the command of gold" could mean the loss of innumerable lives and the piling up of a debt "that the toiling masses that shall come many generations after us will have to pay." Reiterating with variations the theme that the nation was plunging into war at the behest of "wealth's terrible mandate," Norris used many of the phrases and made many of the points that were so enthusiastically received in his Lincoln address. The "war craze," he claimed, had robbed people of their common sense and judgment. Then came the oft-quoted remarks: "I wish we might delay our action until reason could again be enthroned in the brain of man. I feel that we are about to put the dollar sign upon the American flag."

Though he rejoiced at the news of the overthrow of the Russian czar and hoped that a similar event might topple the German kaiser, nevertheless, he insisted that "the troubles of Europe ought to be settled by Europe." The United States, no matter what the sympathies of the American people, ought to remain absolutely neutral.

Senators took exception to his remarks about organized wealth plunging the nation into war. James A. Reed of Missouri accused him "of giving aid and comfort to the enemy on the very eve of the opening of hostilities" and virtually of being guilty of treason. Visitors in the crowded galleries applauded these remarks.[32] Atlee Pomerene of Ohio wanted to know how many more American lives would have to be lost before Norris would be willing to recognize the existence of a state of war. Other senators joined the attack. Norris insisted that it was not his intention to criticize any person but that in the current "war craze" men had lost their judgment and the United States was going to war without adequate reason.[33]

---

items Pinchot cited and which was undoubtedly responsible for Norris's bitter remarks in the Senate was the Feb. 17, 1917, newsletter of W. W. Callahan and Company, investment bankers of Baltimore; it stated that "Wall Street believes" war would be preferable to the uncertainty and confusion then prevailing. "Canada and Japan," the newsletter stated, "are at war and are more prosperous than ever before." A copy of this newsletter is in Box 30, Amos Pinchot Papers.

[32] *New York American,* Apr. 5, 1917.

[33] *Congressional Record,* 65th Cong., 1st sess., Apr. 4, 1917, pp. 212–17. Norris's speech and remarks made in response to questions are included in these pages.

The debate continued after Norris took his seat. LaFollette entered the chamber shortly before 4:00 P.M. and began speaking. He spoke for three hours. His remarks aroused even more bitter and hostile criticism than those of Norris. But speeches could not delay the vote on the war resolution. Senate leaders agreed beforehand to neither adjourn nor recess until war had been declared. The decision came after 11:00 P.M. by an 82-to-6 vote. The six senators who voted in the negative had all opposed the armed-ship bill. Their ranks were depleted by the loss of three "lame-duck" members and by the fact that Albert Cummins of Iowa and William F. Kirby of Arkansas supported the war resolution. Three Democrats (Stone, Lane, and James K. Vardaman) and three Republicans (LaFollette, Norris, and Gronna) voted against the war resolution, but their decision was not marked by any outburst from the galleries. The senators on the floor below were unusually grave and quiet; many answered their names in voices that quivered with emotion. When the clerk announced the vote, there was hardly a murmur of applause.[34]

The House of Representatives considered the war resolution the following morning, April 5, and kept at it doggedly until shortly after 3:00 in the morning of April 6 it was approved by a 373-to-50 vote. Later that day Woodrow Wilson signed the joint resolution, and the collapse of neutrality that Norris fought so determinedly to prevent was completed.

The debates on the armed-ship bill and the war resolution forged further the bonds of friendship between Norris and LaFollette. But at the time Norris was concerned about a Democratic opponent of war, Harry Lane of Oregon, whose health had been broken by the tension and criticism heaped upon him. During this period Norris often rode with Lane from his office to his house. Lane was so weak he could hardly walk and both men felt that it was unsafe to ride streetcars for fear of personal injury. Norris spent many evenings with Lane and went with him to Union Station in September, 1917, when Lane tried to return to Oregon to die. Norris had high regard for Lane, his pointed humor, his calm spirit, his lack of fear, and his concern for the poor and the unfortunate. After Lane's death in San Francisco en route to

[34] *Sioux City* (Iowa) *Journal,* Apr. 5, 1917.

Oregon Norris delivered a moving eulogy on the floor of the Senate.[35]

Having done everything he possibly could to keep the nation out of the European conflict, Norris now had no choice but to submit loyally to any sacrifice necessary for final victory. However, as a U.S. senator, he intended to make certain that the concerns of the American people, as opposed to those of special interests, were guarded and that the close of the conflict would bring "the birth of a world-wide and enduring peace." [36]

[35] *Congressional Record,* 65th Cong., 1st sess., Sept. 16, 1917, pp. 7215–16; Norris to Richard Neuberger, Apr. 13, 1935; to Monroe Sweetland, Mar. 28, 1936.

[36] Norris to I. A. Reneau, Apr. 17, 1917; to "My dear Sir," Mar. 16, 1918; to S. W. Lightner, May 4, 1918.

Taking the Profit out of War

5

The United States was at war for twenty months. During this period it put its economy on a wartime basis, mobilized its resources both natural and human, and developed a line of communication literally extending over 3,000 miles. These factors enabled the nation to place an army in the field that played a decisive role in the military collapse of Germany. In these months the role of government noticeably changed from that of an arbiter of the American scene to that of a manager of the national war effort. Necessarily, the power of government, especially the central government, markedly increased.

To a generation familiar with the charge that big business had to be either curtailed or at least regulated, the war period, with its dollar-a-year men, corporation officials, and technical experts in public service, with government allocation of materials and even actual operation of business enterprises, made some readjustment of focus necessary. By 1920, despite the fact that the fraud and corruption so evident during the Civil and Spanish-American wars were nowhere to be found, Americans in droves were ready to return to what Warren G. Harding called normalcy. However, some progressives, Norris among them, saw wartime developments, particularly in the realm of natural resources and public utilities, as a logical continuum of what had occurred earlier and sought to strengthen these trends by removing all vestiges of private profit from them. Others, usually younger men who served in

the Wilson administration or who had been active Bull Moosers
in 1912, learned much from what occurred during these twenty
months that could be utilized in coping with a more serious crisis
over a decade later.

For all concerned with government, these twenty months necessitated new experiments with few precedents available for guidance. It was a time of trial with tension heightened by the overwhelming demands of war. It was equally a time of experiment
challenging the ingenuity of American leaders and administrators
in all fields of endeavor. For those who served in government in
both the executive and legislative branches, the challenge of these
twenty months would demand a creative response with little besides intuition to serve as a guide. While Norris, a severe critic of
Wilsonian diplomacy, necessarily played a minor role, his views
cast light upon aspects of the war effort and revealed much about
progressivism as old and familiar issues underwent a marked
change or completely disappeared.

The first wartime measure the Sixty-fifth Congress considered,
that of conscription, provoked much discussion before the Selec-
tive Service Act was passed at the end of April. Norris thought a
trained army could be raised quickly by volunteers and preferred
this method to a draft, which he regarded as one step toward a
permanent compulsory system. Since the nation was at war, he
did not feel justified in voting against conscription. But he endorsed an amendment stating that it should cease as soon as the
war was over. As long as the conflict raged, Norris wanted the
nation "to exert every influence and every power and strain every
nerve in order that no stone may be unturned to prosecute this
war to the limit, with a view of successful termination." [1]

Early in the war Norris reiterated the position he had espoused
during the 1915 debate on the ship purchase bill that government-
constructed or -operated means of transportation should not be
turned over to private enterprise at the conclusion of the conflict.
In this instance the suggestion was made that government construct freight cars and then turn them over to the railroads to
prevent an increase of freight rates. Norris preferred that the gov-

[1] *Congressional Record,* 65th Cong., 1st sess., Apr. 28, p. 1496, May 1, 1917,
p. 1623.

ernment take over the railroads, "rolling stock, road beds, and all," if it was deemed necessary.[2]

When the president nationalized the railroads in the last week of 1917 and named William G. McAdoo as Director General of the Railroads, Norris was pleased. Legislation authorized the president to make agreements with the railway companies by which the government would pay for the use of railroad properties their average net operating income for the three-year period ending June 30, 1917. Norris regretted the choice of this particular three-year period because railroad traffic during those years was greater than at any other time in the history of the country.

Since the government was required to keep the roads in repair, and since the companies, if not satisfied with the payment received, could challenge this sum in court, Norris feared that the aggregate paid to the railroads was liable to be in excess of amounts derived from government operation. He also objected to a provision allowing the president, rather than the Interstate Commerce Commission, to fix freight rates. Though the commission could modify the president's decision, the process would be time-consuming, costly, and dubious. This provision only added to the burdens of the Chief Executive and bypassed the Interstate Commerce Commission, an agency well equipped and experienced in determining equitable rates. Norris's position was typical of his attitude throughout these twenty months; while the railroads ought to be paid a fair and just compensation and be protected in all their rights, it was equally important that the already overburdened taxpayer be protected from unjust and unfair taxation.[3]

While effective government operation of railroads interested Norris, it was agriculture in its wartime setting that, as a member of the Agriculture and Forestry Committee, most concerned him. Though Herbert Hoover was not appointed U.S. Food Administrator until August, 1917, at the request of the president he returned to the United States in May and began preparatory work as a voluntary food commissioner. In June, at the request of the National Farmers' Cooperative Association, Norris asked questions of Hoover pertaining to the competition between farmer-

[2] *Ibid.*, May 19, 1917, pp. 2585–86.
[3] *Ibid.*, 2nd sess., Feb. 19, 1918, pp. 2317–19.

owned-and-operated grain elevators and large, privately owned plants and to what the role of government would be. Hoover assured him that the U.S. Food Commissioner did not anticipate operating any grain elevator, packing house, or flour mill. Rather, he felt his job would be to regulate "so as to excise as much as possible wasteful practices, exorbitant profits, and vicious speculation." [4]

All that Norris saw and heard of Hoover impressed him. During the discussion of the bill creating the U.S. Food Administration, wherein it became evident that many senators were not as impressed as he, Norris went out of his way to praise Hoover.

> I think anyone who has come in contact with Mr. Hoover as he has appeared before the committees and at other times before the public or who has been brought in contact with him in any other way must be impressed not only with the man's ability but with his honesty; and I am induced to support some of the provisions of this bill which under ordinary circumstances I would not vote for by the fact that I understand Mr. Hoover is going to be appointed to carry them out. I do not believe there is a better equipped man in the world for that place than Mr. Hoover. I am satisfied. [5]

At the outset of the debate Norris insisted that wasting food in the manufacture of beer was sinful. If the millions of bushels of barley, corn, and rice used every year in its manufacture were diverted to meeting the food shortage, the war effort could be aided. As a sacrifice it was trivial. Only the liquor interests seriously opposed it, though the president felt that inclusion of provisions affecting the manufacture of beer and wine would delay the passage of the food control bill. At his request, however, the committee included clauses allowing the president to change the alcoholic content of beer and to prohibit the use of foodstuffs in its manufacture whenever he saw fit. These items remained in the bill which the president signed on August 10, 1917. [6]

[4] George W. Norris to Herbert Hoover, June 22, 1917; Hoover to Norris, June 29, 1917 (both letters are to be found in *ibid.,* 1st sess., July 12, 1917, p. 5015).

[5] *Ibid.,* July 12, 1917, p. 5008. Despite these remarks Norris admitted under questioning that Hoover was not an outstanding authority on agriculture. He did feel that Hoover would "sincerely protect the farmers of the country" (*ibid.*).

[6] *Ibid.,* July 6, 1917, pp. 4571, 4573; 2nd sess., Aug. 29, 1918, p. 9644.

Several months later Norris observed that the president had not yet exercised this authority. Finally, the Senate Agriculture and Forestry Committee in June, 1918, reinserted the clause prohibiting the use of foods and cereals in the manufacture of intoxicating liquors in a bill coming to it from the House. Though the bill was considered an emergency measure, lengthy hearings and long debate occurred as soon as the prohibitory amendment was added. Norris noted that the liquor interests and their allies were hard at work opposing it; bankers complained that large amounts of money were lent upon whiskey in bond and that if Congress prohibited its sale and insisted that whiskey be taken out of bond, serious financial repercussions would follow. But Norris was assured by the Comptroller of the Currency that while the legislation would tie up some funds, no serious financial difficulty would occur. Whereupon, after mentioning the sacrifices other Americans were making, he asked, "Is it too much to say that the men who have their money invested in whiskey and in breweries must also do their part, even though it may discommode them somewhat in a financial way?" Though the provision again failed to pass, taxation of liquor soon yielded a considerable income. Throughout the debate Norris insisted upon prohibition as a wartime emergency measure and not as a moral issue.[7]

The food control bill was designed to increase production and to control distribution. Its framers also wished to give sufficient reward to the producer and to prevent the consumer from paying exorbitant prices. Norris realized that these aims, necessitated by wartime demands, would repeal "the old law of supply and demand" and would require greater governmental supervision of agriculture than ordinarily would meet with his approval. Once farm prices were fixed, then the government was obligated to consider the interest of the consumer by denying middlemen large and unreasonable profits and by trying to keep the cost of living in check. He insisted that government fix only a minimum price for foodstuffs and take into consideration "the cost of the things that the farmer has to buy." To subject the farmer to control over his product and at the same time allow him to pay exorbitant

[7] *Ibid.*, 2nd sess., Mar. 18, p. 3693, Aug. 29, 1918, pp. 9644–46; *New York Times,* June 19, 1918.

prices for what he had to buy would be a great injustice and a source of grievance.[8]

Possibly taking into account these criticisms, Senate leaders on July 20 introduced a proposition to fix commodity prices. It called for a minimum price of $2.00 a bushel for wheat, which was already commanding $2.50 to $2.60 a bushel. By firmly fixing a minimum price for an entire year, wheat would be dumped on the market as soon as possible, taxing distributing facilities to the utmost. Far better, Norris argued, for a board to investigate and arrive at figures more satisfactory than those so hastily presented to the Senate. The final version of the bill, taking no cognizance of these criticisms, gave the president authority to fix the price of wheat for 1918 and subsequent war years. Congress fixed the minimum price only for the crop that was planted in 1917. Though not satisfied with the price-fixing provisions, Norris voted for the bill as a necessary war measure.[9]

As it turned out, by 1918 the Food Administration, without any statute specifically saying that it had the power, fixed the price of wheat below "what it would have been if the law of supply and demand had run its regular course." Since this agency purchased wheat for the armed forces of the United States and its allies and for people in allied and neutral countries, and since it had the power to license millers and grain elevators, it had the power, indirectly but effectively, to fix the price. While he did not like this development, Norris was concerned lest the minimum price of $2.00 per bushel become the maximum price as well. He said that every farmer who planted wheat in 1917 literally donated $1.00 to the Treasury for every bushel he owned, since wheat was selling at the time for about $3.00 a bushel on the open market. It was unfair because the price of everything farmers had to buy went "soaring to the skies." Furthermore, for the sake of getting a lower price of wheat for the Allies, the price of corn, barley, rye, oatmeal, rice, and every other article of food—except wheat

---

[8] *Congressional Record,* 65th Cong., 1st sess., July 12, pp. 5004–6, 5014, July 19, 1917, pp. 5267–68.

[9] *Ibid.,* July 21, pp. 5347–48, Aug. 6, p. 5836, Aug. 8, 1917, p. 5927; 2nd sess., Mar. 18, 1918, p. 3691.

—increased. None of these items were price-fixed. The American farmer, performing his patriotic duty, was producing wheat at a lower profit than if the same soil were used for another crop. Such a situation, Norris said, was "unfair, unjust, and ought not to be required." [10]

Norris was convinced by 1918 that price-fixing was not necessary for most crops. However, since the 1917 price of wheat had been set at $2.00 per bushel, he felt that Congress ought to make it $2.50 in 1918 to provide some justice for the producer and to insure more wheat for the war effort. Some farmers were already finding it more profitable to feed wheat to hogs because corn commanded a better price. Thus, Norris was forced to conclude, the U.S. Food Administration actually retarded production, heaped injustice upon both producer and consumer, and was not allowing food to play its maximum role in winning the war.[11]

Later in the year the Senate actually fixed the minimum price for the 1918 wheat crop at $2.50 per bushel, but the House conferees, all from cotton-producing states, refused to accept it, thereby provoking further comment from Norris. He noted that the machinery necessary to produce wheat had increased in price anywhere from 25 to 200 percent, thereby insuring that wheat would be produced at a loss compared to nonprice-fixed crops. The more Norris examined the food problem, particularly as it affected Nebraska farmers, the more convinced he became of its importance to the war effort and the more disheartened he was with the injustice accorded farmers who, because of their patriotism, continued to produce wheat. Incidentally, his high regard for Herbert Hoover, who claimed he did not want to fix the price of wheat but only wanted to guarantee the farmer against loss, also underwent a change.[12]

Other wartime agricultural matters also came to Norris's attention. Once he appeared on the Senate floor with samples of dehydrated corn, parsnips, potatoes, and onions. All but the onions

[10] *Ibid.*, 2nd sess., Mar. 18, pp. 3691–92, Mar. 19, p. 3694, July 1, 1918, p. 8547; 3rd sess., Feb. 27, 1919, p. 4442.

[11] *Ibid.*, 2nd sess., Mar. 19, 1918, pp. 3694–95.

[12] *Ibid.*, July 1, 1918, pp. 8546–47, 8552; Norris to James C. Clark, Mar. 22, 1918; to C. F. Graff, July 24, 1924.

had been subjected to the culinary abilities of Mrs. Norris. The proud husband informed his colleagues that "I have never tasted canned corn in my life that I thought equaled in flavor this dried corn." Norris wished to illustrate that by dehydrating vegetables and fruits space could be saved and expenses cut in preparing, packaging, and transporting produce without impairing quality. If the government would construct dehydration plants for the purpose of supplying food to the armed forces, enormous savings could be made and a severe shortage of freight cars would quickly be ameliorated.[13]

But by 1918 Norris's interest in agricultural matters came to center on the meat packers and their profitable wartime activities. Claiming that stockyards were public marketplaces "which ought to be open on equal terms to everybody," Norris noted that they were owned by packers who derived immense revenues from them and made all rules and regulations concerning their use. Cattlemen had no choice but to accept their terms and prices. Norris said that stockyards "ought to be publicly owned, publicly controlled, publicly managed, the same as any other market place, for the benefit of the public, without the view of producing a profit to anybody." [14]

In the summer of 1918 the Senate Agriculture and Forestry Committee listened to testimony showing that farmers and feeders were selling their livestock to the packers at a financial loss. At the other end of the scale the consumer was "paying an outrageous and exorbitant price for the finished product." Through their ownership of stockyards the packers were utilizing this situation to their great advantage. The idea of a marketplace controlled by corporations, Norris felt, involved manipulation that should not be tolerated in a free society. He favored government ownership of stockyards; Nebraska livestock men endorsed his position and, incidentally, his campaign for re-election. While the problem of stockyards at packing centers was not resolved until the Harding administration, it arose during the war period. Norris demanded a

[13] *Congressional Record,* 65th Cong., 2nd sess., Mar. 13, 1918, pp. 3428, 3430.

[14] *Ibid.,* Mar. 19, p. 3699, Sept. 6, 1918, pp. 1072–73.

strong bill, but neither the Wilson nor the Harding administration was willing to consider his views.[15]

Though agriculture was Norris's primary area of legislative involvement, his abiding interest in efficiency and economy was evident as he strove to prohibit profiteering, to curb the cost of living, and, in general, to take the profit out of war and to provide powerful penalties for violators. He opposed wartime construction of permanent buildings in Washington because of inflated prices and material shortages. Unless men at the head of government were willing to economize in wartime, Norris insisted, they could not in good faith ask the American people to do the same.[16]

On the other hand, false economy did not appeal to Norris. He opposed an amendment to an agricultural appropriation bill forbidding employment of men at salaries over $2,500, arguing that the "Agricultural Department ought to have . . . some of the best scientists in the world." Similarly, he fought cuts in appropriations for the Federal Trade and Tariff commissions. Mentioning the Federal Trade Commission's investigation of the meat packers, Norris said that cutting appropriations would camouflage the fact that opponents sought to prevent its functioning as a regulatory agency.[17]

But it was in the area of taxation that Norris made his most vigorous fight to take the profit out of war. He insisted on the premise that an individual with a large income pay a heavier tax than if he had the same income either before the war or after it. He preferred to increase existing tax rates rather than seek new sources of revenue—thus his demand for an increased inheritance tax. It would be easy to administer: no additional expense and no new governmental "machinery" for its collection would be necessary.[18] On the other hand, Norris opposed equalizing charges

[15] Norris to Benjamin C. Marsh, Sept. 6, 1918; Robert Graham to Norris, June 12, 1918; Edward L. Burke to William Kent, June 14, 1918 (the last two items are in the William Kent Papers, Yale University Library).

[16] *Congressional Record,* 65th Cong., 1st sess., Aug. 2, 1917, pp. 5708, 5718–19.

[17] *Ibid.,* 66th Cong., 1st sess., June 26, p. 1820, June 27, pp. 1870, 1872, June 28, 1919, pp. 1959–60.

[18] *Ibid.,* 65th Cong., 1st sess., Aug. 17, 1917, pp. 6130–31.

between express companies and the parcel post and imposing a tax on parcel post packages. Reviewing his previous experience, he observed that government created the parcel post to regulate the express business, which sought only profit and did not service many rural areas. And he also opposed levying a tax on letters because it would harass business. Though it came to only a penny, it was not the only penny tax Congress was considering in the summer of 1917:

> The people will not only pay a tax every time they put a three cent postage stamp on a letter, but they will pay a tax every time they send a parcel post package; they will pay another tax every time they send an express package; they will pay more taxes every time they drink a cup of coffee or a cup of tea or a cup of cocoa; they will pay a tax every time they eat something which contains sugar—all small, all pennies, but in the aggregate amounting to many million dollars.[19]

These nuisance taxes would help make the war unpopular because taxpayers would realize that millions of dollars in profits and incomes were escaping their fair share of taxation. And millions of Americans, beginning to feel the pinch of the mounting cost of living, would resent adding a penny to numerous items. Norris did not think the time had come for such taxes.[20]

In accord with his proposition of taxing income and profits before considering use and consumption taxes, Norris, along with Hiram Johnson, Robert M. LaFollette, and William E. Borah, supported an amendment to the war revenue bill providing a flat rate of 73 percent of excess profits. Though it was defeated, a tax graduated to a maximum of 60 percent on all earnings above the average profits for the years 1911 to 1913 was enacted.[21]

During the debate Norris delineated his views: "Modern warfare has increased the burdens of taxation, and we are confronted today with a necessity of raising more money than was ever before demanded of any people on earth." Yet there were only two

[19] *Ibid.,* Aug. 18, pp. 6153–54, Aug. 27, 1917, p. 6375.

[20] *Ibid.,* Aug. 27, p. 6375, Aug. 28, 1917, pp. 6401–2.

[21] Elting E. Morison, ed., *The Letters of Theodore Roosevelt,* 8 (Cambridge, Mass., 1954): 1228, note 1. Incidentally, Theodore Roosevelt favored an excess profits tax with a maximum of 80 percent as in Great Britain.

sound ways in which this money could be raised: by the issuance of bonds or by increased taxation. Issuing bonds would saddle oncoming generations. Thus, if wartime expenditures were met by taxation, money, like men, could be conscripted and the cost of the war would be met by the generation that fought it. Since taxation was basic, it followed that it ought to interfere as little as possible with the transaction of legitimate business and ought to avoid as long as possible items of consumption. Therefore, said Norris, "if you do not want to interfere with business, and if you do not want to create hardship and dissatisfaction among our people, we must take the taxes from such sources as will not tend to increase the cost of living or create a hardship upon those who have to pay them." A graduated income tax would prove most satisfactory to the patriotic citizen. It would leave him enough money from his income to support himself and his family in a proper and comfortable way.

Thus he introduced an amendment seeking to increase the tax on incomes by a sliding scale. Incomes of $5,000 or less would be exempt. Taxation would increase at different rates beyond this level until it reached 50 percent upon a net income in excess of $1 million. The only objection Norris could foresee was that the rates on large incomes were not heavy enough. While the nation was asking young men to sacrifice their lives, he saw nothing wrong in conscripting the excess of all incomes over $5,000. If it was logical to conscript American youth, why was it not equally logical to conscript American incomes and bring about equality in the distribution of the financial burden? [22]

On the other hand, the war revenue measure proposed to tax food, medicine, and other items necessary to daily life. If adopted, an undue burden would be placed upon those least able to pay. Without Norris's amendment the possessors of war-swollen profits, incomes, and luxuries would escape equitable heavy taxation. But valiant and vigorous though he was in presenting, expounding, and defending his amendment, it was soundly defeated by a 55-to-19 vote. Thereafter, he noticed that "vicious stories" filled with misrepresentations found their way into many large daily news-

[22] *Congressional Record,* 65th Cong., 1st sess., Sept. 6, 1917, pp. 6659–62 (the quote is on p. 6660).

papers. Behind these stories Norris saw the influence of "big business," which opposed his attempt to place a more substantial portion of the financial burden of war upon its profits and surplus income.[23]

In the fight for a more equitable system of taxation a handful of senators, chiefly from the South and West, fought hard and were defeated. Though the 1917 law raised more money by taxation than in any previous war, opponents of the measure were dejected because they had attempted to conscript wealth as well as men. In expressing their sentiments, they came under severe attack and as a result felt some concern for civil liberties in wartime. Should not individuals, consonant with the dictates of a free society, express their convictions even if contrary to the views of the majority? Norris, in particular, with his experience in opposing America's entrance into the war, was concerned about the maintenance of civil liberties.

The Espionage Act of June, 1917, the first major wartime law attempting to curb civil liberties, contained many provisions that he opposed. When men were afraid or were not allowed to speak, Norris said, "our boasted freedom" would disappear "and our great Republic will be in serious danger of degenerating into autocracy." He insisted that no limitation be placed upon the right of any citizen "to voice his honest protest to anything that he considers wrong and is prepared to prove is so." [24]

Norris also protested the power given the Postmaster General to exclude magazines and newspapers from the mails. Though he voted against the Espionage Act, it at least provided for a jury trial to determine whether or not an individual was guilty. How-

[23] *Ibid.,* Sept. 7, 1917, p. 6727; Norris to S. W. Lightner, May 4, 1918; to Amos Pinchot, Sept. 18, 1917 (Box 29, Amos Pinchot Papers, Manuscript Division, Library of Congress). Incidentally, Norris was one of four dissenters to vote against the war revenue measure when it passed the Senate on Sept. 10, 1917. For a discussion of this measure, see Sidney Ratner, *American Taxation* (New York, 1942), pp. 373–83. Ratner says that the 1917 War Revenue Act was "proof of the progress in fiscal justice and democracy by the pre–World War I generation."

[24] *Congressional Record,* 65th Cong., 2nd sess., May 3, 1918, p. 5980; *Akron Journal,* May 22, 1918; Norris to Edward K. West, Apr. 29, 1922; to J. M. Leyda, Dec. 21, 1921.

ever, by provisions of the Trading with the Enemy Act the Post-master General could prevent a publisher from engaging in his business without being guilty of any specific crime against the United States. A newspaper or a periodical might be bankrupted before the publisher or editor could defend himself. Whenever an executive officer secured the power to decide in advance, a blow was struck at the liberties of the people. Contrary to the First Amendment, Norris said it represented a clear violation of the principles of a free press and free speech.[25]

Shortly after uttering these remarks, Norris spent several hours with a southern editor summoned to Washington by Post Office Department officials. He was asked to show cause why his paper's second-class mailing privileges should not be removed. No charges and no specific article had been mentioned. After reading "a large number" of issues, Norris concluded that criticism was always couched in fair language "and that no man could have any just cause for complaint, except to disagree with the arguments that he had made." Yet the editor was denounced for calling for the defeat of those members of Congress who had favored the declaration of war. To Norris this was tantamount to censorship, indicating that the Post Office Department would suppress newspapers that opposed administration policies while editors criticizing opponents of the administration could do so without fear of censorship or loss of mailing privileges.[26]

Then, almost a year after the enactment of the Espionage Act, the Sedition Act, a more severe curtailment of civil liberties, was signed into law. Norris strongly attacked its censorship clause, claiming that the power granted the Postmaster General to withhold mail was too great to give to any official. If the use of the mails were denied to people found guilty of a crime under the Espionage Act, Norris would have had little objection. They would be punished after being found guilty. The danger came from the fact that under the Sedition Act the Postmaster General, in secret, without notice, without any trial or charge, could issue

[25] *Congressional Record,* 65th Cong., 1st sess., Sept. 24, 1917, pp. 7340–42, 7346; *New York Times,* Sept. 25, 1917.

[26] Norris to H. H. Harrington, Oct. 8, 1917.

an order depriving "some individual from getting letters or papers or anything else . . . through the mails." A judgment that was final, from which there could be no appeal, could cause a person to be ostracized or driven out of business without knowledge of what crime he had committed or what law he had violated.

Norris did not object to giving the Postmaster General more authority if it was necessary to the war effort. He did object to granting him power that had nothing "more to do with the winning of the war than the flowers that bloom in the springtime." Even if the Postmaster General never used the arbitrary power at his disposal, Norris insisted that its very existence was "the great evil" and was certain to bring coercion. No good could come from any law that confided "in one man a greater power over all the people of the United States than has ever been possessed by any court in Christendom from the Supreme Court down to a justice of the peace." And Albert Sidney Burleson, the Postmaster General, did not inspire confidence that basic liberties would be respected in wartime. Indeed, Norris charged that Burleson previously had tampered with the Civil Service Commission to make political appointments to postmasterships.[27]

Earlier Norris stood by LaFollette when his expulsion from the Senate was demanded because of a September, 1917, speech the Wisconsin senator gave in St. Paul before the annual convention of the Nonpartisan League. LaFollette had critically discussed the war and the events leading to American participation. To deny a citizen the right to discuss the causes of war and to deduce that the declaration should not have been made constituted an unwarranted attack on free speech and free press, something more dangerous than the war itself:

> No person has a right to advise his fellow citizens to disobey any law of the land, but he has a right to complain of existing law, and to advocate its repeal or change. If he is wrong in his assertion, the best way it seems to me, is to give the fullest consideration, relying on the common sense and sound judgment of the people to reach the right conclusion. Any other course tends to put suspicion in the foreground and cause many of our people

[27] *Congressional Record*, 65th Cong., 2nd sess., May 3, 1918, pp. 5978–80; *New York Times*, May 4, 1918, Sept. 25, 1919.

to doubt the wisdom of our course, because they will claim we are afraid to submit our arguments to public discussion and public test.[28]

Though the expulsion movement was dropped, Norris was shocked to learn that two liberal senators, Republican William S. Kenyon of Iowa and Democrat Henry F. Hollis of New Hampshire, favored LaFollette's expulsion.[29]

The final theme of Norris's legislative experience in wartime, the high cost of living, was related to his overall consideration of taking the profit out of war. While threats to civil liberties affected him indirectly, the high cost of living was a fact he and his family had to cope with every day. Realizing that increases in the cost of living had the effect of reducing the income of people living on fixed salaries, Norris thought the government should increase the pay of all federal employees, particularly those on the lower levels.[30] Increased expenses, combined with wartime shortages, meant deprivation and suffering for citizens with fixed moderate incomes. In Washington, D.C., a fuel shortage developed and a water famine was threatening, owing to the great increase in population. Congestion and overcrowding posed problems in housing and transportation and provided a serious health menace. In December, 1918, Norris reported a conversation with a clerk who watched seven or eight streetcars go by before she was able to board one to go to work. In wet and cold weather the lot of such "strap-hangers" posed a problem that seemed to bother few officials. Norris was so perplexed that he considered moving his family back to Nebraska.[31]

In his own family circle the high cost of living also took its toll. Since both Hazel and Marian worked for the government and Gertrude was going to school, Mrs. Norris did all the housework with what help the girls could give her. Norris helped by running the washing machine, at times into the early morning

[28] Norris to Harrington, Oct. 8, 1917.

[29] Norris to Fola LaFollette, Feb. 15, Mar. 13, 1939.

[30] *Congressional Record,* 64th Cong., 2nd sess., Feb. 21, 1917, pp. 3745–47; 65th Cong., 1st sess., Aug. 27, 1917, p. 6376; 2nd sess., May 15, 1918, pp. 6540–41; 66th Cong., 1st sess., June 26, 1919, p. 1820.

[31] *Ibid.,* 65th Cong., 2nd sess., Dec. 14, 1917, p. 279; 3rd sess., Dec. 12, 1918, pp. 355–56; Norris to I. N. Leonard, Sept. 28, 1918.

hours. Entertainment expenditures almost disappeared and the few forays into Washington society that the Norrises made ended during the war years. Feeding and clothing his family and contributing to a few charities took "practically every cent" of his salary, requiring a stricter economy than the family usually practiced.[32]

Norris complained that he lived on corn bread and other wheat substitutes. For several years after the war the sight of corn bread almost gave him "hysterics." He quit smoking cigars and purchased a corncob pipe to curb his personal expenses. Contributions to charity and subscriptions to periodicals were curtailed, and he canceled at least one of his insurance policies. Though he could not afford a servant, his home in Washington became a headquarters for Nebraskans doing war work. Mrs. Norris met many of them at the train and saw to it that they were suitably placed "in a respectable boarding house." Oftentimes girls stayed with the family for several days and once a week Mrs. Norris met with Nebraska girls in the living room. She also arranged parties for Nebraska soldiers and gave her time and talents to this kind of work in addition to her family responsibilities.[33] During the war years Norris was able to make ends meet only by dipping into his savings. Yet, like millions of other patriotic Americans, he extended himself to aid the war effort. He subscribed $1,000 to the Fourth Liberty Loan and exhorted others to do the same and to support the YMCA and the Red Cross. In May, 1918, he told an audience in Akron, Ohio, why the Red Cross was worthy of support. And in July he sought service in the armed forces of the United States.[34]

Since Marine Corps officials had authority to waive the age requirement with regard to enlistment, Norris wrote the com-

[32] Norris to Leonard, Sept. 28, 1918; to Harrington, Jan. 25, 1917; to R. E. Moore, June 17, 1918 (R. E. Moore Papers, Nebraska Historical Society).

[33] Norris to C. A. Lord, Mar. 18, 1924; to Vernon F. Lohr, Aug. 11, 1919; to "Dear Boys," Mar. 25, 1920; to C. G. Hoag, May 13, 1922; to E. C. Kelso, Mar. 9, 1922.

[34] Norris to Moore, June 17, 1918 (Moore Papers); to Lord, Mar. 18, 1924; *Akron Times, Akron Beacon Journal,* May 22, 1918. The information about his contribution to the Fourth Liberty Loan was obtained from a statement pertaining to his Beaver City properties during the war years in the Norris Papers.

mandant of the corps, Major General George Barnett, inquiring if a fifty-seven-year-old man able to pass a physical examination would be accepted for service. General Barnett was willing to waive the age limit but he could not offer any assurance that Norris would serve in France. Norris was unwilling to enlist unless he would be sent to France. Thus, instead of entering military service, Norris had to prepare for an arduous campaign for re-election. Later he sought overseas service with the YMCA. At the end of the war he requested the chief of the War Personnel Board of the YMCA to withdraw his application; thereafter, except for a brief trip to Panama in 1919, never again did he manifest a desire to travel beyond the confines of the United States.[35]

That Norris sought overseas service in the Marine Corps and with the YMCA because he feared defeat in 1918 is clear from available evidence. A friend who saw him in Washington during the summer reported, "He needs a lot of encouragement, as he has had the nerve pretty well battered out of him." [36] It is equally clear that Norris felt called upon to justify his patriotism because of his opposition to American entrance into World War I. Nothing in his record during the conflict indicated opposition to the war effort. While he preferred to be with the president in support of his legislative program, he voted for or against laws according to his best judgment. Always the theme of taking the profit out of war was uppermost in his conscience. Although his legislative record was singularly constructive, in the public mind he was known as an opponent of war. While many Nebraska citizens had agreed with him in his opposition to American participation, he was impressed with the fact that he would have to justify his actions and record in Congress to his constituents in the coming campaign. This time it would be done in an atmosphere permeated by wartime tensions and heightened partisanship.[37]

[35] Norris to George Barnett, July 24 and 26, 1918; to C. P. Davis, Nov. 14, 1918. For Norris's Panama trip, see Norris to manager, Tivoli Hotel, Mar. 17, 1919; to Katherine F. Worley, May 8, 1920. In the latter letter he admitted that while in Panama he had gone down in a submarine but had no desire to repeat the experience.

[36] Kent to Burke, Aug. 30, 1918 (Kent Papers); Norris to Frank Hitchcock, May 7, 1917. In this letter Norris remarked, "I soon may be looking for a job on a farm, or attempting to renew my acquaintance with my law books."

[37] Norris to Lord, Mar. 18, 1924.

The 1918 Campaign

6

The 1918 campaign was a difficult one for incumbents seeking re-election. For one thing, Congress remained in session throughout the entire period, not adjourning until late in November. For another, the war was still being fought in Europe. Though Germany showed signs of capitulating, an armistice was not achieved until after the election. Thus these candidates had to spend more time in Washington than they wished; in leaving their congressional desks they were vulnerable to the charge of neglecting their patriotic duty at a critical time. Conscientious candidates or those from safe districts resolved this dilemma by continual campaigning from their Washington offices through correspondence, interviews, press releases, and similar devices, departing for the hinterlands as late in October as they dared.

For George W. Norris the 1918 campaign was more difficult. Besides the handicaps affecting all incumbents seeking re-election, he had to bear more serious burdens. His role in opposing America's entrance into the war, despite his support of the war effort, would be denounced on the hustings. He could expect to be called "pro-German" and an obstructionist against the successful conduct of the war. With a capable staff he could have responded quickly to these charges. But until well into the campaign he lacked a competent staff and was unable to present his case adequately. He was discouraged and sought ways of withdrawing his candidacy without openly conceding that he feared defeat. But as circumstances changed, he looked forward to the campaign.

By the end of 1917, once it was known that Norris intended to stand for re-election, several Republicans announced their intention of challenging him. Ross Hammond, a Fremont newspaper publisher, and Congressman Charles H. Sloan indicated an interest. Sloan's entrance muddied Republican political waters, since Sloan, like Norris, opposed administration measures in the crisis leading to the break with Germany. Sloan's candidacy prevented the primary from being one between a pro-war candidate, Hammond, and Norris. It actually enhanced Norris's chances, since the opposition had no unifying issue unless it wished to stress regularity and conservatism against his independence and liberalism. But to Republicans who desired Norris's defeat because of his opposition to war, Sloan hardly commended himself as a logical alternative. Eventually, two other candidates entered the primary race, further compounding the confusion and further enhancing Norris's chances.[1]

Tied down with legislative duties in Washington, Norris had little time to consider these implications. He knew his "war record" would be attacked and he sought to justify it. By March he was writing to constituents:

> While the War Resolution was pending in the Senate, and when it was the duty of every member of Congress to lay bare his heart, I argued my convictions with as much logic as I am given to command, and as a lawyer would argue a case in which he had confidence, to the Supreme Court of the United States. I was speaking before the final verdict had been rendered, and presented facts and arguments that I would not advance after the declaration of war, for fear they might retard enthusiasm and interfere with vigorous prosecution of the contest. When the final verdict was rendered and war was declared by the duly constituted authority, it became my war and it is now my war as much as it is the war of our General Staff.[2]

[1] *Omaha World-Herald*, Jan. 3, 1918; A. E. Sheldon, *Nebraska: The Land and the People*, 1 (Chicago, 1931): 952. A different version of this chapter, originally delivered as a paper at the Fifth Annual Conference of the Western Historical Association at Helena, Mont., in Oct., 1965, appeared in *Pacific Northwest Quarterly*, 57, no. 3 (July, 1966): 113–19.

[2] George W. Norris to "My Dear Sir," Mar. 16, 1918.

Norris then shifted ground and assumed the offensive. He insisted that the most important task confronting the American people was the energetic prosecution of the war to achieve permanent peace based on an Allied victory.[3]

At the outset, however, Norris received a setback that almost ended his political career. His capable secretary since 1905, Ray McCarl, suddenly resigned in the spring of 1918 to work for Senator Simeon Fess, chairman of the Republican Congressional Campaign Committee. Apparently convinced that defeat was inevitable, McCarl sought to salvage something for himself by leaving Norris at a critical juncture in his career.[4] The man Norris had assumed would be his campaign manager "had gone over to the enemy." Years later he still insisted that "it was a case of ingratitude . . . greater than any I have ever met in my life." Reflecting further, Norris added, "This period of my life was the darkest hour I have ever experienced in my public life." By the spring of 1918 opposition to war had cost him the services of his secretary and seemingly was about to cost him his career.[5]

In July, with the primaries only a few weeks away, Norris was discouraged and fearful of defeat. Seeking a means of escape, a way of withdrawing without openly conceding failure, he considered overseas service in the Marine Corps. Shortly before the November election he applied for overseas service with the YMCA. But as a popular World War I song noted, "Every dark cloud has a silver lining"; in Norris's case help came from an unexpected quarter. It is to be doubted that he ever was fully aware of all the aid he received in 1918 from William Kent, a member of the U.S. Tariff Commission and a former congressman from California.

A progressive Republican of independent means, Kent admired Norris's stand "in all the great policies of conservation and de-

---

[3] *Ibid.* There are also two statements by Norris addressed "To the People of Nebraska," n.d., that apply to the primary campaign.

[4] Norris to James E. Lawrence, June 4, 1935; to Lucien B. Fuller, Aug. 8, 1942. McCarl in 1921 became the first Comptroller General of the United States, recommended to Warren G. Harding for the job by Senator Fess and other stalwart Republicans. In 1920, as in 1918, McCarl served as executive secretary to the Republican Congressional Campaign Committee.

[5] Norris to Lawrence, June 4, 1935.

mocratization of our national resources and our national industries." Associated in the lumber, livestock, and grain businesses
for thirty years in Omaha, largely as a silent partner, Kent had
many connections throughout Nebraska. In early June he wrote
Joseph Polcar, editor of the *Omaha Daily News* and a former
LaFollette supporter, that "men like Norris are infinitely necessary at this juncture if we are going to pursue constructive policies and are going to maintain our liberties against prejudice and
passion." With Polcar's support, Kent realized, one large daily
newspaper at least would present the record of Norris's great services in "translating the ideals of democracy into terms of accomplishment." [6]

Kent wrote Norris of his interest in his re-election and thereafter forwarded information about the political climate in Nebraska.
His Omaha business associate, E. L. Burke, traveled constantly
throughout the state preaching Norris's virtues and sounding
out political sentiment. Kent committed himself in a financial
way by helping to organize the Norris League, which prepared
and distributed campaign literature.[7]

Late in July the Republican state convention, meeting in Lincoln, affirmed its loyalty to and support of the war effort. Norris
sent the delegates a message in which he mentioned his opposition
to entering the war and stressed his voting record. But, unlike
previous statements, it focused principally on problems of agriculture and related issues: transportation, irrigation, and prohibition. Concentrating on these issues, Norris struck a responsive
chord with many Nebraska voters. Hereafter his campaign would
stress his wartime fight to aid agriculture, to tax heavily war-
induced wealth, and to curb organized profiteers. Later in the
campaign he interjected foreign policy remarks, insisting that he
stood for a vigorous prosecution of the war in order to secure a
permanent peace.[8]

[6] William Kent to Joseph Polcar, June 5, 1918 (William Kent Papers, Yale
University Library). Kent's interests in the livestock, lumber, and grain businesses
and the packing industry were inherited from his father, who started and expanded them from a base in Chicago.

[7] Kent to Norris, June 17, 1918; draft of 1918 newspaper advertisement about
the Norris League (Kent Papers).

[8] Final draft of convention speech, 1918; Sheldon, *Nebraska*, 1: 952; A. F.

The state primary was held August 20, 1918. On the Republican ballot for U.S. senator were four candidates opposing Norris. Voter inability to unite upon a single opponent allowed Norris to win an impressive victory. He received 23,715 votes to 17,070 for Sloan and 16,948 for Hammond. The other two Republican candidates received less than 5,000 votes apiece. Norris realized that the combined votes for Sloan and Hammond would have defeated him, while the votes for his Democratic opponent, former Governor John H. Morehead, almost exceeded the total vote for the four defeated Republican senatorial contestants. Thus, despite his primary victory, Norris still had reason to fear that his opposition to war would be a potent issue in the coming campaign.[9]

Moreover, at the end of August Norris had neither a campaign manager nor any hope that Congress would adjourn before election day. In Washington, depressed, isolated, and not fully in touch with the Nebraska political situation, Norris needed help if he was to win re-election in November. At this juncture William Kent started to work in earnest, though largely behind the scenes. He provided funds for an impressive campaign broadside which carried supporting statements from prominent political, labor, and farm leaders. Statements by Norris in this broadside and those that appeared in bulletins of the Norris League were reprinted from a series originally published, owing to the efforts of William Kent, in the *Omaha Daily News*.[10]

Immediately after Norris's primary victory Kent wrote Woodrow Wilson requesting that the administration refrain from taking

---

Mullen to J. P. Tumulty, Oct. 24, 1918 (Woodrow Wilson Papers, Manuscript Division, Library of Congress). Mullen's telegram reveals how foreign policy was being used in Norris's campaign.

[9] The primary results are listed in Sheldon, *Nebraska*, 1: 953–54. In an interesting postmortem on the primary Ross L. Hammond delineated efforts made on the part of Republican leaders, including Nebraska National Committeeman Robert B. Howell and National Committee chairman Will H. Hays, to secure a single opponent and a consolidated vote against Norris. Hammond also said Norris told him that he preferred to run against Sloan alone because he felt the prohibition vote would be divided between Hammond and himself; see Ross L. Hammond to the editor, "G. W. Norris: A Post Mortem," n.d. (clipping).

[10] Kent to Robert L. Owen, Sept. 3, 1918. A copy of the broadside and some of the statements that Kent obtained for it, including the draft of his own endorsement of Norris, can be found in the Kent Papers.

sides in the Nebraska contest. Kent indicated that he was prepared to "go the limit" and jeopardize his place on the Tariff Commission to campaign in Nebraska by stressing Norris's efforts to regulate packing houses and stockyards. Kent realized, too, that Norris needed encouragement because, owing to McCarl's departure, "he has had the nerve pretty well battered out of him." Although Kent never went to Nebraska, he provided Norris with both moral and financial support at a critical time.[11]

While Norris remained in Washington, Frank A. Harrison, a former LaFollette supporter, aided by funds from Kent and working through the Norris League, assumed management of the senator's campaign. Under Harrison's direction two men traveled throughout the state during September, visiting an average of eight towns a day, distributing literature, and talking with local workers. Their reports of rural discontent prompted Harrison to urge Norris's early return to the state to capitalize on this unrest.[12]

Farmers throughout the Midwest were dissatisfied. They resented the wartime farm program which limited their profits through price-fixing while other producers or manufacturers were not so restricted. Cattlemen criticized the arbitrary policy of meat packers in setting prices and determining regulations for the use of stockyards. In the trans-Mississippi West, with its populist and progressive heritage, there was strong antipathy to speculation and profiteering, especially when these seemed to be at the expense of men seeking to serve their country. Not only those engaged in agricultural pursuits but townspeople whose businesses were related to agriculture felt that they had grievances against the Wilson administration. Many were ready to express their disapproval by voting for Republican candidates. And in Nebraska Harrison found additional issues to exploit in Norris's behalf.[13]

[11] Kent to Owen, Aug. 29, 1918; to Woodrow Wilson, Aug. 29, 1918; to E. L. Burke, Aug. 30, 1918 (all in Kent Papers); memo, Tumulty to Wilson, n.d. [late Oct., 1918] (Wilson Papers).

[12] Frank A. Harrison to Kent, Sept. 14, 1918 (Kent Papers).

[13] Seward Livermore, "The Sectional Issue in the 1918 Congressional Election," *Mississippi Valley Historical Review*, 35 (June, 1948): 29–60. This article reveals how factors other than Wilson's appeal for a Democratic Congress played a role in this election. Chief among these "other" factors was the administration's agricultural program, centering on farm prices.

In late September Democratic Lieutenant Governor Edgar Howard, owner of the *Columbus Weekly Telegram* and former secretary of William Jennings Bryan, published an editorial that was widely reprinted. In it he denounced the heavy campaign expenditures of John H. Morehead, Norris's opponent, and implied that Morehead's money was coming from railroads, packers, and other "trusts" eager to buy a senator who would follow their policies. He also suggested that voters back a senatorial candidate other than Morehead. Though Norris was not named, the editorial, with its widespread dissemination, meant votes for him among rural Democrats and Bryanites who held Howard in high esteem. Reports received by the Republican State Committee indicated that in rural precincts Norris was leading all candidates on the ticket.[14]

Encouraged by these reports, Norris now made plans to return to Nebraska. The Fourth Liberty Loan drive gave him an opportunity in a nonpartisan guise to judge the situation for himself. In Lincoln he found Harrison in a small room with a "rickety old desk and two broken chairs in it," working harmoniously with the Republican State Committee. Harrison's reports were optimistic and Norris felt renewed confidence in his ability to win. The defeatism and pessimism that had characterized his behavior earlier had disappeared.[15]

Other factors also aided Norris. The large German vote was lining up on the Republican side, chiefly because the administra-

[14] Edgar Howard, "Who Paid the Money," n.d. (editorial), enclosed in Harrison to Kent, Sept. 27, 1918; Harrison to Kent, Sept. 14, 1918, comments on the precinct polls (both in Kent Papers). The editorial, besides being distributed as a circular, was published by Harrison in the *Lincoln Journal, Lincoln Star,* and *Omaha Daily News,* Sept. 27 and 28, 1918. Another factor favoring Norris was that Morehead was a member of the faction of the Democratic party headed by Gilbert M. Hitchcock, while Edgar Howard was a leader of the Bryan faction, whose pacifist and progressive views were not too different from Norris's. As one observer, a Norris critic, remarked, "Leaving the war out of the question, thinking men would choose Norris ten to one over Morehead, for ability, for character, for sympathy, for almost anything you wish to name, not excepting candor and straight dealing"; see H. W. Morrow to the editor, *North American Review,* 209 (Jan., 1919): 142, wherein Morrow explained "Why He Voted for Norris."

[15] Harrison to Kent, Oct. 2, 1918 (Kent Papers); Robert M. LaFollette to Belle Case LaFollette, Oct. 9, 1918 (letter made available through the courtesy of Fola LaFollette); Norris to Lawrence, June 4, 1935.

tion of Democratic Governor Keith Neville and the State Council of Defense had stifled expressions of German sentiment. Moreover, the Democratic party had become a dry party, thus antagonizing beer-, wine-, and whiskey-drinking Nebraskans of German, Bohemian, and Irish stock who resented the loss of their personal liberty to imbibe what they pleased. Finally, in Nebraska as elsewhere, voters would blame the party in power for all the grievances and annoyances they had to endure during the war period.[16]

By early October the Republican State Committee was functioning so well that Harrison remarked, "I have never seen a situation better at this stage of the campaign." Were it not for the money available to Morehead and other Democrats, he felt a Republican victory would have been assured. Harrison also feared "the possible effect of peace moves" in Europe and a fervent appeal to support the president. But with rural sentiment clearly in favor of Norris, he said that more time could be devoted "to educating the town vote—the consumers and the laboring man." After Norris's return he was eager to stump the state with the candidate.[17]

Norris, Harrison, and a friend began an automobile tour, ostensibly to sell Liberty Bonds. At the outset they covered about eight towns a day, but the pace was too much for Norris and had to be slowed down. To attract audiences in small towns, Harrison stopped the automobile, usually in the middle of the main street, and played the cornet until a crowd gathered. One day he appeared with a young lady who beautifully sang "The Holy City," accompanied by Harrison on the cornet, in a dusty street before a

[16] Sheldon, *Nebraska,* 1: 953. It is worthwhile noting that prominent German newspapers in Nebraska, the *Lincoln Free Press* and the *Omaha Tribune,* called for support of the Democratic party on the ground that Woodrow Wilson was the only friend Germany would have at the peace table. That Nebraska Germans would vote Republican in 1918 despite these endorsements was also evident. The *New York Times* in an editorial on Nov. 2, 1918, quoted the *Lincoln Journal* to the effect that, owing to accumulated grievances against the Democratic party, nationally and in Nebraska, reports from all sections of the state seemed to indicate that German-American citizens would support the straight Republican ticket.

[17] Harrison to Kent, Oct. 8, 1918 (Kent Papers). Harrison's impressions were borne out by Kent's business partner, who reported in mid-October that "the livestock interests and farmers seem to be for him strong and I understand that sentiment is growing daily in his favor"; see Burke to Kent, Oct. 17, 1918 (Kent Papers).

large crowd of people. Norris then spoke. Years later he observed
that while Harrison gathered the people with his cornet, he dis-
persed them with his speech. After several days of this routine
Norris began to feel better, and Harrison was convinced he could
"stand up right through the campaign." [18]

At every meeting copies of the Norris broadside containing
endorsements from such distinguished national figures as William
Kent, Senator Robert L. Owen, and Gifford Pinchot were distributed to individuals and deposited in stores and automobiles.
They were also methodically circulated by mail from headquarters
in Lincoln and the material was published in two of Omaha's daily
newspapers. Altogether more than 200,000 copies of the broadside were distributed at a cost of more than $700. Kent assumed
all expenses of this operation.[19]

Harrison's cornet, the automobile tour, and Kent's broadside
combined to make an effective and inexpensive campaign. But
with the election less than three weeks away, an influenza epidemic
brought the campaign to a halt. The State Board of Health issued
an order prohibiting all public meetings. The order was later
rescinded, but it was not until the Saturday before election that
Norris was able to resume speech-making. In the interim he continued to travel, seeing as many people individually as he could
and depending on publicity from friendly newspapers. At this
time Joseph Polcar, whose *Omaha Daily News* had the largest
circulation of any paper in Nebraska, invited him to write a daily
letter for publication. Norris concluded that these articles had
served him well because audiences received his final speeches most
enthusiastically.[20]

Although the influenza epidemic and the order prohibiting
public meetings impaired the efforts of all candidates, Norris's

[18] Norris to G. L. Keith, Dec. 2, 1941; to Fuller, Aug. 8, 1942; Harrison to
Kent, Oct. 14, 1918 (Kent Papers).

[19] Burke to Kent, Oct. 17, 1918; Harrison to Kent, Oct. 17, 1918 (both in
Kent Papers). Kent contributed at least $3,000 to Norris's 1918 campaign, but
it is to be doubted that Norris ever knew just how generous he really was; see
Kent to Harrison, Oct. 14, 1918 (Kent Papers).

[20] Norris to Fuller, Aug. 8, 1942; Harrison to Kent, Oct. 23, 1918 (Kent
Papers).

campaign was affected more than the others. Arrangements had been completed to bring four senators (Albert B. Cummins, William S. Kenyon, William E. Borah, and Hiram Johnson) and several progressive congressmen into Nebraska. The speeches had to be canceled, although Senator Cummins did spend some time in Omaha in Norris's behalf.[21]

Though his opponents labeled him pro-German and emphasized his vote against the war and his opposition to some of the legislative achievements of the Wilson administration, Norris was re-elected on November 5, 1918. He defeated John H. Morehead with a plurality of more than 20,000 votes (120,086 to 99,690). Three Democratic congressmen were unseated, giving the Republicans complete control of the House delegation and leaving Senator Gilbert M. Hitchcock the lone Democrat representing the state in the nation's capital. The 1918 election in Nebraska was a Republican landslide. The party regained the statehouse and won the governorship as well.[22]

Though favored by circumstances, Norris nevertheless won an impressive victory. One of the primary factors responsible for the Democratic defeat was that the Wilson administration fixed a price on wheat but allowed cotton to go unrestrained. Prohibition was another factor. And many Nebraska voters who felt that Norris's vote against war in 1917 was disgraceful as well as disloyal reacted as did the individual who said, "When told that loyalty required that I vote for Democratic dummies, I simply voted for

[21] Norris to C. A. Lord, Mar. 18, 1924; *Nebraska State Journal,* Oct. 25, 1918. Theodore Roosevelt was asked on several occasions to endorse Norris's bid for re-election. Both Roosevelt and Republican National Committee chairman Will Hays decided to do nothing—neither oppose nor endorse Norris's candidacy unless developments necessitated a stand against him; see Theodore Roosevelt to George Harvey, Sept. 19, 1918 (Letters, vol. 183); to David Robinson, Sept. 6, 1918 (Letters, vol. 181); and F. P. Corrick to Roosevelt, Oct. 25, 1918 (Box 413). All items are in the Theodore Roosevelt Papers, Manuscript Division, Library of Congress, and were brought to my attention by Professor Larry K. Smith, formerly of Dartmouth College.

[22] Sheldon, *Nebraska,* 1: 954; *New York Times,* Nov. 6, 1918; Adahbelle Snodgrass, "The Congressional Election of 1918" (M.A. thesis, University of Nebraska, 1944); see also A. B. Keiser to Roosevelt, Nov. 18, 1918 (Box 418, Theodore Roosevelt Papers).

Republicans, just because they were Republicans . . . because I
knew that my duty to self and country required that I do so." [23]

As Norris began to understand the force of these factors, he
emphasized agricultural problems and soon overcame what at the
start of the campaign seemed the most adverse of circumstances.
One editorial writer described his victory as follows: "He is still
unawed, still Norris, still senator, still independent, still victor
over malice and machination." Another editor, a partisan Democrat, concluded in a more colorful but not quite accurate way:

> For downright, dogged, defiant, devilish determination, the an-
> nals of Nebraska politics reveals no rival for Senator Norris. . . .
> Facing a statewide storm of villification [sic] and contempt en-
> tirely deserved on the face of the record, he stood pat. He made
> no apologies, asked no quarter and shed no regretful tears. He
> begged no votes—just demanded them. He never wavered, he
> just lined up the Heinies and fought like the devil. If he [was]
> scared, he never mentioned it. He betrayed no sign of fear. While
> he did a little explanationing [sic], he never appeared on the de-
> fensive. He is a marvelous man.[24]

Victory left Norris little time for rest. Congress had not adjourned and the war was rapidly approaching its end. Important
legislative work remained and new problems, pertaining to peace
and the postwar world, had to be considered. As a progressive
Republican, Norris's influence in party circles was not great;
despite his victory the Senate "Old Guard" showed little disposition to compromise. He understood that harmony was impossible
because "a party that has to compromise to such an extent that
individuals must surrender their conscientious convictions for the
sake of obtaining party success and a division of party spoils, will
sooner or later land on the rocks." But at the end of 1918 Norris
had little time to ruminate on the future of the Republican party,
though he realized that people were disgusted with the Democratic
party and undoubtedly would vote against it in 1920.[25]

---

[23] Morrow to the editor, p. 141, *North American Review.*
[24] *Sioux City* (Iowa) *Tribune, Omaha Nebraskan,* Nov. 7, 1918.
[25] Norris to Gifford Pinchot, Dec. 27, 1918 (Gifford Pinchot Papers, Manuscript Division, Library of Congress).

Returning to Washington, Norris attacked the principle of seniority in committee assignments and thereby threatened a split in Republican ranks just as the party won ascendancy in Congress. The rules change he proposed stated that "any Senator who is Chairman of the Committee on Appropriations, Finance, Foreign Relations, Interstate Commerce, Judiciary, Military Affairs, Naval Affairs or Post Offices and Post Roads, while holding such Chairmanship, shall not be a member of any of the other said committees." His purpose was to prevent the control of conference committees by a handful of Old Guard senators. Because of seniority senators who were chairmen of important committees were also ranking members of other major committees. Thus every significant bill going into conference would have Senate conferees who were chairmen of the major committees named in the amendment. Less than a dozen Old Guard senators could control the fate of every important piece of legislation. While Norris could rely on progressive Republican senators to support his amendment, a two-thirds vote was necessary to amend the Senate rules. Unless Democratic support was forthcoming, his resolution was doomed to failure.[26]

Norris sought to circumscribe seniority in a way the House of Representatives had adopted several weeks earlier. The House had voted that no chairman of a committee should be a member of any other. Since the Senate was a smaller body, Norris provided that the chairmen of the eight major committees should be barred from service on the seven others. Though his amendment would have broadened opportunities for junior senators and, indeed, would have democratized the Senate, it was defeated. In presenting it, Norris again revealed his recognition that the source of Old Guard power was imbedded in the structure of the Senate itself and that a most effective way of challenging it was to secure a rules change.[27]

Since the war came to an end several days after the 1918 election, Norris's anxiety about the Senate rules was not inappropriate.

[26] *New York Times,* Nov. 16 and 19, 1918; *New York Tribune,* Nov. 19, 1918, "Democratizing the Senate" (editorial).

[27] Norris to E. T. Westervelt, Nov. 23, 1918; to M. L. Phares, Dec. 11, 1918.

Now entitled to serve a second term, he realized that progressive voices would count for little in the Senate. Thus while the year 1918 had started with Norris concerned that opposition to American participation in the war might cost him his Senate seat, it ended with Norris aware that his voice would continue to count for little in party circles and in the realm of peacemaking. In between he had overcome a personal and political crisis of some magnitude.

Peacemaking

7

In the debates over the Versailles Peace Treaty Norris was in the irreconcilable camp. His dislike of the treaty and his growing hatred of Woodrow Wilson were evident once the Senate started to consider the treaty. Though Norris was not partisan in his approach, his opposition helped Henry Cabot Lodge and the Old Guard senators to maintain party dominance and to inject partisanship into the discussions. Strife within the Republican party, owing to Lodge's leadership, was not evident during the Senate's effort at peacemaking. Indeed, its noticeable absence helped pave the road toward "normalcy." But before the conflict was concluded in November, 1918, Norris had announced his support of an international organization as a means of remedying grievances among nations.

If the war could "result in the disarmament of nations, in the abolition of secret treaties, and in the promulgation of the principle that no conquest of one people by another shall be recognized by civilization, and in the establishment of a court of international scope to settle international disputes in the future—in other words in the death of militarism and in the establishment of a permanent peace—then the sacrifices made will not have been made in vain." While complete disarmament would be most desirable, Norris said that limitation of armaments supported by enforceable safeguards would achieve the same results.[1]

---

[1] *Congressional Record,* 65th Cong., 2nd sess., Mar. 19, p. 3695, Mar. 29, 1918, p. 4270; George W. Norris to J. A. Kees, Jan. 10, 1918.

During the war period he insisted that the only acceptable peace proposition was one of unconditional surrender. Only when peace was secured could the greatest object of the war be realized, namely, the destruction of militarism. To assist in achieving this goal, the United States, in cooperation with the Allies if possible but without them if necessary, should proclaim definite conditions whereby it could be secured. Norris suggested the destruction of all submarines, the conversion of fighting ships into commercial vessels, the refusal to recognize national title to territory obtained by conquest without the consent of the people involved, and the nonrecognition of secret treaties by any government. A permanent international court should be established which, besides settling international disputes, would resolve such questions as indemnities and the disposition of disputed territories. An official statement voicing these views would demonstrate that the United States was not waging a selfish fight and was striving to make the world safe for democracy. First expounded several months before the president presented his Fourteen Points in January, 1918, Norris reiterated his views at every opportune moment in the remaining months of the war.[2]

With the armistice of November, 1918, and the dominant role of Woodrow Wilson in the peace settlement, Norris no longer needed to talk in generalities. His remarks now focused on the role of the president, the League of Nations, and the Versailles Peace Treaty. His criticisms began shortly after Wilson's departure for Europe as the head of the American delegation to draft the peace treaty with Germany. Norris resented the pomp and splendor surrounding the president's voyage on the *George Washington,* a former German luxury liner, thereby missing an opportunity to present to suffering, war-torn Europe "an illustration of democracy and simplicity." Though he did not criticize Wilson's right to participate in the peacemaking, Norris took serious objection to the president's partisanship and to the fact that he had not taken

[2] *Nebraska State Journal,* Nov. 2, 1917; Norris to "My dear Sir," Mar. 25, 1919; Norris statement about war aims, n.d. The *New York Times,* Sept. 17, 1918, printed a statement by Norris that unconditional surrender was the only peace proposition that could be considered by the Allies. Incidentally, he thought the armistice terms amounted to an unconditional surrender; see *New York Times,* Nov. 12, 1918.

Congress and the people into his confidence about his peace plans. Indeed, throughout this entire period Norris felt the president wanted honor and glory bestowed upon him, leaving the Senate the chore of approving what he had done. In what Norris called the president's "anxiety for power" lay the seeds of serious difficulties.[3]

Having long opposed secret diplomacy and being in complete agreement with the president's "open covenants of peace, openly arrived at," Norris said that Wilson ought to have practiced this doctrine at Versailles. Yet while critical of the president in the late winter and early spring of 1919 when little was known of the work done at Versailles, aside from the fact that provision for a league of nations would be included in the treaty, Norris was further contemplating the nature of the postwar world.[4]

He refused to consider the possibility of maintaining a military force to help support new and independent nations. Among civilized peoples assembled in a league of nations there would be no need for military might to insure peace. Among other peoples, Norris said, it would take years to get them on a higher plane of development and "we should not attempt at the cannon's mouth to establish our civilization upon any people." To be sure, he realized that "permanent, stable civilized Governments" could not be established in many underdeveloped quarters of the globe without strife, revolution, and bloodshed. Such actions, Norris insisted, "would bankrupt the civilized portion of the world" in efforts to impose its "ideas upon the semi-civilized portion." [5]

Norris's comments throughout the period the president was in Europe were chiefly confined to his correspondence. Unlike other members of the Senate, he did not openly criticize Wilson or demand the separation of the league covenant from the rest of the treaty. Nevertheless, by mid-March Norris thought that critical senators had done "a good service for humanity" and were inclined "toward the establishment of a permanent League of Nations." He reached this conclusion as a result of Wilson's response

[3] Norris to M. L. Phares, Dec. 11, 1918; to Walter Locke, Mar. 18, 1919; to "My dear Friend," June 1, 1919.

[4] Norris to Locke, Mar. 18, 1919; to "My dear Sir," Mar. 25, 1919.

[5] *Ibid.*

to the March 3 resolution, signed by thirty-nine Republican senators and senators-elect, requesting that peace with Germany be
concluded before attention was paid to the league. Speaking in
New York the next day, prior to returning to the peace conference, Wilson promised that when the treaty came before the
Senate, the covenant would be tied to it so securely that one could
not "dissect the Covenant from the Treaty without destroying the
whole vital structure." The president's response convinced Norris
that Wilson had not freed his "heart from selfish ambition" and
that he would not allow the Senate an opportunity to aid in establishing the charter of the proposed league.[6]

While critical of Wilson, Norris was not yet hostile to a league
of nations. He understood the necessity of the United States surrendering some freedom of action in international matters and he
realized that the nation could not remain aloof from events in
Europe. Like his Senate colleagues, Norris thought that the
covenant brought back from Versailles needed information, although he was not concerned about including the Monroe Doctrine in it. If disarmament could be achieved, it would be impossible for any European government to seize territory or to conquer
a nation in the western hemisphere.[7]

Norris realized that America's role in the world had changed
and that, "like it or not, we are in European entanglements now."
Nevertheless, in "strictly European" affairs the United States ought
to remain aloof and not try to force its civilization upon unwilling
peoples, "no matter where they are." "I think we owe it to the
world and to those who shall follow us, to lay aside all prejudice,
all ill-feeling, all ambition, and all feeling of resentment or revenge. . . ." If "we reject the proposed League," the next steps
would involve increased armaments and the maintenance of large
armed forces, leading inevitably to another world war.[8]

<hr/>

[6] *Ibid.;* Norris to "My dear Friend," June 2, 1919. See Thomas A. Bailey,
Woodrow Wilson and the Lost Peace (New York, 1944), pp. 205–8, for a discussion of the round robin and the president's response to it.

[7] Norris to "My dear Sir," Mar. 25, 1919.

[8] *Nebraska State Journal,* Mar. 30, 1919, contains a full statement of Norris's
views on a league of nations; see also Norris to "My dear Sir," Mar. 25, 1919; to
"My dear Friend," June 1, 1919. That Norris at this time rarely expressed his
opinions publicly is evident from two May, 1919, letters of William Howard Taft.

On June 9, 1919, Senator William E. Borah, a critic of the treaty, had a newspaper copy of it read into the *Congressional Record* a month before the president formally presented it to the Senate. Norris applauded Borah's action, saying it enabled the Senate to carry out "the newer doctrine" of open covenants openly arrived at. In his first perusals he found nothing in the treaty to drive him into the irreconcilable camp. On May 8, 1919, Norris informed a reporter:

> One thing that I liked particularly about the Treaty of Peace is the disarmament proposition. However, my own idea is that the Treaty should have gone still further in reducing Germany's armament. Germany should not be allowed an army of 100,000 men and her navy is too big. It will follow of course that the size of Germany's army and navy will affect the size of the military and naval organizations of the world. I am greatly pleased with the provision in the treaty, establishing a tribunal which shall try the Kaiser and his military advisers and soldiers. It will be one of the greatest tribunals in history and its award will be of momentous importance.[9]

Earlier he had criticized specific articles in the draft treaty. But in each instance he made it clear that he would not advise rejection because of them. The treaty gave Great Britain and her dependencies much greater power and influence than that possessed by any other nation, while the mandates provision could sanction interference in underdeveloped areas of the world. Though the right of revolution was a desperate remedy, it was also a sacred one and Norris did not want the United States embroiled in such controversies. In short, while he had reservations, Norris believed that detailed debate and constructive criticism would result in a more equitable and humane agreement that would bring order out of chaos and help assure a permanent peace.[10]

On May 10 in a letter to his brother Taft mentioned Norris as an opponent of the treaty; on May 31 in a letter to Gus Karger he said that Norris would vote "for the League as it was" (both in Taft Letterbooks, Box 209, William Howard Taft Papers, Manuscript Division, Library of Congress). Professor Richard W. Leopold first called these letters to my attention.

[9] *Congressional Record*, 66th Cong., 1st sess., June 9, 1919, p. 782; see *New York Times*, May 9, 1919, for the quote.

[10] *Nebraska State Journal*, Mar. 30, 1919.

But by the end of June Norris was in the irreconcilable camp, claiming he would never vote for the Versailles Peace Treaty. What outraged Norris was the Shantung provision. It granted Japan control of Germany's concessions on this peninsula, including extensive railroad and mining privileges and a leased area at Kiaochow Bay which Japan already had promised to return to China. Unless this provision were eliminated, Norris would not vote for the treaty, announcing to his colleagues, "I am going to cast . . . every possible vote that I can cast anywhere along the line in the hope of defeating" it.[11]

On July 5, 1919, five days after the president formally placed the Versailles Peace Treaty before the Senate, Norris delivered his first speech against it. His remarks were confined almost entirely to the Shantung provisions, which he considered "so indefensible, so unjust and so wicked" that they alone would be sufficient "to reject the treaty even though every other word contained in it were entirely satisfactory." If accepted, seeds would be sown for a future war as surely as the German acquisition of Alsace and Lorraine kindled in Frenchmen a hope to overthrow German rule someday in these French-speaking provinces. Since the treaty needed to be changed, modifying his earlier vow, Norris announced his intention of voting for any amendment that improved it. He then suggested articles that might improve it, mentioning disarmament and a provision that would recognize the transfer of people from one nationality to another only with their consent. The league covenant also should require all League of Nations business to be done in public and should provide for arbitration of international disputes and abrogation of secret treaties. Moreover, if international arbitration prevailed, the necessity for the use of force among civilized nations should disappear. With effective disarmament, an economic boycott could compel recalcitrant nations to accept decisions of the international tribunal.[12] Norris made these suggestions in conjunction with his opposition to the Shantung section. If approved, Norris would resolve his doubts in favor of

11 *New York Times,* June 29, July 3, 1919; see Frederic L. Paxson, *Post-War Years: Normalcy, 1918–1923* (Berkeley and Los Angeles, 1948), p. 120, for the Norris statement.

12 *Congressional Record,* 66th Cong., 1st sess., July 15, 1919, pp. 2592–93.

the treaty. But since he could not sanction the transfer of a portion of the Chinese empire to Japan, he balked at the rest of the treaty as well.

Section 156 of the treaty provided that all rights, privileges, and possessions of Germany in China be turned over to Japan. Norris objected:

> The practical effect of this provision is to give Japan control over the Chinese nation and to turn over to her the control of more than thirty-six millions of the Chinese population. Japan is given railroads, mines, submarine cables, together with the right and privilege of exploiting, all free, without compensation, and without limit. There is not a word anywhere in the Treaty, of Japan under any circumstances, ever being required to turn anything back to China. It must be remembered that Germany had no right in China that any honest man was bound to respect. What rights she obtained there she obtained at the cannon's mouth because China was unable to defend herself.

China was an ally who had contributed to the full extent of her limited ability in the war against Germany, while Japan, also an ally, "was perhaps the only one that made any financial gain out of the war." Since the Allies granted that France was entitled to the return of Alsace and Lorraine, by the same logic territory and property Germany wrested from China should be returned. But China, a helpless and weak nation, was being betrayed while Shantung, the burial place of Confucius and the home of over 30 million of her people, was placed "in the control of the last nation on earth that China would have selected to control her had she been given a voice in the decision of her own destiny."

The plight of China's neighbor, Korea, provided an illustration of what could be expected when the Japanese gained power to rule a foreign people. Aspects of the history of Korea under Japanese rule were discussed by Norris with particular emphasis on the maltreatment of Christians. The implication was that "they will do in China like they are doing in Korea," trying to "blot off the face of the earth" every possible vestige of Korean culture and civilization. For the Senate to approve "this unjust judgment" would sanction an international tribunal founded upon the betrayal of the Chinese people: "And whatever structure we build, however powerful we may be when we build it, founded upon such an outrageous and unjust judgment, it will, in God's own time, bring about its own destruction. We are only planting the seeds of future wars that will be just as certain to come as the universal law of creation remains intact."

Moreover, Norris asserted, this attempt to rob China of her "birthright" was preceded by a secret agreement between the Allies and Japan made shortly before the United States entered the war. He claimed that "in all the annals of history I do not believe there is recorded an instance of a more disgraceful and dishonorable agreement to carve up the territory not of an enemy but of an allied friend." Agreeing to a treaty approving such an arrangement "would give the lie to every principle or declaration of justice that was ever made by our Government or any of our allies during the progress of the war." Greed, avarice, and hypocrisy would predominate over justice, equality, and good will; the poor and the weak could expect little comfort and help in the postwar world.[13]

Norris's speech, making public the secret pledges between Japan and the Allied governments, received much attention. But officials of the State Department declined to comment. Several days later Norris received a note from the president inviting him to the White House to discuss the Versailles Peace Treaty. He declined Wilson's invitation, feeling that he could not consistently accept in view of his uncompromising opposition to portions of the treaty. Norris concluded, "I most respectfully suggest that you follow the method prescribed in the Constitution in communicating to the Senate any information that in your wisdom is deemed advisable. Such a course would not only conserve your time and energy, but would give to all our countrymen, as well as to the Senate, the benefit of your valuable argument and advice." [14]

The Shantung speech and the letter of refusal placed Norris

[13] *Ibid.,* pp. 2592–97 (the entire speech; pp. 2594–97 concentrate on the Shantung provisions); see also *New York Times,* July 16, 1919.

[14] *New York Times,* July 16, 21, 22, and 24, 1919; Woodrow Wilson to Norris, July 19, 1919 (File VII, Box 30, Letterbook 57, Woodrow Wilson Papers, Manuscript Division, Library of Congress). Norris's letter of July 21, 1919, refusing the president's invitation was printed in the *New York Times,* July 24, 1919; see also Box 181, Wilson Papers.

in the camp of senators opposed to the acceptance of the covenant without amendment or reservations. Thus he moved from the moderate into the irreconcilable camp. Throughout the entire debate on the Versailles Peace Treaty he devoted most of his energies to criticizing the Shantung provisions, reiterating the points first made in his July 15 speech.[15]

In September, while Wilson was on his ill-fated western tour, Norris presented an allegorical dissertation on the Shantung settlement that embodied a covert attack on the president. It concerned characters whose identity was clear from the descriptive names applied to them. Bill Kaiser, John Chinaman, Mr. Jap, Miss Korea, John Bull, Mr. French, Mr. Italiano, and Miss Columbia War I; it was devoted primarily to the seizure of Shantung by Bill Kaiser who instigated difficulties when he started preying on his neighbors. But Norris's tale touched only incidentally on World War I; it was devoted primarily to the seizure of Shantung by Bill Kaiser and the subsequent course of Mr. Jap in evicting Bill Kaiser and taking possession for himself. Mr. Jap was represented as a desperado who previously had been guilty "of an unprovoked and outrageous assault upon an old maiden lady," Miss Korea.

In this way Norris recounted the history he had previously presented in his July speech. It soon became apparent that the Miss Columbia of the allegory was Woodrow Wilson. Once members of "the Troubled Community" had arrested Bill Kaiser, the question arose as to how he should be tried. Finally a tribunal was established and the three male judges, John Bull, Mr. French, and Mr. Italiano, were joined by Miss Columbia. Analyzing the Shantung settlement within this allegorical framework, Norris castigated

---

[15] *New York Times,* July 21 and 22, 1919. While public figures, including administration leaders and senators, were critical of the Shantung settlement, many did not wish to reject the treaty only because one or two clauses did not measure up to the standards proclaimed by Wilson. Among the critics Norris was the only senator to base his opposition almost exclusively on the Shantung settlement. For more moderate views on the Shantung situation, see John Sharp Williams to Wilson, July 9, 1917 (Presidential Series: 1918–1923, Box 4, John Sharp Williams Papers, Manuscript Division, Library of Congress); Taft to G. M. Hitchcock, July 21, 1919 (Gilbert M. Hitchcock Papers, Manuscript Division, Library of Congress); and Thomas A. Bailey, *Woodrow Wilson and the Great Betrayal* (New York, 1945), pp. 161–64.

Wilson for abandoning his previously pronounced principles. He concluded by observing that "the Troubled Community" would remain troubled, since peace could not be built upon "such a wicked judgment." [16]

Later Norris delivered a lengthy speech denouncing the award of economic privileges on the Shantung peninsula to Japan. He started on Friday, October 10, 1919, and concluded the following Monday. He began with an attack on the president, who in St. Louis on September 5 had said that the secret treaties Japan made with Great Britain and France were necessary to induce Japan to enter the war on the side of the Allies. This statement, subsequently repeated by Wilson at least three more times on his western trip, Norris claimed was inaccurate because Japan declared war on Germany on August 23, 1914, and the first of these secret treaties was not negotiated until March, 1917. Though Wilson in a telegram to Norris admitted his error at St. Louis, the president never gave any publicity to the correction.[17]

Norris spoke in favor of an amendment which "would give to China what belongs to China," thereby relieving the treaty "of one of its very many serious objectionable features." Denouncing the argument that since Japan would keep Shantung, the United States ought to accept the situation, Norris was unwilling to give official sanction to what he called "this disgraceful rape of an innocent people." He quoted with approval Secretary of State Robert Lansing's testimony that if the United States refused to agree to the "Shantung crime," it would not mean the demise of the treaty or the failure of the League of Nations. Norris excoriated the president for his twin failure in not denouncing the Shantung settlement and in not condemning the secret treaties.[18] Approving

[16] *Congressional Record*, 66th Cong., 1st sess., Sept. 6, 1919, pp. 4960–63; *New York Times*, Sept. 7, 1919.

[17] *Congressional Record*, 66th Cong., 1st sess., Oct. 10, pp. 6789–90, Oct. 13, 1919, pp. 6811–12; Norris to Herman Aye, Mar. 5, 1920; to H. R. Todd, Mar. 4, 1920.

[18] That Norris was unfair to the president and his work at the Paris peace conference is evident from the overwhelming mass of recent scholarly material on this subject. For earlier studies, available while Norris was still alive, which critically but favorably evaluate Wilson's work, see Paul Birdsall, *Versailles:*

the treaty with the Shantung provision would only compound the error. Rejecting it was a necessary step toward permanent peace, since people everywhere would know that America demanded "a genuine treaty based upon absolute justice." Moreover, rejection did not necessarily mean that America would be left out of the League of Nations. Though he had reservations about particular provisions, he claimed that "a league without America will not succeed."

Carefully reviewing the situation, Norris argued that the inequities of the Shantung arrangement would sow the seeds of future conflict. The Paris peacemakers, instead of overthrowing "the old methods of diplomacy," re-established them "and thereby gave license to any nation to go out and practice the same old cruel methods that they have practiced since the days of barbarism." Doubts and hesitations over Shantung led Norris to conclude that the peacemakers were "dishonest," "unfair," and "wicked." He sympathized with the newborn Chinese republic in its struggle for survival and evinced distaste for Japan, a nation which he felt was embarked on a career of conquest. Japanese expansion would drive the Christian religion and the American business community out of East Asia. The peace treaty with its Shantung provision would encourage paganism over Christianity; it would retard progress, representing "a crime against humanity" and a dishonor to the United States. The failure of the Shantung amendment to gain Senate approval placed Norris among the irreconcilables, the group unalterably opposed to the Versailles Peace Treaty.[19]

His further remarks were relatively brief and always critical, clearly indicating that his vote would be cast in the negative when

Twenty Years After (New York, 1941), and Allan Nevins, *Henry White: Thirty Years of American Diplomacy* (New York, 1930), Chapters XIX–XXIII. Russell H. Fifield in his careful monograph *Woodrow Wilson and the Far East: The Diplomacy of the Shantung Question* (New York, 1952) concludes that Wilson, fearful that the Japanese would not sign the treaty if they were not given satisfaction in Shantung, reluctantly agreed to Japanese control after hedging it with stipulations. All authors agree that Wilson was unhappy with this part of the treaty.

[19] The entire speech can be found in the *Congressional Record*, 66th Cong., 1st sess., Oct. 10 and 13, 1919, pp. 6788–6826; see also *New York Times*, Oct. 11 and 14, 1919.

the Senate decided the fate of the peace treaty. Norris criticized overrepresentation of the British empire in the league covenant, the failure to achieve definite disarmament, and Article 10, which he now felt ought to be stricken from the treaty. The prime object of Article 10, he maintained, was to insure world supremacy of the British and Japanese empires, since it tended to guarantee territory acquired during the war by the various secret treaties: "By its terms we are bound to turn a deaf ear to the struggling cry of freedom, no matter from what part of the world it may come, and we mortgage thereby the life blood of unborn American boys to stifle this cry and uphold the cruel aristocratic reign of greedy kings and pagan monarchs the world over." [20]

In the last days of the session Norris espoused the cause of Egypt; he saw it as another Shantung with Great Britain replacing Japan as the oppressor nation. His remarks were brief but pithy. While Japanese expansion was more cruel and represented a triumph of paganism over Christianity, British expansion was directed toward control of trade routes. In each instance an oppressed people who had supported the Allied cause and who had been promised freedom during the war found themselves under new rulers whose control was sanctioned by the Versailles Peace Treaty.[21] He returned to the plight of Egypt when the second session of the Sixty-sixth Congress again discussed the treaty in 1920; it should be noted, however, that the Senate reconsidered the treaty over his strenuous opposition.

On February 9, 1920, when Henry Cabot Lodge moved to reconsider the vote by which the Senate on November 19, 1919, tabled the motion to reconsider the vote rejecting ratification of the peace treaty with Germany with reservations, Norris rose to make a point of order. The senator from Massachusetts, having voted with the prevailing side, was not entitled to make the motion to reconsider. He insisted that the treaty had already been reconsidered when a second vote on November 19, 1919, considered the treaty without reservations. Consequently, it now was too late

---

[20] *Congressional Record,* 66th Cong., 1st sess., Oct. 29, p. 7689 (British empire representation), Nov. 15, p. 8567 (disarmament), Nov. 11, 1919, pp. 8274–75 (Article 10).

[21] *Ibid.,* Nov. 17, p. 8643, Nov. 18, 1919, p. 8758.

under general parliamentary law to reconsider. The vice-president overruled this point of order, whereupon Norris unsuccessfully challenged Vice-President Thomas R. Marshall's decision.[22]

In the ensuing debate Norris was concerned with the plight of oppressed peoples who were losing opportunities for freedom and liberty under various provisions of the peace treaty. On February 27, 1920, he delivered a lengthy speech devoted almost entirely to that part of the treaty (Article 147) referring to Egypt. England's course in Egypt since the armistice, Norris claimed, paralleled Japan's in Korea and China before the armistice. Both violated pledges and used force to consolidate their positions. Approval of the treaty would seal the fate of Egypt, "an ally who lost more men than America did in the war." The case of Egypt, like that of Shantung, revealed to Norris how far the peacemakers had departed from the famous Fourteen Points "and the other addresses of the President on that subject." The pledges made by the Allies to subject peoples were doomed by secret treaties which vitiated them. In calling for the defeat of the treaty, Norris asked, "Can we long boast of our freedom and our honor if by our act we hold as chattels and slaves millions of helpless and innocent people and in this civilized day divide up the earth to suit the autocrats of Europe and Asia, without considering the wish or the will of the people whose freedom and liberty are thus denied?"[23] A permanent peace could not be built upon a foundation of broken pledges and unjust treatment of subjected peoples who were clamoring for freedom and independence. History revealed that all such ventures "must end in disaster." The Versailles Peace Treaty, "containing these inhuman and dishonorable things," could only bring misery, suffering, and war in its wake. Fair-minded people, Norris claimed, were beginning to comprehend these injustices and to condemn the self-appointed autocrats "who sat in secret judgment at Versailles." To prove his point, he noted that "Orlando has been defeated in Italy; Clemenceau has been overthrown in France; Lloyd-George sees the handwriting on the wall; and Woodrow

22 *Ibid.,* 2nd sess., Feb. 9, 1920, pp. 2629, 2636–37; George F. Sparks, ed., *A Many-Colored Toga: The Diary of Henry Fountain Ashurst* (Tucson, Ariz., 1962), p. 123.

23 *Congressional Record,* 66th Cong., 2nd sess., Feb. 27, 1920, p. 3576.

Wilson is 'watchfully waiting' the coming condemnation of the American people." [24]

To the charge that he was an irreconcilable, a senator unalterably opposed to the treaty, Norris replied, "I think it is an honor on the matter of this treaty to be an irreconcilable." To the further charge that the Shantung situation would not be changed one iota by U.S. rejection of the treaty, whereas if it entered the League of Nations, an opportunity to help meliorate the situation would arise, Norris insisted that the Versailles Peace Treaty wove inequities into the very fabric of the peace, guaranteeing to England, France, and Japan title to areas promised independence and freedom. Under the covenant Shantung and Egypt, for example, could not initiate a plea that they ought to be freed from the control of Japan and Great Britain. Indeed, the reverse was true: "The approval of this treaty puts the nail into every one of these coffins and drives it down and clinches it." Instead of moving into a new era wherein open covenants would be openly arrived at and secret treaties would be a thing of the past, the precedents and crimes already established would prevail, despite the fact that the victorious Allies supposedly had turned over a new leaf. [25]

With his concern for oppressed peoples and their inability to achieve independence, it is not surprising that Norris devoted some attention to the Irish question, despite its not being mentioned in the treaty. He saw the same pattern: a spirited people dominated and controlled against their consent. Thus Norris supported a reservation about Ireland because he felt that acceptance of the treaty without it would seal the doom of a free and independent Ireland. If the revolutionary tradition of the American people, expressed in the basic ideas of the Declaration of Independence, still meant anything, Norris felt it meant that the United States must support struggling peoples in Ireland and elsewhere whose ability and desire for self-government were unquestioned. [26] But his efforts came to nought: reservations pertaining to Egypt and Ireland were tabled on March 18, 1920. Norris voted his convictions and denied he was playing politics. If he was a demagogue

[24] *Ibid.* (the entire speech can be found on pp. 3564–76).
[25] *Ibid.,* Mar. 4, 1920, p. 3854.
[26] *Ibid.,* Mar. 18, 1920, pp. 4501–2.

courting the Irish vote, to what group in Nebraska, he inquired, was he appealing when he voted for the Shantung amendment and the Egyptian reservation? [27]

That Norris's opposition to the Versailles Peace Treaty was based on conviction and not opportunism can be taken for granted. That his view of international relations was moralistic and predicated almost exclusively upon concern for oppressed peoples is evident from his Senate speeches; they exhibited no understanding of the realities of power and its shifting balance as a result of World War I. Nor did his remarks reveal any understanding of the realities of the political situation in countries whose peoples he championed. That his idealism was utterly naive is not so evident. The violence attending the withdrawal of colonial powers in later years would prove that there was more than an element of wisdom in his remarks about the results of policies of keeping peoples in subjection against their will. That his opposition to the Versailles Peace Treaty was tinged with partisanship is something Norris would have denied, though his denunciations of Wilson, let alone his irreconcilable position, aided the Republican cause and helped to heal divisions that had split the party for many years.

Some argued that, despite inequities in the treaty, the only hope for remedying them and for promoting peace and idealism in international relations was in the League of Nations and American participation. Norris answered this argument by asserting that in approving flagrant inequities, the treaty provided a faulty base on which to promote peace. The very principles it was designed to promote had been violated through secret treaties and actual clauses embedded in the Versailles Treaty itself.[28]

After the Senate on March 19, 1920, refused, this time by only seven votes, to approve the treaty with reservations, Norris did not withdraw into a nationalist shell and forget the plight of oppressed peoples. Throughout the rest of his career an anti-Japanese bias could be noted in his remarks. And he remained suspicious of Great Britain and other imperialist powers, including the United

[27] *Ibid.,* Mar. 25, 1920, p. 4801.

[28] Norris's position on the Versailles Treaty is conveniently summarized by Edward G. Lowry in "Norris: A Native Product," in *Washington Close-Ups* (Boston and New York, 1921), pp. 112–15.

States, whenever they interfered in the affairs of other nations, no matter how underdeveloped the nation or how poverty-stricken and plagued by dictatorship, graft, and corruption the people were. In June of 1920, for example, Norris championed the Irish in their struggle for independence, claiming that British forces had been guilty of "cruelties and inhuman punishment without parallel in the history of civilization." He introduced a resolution expressing Senate sympathy for the efforts of the Irish to secure a government of their own choosing. The resolution was a companion to one by Senator LaFollette recognizing the independence of the Irish republic. Both measures were before the Foreign Relations Committee and Norris sought to force action on them by his remarks.[29]

To champion the cause of oppressed peoples denied liberty and freedom, Norris joined with Fred C. Howe, Jane Addams, Norman Thomas, Senator David I. Walsh, and others in the American Commission on Conditions in Ireland. In December, 1920, it was announced that he would take an active part in a commission organized by Oswald Garrison Villard to inquire into the situation in Ireland. In the same month he spoke at a meeting held by the Friends of Freedom for India at the Lexington Theatre in New York and demanded that President Wilson and others responsible for sending American troops to Russia be impeached. Pandemonium followed these remarks. The audience rose en masse, the colors of Ireland and India were waved, and people cheered lustily. Norris's denunciation of the Versailles Peace Treaty, particularly when he asserted that no reservation would do when only one amendment could be effective, "and that amendment is to strike the whole thing out," provoked a similar response.[30] Examining conditions in Korea, Egypt, Ireland, and India, Norris reluctantly concluded that "the most enlightened nations of the world are now almost barbarous." They were responsible for atrocities previously unknown to civilized nations. Great Britain and Japan, he was convinced, "were determined to rule the world, and have the erroneous idea that they can get the confidence of honest people by

[29] *Omaha Bee*, June 21, 1920; Norris to "Dear Boys," Dec. 30, 1920. On Apr. 7, 1920, Norris spoke at a dinner in Washington honoring Eamon DeValera; see Norris to Will Owen Jones, May 8, 1920.

[30] *Omaha Bee*, June 21, Dec. 7, 1920; *New York Times*, Dec. 4, 1920.

shooting down, murdering and flogging innocent folks, and terrorize them into submission." [31]

Several of Norris's friends were upset by his remarks calling for the impeachment of the president. Since ardent supporters of the new Soviet government of Russia were prominent at the New York meeting, Norris explained his position. Officials responsible for sending an army into a country on which the Congress had not declared war and where the rights of no American citizen were curtailed should be impeached and removed from office. While he condemned the Versailles Peace Treaty, he insisted that he had never mentioned Lenin or Trotsky and did not discuss the government of Russia. If the Russians wanted a Soviet government, it was not "any of our business." Norris was in favor of establishing trade relations with Russia, as with other countries regardless of their form of government. Bolsheviks, he said, appeared in Russia because of the tyranny of its former rulers. They would appear in other countries where the rule of an autocracy was pitted against the rule of the people. To prevent the spread of such a system, Norris announced, the rights of all people must be observed. Laws that treated all alike and did "not give advantage to men of wealth over those who are poor" would have to be enacted in all countries. Thus Norris's internationalism was merely his progressivism writ large. [32]

[31] Norris to "Dear Boys," Dec. 30, 1920.
[32] Norris to C. E. Hopping, Dec. 30, 1920; to "Dear Boys," Dec. 30, 1920.

End of an Era?

8

On the domestic scene the last years of the Wilson administration witnessed a marked departure from the values for which Norris, as a progressive, had fought. Extravagance and lack of economy in the public interest, corporate control tightening its vise, a Sedition Act and wholesale interference with free speech and free press tending to annihilate civil liberties—all exerted their influence and helped disillusion Norris about progress in postwar America. The blame for much of what he disliked about the course of events Norris placed on the Wilson administration and upon the president himself. That this blame had erupted into a bitterness that passed the bounds of mere political opposition was revealed when Norris commented upon the resignation of Robert Lansing as Secretary of State. The correspondence exchanged between the two men revealed, Norris claimed, that "first, the President was incapacitated, and it was necessary for someone to look after the Government; second, the mental expert that was employed at the White House was discharged too soon." [1]

While the president alone could not be charged with the high cost of living, Norris believed that the nation's leaders should set examples of probity and moderation. Instead the president "spent money like a drunken sailor" in connection with the peace conference while food and materials no longer needed by the armed

[1] *New York Times,* Feb. 15, 1920.

forces were not used to relieve shortages and to reduce the cost of living in the United States.[2]

Norris also blamed the president for the Senate's delay in passing appropriation bills. While he did not absolve the Senate from responsibility, he said that since Wilson had been in the White House, appropriation bills never passed Congress before March 4 because in the short session, just before Congress was to adjourn, the president "invariably attempted the passage of legislation of great importance." Attempts to discuss either the appropriation bills or the important measure always brought forth the cry of filibuster along with criticism of members who asked questions. While Wilson in 1919 had reasons for delay, Norris noted that the appropriation bills, containing primarily lump-sum allocations, were the largest in history. He felt they ought to be analyzed and discussed, thereby necessitating a special session.[3]

He favored this approach because of "wild extravagance" prevailing in the executive branch. In March, 1919, the president, several cabinet members, and numerous lesser officials were in Europe while there was "almost complete demoralization in every Department of Government here." All of this "wild and mad extravagance" added to the war-swollen public debt. It helped to cause dissatisfaction and further increases in the cost of living.[4]

Paradoxically, Norris agreed in several instances that economy could be practiced by increasing government expenditures. Paying pensions to civil service employees actually would promote efficiency and economy in the government service. But it did pose a dilemma in 1920 when the nation was paying interest "greater than was the entire expense of the Government five years ago." Government employees, hard hit by the high cost of living, needed an increase in salary,[5] and large sums would have to be paid to returning soldiers. Between the veteran and the civil servant, Norris

---

[2] *Congressional Record,* 66th Cong., 1st sess., Sept. 10, 1919, pp. 5158–61, 5163; 3rd sess., Feb. 26, 1921, p. 3948; *New York Times,* Sept. 11, 1919.

[3] George W. Norris to Walter Locke, Mar. 18, 1919; *Congressional Record,* 66th Cong., 1st sess., June 17, 1919, p. 1212.

[4] Norris to Locke, Mar. 18, 1919; to A. R. Whitson, Apr. 9, 1920; to S. F. Sanders, Jan. 31, 1921; *Congressional Record,* 66th Cong., 3rd sess., Jan. 4, 1921, p. 923; 2nd sess., Mar. 23, 1920, pp. 4728–30.

[5] Norris to Florence E. Miller, Feb. 2, 1921.

chose the former in the situation where not enough money was available to pension them both. Reluctantly, therefore, he insisted that a bill providing pensions for retired civil servants be turned down until conditions improved. People would have to sacrifice and worthy citizens would have to go without, lest the government be bankrupted.[6]

As long as federal funds were dispensed to soldiers in the process of severing them from the service, Norris refused to yield to persistent pressures from Nebraska veterans and their organizations that he support a bonus bill. The arguments he made in the Senate—fear of further inflation, the high cost of living, the financial plight of the government—were reiterated in his correspondence:

> . . . the issuing of more bonds will increase further the already inflated currency, and very materially increase the cost of living, and I fear that in this respect, we have now almost reached the breaking point. In fact, I do not see how we can very long continue under present conditions of living costs. Another issue of bonds will increase taxation, and the further increasing of the cost of living is fraught with very great danger to the stability of the Government itself.[7]

He appealed to the patriotism of the soldiers "who won the war, who saved the situation, and protected the country" to refrain from taking steps that might bring financial disaster.[8]

But economy carried too far could bring ruin in its wake as easily as extravagance could. As a member of the Agriculture and Forestry Committee, Norris voted to leave only a nucleus sufficient to administer the department until more propitious times appeared. Though agriculture in the past had not had "its fair share," Norris was willing for the agricultural part of the government to assume the burdens of rigid economy. But when credit sources available to farmers were curtailed, he protested, noting that when the

[6] *Congressional Record,* 66th Cong., 2nd sess., Feb. 11, pp. 2755–56, Mar. 23, 1920, p. 4729.

[7] Norris to Archie Z. Myers, Apr. 1, 1920 (for quote); to Kendall Hammond, Mar. 23, 1920; to E. P. McDermott, May 12, 1920.

[8] Norris to Myers, Apr. 1, 1920; to A. R. Davis, May 4, 1920.

farmer "wanted to buy something which was manufactured and handled and owned by a businessman, if he wanted to buy a new automobile for a joy ride, he could get all the money he wanted." [9] Unable to secure adequate credit, farmers by 1920 were selling their produce at ruinous prices. Speculators bought crops to hold off the market until more advantageous prices could be secured. Norris insisted that the government extend credit to the farmer to allow him, rather than the speculator, to retain his crop until agricultural prices rose. Thus, before Wilson left the White House, Norris was considering a problem that would plague him and his colleagues throughout the following decade.[10]

To complicate and compound the plight of the farmer, the Federal Land Bank System, the heart of the administration's agricultural program, was being subjected to a rising barrage of criticism. Under the terms of the Federal Farm Loan Act of 1916 there were established two basic methods of lending money to farmers. One was through Federal Farm Loan banks, whose loans, limited to $10,000, were made to resident farmers for specific purposes. The other method, the Joint-Stock Land Bank System, permitted the creation, by private individuals for private profit, of corporations which could lend larger amounts without restrictive conditions. Their bonds, like those of the nonprofit Farm Loan banks, would be tax-free. At the outset the issuing of tax-free bonds did not materially interfere with governmental operations and little criticism arose. But by the end of 1919 these bonds had become a source of contention to Norris and many Nebraska farmers.

It hardly seemed fair that the government should aid through tax-free bonds large corporations whose operations tended to have an effect opposite to what Norris considered the main purpose of the law: to keep people on the farm and to encourage others to engage in agriculture. Instead of increasing the number of farms, the law helped reduce their number by permitting loans on large tracts, thereby allowing a person possessing large amounts of land

[9] *Congressional Record,* 66th Cong., 2nd sess., Mar. 23, pp. 4728, 4730, May 31, 1920, p. 7976; Norris to Whitson, Apr. 9, 1920.

[10] *Congressional Record,* 66th Cong., 3rd sess., Dec. 13, 1920, pp. 264–65.

to obtain a mortgage, possibly to purchase more land. Instead of having more farmers with modest means, fewer farmers with greater wealth and an increase in tenancy were the results.[11] Norris was unhappy about this situation, aggravated for the small farmer by the high cost of living and mounting taxes. To remedy it, Norris sought the repeal of the tax-exemption status of bonds issued by the Joint-Stock Land banks. But objections emanating from those who had organized these banks were powerful and the measure failed. Moreover, Norris was concerned because some Farm Loan banks were making loans illegally for more than $10,000 to men who were not farmers. The law, he felt, was being used to benefit land speculators.[12]

As a solution to this inequity and to the problem of farm credit, Norris again proposed, but the Senate did not accept, a federal bureau of farm loans. Long-term loans on farm land would be made payable to this bureau and secured at a modest rate of interest. The bureau could help tenants become proprietors and other individuals become farmers. To secure funds, it would issue bonds; "it would be a clearing house where the middleman's profit and where the overhead machinery of loan companies would be almost entirely eliminated." This plan, Norris believed, would add to the prosperity of citizens with no risk or danger to the government and "it would build buildings and houses in the country, to be occupied by owners, where now the homes are few and too many of them occupied by men who do not own them." [13]

To other problems emanating from the war Norris likewise suggested solutions, but in no instance did the Congress accept them. The problems persisted on into the Harding administration. Rather than sell ships owned and operated by the Shipping Board during the war, Norris suggested leasing them to the Panama Railroad Company, a government corporation already operating a fleet of its own. With regard to internal transportation, Norris was not pleased with the president's proposal for compensating railroad companies while the government held possession. He thought the

[11] Norris to S. Fuhrman, Jan. 9, 1920; to W. E. Barclay, Jan. 17, 1920; to Elmer E. Strain, Dec. 22, 1920.

[12] Norris to L. S. Herron, Dec. 27, 1919; to Anton Wallinger, Feb. 3, 1920.

[13] Norris, "A Federal Bureau of Farm Loans," n.d. (draft); draft article for *Farm and Fireside,* n.d.; statement about bureau of farm loans, n.d.

plan would pay railroad companies an income very much in excess of what they had received in normal times.[14]

On December 24, 1919, the president announced the return of the roads to their owners on March 1, 1920. Earlier Senator Albert B. Cummins had introduced a measure, which Norris opposed, outlining conditions by which the railroads would function under private ownership. Though Norris favored government operation, he did not equate effective public ownership with the wartime administration of the railroads. He proposed instead a federal railroad corporation with five directors appointed by the president. It would have $10 billion worth of stock with additional amounts subject to subscription only by railroad employees. Norris's measure provided for the issuance of government bonds at no more than 4.5 percent interest and limited dividends to 6 percent with excess earnings reverting to the government.[15] Norris also made provision for the corporation to acquire government-owned merchant ships for foreign and interstate commerce. All boats and barges owned by the government on inland waters were to be operated by the federal railroad corporation in connection with its railroad business. The corporation could construct dams to generate electricity for power and acquire coal mines for the same purpose.[16]

Norris said his measure would coordinate transportation upon the nation's rivers and rails, thereby reducing freight rates; the corporation could regulate passenger and freight traffic without any undue expense. It would likewise reduce rates upon shipments

[14] *Congressional Record,* 66th Cong., 2nd sess., Feb. 13, 1920, pp. 2830, 2843. A chart presented by Norris listing almost all the nation's Class I railroads, their capital stock outstanding, their average net income for the three years ending June 30, 1917, and the average percent of net income to capital stock can be found in *ibid.,* 65th Cong., 2nd sess., Feb. 19, 1918, pp. 2317–18. Frank H. Dixon in *Railroads and Government* (New York, 1922), p. 130, noted that while operating income in 1915 was low, "1916 surpassed any previous year in railroad history in the aggregate of net operating income, being $300,000,000 greater than 1915, and 1917 was less than 1916 by only $100,000,000." Dixon, unlike Norris, concluded that the bargain was "a fair one, equitable from the standpoint of both Government and carriers."

[15] *Congressional Record,* 66th Cong., 2nd sess., Dec. 4, 1919, p. 123; *New York Times,* Dec. 16, 1919.

[16] Norris statement about railroad bill, n.d.

to and from the United States.[17] Thus by the end of the Wilson era Norris favored government operation of most public utilities. Early in the New Freedom he had asked for government development of water resources. At the end of the Wilson administration he was calling for federal operation of transportation facilities.

Before Wilson left office, Norris broadened his definition of "public utility" to include stockyards. In an article entitled "Some Sidelights on the Packers" he examined the activities of the "multitude of unnecessary profiteers who are living in luxury upon the toil of the two extremes of this great equation," namely, underpaid producers and overcharged consumers. His facts were garnered from Senate hearings and a Federal Trade Commission investigation of the meat-packing industry which the packers were trying to counterbalance by an active advertising campaign.[18] Throughout the article Norris stressed the theme that the toil of the producer and the exorbitant prices paid by the consumer made possible the luxuries and indulgences of the great packers. They helped packers gain funds to attempt the control of legislation, to appoint officials, and to deceive the public. Though the Federal Trade Commission recommended prosecutions, Attorney General A. Mitchell Palmer decided not to institute criminal proceedings. Instead, he commenced a civil suit; this meant that the packers could be fined but that they would not be criminally liable. No common thief, Norris observed, could expect such merciful treatment. Thus the activities of the packers, like those of the government in its operation of the railroads, added to the high cost of living and helped to throw the times out of joint.[19]

The plight of the ordinary citizen in the postwar period dis-

[17] *Ibid.*

[18] The article was originally published in two installments in the *Nebraska Farmer*, May 15 and 22, 1920. It was also inserted in the *Congressional Record*, 66th Cong., 3rd sess., Jan. 22, 1921, pp. 1877–81 (quote is on p. 1878).

[19] *Congressional Record*, 66th Cong., 3rd sess., Jan. 22, 1921, p. 1881; Norris to Benjamin C. Marsh, Sept. 6, 1918. Norris specifically called for public ownership, control, and operation of stockyards "without any idea of profit": "The idea of having a market place owned and controlled by the corporations that do practically all of the buying at such a market place, is in itself a direct manipulation and control of the market by these special interests, and should not be tolerated in a free country." For a discussion of Palmer and the packers, see Stanley Coben, *A. Mitchell Palmer: Politician* (New York, 1963), pp. 189–92.

turbed Norris enormously. Victimized by the high cost of living and extraordinary examples of both public and private extravagance, Norris was more concerned with the citizen's loss of civil liberty than with his economic difficulties. In both instances he held the Wilson administration responsible.

During the war Norris had hoped that the Constitution could be held intact and that any citizen could criticize anyone or anything he considered wrong and was so prepared to prove. Thus he opposed an amendment to the Espionage Act enabling the Postmaster General to stop the mail of people suspected of violating the act; he thought it an arbitrary interference "with the very fundamental principles of human liberty and human freedom on which our great Commonwealth is founded." It placed in the hands of an individual a power far greater than that possessed by any American court, a power that in the past had impelled men to rebel against autocracy and monarchy. For a people seeking to make the world safe for democracy, it seemingly was of little consequence if, in the process of establishing democracy elsewhere, autocracy was maintained at home. Norris queried, "What doth it profit a man if he gain the whole world and lose his own soul?" [20]

Thus Congress, responding to demands of the executive branch, allowed officials to interfere with basic civil liberties. Rumblings and dissatisfactions pervaded the postwar period and helped "to put everybody on edge" against radicals and other critics of prevailing conditions. "Wrongs, profiteering, and inefficiency are overlooked," Norris asserted, but "when criticism is made, the critic is condemned as being a bolshevist." Though he did speak out against the "Red scare," his voice was not heard as the Wilson administration entered its last full year in office.[21] In January, 1920, Norris argued unsuccessfully against extending wartime sedition measures. He said that free government would perish if free speech was not preserved. Criticizing the power granted the Postmaster General, he mentioned the doleful effect such laws had in intimidating citizens into silence, noting that whenever and wherever officials had been given power to interfere with the liberty and the freedom of

[20] *Akron Beacon Journal,* May 22, 1918; *Congressional Record,* 65th Cong., 2nd sess., May 3, 1918, pp. 5978, 5980.
[21] Norris to Locke, Mar. 18, 1919; to A. T. Seashore, Dec. 27, 1919.

citizens "without trial, without cause, without a charge," free government based on free speech and a free press disappeared. Citing numerous examples, Norris showed how free government in the United States was disappearing, that in 1920 a man would be afraid "to talk to his neighbor, to speak his sentiments, to honestly criticize public officials." [22]

While Norris blamed the administration for this sad state of affairs, he recognized that the Republican-controlled Congress which followed the president's bidding was not entirely blameless. At the minimum he urged that suspect citizens should have the same basic rights universally accorded to criminals—a trial before being deprived of property or liberty, a hearing before a tribunal with an opportunity to defend oneself and where a written charge had to be filed. If Congress made the publication of seditious matter a crime, then an individual would come under the jurisdiction of the criminal code and the arbitrary procedures of government officials would disappear.[23]

Rather than curb free speech, Norris would encourage it; "instead of stopping a man from making a speech on a street corner, I would buy him another soap box and put it out on the street and tell him to go to it." His faith in the American way was so great that he was not afraid to let any man criticize it. Yet under wartime legislation, continued in time of peace, criticism was effectively stifled. Suffer abuse before curbing the right of free speech and free press because, Norris insisted, if you place in any man's hands the power to suppress, you eventually destroy free government. Moreover, given an intelligent, satisfied citizenry, radical criticism would not have "any more harmful effect than the blowing of the north wind." [24]

In another matter, while some senators acted as if "immigrant" and "radical" were almost synonymous terms and favored compulsory adult education to teach all recent arrivals the English language, Norris did neither. Though he favored compulsory education, it ought to be confined to children. Realizing that adults

[22] *Congressional Record,* 66th Cong., 2nd sess., Jan. 8, pp. 1253–57, Jan. 9, pp. 1259–60, Jan. 20, 1920, pp. 1772–73.

[23] *Ibid.,* Jan. 8, 1920, p. 1258.

[24] *Ibid.,* Jan. 9, 1920, p. 1261.

had to work to support themselves and their families, he would rather offer them special inducements—free tuition, free books, night classes—to learn the language. But it would be a mistake to force the English language on adult immigrants. And it would be using public funds in a way that Norris felt ought to be avoided.[25]

That he was far from enthusiastic about the Wilson administration in its last years in office is further evident from the fact that by the end of 1919 Norris announced his support of Hiram Johnson as the most suitable Republican to succeed Woodrow Wilson in the White House. Their views on both the incompetency and the extravagance of Wilsonian policies were similar.[26] Norris went further and insisted that in the campaign the Republican party capitalize upon the strength of its position rather than upon the weakness of the Democratic party. He observed, "We ought to be more anxious to be right than to be successful."

To be both right and successful, the Republican party would have to repeal legislation that Congress "in subservient obedience to the Executive" enacted impairing free speech and free press. It should favor a more equitable tax system, including a progressive inheritance tax and a better-structured income tax. In the realm of foreign policy Norris wanted the Republican party to support a league among civilized nations that would endorse disarmament and the end of conquest and would establish an international court for the settlement of disputes between nations, things the League of Nations did not do. The Republican candidate most in accord with these views was Hiram Johnson, on whose behalf Norris spoke in the Nebraska, Indiana, and New Jersey primary campaigns.[27]

Johnson, he told his listeners, stood fearlessly for efficiency and honesty in public service. He had fought political machines and a powerful monopoly in California and left it "one of the most progressive and efficiently administered governments in the world." In the Senate he stood for the things Norris favored. In short, Johnson was opposed to monopolies and political machines and championed the aspirations of rank-and-file voters. If the people

25 *Ibid.,* Jan. 22, pp. 1885–87, Jan. 23, 1920, pp. 1941, 1944, 1946.

26 Norris to Johnson Club Committee, Dec. 13, 1919 (published in the *Nebraska State Journal,* Dec. 17, 1919).

27 Norris statement about campaign of 1920, n.d.; Norris to William Armstrong, Apr. 10, 1920; to Will Owen Jones, May 8, 1920.

had a full and fair opportunity through a presidential primary to express their choice, Johnson would be nominated and then elected because of his personal popularity and the principles for which he stood. But, alas, Norris knew that Republican voters would not have a full and fair opportunity to express their choice and that party bosses would choose their presidential candidate for them.[28]

So little enthusiasm did Norris show for politics once it became evident that Hiram Johnson could not win the nomination that he wished Congress to remain in session until September to "clean up" legislative business.[29] He did not actively participate in the campaign and it was with misgivings that he voted for Harding and Coolidge. A "return to normalcy," Norris realized, would be a return to the machine politics and monopoly control that had characterized the political and economic scene during the Taft administration. His role, as it had been since the presidency of William Howard Taft, would be that of a progressive critic, harassing the administration and its policies but never enjoying enough power and influence to enact a progressive program. At the very best Norris could hope to hold the balance of power, preventing excesses and serving as an embarrassment to his party and its program.

He immediately assumed the latter role when after the election he called upon his colleagues to curb their enthusiasm and keep the appropriation for the inaugural ceremonies at a minimum. With the benefit of hindsight his remarks reveal a touch of sardonic humor:

> It is said that even when Lincoln was inaugurated there was extravagance; and to fortify that assertion the claim is made that Lincoln kissed thirty-four girls on that occasion. Nobody, however, has claimed that the Government had to pay for that osculatory process; the taxpayers were not burdened by it. Nobody

[28] Norris statement about Hiram Johnson, n.d. Norris approved of a plan by Gifford Pinchot and others to secure progressive delegates to the Republican convention, but nothing came of it; see Pinchot to Harold L. Ickes, telegram, July 16, 1919 (Box 7, Harold L. Ickes Papers, Manuscript Division, Library of Congress).

[29] *Congressional Record,* 66th Cong., 2nd sess., June 3, 1920, p. 8310. Congress adjourned on June 5, 1920, and agreed to reconvene after the election in December for the final or lame-duck session of the Sixty-sixth Congress.

will deny the same privilege to President-elect Harding, if he can find girls who are willing—and I presume he can—so long as it is not charged up to the taxpayers of the country and they do not have to pay for it.[30]

For the very reasons that Norris was unenthusiastic about Warren G. Harding's election, regular Republicans were delighted. William Howard Taft, for example, found the results most gratifying. The increased number of Republicans in the Senate particularly pleased him because the party now could prevent "LaFollette and Johnson and Borah and Norris" and one or two others from defeating Harding's tax, tariff, and other measures. The election minimized the importance of the progressives because they were not essential to a Republican majority; or, as Taft said, "it prevents their exercising that instrumentality of blackmail with which they love to manifest their nuisance importance." [31]

Thus the end of the Wilson era brought no joy to Norris; he envisioned further excesses and extravagances and a continuation of boss rule and monopoly control. Economy and efficiency cast within a progressive mold could not be expected. His frame of mind was accurately reflected in the anonymous article Norris published in 1920 in a popular national magazine. "A Senator's Story" related the trials and tribulations of maintaining a family in Washington on a senator's salary. The high cost of living and the belief that the Senate was still a millionaires' club made it difficult for a poor man to maintain himself in the nation's capital. The article did end on an optimistic note indicating Norris's ultimate belief that free government would triumph once the independent voter realized his power. Political machines could be overthrown once independent citizens acted so that "fundamental laws and facts of government, both state and national, are simplified so that the power shall rest directly in the hands of the people, thus giving them the opportunity to overthrow and keep out of office the public servant who serves the bosses rather than the states and

[30] *Ibid.,* 3rd sess., Jan. 4, 1921, p. 924.
[31] William Howard Taft to Mabel T. Boardman, Nov. 3, 1920; to William Hooper, Nov. 8, 1920 (both in Letterbooks, Box 128, William Howard Taft Papers, Manuscript Division, Library of Congress). These items were called to my attention through the courtesy of Professor Richard W. Leopold.

nation." The article was written before the 1920 conventions and was published as the campaign was getting underway. The election of Harding made its optimism seem false and hollow. The following years would prove it so.[32]

In an age of excess and indulgence Norris was the very model of probity and economy to which he wished the nation to return. Approaching his sixtieth birthday in 1920, he was well muscled and wiry and his hair was not yet completely gray. At times he would walk from his home in the Cleveland Park section to his Senate office and back, a distance of ten miles. His quiet manner had not changed either; his face was open, frank, and friendly. He was busier and more industrious than most of his colleagues on Capitol Hill. "He is," wrote Edward G. Lowry, "the average American born of clean stock in a farming country who has lived all his life upon a plane of perfect equality and upon terms of absolute democracy with his neighbors." His favorite poem, "Abou Ben Adhem," which at times without any self-consciousness he recited on the Senate floor, contained his basic creed. Norris wished to be classed as one of the followers of the religion proclaimed by the Oriental sage: one who loved the Lord by loving his fellow men.[33]

Other views, like his religious beliefs, were equally simple and straightforward, unmarred by complexities and nuances of a theological or philosophical nature. His convictions were for the most part based on experience. Once arriving at a conclusion, Norris was not afraid to express it though it might run counter to majority sentiment. He wore his party label lightly, but he believed that the Democratic party under Woodrow Wilson was more machine-dominated than his own. While personal animus and partisanship appeared in his public expressions, these instances were exceptions; the general rule of his official behavior gave the impression of a disinterested person striving to promote the general welfare.[34]

[32] "A Senator's Story" appeared in the *Saturday Evening Post,* in two installments: Aug. 7, 1920, pp. 22–23, 125, and Aug. 14, 1920, pp. 22–23, 170.

[33] Edward G. Lowry, *Washington Close-Ups* (Boston and New York, 1921), p. 115; *Congressional Record,* 66th Cong., 2nd sess., June 3, 1920, p. 8359.

[34] For his views on happiness, see Norris to Mr. and Mrs. H. F. Merwin, Mar. 26, 1914. Norris wrote, ". . . I have learned one thing that I do not believe can ever be successfully controverted, and that is that true happiness is found in

"In his manner, in his processes of mind, and in his mode of living he is as simple, as plain, as direct, and as unassuming," Lowry observed, as when he was teaching school in Ohio. Consequently, he was uncomfortable coping with the high cost of living and the excesses of the cynical and sophisticated postwar American scene. Nevertheless, he continued to speak as one who loved his fellow man well enough to do battle for his cause against corporate and governmental domination. Following this course in the 1920s, Norris would become a major figure on the American political scene.[35]

the contented home of moderate circumstances. No true enjoyment ever comes to those who never struggle, who never sacrifice, and who never are compelled to work. . . . Those who struggle for money or power or for prestige simply for the sake of the power or the wealth, never see real happiness." With regard to death, Norris believed in existence beyond the grave and he could not "conceive how the transition should be any other than an advancement" in which those who passed into "the unknown realms" were living in "a happier and more blissful state." "If those we love," he wrote, "have passed into that existence, then we ought to temper our sorrow even with gladness." These views differed from his depressed feelings at the time of the deaths of his mother and first wife. For an expression of Norris's more optimistic view of death, see Norris to F. N. Merwin, Sept. 9, 1914.

[35] Lowry, *Washington Close-Ups*, p. 118; Norris to Harper Overland Company, Nov. 25, 1919; to C. B. Gray, Apr. 7, 1920. "A Senator's Story," Part I, pp. 22–23, 125, gives examples of Norris coping with the high cost of living in Washington, D.C.

Normalcy: Foreign Affairs

9

Normalcy officially began with the inauguration of Warren G. Harding on March 4, 1921. For George W. Norris it meant little. His party now occupied the positions of power and prestige in government. He would continue in the role of critic, although achieving much more attention than during the Wilson era. The retreat from responsibility that historians have noted as characterizing the decade Norris merely saw as a continuation of what he had experienced during the Wilson administration. Seniority now gave him a prominence he had not formerly enjoyed. His support was needed by a Republican party whose control over Congress was very precarious throughout the decade. Thus the scope of his criticisms, the power and influence he enjoyed, and the attention he received were greater than ever before. Norris became a national figure during the decade in the role of a constructive critic, suggesting alternatives more in tune with the public interest as he viewed it.

Selfish concern with profits at public expense dominated the American scene, as it did during the later Wilson years. In doing battle with private wealth seeking public favors, Norris shifted his concern from procedural to economic reform. Not that his interest in improving the machinery of government declined during the 1920s. Rather, other issues came to the center of his attention. While the nation was focusing on social themes—prohibition, immigration restriction, flappers and their foibles, Lindbergh, Leo-

138

pold and Loeb, and the Scopes trial in Tennessee, to mention but a few—Norris was aroused by economic concentration and exploitation, especially in the field of hydroelectric power, and by his old progressive interest in improving the efficiency of government.

In short, he was during the era known as normalcy a progressive in transition. During the Wilson years Norris's attention had been attracted to economic matters in the realms of agriculture, taxation, and hydroelectric power, among others. To be sure, some of these issues, agriculture and the tariff, for example, had concerned him as a congressman. But his congressional fame related to his role in overthrowing the power of the Speaker. As a senator his interest in economic issues grew. His opposition to war was followed by a desire to curb the influence of private groups that placed profits above patriotism. In the twenties his perseverance paid off. His views gained increasing recognition and eventual acceptance as the country coped with the crises of the Great Depression.

As the Sixty-seventh Congress convened, Norris was still in the process of getting his office staff to function effectively. Ray McCarl received his reward for deserting Norris in 1918 by being made Comptroller General in the Harding administration. Presumably Senator Simeon Fess, who had lured McCarl from Norris with the attractive offer of executive secretary of the Republican Congressional Campaign Committee, was responsible for the promotion. McCarl's replacements in the Norris office were a young Army veteran, Thomas Hudson McKee, who served for a year and a half before moving across the hall to join the secretarial staff of New York Senator James W. Wadsworth, and Harrie Thomas from Harvard, Nebraska, who had devotedly campaigned with Norris in 1912. He served as private secretary and as clerk of the Agriculture and Forestry Committee. He remained until family problems and his own strained financial circumstances necessitated his resignation in 1922.[1] Until Norris's son-in-law came to Washington in 1926, he could not resolve the crisis that occurred when McCarl left the office in 1918. Devoted clerks, particularly Mabelle J. Talbert and Lois Wickham, performed yeoman service. But until

[1] Thomas Hudson McKee to George W. Norris, Nov. 15, 1941; Norris to Harrie G. Thomas, Dec. 14, 1921.

John P. Robertson assumed the role of chief assistant and private secretary, he never had a person who could replace McCarl and leave him free to devote all his time and attention to senatorial responsibilities. Until his office staff functioned effectively, neither could Norris.

During most of the lame-duck session of the Sixty-sixth Congress Norris had been ill. He took little part in the proceedings of the Senate and virtually ignored his correspondence and office details.[2] But when the first session of the Sixty-seventh Congress convened on April 11, 1921, Norris was ready to continue as a progressive critic now of his own party, fully returned to control of the government for the first time since the election of William Howard Taft in 1908.

The Sixty-seventh Congress gave distinction to the Harding administration. It was the first Congress to hold four sessions and it surpassed all previous Congresses by the number of days—415—on which it convened. It passed 600 bills and 90 resolutions and when it finally adjourned *sine die* in March of 1923, for the first time in nine years Congress did not function through the summer months. At its outset Norris sought with little success to secure able appointments. At his request the injunction of secrecy was removed from the vote on the confirmation of George Harvey as ambassador to Great Britain. Revealing himself as the lone Republican in opposition, Norris claimed that Harvey had pursued methods both disreputable and dishonorable in driving his enemies from public life and that despite great abilities and passionate patriotism he could not function as an effective diplomat. Norris said other Republican members of the Senate privately agreed with him. Later, in 1923, Norris and eight others, including both Minnesota senators, voted against Harvey's successor, ex-Senator Frank B. Kellogg of Minnesota.[3] In another instance Norris sought the appointment of James Wickersham, former territorial delegate from Alaska, as governor of the territory to prevent a representative of the Guggenheim interests from receiving the post. Though

---

[2] Private secretary to William Armstrong, Feb. 14, 1921.

[3] Frances Parkinson Keyes, *Letters from a Senator's Wife* (New York, 1924), p. 322; *Congressional Record,* 67th Cong., 1st sess., Apr. 16, p. 369, Apr. 21, 1921, p. 539; 68th Cong., 1st sess., Dec. 11, 1923, p. 235.

Wickersham was not appointed, Gifford Pinchot informed Norris that neither would the "Guggenheim candidate" secure the job.[4]

So hungry were Republicans for the spoils of office that there was little that Norris, deprived of party patronage since 1910, could do to stem the partisan tide. Appointees brought under the blanket of civil service late in the Wilson administration were removed. Objecting to this process and to some of Harding's appointees, Norris claimed, following Lincoln, "that he was for anybody as long as he believed they were right; that he would stay with them as long as he thought they were right; and that he would leave them whenever he thought they were wrong." [5]

Out of step with the Harding administration in the matter of appointments, Norris soon was opposed to its diplomacy as well. He saw the spirit of revenge and hatred being inculcated into the hearts of men and women by deceiving statesmen and selfish leaders on both sides of the Atlantic. Only David Lloyd George, who insisted that it was impossible for Germany to pay reparations, received Norris's praise. But prospects for peace would not improve until the deceptions and falsehoods of most national leaders were exposed and their policies defeated by an aroused electorate.[6]

Applauding Lloyd George for telling the truth about German reparations, Norris took what he considered a realistic position on war debts owed the United States. As long as debtor governments met their interest payments, he would not collect the principal until the nation could pay without undue hardship. Extensions should be freely given. But Norris was unwilling to forgive or forget the debts, since he regarded them as essentially a contractual obligation. In the case of Great Britain and France Norris felt no sympathy. Since the armistice Britain had spent more money subduing the people of Ireland "than would pay all the interest she owes to the Government of the United States." Both Britain and France, he claimed, "have been spending more money in warfare, after this great League of Nations was installed to give peace and

[4] Norris to Gifford Pinchot, Mar. 11, 1921; Pinchot to Norris, Mar. 15, 1921 (both in Box 240, Gifford Pinchot Papers, Manuscript Division, Library of Congress).

[5] Norris to John P. Robertson, Feb. 22, 1921; to Harry A. Billany, Dec. 21, 1922; to James C. Kinsler, Feb. 20, 1923; to George C. Dyer, Jan. 4, 1923.

[6] Norris to Norman Thomas, July 20, 1923.

harmony forever, than would pay all the interest that they owe to the Government of the United States." [7]

Money collected in the form of interest on the war debt, Norris said, should provide a bonus for overseas veterans. But when Congress in 1922 considered using funds collected in connection with war debts for paying doughboys stationed on the Rhine River, Norris objected. Unable to understand why American soldiers need remain abroad, he criticized America's allies for requesting that they stay in Europe while their governments were collecting reparations from Germany and at the same time reneging on obligations owed the United States.[8]

In his attitude toward European nations his views ran counter to those of the administration. On April 16, 1921, he introduced a resolution protesting violations and indignities committed by British forces against the Irish people in their struggle for independence. In June he offered evidence documenting his charges. It took him two days to present this material; it filled a fifty-four-page pamphlet which he sent to constituents. The situation in Ireland, he insisted, was making it difficult to maintain good will and common understanding between the United States and Great Britain. Violating the dictates of humanity and the laws of war, British troops were preventing the Irish from achieving a government of their own choice. Although Norris insisted that his remarks had as their primary object the alleviation of suffering in Ireland, they actually revealed the essence of his hostility toward imperialism and provided a touchstone for his criticism of aspects of American foreign policy.[9]

Norris criticized Great Britain for violating the Wilsonian principles of self-determination and the rights of weak nations. These principles, supposedly secured as a result of the Allied victory, were proclaimed "by British statemen to their people, to the people of Ireland and to the world." Then in shocking "violation of every rule of war, peace or humanity" British armed forces subjected the Irish people to conditions of brute force, intimidation, and ter-

---

[7] *Congressional Record*, 67th Cong., 1st sess., July 11, 1921, pp. 3531–32; 2nd sess., Jan. 24, p. 1631, Jan. 30, 1922, p. 1901.

[8] *Ibid.*, 1st sess., July 11, 1921, pp. 3528, 3534; 2nd sess., Mar. 17, 1922, p. 4003.

[9] *Ibid.*, 1st sess., June 20, 1921, p. 2803.

ror that trampled human rights and flagrantly destroyed property. He championed the cause of Irish freedom and called upon the Senate to express the sentiment of the American people by demanding for the Irish "the same freedom, the same liberty that by the will of Almighty God and the sacrifices of our forefathers we ourselves enjoy." [10]

Analysis of the situation in Ireland and his earlier examination of the Shantung question convinced Norris that Great Britain and Japan were determined to rule the world. He saw no similar determination on the part of the Soviet Union and favored recognition, an action most Americans opposed. Norris argued that "if the Russians want a Soviet Government, I do not believe it is any of our business." He disputed the value of aid previously extended to the Kerensky government, claiming that the Soviets acquired most of the clothing, munitions, and guns supplied to the troops of Generals P. N. Wrangel and A. I. Denekin when their forces were captured or surrendered. All ventures in bolstering governments not having the support of the people were bound to fail and to increase the American taxpayer's burden.[11]

On the other hand, he wished to help victims of famine and war in Russia, claiming that "millions of people have died of starvation." The Agriculture and Forestry Committee with Norris as chairman endorsed a resolution, which Congress enacted, authorizing the president to expend not more than $20 million to purchase foodstuffs for the relief of distress in Russia. Norris was disturbed by rumours of friction, revolving around Secretary of Commerce Herbert Hoover, which supposedly was responsible for the delay in sending relief shipments. While he claimed no knowledge of these controversies, he thought the delay unfortunate, stemming in part from the fact that "our Government has not recognized the Soviet Government." [12] Recognition, he said, would allow for trade in which American machinery could find an ex-

[10] *Ibid.*, June 20 and 21, 1921, pp. 2803–30 (for the entire speech).

[11] Norris to "Dear Boys," Dec. 30, 1920; to H. Gifford, Apr. 17, 1922; to O. H. Johnson, Apr. 18, 1922.

[12] Norris to H. E. Wekesser, Feb. 18, 1922; to Herbert Hoover, Dec. 29, 1921; to E. S. Miller, Dec. 28, 1921; to Johnson, Apr. 18, 1922. Benjamin C. Marsh, *Lobbyist for the People* (Washington, D.C., 1953), pp. 78–79, presents an incident indicating Hoover's opposition to Russian relief.

panding market and jobs for American technicians to install and operate this equipment. Russian raw materials and foodstuffs could find ready markets in many lands. But because outside parties had not been allowed to dictate the form of government in Russia, recognition was withheld. Since 1917 the demise of the Soviet system had been continually predicted, yet it still endured and the United States refused recognition. Such a policy to Norris was not only "foolish and silly"; it was fundamentally wrong. Taxpayers lost money and American soldiers died "simply because our Government says that the Russians have not set up a government there according to our liking." [13]

That Russian agents were plotting to overthrow the American government Norris found inconceivable. Such a view had prevailed "under the palmy days of Palmer," and millions of dollars had been spent to arrest thousands of suspected aliens. Yet the records of only a minute number revealed anything of a suspicious or criminal nature. Norris had been told by a man who watched Palmer's agents that they arrested "every man who had any whiskers." With Charles Evans Hughes in mind, he commented, "If the Department of Justice, now under Daugherty, are going to make that kind of raids, they ought at least to give the Secretary of State notice before they make them." [14]

Critical of administration policies with regard to Europe, Norris found even less to praise when he turned to Latin America. While he considered the treaty payment of $25 million to Colombia as indefensible, the provision allowing Colombia to transport troops and war supplies through the Panama Canal without paying tolls bothered Norris more than the lump sum designed to soothe her for the loss of her territory. These special privileges could have repercussions affecting American trade throughout the world. Moreover, Harding's admonition regarding economy would be cast aside with ratification of this treaty.

Acknowledging that the United States had done a wrong to Colombia, Norris said it was illogical to strike out the apology

[13] Norris statement on recognition of Russia, n.d. [1920s].

[14] *Congressional Record*, 68th Cong., 1st sess., Dec. 20, 1923, p. 447. Secretary of State Charles Evans Hughes had a trim, dignified, and full beard. He and Henry Cabot Lodge, also included in Norris's remarks, sported the most famous beards in Washington.

originally contained in the treaty. But upon the insistence of Henry Cabot Lodge, intent on avoiding any slur upon the actions of Theodore Roosevelt in 1903, this clause was deleted. Norris insisted that the United States, desirous of friendship with all countries, could not afford to buy the friendship of any country. If American oil interests seeking concessions in Colombia wanted a favorable climate in which to operate, then, Norris said, "let the oil, rather than the Treasury of the United States, pay for the smiles we are trying to get." The treaty with Colombia squandered American funds and partially surrendered American rights to the canal. But Norris's vote, along with those of eighteen other senators, was not enough to defeat it.[15]

Elsewhere in Latin America bolstering of governments in Haiti, Nicaragua, and Santo Domingo aroused vociferous opposition in which Norris participated. Not only did American interference harm the country involved but other governments believed the United States intent upon conquest. In June of 1922 Norris charged, "We put our Army into Nicaragua . . . changed their Government officials entirely by the force of arms, established a Government contrary to the wishes of the people of that country and then proceeded to make an agreement with ourselves by which we could say that we had the consent of that Government to continue in our occupation of the country." It seemed to him that the United States had done practically the same thing in Haiti.[16]

In both instances invasions had occurred without the matter having been decided by Congress. They had happened, Norris believed, simply because executive authority desired it, and they brought the United States disrepute in the eyes of other nations. Though the Haitian invasion occurred during the Wilson administration, Norris's remarks were prompted by an amendment to the naval appropriation bill seeking to end the occupation. It was clear that Harding's administration proposed to continue it. American bankers benefited because a financial adviser, one of William Jennings Bryan's "deserving Democrats," was foisted on the Haitian government and also because "the American Navy and

15 *Ibid.*, 67th Cong., 1st sess., Apr. 19, 1921, pp. 465–69.
16 *Ibid.*, 2nd sess., June 19, 1922, p. 8967.

the American Army are the guaranties that the bonds shall be paid in full." Investors benefited from American insistence upon removing the clause in the Haitian constitution prohibiting alien land ownership.

As an American citizen, Norris was ashamed of a Haitian policy predicated upon neither legal nor moral grounds. He said:

> When we stand before the world as one of the leading nations of civilization and take advantage of a poor, weak, ignorant nation . . . and perform the little tricks that we have been performing there, we ought to withdraw in shame and humiliation. All these things are being charged up in history against us. All over South America they know about it, and we are gaining every day in the reputation . . . that we are trying to conquer the balance of this continent, and that we intend in the end to take all without their consent under our flag and under our jurisdiction. It is no defense to say that these people are barbarous, not fit for self-government, and therefore we must take charge of them.[17]

Surprisingly, given his indignation about American policies toward Europe and Latin America, Norris had little to say about the treaties emanating from the conferences conducted in Washington seeking a new balance in the Far East. When he did speak, he favored Japan securing a mandate over former German outposts in the Caroline, Marshall, and Mariana archipelagoes. Formerly in bitter opposition to Japanese retention of the Shantung peninsula, Norris now favored the Japanese. He did so because he felt a mandate better than Japan owning the islands outright. According to the mandate terms missionaries could pursue their calling and Japan would have to make available an annual report delineating her treatment of the native population. Unless the United States wished to go to war with Japan over these coral atolls, there was little that could be done to change the situation.[18] Because of the atolls he would not oppose a treaty; thus, finding no moral issue to arouse his already keen antagonism against Japan, Norris voted for the Four-Power Treaty in the Senate. For

[17] *Ibid.,* pp. 8956–57, 8968–69 (quote is on p. 8969). An open letter to the Secretary of State of Apr. 27, 1922, condemning American policy in Haiti was inserted by Norris into the *Record* as part of his remarks; see *ibid.,* pp. 8969–73.
[18] *Ibid.,* Feb. 25, 1922, p. 3052.

the first time on any important issue he did not agree with Robert M. LaFollette. While they spoke no words about their difference, LaFollette felt "a great personal tug" not to have Norris siding with him when the treaty came to a vote.[19]

Central to Norris's criticism in the realm of foreign affairs was his firm opposition "to any civilized people being governed by any other people without their consent." In the case of the Philippine Islands he favored granting Filipinos their independence, having concluded that they were competent to govern themselves. On this premise he based his denunciation of the "disgraceful and barbarous practices" of the Turks in Armenia, the Japanese in Korea and China, and the British in Ireland, India, and Egypt. At times since the end of the war it seemed as if the world had gone mad, the victors engaging in the very practices they had condemned their opponents for during the conflict. Yet deplorable as conditions were, Norris did not see how the United States could take remedial action short of sending an army abroad. And that he was unwilling to do. While his sympathies were with oppressed peoples, he recognized that barbarism encouraged barbarism and that the oppressed would respond in kind against their oppressors. He sided with subjugated peoples and criticized his own government whenever it cast principle aside. He first acted on these premises during the Wilson administration and continued to do so during the Harding administration. In this area, as in others, he found no break in continuity between Wilson and Harding.[20]

If civilization was to end the oppression of one people by another, Norris said that a first step would be to let investors in a foreign country take the risk of whatever might happen in that country. Regardless of what other nations might do, the American "Government at least ought to announce once and for all that under no circumstances would it send warships or men to make valid any agreement that speculators may make." If the United States would renounce advantages secured at another country's expense, it could conduct its foreign policy based on "honorable

[19] *Ibid.*, Feb. 27, 1922, p. 3089; Belle Case and Fola LaFollette, *Robert M. LaFollette*, 2 vols. (New York, 1953), 2: 1038.

[20] Norris to Fred G. Bale, Jan. 28, 1922; to Walter N. Giles, July 18, 1921; to Mabel Dickinson, June 11, 1921, Dec. 10, 1922.

dealings." Popular control of foreign affairs, by eliminating secrecy and assuring publicity, could achieve the honor and integrity Norris believed should characterize American policies.[21]

While diplomats should conduct negotiations in secrecy, full publicity of the proceedings once negotiations were concluded would raise the standard of American diplomacy and promote good will with other nations. Comparable to the British method of subjecting ministers to the House of Commons, an opportunity for public questioning of officials was necessary. If publicity could be detrimental to the national interest, once the point was established, Norris was willing that information then be withheld from the public. Even more important, public negotiation was vital in securing or protecting private privileges. "We should as a nation," Norris said, "cast aside forever the idea that when civil contracts are entered into by individuals or corporations with individuals or groups in the government of another country, our nationals can expect to have their claims against the nationals or the government of that other country backed up by diplomatic pressure or by show of force." Full publicity of the doings of diplomats and investors could end the confusion between national honor and private business which permeated foreign relations. While not guaranteed to change policies, publicity offered an opportunity for resolving rumors and conflicting viewpoints in diplomatic dealings. The enforcement of publicity over a period of time, involving, incidentally, a minimum of expense, could help develop an intelligent popular interest in foreign relations and thereby, Norris hoped, bring the conduct of foreign affairs "perceptibly nearer to popular control." [22]

[21] Norris to Judson King, July 20, 1923; Norris, "Popular Control of Foreign Affairs" (draft), *The World Tomorrow,* vol. 7, no. 1 (Jan., 1924).

[22] Norris, "Popular Control of Foreign Affairs" (draft).

Normalcy: Domestic Problems

10

Publicity was a weapon for bringing light into dark places where selfish groups sought to evade the public interest and promote private profits. It had been championed by progressives in their period of prominence before World War I. So, too, were economy and efficiency weapons that progressives had used with telling effect in seeking governmental reform. Throughout the Harding administration Norris fought for a fuller understanding of American foreign policy by revealing its hidden dimensions and the contradictions between proclaimed policies and actual facts. When he turned to domestic issues, he continued to criticize the administration, espousing these same progressive virtues but with greater emphasis on economy and efficiency.

Only once, in opposing a joint resolution granting $5 million to Liberia, presumably for her help in the war, did Norris principally use the theme of economy in a matter pertaining to foreign policy. Usually he felt the greatest opportunity for reducing governmental expenses to be in connection with military might. In 1922, for example, he saw no need for a standing army of 150,000 men. It could be reduced to 100,000, and he would cut naval strength as well. Greater reliance on the National Guard, at a peak of readiness with its recent wartime experience, would obviate the necessity of a large standing army, as did the numbers of discharged veterans who in effect comprised a well-trained citizen soldiery. Thus military strength could be reduced, the taxpayer's burden lightened, and the nation's security remain at a high level of efficiency.[1]

Norris was not incapable of viewing a national debt as an asset, and he could understand an individual, like a nation, going into debt "for the purpose of doing some useful thing, creating some new product, developing some new invention of use and benefit to mankind. . . ." But at the end of a holocaust that had taxed the capacities of the American people, he believed increased military expenditures could bankrupt the nation. In 1921 taxpayers were paying more interest on the nation's debt than it cost to run the government before the war.[2]

Moreover, with the scuttling of the German navy there was no need to increase what was already the second largest navy in the world. To keep this force in a condition of readiness, Norris said that in the interest of economy and efficiency the federal government "ought to do its own work, ought to make its own guns, ought to build its own ships of war, and ought to do everything that is necessary to be done in the maintaining of its Navy." Recent revelations showed how private parties "had passed off on the Government worthless armor plate" that might have jeopardized victory on the high seas. If Secretary of the Navy Edwin Denby persisted in calling for a navy second to none, another arms race could start, bringing with it burdensome debts and increased taxation. Norris also realized that no sooner would the new navy be completed than it would be outdated, given accelerating changes in technology and the conduct of war. Economy in the public interest so that taxpayers might be lightly burdened was a Jeffersonian precept that Norris accepted. Like Jefferson, he believed that curtailing military expenditures was one way to achieve it.[3]

Another way of achieving economy was by eliminating subsidies not in the public interest. Coastwise shipping, for example, already benefited in several ways without a subsidy. Foreign ships

[1] *Congressional Record,* 67th Cong., 3rd sess., Nov. 24, 1922, p. 127; 2nd sess., June 2, 1922, p. 8029; George W. Norris to G. B. Welch, June 17, 1922; to W. Ritchie, Jr., June 10, 1922.

[2] *Congressional Record,* 67th Cong., 1st sess., May 13, 1921, pp. 1412–13.

[3] *Ibid.,* pp. 1413–15, May 17, 1921, p. 1504; 2nd sess., Feb. 11, 1922, pp. 2430, 2433; 4th sess., Mar. 1, 1923, p. 5000.

were prohibited from engaging in this trade, and the Panama Canal toll did not curb competition with railroads. So, too, Norris opposed the ship subsidy measure favored by the Harding administration. This bill, which incidentally provoked a Senate filibuster and never came to a vote, proposed to sell about 1,400 government-owned merchant vessels costing about $4 billion to private ship owners. Until they were sold, the government would compensate the U.S. Shipping Board for losses incurred in their operation.[4] Norris favored the government retaining its merchant fleet at a loss, if necessary, rather than selling ships "at gift prices" and then subsidizing private persons to operate the vessels. In the event of another war the government would have to buy them back at an enhanced price. If, instead, the vessels were turned over to the Panama Railroad Company or some other government agency and kept in operation, they would help reduce freight rates. In the interest of economy Norris also opposed the expenditure of $2,500,000 for the construction of an archives building. Since all officials proclaimed the necessity of economy in government, he thought it best to postpone the project.[5]

In part because of economy, he opposed monopoly and favored effective enforcement of the Sherman Antitrust Act. What aroused Norris's ire was an article appearing in the *Washington Herald* for February 16, 1922. Because this paper was purported to be owned entirely or in part by Secretary of Commerce Herbert Hoover, the article, Norris claimed, had "a semi-official appearance." Its gist was that "concerns that want to combine and form a trust or a monopoly have only to announce that their combination is not in restraint of trade and is not a monopoly." The article included portions of a letter from Hoover to Attorney General Harry Daugherty in which the Secretary called for standardization and uniformity in areas ranging from systems of cost accounting to the use of trade names and for the representation of trade associations in matters affecting legislation, litigation, and

---

[4] Norris to Gilbert Henline, Feb. 6, 1922; John D. Hicks, *Republican Ascendancy, 1921–1933* (New York, 1960), p. 61; Frances Parkinson Keyes, *Letters from a Senator's Wife* (New York, 1924), pp. 284–85.

[5] Norris to William L. Cartledge, Dec. 19, 1922; to E. E. Spafford, Feb. 16, 1923; to Frank Fiscus, Mar. 8, 1923; *Congressional Record*, 67th Cong., 4th sess., Jan. 20, 1923, pp. 2064, 2067.

transportation. One sentence in the article championed "closer relations between an industry and the Federal and State Governments through trade associations." These practices, Norris said, would make the Sherman Antitrust Act meaningless; competition would become "as dead as a doornail." What was efficiency to Herbert Hoover seemed to be anything but economy in the public interest to George W. Norris.

Norris realized that the question of monopoly was one that well-intentioned men might debate. If the American people desired monopoly, "then we must take the other horn of the dilemma and regulate them, and have prices fixed, and so on, by somebody who is not directly interested in either side of the matter." But such was not the theory behind the Sherman Act. As long as competition was to be retained, what Herbert Hoover proposed should be prohibited.[6]

Nor was Norris satisfied with the method pursued in contracting the currency to curb inflation. When the Sixty-seventh Congress convened, he introduced a resolution calling upon the Federal Reserve Board to be more lenient in its reserve requirements so that member banks might extend additional credit to farmers. With the rising number of rural bank failures, Norris hoped the Federal Reserve System might adopt a guarantee-of-deposits law similar to those in effect in some states. But his efforts were in vain because the Harding administration did not lend its support.[7]

Norris agreed with the harsh criticisms of Andrew Mellon's reductionist tax policies leveled by Senator James Couzens of Michigan. He supported Couzens's resolution calling for an investigation of the Bureau of Internal Revenue. Rather than merely agreeing with his criticisms, Norris joined in attacking the conference report embodying the Secretary of the Treasury's tax-reduction program. He opposed the deletion of Senate amendments calling for a graduated corporate income tax and for publicity of income tax returns, stressing that in "a democratic form of government there is no place for secret public business." Not pro-

[6] *Congressional Record,* 67th Cong., 2nd sess., Feb. 16, pp. 2645–46, Mar. 2, 1922, p. 3279; Norris to John L. Mechem, Mar. 2, 1922.

[7] Norris to Frederick C. Howe, Dec. 11, 1922; to E. Duane Pratt, Apr. 27, 1921; to C. E. Burnham, July 15, 1921; to C. W. McConaughy, Dec. 16, 1921.

viding a graduated corporation tax would benefit big business and work to the detriment of small firms, since all corporations would pay a flat rate of 14 percent.[8]

In one instance where Norris viewed as valid the expenditure of public funds, the president vetoed the proposal. Norris believed a reasonable bonus was due "those who in most instances sacrificed much to serve their country in its time of need." Aware that "adjusted compensation" would add an additional burden to tax-payers, he rationalized by arguing that "if the wealth of the country had been properly taxed," there would be no difficulty in meeting governmental expenses and obligations. A progressive inheritance tax, insistence upon interest payments by foreign governments on their American indebtedness, proper levies upon profits and incomes of both individuals and corporations—if all or most of these proposals were considered, if Andrew Mellon's monetary policies were reversed, funds soon would become available to meet government needs and to aid those who "bore the heaviest burden and were deprived of any opportunity to make money during the War." [9]

Criticism was also leveled by Norris at another area of progressive interest: procedural reform and administrative efficiency. Though it is difficult to separate the themes of economy and efficiency, Norris's concern for procedural reform was designed to simplify sectors of government so that archaic structures and antiquated procedures could be overhauled to operate effectively and efficiently. His fame as a congressman rested upon his spectacular but only partial victory in reforming the House rules in 1910. Criticism of partisan procedures and unwieldy practices continued throughout his first term in the Senate with little success. Nevertheless, he now accelerated his attack and, as was the pattern in all of his great achievements, sowed some seeds of future triumphs.

Expanding civil service to include postal employees was a theme that had long interested Norris. Thus he viewed Harding's action

[8] *Congressional Record,* 68th Cong., 1st sess., May 6, pp. 7916–19, May 24, 1924, pp. 9403–6; Norris to H. Hemmingsen, Feb. 26, 1924.

[9] Norris to William J. Weinhenmayer, Apr. 11, 1924; to Frank A. Warner, June 9, 1924.

as a step backward when he removed postal positions placed in civil service by Woodrow Wilson. The Post Office Department now would submit the three top names to the chief Republican official in the district, who would make the selection. His choice would then be certified by the Post Office Department and forwarded to the president for appointment.[10] This process nullified the spirit of civil service appointment of postmasters and Norris called it to the attention of the Postmaster General.[11] The shift, he felt, would do great harm to the public service, since Republicans had not campaigned on a plank promising to reinstate partisanship in the Post Office Department. Indeed, Norris admitted that Woodrow Wilson "on the whole . . . did a great deal for civil service" and that the Republican party in this respect was worse than the Democratic. Civil service was necessary for efficient government. But if the majority disagreed on this point, they ought to strike the civil service law from the statute books and stop claiming as a virtue something they did not believe.[12]

While progressives favored civil service reform and were critical of partisanship in the Post Office Department, not all agreed with Norris in calling for the abolition of the Electoral College. In 1916 he had introduced a joint resolution which proposed a constitutional amendment abolishing the College of Electors and providing for direct election of president and vice-president. In 1922 he introduced it again, indicating that "the people have very little, if anything, to say in regard to the nomination of presidential candidates." If the Electoral College were abandoned, independent presidential candidates conceivably could be elected. In addition,

---

[10] Under the Wilson order the Postmaster General would appoint the candidate with the highest score on the civil service list. Norris was aware that Postmaster General Burleson did not always act in good faith; see Norris to J. H. Harrison, June 2, 1923.

[11] Norris to Will H. Hays, Mar. 21, 1921. Norris claimed that Postmaster General Hays agreed with him and did not favor the modification; see Norris to Harrison, June 2, 1923.

[12] Norris to Lew D. Holston, Aug. 18, 1923; to M. R. Halker, Sept. 21, 1923; *Congressional Record,* 67th Cong., 2nd sess., Apr. 4, pp. 4968–69, 4971, Feb. 11, 1922, p. 2442; 4th sess., Jan. 26, 1923, p. 2485. In an article entitled "My Party, Right or Wrong" published in *Collier's,* June 21, 1924, pp. 5–6, Norris presented a long peroration against partisanship, recounting and distorting his previous battles and expounding on the situation during Harding's administration. Draft of the article is in the Norris Papers.

"such change would have the beneficial effect of restraining political leaders and machines from imposing upon the party and the people unworthy candidates for office." By allowing the people the "free and untrammeled right" to vote for president and vice-president, the Constitution then would grant citizens another fundamental right. Every voter could decide whether he would be partisan or not in presidential matters. Better candidates would appear, expenses would be reduced, and the people would benefit, Norris believed, if the Electoral College were abolished.[13]

In calling for a further amendment fixing the presidential term, Norris sowed a seed that eventually bloomed. At the outset everybody laughed when a resolution introduced by Senator Thaddeus Caraway on behalf of a Farmers Union group in Arkansas repudiating "lame ducks" was referred to the Agriculture and Forestry Committee rather than to the Judiciary Committee. As chairman of the former committee, Norris did not wish the resolution sent to his group, and he claimed he "had an impulse to object." He remained silent, however, and everybody thought it would never be considered in committee. But, Norris remarked, "the Committee on Agriculture [and Forestry] took it up seriously." He was directed to report a measure resolving the difficulty. The joint resolution drafted by Norris had two parts and necessitated a constitutional amendment to accomplish its purpose. One part pertained to presidential electors; the other proposed beginning on the first Monday in January the term of the new Congress elected the previous November. The short or lame-duck session would thus be eliminated. The resolution was read at a meeting of a subcommittee and was then referred to the full committee; by a unanimous vote the committee directed Norris to report it to the Senate. For the only time in the nation's history a proposed amendment to the Constitution was reported from a committee other than Judiciary.[14]

The part pertaining to presidential elections, calling for the abolition of the Electoral College, failed to attract serious atten-

[13] *New York Times,* Jan. 25, 1916; *Congressional Record,* 67th Cong., 2nd sess., Jan. 4, 1922, p. 749; Norris to B. Brewer, Dec. 16, 1923.

[14] *Congressional Record,* 67th Cong., 4th sess., Jan. 29, 1923, pp. 2679–80; Norris to Joseph Polcar, Mar. 17, 1924.

tion. In February, 1923, Norris agreed to separate the two propositions and eliminate this part of the resolution. The other part did attract serious attention. It called for the commencement of a congressman's term two weeks prior to those of the president and vice-president, giving Congress ample time to organize and to canvass the electoral votes as provided in the Constitution. Inauguration day would be in January instead of March. When the proposed amendment went into effect, members of Congress would begin to serve two months after they were elected, eliminating the current delay of over a year. The occupant of the White House would serve six weeks less than his full four-year term.[15]

Norris devoted much time to denouncing lame-duck sessions because important measures were given scant consideration in them. If congressional business was not completed in the short session, and in the Senate it rarely was, a special session was called. This involved additional expense to the taxpayers and additional work for members of Congress when the weather was at times almost unbearable. While the delay in commencing legislative service was valid in the eighteenth and nineteenth centuries owing to poor transportation, it made little sense in the 1920s when automobile and railroad and soon the airplane could bring members to Washington with relative speed and comfort. Since the ratification of the Seventeenth Amendment in 1913 senators no longer had to secure the approval of state legislatures, which usually met after the first of January, thereby removing a further cause for delay.

The failure of Norris's proposal to secure immediate adoption had nothing to do with technological improvements or administrative efficiency. The lame-duck session allowed the president to exert overpowering influence on the legislative process. Defeated members of the president's party were dependent upon him for a patronage prize if they wished to continue in public service. Norris observed that "ninety per cent of the successful filibusters which have been carried on have been in the short sessions of Congress,

---

[15] Unless the president called a special session, a member elected in November would wait a year from the following December before starting his service. No state legislature or other civilized government required its newly elected members to wait a year and a month before assuming their responsibilities.

made possible entirely by the ending of Congress on the fourth day of March." The short session could be used by the president to push through his programs and by determined minorities to thwart effectively the legislative process. Thus while public sentiment favored the proposed amendment and majorities in both houses of Congress were for it, nevertheless, Norris said in March, 1923, "we cannot get it." [16]

In the Sixty-seventh Congress the amendment passed the Senate by an almost unanimous vote. In the House, where Norris felt there was overwhelming support, the matter never came to a vote because powerful members, including the Republican leader and acting Speaker, opposed it. Throughout the fight for this amendment opposition in the House of Representatives, where party discipline was stronger and lame-duck members existed in relatively large numbers, was always greater than in the Senate.[17]

William Jennings Bryan, who sympathized with the fight Norris was making, suggested passing a bill rather than amending the Constitution to achieve the same end. Norris agreed that the regular meeting day of Congress could be changed without an amendment, since the Constitution prescribed that Congress should meet on the first Monday in December annually unless it fixed a different time. But little relief could be achieved by changing the meeting time unless the dates of commencement and expiration of congressmen's terms were officially changed. This could not be done without an amendment to the Constitution.[18]

[16] *Congressional Record,* 67th Cong., 4th sess., Feb. 12, pp. 3492, 3504–5, Mar. 2, 1923, pp. 5085–86. In the draft version of "Lame Duck vs. People's Representation," prepared for the Jan., 1923, issue of *LaFollette's Magazine,* Norris fully discussed both parts of his proposed amendment.

[17] Norris to William Jennings Bryan, Mar. 6, 1923 (Box 37, William Jennings Bryan Papers, Manuscript Division, Library of Congress). In the first session of the Sixty-eighth Congress Norris renewed the campaign for this amendment; see *Congressional Record,* Mar. 14, pp. 4142, 4149–50, Mar. 6, 1924, p. 3673.

[18] Norris to Bryan, Mar. 6, 1923 (Bryan Papers). Under the Twelfth Amendment to the Constitution the terms of the president and vice-president impliedly end and the terms of their successors commence on Mar. 4. Furthermore, the Constitution provides for a presidential term of four years (Article II, Section 1), a senatorial term of six years (Seventeenth Amendment), and a term of two years for members of the House of Representatives (Article I, Section 2). Norris's amendment involved shortening the terms of the incumbents when it went into effect, something that a law could not do.

At the time he began this fight, Norris launched another endeavor which, like the proposed lame-duck amendment, involved a procedural reform and came to fruition in the next decade. In the *New York Times* on January 28, 1923, there appeared an article by Norris entitled "A Model State Legislature" which argued for a unicameral legislature. "The experience of more than 100 years has demonstrated," he wrote, "that the two branch legislature, at least so far as the various States are concerned, has been very unsatisfactory in its results" because it was almost impossible to place responsibility properly for the success or failure of legislation. Again secrecy was responsible. In a bicameral legislature it was in conference committee that the "finishing touches" were placed on legislation. When the bill emerged from committee, it was no longer subject to amendment and had to be accepted or rejected as a whole. In a one-branch legislature "buck-passing" from one house to the other would end, and praise or blame could easily be pinpointed. "Every act would be performed in the open, and the record would be simple and easily understood." If the unicameral legislature were kept relatively small, even greater efficiency would result. Equating, in the fashion of progressivism, competitive business with efficiency and politics with possible corruption and inefficiency, Norris felt that limited membership in the unicameral legislature "would give to the State a business administration" resulting in fuller discussion and "the highest possible wisdom in the enactment of laws."

From such a plan almost all the desirable things Norris wished to see in American government would result. Secrecy would be eliminated and the benefits thereof would quickly appear. Better legislation would result and at the same time the taxpayer would save money. Abler men, less prone to deception and corruption, would be attracted to politics; partisanship could be virtually eliminated, particularly if members were elected by districts on a nonpartisan ballot. Since a state legislator's duties had nothing to do with the national administration or with the welfare of any political party, qualifications and not politics could become the chief criterion for public service. Though he found much to criticize in the way corporate business was conducted, Norris could still write that "the State would be similar to a gigantic corporation and the members of the legislature would be members of the board of directors." Such a legislature would look "solely after the interests and welfare of the people of the State." The irony of such statements was never pointed out to Norris, and he continued championing procedural reform on the grounds of efficiency and good business practice during the 1920s while finding much to criticize in the practices of outstanding corporations.[19]

In a 1927 article entitled "Government on a Business Basis" Norris called for nonpartisan officials on the county and state levels because divisions along party lines had little application to state and county affairs where many offices required technical skills or had duties defined by law and required no discretion. If partisanship were eliminated, a state could be "managed entirely upon business principles and upon a business basis." The governor could be compared to a corporation president while the legislature would constitute the board of directors: "The object of this corporation would be the welfare, the happiness and the prosperity of the citizenship within the State." Since government was the biggest business of all, Norris insisted it should be the most efficient and modern.[20] While interest in such reform in Nebraska was not great, in 1927 he was delighted to learn that a state senator, Dwight P. Griswold, introduced bills to remove the party circle and to provide for the election of county officials upon a nonpartisan ballot. At times Norris expressed the view that he might retire from the Senate and devote his energies to bringing better business practices to the state of Nebraska.[21]

While reform of state government and elimination of the short session of Congress were expressed by Norris for the first time

[19] "A Model State Legislature" also appeared in *Congressional Record,* 67th Cong., 4th sess., Feb. 5, 1923, pp. 2999–3000. Norris sent copies of the article to his constituent mailing list.

[20] Norris, "Government on a Business Basis," Apr. 1, 1927 (draft article). In an article appearing in the *Grand Island Independent* on May 19, 1927, entitled "A Plan for State Government," Norris called for placing the state government of Nebraska on a business basis.

[21] Norris to Otto Mutz, Feb. 10, 1924; to Charles P. Croft, Nov. 15, 1926; to Dwight P. Griswold, Feb. 13, May 6, 1927; to Kenneth S. Wherry, Dec. 2, 1931; to H. W. Dodds, July 15, 1927. In Norris to G. E. Thompson, Dec. 28, 1928, he expressed an interest in reform of municipal government.

during the Harding administration, championing a national primary dated back to his years in the House of Representatives. A 1922 speech by Secretary of War John W. Weeks bemoaning the tendency of Americans toward reform and specifically attacking primaries aroused Norris and led him to assert their value as an instrument of direct democracy. Many of the evils he found in government—boss rule, machine politics, arbitrary partisanship—related to the lack of a national primary system. He perceptively noted that Weeks, originally chosen to serve as U.S. senator by the legislature of Massachusetts, was defeated when the people had the opportunity to decide if he should serve another term. Harding was defeated "when he was running for President wherever there was a presidential primary." Admitting that the primary system had faults, Norris insisted that "instead of abolishing it, we ought to devote our minds and our intellects and our powers toward improvements." [22]

One of the difficulties with the primary was that candidates often entered a race merely to weaken another by helping divide the vote. A way of relieving the situation "would be to provide for a first and second choice in all primary elections. Another method would be to call a second primary in which the two highest would be the only candidates allowed." While the latter approach usually proved more satisfactory, it was also more expensive.[23] Nevertheless, as a method for ascertaining the will of the people, the primary with its faults was infinitely superior to the convention system and the Electoral College. In correspondence, articles, and speeches Norris throughout the decade reiterated his views in favor of the primary system.[24]

[22] *Congressional Record,* 67th Cong., 2nd sess., June 16, 1922, pp. 8806–7, 8809–10. The essence of Norris's remarks were later published in *Congressional Digest,* 5, no. 10 (Oct., 1926): 267–68.

[23] As in business so, too, in politics: the man with money had an advantage over the man without. The remedy, Norris thought, involved the enactment of a stringent corrupt practices act. In 1923 he claimed he had spent less than $500 each time he had sought the senatorial nomination, whereas it would have cost him much more to secure nomination by a convention with much less chance of success.

[24] Norris to Olney Newell, June 30, 1922; to H. C. Trisler, June 30, 1922; to J. J. Jensen, Dec. 19, 1926; to Meyer Rothwacks, Mar. 19, 1927. "Why I Believe in the Direct Primary," an article by Norris, appeared in *The Annals,*

During the Harding years Norris considered one election flagrant and fraudulent enough to comment upon, though he never cited it when discussing the primary in general. In 1918 Truman H. Newberry, Secretary of the Navy during the Taft administration, defeated Henry Ford for a Senate seat. Having spent more than the $3,750 allowed under the Michigan Corrupt Practices Act, Newberry was indicted on charges of fraud, corruption, and conspiracy. How much money had been spent in Newberry's campaign was a matter of speculation, but estimates ran as high as a million dollars. Ford also brought suit against Newberry and the Senate conducted hearings before voting 46 to 41 (Norris in the negative) to admit him in January, 1922.[25] Norris's remarks were sarcastic. To the argument that Newberry's confirmation would establish a precedent by which the poor man might be eliminated from the Senate, he replied that selling seats to the highest bidder would insure "a highclass membership." Better to choose men of means and make Washington the social center of the world; "we can then employ experts to do our thinking and Senators will have more time to give to golf and other kindred social duties." [26]

As a former judge and lawyer, Norris had always been interested in efficiency and economy in court practices and procedures. It wasn't until he gained a seat on the Judiciary Committee after his re-election in 1918 that he could afford a more than casual interest in this topic. During the Harding years he expounded views which he would reiterate through the period of Republican ascendancy.

Excessive delay on the part of the Supreme Court in rendering decisions concerned Norris. Until the Court decided, Congress, executive agencies, and involved citizens, for example, would be uncertain about how to proceed. Though he didn't elaborate,

106 (Mar., 1923): 22–30. Another article entitled "The Primary," appearing originally in the *Locomotive Engineers' Journal,* was reprinted in *Congressional Record,* 68th Cong., 1st sess., Apr. 12, 1924, pp. 6180–84.

[25] Mark Sullivan, *Our Times,* 6 (New York, 1935): 521–23.

[26] *Congressional Record,* 67th Cong., 2nd sess., Jan. 11, 1922, pp. 1052–53. Norris in his autobiography said he knew that "in the atmosphere of Washington any orthodox attack upon Newberry would be futile." To attract attention to the Michigan election, he tried sarcasm in order, hopefully, to laugh Newberry out of public life; see *Fighting Liberal* (New York, 1945), pp. 215–20. After serving ten months, Newberry resigned and retired to private life.

Norris believed the Supreme Court ought not hold an act of Congress unconstitutional for some technicality only with a bare majority. More central to his criticism was the fact that taking a case through the federal court system would bankrupt all but the wealthiest of individuals. When federal court dockets were over-crowded, a delay meant a denial of justice. When a litigant be-came involved with the federal courts, besides delay in coming to trial, he might have to travel several hundred miles to the court. Thus he often found it less expensive to settle than to get involved in excessive and costly litigation. What Norris desired was legis-lation allowing federal cases to be tried in state courts where evidence and circumstances were available and applicable. The change would involve breaking precedent, but because a practice was old was not sufficient reason to follow it blindly under all circumstances.[27] Norris also said that life tenure for federal judges was not desirable. While in theory a judge appointed for life was removed from temptation, too often security made some men in-different to "the common run of humanity." More important than judicial tenure was the duplicate system involving U.S. courts and judges, state courts and judges, all the way down to duplicate sets of court clerks, with the taxpayer footing the bill. These fac-tors helped make justice too expensive, "so expensive, in fact, that the poor man cannot afford to buy it." [28]

Armed with evidence from lawyers, judges, students, and phi-lanthropists, Norris asserted that the American court system was expensive and inefficient. Indeed, it was "the most inefficient sys-tem in the world." And it violated the basic common-law prin-ciple that a man must be tried by a jury of his peers when it hauled a man for trial to a distant place before a judge who might have traveled an even greater distance to hear the case. Federal judges usually were not as familiar with local conditions as state judges. Abolish the duplicate court system: economy, efficiency, and a fairer dispensation of justice for "the common run of humanity" would follow.[29] The fact that federal judges were re-

[27] Norris to Bryan, Jan. 11, 1921 (Box 43, Bryan Papers); to Albert F. Coyle, June 2, 1923; *Congressional Record,* 64th Cong., 1st sess., Feb. 29, 1916, p. 3287; 67th Cong., 2nd sess., Apr. 6, 1922, p. 5107.

[28] *Congressional Record,* 67th Cong., 2nd sess., Apr. 6, 1922, p. 5107.

[29] *Ibid.,* pp. 5107–13.

moved from the people through tenure and comfortable incomes disturbed Norris. The elegant social life of Chief Justice Taft antagonized him. While a congressman, Norris had opposed Taft as president, but he had not voted against Taft's confirmation as chief justice in 1921. He did feel that Taft's well-publicized social life "was bound to influence his decisions." If federal judges emulated the social life of the chief justice, the court system would be further weakened.[30]

Views expressed during the Harding administration were expounded and expanded by Norris throughout the New Era. Postulating the progressive virtues of economy and efficiency, he found much to attack during the Harding years when his own party was in power. As during the Wilson years, his place in the Senate power structure was on the periphery, though his voice became more strident and his presence more noticeable. His principles, nevertheless, remained the same. He continued to be guided more by conscientious conviction than by partisan consideration and political expediency. In the past conscientious conviction rarely had run contrary to political expediency. Thus he had been able to oppose, for example, American participation in the war and the Versailles Peace Treaty and still maintain the support of his constituency. For George W. Norris the return to normalcy called for by President Harding again tested whether conscientious conviction could run counter to political expediency.

[30] *Ibid.,* p. 5113; Norris to Coyle, July 10, 1923; to R. C. Grubb, Dec. 14, 1922. Norris voted against the confirmation of Pierce Butler, Harding's next appointment to the Supreme Court; see *Congressional Record,* 67th Cong., 4th sess., Dec. 21, 1922, p. 813. A fascinating study of the Butler confirmation is David J. Danelski, *A Supreme Court Justice Is Appointed* (New York, 1964).

Aid to Agriculture

11

As chairman of the Senate Agriculture and Forestry Committee, Norris had to cope with a growing farm problem. Constructive criticism of past policies and penetrating comments on the plight of the farmer were not enough. In this area, one directly and immediately affecting his constituents, Norris had to offer a program that would meet the situation. To be sure, he had offered programs to meet other situations but none had gained executive approval or party support. In the case of agricultural legislation Norris faced the same problem and met the same rebuff, a situation that prevailed throughout the decade.

The 1920 election, besides bringing Warren G. Harding to the White House, brought George W. Norris to the chairmanship of the Agriculture and Forestry Committee at a critical time. With the end of the war, the farmer's economic well-being was subjected to severe shocks. Price supports and the boom market for agricultural produce disappeared. Food production in war-ravaged nations started to increase while the demands of the armed forces drastically decreased. The farmer who had increased his production, extended his operations, and started to partake of some of the consumer benefits of a mass-production society found himself in a tight spot. His costs either remained the same or increased, but prices received for produce drastically declined. The dilemma of the surplus, a problem that had not seriously bedeviled the farmer since the 1890s, returned to plague him after a period of war-induced prosperity which other sectors of the American economy continued to enjoy.[1]

Wheat, selling in Nebraska for more than $2.00 a bushel at the end of 1919, brought about $1.30 a year later. Corn during the same period dropped from $1.22 to $.41, barley from $1.00 to half this sum at the end of 1920, oats from $.65 to $.37. Burdened with such fixed costs as mortgage payments and interest on loans, farmers suffered heavy losses as they marketed their crops in the election year of 1920. The situation did not improve during the following year as livestock prices also tumbled. Nebraska beef cattle brought $9.53 per hundredweight in 1920 and only $6.13 in 1921, while hogs fell from $12.62 to $7.52. In most instances the price of farm products decreased nearly 50 percent, compared to a decrease of about 15 percent in other commodities during this same time. By June of 1921 farmers had lost between $5 and $6 billion in the slump of agricultural prices. Though they recovered during the decade, production costs always were higher relative to income from farm products. While agricultural prices dropped below the prewar level, most others remained near the wartime level. Combined with further problems that beset citizens of predominantly rural Nebraska (68.7 percent in 1920), the golden glow of the decade eluded the state and posed a dilemma for George Norris.[2]

Since the president was not interested in effective agricultural legislation, suggestions usually originated outside the executive branch. Norris found that his proposals added to tensions within the Republican party which threatened to revive the antagonisms and bitterness of the pre–World War I period. The first agricultural concern commanding his attention was the activities of meat packers. The packers had been investigated and regulated continually since Theodore Roosevelt's administration, and Norris late

[1] James H. Shideler, *Farm Crisis, 1919–1923* (Berkeley and Los Angeles, 1957), presents a comprehensive analysis of the critical situation.

[2] James C. Olson, *History of Nebraska* (Lincoln, Nebr., 1955), pp. 296, 299, presents an excellent brief discussion on the farm situation in Nebraska; Verne S. Sweedlum, "A History of the Evolution of Agriculture in Nebraska, 1870–1930" (Ph.D. thesis, University of Nebraska, 1940), pp. 287–88; Benjamin C. Marsh to Warren G. Harding, June 18, 1921 (Box 1, Benjamin C. Marsh Papers, Manuscript Division, Library of Congress).

in the Wilson administration had criticized their monopolistic practices and demanded either government ownership or regulation of stockyards. But no legislation was enacted, and in June of 1921 Norris renewed the demand. With recent congressional hearings and a Federal Trade Commission investigation, the Agriculture and Forestry Committee unanimously decided against further hearings and proceeded immediately to consider a bill.[3]

The measure Norris presented, while similar to the previous Senate bill, called for a commissioner instead of a permanent commission, removed from politics. The House bill, on the other hand, put its regulatory power in the hands of the Secretary of Agriculture; Norris claimed that it was not as effective or as comprehensive in its proposals. In debate Norris denounced the packers, reiterating material unearthed in earlier hearings. He said that until the packers, like the railroads, were made to adopt a uniform system of bookkeeping, full knowledge of their activities could not be obtained. He concluded, seemingly for good measure, "If we are going to control the packers at all we ought to control them in their by-products as well as in their food products, because if we do not they can make an apparent loss on one and make it up, and a good deal more, on another." [4]

The resulting legislation represented a defeat for the Senate Agriculture and Forestry Committee. The House provision empowering the Secretary of Agriculture to enforce the law was part of the Packers and Stockyards Act of 1921. The Agriculture Department now assumed substantial powers over the meat-packing industry, though the authority of the Federal Trade Commission to investigate and the Interstate Commerce Commission to supervise the transportation of cattle to stockyards was not impaired by the act.

Norris was a member of the conference committee that met to reconcile differences between the House and Senate bills. He had an agreement with the Senate Republican conferees that no report

[3] *Congressional Record,* 67th Cong., 1st sess., June 9, 1921, pp. 2322–23. See also discussion in Chapter 5.

[4] *Congressional Record,* 67th Cong., 1st sess., June 9, pp. 2323–24, 2486, 2487, 2492, June 16, 1921, p. 2667; George W. Norris to William Kent, Jan. 5, 1922 (packer investigation, Addition 3, William Kent Papers, Yale University Library).

be approved unless the House made concessions. But at the time of the crucial committee meetings Norris was seriously ill and the Senate conferees receded from practically all amendments, including one for regulation of municipally owned slaughterhouses, which in Norris's judgment would have strengthened the bill. The conference report was adopted by Congress and became law in August with Norris still in his sickbed. The fight left him more critical than ever of the president who had called for curbing the packers but who balked at what Norris considered effective legislation.[5]

He made one last effort when at the end of 1922 he introduced a resolution protesting the proposed merger of Morris and Company with Armour and Company, two of the largest packing establishments in the world, because it was detrimental to the public interest and would unlawfully restrain trade. Norris wanted the Agriculture and Forestry Committee to call J. Ogden Armour, Nelson Morris, and the bankers involved in the proposed merger to testify. Although the Washington representatives of the National Grange and the National Board of Farm Organizations endorsed Norris's resolution, nothing came of it. On March 9, 1923, the $500-million merger was completed, though Secretary of Agriculture Henry C. Wallace had tried to prevent the combination as a violation of the Packers and Stockyards Act.[6]

More important than curbing the monopolistic meat packers was relief for agriculture. On May 31, 1921, Norris introduced a bill to create a farmers' export financing corporation, an effort to resolve part of the farmers' dilemma. But the Senate, involved with revenue and tariff legislation, was in no frame of mind to consider new legislation. Norris had to urge continuation of the session, despite the hot weather, until some of the bills relating to agriculture had been considered.[7]

[5] *Congressional Record,* 67th Cong., 2nd sess., Feb. 3, 1922, p. 2105; Norris to Kent, Jan. 5, 1922 (Kent Papers).

[6] Norris introduced S. Res. 389 on Dec. 30, 1922; see *Congressional Record,* 67th Cong., 4th sess., p. 1104; Marsh to Harding, Feb. 16, 1923 (Box 2, Marsh Papers); Shideler, *Farm Crisis,* p. 239. Norris to H. L. Williams, Jan. 6, 1924, reviews the situation.

[7] Harry Slattery to Gifford Pinchot, June 10, 1921 (Harry Slattery Papers, Manuscripts Collections, Duke University Library); *Congressional Record,* 67th

Presenting his measure, Norris examined the plight of farmers unable to finance satisfactorily the sale of surplus agricultural products abroad without governmental assistance. On the other hand, European peoples faced with staggering problems of rehabilitation, including famine, would buy American surplus food if it were available on relatively easy terms. If not, each new harvest would add to American farmers' problems. Clearly, Norris argued, an emergency situation existed and his bill, endorsed by the Agriculture and Forestry Committee, was framed to meet these abnormal conditions. It provided for a governmental corporation controlled by a board of directors with a capital stock subscribed from the public treasury of $100 million. The Secretary of Agriculture would be chairman; other members would be appointed by the president and confirmed by the Senate. The corporation would have the power to purchase American farm products for sale on time in foreign countries. Its other powers, similar to some exercised by the War Finance Board, would allow the corporation to act as agent for farmers and help finance those exporting agricultural products.[8] The measure further provided that when the products were sold on time in foreign countries, the directors could accept securities to be held by the corporation. On the strength of these securities, bonds not exceeding ten times the amount of the paid-up capital stock would be sold and the

---

Cong., 1st sess., July 5, 1921, p. 3329. According to an undated memorandum in the Slattery Papers (Mar., 1929, letters folder), Carl Vrooman of Illinois, Assistant Secretary of Agriculture in both Wilson administrations, was the author of the farm relief measure Norris introduced. Shideler, *Farm Crisis,* p. 160, says Vrooman aided in drafting the Norris bill. Norris recalled that Louis Crossette, an aide of Hoover, helped him on the bill along with Vrooman; see Norris to James E. Lawrence, Mar. 13, 1944; Norris, *Fighting Liberal* (New York, 1945), p. 279.

[8] *Congressional Record,* 67th Cong., 1st sess., July 5, 1921, p. 4043. Norris claimed that originally the Secretary of Commerce was to be chairman of the board and that Hoover was receptive to the idea even though Harding was opposed to it. Just before the hearings on the bill Norris learned that Hoover would speak against it. Presumably at this time it was decided that the Secretary of Agriculture should be the chairman, though in his autobiography Norris leaves the impression that the bill, when introduced, called for the Secretary of Commerce to be chairman; see Norris to Lawrence, Mar. 13, 1944; Norris, *Fighting Liberal,* pp. 278–81.

operation repeated. Another provision allowed the corporation or any other shipper to appeal to the Interstate Commerce Commission for reduced rates upon agricultural products destined for export. Thus railroads, beset with empty freight cars because farmers could not afford the rates, would benefit as well.

While Norris admitted that his bill would not fully resolve the problem, he did believe that it would help farmers make a fair and reasonable profit and that, consequently, the rest of the economy would prosper. "If we drag down the farmer and ruin the producer, the grass will grow in the streets of our cities. Elevate him, put agriculture on a fair paying basis, and he lifts with him the entire superstructure of civilization." [9]

The surplus was central to the farmer's dilemma. If surpluses disappeared, farm prices would rise. But with the end of the war and the restoration of European agricultural production, the dilemma of the surplus reappeared with increasing intensity. Norris's bill represented an attempt to deal with it; in the hearings held by the Agriculture and Forestry Committee most witnesses agreed. Herbert Hoover, Secretary of Commerce, was one witness who did not. He thought that Europe in 1921 was producing approximately all the food it wanted. Moreover, according to Norris, Hoover said that foreign countries would buy anything on time from the United States and believed that private initiative and private agencies could best transact whatever business of this type was available.[10]

Norris disagreed. Recalling the testimony of the Polish government agent who said it might take the Polish people from nine months to three years to pay for American farm products, Norris believed a government corporation could better handle these transactions. Certainly private agencies in 1921 were not engaging in such activities. Further, Norris doubted that European countries, as Hoover implied, would seek to take advantage of the United States. "They know that there is only one hope for their countries, for their civilization, and that is to become rejuvenated,

[9] *Congressional Record,* 67th Cong., 1st sess., July 19, 1921, p. 4044; Norris to Ralph N. Baker, July 22, 1921.

[10] *Congressional Record,* 67th Cong., 1st sess., July 19, 1921, pp. 4045–46.

to build themselves up; and they cannot do that unless they get a start, unless somebody will trust them for a while." Their salvation depended upon it. "If they build up," Norris remarked, "they will pay us. If they fail, then we have lost our market anyway, whether we sell to them or whether we do not." [11]

Though his bill was not a cure-all, he believed it would help both American farmers and people in war-ravaged Europe. It would provide a means whereby European nations could receive surplus American produce in return for securities, which would satisfy those who cared to consider the world situation. If anarchy prevailed, if Europe went "bolshevik," if revolutions took place, securities of the proposed corporation would be worthless and the market for American farm products would disappear. But barring these catastrophes and with the demand for food and efforts toward recovery already underway, Norris believed the risks involved were minimal.[12]

Others disagreed. Rumor had it that President Harding himself was opposed. Secretary of Commerce Hoover and Eugene C. Meyer, chairman of the War Finance Corporation, testified against it. Secretary of Agriculture Wallace believed the War Finance Corporation could promote agricultural exports without the creation of a new board. A substitute measure encompassing administration views was introduced by Senator Frank Kellogg on July 26, 1921, though neither Hoover nor Meyer in their testimony indicated that a substitute was being prepared. The measure broadening the powers of the War Finance Corporation was prepared in secret; members of the Agriculture and Forestry Committee had not been consulted and, according to Norris, were unable to secure a copy.[13] But Norris's bill did have wide support. Representatives of farm organizations had testified in its favor and Norris was determined to battle for it, though it necessitated a break with the administration and Herbert Hoover in particular. The dislike that the two men developed for each other emanated

[11] *Ibid.*

[12] *Ibid.,* pp. 4046–47, 4050.

[13] *Ibid.,* July 26, p. 4289, July 27, 1921, p. 4375; Marsh to Harding, June 28, 1921 (Box 1, Marsh Papers). Shideler, *Farm Crisis,* p. 161, says that Hoover and Meyer drafted the substitute bill.

from this incident, Norris having previously held Hoover in high regard.[14]

On July 26 Norris launched a three-day tirade against the Kellogg bill and the Harding administration. Acknowledging that he would rather have the new bill than no bill at all, he noted that while his bill called for a corporation as a link between the producer and the consumer, the Kellogg bill did not consider the producer. Bankers, middlemen, and trust companies would benefit while the producer would pay them tribute in the form of added service charges. The War Finance Corporation, which under the terms of the substitute measure would extend credit to farmers, knew nothing about agriculture. Among its publications there was only one dealing with a farm topic, and that told about collecting money for a wheat sale made in Belgium during the war. Thus an agency without a farmer on its board would decide whether individual farmers were to be lent funds, by means of a substitute measure that had never been referred to a committee of Congress.[15]

Norris's bill was primarily a marketing measure; Kellogg's was a financing proposition, which meant holding agricultural products until a market suitable to the holder was found. Yet what was needed most was a market for surplus products. The committee bill tried to resolve this problem; the substitute measure never considered it. Lending money to farmers unable to market their produce meant ultimate ruin for agriculture. It would increase the farmer's burden by postponing the day of liquidation, adding interest for the banker in the meantime. The farmer could get nothing for his efforts and might be in debt when the transaction was concluded. Under the provisions of Norris's bill this situation could not occur. Certainly agricultural prosperity could not be restored simply by lending money and having everything held in status quo.[16]

[14] See Shideler, *Farm Crisis,* pp. 160–62, for evidence of support for the Norris bill.

[15] *Congressional Record,* 67th Cong., 1st sess., July 26, p. 4289, July 27, 1921, pp. 4375–76, 4379–80

[16] *Ibid.,* July 28, 1921, pp. 4380–85, 4387–91; Norris to C. W. McConaughy, Nov. 14, 1921; to Harry N. Owen, Jan. 14, 1922; to G. B. Welch, Jan. 5, 1923.

On Thursday, July 28, after noting that his bill provided a more realistic appraisal of and solution to farmers' problems, Norris collapsed. He had been speaking for two and a half hours. He walked into the Senate cloakroom and crumpled up on one of the couches. Colleagues noticed his condition and half carried, half dragged him into an adjoining room where Senator L. Heisler Ball of Delaware, who was a doctor, attended him. A combination of overwork and heat exhaustion was responsible for his collapse. On the Senate floor Norris had appeared pale, but his voice was strong and he spoke vigorously. While Ball was attending Norris, Senator Kellogg, sponsor of the substitute measure, was sharply criticizing him on the Senate floor.[17]

Earlier in the day the Agriculture and Forestry Committee, under pressure from the administration, decided to displace the Norris bill with another composed of parts of both bills. The committee insisted on adding several provisions of the later bill, thereby allowing the War Finance Corporation to perform some functions of the government corporation that Norris favored. The vote was 10 to 2 with only freshman Senator Edwin F. Ladd of North Dakota supporting Norris in opposition. Thus it was the substitute, further amended but not along the lines of the Norris bill, that became law a month later while Norris was absent, seeking to regain his strength.[18]

He spent the summer at his cottage in Wisconsin. His collapse had been due to his inability to withstand work in hot weather. Well rested and feeling trim, he returned to the Senate in October, where the situation had changed considerably. The initiative had been taken from him and the Agriculture and Forestry Committee. In the process the farm bloc had been revealed as a weak and ineffective group that bowed under administration pressure.[19]

Concerned with the farm situation, a bipartisan group of senators banded together to promote legislation beneficial to agricul-

---

In the latter two letters Norris surveyed the farm situation and his legislative efforts to obtain an effective farm bill.

[17] *Washington Post,* July 29, 1921.

[18] *Ibid.;* Shideler, *Farm Crisis,* p. 162.

[19] Clerk to John F. Cordeal, Oct. 3, 1921; Norris to A. B. Allen, June 14, 1922 (comments about Norris's health); to W. R. Farnsworth, Dec. 31, 1922 (comments on the farm bloc).

ture. It had no formal organization, no written statement of principles, and no bylaws. Its membership did not agree on specific measures. Rather, they proposed to discuss problems, exchange ideas, and fight for farm legislation. William S. Kenyon of Iowa was selected as chairman at the first meeting in May, 1921, and, according to Norris, newspapers immediately dubbed him leader of the farm bloc. Whereupon Kenyon accepted the designation and assumed the leadership so far as there was any, receiving publicity as the head of an organization influential in the control of national legislation. Other senators announced themselves as members with the hope of assisting their political fortunes. While the press helped establish the notion that farm bloc leaders exercised power and influence in the control of legislation, so-called leaders actually controlled no vote but their own and Kenyon, Norris claimed, changed his several times at the behest of the Harding administration.[20]

Norris did not believe that the farm bloc influenced the vote on any measure, though its members were all sincere in their desire to help the farmer. They disagreed widely as to how this could be accomplished. At the outset most members had supported Norris's bill for agricultural relief; by the end of the battle almost all sided with the administration and supported the Kellogg substitute. The Minnesota senator, incidentally, was usually listed along with Norris as a member of the farm bloc, while the putative leader, Senator Kenyon, at the outset supported Norris and then voted for the substitute measure. Shortly thereafter he was appointed by Harding as a judge of the U.S. Circuit Court of Appeals, Eighth District.[21]

Before he left the Senate, Kenyon called together a few farm bloc friends and had Senator Arthur Capper elected in his place. Norris did not believe there were more than a half-dozen senators present, including some who had never before attended a meeting. Most members remained away because they, like Norris, had reached the conclusion that the farm bloc was being used for

[20] John P. Robertson to Gilbert Fite, Feb. 25, 1941; Norris to N. B. Updike, Mar. 17, 1922; to Dante M. Pierce, May 31, 1922.
[21] William Kenyon was appointed to the federal judiciary by Harding on Jan. 31 and resigned his Senate seat on Feb. 24, 1922.

partisan political purposes. By the end of the first session of the Sixty-seventh Congress the farm bloc was voting with Republican leaders and capitulating to administration wishes.[22]

Thus unable to aid the farmer through effective legislation, critical of the farm bloc, and hostile to administration efforts at meliorating the farm crisis, Norris was unhappy in his position as chairman of the Senate Agriculture and Forestry Committee. He wanted to quit but Charles McNary of Oregon, his would-be successor, "begged him to hang on" for a while.[23]

In his analysis Norris complained that the price spread between producer and consumer was outrageously large. The farmer had not been getting enough to pay the cost of production while the consumer was charged high prices. The historic explanation for this discrepancy was too many middlemen taking "unconscionable profits." Add to this factor a surplus which could not be sold, though people in Europe were willing to purchase on time, and the American farmer in the early 1920s was in serious economic trouble. Because Congress failed to take effective action, a foreign market for surplus agricultural produce was out of the question. Therefore, only middlemen remained as villains in the farmer's dilemma. The greatest of these, according to Norris, was the railroad with its unreasonable freight charges. As he saw it, two things were necessary to put agriculture on a profitable basis: one was a substantial reduction in freight rates; the other was a foreign market for surplus products. In his bill Norris had tried to consider both of these aspects. With its failure, he devoted his energies to the problem of freight rates. The Kellogg substitute, allowing the War Finance Corporation to lend money to banks and trust companies which in turn could be lent to farmers, did not resolve any of these difficulties. Norris concluded that unless

[22] Norris to Updike, Mar. 17, 1922; to Pierce, May 21, 1922 (further evidence of farm bloc leaders voting against the interests of the farmer); to F. A. Ansberry, Jan. 20, 1922; to C. V. Nelson, June 14, 1922. Arthur Capper in *The Agricultural Bloc* (New York, 1922) presents a very favorable picture of the farm bloc and its activities.

[23] Charles L. McNary to John H. McNary, July 24, 1922 (Charles L. McNary Papers, Manuscript Division, Library of Congress). Norris finally resigned as chairman in 1926.

markets for the surplus could be found, agriculture was doomed. All other efforts could not truly succeed.[24]

In all of Norris's remarks pertaining to agriculture was a central value. Genuine material well-being could not be secured until agriculture was on a profitable basis: it was the foundation of all prosperity. Every nation that neglected it sooner or later came to ruin and decay. Agriculture was the fundamental industry, "not of our country alone but of the world." "When we lift up agriculture we lift up everybody dependent upon agriculture, which includes everyone except those who make their money out of the products which are consumed, as such products travel from the producer to the consumer." Having faith in values with little meaning to an urban nation where an unfolding mass-consumption society was developing new tastes and standards, Norris, unlike Calvin Coolidge, never appeared quaint or outdated. The battles he fought concerned real and vital problems. Rarely for middlemen or their allies in the fields of finance and industry, Norris's battles were meaningful to producers, small businessmen, working people, and consumers concerned with maintaining their entity as entrepreneurs and individuals in an age when mass production and mass consumption, while improving the lot of many people, also tended to destroy traditional bases of the democratic faith: a belief in the free individual and the moral law.

Norris believed, along with most Americans, that loss of competition usually meant a rising cost of living. In raising the specter of monopoly, in attacking private wealth in terms reminiscent of an earlier era, Norris aroused little antagonism on the part of citizens, particularly those from small-town or rural backgrounds. Moreover, in improving the lot of the farmer, he was willing for government to spend money. It was no argument to say that because in the past people knew nothing about a problem and therefore suffered its consequences, people in the present likewise should sit idly by and do nothing. While he recognized that much money

[24] Norris to McConaughy, Nov. 14, 1921, Jan. 30, 1922; to Owen, Jan. 14, 1922. See *Congressional Record,* 67th Cong., 4th sess., Feb. 2, 1923, p. 2895, for an example of Norris arguing that proposed legislation (rural credits) could not accomplish any great or material good for the farmer.

was foolishly spent, he was not in favor of limiting advances and delaying progress.[25]

Early in 1922 Norris was impressed when two representatives of labor organizations testified before his committee in behalf of a bill to stabilize prices of agricultural produce. While they did not pretend to be informed, they did advocate that something be done so that farmers could produce crops at "a living profit." They remarked that when farmers were losing money, wages were not sufficiently remunerative. Unless the farmer was prosperous, labor could not prosper. Such remarks as these further convinced Norris of the truth of his values. In improving the lot of the farmer, Congress would be legislating to promote the prosperity of all.[26]

To help the farmer curtail the incursions of middlemen on his declining income, Norris supported legislation to relieve agriculture from the effects of the Sherman Antitrust Act. Farmers could then cooperate, eliminate some middlemen, and possibly lower prices for consumers. Such legislation could offer the farmer a way out of the trust-controlled market: "He buys his binder from the Harvester Trust. He sells his hogs and his beef to the Packer Trust. He sells his hides to a trust, and he buys them back from the same trust at a profit of about 10,000 percent. He has nothing to do with fixing the price of what he sells. He has nothing to do with fixing the price of what he must buy. The trusts control him in all he buys and control him in all he sells. . . ."[27]

At the end of 1922 Norris made another major effort to secure legislation more central to the farmers' dilemma. During the debate on Harding's so-called ship subsidy bill he proposed a new method of regulating combinations dealing in food products. Like his earlier bill, this one also called for a governmental corporation with a board of directors, chosen by the president with the advice and consent of the Senate, to direct its affairs. The corpora-

[25] *Congressional Record,* 67th Cong., 2nd sess., Feb. 8, p. 2257, Apr. 12, 1922, p. 5397; Norris to E. O. Hackenburger, Dec. 9, 1923.

[26] *Congressional Record,* 67th Cong., 2nd sess., Feb. 8, 1922, p. 2257. One of the union men was a representative of the American Federation of Labor and the other from the International Association of Machinists.

[27] *Ibid.,* pp. 2257, 2259–60 (the quote is on p. 2257). The Capper-Volstead Act, authorizing the formation of associations of producers of agricultural products, became law on Feb. 18, 1922. It had passed the Senate on Feb. 8, 1922.

tion could build, buy, lease, and operate elevators and storage warehouses. It would buy and sell agricultural products within the United States and, if desired, grant assistance to any person or organization engaged in similar practices. One proposition provided that the government turn over to this corporation ships it owned for use in transporting agricultural products to foreign ports with compensation merely to meet the cost of operation.

Norris envisioned this measure as providing a market for the sale of agricultural products and eliminating many charges extracted by middlemen. It would have the double effect of increasing the producer's price and decreasing the consumer's cost. In calling for a gigantic publicly owned and operated middleman, Norris's approach went beyond regulation, which he asserted was a costly failure. The government corporation would compete with trusts and seek justice instead of profit in alleviating difficulties confronting both producers and consumers.[28] Again Norris did not see the measure as offering a complete solution to the farm crisis. It neither fully grappled with the surplus nor confronted the problem of freight rates. However, if the railroad difficulty were remedied, the farmer provided with adequate credit facilities, and the surplus reduced, "there would still be the enormous expense connected with the sale of the farmer's products, all of which must be paid by the consumer or lost by the producer." As expected, Norris's measure did not prevail, though it grappled more effectively with important aspects of the farm problem than anything the Harding administration proposed.[29]

Norris next turned his attention to that "most important single question" of freight rates. Starting with the premise that "every dollar charged for freight must be paid by the consumer in the end," he noted that freight charges were part of the cost of living, representing in effect taxation without representation. Rates were

[28] *Ibid.*, 4th sess., Dec. 19, 1922, pp. 666–67. The *New Republic,* Feb. 20, 1924, pp. 326–27, in an editorial, "Relief for the Farmer," commented on the proposal. Like Norris, the author did not see the bill as a final solution to the farm problem.

[29] *Congressional Record,* 67th Cong., 4th sess., Dec. 19, 1922, p. 667. Norris envisioned cooperative organizations of both producers and consumers eventually replacing the government as the owner and operator of grain elevators and storage warehouses created under the terms of his bill; see Norris to H. B. Sheppard, Nov. 25, 1923.

so high that some means must be found to reduce them or "we must reconstruct our civilization . . . using the railroads of the country as a basis for our operations." [30] To be sure, more efficiently managed railroads might help the situation. Though never one to demean the virtues of competition, with a public utility such as a railroad he believed consolidation more efficient. In this respect Norris's views differed not one iota from those of most businessmen and railroad managers. But he understood that unless managed in the public interest with service and not profits as the chief criterion, consolidation could not guarantee lower rates. [31]

Listening to comments on the plight of the farmer before the Agriculture and Forestry Committee, at times Norris became so depressed that he wanted to escape from the committee room. Continuously in session, at times until late in the evening, he was so overwhelmed with work that he was unable to read mail coming into his office. While committee members were overburdened, country bankers complained that owing to the plight of the producer they, too, were facing ruin. Newspapers contained nine or ten pages filled with notices of farms for sale, every one of them mortgaged. Norris heard of farmers committing suicide while others went insane because of their inability to free themselves of the nightmare of debt. He heard of farmers unable to care for their families, losing their homes under foreclosure proceedings. Virtually all farmers producing crops were finding themselves worse off than if they did not produce any. [32]

To contrast the misery of the farmer, Norris noted the prosperity of the middleman. He mentioned the freight ($508.83) on a carload of apples shipped from Idaho to a station in western Nebraska to illustrate his point. Then he cited statistics indicating the prosperous condition of big business, contrasting it with the deplorable condition of the farmer. That American civilization

---

[30] *Congressional Record,* 67th Cong., 4th sess., Dec. 19, 1922, p. 667.

[31] *Ibid.,* p. 668.

[32] *Ibid.,* pp. 668–69 (the quote is on p. 668); 68th Cong., 1st sess., Jan. 15, pp. 982–83, Jan. 17, p. 1084, Mar. 10, 1924, p. 3873. For extended comments by Norris on the plight of the wheat farmer, see Mar. 4, pp. 3536–37, 3539–40, Mar. 10, 1924, pp. 3893, 3899. See Norris to E. Bossenmeyer, Jr., Feb. 20, 1920, for earlier comments on wheat farming.

could not proceed at this pace, where one class enjoyed enormous wealth and paid minimum taxes while another class toiled and lacked the very necessaries of life, Norris was certain. History had recorded other governments collapsing under such a top-heavy burden. Since traditional responses had failed, a new approach was necessary. While the two bills Norris proposed, one dealing with the surplus, the other with middlemen, were not cure-alls, they did represent efforts to meet the crisis with remedies that were central to existing conditions. They would have gone further than any other suggestion under consideration during the Harding era.[33]

Early in the next session of Congress, with Calvin Coolidge now in the White House, Norris reintroduced his middleman measure, calling for a farmers' and consumers' financing corporation. But this time the Agriculture and Forestry Committee had before it another measure of general scope, the McNary-Haugen bill. After extensive hearings the committee reported the McNary-Haugen bill. A minority report, while not antagonistic to the majority measure, showed a preference for the other item, known as the Norris-Sinclair bill. While Norris, of course, favored his measure, he realized that its chances of approval were nonexistent.[34]

The majority measure, sponsored by McNary in the Senate, Norris believed to be the best bill introduced aside from those he had sponsored. It had many beneficial features and would do much good. However, he cautioned, it provided for "a very intricate and complex lot of machinery." In no way did it interfere with middlemen's profits and with freight charges or in any way benefit the consumer, though its two-price system sought to dispose of surplus produce.[35] However, the Senate at this time never seriously considered the McNary-Haugen bill. The House of Representatives defeated the measure and it never reached the Senate floor. But with the injection of the McNary-Haugen proposal into the legislative hopper, a new dimension of the battle to aid the farmer developed. Other proposals were quickly eliminated; this one drew

[33] *Congressional Record,* 67th Cong., 4th sess., Dec. 19, 1922, pp. 668–71.
[34] *Ibid.,* 68th Cong., 1st sess., Apr. 24, pp. 7011–13, May 8, 1924, p. 8129; Norris to Sam W. Teagarden, Mar. 1, 1924.
[35] Norris to W. J. Hammond, Feb. 17, 1924; to Teagarden, Mar. 1, 1924.

together numerous groups seeking to aid agriculture. Though it did not have administrative approval, it had support from many farm spokesmen, including some in the Agriculture Department. It dominated the legislative scene for the next four years and emerged as a symbol of the farmers' need for relief.

Producers and Consumers

12

Having lost his battles to aid agriculture directly, Norris sought to relate other issues to the farm problem. But the plight of the farmer was not easy to isolate. The consumer, let alone the middleman, was equally involved. Thus when Norris considered transportation, the tariff, and other matters, he was able to refer to agriculture. Without a chairman's responsibility of guiding legislation or speaking for favored proposals, Norris could criticize and comment more freely and more at random.

The Federal Reserve Board, for example, he blamed "to quite an extent" for the credit difficulties of farmers. Convinced that the board wished to contract credit, Norris said the contraction adversely affected farmers more than businessmen. He was equally dubious about the newly created American Farm Bureau Federation. James R. Howard, president, and Gray Silver, legislative representative, usually supported administration measures. In the fights that he waged on behalf of the farmer and in the Muscle Shoals controversy, the leadership of the Farm Bureau was always on the other side. To Norris it seemed that the leadership operated in opposition to the interests of the farmers they represented.[1]

But the leadership of the American Farm Bureau Federation never aroused Norris as much as the railroads and their freight rates. He devoted more time to these questions in his fight to aid

[1] George W. Norris to Frederic C. Howe, Dec. 11, 1922; to W. T. Farnsworth, Dec. 10, 1922; to W. B. Yeary, Jan. 4, 1923.

the farmer than to any other matter except the bills he sponsored, in which, incidentally, the question of freight rates was inextricably involved. In the second session of the Sixty-seventh Congress Norris reported a conversation he had with a prominent railroad president about farmers unable to ship produce owing to excessive freight rates. The president agreed that from a "patriotic stand-point" there was much validity to the points Norris presented. But from the standpoint he had to take as an executive required to run a railroad at a profit, rates were set to secure the greatest profits. And more money could be made from higher than lower rates. In this situation Norris thought that government would have to help.[2]

Because of excessive railroad rates farm products could not be marketed with any profit to the producer. Norris learned of Nebraska farmers receiving less for their shipments than the freight they had to pay, of tons of hay rotting in fields because the market price was not sufficient to pay the expenses of baling and shipping, of farmers receiving less for a lamb in the Chicago market than one would pay for a lamb chop in a restaurant. At the same time he read that the Burlington railroad which crossed Nebraska had declared an extra cash dividend of 15 percent or $60 million in addition to its regular 10 percent annual dividend. To Norris both producers and consumers were in the same situation, "both of them harassed, both of them annoyed, both of them robbed by the corporations and the profiteers that exist between them. . . ."[3]

Launching an attack against the Burlington railroad in an article, "High Rates Fatal to Midwest," that appeared in the *Omaha Bee,* Norris examined the role of the railroad as a middleman whose

[2] *Congressional Record,* 67th Cong., 2nd sess., Feb. 16, 1922, pp. 2650–51. That the railroad president had his problems too is evident from a contemporary account, "Our Transportation Strangling," *Literary Digest,* Dec. 30, 1922, pp. 8–9. The problem of Nebraska shippers can be illustrated by brief quotes from two letters Norris received: "This can perhaps be best illustrated by comparing this morning's quotations. New York, corn $.69, Omaha $.40. Prices throughout the state of Nebraska at local elevators vary from $.17 to $.25" (J. A. McCammon to Norris, Dec. 10, 1921) and ". . . our competitors located in New York and Waynesboro, Penna., can ship via the Panama Canal to the West Coast for $1.32 per cwt., whereas our rate from Omaha to Los Angeles is $1.74 per cwt. . . ." (J. L. Baker to Norris, Mar. 10, 1926).

[3] Norris to J. A. Little, Dec. 16, 1921; to S. E. Solomon, Jan. 4, 1923; *Congressional Record,* 67th Cong., 2nd sess., Feb. 8, 1922, p. 2261.

charges were added to everything a producer shipped and a consumer purchased. While these charges could not be eliminated, railroad malpractices could be curbed. Focusing on the $60 million extra stock dividend of 1921 and the Burlington's lucrative annual dividends, Norris remarked, "What would have been fairer and what would have been honest as between the public and the railroad, would have been to use this $60,000,000 to pay off some of its bonds or cancel some of its stock"; such a plan would reduce capitalization and allow the public to receive the benefit of the overtaxation of the past.[4] Recognizing the railroad's right to a legitimate profit and its ability to pass costs on to others, Norris noted that the farmer was denied this privilege, being unable to fix the price of the product he sold to the middleman. Whether it would be possible for the farmer to do this by proper organization was a debatable question during the twenties. But Norris was certain that if freight rates were properly adjusted, the farmer's venture could be a more profitable one.[5]

A vice-president of the Burlington answered Norris, arguing that the Nebraska farmer was fairly prosperous and that his analysis was mistaken in its viewpoint. In his reply Norris delineated the depressed condition of western farmers and again emphasized freight rates as an important item in the enormous stretch between producer and consumer. In this response as in his other remarks Norris insisted that he was anxious to protect both consumer and producer. In this respect his approach was broader than those of most spokesmen for agriculture. His concern about middlemen and freight rates encompassed both urban workers and rural residents.

[4] Richard C. Overton, *Burlington Route* (New York, 1965), pp. 322–23, explains these developments as part of a grand strategy in the twenties to consolidate and strengthen the Burlington system. He notes that "the Burlington made money consistently through the 20's" (p. 353). In a brief discussion of "Agricultural Development" in the twenties (pp. 347–49) he mentions efforts made by the Burlington system toward more efficient production and diversification to foster regional stability. Nowhere in his discussion does he examine the things that concerned Norris and numerous Nebraskans about railroads and their practices; see for example, the quote cited in note 7 below.

[5] *Omaha Bee,* Sept. 23, 1923. Norris concluded this lengthy article with a history of the two bills he introduced to meet the farm situation. A similar analysis can be found in another draft article written by Norris at this time entitled "The Cost of Wheat and the Price of Bread."

Producer and consumer could be brought closer by lessening the cost of distribution. The Chicago, Burlington & Quincy Railroad, with its high dividends accumulated from rates charged the public, was not helping to close this gap by reducing freight rates to as near actual cost as possible. Unless the approach changed and the public benefited from excess profits by the reduction of bonds, "and through this means the reduction of rates," Norris said, the result eventually would be public ownership and operation for service rather than for profit.[6]

Reduce freight rates, and other costs would be lowered. If the cost of living were reduced, wages would not have to be increased. If government owned the railroads and it was thus possible to reduce rates, Norris would have rolled them back to their prewar levels: "This would enable everybody along the line to reduce." With the cost of distribution reduced, farmers could sell some of their crops at a reasonable profit. With lower freight rates, the margin between success and failure in farming might be eliminated.[7]

Because few railroads were making money, it was evident that high freight rates were not benefiting them. Norris said that they ought to be owned by the government or by a few large corporations. Meaningful competition in this industry had long ago "changed into fiction." Transportation was a monopoly and, if operated in the public interest, excess earnings could be taken out of capital stock instead of added to it. The Interstate Commerce Commission, directed by the Esch-Cummins Act of 1920 to fix

[6] W. W. Baldwin's reply to Norris appeared in the *Omaha Bee,* Oct. 11, 1923, Norris's answer in *ibid.,* Oct. 19, 1923. The entire correspondence was published in pamphlet form, a copy of which is to be found in the Norris Papers. That Norris did not use the Burlington system as the sole example of what he considered railroad malpractices is evident from his correspondence a year earlier. He had criticized the Missouri, Kansas and Texas Railroad, which, with the approval of the Interstate Commerce Commission, had recently issued large amounts of "watered" stock. The pyramiding of railroad capitalization, it seemed to Norris, could go no further without "the collapse of an entire structure"; see Norris to J. J. Halligan, Jan. 4, 1922.

[7] Norris to Sydney Anderson, Oct. 4 and 22, 1923; to Halligan, Jan. 4, 1922. See S. J. Franklin to Norris, Dec. 20, 1923, wherein was a freight bill for corn shipped 100 miles from McDonald, Kans., to Beaver City, Nebr. Franklin wrote that "the cash value of the corn today is forty-eight cents per bushel, but the Burlington took fifty cents for freight."

rates that would give railroads a reasonable income, was incapable of determining valid rates because "nobody knew just what the railroads were worth." Stocks and bonds as the basis of determining value were unfair and unjust because they gave "life to every part of water that had been put into the stock." Thus rates were so high that in many instances they alone caused business failures; many people, like drowning men grasping at straws, favored increasing the power of state commissions as one way of reducing them.[8]

In another approach Norris suggested that partial relief could be achieved by attention to rivers and harbors. Legislation that went beyond the pork-barrel approach could encourage barge transportation on inland waterways and thereby offer some competition to railroads. At times barges could supplement railroads as carriers of freight. In all instances shippers and ultimate consumers would benefit: one by increased profits and the other by reduced costs.[9]

The ultimate answer to the problem of freight rates was similar to the answers Norris proposed for the problems of agriculture; namely, have the government go into business to bring the producer and the consumer together. With this end in mind he called for a government corporation to build, buy, and operate railroads. Only consolidation could lower overhead expenses and reduce freight rates, and it could best be achieved under government auspices. Then in an emergency situation some products might be carried at a loss, while at the same time the incentive for profits would be reduced. Though the Transportation Act did not specifically guarantee railroad operators a profit, it authorized the Interstate Commerce Commission to fix a rate that would give a profit. But farmers found no way by which they could be given a profit by law. Suggesting that government go into business to aid agriculture was considered almost a sacrilege and helped make Norris a political outcast from Republican ranks during the 1920s.[10]

In another important area where the Harding administration

[8] Norris to C. D. Marr, Apr. 11, 1922; to J. G. Payne, Nov. 16, 1923; to W. H. Young, Apr. 15, 1922; to Nelson C. Pratt, May 26, 1924.

[9] *Congressional Record,* 67th Cong., 4th sess., Feb. 8, 1923, pp. 3243–45.

[10] Norris to Payne, Nov. 16, 1923; to Wallace E. Linn, Dec. 9, 1923; to Nathan L. Amster, Feb. 10, 1924; to C. J. Osborn, Aug. 12, 1924.

talked of aiding the farmer, Norris found himself in strong opposition. Like other progressives, he was initially convinced of the virtues of a protective tariff, believing that domestic competition would reduce the prices of American-made goods consistent with the maintenance of American wages. But during his service in the House of Representatives, as he became aware of monopoly as a threat to competition, he accepted the nebulous premise that tariff schedules should measure the difference in cost of production at home and abroad, thereby taking into account the nation's higher standard of living. While almost impossible to apply specifically, this view made Norris suspicious of the rigid application of the protective principle and therefore at odds with Republican leaders.

A critical situation arose when the Harding administration decided to reverse the low-tariff pattern of the Wilson years. Farm crisis combined with industrial depression to provide an opportunity, and in the spring of 1921 an Emergency Tariff Act, which Norris supported, imposed high duties on agricultural items with the hope of benefiting the domestic producer. Within a year the protective principle was applied more pervasively in a general tariff act. Most farm spokesmen who had called for emergency tariff legislation in 1921 now supported higher rates on manufactured items in 1922. The Democrats, hopelessly outnumbered in the Sixty-seventh Congress, could not effectively protest; indeed, not a few of their number had supported the emergency tariff in 1921. When the Fordney-McCumber tariff came to a vote in August, 1922, Norris, unable to stand the Washington weather, had fled to his summer cottage in Wisconsin, leaving Borah and LaFollette as the lone Republicans to oppose the measure.[11]

In an article drafted at this time, Norris wrote that "the farmer ought not be compelled to sell his product in a free trade market" while everything he consumed and used was purchased in a protected market. But the only asset he could cite in favor of a tariff on wheat was that it would have a stabilizing effect and prevent dumping of the surplus produced by other countries. Never-

[11] *Congressional Record,* 67th Cong., 2nd sess., Dec. 8, 1921, p. 131. James H. Shideler, *Farm Crisis, 1919–1923* (Berkeley and Los Angeles, 1957), pp. 183–87, and John D. Hicks, *Republican Ascendancy, 1921–1933* (New York, 1960), pp. 54–58, have succinct discussions of these tariff measures.

theless, in principle Norris supported tariff protection because involved in it was a set of mythical values which glorified the farmer: ". . . in the country, in the agricultural communities and in the small villages, we find a stronger and more patriotic citizenship, and in case of danger and need, it is to the farm that the Government must go for the strong arm of protection and defense." Since the farmer was the foundation of all true prosperity, it was incumbent upon legislators to take heed and treat him "with honesty and fairness in order to promote the welfare and experience of humanity." Otherwise farmers would flock to the cities where they would add to urban congestion and its attendant manifestations. They would become consumers rather than producers and help weaken the moral fiber and tone of American life.[12]

In expounding these views, Norris reaffirmed his commitment to an agrarian democratic faith, a proper affirmation for the new chairman of the Senate Agriculture and Forestry Committee. But, unlike most farm spokesmen, he also manifested concern for oppressed consumers; in so doing he challenged entrenched and powerful interest groups allied with the Harding administration. It was the old fight in a new guise, and Norris did not shirk from differing with the leaders of his party at this time.

In fighting for the farmer, he sought "honesty and fairness," not special privileges. He explained, "I am in favor of protecting the farmers to the same extent and in the same way that men in other occupations are protected." He favored a tariff that would not be so high as to encourage monopoly but at the same time high enough that the domestic market would absorb reasonably priced American products. But framing a satisfactory tariff proved to be impossible in 1922. The Fordney-McCumber tariff Norris considered "the worst tariff bill ever brought out of Committee." [13]

Particularly disappointing was the fact that the bill was blindly supported by "the Republican machine," including so-called farm bloc members who continually voted against what Norris con-

[12] These views are expounded in the undated draft article written by Norris early in the twenties, "The Necessary Tariff Protection for the Farmer." The article was included in the *Congressional Record,* 67th Cong., 2nd sess., July 1, 1922, pp. 9889–90, as part of his remarks.
[13] Norris to A. J. Plumer, Feb. 23, 1922; to H. H. Harrington, May 29, 1922; *Congressional Record,* 67th Cong., 2nd sess., May 18, 1922, p. 7185.

sidered the farmer's best interests. Too few senators gave the measure any attention, merely coming on the floor for a roll call and voting "with the Committee." Long before debates were concluded, Norris realized that the tariff would pass with little criticism of its schedules. He was appalled that hard-pressed farmers would have to pay prices that would add significantly to their burdens while increasing manufacturers' profits.[14]

On plank after plank Norris voiced his opposition. The tariff was being framed "in accordance with the opinions and evidence of men who had a direct interest one way or the other in the legislation to be enacted." At one point Furnifold Simmons, the leading Democratic authority on tariff matters in the Senate, interrupted him to remark:

> . . . I want to say that I have heard quite a number of good tariff speeches, but I think the speech just delivered by the Senator from Nebraska is the best tariff speech that I have ever heard. It is the best indictment of this bill that has been made. It is the best indictment of the application of the principle of protection so as to help those who do not need help and oppress those who are already overburdened that has been made.[15]

Crystallizing his objections, Norris announced that the tariff bill could not get his vote "unless it was reconstructed from bottom to top." Early in July he left Washington to escape the oppressive heat and was not on hand in August when the bill passed the Senate. Defeated at every turn in an attempt to aid agriculture and to lower the cost of living, Norris had reason to feel discouraged: in no way did the consumer, including the farmer, benefit from the Fordney-McCumber Tariff Act. The law was a hindrance in assisting farmers seeking markets for their surplus because it encouraged other nations to retaliate.[16]

[14] Norris to Harrington, May 19, 1922; to William Kent, May 29, 1922 (Addition 3, William Kent Papers, Yale University Library); *Congressional Record,* 67th Cong., 2nd sess., May 18, 1922, pp. 7168, 7185–86.

[15] *Congressional Record,* 67th Cong., 2nd sess., May 19, p. 7245, May 23, p. 7449, June 30, pp. 9372–73, June 7, 1922, pp. 8304–5 (Simmons's remarks are on p. 8304).

[16] Norris to George Bischel, June 30, 1922; to Arthur D. Dunn, June 30, 1922; to F. S. Frisbie, June 30, 1922; to Carl Gutmann & Co., July 6, 1922; to Solomon, Dec. 8, 1922; to William R. Patrick, Oct. 7, 1923; *Congressional Record,* 67th Cong., 2nd sess., July 6, 1922, pp. 10025–26.

In surveying this situation and in analyzing his reaction to it, Norris did not start with a political philosophy that determined his views. Instead, he began, with the patience and fortitude already evident to observers of his career, to battle against overwhelming odds and to adapt his methods without compromising himself. Throughout the controversies on behalf of agriculture Norris revealed a sense of justice that encompassed more than the rural sector of the population, though he was unabashedly biased in its favor. Having fought and lost, most men would have been content to retire from the fray and seek to re-evaluate or compromise their position, as Norris felt members of the farm bloc did. But he continued to battle, shifting his focus to the field of natural resources, arousing further animosity among the leaders of his party, and challenging interests far more powerful than the middlemen and credit agencies central to many aspects of the farm crisis.

Like most progressives, Norris was willing to use government authority as a countervailing balance on behalf of unorganized and therefore powerless producers and consumers. Government corporations to operate railroads, to build storage warehouses and grain elevators, or to ship surplus produce abroad were suggested by Norris in his battles during the Harding years. Yet he had no preconceived notions about government operation being either good or bad; it was a tool that could be suggested when circumstances warranted. Unlike a colleague who was so opposed to government operation that he would not eat in the Senate restaurant,[17] Norris preferred to examine and weigh each situation on its own merits before coming to his conclusions. It was in the field of natural resources that his conclusions, formulated over a period of years stretching back to his earliest days in the Senate, were going to have an impact on the history of his times.

[17] *Congressional Record,* 67th Cong., 4th sess., Feb. 6, 1923, p. 3117.

The Proper Use of Natural Resources

13

While the Muscle Shoals controversy was the most important example of Norris's interest in the proper use of natural resources, it was not the only one. In the case of coal, for example, his interest was aroused during the strike that began in the bituminous coal fields in April, 1922. The situation was similar to that of agriculture: the miner received too little, the consumer paid too much. In addition, governmental authority in the form of federal judges granted injunctions either restraining labor or preventing effective state supervision on the ground that the coal business was interstate. The plight of the farmer was not too different from the plight of the coal miner.

John L. Lewis, Norris said, was not seeking higher wages so much as an opportunity for miners to work more. With the mines shut down two-thirds of the time, consumers were still paying an exorbitant price for coal. Understanding the plight of the farmer, Norris saw similarities in the condition of the coal miner. He quickly extended his concern to include the miner in particular and the working man in general. All were underpaid and overcharged.[1]

The answer to this dilemma was similar to some suggested with regard to the farmer, namely, government ownership. As in the case of foodstuffs, the cost of coal to the consumer included transportation charges while the miner had freight costs added to everything he used. In mining, as in agriculture, freight rates were a

[1] *Congressional Record,* 67th Cong., 2nd sess., Apr. 6, 1922, p. 5113; George W. Norris to D. H. Barger, Apr. 12, 1922.

basic factor in the high cost of living and one of the reasons necessitating government's operative role. Later, as the Muscle Shoals controversy developed, Norris felt that state operation of coal mines in some instances, such as in Illinois, could give the people the blessings of cheap electricity as well as water power could elsewhere.[2]

Basically, the settlement of the coal question involved government operation of at least a portion of the mines. Those who studied the problem almost always concluded that mines were not operated efficiently and that there were continual coal shortages, usually in the winter months. The fact that coal existed in great abundance made these conditions seem more deplorable. Mines operated at less than half capacity and miners, often out of work, lived under the most adverse of conditions, leading Norris to believe that the only people who benefited were the operators. Strikes did not disturb them because consumers always paid the bill in the form of higher coal prices. Government operation, by eliminating the stress on profits, would remedy inequities and promote efficiency. By 1925 Norris was comparing private ownership in the coal industry "with the dark ages": "It is inefficient. It is expensive. It is absolutely indefensible." [3]

Earlier, during the Wilson years, he had reached the same conclusion with regard to water power. One of the controversies of that period, developing water power at Great Falls in the Potomac near Washington, continued throughout the twenties. Defeated at every turn, he continued in his efforts to activate it for the dual purpose of increasing Washington's water supply and developing its hydroelectric power resources. Yet despite Senate approval on four different occasions and numerous reports recommending the Great Falls project, the House of Representatives never gave its approval.[4] Norris suggested why:

[2] *Congressional Record,* 67th Cong., 2nd sess., June 8, 1922, p. 8379; Norris to the editor, *Omaha Bee,* Oct. 19, 1923; to Frank Farrington, Dec. 19, 1925.

[3] Norris to Farrington, Dec. 19, 1925; to Murray E. King, Dec. 26, 1925.

[4] *Congressional Record,* 67th Cong., 1st sess., June 8, 1921, pp. 2232–34; Norris to Thomas R. Keith, Oct. 5, 1929; Norris, "A Brief History of the Proposed Water Power Development at Great Falls," Nov., 1923 (draft); Norris to William C. Hammer, May 30, 1924. See Chapter 2 for a discussion of the Great Falls controversy during the Wilson years.

There are too many men of wealth in Washington who are interested in the street railway companies, who are interested in the gas company, who are interested in the electric light company. There are too many and too powerful men all over the country interested in similar institutions who do not want the example set before the country of the development of Great Falls in the Capital City, where it will stand as an illustration to the whole country, and so it must be killed. Some way, somehow, there is always a way to kill it.[5]

He considered it both a moral and an economic sin that water flowing down the Potomac River, which could do so much good at so little cost, was going to waste. The time would come, he concluded in 1921, "when you fellows who think more of big business than you do of your religion will be on your bended knees to such men as shall follow me—because I shall not be here then—praying for protection against the mob. The men who are called radicals and progressives now will be the conservatives to whom the weeping, suffering world will plead for justice; and it may be that the pendulum will have swung so far that justice will be impossible." [6]

In 1924 the Senate for the fourth time approved the proposition. Earlier Norris had won over businessmen in the District of Columbia who endorsed and urged its passage. This time Norris added a clause granting the Federal Power Commission authority to increase the amount of hydroelectric power that could be developed. Though the secretary of the commission, O. C. Merrill, was a proponent of publicly regulated private utilities, he favored public development of the Great Falls site. But again the House of Representatives refused to approve the measure. Though Norris never introduced another specific bill, he continued to support the idea. In 1927, for example, he bitterly opposed a request by the Federal Power Commission permitting private interests to develop Great Falls.[7]

[5] *Congressional Record,* 67th Cong., 1st sess., June 22, 1921, p. 2885.

[6] *Ibid.,* pp. 2887–89; 2nd sess., Apr. 19, 1922, pp. 5699–5700. Later Norris called it a "legislative sin" because with an abundance of favorable expert testimony, Congress still refused to act; see Norris to Hammer, May 30, 1924.

[7] *Congressional Record,* 68th Cong., 1st sess., Apr. 10, pp. 6008–9, Apr. 12, 1924, p. 6291, wherein Norris inserted a letter by O. C. Merrill delineating his

His study of the potential use and development of Great Falls, which, incidentally, had begun long before he became interested in Muscle Shoals, helped convince Norris that an electrical age was dawning. Other rivers than the Potomac were being developed. Pennsylvania in 1924, under the direction of Governor Gifford Pinchot, was making a survey of the power possibilities of the commonwealth, including both coal and water. Norris thought the time was not far distant when vast numbers of power units would be joined into one giant system. Already, senatorial hearings revealed, North Carolina during a dry season had received power through interconnected transmission lines from the government-owned steam plant at Muscle Shoals, thereby dramatically suggesting the possibilities of a giant power plant. The great challenge would be to prevent monopoly from garnering benefits that could accrue directly to the people.[8]

Concern about private monopoly seeking its own selfish purposes was accentuated by the Teapot Dome controversy. Norris's interest in naval oil reserves was evident in 1922 before the scandal erupted. He had strongly defended Josephus Daniels, Wilson's Secretary of the Navy, for maintaining naval oil reserves while under heavy pressure from associates within the Wilson administration and from private companies, some of whom were beginning to bore wells in adjoining areas to tap oil pools under government land. Daniels had met these challenges by securing an appropriation to drill wells to drain oil from adjacent lands. Norris now wanted the Senate to allow the Secretary of the Navy to sink similar wells on reserve lands in California at Elk Hills and in Wyoming at Teapot Dome without special appropriations.[9]

At the time the Senate was considering Robert M. LaFollette's

views; Norris to Gifford Pinchot, June 11, 1924 (Box 251, Gifford Pinchot Papers, Manuscript Division, Library of Congress); to E. E. Browne, Jan. 20, 1925; to Federal Power Commission, May 19, 1927; *Washington News, Washington Times,* May 23, 1927. See *Washington Herald,* Feb. 21, 1924, for an account of a talk by Norris to the Connecticut Avenue Citizens Association. A private corporation filed an application with the Federal Power Commission for permission to develop the power resources at Great Falls. Its backers planned to spend $60 million.

[8] Norris to Hammer, May 30, 1924; to Pinchot (Box 251, Gifford Pinchot Papers).

[9] *Congressional Record,* 67th Cong., 2nd sess., Apr. 29, 1922, pp. 6099–6101.

resolution calling for an inquiry into the "entire subject of leases upon naval reserves." The Wisconsin senator supported it with a scathing attack, noting that under Harding the Teapot Dome naval oil reserve had been leased to private oil interests. Norris resented LaFollette's criticism, which implied that as a member of the Public Lands Committee he had endorsed the leasing bill enacted in 1920. By the same token, Norris said, LaFollette should be held responsible for the Esch-Cummins law and the pending tariff bill, since he was a member of the committees that reported these measures. LaFollette quickly apologized and what seemed to be the beginning of a rift was quickly breached. More important, the Senate unanimously approved LaFollette's resolution.[10]

As the investigation unfolded, Norris took more than a casual interest in it. As a member of the Public Lands Committee he attended the Teapot Dome hearings. Early in the Sixty-eighth Congress, though no longer a committee member, Norris commended the chairman, Reed Smoot of Utah, for his handling of the investigation. He was open and fair and "no one was denied an opportunity to secure any evidence anywhere." In fulfilling its function of inquiry without at the same time denying witnesses basic rights, Norris told his colleagues, the committee under Smoot's guidance was doing an admirable job.[11]

On January 30, 1924, the Senate plunged into bitter debate over the oil leasing scandals. Norris admitted that while senators disagreed on the status of the Navy, all were desirous of maintaining naval oil reserves either in the ground or in storage tanks above ground. It was shocking to report that some people high in public life utterly disregarded government policy and the laws enacted to carry out that policy.

Congress had placed jurisdiction of the naval oil reserves with the Secretary of the Navy. When President Harding transferred these reserves to the Secretary of the Interior, he did so, Norris said, in open defiance of the law. Such action, evident in other areas of government as well, was bound to weaken the moral fiber

10 *Ibid.*, p. 6104; Belle Case and Fola LaFollette, *Robert M. LaFollette*, 2 (New York, 1953): 1048–50. J. Leonard Bates, *The Origins of Teapot Dome* (Urbana, Ill., 1963), presents a comprehensive study of the development of a federal leasing policy.

11 *Congressional Record*, 68th Cong., 1st sess., Jan. 14, 1924, p. 935.

of the nation because now ordinary citizens were encouraged to flout the law. More than the proper use of natural resources was involved. Violations of the law, however harmless they might seem, could create precedents that would be cited "by despots and tyrants in order to crush the life out of our liberties." [12] Flowing from what Norris considered the president's illegal order transferring control of oil reserves from the Navy to the Interior Department came the leasing contracts made by Secretary Albert B. Fall with the Doheny and Sinclair interests. Norris insisted further that no law of Congress authorized the construction of storage tanks, the building of docks, and the dredging of channels; yet all were provided for in these contracts. The leases, therefore, were "illegal and void," and the value of every drop of oil taken from the reserve lands should be paid back to the government.

Norris stressed the fact that the original transfer order was illegal. Charles Evans Hughes, Secretary of State and former associate justice of the Supreme Court of the United States, and other department heads were criticized for not protesting when it supposedly was discussed at cabinet meetings. Finally, Norris was convinced from his reading of the testimony that fraud was involved. The testimony about a $100,000 loan by Edward B. McLean to Secretary Fall was a "cock and bull story," planned when Fall found it necessary to explain the source of his sudden wealth. "It was an attempt of Fall to shield himself from further investigation, which would show," Norris declared, "that he was a liar all the way through." The sordid tale was a terrible nightmare that could weaken the moral fiber of the nation because it violated respect for the law.[13]

The American people, Norris claimed, were indebted to Senator Thomas J. Walsh of Montana for his careful and thorough conduct

12 *Ibid.,* Jan. 30, 1924, pp. 1668–69. Norris's views suggest that there was more involved than controversy over conflicting views on conservation, a point that recent scholarship stresses. See Burl Noggle's monograph, *Teapot Dome* (Baton Rouge, La., 1962), for a careful and thorough analysis that makes much of this point.

13 *Washington Evening Star,* Jan. 30, 1924; *Congressional Record,* 68th Cong., 1st sess., Jan. 30, 1924, pp. 1668–71. Norris later said that as a result of his remarks he learned from "three different sources" that detectives hired by McLean were going to Nebraska to unearth evidence that could be used against him; see Norris to B. F. Eberhart, Mar. 16, 1924.

in the Teapot Dome investigation. Yet Walsh was ignored by Calvin Coolidge when he chose special counsel to investigate the matter further. Norris was "dumbfounded," "amazed," and "nearly brokenhearted" when he read that the president had not consulted Walsh in the selection of Atlee Pomerene and Owen J. Roberts. Mere courtesy, Norris said, required the president to consult Walsh in his effort to restore confidence in the honor and honesty of the government. By not consulting Walsh, the president had raised doubts about the senator's ability and integrity and about what he wished to accomplish by the investigation.[14]

Though Coolidge had succeeded Harding in the White House, Norris saw no change in policy toward agriculture or the proper use of natural resources. His views were rebuffed and unaccepted by his party. In one area affecting natural resources, the proper use of hydroelectric power, Norris had evinced an interest during the Wilson era. When the issue focused on Muscle Shoals, Norris became the leading advocate of a position he had formulated during the Wilson years.[15] The first phase of this controversy must now be examined.

[14] *Congressional Record,* 68th Cong., 1st sess., Feb. 16, 1924, pp. 2555–57. That Walsh was pleased with Norris's remarks is evident in the letter he wrote thanking him shortly thereafter. Walsh also mentioned his disappointment when circumstances compelled Norris's retirement from the Public Lands Committee: "Until you came, I never had . . . one word of encouragement or even of sympathy from the majority side . . ."; see Walsh to Norris, Feb. 18, 1924.

[15] In "A Neglected Aspect of the Progressive Movement: George W. Norris and Public Control of Hydroelectric Power, 1913–1919," *The Historian,* 27 (1965): 350–65, I focus on this point.

The Greatest Gift since Salvation

14

"Let me have this," said Henry Ford of Muscle Shoals, "and I will make it a wonderful development—something that will open the eyes of the world." Norris called the Ford offer ". . . the greatest gift ever bestowed upon mortal man since salvation was made free to the human race." In both instances, the potential of Muscle Shoals and the grant of salvation, the gift originally came from God. While Congress created the states, God had made the rivers; usually there was little harmony between them. It was reserved for George W. Norris to battle for a concept, capping the work of numerous pioneers in the field of conservation and calling for an economic life in harmony with nature and geography through utilization in the public interest of the manifold resources of a great river valley system.[1]

The focus of the motor magnate's and the senator's attention, Muscle Shoals, is situated on the Tennessee River in northern Alabama and owes its existence to a long series of rapids with a swift current having a fall equal to four-fifths the height of Niagara, about 134 feet, and spread out in scenic beauty over a distance of thirty-seven miles. Located at the foot of the rapids and at what was then the head of navigation on the Tennessee River are the "tri-cities" of Florence, Sheffield, and Tuscumbia. To partially overcome this

---

[1] Littell McClung, "Muscle Shoals," *Illustrated World*, 36, no. 6 (Feb., 1922): 825 (the Ford quote); the *Omaha Daily News*, May 11, 1924, carried the statement by Norris.

barrier to navigation, canals on both banks of the river were completed and in operation in 1890.

The Tennessee River twists and wends its way for 650 miles through four states. Including tributaries, it makes a valley involving six states, about 40,000 square miles or 26 million acres. In 1920 there were approximately 2 million people in the valley, living mostly on small farms, producing cash crops: corn, cotton, and tobacco. These yielded their cultivators inadequate returns to provide food, processed goods, housing, and health, educational, and other local government services. For almost a hundred years before Norris became involved with Muscle Shoals, it had been continually brought to the attention of Congress.

As early as 1824 John C. Calhoun, then Secretary of War, urged Congress to provide a survey, on the grounds of military necessity, of the Muscle Shoals section of the Tennessee River. Periodically since that time the federal government had concerned itself with Muscle Shoals: in the nineteenth century to improve navigation and in the twentieth to develop hydroelectric potential as well. Basically, the controversy over Muscle Shoals was a legacy of World War I. Had it not been for the war, about $160 million (as of 1927) of the taxpayers' money would not have been invested in the tri-cities area. Anticipating the need for enormous quantities of nitrates, necessary for explosives, Congress in Section 124 of the National Defense Act of 1916 authorized the construction of nitrate plants and appropriated $20 million for the purpose. By this action Congress recognized that in the event of war the availability of Chilean nitrates, upon which the nation formerly depended, would be in jeopardy. As an alternative, Congress authorized the president to select one or more sites in the United States where an abundance of cheap water power could be utilized for the purpose of extracting nitrogen from the atmosphere. In September, 1917, President Wilson chose Muscle Shoals. Shortly thereafter the construction of a nitrate plant was begun and arrangements were made with the Alabama Power Company to build a government unit at its Gorgas Power Plant at the mouth of a coal mine, ninety miles south of Muscle Shoals, for the production of electricity to be used at the nitrate plant.

In 1918 two nitrate plants at Muscle Shoals were completed

and work had started on Dam No. 2 (eventually Wilson Dam), for which $12 million of the $20-million appropriation had been set aside.[2] After the armistice the question of what to do with this vast project arose. Unsuccessful in efforts to interest private concerns in the production of nitrates, a plan was submitted to Congress calling for government operation of the second nitrate plant. The Wadsworth-Kahn bill embodying this suggestion was approved by the Senate in May, 1920, but was lost when Congress adjourned without the House having considered it.

Shortly after the inauguration of Warren G. Harding, Secretary of War John W. Weeks announced that if an offer representing a fair return to the government were received, it would be sent to Congress. The War Department then asked for bids. Henry Ford and the Alabama Power Company submitted the principal bids with the motor magnate's offer coming first. Immediately Muscle Shoals became a matter of controversy which for over a decade absorbed the attention of George W. Norris. Three divisions or categories were involved: nitrogen and the production of nitrates and fertilizer, navigation, and power. In deciding to send Muscle Shoals measures to the Agriculture and Forestry Committee, the Senate signified that it considered the military aspects secondary to the production of fertilizer. Thus Muscle Shoals became a primary concern of Norris, though the House measures emanated from the Military Affairs Committee.

On July 8, 1921, the proposal of Henry Ford was signed, sent to Secretary Weeks, and its terms made public. The American Farm Bureau Federation endorsed it in November and on February 1, 1922, the Secretary of War transmitted the offer to Congress. Before the Senate Agriculture and Forestry Committee began its hearings, Norris and a coterie of congressmen, their families, and staff members junketed to Muscle Shoals to inspect the properties. When Norris came to consider Muscle Shoals, he had a clear notion of the history and the dimensions of the project.[3]

[2] Wilson Dam was completed in 1925, at the time the largest concrete dam in the world. It was designed by Hugh L. Cooper, a distinguished American engineer, and built and administered by the Engineer Corps of the U.S. Army. It represented an investment of about $47 million and was capable of generating about 240,000 horsepower. At the time of the Ford offer it was less than one-third completed.

[3] Background information on Muscle Shoals was secured from the following

Henry Ford agreed to purchase the two nitrate plants for $5 million and to lease the water power plant for 100 years, provided the government constructed and included in the lease a dam and power plant at Site No. 3, fifteen miles above Muscle Shoals, and installed additional horsepower at Dam No. 2 (Wilson Dam). Ford proposed to pay annually 4 percent interest on the cost of the power plants, exclusive of about $17 million of wartime funds expended on the Wilson Dam power plant, and an additional $66,746, which if compounded at 4 percent semiannually would amortize the cost of the power plants in 100 years. Ford further agreed to produce annually, after six years, fertilizer containing 40,000 tons of nitrogen which would be sold commercially at 8 percent profit. If unable to sell this amount, Ford would maintain in storage ready for sale a minimum quantity of fertilizer containing 2,500 tons of nitrogen. The proposal also would grant Ford title to a transmission line extending 100 miles from Muscle Shoals to one steam plant on the Warrior River and to another of 30,000 kw, including the Alabama Power Company lands on which these facilities were located.[4]

Shortly after the Ford offer was submitted, Secretary Weeks approved and sent to Congress another offer. This one was by the Alabama Power Company. It proposed to complete the power plant at Muscle Shoals at its own expense, operate it under a

---

sources: National League of Women Voters, *Facts about Muscle Shoals* (Washington, D.C., 1927), pp. 5–7; "The Muscle Shoals Controversy in Congress," *Congressional Digest*, 9, no. 12 (Dec., 1930): 295–96; "Present Status of Muscle Shoals," *ibid.*, no. 5 (May, 1930): 135–36; "Chronological History of Muscle Shoals Developments," *ibid.*, 2, no. 1 (Oct., 1922): 7. There are two excellent volumes examining the Muscle Shoals controversy in Congress. Judson King, *The Conservation Fight* (Washington, D.C., 1959), analyzes the controversy from the viewpoint of a devoted follower, confidant, and aid of Norris. Preston Hubbard, *Origins of the TVA* (Nashville, Tenn., 1961), in a painstaking and careful monograph, presents a more balanced account. Both volumes are well-written, fully documented, comprehensive accounts. My purpose is not to duplicate them but rather to focus on Norris's role in the controversy.

[4] Colonel Joseph I. McMullen, "Brief Review of Muscle Shoals Legislation," Mar. 8, 1933 (memorandum in the Franklin D. Roosevelt Papers (OF 44), pp. 5–6, Franklin D. Roosevelt Library, Hyde Park, N.Y.). In his final modified offer Ford omitted the provision to acquire the transmission line and steam plant, since the Secretary of War had previously sold these facilities to the Alabama Power Company. The *Congressional Digest*, 2, no. 1 (Oct., 1922): 8, presents a convenient summary of the Ford offer.

license from the Federal Power Commission, and supply power for the operation of the nitrate plants for national defense and the production of fertilizer.[5] Other proposals were later submitted to Congress by Secretary Weeks but these two were the most important.

The Senate Agriculture and Forestry Committee, chaired by Norris, began hearings on February 16 and continued intermittently until June 22, 1922. Before the hearings were launched, the country was deluged with propaganda in favor of the Ford offer. Relief to agriculture and patriotism were stressed. Ford would sell fertilizer at low cost and would maintain the larger of the nitrate plants in constant readiness for war work. The offer, it should be noted, was made at a time when the Harding administration was seeking to sell numerous wartime facilities, including merchant vessels, for low salvage prices.[6]

Great benefits from Ford's offer to develop Muscle Shoals were envisioned. One writer, carried away by the prospects, wrote:

> His will be a conquest such as Alexander, Caesar, or Napoleon never visioned—a conquest of science by scientists for the benefit of millions who have never seen, and may never see, Henry Ford. His is an ambition unique in conception, humanitarian in purpose, staggering in proportions. In comparison, boring through the Alps, tunneling under the English Channel, or uniting two oceans by the Panama Canal are but mechanical engineering triumphs.
>
> Ford will forge far beyond these—beyond anything previously conceived by engineer, chemist or electrician. He will cross the borderland into a new realm of endeavor. Henry Ford, with Thomas A. Edison, will inaugurate—for the common folk of America—the Hydro-Electric-Chemical Age. At Muscle Shoals we will witness the culmination of centuries of patient research into the mysteries of Nature. Muscle Shoals, under Ford, will be a

[5] McMullen, "Brief Review," p. 6.

[6] National League of Women Voters, *Facts about Muscle Shoals,* p. 17. The discussion in Allan Nevins and Frank Ernest Hill, *Ford: Expansion and Challenge, 1915–1933* (New York, 1957), pp. 305–11, is revealing. The terms of the Ford offer stated herein differ somewhat from those in the text. The authors conclude that "while unquestionably Ford's motives were mainly public spirited, it is clear that he hoped for a certain amount of personal glory from the enterprise" (p. 310).

revelation to this generation. Mr. Ford has said he "will open the eyes of the world"—and he will.[7]

Not everyone was so enthusiastic about the wonders yet to come. Gifford Pinchot observed "that for the water-power itself Mr. Ford would pay nothing, and that he would be free from all taxes on the property." Overall, it was a proposition that was "seven parts waterpower to one part fertilizer." As a water power proposition, Pinchot found it contrary to the Roosevelt leasing policy included in the Federal Water Power Act of 1920, wherein at the end of fifty years the property reverted to the government. The Ford offer asked for 100 years with indefinite renewals. The Roosevelt policy demanded regulation of consumer rates and a return to the public; the Ford offer had no such provisions and called for government construction of additional generating units. Pinchot did not summarily reject the Ford offer. He only wished it to fit the Roosevelt power policy and to pay something approaching what the property was really worth. But the proposal presented to Congress literally gave Ford all the water power available at Muscle Shoals for nothing. Thus Pinchot saw, before Norris had uttered his first words on the controversy, that it revolved around cheap power, that concern for agriculture and improved navigation were fronts for the chance to control and exploit the power potential at Muscle Shoals.[8]

In February, 1922, before the Agriculture and Forestry Committee started hearings on the proposals, Norris turned his attention to the subject. He said his committee should consider the Ford offer because "the fundamental proposition involved . . . at least in times of peace, is the making of fertilizer for farmers." At the outset he realized that the question of improving navigation was

[7] Littell McClung, "What Can Henry Ford Do with Muscle Shoals," *Illustrated World,* 37, no. 2 (Apr., 1922): 185. Ford envisioned, to the delight of real estate promoters, a wonder city some seventy-five miles long, smokeless, and offering all the advantages of electricity.

[8] Statement by Gifford Pinchot, Aug. 25, 1921 (copy in Harry Slattery Papers, Manuscripts Collections, Duke University Library). Slattery, who played a key role in unearthing the Teapot Dome scandal, originally considered the Ford offer an unusually "liberal one" for the government; see, for example, Harry Slattery to Pinchot, Aug. 8, 1921; to James A. Frear, Aug. 8, 1921 (both in Slattery Papers). A month later, however, Slattery was having doubts about his initial enthusiasm; see Pinchot to Slattery, Oct. 5, 1921 (Slattery Papers).

only incidental. Norris admitted that although he had read the Ford proposal twice, he had not yet come to any conclusions. He acknowledged that the committee had much to do and that he would "be glad to be relieved of any additional work that might come to the committee on this account." [9]

At this time Norris requested that committee members make a trip to Muscle Shoals. Before the senators visited the area late in March, there were indications that Norris had come to a conclusion about the validity of the Ford offer. At the end of February Harry Slattery reported a conversation in which Norris said that Ford could not live for more than twenty years and questioned what would become of the proposal then. Slattery suggested government operation and thought that Norris was interested.[10]

On March 10, 1922, Norris announced that he was preparing a government operation bill which would provide for both power and fertilizer. Not that he favored this view; he merely wished to place before the Agriculture and Forestry Committee alternative avenues of investigation, "based upon the fact that we have already done a great deal of work and have partially completed the work that is necessary for the development of power there." In considering the Ford, Alabama Power Company, and other offers, Norris felt that committee members ought to know how much money had already been spent (over $105 million by November, 1918) and how much more would have to be spent for the government to develop and operate Muscle Shoals. Congress could then "face this proposition squarely" and "with intelligence, with absolute fairness, without any bias and without any prejudice." [11]

On April 10, 1922, Norris introduced his bill for a government corporation to control and operate the Muscle Shoals properties. The board of directors, appointed by the president and confirmed by the Senate, would operate the properties "for the purpose, first, of supplying explosives in time of war, and, second, fertilizer in time of peace." Surplus power could be sold, providing preference was given to states, counties, and municipalities. The smaller ni-

[9] *Congressional Record,* 67th Cong., 2nd sess., Feb. 7, 1922, p. 2210.

[10] *Ibid.,* Feb. 16, 1922, p. 2635; Slattery to Pinchot, Feb. 28, 1922 (Slattery Papers).

[11] *Congressional Record,* 67th Cong., 2nd sess., Mar. 10, 1922, pp. 3659–60.

trate plant would be devoted to improving methods for the extraction of nitrogen from the atmosphere. In case of war the larger plant would be operated for the benefit for the government.[12]

On April 20 Norris submitted a report from the committee unanimously rejecting all bids except that of Henry Ford. He said that the committee stood seven in favor of Ford's offer and nine for its rejection. Five members favored Norris's bill for government operation. Thus the report was unanimous only so far as a rejection of all other bids was concerned, while a bare majority favored the rejection of all bids sent to the Senate by the Secretary of War.[13]

Early in June, with the matter at a stalemate in the Senate, Norris offered an amendment to the Army appropriation bill calling for an outlay of $7,500,000 for continuing work on Dam No. 2. It was estimated that the dam could be completed in three years if funds were appropriated. Norris concluded that it would be "an economic crime to delay a moment in going ahead." The Senate and later the House approved this amendment, and by the end of 1922 work on the construction of Dam No. 2 was again under way.[14]

Meanwhile, Norris was carefully investigating the Ford offer. The more he learned, the more critical he became. Once the House Military Affairs Committee on June 9 had reported the McKenzie bill to accept the Ford offer, Norris voiced misgivings lest the movement to sell the properties to the motor magnate gain too much headway in Congress.[15] On June 17, 1922, he launched a major assault against the proposal. Never criticizing Ford or any other individual or corporation, all of whom, he insisted, acted in good faith, Norris mentioned groups of individuals, aside from the bidders, who were interested in Muscle Shoals. Real estate agents and speculators expected to make millions. Others were seeking

[12] A convenient summary of Norris's bill can be found in the *Congressional Digest*, 2, no. 1 (Oct., 1922): 8.

[13] *Senate Calendar 817*, 67th Cong., 2nd sess., Report 831, Part 1, Muscle Shoals, p. 1.

[14] *Congressional Record*, 67th Cong., 2nd sess., June 2, 1922, pp. 8036–37; National League of Women Voters, *Facts about Muscle Shoals*, p. 18.

[15] In August Senator Edwin F. Ladd for himself and six other members of the Agriculture and Forestry Committee submitted a minority report (*Senate Calendar 817*, 67th Cong., 2nd sess., Report 831, Part 2) calling for the adoption of his bill accepting the Ford offer.

cheap fertilizer or to have the river developed, principally by improving navigation. While the bulk of the propaganda favored the Ford proposal, everybody concerned with Muscle Shoals envisioned the development of the area. And this consideration, Norris agreed, was worthy of the attention of all honest men.[16]

First, Norris examined the question of fertilizer. While everyone hoped to reduce the cost of fertilizer, nobody actually knew how to do so. Ford had not agreed to do it, and government chemists could not agree. Yet so great was the prestige and influence of Henry Ford that millions of people believed that if he received Muscle Shoals, he would reduce the price of fertilizer.

The government corporation in Norris's bill would develop the properties in the interests of the American people, instead of making a profit venture out of it. And profit is what Norris saw in the Ford proposal. The government had spent $106 million on the property at Muscle Shoals. Ford offered to buy it for $5 million, and for all except the land adjacent to the dams he was to get a deed in fee simple. Opposing this give-away, Norris also resented leasing the dams for 100 years: "I am against any corporation or any man getting for a mere bagatelle what cost the taxpayers of the United States $106,000,000. . . ." Moreover, until a new discovery was made to manufacture nitrates inexpensively, Norris said, "we must maintain nitrate plant No. 2 as a war proposition, even though we cannot make any fertilizer out of it." Under the terms of his offer Ford would secure property worth more than twenty times his $5-million payment and, in addition, would obtain a lease for 100 years on the water power to be generated. But the government would provide all the money for the dams, with Ford paying 4 percent interest and agreeing to repay the principal in 100 years.

Citing his own bill calling for a government corporation, Norris claimed it would develop the properties at Muscle Shoals, generate power at Dam No. 2 and at proposed Dam No. 3, and with that

[16] *Congressional Record,* 67th Cong., 2nd sess., June 17, 1922, p. 8892. Senate debate on Muscle Shoals was interspersed with discussion of proposed tariff legislation. For an example of Norris's investigation of facets of the Ford offer, see Norris to Hugh L. Cooper, June 12, 1922; Cooper to Norris, June 20, 1922 (both letters in Box 17, Judson King Papers, Manuscript Division, Library of Congress).

power help reduce operating costs. It would make fertilizer; if new discoveries were made, the farmer would get the benefit of them. It was unfair and ungracious to insinuate with some senators that only Henry Ford stood between the American farmer and ruin.[17]

Then Norris came to the heart of the matter. Over 4,600 acres of government-owned land would go to Henry Ford if his bid were accepted. In addition to gaining title to this property, all the power developed at Muscle Shoals would be his with the exception of enough to run the second nitrate plant. Ford could not lose anything on that because his proposal provided for not more than 8 percent profit on the fertilizer produced at this plant. With land and hydro-electric power available in abundance, Ford propaganda envisioned a center of industry and real estate agents boomed the area as a future metropolis. Yet, Norris noted, Ford, almost sixty years of age, would have 100 years in which to pay back less money than the government had already spent in developing the properties. His offer did not contemplate repayment of $17 million spent on Dam No. 2 or any part of the money spent on Dam No. 3,[18] or any interest on the money the government would advance to complete these dams. True, Ford promised to pay 4 percent interest, but this would not commence until after the dams were completed. Until that time Ford's proposition did not provide for the payment of a cent of interest. Further, on the more than 4,600 acres to be deeded to Ford, there were two towns, one at each of the nitrate plants. There existed macadamized streets, furnished houses for several thousand people and a larger number of temporary houses, a lighting, sewerage, and water system in each of the towns, the Gorgas transmission line, and an interest in the Gorgas steam plant on the Warrior River ninety miles from Muscle Shoals, costing the government in all over $100 million.[19] All of these installations had been provided by the government, and all would go to Henry Ford for the $5 million he agreed to pay for the two nitrate plants at Muscle Shoals.

Nitrate Plant No. 2, Norris said, was in first-class condition and

[17] Thomas J. Heflin of Alabama voiced this view.

[18] Several hundred thousand dollars had been spent on Dam No. 3.

[19] In 1923, before Ford withdrew his offer, the government sold its interest in the Gorgas steam plant. The government had spent about $5 million on this property, originally owned by the Alabama Power Company.

ready to function. A modern steam plant capable of generating 130,000 horsepower, twenty-six miles of standard-gauge railroad, engines and cars, machinery, one of the largest cement-mixing plants in the world, a stone quarry—all furnished with the best equipment—would be included in the Ford offer with this nitrate plant. Nitrate Plant No. 1, while housed in a fireproof building, had machinery in it that was of little value, since it had been devised as something of an experiment. But by citing all the equipment, machinery, and other property involved, Norris made it abundantly clear that Ford in offering $5 million was not animated by altruistic motives.

Under the provisions of Norris's public ownership bill, the government would continue to experiment at Nitrate Plant No. 1. Several million dollars, he admitted, would have to be spent to make a modern nitrate plant out of it. On the other hand, the Ford offer granted title to the plant and did not specify what was to be done with it. Ford did agree to operate Nitrate Plant No. 2. And that was the only thing he agreed to do with the $106 million worth of property he would receive for his $5 million. In addition, Ford or his corporation would secure a 100-year lease on two dams. He would benefit from the $17 million already spent on dams and he would not pay any interest on the money the government provided for completing them. When completed, he would pay the government, on an amortized 100-year basis, a yearly fee covering the money spent on these dams since the date of the acceptance of his bid.

Out of the power developed at the dams, Ford would be obligated to use enough of it, around 100,000 horsepower, to operate Nitrate Plant No. 2. He would have to make fertilizer which he could not sell at more than 8 percent profit. The balance of the power was Ford's to use as he saw fit. Moreover, the government would be obligated to keep the dams in repair for the 100-year period, "with no redress, no interest, and no return of anything." For these services Ford agreed to pay a minimum fee that Norris estimated would not be one-tenth of what was necessary to keep the dams in repair.

Nor, Norris next noted, was this all. "None of this concession," he said, "will go to Ford." It would go to a corporation organized by Ford; there was no guarantee that he would own or control it during the remainder of his life. After his death he could not bind it in any way. Many of the processes utilized at Muscle Shoals would soon be obsolete and incredibly expensive. Nitrate Plant No. 2, necessary in case of war, could be scrapped as new methods of producing nitrates came into use. Under government ownership this could be done; under the terms of the Ford proposal it would have to be kept on a "standby" basis for 100 years. Then, too, with Ford's plan to build a city at Muscle Shoals, the bulk of the electricity generated would be used within the vicinity for manufacturing purposes. Little would be distributed among states, counties, and municipalities; little would get into rural homes at a cheap rate. Norris's proposal, on the other hand, with its preference clause, would scatter electricity within a 300-mile radius and insure its wide distribution at an inexpensive rate. He regarded "as a sin against unborn generations" the granting of this great inheritance to one corporation for 100 years without any regulation whatsoever, particularly when the electricity would come from a river developed with taxpayers' money.

The Muscle Shoals site, Norris concluded, was one of the most valuable gifts ever given to man. The engineer in charge of the construction of Dam No. 2 estimated that Ford could sell it on the market for $200 million. While Norris did not think there was any deception in the offer, he thought Ford would make "hundreds of millions." He would build a huge city, construct great manufacturing plants, and with cheap power would have an extraordinary advantage over every competitor. Considering the public money already spent, the money Ford would use for other purposes while government built the dams, and the puny interest he would pay, nobody could compete. The difference, then, between Norris's proposal for public ownership of Muscle Shoals and the Ford bid was the difference between letting the people who put up the money get the benefit and giving all the benefit to one corporation. If the Ford offer were accepted, the fight for conservation would be lost and the public, Norris said, would be taxed for a century to make the gift more profitable.[20]

[20] *Congressional Record,* 67th Cong., 2nd sess., June 17, 1922, pp. 8893, 8895–96, 8900–8904.

These extemporaneous remarks to the Senate in June, 1922, constituted Norris's first major address on Muscle Shoals.[21] Starting with the concrete fact that the government had invested over $100 million, he soon was convinced that all offers for the property were grossly unfair to the government and the American people. Public ownership was by far the fairest way to resolve the question. Norris quickly discerned that the power potential at Muscle Shoals was the prize bidders desired, that the production of fertilizer was a front to assuage the sentiments of farmers and farm spokesmen, particularly in the distressed rural regions of the South. Since the Ford offer stood the best chance of being approved, Norris devoted most of his attention to it. In speeches, statements, letters, and articles he reiterated the points he made in this speech.[22]

So strong were the proponents of the Ford offer and so great was their belief in his ability to provide cheap fertilizer that a bill to investigate ways and means of producing cheap fertilizer could not be considered by the Senate Agriculture and Forestry Committee. Norris said that Ford ought to be able to produce cheap fertilizer within the 100 years provided in the lease he sought. He reiterated, however, that cheap fertilizer was still a question of experimentation. Furthermore, his bill had the virtue of considering fertilizer, navigation, flood control, and hydroelectric power while the Ford proposal did not comprehensively consider multiple-purpose aspects. Such a program, Norris said, would do more for the development of the South than anything Henry Ford had proposed.[23]

Throughout this controversy Norris insisted that his political

[21] *Ibid.,* July 5, 1922, p. 9933. Commenting on his June 17 speech, Norris said, ". . . my remarks on that occasion were entirely extemporaneous; I spoke entirely from memory." Norris rarely spoke from a manuscript; at best he would have before him an index card with several points jotted on it.

[22] See, for example, Norris to the editor, *Madison* (Wis.) *Capital Times,* Nov. 2, 1922. The *Washington Times,* Mar. 12, 1924, and the *Omaha Daily News,* May 11, 1924, both contain statements by Norris. See also the two-part article Norris wrote, "Shall We Give Muscle Shoals to Henry Ford?" *Saturday Evening Post,* May 24 (Part I), May 31 (Part II), 1924.

[23] *Congressional Record,* 67th Cong., 4th sess., Dec. 7, 1922, pp. 174–76, Feb. 9, 1923, pp. 3296–99. In his remarks on Feb. 9, 1923, Norris dealt extensively with the question of producing fertilizer and the different methods involved.

fortunes were not involved with the fate of the Ford proposition. He was animated only by a sense of duty to aid the American farmer, announcing in February, 1923, that "I do not seem to have pleased the Ford men any better than I have pleased the administration." He might have added that his actions did not please the lower house of the Nebraska legislature; it requested members of the state's congressional delegation to support the Ford offer. It also extended an invitation to Henry Ford to make an industrial survey of hydroelectric power in Nebraska with a view to its development.[24]

In a sharp reply Norris remarked, "The reasons you give in your resolution confirm me in the righteousness of my opposition to the acceptance of the Ford offer. I am unwilling to give away the birthright of millions of unborn citizens for the enrichment of private corporations at the expense of the taxpayers of America, and I am unwilling to do this even when requested to do it by so high and honorable a body as the House of Representatives of the Nebraska legislature." [25] William Kent in California, upon reading this open letter, surmised correctly that, as a result of Norris's efforts, the Ford offer was dead as far as the Sixty-seventh Congress was concerned but would be renewed in the next session. Like Norris, Kent understood that water power was "the biggest economic and progressive factor of the future and upon its proper solution depends the public welfare more than any other single matter." [26]

While propaganda for the Ford offer continued after the Sixty-seventh Congress adjourned on March 3, 1923, the climate of opinion gradually changed. When the first session of the Sixty-eighth Congress convened in December, 1923, Harding had been dead four months; evidence of scandal in his administration, particularly involving the naval oil reserves, helped cast doubt on private entrepreneurs developing natural resource sites. The labors of Norris and the handful of senators who agreed with him were slowly convincing other colleagues and prominent citizens that

[24] *Ibid.,* Feb. 9, p. 3307, Feb. 20, 1923, p. 4056. The resolution of the Nebraska House of Representatives was dated Feb. 16, 1923.

[25] The resolution and Norris's letter of Feb. 20, 1923, in response can be conveniently found in *ibid.,* Feb. 20, 1923, p. 4056.

[26] William Kent to Norris, Feb. 26, 1923 (water power, 1st Lot); to Pinchot, Feb. 26, 1923 (both in Addition 4, William Kent Papers, Yale University Library).

legitimate questions could be raised about the Ford offer, especially the 100-year lease, which violated the basic canon of conservation policy promulgated during the presidency of Theodore Roosevelt. The efforts of Gifford Pinchot and his associates were likewise beginning to convince citizens, despite President Coolidge's message to the new Congress on December 6, 1923, recommending that the Muscle Shoals properties be sold.[27]

In January, 1924, Secretary of War John Weeks submitted to Congress three separate offers to lease the Muscle Shoals properties. One was from the Alabama Power Company and two associates, the Tennessee Electric Power Company and the Memphis Light & Power Company. They proposed a fifty-year lease on Dam No. 2 and agreed to furnish up to 100,000 horsepower at cost for the production of fertilizer by others. The Union Carbide Company proposed to lease the properties for fifty years and to use part of the power generated for the production of nitrates. The third bid was submitted by a group of prominent individuals. They proposed to organize a million-dollar management corporation to operate the properties at government expense with a division of the net profits.[28]

In February Norris introduced, for the second time, his bill calling for government operation of the Muscle Shoals properties; in the House of Representatives the Military Affairs Committee already had endorsed a measure accepting the Ford offer. It was debated and accepted by the House on March 10 and then sent to the Senate, where it was referred to the Agriculture and Forestry Committee and was never voted upon.[29] The administration was

27 See, for example, Philip P. Wells to Kent, Mar. 22, 1923 (water power, 1st Lot, Kent Papers); Frank L. Greene to Bruce R. Buchanan, Dec. 5, 1923 (Box 20, Frank L. Greene Papers, Manuscript Division, Library of Congress). Greene, a former Vermont congressman, was starting his service in the Senate. He wrote his constituent, "I am glad you are suspicious of the Henry Ford Muscle Shoals proposition." Greene himself regarded it as "bunk." In his judgment "professionals who have been so long 'farming the farmer' are using this Henry Ford propaganda in their own interests, and that Ford is just childlike enough—away from automobile engines—to be used as a decoy." Greene regarded himself as a conservative but insisted that "a conservative is not necessarily a reactionary by any means." See also the editorial, "Changing Times; Changing Mind," in *Washington Daily News*, Apr. 9, 1924.

28 National League of Women Voters, *Facts about Muscle Shoals*, p. 18.

29 This was the last recorded vote on Muscle Shoals in the House of Representatives until the Norris bill passed Congress in May, 1928.

determined to sell the properties, Secretary Weeks explaining that the entrance of the government into an industrial field would deter private capital from similar enterprises. But Norris, focusing attention not on general premises but on a specific situation, could not agree to granting any corporation over $100 million worth of government property for an insignificant sum.[30]

Increasing numbers of influential citizens were beginning to agree with him. Newton D. Baker, despite earlier disagreements about Great Falls on the Potomac River, was one. As Secretary of War during the Wilson administration, Baker claimed responsibility for the selection of the Muscle Shoals site and the building of the dam. He wrote that "safety lies alone in the Government's retaining this property and others like it, rather than passing it . . . to any private corporation whatsoever." Recognizing that Muscle Shoals was the greatest water power site east of the Rockies, capable of generating more electricity than was produced on the American side of Niagara Falls, Baker said that "no project to take that power out of the hands of the Government would interest me." [31]

Meanwhile, aided by the Public Ownership League of America, Norris and Representative Oscar E. Keller of Minnesota introduced a general measure providing for the conservation of natural resources. It called for the coordination of flood control and navigation, the development and distribution of hydroelectric energy, and other items, all functioning under government control. It provided for a public service commission to cooperate with states, municipalities, counties, and other subdivisions in developing an integrated, publicly owned power system. The measure diverted attention from the McKenzie bill, containing the Ford proposal, but it also detracted somewhat from Norris's bill for government opera-

[30] John W. Weeks to Norris, Mar. 3, 1924; Norris to W. A. Hammond, Mar. 28, 1924; to H. M. Merrill, Apr. 25, 1924.

[31] Rixey Smith and Norman Beasley, *Carter Glass: A Biography* (New York, 1939), p. 279, present a 1924 letter from Newton D. Baker to Carter Glass; see also Baker to Ernest Greenwood, Apr. 3, 1924 (Box 160); to Norris, Apr. 11, 1924 (Box 177, Newton D. Baker Papers, Manuscript Division, Library of Congress). Incidentally, Carter Glass in 1924 also "thought it would be better for the Government to complete and operate the plant"; see Smith and Beasley, *Carter Glass*, p. 280.

tion of the Muscle Shoals facilities. In April the Senate Agriculture and Forestry Committee held hearings on the House-approved McKenzie bill and substituted the text of the Norris Muscle Shoals bill for it. Though the measure was debated in the Senate, no vote was taken before the first session of the Sixty-eighth Congress adjourned in June.[32]

By the end of April Norris thought the Ford offer could be defeated. The *Chicago Tribune,* commenting editorially on its failure to conform "to America's power conservation policy," said "for this reason it is promised defeat in Congress." The *Washington Star,* never before in sympathy with Norris, felt he had performed a patriotic service by challenging the "astonishing proposition" presented to Congress in the bid of Henry Ford. "Many conscientious and honest advocates of the Ford proposition," Norris wrote, "are beginning to see the truth." So effective was he in exposing what Harry Slattery called "the 'holy and sacred' atmosphere around this crooked deal between Henry and many other politicals, land speculators, and others Most High" that Slattery felt "Uncle George" was about "to lay it away in lavender for this session." While a majority of the Senate Agriculture and Forestry Committee were already in accord with Norris's views on the Ford offer and Muscle Shoals, the Coolidge administration, Republican leaders, and their allies in and out of Washington were united in opposition to them.[33]

Norris was convinced that the president for political reasons wanted Ford to get Muscle Shoals. Earlier animosity by the motor magnate toward the administration had been converted into friendship. Norris recognized that he had incurred the wrath of the ad-

[32] *Taloga* (Okla.) *Advocate,* Apr. 17, 1924; *Chicago Tribune,* Apr. 30, 1924 (both papers' editorials supported the Norris-Keller measure); Norris to Merrill, Apr. 25, 1924. On May 27, 1924, the Agriculture and Forestry Committee by a vote of 11 to 4 favorably reported the Norris government-ownership plan for the operation of Muscle Shoals. A motion to report the Ford offer favorably was defeated 11 to 5. No action was taken concerning other pending offers; see *Wall Street Journal,* May 28, 1924.

[33] *Chicago Tribune,* Apr. 30, 1924; *Washington Evening Star,* n.d. [1924], "Farm Bureau Criticism of Norris" (editorial), appears as a clipping in the Norris Papers; Norris to Carl D. Thompson, Apr. 27, 1924; Slattery to Kent, May 5, 1924 (Slattery Papers).

ministration and its supporters in Nebraska. The *Omaha Bee,* formerly friendly to him, now carried editorials favoring the Ford proposal. Backfires were being built against him and their intensity would increase as the campaign of 1924 got underway. But such maneuvers, besides indicating desperation on the part of Ford's supporters, served to reinforce Norris in his opposition to the proposal.[34]

Meanwhile, as the first session of the Sixty-eighth Congress moved toward adjournment in June before the national nominating conventions met, obstructionist charges were leveled against Norris because the Senate did not act upon the Ford offer. He denied them, pointing to the fair and comprehensive hearings that had been conducted. No senator publicly challenged his statements. On June 3, 1924, he admitted that the Senate could not dispose of Muscle Shoals unless the resolution calling for adjournment on June 7 was defeated. Realizing this was impossible, he announced his intention of submitting a unanimous-consent request fixing a definite date shortly after the reconvening of Congress to dispose of the Muscle Shoals proposition.[35] But Senator Oscar Underwood of Alabama was quicker than Norris. On June 4, 1924, the Senate approved his resolution to resume discussion of the McKenzie bill as amended by the Senate Agriculture and Forestry Committee on December 3, at the opening of the second session of the Sixty-eighth Congress, and to continue considerations until the Norris amendment calling for public ownership and operation of the Muscle Shoals properties was disposed of.

On October 18, 1924, Henry Ford withdrew his offer for Muscle Shoals. The first phase of the controversy had ended with a victory for Norris in the sense that a flagrant give-away of a prime natural resource site had been staved off. Other fights and a more serious threat were yet to come. But out of the fight over the Ford

[34] Norris to I. D. Evans, May 13, 1924; *Congressional Record,* 68th Cong., 1st sess., May 6, 1924, pp. 7919–20. In both citations Norris discussed the growing friendship between Coolidge and Ford. In the Senate, speaking of Ford supporters, he said, "Coolidge, Ford, Heflin, Harrison, Cal, Hank, Tom and Pat, all mixed up together like a scrambled egg. Result: Fertilizer."

[35] Norris to John Humphreys, May 19, 1924; *Congressional Record,* 68th Cong., 1st sess., May 14, pp. 8501–3, June 3, 1924, pp. 10278, 10280–81.

offer Norris emerged as a leading advocate of public ownership and operation of Muscle Shoals not only for national defense but for the improvement of rural life in the South. The fight over the Ford offer also indicated that water power was one of the great national questions of the decade. Muscle Shoals, Boulder Canyon, the St. Lawrence, and Great Falls projected the issue onto the national scene. Whereas many earlier fights had been waged to prevent the granting of power sites in perpetuity to private interests, by the 1920s the issue revolved around the question of public versus private development.

Norris helped define the issue almost single-handedly. Judson King aided by researching and by presenting to interested citizens information about Muscle Shoals and Norris's position.[36] On another level Harry Slattery, once he clearly saw what was involved, lined up "many of the old conservation crowd back of Norris in his fight." Many others, like William Kent, lent what support they could.[37] In the Senate, interestingly enough, many Republican conservatives saw validity in Norris's arguments against the Ford offer. Republican progressives went the entire route with Norris. They not only regarded the Ford proposal as a give-away scheme; they favored public ownership. A majority of Senate Democrats, on the other hand, favored the Ford offer. Chiefly southerners concerned with the plight of their rural constituents, they sought cheap fertilizer and accepted the premise that if anyone could provide it, Henry Ford was the man. It was only when this group in both houses of Congress accepted the validity of Norris's position that a public ownership proposal was approved by the Congress of the United States.

But when Congress adjourned in June, 1924, Ford had not yet

[36] The King Papers delineate his interesting career.

[37] Slattery to Kent, May 23, 1924 (Slattery Papers). Gifford Pinchot thought Ford "was attempting to put over one of the most outrageous pieces of piracy against the property of the people" he had ever seen. In June Pinchot thought Ford was beaten "and beaten for good, and for that the chief credit belongs to Senator Norris"; see Pinchot to W. A. Lloyd, June 12, 1924 (Box 250, Gifford Pinchot Papers, Manuscript Division, Library of Congress). In a letter to Norris on July 2, 1924, Pinchot congratulated the senator for his handling of the Ford offer, concluding with ". . . my hat is off to you" (Box 251, Gifford Pinchot Papers).

withdrawn his offer. Immediately upon adjournment, if not before, politics came to the forefront as both parties prepared for the presidential election in November. Politics also concerned George Norris. He had to consider his campaign for a third term in the U.S. Senate.

1924: Personal and Political

15

When the first session of the Sixty-eighth Congress concluded in June of 1924, Norris was one month short of his sixty-third birthday. Aside from Robert M. LaFollette, he was recognized as the outstanding progressive member of the U.S. Senate. On the floor he was rarely bitter or vindictive in his remarks and was never given to oratory. He was not radical in the sense of conviction that the capitalist system of production and distribution should yield to a cooperative commonwealth. Rather, he reflected or articulated the progressive views of a segment of the citizenry interested in efficiency and integrity in the operation of government. He was merciless in exposing the hypocritical pretenses of colleagues and incumbent administrations, Democratic or Republican. Always ready to concede the most sincere motives to his opponents until proven otherwise, his attacks were normally against policies rather than persons. At times, usually when an election was in the offing or when tired and overworked, he would get despondent and discouraged. But he had a mercurial temperament and, with a satirical jingle or an amusing limerick at the expense of a pretentious colleague or prominent official, he would usually snap out of it. Harry Slattery recalled that on several occasions in the long contest over Muscle Shoals Norris would have a fire built in his committee room on some bleak day at the Capitol and would refresh himself by reminiscing and swapping tales with his visitor.[1]

[1] Harry A. Slattery, "Autobiography" (unpublished), p. 127 (typescript in the Harry Slattery Papers, Manuscripts Collections, Duke University Library).

217

No one claimed that Norris was a brilliant senator. No one regarded him as eloquent or witty or polished. There were senators more profound than he, some with better minds, some with larger powers of expression and deeper knowledge of constitutional law. Not that Norris was noticeably deficient in any of these attributes, but they were not the qualities that made him stand out among the small number of senators who, no matter how greatly one differed with their views, nevertheless compelled respect.

The outstanding things about Norris were his perfect sincerity, his utter fearlessness, his almost complete lack of partisanship, and his almost complete personal disinterestedness. Most senators are honest, but not many are honest in the way Norris was, or as independent, or as free from pretense, or as completely disregardful of personal political consequences. He seemingly had not a particle of self-consciousness in his political being and, again in a political sense, he did not know what fear meant. Having won re-election easily in 1918 despite great fear about his chances, Norris had gained a feeling of security that his constituents, if given an opportunity to know the truth, would endorse his record. That he was of an age when most men were ready to retire and viewed their careers as almost completed reinforced Norris in the view that he now had little to lose if he followed his conscience more than his constituents when a controversy occurred.

Dressed in a plain business suit and usually smoking either a cigar or a corn-cob pipe, Norris seemed more belligerent in print than on the floor of the Senate. He spoke in a quiet, patient, conversational tone, putting force into his words rather than into gestures. He was an easy, clear, impressive, and frequent speaker. He handled himself well in debate and when the necessity arose, he could be brutal in the force of his remarks or adroitly sarcastic. He could be pitiless to an unscrupulous foe, yet he was rarely inconsiderate to those who offered him no quarter. Having deep respect for his own convictions, he had equal respect for the convictions of others. He would attempt to change a colleague's opinion by argument, rarely by abuse or by what Raymond Clapper called "the tactics of the cloak room." [2] Norris always thought in

2 *Christian Science Monitor,* Dec. 22, 1927.

terms of the particular rather than the general. When he saw something to be done or undone, he saw that almost exclusively. His purpose was to use government, so far as necessary, to make life decent for plain people.

His family, his books, and his summers on the shore of a Wisconsin lake constituted his chief interests, aside from politics. He saw his principal friends of these years, Senators Borah, Johnson, Smith Brookhart, and LaFollette, mostly at the capital. His desk in the Senate was at the back of the chamber next to Borah's. For relaxation he liked to walk, enjoyed swimming, and occasionally would watch a baseball game. More frequently, he would listen to radio reports of games. He had a good baritone voice and knew the words of most of the old-time songs. He enjoyed reading and was very fond of Shakespeare, though he thought Dickens one of the greatest of novelists. He read Emerson, Whitman, Twain, Victor Hugo; he delighted in *Cyrano de Bergerac* by Edmond Rostand, his favorite play. In reading, if he came across a phrase or an expression that appealed to him, he usually wrote it on the inside cover. He was also a crack shot, though he rarely exercised this talent. While William Kent was a member of the Tariff Commission, occasionally he would practice on the range in Kent's yard on F Street, and once Harry Slattery got him to go to the pistol range in the FBI headquarters on Pennsylvania Avenue.[3]

During the early 1920s Norris tried a new way of relaxing. He wrote short stories, based in most instances on his own political career. Though they were rejected, editors seemed impressed with their potential. "The Congressional Christmas Tree," written in 1923, dealt with special privileges enjoyed by wealth, the power of the Speaker, the liquor lobby, and other themes relevant to his career. It had an ironic tone but ended on a moral note: "And thus while they are both satisfied, both contented and both happy, let us quietly take our leave." [4]

In appearance Norris had not changed much from his last campaign for re-election. He was well built, with a square jaw and a

[3] Slattery, "Autobiography," p. 128.
[4] A copy of "The Congressional Christmas Tree" is available in the Norris Papers.

high forehead below a shock of grey hair. His mustache, a trade-
mark of over twenty years' standing, was shaved after his re-election
in 1924. A man of heavy-lidded eyes with a wry, tired smile and a
somewhat indifferent manner, Norris went his own way. Never a
wealthy man, he had simple tastes and no regular source of income
save his salary.

In 1924 two of his daughters were married. Hazel, the oldest,
was married to John P. Robertson, the assistant cashier of the
Custer State Bank in Broken Bow. Marian was married to Harvey
Nelson, also a native Nebraskan. They were living in Long Beach,
California, where he was active in the building and loan association
business. The youngest daughter, Gertrude or DeWitt, as she was
called in the family circle, resided with her parents in their Ross
Place home in Washington. A recent graduate, like her sisters, of
the University of Nebraska, she had eagerly sought an exciting
government job in her final semester in the spring of 1923. She was
aware that her father would not help her, Norris insisting that "he
wouldn't put his family on the pay roll." When an opportunity to
teach grade school in Kalamazoo, Michigan, developed, she phoned
her parents for advice. Her father responded that she would have to
decide for herself and hung up the receiver. Gertrude took the job
but at the end of the school year in 1924 she was in Washington,
having accepted a job with the Board of Children's Guardians.[5]

The Washington residence in the attractive Cleveland Park section with only one daughter at home was beginning to seem too
large. The senator and Mrs. Norris considered selling it and moving
into an apartment. Meanwhile, their home in McCook was rented
continually. This arrangement was not entirely satisfactory. Repairs
had to be made; family possessions were damaged by careless
tenants; new tenants had to be found; and if the Norrises returned
to McCook when the house was occupied, they had to stay at the
Keystone Hotel. By 1924 the house was in such a state of disrepair
that Norris was considering tearing it down and rebuilding on the
property.[6]

[5] John P. Robertson to George W. Norris, Feb. 16, 1921; Norris to Frans
Nelson, Mar. 23, 1922; Gertrude Norris to Mabelle Talbert, Mar. 16, Apr. 3 and
27, 1923; Talbert to Gertrude Norris, Sept. 21, 1923; Mrs. George W. Norris to
Talbert, Aug. 10, 1923.
[6] Norris to John E. Kelley, May 18, Nov. 28, 1924, Apr. 1, Nov. 25, 1925. In

At the end of 1920 Norris proposed to change his will in accordance with his modified financial condition brought about by the investment of nearly all of his assets in Liberty Bonds. He continued to invest money in bonds, thereby assuring himself a modest return and a minimum of responsibility. The evaluation he prepared at the time can serve as a profile of his financial status in the early 1920s. Besides his Washington home, Norris owned a half lot in Waupaca, Wisconsin, on which his summer cottage was located, and some Texas land which he hoped to sell. He had several life insurance policies which would yield a total of about $11,000. Other policies would bring each of his daughters $200 per year for life. Aside from a few shares of stock in a fraternal organization, this was the extent of his wealth as he sought a third term in the U.S. Senate, still occasionally called a rich man's club.[7]

Vacations meant summers at the Wisconsin cottage. It was the most restful place Norris ever found. Here he puttered about the cottage, installing in 1923 electric lighting and a water system. He had actually built most of the cottage earlier and by 1925 had spent "perhaps more than ten thousand dollars in its improvement." He chopped wood, went swimming, enjoyed the company of the L.U.N. families, and relaxed in general. It was, he said, "the one place in all the world where I can rest and work at the same time." In this way he escaped the hot weather and compensated for his inability to work in Washington during summer months. After his collapse in the Senate in July, 1921, he vowed that he would never spend another summer in Washington.

At Waupaca in the summer of 1924 Norris considered his own campaign and that of Robert M. LaFollette, seeking the presidency on a third-party ticket. As a result of the 1922 elections, progressives in Congress had increased their membership and had begun to hold strategy meetings.[8] Throughout the Harding years the Re-

1925 Norris moved into an apartment in Washington. His home at 3300 Ross Place was sold for $16,500; he had purchased it in 1914 for $7,000.

[7] Norris to W. E. Barkley, Nov. 23, 1920; to John F. Cordeal, Dec. 29, 1920. By 1920 Norris had purchased at least $13,000 worth of Liberty Bonds. In 1924 he purchased $5,000 worth of U.S. Notes; see Liberty Bond Folder, Box 33.

[8] In 1922 progressive Republican Robert B. Howell defeated Gilbert M. Hitchcock in the Nebraska senatorial race with a plurality of about 72,000 votes. Howell claimed that Norris's support was "certainly effective"; see Howell to Norris, Nov. 24, 1922.

publican party was so beset with inner tensions and contradictions, especially in the Senate, that its ability to achieve a legislative program was jeopardized. The tensions and contradictions were not exclusively between progressives and conservatives within the party. By August, 1921, for example, Senator Irvine Lenroot, a former LaFollette supporter, confessed that he was "not at all optimistic over the future" because there was "no leadership in the Senate." [9]

By 1924 other conservative Republican senators agreed. "Speaking personally," Walter Edge of New Jersey remarked, "I would have preferred defeat than to go back to the Senate for six years, if they were to be anything like a repetition of the last two." The chief difficulty was the majority leader, Henry Cabot Lodge, who would not delegate any of the power and authority he wielded. In November, shortly after the election, Lodge died, causing further uneasiness among administration supporters in the Senate. This situation, combined with the death of Harding in August, 1923, aided progressive Republicans in that august body.[10]

Under the leadership of Robert M. LaFollette an invitation was extended in November, 1922, to progressive senators and representatives of both parties to attend a meeting to plan for more united and effective cooperation. LaFollette made a point that Norris knew from experience to be true when he wrote, "It cannot be expected that all progressives should be in agreement on all the details of any legislative program." Nevertheless, they agreed to propose practical and constructive legislative plans and resolved to launch a campaign "for direct, open primaries for all elective offices, including the presidency and for effective federal and state corrupt practice acts." At the outset the progressives did little but oppose administration policies with little success. Norris, who participated in these proceedings, was discouraged and privately talked of retiring.[11]

[9] Irvine Lenroot to J. L. Sturtevant, Aug. 8, 1921 (Box 4, Irvine Lenroot Papers, Manuscript Division, Library of Congress).

[10] Walter E. Edge to James W. Wadsworth, Jr., Nov. 8, 1924; Wadsworth to Edge, Nov. 10, 1924 (both in Box 19, Wadsworth Family Papers, Manuscript Division, Library of Congress).

[11] Robert M. LaFollette to Norris, Nov. 24, 1922; Norris to B. Brewer, Dec. 8, 1923; William Kent to Gifford Pinchot, Feb. 26, 1923 (Addition 4, William Kent Papers, Yale University Library). Kent commented to Pinchot that Norris "has been threatening to get out." The meeting of the progressives was officially called by the People's Legislative Service, an organization founded after the

Norris was discouraged because progressives in Congress often were divided among themselves. Though ordinarily he would have accepted this point as a truism, he found it disturbing when measures he strongly advocated received little support from members usually labeled progressive. Furthermore, he understood that a reform program could never be achieved with Warren G. Harding and now his successor, Calvin Coolidge, in the White House.[12]

But by the end of 1923 progressive Republican senators had achieved some cohesion and were ready to battle for a stronger voice in the Sixty-eighth Congress. Upon the ascendancy of Calvin Coolidge to the presidency on August 3, 1923, Senator Albert B. Cummins of Iowa, president pro tempore of the Senate, became its presiding officer, with vice-presidential prestige and salary. In November, as preparations for the convening of the new Congress got under way, at least four candidates were competing for the coveted job of presiding officer. Albert Cummins sought re-election to the post he had held since 1919. Charles Curtis, the majority whip, George H. Moses, and Norris were also candidates. Supporters of Senator Cummins insisted upon his re-election to the Senate presidency and retention of his chairmanship of the powerful Interstate Commerce Committee. Progressives hoped to force Cummins out of the committee chairmanship, in which event Robert LaFollette would succeed him.

The progressives were well organized, the Republicans were divided, and it soon became clear that the former group held the balance of power. If Cummins wished to serve as president pro tem of the Senate, with its prestige now second to that of the Chief Executive, he would have to relinquish the chairmanship of the Interstate Commerce Committee to be assured of at least seven votes controlled by the progressive faction. On the other hand, party stalwarts, fearing the influence of LaFollette as committee chairman, sought to persuade Cummins to retain the chairmanship and to relinquish the other office.[13]

election of 1920. Robert M. LaFollette was chairman and Congressman George M. Huddleston of Alabama was vice-chairman.

12 Norris to Kent, Mar. 5, 1923.

13 *Omaha Bee*, Nov. 24, 1923; *New York Evening Post*, Nov. 26, 1923; *New York Times*, Nov. 27, 1923. A similar battle occurred in the House, where progressive Republican members sought additional committee chairmanships. In the

LaFollette, who was ill and at home as the group worked out its strategy, hoped they might insist that progressives fill the vacancies on the Republican side of the Interstate Commerce Committee. With their strength thus concentrated, strong bills could be reported. If Republican leaders refused this proposal, LaFollette suggested overtures to the Democrats, urging them to join the progressive group in organizing two committees, Interstate Commerce and Finance.[14]

Norris, who played a key role in the strategy meetings of the progressives, was not in complete accord with LaFollette's ideas. The most desirable thing, he felt, would be to secure the chairmanship of the Interstate Commerce Committee for LaFollette. While all agreed to urge progressives to seek places on this committee, Norris claimed that if every vacancy was filled with a progressive, they would still be in the minority. But with LaFollette as chairman, minority reports would receive national attention and floor fights could be waged. With their organization, Norris said, the group could "make whatever record we think ought to be made with reference to any measure upon which we desire a record vote." [15]

For more than a month after the convening of the Sixty-eighth Congress, the Senate was in turmoil as the Republican party sought to elect Senate leaders. Norris declined to become a candidate for president of the Senate, though he had been urged to do so. He was for Cummins, confident that the Iowa senator would yield his committee chairmanship and that LaFollette would succeed him. Usually each party chose its leaders in caucus and the Senate formally approved them. On this occasion the Senate itself would decide the matter. On December 12, 1923, when balloting began for the chairmanship of the Interstate Commerce Committee, a deadlock developed and the progressive bloc broke ranks. Cummins, supported by the administration forces, received forty votes, as did the ranking Democrat on the committee, Ellison D. Smith of South Carolina. Rather than see Cummins elected, progressive Republicans supported Smith. Only Norris, his Nebraska colleague, Robert B.

Senate the progressive group included LaFollette, Shipstead, Magnus Johnson, Ladd, Frazier, Brookhart, and Norris.

[14] LaFollette to Norris, Nov. 30, 1923.

[15] Norris to LaFollette, Dec. 1, 1923.

Howell, and Edwin F. Ladd of North Dakota, who, incidentally, had actively backed the Ford proposal for Muscle Shoals, supported LaFollette. On the second ballot Smith fell one short of the necessary majority, receiving forty-one votes to thirty-nine for Cummins and two for LaFollette, Ladd now voting for Smith. On the third ballot Cummins gained one vote while the Smith and La-Follette tallies remained the same. These votes occurred on a Wednesday and the Senate agreed to resume balloting the following Monday.[16]

On Thursday, December 13, 1923, progressive Republicans met in Norris's office in Room 433 of the Senate Office Building. They decided to overthrow seniority and support freshman Senator R. B. Howell. If this effort failed, they would back another freshman, James Couzens of Michigan. In their effort to prevent Cummins from becoming chairman of the Interstate Commerce Committee, progressives discarded both Smith and LaFollette in the hope of breaking the deadlock with either Howell or Couzens. Observers thought the strategy would not work and LaFollette, absent because of illness, still favored Senator Smith.[17]

The progressive strategy failed. Administration supporters voted for Cummins; Democrats, with the exception of William Cabell Bruce of Maryland, supported Smith. Norris and other progressives voted for Howell and threatened to throw their strength to Senator Smith. While the machinery of the Senate was blocked by this deadlock, the president was not pushing any legislative matters and there seemed little prospect of resolving the crisis until after the Christmas recess. Finally, on the thirty-third ballot on January 9, 1924, with Senator LaFollette now in command of the progressive group, six members voted for Smith, thereby electing him chairman of the Interstate Commerce Committee with one vote to spare. Norris, however, voted for Couzens.[18]

[16] *Omaha Bee,* Dec. 12, 1923.

[17] *Omaha World-Herald, Omaha Daily News,* Dec. 15, 1923.

[18] *Omaha Bee,* Dec. 17, 1923; *New York Herald,* Dec. 18, 1923; Belle Case and Fola LaFollette, *Robert M. LaFollette,* 2 vols. (New York, 1953), 2: 1090–91; *Congressional Record,* 68th Cong., 1st sess., Jan. 9, 1924, p. 747. The LaFollette bloc that voted for Smith were Brookhart, Frazier, Ladd, Magnus Johnson, and Shipstead. The six Republicans who voted for Couzens were Norris, Howell, Peter Norbeck, Capper, Frank Gooding, and Wesley Jones of Washington. The final vote was Smith 39, Cummins 29, Couzens 6. For an interesting analysis of

As the progressives had prepared to challenge the party leadership in the Senate, Norris decided to define his relationship with the president of the United States. He wrote Coolidge explaining his position on political patronage. Emphasizing efficiency and economy, he called for a nonpartisan administration with no consideration given to political affiliation in filling offices or making promotions. Though the exchange yielded little, Norris had expressed a standard by which to evaluate Coolidge's appointments and, possibly, to justify his position in the forthcoming election year.[19]

As early as September, 1923, Norris began receiving petitions requesting him to seek a third term in the Senate. In mid-September he called upon the chairman of the Republican State Central Committee in Lincoln and arranged for speaking dates. He intended to report on his stewardship as senator, insisting on his right to follow conscientious convictions and to criticize wrong in his own party or elsewhere: "If I am wrong, I do not deserve the support of members of my party. Since I was nominated at a state-wide primary, when my public record was an open book and fully understood by the voters of the state, I think I have a right to proclaim that the doctrines for which I have stood and which I have promulgated are the doctrines of the Republican party, at least in Nebraska." [20]

While in September Norris had appeared eager to seek the Republican nomination for another Senate term, in November in Washington he declared he would not seek re-election under any circumstances. The belief that little could be accomplished in Congress disillusioned Norris, but he did not completely close the door. He said that if he decided to run, he would have no opposition on the Republican ticket; other candidates would withdraw if he sought the nomination. Less than two weeks later newspaper reports confirmed that Norris had changed his mind, claiming the refusal was

---

Cummins, whom Norris formerly admired, see Norris to Elbert W. Harrington, May 14, 1937. Norris thought Cummins an exceedingly able lawyer with a logical mind and unlimited reasoning power. Susceptibility to flattery was his great weakness, leading him away from the progressive fold. In addition, Norris thought he might have presidential ambitions. These factors led him into the conservative camp.

[19] Norris to Calvin Coolidge, Dec. 6 and 26, 1923.
[20] *Nebraska State Journal*, Sept. 18, 1923.

due to poor health which had now greatly improved and that he was being deluged with mail urging him to make the race.[21]

If Nebraskans thought the matter settled, they were doomed to disappointment. On Sunday, December 9, 1923, the *New York World* in its editorial section carried a story by Paul Y. Anderson wherein Norris reaffirmed his earlier decision: "I have been bucking this game for twenty years and there is no way of beating it. I've done all I could. Now I'm through." Anderson commented that "his lined face, his tired eyes, his hair grown white, the resignation of his speech and gesture, all testify to the utter weariness, and his words are almost despairing." To the suggestion that some people might interpret his retirement as tantamount to running away from the fight to aid agriculture, to save Muscle Shoals, and to secure more efficient and hence effective government, Norris replied, "Let them say it. Twenty years is enough. I'm done." [22]

Meanwhile, petitions for Norris's candidacy were being distributed. On December 18 Lincoln attorney C. A. Sorensen announced that they soon would be filed with the Secretary of State and that he "felt quite sure" Norris would run again. By the end of the year Norris supporters had formed a committee and were busy circulating petitions in every voting precinct in Nebraska. Prominent conservative Republicans also announced for Norris. Walter W. Head, president of the Omaha National Bank and of the American Bankers Association, announced that "Senator Norris is needed in the Senate." [23] In Washington Judson King reported that Norris's secretary told him that Norris inquired constantly about letters questioning his decision and that he was pleased at the large number protesting

21 *Omaha World-Herald,* Nov. 9, 1923; *Hastings Daily Tribune,* Nov. 20, 1923.

22 Whether Anderson interviewed Norris at the time he originally announced his decision to retire (early in November), or after he said he would run again (Nov. 20), was impossible for me to determine. There is a distinct possibility that Anderson interviewed him earlier and that Norris did not announce his retirement, agree to run again, and then for the second time in a month say he would not seek another term, as the sequence of newspaper stories indicates. At the time the Anderson story appeared, Norris was deeply involved in the battle to prevent Senator Cummins from becoming chairman of the Interstate Commerce Committee.

23 *Omaha World-Herald,* Dec. 19, 1923; *Omaha Daily News,* Dec. 30, 1923. Conservative Republican leaders had little choice but to support Norris. They needed him on the ticket to insure carrying the state for Coolidge.

it. But in a letter to William Kent early in January, 1924, Norris reaffirmed his intention to return to private life. While Norris was pondering his decision in Washington, on January 25, 1924, C. A. Sorensen handed a petition signed by over 6,000 registered Republicans to the Nebraska secretary of state, requesting the name of George W. Norris on the official primary ballot of the Republican party as a candidate for the office of U.S. senator. Sorensen also handed him a receipt showing that the $50 filing fee had been paid. Norris now had five days to decide about seeking a third term in the Senate.[24]

On Saturday afternoon, January 26, 1924, Senator Howell spent two hours with Norris and secured his signature on a statement accepting nomination. Howell admitted that at the last moment he was inclined to say "no." But not much more than twenty-four hours after the nominating petition had been filed, Norris accepted. The thousands of individual letters and telegrams urging him to make the race, the more than 6,000 signatures on the petition filed in Lincoln, plus Howell's urging convinced Norris to accept the nomination.[25] Norris quickly announced that he would not participate in

[24] Judson King to Kent, Dec. 20, 1923 (Addition 1); Norris to Kent, Jan. 6, 1924 (Addition 4, Kent Papers). At this time Norris, though sympathetic with what they were trying to do, doubted that anything could be accomplished by forming a third party dedicated to progressive principles. In fact, it might have a tendency to increase "the already outrageously powerful partisan spirit" which Norris believed was one of the greatest deterrents to progressive government; see Norris to J. A. H. Hopkins, Jan. 6, 1924; committee to A. Buechler, Jan. 5, 1924; C. A. Sorensen to Charles W. Pool, Jan. 25, 1924 (C. A. Sorensen Papers, Nebraska State Historical Society).

[25] Howell to Sorensen, Jan. 26, 1924 (Sorensen Papers); *Bloomington* (Nebr.) *Advocate Tribune,* Jan. 31, 1924; *Omaha Daily News,* Jan. 27, 1924. I have been able to find little evidence for the incident recounted by two of Norris's earlier biographers that Paul Y. Anderson intercepted a Western Union messenger in a Senate corridor with a telegram from Norris declining the nomination. Anderson supposedly told the messenger that Norris had decided not to send it and thereupon pocketed it, not informing the senator of what he had done. See Richard L. Neuberger and Stephen B. Kahn, *Integrity: The Life of George W. Norris* (New York, 1937), pp. 152–53, and Alfred Lief, *Democracy's Norris* (New York, 1939), pp. 266–67. Norris in his autobiography, *Fighting Liberal* (New York, 1945), never mentioned sending such a telegram. The fact that, despite misgivings, he accepted the nomination as quickly as he did once the petition was filed raises some doubt about the validity of such a telegram. The story in the *Omaha Daily News,* Jan. 27, 1924, said that "Norris had actually dictated a letter refusing to

the primary. But this statement cannot be cited to indicate doubts or anxiety about his decision. He had not directly participated in the primary in his two previous senatorial campaigns, using the excuse of pressing congressional business and thereby immeasurably reducing his campaign expenses. Though a strong believer in the efficacy of the primary, Norris in campaigning for the Senate had not yet directly participated in one. His opponent, Charles H. Sloan, a former congressman, had been defeated by him in the 1918 primary.[26]

To help his cause, Norris asked William Kent to write prominent Nebraska editors on his behalf. He was concerned about the *State Journal,* which had not mentioned him in an editorial since his opposition to the Versailles Peace Treaty. The *Omaha Daily News,* edited by a student of Woodrow Wilson's at Princeton, had a statewide circulation and was not ardent in his support. The *Omaha Bee,* the leading Republican paper in the state, Norris thought would not oppose him but would not enthusiastically endorse him either. The two other dailies in the state, the *Lincoln Star* and the *Omaha World-Herald,* were both Democratic and against him. Though Norris feared he had enemies in the editorial ranks of the leading newspapers of Nebraska, his request to William Kent indicates that he was interested in winning the coming campaign. He had won in the past with most newspapers against him and he realized he could win this time.[27]

In Nebraska, meanwhile, friends were planning the primary campaign and inquired of Howell whether Norris would return for

permit his name to go on the Republican primary in Nebraska, when Senator Howell arrived at his office." The only account by Norris of this incident that I have been able to locate is a letter he wrote to Harvey Newbranch, editor of the *Omaha World-Herald,* Aug. 28, 1929. Norris said that "when the election was over, the story which I have narrated above was told to me by Mr. Anderson and my secretary." From contemporary evidence available in the Norris Papers and elsewhere and cited in the footnotes of this chapter, I have doubts about its validity. Norris was suggesting to Newbranch that he possibly intended to retire in 1930 and really wished to do so in 1924.

26 *Omaha Daily News,* Jan. 27, 1924; Norris to Kent, Feb. 10, 1924 (Addition 4, Kent Papers).

27 Norris to Kent, Feb. 10, 1924 (Addition 4, Kent Papers). Norris erred in that the *Omaha Bee* actively opposed him in the primary campaign.

a few speeches on his own behalf. They realized if Norris were victorious against Sloan, chances of winning in November were almost assured. Sorensen and others felt his chances would be enhanced if he dissociated himself from Hiram Johnson's effort to capture Nebraska delegates' votes at the national Republican convention and from any third-party organization. Registered Democrats then would cross party lines to vote for him. In Washington Norris devoted all of his efforts to the Muscle Shoals controversy and explained that the primary would depend upon his friends, "those who believe in me and wish me to remain in the Senate." [28]

If Norris did not campaign in the primary, he still wrote letters to constituents. In some of these letters he did what Sorensen and others hoped he would not do: he commented on campaigns other than his own. Although in 1920 he had canvassed Nebraska and several other states on behalf of Hiram Johnson, he now was discouraged about the Californian's candidacy, thinking, "together with a great many other progressives," that "he did not measure up to what his prior record indicated he ought to be." On the other hand, Norris found nothing in Coolidge to satisfy him. The president was partisan; to Norris this meant that he sought to cover up Republican rascality in the oil scandals. The president's repeated declarations that he intended to see the guilty quickly brought to punishment seemed the height of hypocrisy, since Coolidge still associated with Edward B. McLean, a wealthy reprobate, who had been shown "to be one of those trying to cover up the truth when we are attempting to save the natural resources of the Nation." The president's outlook helped explain Norris's discouragement and desire to retire. "I have never felt so humiliated," he wrote, "since I have been in public life, and when I think that the people over the country are in conventions endorsing this man for renomination

[28] Sorensen to Howell, Feb. 11, 1924; Mrs. C. T. Gutzka to Sorensen, Jan. 11, 1924 (both in Sorensen Papers); Talbert to Carl D. Thompson, Feb. 12, 1924. At this time William Kent was writing that Hiram Johnson had been brought into the private power fold in California and had long since departed from his progressive stance, thereby suggesting that Norris dissociate himself from Hiram Johnson in this campaign; see Kent to Norris, Feb. 26, 1923 (water power, 1st Lot, Kent Papers). The *Grand Island Herald,* Mar. 13, 1924, printed a letter from Norris to a local resident.

and reelection, it almost makes me feel that democracy is a failure." [29]

Throughout the primary Norris was consistent in his position. He had intended to retire, disheartened at the prospect of achieving reform within the context of the degraded moral tone of American political life. He had become a candidate only when compelled by thousands of letters, telegrams, and signatures on petitions to cast aside personal wishes. He was consistent, too, in his decision not to participate directly in the primary, remarking, "If the people of Nebraska do not appreciate the fact that I stay here and do the best I can to improve our governmental conditions, rather than to go out in a primary fight and make a contest for my personal advancement, then I am not sure whether I want to stay here." [30]

Others prominent in national life, usually associated with the progressive group, assisted by supporting Norris's candidacy. Sorensen received endorsements from Senators LaFollette, Borah, Lynn J. Frazier, Ladd, Capper, Burton K. Wheeler, Owen, Howell, Henrik Shipstead, Brookhart, and Magnus Johnson which were widely distributed. The Public Ownership League of America circularized its Nebraska membership on Norris's behalf. Sorensen, in charge of the campaign in Nebraska, exuded confidence. Funds were forthcoming and advertisements were placed in various periodicals. In addition, citizens were urged to vote in the Republican primary through a widely distributed form letter to "Dear Friend of Clean Government," signed by Sorensen. In all, the committee headed by Sorensen spent $1,028.45 on Norris's behalf. The weekend before election he claimed, "I am confident that Senator Norris will be nominated." Though concerned about the active campaign of Fred Johnson, a third entry in the primary race, among the Scandinavian

[29] Norris to B. F. Eberhart, Mar. 8 and 16, 1924; to W. L. Crom, Apr. 7, 1924. In these letters Norris also expressed grave reservations about Bascom Slemp, who had "for years been trafficing in public office through the South, in a way that would make any honest citizen blush with shame." His appointment as Coolidge's private secretary, Norris felt, was for the primary purpose of controlling southern delegates at the Republican national convention.

[30] Norris to James T. Whitehead, Mar. 14, 1924; to J. F. Lawrence, Mar. 16, 1924; to Sorensen, Mar. 16, 1924; to John G. Maher, Mar. 16, 1924. Maher, a wealthy insurance man in Lincoln, was working with Sorensen on Norris's behalf.

farmers, Sorensen still believed the farm vote would give Norris his strength.[31]

On the day before election telegrams endorsing Norris by Governor Gifford Pinchot and Senator Charles L. McNary were published in the *Omaha Bee,* and Sorensen wrote Norris offering his analysis of the outcome.[32] To begin with, good weather was predicted. This meant a large turnout in cities and towns and in the rural districts, though some farmers might be unwilling to leave their work. While the opposition criticized Norris's independence, his minority role, his vote against the war, his reluctance to run, and his record in Congress, Sorensen said that his political independence was driving thousands of voters "not from you, but to you." While the *Omaha Bee, Fremont Tribune, Lincoln Star,* and a number of county papers were hostile, other dailies like the *Omaha Daily News* and the *Grand Island Independent* plus a large number of rural weeklies supported Norris. The editor of the *Ord Quiz,* for example, accepted a large ad for Sloan but in the same issue printed a long editorial and other material favorable to Norris. In addition, 1,600 farmers scattered over ninety counties who had circulated Norris petitions were contacted to organize their precincts and to turn out the farm vote. Sorensen concluded, "It is my conviction that you will get as many votes as Johnson and Sloan put together and as many more." [33]

And his prognostication was accurate. When the Republican ballots for senator were tallied, Norris received 71,974 votes to 30,768 for Charles H. Sloan and 15,970 for Fred Johnson. In the presidential primary Calvin Coolidge easily defeated Hiram Johnson, 79,676 to 45,032. Coolidge ran ahead of his ticket, though Norris had more than twice the number of votes for his nearest opponent and carried all but four counties, two of which were the home counties of his opponents. He carried Red Willow County, his own, by eight to one, despite the opposition of the *McCook Daily Gazette,* while Douglas, Lancaster, and Dawes, the most pop-

[31] Sorensen to Thompson, Mar. 13, 1924; to Charles Skalla, Apr. 1, 1924; to J. L. Burke, Apr. 5, 1924; to Edward L. Burke, Apr. 5, 1924; to "Dear Friend of Clean Government," n.d.; statement by Edward L. Burke, treasurer, Norris campaign committee, Apr. 1, 1924 (all in Sorensen Papers).

[32] *Omaha Bee,* Apr. 7, 1924.

[33] Sorensen to Norris, Apr. 7, 1924 (Sorensen Papers).

ulous counties in the state, all went for him.[34] An editorial in the
State Journal succinctly summed up the situation:

> Norris goes contrary to most of the established rules for hold-
> ing political popularity. He has made no effort to secure and hold
> party support. Politically he is probably the most independent
> member of the American senate. He seems to make no particular
> effort, either, to appease popular opinion. . . . At the time of
> these primaries he is making a fight on the Ford Muscle Shoals
> lease, a measure which has been popular with Nebraska farmers.
> He supports the short ballot and the one house legislature, mea-
> sures not popular with the Nebraska majority, yet we go on voting
> for him.
>
> Meanwhile Norris appears to grow on the senate and country
> at large. In *Collier's* two Democratic senators, one eastern, the
> other western, are quoted as saying that if the Republicans would
> nominate Norris for president, they would support him. Yester-
> day the *Search-Light on Congress* designated Norris as "perhaps
> the clearest, straightest thinker on political and governmental
> questions in America." Senator Howell has reported the Senate
> press gallery as voting Norris the most honest man in the Senate.
> When a public official convinces the hard boiled gentlemen of the
> press gallery that he is sincere and honest, it is time for the sky to
> fall. . . . He does what he thinks ought to be done and says
> what he thinks ought to be said, and then we can take him or
> leave him as we please. This independence and sincerity the vot-
> ing public obviously likes.[35]

[34] Addison E. Sheldon, *Nebraska: The Land and the People* (Chicago, 1931),
1: 1013; *Nebraska State Journal,* Apr. 11, 1924.
[35] *Nebraska State Journal,* Apr. 11, 1924.

"My Party, Right or Wrong"

16

The primary victory was gratifying to Norris because it indicated that a majority of Nebraska Republicans wished him to continue in the U.S. Senate. He looked forward to the coming campaign but realized that it would bring to the fore bitterness, strife, and ill will, especially since Robert LaFollette and the newly organized Progressive party would attract progressive Republican voters. Since Norris was in the process of shedding whatever partisanship remained in him, he realized that many Democrats sympathetic to his criticisms of the Coolidge administration could vote more easily for him if he loosened his ties with the Republican party. Thus the way was cleared for Norris to support LaFollette and a third party.[1]

C. A. Sorensen, flushed with optimism after the primary victory, was confident Norris would get a 50,000-vote majority in November. Nor did his confidence falter when Norris refused to stump the state for the entire Republican ticket. The decisive defeat of Hiram Johnson in the presidential primary caused him no concern about a lack of progressive sentiment in Nebraska: "A man like Borah or LaFollette could probably have carried the state over Coolidge." Sorensen insisted the Republican party could hold the Middle West in November only if a progressive from the region was chosen for vice-president.[2]

[1] George W. Norris to Henry F. Lehr, Apr. 16, 1924; to Charles A. Goss, Apr. 15, 1924; to John McClellan, Apr. 29, 1924; to C. A. Sorensen, Apr. 20, 1924 (C. A. Sorensen Papers, Nebraska State Historical Society).
[2] Sorensen to R. B. Howell, May 1, 1924 (Sorensen Papers).

Norris, meanwhile, was heavily involved in Senate business, with little time to think about politics or conditions in Nebraska. One thing he did consider: he would not extend a blanket endorsement to all Republican candidates. If any voter felt that his views were not for the best interests of the people, Norris hoped such a person would not support him because he intended to continue denouncing "wrong or evil" in public office whether Republicans or Democrats were to blame, "from President down to janitor." He insisted that this approach was in accord with the best Republican principles. Those who frowned upon it and would expose wrong only if committed by Democrats were neither good Republicans nor good citizens.[3]

With Coolidge certain to receive the nomination, Norris's principles would be put to the test. Nevertheless, he announced, "I am not going to try to conceal anything that I believe ought to be exposed regardless of what may happen to me in the coming campaign." Expecting condemnation and abuse, he resolved to sacrifice his career rather than be a party, for example, to turning Muscle Shoals over to Henry Ford. His activities in Congress and his political predicament played a major role in Norris's rapidly emerging independent stance. The dimensions of his primary victory, especially considering his initial decision to retire and his virtual silence during the campaign, assured Norris that he would have strong support during the coming campaign.[4]

Having formulated his views, he now decided to publicize them. In an open letter to the chairman of the Republican State Committee Norris acknowledged criticism of his candidacy on the part of "self-alleged Republican leaders." Though legally nominated, he was willing to submit to another primary. If at this time a majority were against him, Norris promised to tender his resignation immediately. To insure that the issue was fairly presented and to embarrass Republican leaders as much as possible, Norris insisted that all Republican candidates, including members of the state committee, opposed to his candidacy agree in writing to resign their respective

[3] Norris to C. A. Randall, May 14, 1924.

[4] *Ibid.* In this letter Norris also said, "Never in my lifetime have I cared so little about what these people [partisan Republicans] did or what they felt, and never in my life have I been so free of any ill will or feeling against them."

positions if his candidacy was vindicated.[5] In a confidential letter
to the chairman Norris further explained his position, reiterating
his judgment that the nation owed much of its political progress to
the independent voter. While his enemies claimed that he intended
to oppose some Republican candidates, that he favored lessening
party responsibility and increasing personal responsibility, Norris
denied the first premise but admitted the others. But these beliefs
would not be applied to particular individuals, since he had no intention of opposing anyone on the Republican ticket.[6]

Harry Sackett, chairman of the Republican State Committee,
quickly deflated Norris's self-righteous pose. Besides there being no
legal basis for calling a special primary, something Governor Keith
Neville had told Norris in 1917 when he suggested a recall election
then, Sackett could see no reason for one. No candidate on the state
ticket had either intimated or suggested that he withdraw. On the
contrary, "you will have," Sackett wrote, "the support of the Republicans in this State who believe that the choice of the voters
expressed in the primary shall not be nullified." [7]

Though deflated, Norris's pose was genuine. He would not remain in public life and stultify his conscience. He claimed that
everybody had known this when he was nominated, having admitted
his work in Congress to be "the most burdensome of any" since the
beginning of his public service. Norris had compromised with his
conscience in previous elections, particularly in 1918. Hereafter,
however, his independent stance would predominate. While it did
not attain widespread national attention in this campaign, in future
ones it would be noticed. Norris himself recognized one reason for
it. The progressive group in the Senate was small, while the constituency of a man who believed as he did extended over all the
country.[8]

In June, 1924, Norris did receive some national recognition as

[5] Norris to H. E. Sackett, May 18, 1924.

[6] Norris to Sackett, May 18, 1924 (a second letter).

[7] Sackett to Norris, May 22, 1924. In his response Norris insisted that he had
acted in good faith. Part of his complaint, he admitted, stemmed from the bitterness expressed by ex-Congressman C. H. Sloan after his defeat by Norris in the
primary; see Norris to Sackett, May 29, 1924.

[8] Norris to Sackett, May 29, 1924.

political passions ignited with a presidential campaign in the offing. The *New Republic,* in an article entitled "Norris, the Discouraged," reiterated the theme of his earlier interview with Paul Anderson: dogged determination to battle for worthwhile but lost causes in opposition to the partisan and conservative leadership in Congress and the White House. Later in the month *Collier's* carried an article by Norris entitled "My Party, Right or Wrong." It was a denunciation of partisanship and an affirmation of his insistence that "progress is independent"; "no man could serve a political party and his country at the same time." He concluded, "To vote for a candidate for office simply and solely because he is on a particular party ticket is to put party above country and to subvert patriotism to partisanship." [9]

These articles reflected Norris's outlook as the Republican convention in Cleveland chose Calvin Coolidge as the party standard bearer. So great was Norris's dilemma that he contemplated withdrawing as a candidate. Since he could not support Coolidge, he felt he ought to get off the ticket. Undecided about what course to follow, he remained in Washington for a month after Congress adjourned, assessing the political situation and the results of the Cleveland convention. But he was able to get little solace. At Cleveland Norris had received a few votes for vice-president from western delegates. With the calling of these votes his name was hissed, more so, a hostile newspaper reported, than that of LaFollette. [10]

Norris discussed his predicament with friends. If he withdrew as a candidate, he could participate in the presidential campaign and support Robert M. LaFollette. But the senator's son said his father would be opposed to Norris taking such a course. Nevertheless, Norris decided to withdraw and prepared a statement which he sent

[9] John W. Owens, "Norris, the Discouraged," *New Republic,* June 11, 1924, p. 68; *Collier's,* June 21, 1924. In the *Collier's* article Norris admitted he was a bitter partisan when he entered Congress and mentioned for the first time the Washington's birthday incident (the House adjourned and the Senate did not, though both houses were controlled by the Republican party) as the beginning of his doubts about the efficacy of partisanship. This incident, as far as I have been able to determine, is fictitious; see my *George W. Norris: The Making of a Progressive, 1861–1912* (Syracuse, N.Y., 1963), p. 297, note 8.

[10] Norris to E. E. Smith, June 4, 1924; *Omaha World-Herald,* June 14, 1924.

to friends in Nebraska who had strongly supported his candidacy. All protested his proposed action, as did all but one person with whom he conferred in Washington. Several suggested rising resentment if he did withdraw, that he would not be true to obligations assumed after his name had been placed in nomination. Though Norris regretted permitting his name to go on the ballot when he left Washington in July, he was determined to follow through with his candidacy and his independent course.[11]

In correspondence at this time one can discern Norris's attempt to rationalize and justify an independent stance. Using Woodrow Wilson as an example, he observed that planks placed in party platforms often were repudiated after election.[12] But in his own case no deception had been practiced in securing the Republican nomination. No action of his would be controlled by the president or any other leader. If re-elected, he intended to pursue the same policy. "I will be glad to get advice . . . but in the end, when I come to make a decision or any other official action, it is my own convictions that will control." Those who felt he was not a good Republican, who demanded greater fidelity "to party machines and self-appointed leaders," Norris requested to vote against him in November. He did not want any man's vote under false pretenses.

Fueling the determination to go his own way was Norris's detestation of the policies of the Coolidge administration, an animosity that went beyond opposition to the Ford proposal for Muscle Shoals. The president's friendship with Edward McLean after he had been exposed as a liar, the farce of prohibition enforcement, the mess in the Justice Department which continued after Harry Daugherty resigned, plus the fact that Daugherty "went out still retaining the friendship of the leader of our party and is now in Cleveland as one of the official delegates pledged to secure the nomination of this same leader"—all appalled Norris. All helped confirm for him the validity of his independent position as the campaign got under way. He remarked that "if there had been a Roosevelt in the White

---

[11] Norris to Ralph G. Sucher, July 12, 1924.

[12] Norris cited the Panama Canal no-tolls plank in the 1912 Democratic platform as his chief example. If he had examined Wilson's first inaugural address, he would have been able to note a remarkable record of achievement.

House," there would have been a house cleaning before the investigating committees ever got a start.[13]

Norris left Washington for a summer vacation at his lakeside cottage in Wisconsin, insisting that he would take no new stand in the campaign. The hesitancy and doubt of his earlier letters were now replaced by positive assertions of his position. While he would not endorse the Coolidge administration, neither did he expect to criticize Republican candidates. He intended to explain the principles of government he favored, hoping the voter would apply those principles and vote as he saw fit. He would not endorse Robert M. LaFollette in his third-party bid for the presidency. After the interview with the senator's son in Washington Norris was convinced that LaFollette did not expect him to speak on his behalf. Though Norris intended whenever possible to say friendly things about LaFollette, it did not seem valid for a Republican candidate to support the presidential nominee of a third party.[14] As for the Democratic candidate, John W. Davis, he possessed too many "eastern corporate connections" and had the belief of party subservience. Recalling his earlier acquaintance with Davis, Norris admitted his high personal character and great ability.[15] Despite his serious reservations about the major party candidates, Norris recognized that either Davis or Coolidge, creatures of boss-dominated conventions rallying partisan support, would be elected president. He was disturbed because through "the unreasonable and almost unexplainable power of partisan politics" many honest-minded citizens had been duped into demanding party regularity of him.[16]

On September 24, 1924, Norris opened his campaign in Grand Island, stressing his record in Congress and calling for the nonpartisan election of state and county officials. In this speech and in all others he followed a straight course: he did not directly criticize Coolidge nor did he boost any other candidate. Thus he maintained

[13] Norris to James E. Wagner, June 11, 1924. In this long letter, written while the Republican convention was meeting in Cleveland, Norris presented a precise formulation of his position.

[14] Norris to C. O. Talmage, July 24, 1924; to C. W. McConaughy, July 24, 1924.

[15] See Lowitt, *George W. Norris: The Making of a Progressive,* p. 269.

[16] Norris to Talmage, July 24, 1924; to Fred Carey, July 24, 1924.

the support of the Republican organization in Nebraska. In early October members of his campaign committee thought he was succeeding admirably and would be elected by a heavy majority. They noted that both the state and Douglas County (Omaha) organizations supported him, but how effectively was a matter of dispute.[17]

Sorensen, who was active for LaFollette as well as for Norris, said that many prominent Republicans, apparently with the knowledge of the state committee, were openly urging the election of his opponent, John J. Thomas. In Lincoln, for example, a local Republican politician distributed leaflets at a LaFollette meeting urging the election of the Republican candidate for governor and the Democrat for senator. But other politicians were linking Norris's name with the Republican candidates to insure their election. Besides keeping Norris abreast of political developments, Sorensen ordered 10,000 copies of his speech at Grand Island for widespread distribution.[18]

On October 20, 1924, Robert M. LaFollette spoke in Omaha. When he mentioned Norris's name, the audience applauded, whereupon the Wisconsin senator remarked, "You can't applaud George Norris too roundly to suit me. Nebraska has never sent a man to the United States Senate to match him. Norris can take his rank with the senators of the highest stature who have been in Congress throughout the history of our country." [19] Earlier the Nebraska Conference for Progressive Political Action had recommended several candidates from those nominated by the major parties. For U.S. senator they endorsed Norris, whose name topped the list they widely distributed. Senator Robert Howell also specifically endorsed him. But by the end of October the anti-Norris fight within the Republican hierarchy suddenly burst into the open with a bitter attack by H. H. Wilson, a Lincoln attorney, who asked Republicans to vote

[17] Robert Smith to Norris, Oct. 3, 1924. Apparently the Old Guard politicians were at first inclined to make an open fight against Norris, but after some deliberation they concluded that a fight would hurt other Republican candidates, including Calvin Coolidge, more than it would hurt the senator. Though organized opposition subsided, individuals continued to try to embarrass Norris; see *Hastings Daily Tribune*, Oct. 16, 1924.

[18] Sorensen to Norris, Oct. 11, 1924 (Sorensen Papers). At the end of the campaign Sorensen had about sixty copies of Norris's Grand Island speech left; see Sorensen to Norris, Nov. 10, 1924 (Sorensen Papers).

[19] *Omaha Daily News*, Oct. 21, 1924.

for the Democratic candidate. His remarks were regarded as the opening barrage in a last-minute statewide anti-Norris campaign. Norris supporters said they were glad his enemies were openly instead of secretly attacking him. And Norris, campaigning in the southwestern part of the state, was too busy to take cognizance of Wilson's speech.[20]

As usual, he concluded the campaign in his old congressional district with his final speech in McCook. While Sorensen and other friends in Lincoln were attending to details, Norris had stumped the rural areas, stating his views on agriculture, partisanship, honesty and efficiency in government, and other national issues. He avoided personalities, sticking to the issues as he saw them. Large crowds received him warmly as he appeared in the towns of the fifth congressional district; in every audience were numerous personal acquaintances, some dating back to his career as a district judge and congressman.[21]

In the election Norris won an impressive victory, polling more votes than any other major candidate on the ballot.[22] He defeated his Democratic opponent, John J. Thomas, by over 100,000 votes: 274,647 for Norris to 165,370 for Thomas. He polled 56,000 more votes than Calvin Coolidge and became the first Nebraskan to be elected to a third term in the U.S. Senate. C. A. Sorensen summed up its significance: "You are entitled to something more than formal congratulations on your victory. The Republican organization did not want you. Your election was a conspicuous victory for the common people. You have been elected without becoming obligated to any person, group or corporation." [23]

Norris spent less than $500 and concluded that the expenditure

[20] *Alma* (Nebr.) *Record,* Oct. 24, 1924; *Omaha Daily News,* Oct. 29, 1924. Norris did not campaign in the most populous, eastern part of Nebraska, a pattern he usually followed. If the rural areas strongly supported him, Norris knew he would win as many votes as he would lose in Douglas County and preferred to let the politicians turn out the Republican vote there.

[21] *Omaha Daily News,* Oct. 29, 1924; *McCook Daily Gazette,* Oct. 31, 1924.

[22] Norris's majority was not as large as that of the candidate for attorney general, though he secured more votes than any other candidate on any ticket.

[23] Sorensen to Norris, Nov. 10, 1924 (Sorensen Papers). See Addison E. Sheldon, *Nebraska: The Land and the People* (Chicago, 1931), 1: 1017–18, for election results. In 1924 Norris probably voted for Robert M. LaFollette, though he never revealed for whom he voted.

of large sums of money in politics was unnecessary. While Norris saw no need for spending large sums, he also saw no need for declaring himself an independent and severing his Republican ties. He knew that most regular Republicans had supported him if not out of conviction, then out of loyalty.[24] While he would maintain his independence, he would do so within the framework of party lines. Sorensen, his campaign manager, commented, "Had Norris run as an Independent, he would in all likelihood have been defeated; but on the Republican ballot, nothing could stop him." A third party, while fine for educational purposes, was not the best way to elect men to public office.[25]

Norris prepared his analysis of the campaign two months after it was over. He had occupied an embarrassing position. He had not wanted to be a candidate at the outset and in January, 1925, still had misgivings about it. Staying within the Republican fold made him feel that he was not "as frank and free with the people" as he should have been. Though he did not support Coolidge, he had waged no fight against him, explaining that if he had been asked his views of any candidate, he would have been frank in answering. He expected questions about his attitude toward Coolidge but they were never raised during the campaign. Though dissatisfied with his position, Norris said he could not have retained the nomination and pursued any other course. Nevertheless, the 1924 election was of prime significance in further weakening Norris's party ties and weaving his independent stance into the very fiber of his political being. Reservations about independence would disappear, never to return again, once the second session of the Sixty-eighth Congress began.[26]

Entitled to serve another six years in the Senate, Norris was

[24] By the same token Norris's name strengthened the Republican ticket in Nebraska and brought into the fold many voters who supported the party carrying his name on the ballot.

[25] Norris to W. T. Rawleigh, July 20, 1926; Sorensen to Frank A. Harrison, Dec. 2, 1924 (copy in the Norris Papers).

[26] Norris to Sorensen, Jan. 18, 1925. Reflecting later about the campaign, Norris expressed essentially the same views but was stronger in his insistence that he should have run as an independent candidate. If he had done so, he believed he could have helped carry Nebraska for LaFollette. The Wisconsin senator ran 30,000 votes behind Davis and over 100,000 votes behind Coolidge; see Norris to Edward Keating, Sept. 8, 1927; to Harvey Newbranch, Aug. 8, 1929.

anxious to return to Washington for the forthcoming session. Before he left Nebraska, he went to Omaha, where he had a growth removed from one of his eyes. The doctor, though skeptical, consented after several days to allow him to drive to Washington. And his forebodings proved correct. Norris drove from Omaha to Washington with the use of only one eye. During the trip he caught cold and both he and Mrs. Norris worried that it might disturb the injured eye. Every night Mrs. Norris put hot cloths over the eye and kept changing them for an hour or two. With this treatment the eye improved and soon after Congress convened, it was as good as ever. Driving through southern Iowa, they were caught in a heavy downpour; Norris boasted that while farmers along the road were getting rich pulling other cars out of the mud, "the old Dodge went right through." Though the car skidded "all over several counties," the senator and Mrs. Norris returned safely to Washington shortly before the short session of the Sixty-eighth Congress convened on December 1, 1924. In this session Norris faced the most serious challenge to public ownership of Muscle Shoals in the entire history of the controversy.[27]

[27] Harold Gifford to Norris, Nov. 25, 1924; Norris to "Dear Boys," Jan. 18, 1925.

The Coolidge-Underwood Coalition

17

On December 2, 1924, the second day of the session, Senator Oscar W. Underwood of Alabama introduced a Muscle Shoals measure replacing the withdrawn Ford offer. Authorizing the president to lease the plants for private operation, it required their maintenance for national defense and called for an annual production of fertilizer containing 40,000 tons of nitrogen. Surplus power would be sold for general distribution under local regulations. Failing to secure a satisfactory lessee, the measure authorized operation by a government corporation to the same extent as required of a lessee. At the outset Underwood said the measure had Coolidge's approval, but it soon attracted bitter opposition and the president withdrew his support.[1]

The Ford offer, approved by the House in March, 1924, was replaced by the Senate Agriculture and Forestry Committee with a government operation bill proposed by Norris, which was recommended to the Senate. The Norris bill, then, would have to vie with the Underwood leasing measure. Under a unanimous-consent order, agreed to in the closing days of the first session of the Sixty-eighth Congress, Muscle Shoals legislation was to be the first order of business when Congress reconvened.

On December 4 Norris carefully discussed his public ownership

[1] The full text of the Underwood bill (S. 3507) can be found in the *Congressional Record*, 68th Cong., 2nd sess., Dec. 8, 1924, pp. 259–61.

measure. He reviewed the history of the project, examined the fertilizer question, discussed power possibilities, and observed that there were two definite and distinct propositions which had no precise connection with each other: "the question of power and the question of explosives and of fertilizer material."

Norris said that power at Muscle Shoals, developed from a navigable stream over which the federal government had jurisdiction, "should not be given away to any private individual or corporation for his or its own personal financial benefit." Moreover, he believed that the entire stream including its tributaries should be considered as a whole: "Every dam should be selected with reference to all other dam sites, keeping always in view the question of navigation." Besides maintaining the even flow of the river, storage dams would help increase the amount of hydroelectric power to be generated and would play an important role in flood control. Finally, Norris envisioned a system of interchangeable transmission lines so that the maximum amount of power could be developed and the maximum amount of secondary power could be converted into primary power.[2]

The one possible danger in such a scheme was that of monopoly and the most effective way "to help save the people from such a monopoly would be to have the Federal Government own at least some of the power-producing elements that enter into such a system." With this premise as a base, Norris argued for government ownership and management. At the same time he envisioned a "new electric age" which would decentralize manufacturing areas and make it possible for the small producer in the vicinity of his raw materials to compete successfully with larger concerns. The South, of course, stood to gain more than any other section. Not that Muscle Shoals could generate enough power for the entire South, but it was the central focus of any system that might develop. If the properties were leased, a favored corporation would receive an

---

[2] Primary power is the power that can be utilized every hour in the day and every day in the year; secondary power is that which is developed only during a portion of the year. For most purposes primary power is required; its value is much greater than secondary power. Through steam plants, storage dams, or interchangeable transmission lines much secondary power can be converted into primary power. Whenever such a conversion occurs, economy and great gain in power result. My definitions follow the discussion by Norris of these two terms; see *ibid.*, Dec. 4, 1924, p. 114.

undue advantage over every manufacturing establishment of a similar nature in the entire South.

While the question of hydroelectric power and how to deal with it was "quite simple" according to Norris, the question of fertilizer was complicated. It was basic to the preservation of agriculture and thus to "the maintaining of our civilization." The expenditure of public funds in an endeavor to cheapen the manufacture of fertilizer was easily justified. Any process that would cheapen the extraction of nitrogen, a necessary ingredient of fertilizer, from the atmosphere would at the same time cut the cost of fertilizer to the farmer. Largely through the efforts of government scientists, the extraction of nitrogen from the air, Norris said, eventually would be depreciated by at least one-half the prior cost. Moreover, their discoveries were freely available to the public. But no one had yet demonstrated that fertilizer costs could be greatly reduced by prevailing methods. Scientists believed improvements would be made and that cost reductions would follow.[3] If the nitrate plants at Muscle Shoals were placed at the disposal of government chemists, Norris and the members of the Agriculture and Forestry Committee claimed, further progress would be made. The indications were that every improvement would consume less power.

The provisions of Norris's government operation bill reflected the gist of his remarks. It separated the two propositions involved at Muscle Shoals: power and fertilizer. It called for a government corporation to handle the power proposition: to build transmission lines; to sell the current, giving preference to states, municipalities, and public corporations; to connect with lines of other concerns; to perform all the other functions the owner of a power plant would perform. It would not be necessary, furthermore, to use most of the power generated for the production of fertilizer "because the scien-

[3] In 1924 the factory cost of nitrogen in a ton of completed "2-8-2" fertilizer was about $4.80. Two parts of nitrogen, eight parts of phosphorus, and two parts of potash by weight made up the ordinary fertilizer available on the market. If the cost of nitrogen were reduced one-half, the cost of the completed fertilizer would only be reduced $2.40 per ton. The cost both of completed fertilizer and of nitrogen alone would have to be substantially lowered before the price to the farmer could be reduced. While Norris was hopeful that this would occur, it had not yet happened at the end of 1924; see Norris's remarks in *ibid.*, p. 116.

tific people of the world know that it would be useless." Producing large amounts of nitrogen would neither cut the cost of fertilizer nor make it more easily available. Vast amounts of power were not necessary to lower the cost of fertilizer, while every new invention lessened the amount of power necessary to produce fertilizer. The cyanamide process used at Plant No. 2, to be sure, required a vast amount of power, but the Haber process, developed in Germany during World War I, materially reduced the power requirement. And it was a better process. What was necessary was to develop the best process "so that everybody everywhere can have the benefit of the knowledge thereby gained and go into the fertilizer business if they want to." Under the Norris bill researchers could utilize any approach and follow any clue in their efforts to reduce the cost of producing an effective commercial fertilizer.

The Norris bill also called for the development of the Tennessee River, seeking in the most economic way the maximum amount of hydroelectric energy. The Secretary of War was directed to survey the river and its tributaries to ascertain the best sites for the location of storage reservoirs and power dams or a combination of both. Thus it eventually would be possible at Dam No. 2 (Wilson Dam) to convert secondary power into primary power. "Instead of being able to sell practically 100,000 horsepower every hour in the year at this great dam, they will then be able to sell five, six, or seven times that amount; and when you at once develop the power and multiply its capacity by seven without any material addition to the cost, thereby you divide the cost to the consumer by seven."

The revenue for the government corporation called for in Norris's bill would come from funds paid by the Alabama Power Company in 1923 when it purchased the government interest in the Gorgas steam plant on the Warrior River. With these funds, almost $4 million, as a starter, the corporation could retain its entire income until a sum of $25 million was secured; thereafter, all profits would be turned over to the U.S. Treasury. Norris thus envisioned a long-term proposition to make the Tennessee River the only "scientifically developed" river in the nation, whose resources would be developed "for the benefit of humanity," providing "the most benefit for the most people at the least cost possible."

Recognizing that though people in the South would benefit most, eventually people in other sections would benefit as well, Norris said:

> . . . the time is coming when this whole country will be under one giant power scheme. The development of such a scheme would be the economic way to get all the power possible at the minimum cost from our great streams, and if we are wise, we will not do anything that will interfere with the extension of this giant power scheme, which as time progresses and things develop will more and more hook one system into another, so that we can turn the power of the Tennessee River into the State of California some day by the pushing of a button. You can do it now all through the South.[4]

These lengthy remarks represented Norris's major effort to present his position. He was firm in his opposition to private development, offering instead a full explanation of how multi-purpose development would emanate from the full-scale generation of hydroelectric power on the Tennessee River. He also made clear that fertilizer was not central to the Muscle Shoals proposition. It had been used as a shield by those interested in acquiring hydroelectric power while talking of aiding agriculture by producing fertilizers. By permitting the Agriculture Department to experiment with methods of producing cheaper fertilizers, Norris hoped to insure public benefit in this area as well. These extemporaneous remarks represented a notable statement of Norris's position. Most of the positive points that he would reiterate throughout the controversy were stated or suggested in this speech. But in Senator Oscar W. Underwood of Alabama he faced an antagonist and parliamentarian of great ability.

Underwood remarked that Norris's "is a good bill if what you want is only hydro-electric power." He suggested that it would turn the operation of a business proposition over to "theorists" and bureaucrats, the last people from whom to expect efficient and practical business results. His bill, on the other hand, dedicated "all the property at Muscle Shoals to the national defense and to

---

[4] *Ibid.*, p. 122 (the quote), pp. 113–22 (Norris's lengthy remarks explaining and supporting the bill for public ownership of Muscle Shoals); see also *New York Evening Journal,* Dec. 5, 1924.

the production of fertilizer." Stressing aid to depressed agriculture, the Underwood measure called for fertilizer production as its chief aim. Patriotism pervaded it as well. In time of war a lessee on five days' notice would have to return the property to the government for the production of nitrates. While the Underwood proposal did not name a specific lessee, the Alabama Power Company was a prospective bidder.[5]

In his remarks Norris stressed the fact that the Alabama Power Company was the only possible bidder, since there was no provision for building transmission lines in the Underwood measure. Any other bidder would have to build lines. That power was central to Underwood's bill Norris firmly believed. Nobody, "even if supplied with power absolutely free," could use it to make fertilizer at Muscle Shoals and compete successfully with commercial firms. Unless it could be produced at a price the farmer could afford, the fertilizer proposition served primarily as a cover to gain control of the prodigious power resources.[6] He hit hard at the fact, central to the Underwood bill, that fertilizer production was not commercially feasible at Muscle Shoals with the scientific knowledge available at that time.

Then on December 17, in criticizing the Underwood bill, Norris assailed President Coolidge for supporting the measure. Conceding the honesty and integrity of the president and granting the conscientious ability of Senator Underwood, "his officer in command," in their desire to grant Muscle Shoals to private interests, Norris went on:

> . . . it seems to me that the inevitable conclusion must be that if this administration measure, fathered here by the Senator from Alabama, shall be enacted into law, it will ultimately be recog-

[5] *Congressional Record*, 68th Cong., 2nd sess., Dec. 4, 1924, pp. 127–28. The *New York Evening Journal*, Dec. 5, 1924, said that four firms were anxious to submit bids but could name only two: Hamble & Company of New York and the Alabama Power Company.

[6] *Congressional Record*, 68th Cong., 2nd sess., Dec. 10, 1924, p. 400. Senator Kenneth McKellar of Tennessee was even more sharply critical than Norris in charging that the Underwood bill "would give Muscle Shoals over to the Alabama Power Company." Underwood, hard pressed in debate, agreed to several amendments, including one by Norris eliminating a qualifying phrase and thereby requiring the conversion into fertilizer of nitrogen not needed for national defense; see *New York Times*, Dec. 11, 1924.

nized as a rape upon the Treasury of the United States, a gold brick to the American farmer, and the giving of a concession of untold value to some corporation, whose identity has not yet been disclosed; a concession so great that it will make Tea Pot Dome look like a pin head. Doheny and Sinclair will soon realize that they were only pikers when they spent hundreds of thousands of dollars for the corrupting of public officials and the hiring of ex-public officials when a greater property is going to be conveyed to some private interest through the legislative channel without the expenditure of a dollar and without the necessity of any fraudulent methods.[7]

Norris was convinced that if Muscle Shoals were leased to "the Alabama Power Company or some similar institution," it would become part of the "water power trust," a term he often used throughout the twenties and which he defined as property dominated by the General Electric Company, "either through the control of stock ownership or through the control of directors holding places upon the directorates of several corporations of this kind, all of which are in one way or another subsidiary to the General Electric Corporation." In regulating these properties, state commissions had never truly lowered electric rates. In many instances members of regulatory bodies had fallen under the sway of the interests they were supposed to regulate, convincing Norris that the only effective way to reduce rates was through public ownership.[8]

For more than two years the Agriculture and Forestry Committee had investigated Muscle Shoals, devoting "weary days . . . and weary nights to listening to volumes of testimony, reading volumes and volumes of authority on the various elements that enter into the equation." While some of this effort was useless, a

[7] *Congressional Record,* 68th Cong., 2nd sess., Dec. 11, pp. 456–57, Dec. 12, pp. 519–20, Dec. 17, 1924, p. 703 (the quote); see also *New York Evening World,* Dec. 18, 1924. Norris in his remarks implied that Coolidge, after a sail on the Potomac aboard the presidential yacht, the *Mayflower,* with Underwood as his guest, approved the Underwood bill and suggested minor amendments to it. Harry Slattery confirmed what Norris only implied: "After Underwood had returned from a week-end sail with the President," several minor amendments were added to Underwood's proposal; see Slattery to Mrs. Gifford Pinchot, Dec. 18, 1924 (Harry Slattery Papers, Manuscripts Collections, Duke University Library).

[8] For ramifications, see George W. Norris to Carl D. Thompson, Mar. 6, 1925.

great deal was of inestimable value. But it was only after patient and conscientious consideration of the subject in committee, where individuals who wished to be heard were allowed to speak "without limitation of time," that their deliberations were presented to the Senate. And what happened? Norris asserted, "We are confronted now not with an analysis of our proposition, not with a fair and open debate in the forum of discussion of the things that we asked, but we are confronted with a control of senatorial votes by the administration in power, votes that are going arbitrarily according to the demands and wishes of the Administration without regard to argument, without regard to logic; and I confess, Mr. President, that it is not a very pleasant experience." [9]

The result would be to give Muscle Shoals, where the government had already spent millions of dollars, to private interests "having no other incentive than the making of the almighty dollar." It would become the key site controlled by the power trust. At the dawn of an electric age, when every citizen would seek to take advantage of the blessings of electricity, "the whole thing" would be "in control of Wall Street through one company either directly or indirectly." To prevent this predicament, Norris suggested what had been done in a small way in municipalities: ". . . save enough of the energy, keep our hands on enough of the power, so that through its instrumentalities we will be able to control, by competition . . . the price of all power, and when these mighty projects are hooked up together and the entire United States [*sic*] perhaps at least under one control we will hold the key to the situation." The government should be able to say that the energy generated and distributed by private interests "must do justice to the people or that they they shall not have it." [10]

[9] *Congressional Record,* 68th Cong., 2nd sess., Dec. 17, 1924, pp. 704–5.

[10] Later in the session Norris spoke in favor of a Senate resolution he introduced calling for an investigation by the Federal Trade Commission of the so-called power trust. Investigating the dimensions of a power monopoly was so gigantic a task that Norris felt a responsible government agency could gather the facts and explore the surrounding circumstances better than he could. Norris claimed he was "dumbfounded and amazed" in his brief investigation to learn how subsidiary corporations reaching into every section of the country were controlled in one way or another by the General Electric Company. He had inserted into the *Congressional Record* a map and a chart illustrating its dimensions. In modified form the resolution Norris supported was approved by the Senate on Feb.

Though critical of Coolidge in his remarks on December 17, Norris admitted to a high regard "for the great office of President of the United States." He simply could not understand how a congressman could perform the functions of his office if he permitted a president, "no matter how great, no matter how wise, to control his official action by a wish, by a sign, or even by a request." With the transcending importance of Muscle Shoals affecting resource development and the happiness of future generations, Norris said that the Senate could at least carefully examine both measures before coming to a conclusion, "because something fundamental is involved here." After nearly two hours on the floor Norris concluded his lengthy and at times embittered remarks.[11]

Thereafter his comments until the final battle on the Underwood bill were briefer and usually repetitious. Occasionally he injected a new theme or idea, so that by the end of this phase of the controversy Norris had expressed virtually every idea and suggested every point that he would make throughout the remainder of the decade. On December 20, 1924, for example, Norris presented for the first time data and information on Ontario water power and electric development, relating them to the Muscle Shoals proposition.[12]

During debate on the Underwood bill Norris spent much time preparing for the floor fight. Night after night he was up until after midnight, sometimes in conference with supporting senators. Most of the brief Christmas recess was consumed in a similar way. His correspondence was neglected in December and January. In the few letters he did write his concern about "the greatest combination or

---

9, 1925; see *ibid.*, Jan. 2, pp. 2073–86, Jan. 20, pp. 2126, 2129–30, Feb. 9, 1925, pp. 3282–83, 3285–86, 3300, 3303; 69th Cong., 1st sess., July 3, 1926, p. 12903; Norris to C. O. Biggs, Feb. 18, 1925.

[11] *Congressional Record,* 68th Cong., 2nd sess., Dec. 17, 1924, pp. 703–13; *New York Evening World,* Dec. 18, 1924. The *Washington Herald,* Dec. 18, 1924, instead of mentioning the Underwood proposal, called it "the Coolidge bill." Harry Slattery thought Norris's speech "able" but still expected the Underwood proposal to pass the Senate, although "not by a large vote"; see Slattery to Mrs. Pinchot, Dec. 18, 1924 (Slattery Papers).

[12] *Congressional Record,* 68th Cong., 2nd sess., Dec. 20, 1924, pp. 868–69. See W. R. Plewman, *Adam Beck and the Ontario Hydro* (Toronto, 1947), for an interesting biography of the chief architect of the system. Beck died in 1925. See also my article, "Ontario Hydro: A 1925 Tempest in an American Teapot," *Canadian Historical Review,* 49, no. 3 (Sept., 1968): 267–74.

trust in the world" was clearly evident. The fact that the power trust had as its allies the national leader of the Republican party and the senatorial leader of the Democratic party grieved Norris and served to reinforce his conviction of the efficacy and necessity of pursuing an independent role.[13]

However, during the Christmas recess the press announced that the president had withdrawn his tacit support of the Underwood bill and that the measure was presumably doomed to defeat. Many southern Democrats quickly announced their opposition to the Underwood bill, and Senate sentiment seemed to be supporting an amendment offered by Wesley L. Jones of Washington calling for a commission to recommend to Congress a plan for the disposal of Muscle Shoals. On the day after Christmas Norris released a statement denouncing the Jones amendment and reaffirming his public ownership position.[14]

On January 8 the Underwood bill, slightly amended, was reported from the committee of the whole. In the complicated and climactic proceedings that lasted until January 14, 1925, Norris played a considerable part. The parliamentary maneuverings were complex. The Underwood bill was substituted in H. Res. 518 for the Agriculture and Forestry Committee's substitute providing for government operation. The Jones amendment, striking out all of the Underwood amendment and creating a commission to recommend a plan for disposing of Muscle Shoals, was then adopted. Immediately Norris offered in place of the Jones amendment his revised committee substitute providing for government operation; it was adopted. Senator Underwood then changed his bill somewhat by accepting an amendment offered by Senator Kenneth McKellar. He now offered it as a revised amendment, substituting for the Norris amendment. Norris objected and appealed the ruling of the chair permitting Underwood's action, but the chair's ruling was confirmed. The Underwood amendment then was approved and the bill went to conference on January 27, 1925.[15]

---

13 Norris to John J. Thomas, Dec. 23, 1924. Thomas had been Norris's Democratic opponent in the recent senatorial campaign.

14 *New York Evening Journal*, Dec. 26, 1924.

15 My guide through this legislative maze was a pamphlet, *Facts about Muscle Shoals*, published by the National League of Women Voters in Aug., 1927; see p. 19.

In his remarks Norris suggested to Democratic supporters of the Underwood bill that they were being used by the Coolidge administration, which would drop them once they had served its purpose. Lame-duck and Underwood Democrats were voting with Coolidge Republicans despite the fact that a 1924 Democratic National Committee campaign document specifically denounced the power trust. So bitter was Norris in his opposition that sarcasm, after every other approach had been tried, came to the fore:

> This has been really a wonderful combination of the two great political machines. There are Silent Cal at the head, Smiling Oscar, Happy Pat, Jovial Joe, and "Me Too" Tom, all bound up together by sacred ties of fertilizer, five souls with but a single thought, five hearts that beat as one. What a glorious time, what a glorious banquet they could have. Going into the banquet hall, the dinner would be furnished by the Electric Trust, the General Electric Co., the seasoning for the meats and soups supplied in the shape of fertilizer by the Alabama Power Co., the liquid refreshments given to them by the Republican National Committee. What a glorious jubilee they could have! . . .[16]

On January 14, 1925, before the Senate voted on the amended Underwood bill, Norris was granted the floor "to say a few words." He repeated his belief that the Underwood bill was not a fertilizer proposition, noting no provisions for investigating and experimenting in order to cheapen the cost of fertilizer. There was now no humor or sarcasm in his remarks. He was in earnest as he indicated that essentially the bill was a power bill. He realized, too, that he would be defeated in the forthcoming vote: "Personally I feel it

[16] *New York Commercial,* Jan. 10, 1925; *Congressional Record,* 68th Cong., 2nd sess., Jan. 9, 1925, p. 1507 (Silent Cal Coolidge, Smiling Oscar Underwood, Happy Pat Harrison, Jovial Joe Robinson, and "Me Too" Tom Heflin). All the senators were southern Democrats supporting the Underwood bill. Norris in his remarks of this date also observed that Coolidge was *now* trying to reach the same goal of giving away Muscle Shoals but by the Jones amendment "or some shifting arrangement of that kind." Norris thought Senator Robinson was responsible for lining up standpat Democrats to vote with Coolidge Republicans to substitute Underwood's proposal for his public ownership bill. It was Judson King who called Norris's attention to the 1924 Democratic campaign document which King had written; see King to William Kent, Jan. 9, 1925 (Addition 1, William Kent Papers, Yale University Library).

very sincerely and deeply." He was not sorry he had made the fight, devoting over two years of his life "to almost continual labor for an unselfish purpose." While he found no fault with Senator Underwood for securing Republican votes and allying himself with the administration, he feared the precedent of using public funds to develop valuable properties which then would be granted to private interests, to someone associated with "the great Electric Trust." [17]

The Underwood bill passed the Senate with fifty members in favor of it and thirty opposed. After the vote Norris attended to his correspondence; after doing little else for four days, he confessed that the Muscle Shoals fight was the hardest he had ever been in and, though he knew he was going to lose, he was not sorry he made it. To be sure, eliminating the Ford proposal was worth something, but Norris was not sure exactly what, now that "monopoly is going to get it." [18]

One thing Norris's fight did achieve. It encouraged segments of the public to think about natural resources and how they could be utilized. His efforts called attention to the potential involved in granting to private interests an energy source of tremendous value, while those of Senator Thomas J. Walsh on Teapot Dome revealed an accomplished fact. In both instances a great public resource of increasing worth in an emerging power age was involved. In both instances prominent business leaders sought to own the resource and exploit it for their own advantage. In both instances there were prominent politicians willing to let them do it. And the

[17] *Congressional Record,* 68th Cong., 2nd sess., Jan. 14, 1925, pp. 1807–8. In his remarks Norris said he voted for an abortive effort to substitute Jones's amendment for the Underwood proposal, made shortly before the final vote was taken, as a choice between evils, chiefly because in having a commission recommend to Congress a plan for disposal of Muscle Shoals, time would be gained to attempt to arouse public opinion. He felt the amended Underwood bill, with its proposal to build Dam No. 3, with no statement about what should be done with it when finished and with no provision for converting secondary power into primary power, was a poorly drawn measure that did nothing cheaply in developing the Tennessee River.

[18] Norris to "Dear Boys," Jan. 18, 1925; to C. H. Boyle, Jan. 18, 1925. The overwhelming vote of confidence given to Coolidge in the 1924 election, Norris felt, served as a force in gaining support for anything Coolidge favored.

politicians and their business allies were seemingly successful.[19]

The Underwood bill, after passing the Senate, remained on the Speaker's table for almost two weeks until a special ruling permitted it to be sent directly to a conference committee, never having been considered by the House itself. Norris questioned this procedure, insisting that "the concurrence of both branches is necessary for the enactment of a law or for any other action." The principle underlying the appointment of conferees is that they represent the action taken by the body from which they were appointed. Since Norris did not approve the action taken by the Senate, he did not want to be on the conference committee. Some senators were disturbed by the possibility that, as chairman of the committee which had considered Muscle Shoals legislation, he would be appointed. If appointed, Norris assured his critics, he would represent the views of the Senate majority.

Technically, there were two bills in dispute. The House had approved the Ford offer, which nobody would accept since the auto magnate had withdrawn his offer; the Senate had passed the Underwood bill. In effect, there was no House bill and the House took no action except to ask for a conference on the Underwood bill. Thus a bill approved by the Senate but never considered by a standing committee of the Senate was sent to the House, where it was never considered before going to conference.[20]

Despite misgivings, Senator Cummins, the presiding officer of the chamber, chose Norris to head the Senate conferees. His associates were Senators McNary and E. D. Smith, ranking members of the Agriculture and Forestry Committee. All three had voted against the Underwood bill. Both McNary and Norris requested unanimous consent to be relieved of their assignment. No objection was raised, and Cummins replaced them with Senators Henry Keyes and Edwin Ladd, both Republicans and supporters of the Underwood bill. Senator Underwood, who as a member of the

[19] See *Omaha Daily News,* Jan. 15, 1925, "Norris Lost, But It Was a Good Fight" (editorial). Norris published an article, "A Powerless America," in which he reviewed the history of the Ford proposal and attacked the Coolidge-Underwood plan as a "thrust in the dark" wherein the government's own property would be used against the people. It appeared in *Labor Age* (Feb., 1925), pp. 4–6.

[20] *Congressional Record,* 68th Cong., 2nd sess., Jan. 28, 1925, pp. 2555–56; Norris to J. A. H. Hopkins, Feb. 1, 1925.

Democratic minority was precluded from serving on the conference committee, complimented McNary and Norris on their position: "It is playing true to form." [21]

The conference report, which approved the Underwood measure with some modifications, was submitted on February 7, 1925. It was not until February 19 that Norris offered objections similar to those he had made when the bill went into conference. Then, comparing provisions in the Senate bill and the Ford proposal which had passed the House, he criticized those which departed from the guidelines of the Ford proposal on the one hand and the Underwood bill on the other. For example, the conference report excluded the construction of navigation locks. Locks had been included in both bills; consequently, Norris insisted, the conferees had no right to exclude them. In another instance the conference committee provided for an annual rental fee less than the amount mentioned in either bill. Since the conference report contained new material, Norris suggested that it was out of order.[22] President pro tem Cummins agreed with him.

On February 23, 1925, Norris presented his objections more formally and in greater detail as the Senate decided whether to sustain the ruling of the chair. The argument shifted to a discussion of the rules, to questions of parliamentary law. Norris's criticism was based on paragraph 2 of Senate Rule XXVII: "The conferees shall not insert in their report matter not committed to them by either House, nor shall they strike from the bill matters agreed to by both Houses. If new matter is inserted in the report, or if matter which was agreed to by both Houses is stricken from the bill, a point of order may be made against the report, and if the point of order is sustained the report shall be recommitted to the committee of conference." [23] On as clear a proposition as the one under discussion, if the chair were overruled, then henceforth, Norris asserted, no one would pay attention to the rules. Conferees, who ought to have no legislative authority, would become the most powerful of legislators, deciding in secret for the Ameri-

21 *Congressional Record*, 68th Cong., 2nd sess., Jan. 28, 1925, p. 2561.

22 *Ibid.*, Feb. 19, 1925, pp. 4124–25, 4132, 4135.

23 Norris observed that a conference report on a recent immigration bill was defeated mainly because the conferees put in a provision that neither house had inserted, even though it was done at the request of the president.

can people. Some senators, he realized, would follow the wishes of the president and seek to overrule the chair, despite the fact that the conference committee had overstepped its rights, duties, and privileges.[24]

By a vote of 45 yeas to 41 nays the decision of the chair was sustained. The report was referred back to conference committee.[25] On February 26, 1925, the conference committee reported an agreement on the Underwood bill designed to meet the objections raised against it. But when the Senate adjourned *sine die* on March 3, 1925, the disposition of the Muscle Shoals properties was still unsettled. Thus, as in the fight against the power of the Speaker in 1910, Norris won an outstanding victory on a point of parliamentary procedure. The threat posed by the Underwood bill, the most serious in the history of the controversy, was turned back by his stress on parliamentary procedure after Norris had considered it lost.

At the end of February Norris felt he had won. He confessed hope that the Senate leadership would present the conference committee report so that he could use some of the information he had been collecting. Norris also reported that he had led majority leader Charles Curtis to understand that "if Curtis would lay off Muscle Shoals, he would lay off the rest of the Administration program." Otherwise he would discuss every bill Curtis presented in order to consume time. The necessity did not arise, partly because of the death of Medill McCormick, erstwhile progressive, who was a staunch supporter of the Coolidge administration in the Muscle Shoals fight. Judson King remarked that there were two

[24] *Congressional Record*, 68th Cong., 2nd sess., Feb. 23, 1925, pp. 4395–97, 4403. Paragraph 2 of Senate Rule XXVII was adopted unanimously on Mar. 8, 1918, as S. J. Res. 103.

[25] Now Underwood and the Coolidge administration were placed in a dilemma. The conference committee could prepare a new report which would take time and probably be filibustered to death, or the House could pass the original Underwood bill and no conference would be necessary. At this point Underwood was caught in his own trap. In the original bill he fixed the profits that could be made on fertilizer at 1 percent in order to gain Senate support, realizing that no lessee would accept a contract on that basis even though they could develop the hydroelectric power. So the measure went back to conference committee and the battle was lost.

funerals: "I only wish that Muscle Shoals were as dead as Medill." [26]

As if to prove King's point, on March 26, 1925, President Coolidge, complying with a House resolution approved at the end of the session, appointed a committee, with Representative John C. McKenzie as chairman, to assemble reliable information about the best method of utilizing the Muscle Shoals properties. Norris felt that the makeup of the committee meant public funds would be spent to present an argument against retention and development of Muscle Shoals. Norris intended to spend his own money to develop arguments on the other side by visiting Ontario and its great hydroelectric system. [27]

In the Sixty-eighth Congress Norris had faced his most severe test in preventing the leasing of Muscle Shoals to private interests. Other tests, to be sure, would be forthcoming but hereafter, when the Senate approved a measure pertaining to Muscle Shoals, it would always be a public ownership bill submitted by George W. Norris. Meanwhile, other important measures and incidents pertaining to resource development concerned Norris in the Sixty-eighth Congress. Since some of these items had important or interesting ramifications, we will examine them in the next chapter.

[26] Norris to Bruce Bliven, Mar. 4, 1925; King to Slattery, Mar. 2, 1925 (Slattery Papers). Medill McCormick died on Feb. 25, 1925. Norris's secretary, Mabelle Talbert, made the interesting point that had Congress not had to adjourn at noon on Mar. 4, 1925, the chances for working out an arrangement to dispose of Muscle Shoals would have increased. If Norris's lame-duck amendment to the Constitution had been in effect, the Underwood-Coolidge coalition no doubt would have succeeded; see Mabelle Talbert to John F. White, Sept. 9, 1925.

[27] Norris to J. G. W. Lewis, Mar. 31, 1925; to Thompson, Apr. 1, 1925. During the summer Norris wrote to Congressman McKenzie reiterating his views and calling for the multiple-purpose development of the Tennessee and Potomac rivers; see Norris to John C. McKenzie, July 11, 1925. In November, as Norris had anticipated, the president's Muscle Shoals Inquiry Commission reported and recommended that Muscle Shoals be leased for private enterprise. If no satisfactory lease could be made, then the government should operate the properties.

Multiple-Purpose Developments

18

The Smithsonian Institution, largely supported by federal funds and under federal direction, has as its motto "For the Increase and Diffusion of Knowledge among Men." In January, 1925, in the midst of the fight on the Underwood bill, it issued a handsomely printed pamphlet purporting to be an examination of *Niagara Falls; Its Power Possibilities and Preservation*. It was written by Samuel S. Wyer, whose title was given as "Associate in Mineral Technology, United States National Museum." Seemingly it was a report by a reputed government scientist who had made an investigation at the direction of the Smithsonian Institution. Ordinarily, it would never have come to the attention of George W. Norris. But the greater part of this pseudoscientific pamphlet was a diatribe against the publicly owned and operated Ontario hydroelectric system. Figures were presented to prove that the enterprise was not solvent, that it was almost $20 million short of the actual cost of the service furnished by it, though the source of these figures was not mentioned. Moreover, Dr. Charles D. Walcott, secretary and head of the Smithsonian Institution, had written an introduction in which he called special attention to Wyer's assertions of the superiority of private over public ownership.[1]

The pamphlet was widely distributed to newspapers, members of

[1] Investigation revealed that Samuel S. Wyer was not an employee of the Smithsonian Institution and not on its payroll. He was a private consulting engineer, a resident of Columbus, Ohio, who was very actively opposed to public power programs. Most of his statements, Norris felt, were fallacious, misleading, and unfounded; see National Popular Government League, Bulletin 96, Jan. 20, 1925. Judson King was director of the league.

Congress, and numerous other officials. The U.S. Chamber of Commerce republished it in its official journal, *Nation's Business,* and also in pamphlet form; more than 170,000 copies were in circulation in February, 1925. Norris was appalled. He thought the action of the Smithsonian Institution disgraceful and he wrote, virtually apologizing for the pamphlet, to Sir Adam Beck, chairman of the Ontario Hydroelectric Power Commission. "To me," he observed, "it is rather humiliating that we have any Institution connected with our Government, that will issue a pamphlet similar to the Wyer pamphlet, criticizing in language that is hardly respectful, a great governmental activity of a friendly nation." So disturbed was Beck by the pamphlet that he prepared a rejoinder refuting its misstatements and misrepresentations. Appearing when it did, the pamphlet served as a propaganda weapon in favor of private operation of Muscle Shoals, the view that supporters of public ownership imputed to it.[2]

That the imputation contained more than an element of truth is evident from a January, 1925, letter from Charles Walcott in his capacity as secretary of the Smithsonian Institution to Calvin Coolidge. Walcott suggested that "in continuation of the Smithsonian Institution's study of natural resources" there had been no thorough study nor "a concise statement of the outstanding features of the Muscle Shoals power situation." Writing while the controversy over the Underwood bill was at its height, Walcott proposed a "concisely summarized" statement "so that the average intelligent American citizen" could readily "comprehend the energy possibilities and what has been and is now involved in their development and utilization." Within this context and coming after the Wyer report, Walcott's letter indicated that the secretary of the Smithsonian Intsitution was prepared to print more propaganda to help the hard-pressed Coolidge administration get rid of Muscle Shoals.[3]

2 George W. Norris to Bruce Bliven, Mar. 4, 1924; to Adam Beck, Feb. 11, 1925; see also Judson King to Charles D. Walcott, Feb. 25, 1925 (copy in the Harry Slattery Papers, Manuscripts Collections, Duke University Library).

3 Walcott to Calvin Coolidge, Jan. 31, 1925. The president's secretary responded that the president thought Walcott's idea "an excellent one"; see Everett Sanders to Walcott, Feb. 2, 1925 (Box 127, Folder 44, Calvin Coolidge Papers, Manuscript Division, Library of Congress).

On his part Norris intended to discuss the Wyer pamphlet to help avoid a final vote on the Underwood bill if it came to the floor again at the end of the Sixty-eighth Congress. Instead, he waited until the brief special session of the Senate in the new Congress in March, 1925. Then he denounced the pamphlet as propaganda, "pure and simple," and called for the removal of Walcott by the trustees of the Smithsonian Institution. The pamphlet, besides being an indefensible attack on the business methods of a friendly nation, contained facts and figures differing from those found in official sources. While Norris felt Samuel Wyer was acting within his rights as a "professional propagandist," the role of Walcott in printing the pamphlet as a scientific document under government auspices seemingly called for his expulsion. Norris suspected he was acting in accordance with administration wishes, supporting it in the Muscle Shoals controversy. The incident served only to lower the standards of the Smithsonian Institution by using its name on behalf of private interests.[4]

In the early summer of 1925 Norris went to Ontario to see for himself. He traveled by automobile, visiting the principal towns. He went out into the country, talked with farmers, and made as thorough an investigation of the system of generation and distribution of electrical energy as possible. And he acquired a mass of documents. All of this travel and analysis of documents was designed to help him in presenting "as good a front as possible in the Muscle Shoals fight."[5]

At the invitation of a United Press vice-president Norris prepared an account of his trip. The Ontario operation offered an opportunity to compare costs involved in the generation of electricity, something with which private corporations, "interested solely in the almighty dollar," were not always concerned. To maintain their high profits, the "gigantic electric-trust" influenced both political contests and political parties. Magazines and newspapers came under its control, and "the real truth" about costs was withheld

[4] Norris to Bliven, Mar. 4, 1925; to M. L. Cooke, May 13, 1925; *Chattanooga News,* Mar. 19, 1925; *Congressional Record,* 69th Cong., special sess. of Senate, Mar. 18, 1925, pp. 332–61 (Norris's remarks and the voluminous material he inserted pertaining to Ontario Hydro and the Wyer report).
[5] Norris to Carl D. Thompson, July 10, 1925.

from the people. If this power were properly converted into electricity, Norris believed, the labors of man would be lessened and the drudgery of every housewife would be relieved by the efficient work of a universal servant. Through transmission lines the power not in use in one system could be transferred to another so that its blessings would become manifold.

Since electricity was usually generated by property that belonged to the public, Norris felt it should not be converted to private ownership where profit became the primary incentive and the consumer payed exorbitant bills. Since universality in the use of electric current depended upon its price, the lower the price, the more widespread would be its use. To Norris a most wonderful demonstration of the possibilities for the generation and distribution of electric current had been given to the civilized world by the province of Ontario.[6]

While in the United States people paid from 8 to 12 cents per kilowatt-hour for electricity, the cities of Ontario were getting their current at from 2 to 5 cents per kilowatt-hour, "and in many instances at less than two cents." Included in these rates were all items necessary to continue the system indefinitely: maintenance, a sinking fund, repairs and upkeep, emergency expenses, interest, indebtedness, and cost of construction. In the United States, Norris noted, private utility companies made no provision for sinking funds to cancel debts and eventually place the property in a position where the only items of expense would be cost of operation and management. American rates were not likely to be reduced, whereas the prevailing low rates in Canada would go still lower when the original investment could be charged off the books.

Norris suggested that as rates were reduced, current consumption increased materially. "The ordinary home in Ontario," he wrote, "consumes from twice to three and four, and sometimes ten times as much current, as is consumed in similar homes in the

[6] Writing about Sir Adam Beck, founding father of the Ontario system, shortly after his death, Norris said, "The time will come when the natural resources of civilization are in the hands of the people, and when the common folks begin to realize the God-given gifts that can come from the handling of these resources, they will revere the memory of Sir Adam Beck as the slave reveres the memory of his emancipator"; see Norris to Frederick L. Gaby, Aug. 18, 1925.

United States. . . ." In the Canadian home electricity was the ever-available servant, relieving the housewife of labor and saving money for the head of the household at the same time. If the American housewife could see "the lighting, the cooking, the heating, the ironing and the washing, all being done in the Canadian home by this silent and uncomplaining servant," Norris was convinced there would be a clamor that would make Congress and the state legislatures "sit up and take notice." But the benefits of electricity witnessed in Ontario could not occur in the United States until the cost was cheapened. In the United States people paid not only for the actual cost of electricity but also for "premiums on watered stock, profits on fictitious values," and for propaganda, circulated by utility companies, informing the public of benefits they offered while vehemently denouncing publicly operated systems. In short, the American user of electricty paid the cost of his own deception.[7]

Ontario Hydro thus served as an important weapon in Norris's arsenal of information. Again and again he mentioned it as a prime example of the efficacy and efficiency of a publicly owned and operated system. Initially cited in the battle to save Muscle Shoals for public use, Norris constantly referred to Ontario Hydro in his war against utility companies. He continually compared rates, examining typical utility bills always to the marked disadvantage of the American customer.

Besides Muscle Shoals Norris also became involved in another battle for public ownership. While his knowledge of the Ontario system could not be applied at the outset, as the dimensions of the Boulder Canyon project became clear, Norris would find opportunity to use it. His initial comments were made in 1924 when he discussed the danger from floods that continually challenged the farmers of the fertile Imperial Valley, a large portion of which is below sea level and thus has no outlet. Whenever the Colorado River at its lower end spilled over its banks, floodwaters would

---

[7] Draft article written by Norris for the United Press at the request of Paul Mallon, n.d. [June, 1925?]. In Norris to John T. Duncan, Mar. 25, 1926, he tried to explain the system to an interested correspondent. In "Ontario Hydro: A 1925 Tempest in an American Teapot," *Canadian Historical Review*, 49, no. 3 (Sept., 1968): 267–74, I have further developed this account.

pour into the Imperial Valley. A projected canal to carry water for irrigation to the valley would ease the situation. But Norris thought the construction of a dam many miles farther up the Colorado River, at a place known as Black Canyon, would keep waters in check and let them out in such volume as would supply irrigation ditches without causing damage elsewhere.[8]

The Boulder Canyon project immediately faced difficulties. The Yuma reclamation project in Arizona, not too far from the Imperial Valley, was supposed to generate electricity, threatening some of the water used by Imperial Valley farmers for irrigation purposes. Their plight was either too much or too little water. Without an effort to control the Colorado River, their difficulty could not be resolved. The controversy between Imperial Valley farmers and residents of the Yuma project was merely a microcosm of the conflict between Arizona and California, vying for the use of the waters of the Colorado River. Southern California would not realize its development potential without adequate water and Arizona could not exist without it. Water for flood control, irrigation, and power involved conflicting claims between citizens throughout seven states and Mexico. Besides an arrangement between states of both upper and lower basins of the Colorado River, involving the federal government, Mexican interests were also at stake. In the Sixty-eighth Congress a bill introduced by Congressman Philip Swing and Senator Hiram Johnson, both of California, proposed to utilize the resources of the Colorado River effectively. Calvin Coolidge, believing the project a feasible one, favored it.[9]

In February, 1925, a year after his initial remarks on the Boulder Canyon project, Norris again devoted attention to it. Focusing on the Imperial Valley, he said it was one of the most fertile in the world. Created over the centuries by silt coming down the Colorado River, its soil was hundreds of feet deep, easy to farm

[8] *Congressional Record,* 68th Cong., 1st sess., Feb. 21, p. 2895, Feb. 23, 1924, p. 2989.

[9] Paul Kleinsorge, *The Boulder Canyon Project* (Stanford, Calif., 1941), carefully examines its historical and economic aspects. See also Carl Hayden and John E. Raker to Harry Slattery, Aug. 8, 1924; Slattery to William Allen White, May 4, 1933 (both in Slattery Papers). Slattery provided White with conservation material for his biographies of Calvin Coolidge.

and easy to work.[10] Needing only water, a system of irrigation had been developed, and 60,000 people now lived in the valley. Towns, roads, homes, and public buildings revealed a thriving civilization, sustained by an intensive system of cultivation, the products of which were shipped throughout the United States. "It is," Norris asserted, "a veritable empire, made by the toil and the brawn of American citizens." But this empire was beset with problems. Water for its irrigation system was taken from the Colorado River on American soil. The irrigation ditch then ran through beautiful country for many miles in Mexico before reaching the Imperial Valley, its lowest point. Farmers in Mexico, chiefly American citizens, irrigated their lands from the ditch and were not interested in the creation of a canal, called for in the Swing-Johnson bill, passing entirely through American territory.

The residents of the Imperial Valley were absolutely dependent for their existence upon this irrigation ditch. If it were to be destroyed in Mexico, Norris said, "every farm, every home in the entire Imperial Valley would become a desert waste." And if the banks of the river in the lower basin were broken and the channel changed, the Imperial Valley with its cities and farms "would be many feet under the sea." An irrigation company owned and maintained the ditch. While millions of dollars were spent to keep the river in its banks, American farmers, chiefly in the Imperial Valley, paid for the improvements in the form of increasing water rates. They also had to keep expensive equipment in constant readiness in case the Colorado River broke its banks and threatened them with inundation.

A more permanent solution, endorsed by Norris, would be a new irrigation canal that would take the water out of the river on American soil and never cross Mexican territory. Moreover, an all-American canal could irrigate more land because higher levels in the Imperial Valley could be reached, something that could not be done with the winding irrigation ditch then in use. What interested Norris particularly about this proposal was that it called

---

[10] Kleinsorge, *Boulder Canyon Project,* p. 11, writes: "The Colorado has a silt content three times that of the Ganges and ten times that of the Nile. With the possible exception of the Tigris, it is the greatest silt-bearing stream in the world."

for a dam to hold back floodwaters. The hydroelectric power that could be generated "would be equal to the largest water-power development in the United States." Flood control, irrigation, and power development were all involved. It was as a multi-purpose project that Norris endorsed the all-American canal.

However, there was opposition. Power interests were opposed, as were American citizens owning land in Mexico served by the irrigation ditch. Though not a member of the committee concerned with the proposal, Norris examined enough information to justify it in his own mind, claiming an assured market in Los Angeles for the electricity generated if it could not be sold elsewhere. Further surveys and investigations were regarded as dilatory tactics to aid groups opposed to the project; "in the meantime the Colorado River is flowing along, and a flood may at any time break out and drown all those beautiful farms and 60,000 American citizens." Congress, Norris said, was derelict in its duty because it had failed long ago to enact legislation "that would protect these people." [11]

In some respects the Boulder Canyon proposition was more interesting and far reaching than Muscle Shoals. Both were multiple-purpose projects, Boulder Dam bearing the same relation to the Colorado that Muscle Shoals had to the Tennessee River. It would be within transmission distance of many cities, including Los Angeles, while control of floodwaters on the Colorado River would remove the ever-present threat of inundation to its lower basin. The construction of an all-American canal would insure the Imperial Valley continuous water for irrigation without farmers in Mexico first using it. These dramatic aspects were lacking in the Muscle Shoals controversy, though in both instances private power interests opposed the projects. And it was these aspects that challenged Norris's imagination. They were reiterated almost every time he spoke on the subject, and Norris proved a staunch ally to Hiram Johnson in Senate battles on this subject.[12]

Meanwhile, constituents and critics charged Norris with ignoring Nebraska while he fought for programs that would aid the South and save California farmers from destruction. As a senator, they said, he did not truly represent Nebraska. Norris could have re-

[11] *Congressional Record,* 68th Cong., 2nd sess., Feb. 27, 1925, pp. 4805–8.
[12] Norris to Walter Lippmann, Jan. 19, 1925.

sponded by pointing to his fight to aid the farmer and by noting that the Harding and Coolidge administrations had to be prevented from granting the heritage of all citizens to private and privileged groups. In addition, beginning in the Sixty-eighth Congress, he could have mentioned efforts to provide supplemental water for a large area in Nebraska.

Comprising about 500,000 acres of irrigable land covering portions of Adams, Kearney, Phelps, and adjoining counties, the area of the proposed Tri-County project was roughly sixty-five miles long from east to west and ten to twenty miles wide from north to south. It was located in a subhumid region where on an average once in every five years profitable crops were produced. Little rainfall and frequent droughts made agriculture a haphazard proposition for the hardy farmers who persisted in the area. Supplemental irrigation, the concept favored by the promoters of the project, would add sufficient water to the soil to diminish the difference between crop requirements and rainfall. Great Plains farmers had learned that when there was considerable water in the soil at seeding time, either as a carry-over from the previous year or from early spring rains, they were more certain of satisfactory yields. Otherwise the crop would be totally dependent upon opportune rains. Supplemental irrigation would provide water for annual crops and allow for more diversified agriculture as well.[13]

Though Norris was not one of the men who originated the idea, he was their man in Washington. In 1914 he had helped secure a congressional appropriation of $10,000 for a study of the water resources of Nebraska. It resulted in an adverse report. Then in 1922 he introduced a resolution providing for a $5,000 appropriation for further investigation. As approved, it called upon Nebraskans interested in the proposal to furnish funds for the survey. Both instances indicated concern on Norris's part for the intelligent development of Nebraska's water resources. These efforts merely

[13] An excellent history of the Tri-County project is Gene E. Hamaker's Ph.D. thesis (1958) at the University of Nebraska, "Irrigation Pioneers: A History of the Tri-County Project to 1935." It was published in 1964 for the Central Nebraska Public Power and Irrigation District by the Warp Publishing Company of Minden, Nebr. See Norris to Hubert Work, Dec. 10, 1923, for a succinct explanation of the concept of supplemental water.

reflected the concern of Norris's constituents who supported these surveys. Like them, he was convinced that if it were possible to supply supplemental water, a vast area in Nebraska and elsewhere in the semi-arid West could be brought under cultivation.[14]

In June, 1924, the Senate approved a resolution introduced by Norris appropriating funds for a visit to Nebraska of a subcommittee of the Irrigation and Reclamation Committee. Norris hoped the chairman of the House Irrigation and Reclamation Committee could join them. The members would then ascertain for themselves whether the soil could store moisture. The problem, however, was to get to Nebraska. With both parties holding nominating conventions, many members would wish to attend. Norris wrote each western member of the subcommittee that they would be delayed "but a day or so" if they stopped in Nebraska, where a committee of citizens were anxious to show them the "wonderful possibilities in connection with this project." While few found it possible to make a personal inspection, a majority indicated interest in the project.[15]

Confident now of some support, Norris on January 24, 1925, introduced a bill for the construction of the Tri-County project. It was the first Nebraska irrigation bill introduced in Congress. It called upon the Interior Department to construct works for the storage of water and the irrigation of lands which would reclaim initially about 500,000 acres of farm land and eventually up to 4 million acres. Opposition developed because a power proposal was part of the plan and would help pay the expense of the entire project, estimated at $15 million. Nevertheless, the bill was approved by the Senate on February 27, 1925, but at this late date there was no chance that the House would act before Congress adjourned on March 4. However, the matter had been brought to the

[14] Norris to Work, Dec. 10, 1923. For the decade ending in 1922 the average annual gross income per acre in the Tri-County project area, including high prices brought on by the war, was less than $15. It was estimated that with the conclusion of the project some 3 to 4 million acres of land, with an annual gross income of about $40 an acre, would be reclaimed; see *Omaha Bee*, Jan. 25, 1925.

[15] Norris to Elwood Mead, June 3, 1924; to C. W. McConaughy, June 7, 1924; to Lawrence C. Phipps, June 17, 1924; to J. H. Clearman, Dec. 3, 1924.

attention of Congress and Norris had sown seeds which in the following decade would yield sweet results.[16]

Another multi-purpose proposal that caught Norris's attention was the St. Lawrence Waterway. He favored it for two reasons: it would have a tendency to lower freight rates upon western products, and an immense amount of hydroelectric power would be generated. While Nebraskan freight rates would not be directly affected by the seaway, by providing competition, it would reduce rates on some railroads without bankrupting them. History demonstrated, Norris claimed, that competition actually benefited railroads in the form of increased business, much of which would never have come about had it not been for waterway development. The fact that construction of a waterway was necessary before freight rates might be reduced was an indication that "instead of Government regulation of railroads we have railroad regulation of Government." [17] At the outset Norris was interested in the St. Lawrence Waterway as a factor in transportation, particularly in the reduction of freight rates. Later he would consider it in terms of hydroelectric power. It was the only instance where Norris's concern for the intelligent development of a water resource did not quickly lead him to consider the hydroelectric power aspects of the proposal.

By the end of the Sixty-eighth Congress he was the best-informed person in Congress and possibly in Washington on the question of public development of hydroelectric power. Newton D. Baker, for example, informed him about the municipal electric light plant in Cleveland. Norris was a member of the Committee on Coal and Giant Power, composed of citizens who believed that in the development of these resources the interests of consumers and workers should be considered. He was continually interested in hooking up various systems, thereby securing the largest output of electric energy at the least cost. This did not mean that government should

[16] *Omaha Bee*, Jan. 25, 1925; Norris to J. S. Funk, Feb. 4, 1925; to L. Newell, Mar. 4, 1925; *Congressional Record,* 68th Cong., 2nd sess., Feb. 27, 1925, pp. 4846–47. No record was taken. A motion by Senator William King of Utah to reconsider the vote was made and then withdrawn. This action consumed several days. C. W. McConaughy, president of the Central Nebraska Supplemental Water Association, and George B. Kingsley, vice-president, were in Washington at the time Norris introduced the bill, conferring with officials of the Interior Department and members of the Nebraska congressional delegation.

[17] Norris to I. I. Femrite, Nov. 25, 1923; to H. M. Harden, June 23, 1927.

own all the systems involved; rather, Norris believed, "if it held the key situations it would be able to control the cost of electricity throughout the entire country."[18]

A confirmed believer in public ownership, Norris was not disposed to further his position unfairly. In the case of municipal ownership of waterworks, for example, he did not see why municipal, county, and state bonds, which might provide for the local system, should be exempt from taxation.[19] He realized, however, that one of the arguments effectively used against municipal ownership was taxation. To meet this argument, which usually had a great impact on voters, Norris was willing that public property be subject to the same taxation as privately owned property because of the benefits he envisioned from public ownership.[20]

Basic to his involvement in these fights was the fact that agriculture eventually would benefit. Only when the farmer enjoyed "this modern method of relieving human toil," when the farm home was equipped with facilities that electricity made possible, could the farmer begin to live on a par with the comfortable city dweller. Electricity, Norris said, would do more than any other single thing to keep people in rural areas.[21] The plight of the farmer was never far from Norris's thoughts in the battles he waged in the Harding-Coolidge era. As he returned to the Senate for the Sixty-ninth Congress, secure in his third-term victory, to meet the challenges posed by an equally secure president, fortified by an overwhelming vote of confidence from the American people, Norris was convinced of the righteousness of his views. And he was strong enough in his independent stance to be unconcerned about the political consequences of his actions.

[18] Newton D. Baker to Norris, Feb. 21 and 27, 1925 (Box 177, Newton D. Baker Papers, Manuscript Division, Library of Congress); Norris to Lippmann, Jan. 19, 1925. At this time Baker favored Norris's position on Muscle Shoals and seemed to have some doubts about his previous opposition to the Great Falls proposal.

[19] Norris to Thompson, June 13, 1924.

[20] Norris to Charles K. McClatchy, Apr. 3, 1925.

[21] *Ibid.*

The Business of the United States Is Business

19

Though the Coolidge administration was devoid of significant legislation, it represented a triumph of Republicanism in a period of partial prosperity. The party was rife with tensions that threatened to wrench it asunder. But the Democratic split, more serious than the Republican, usually attracted the attention. Ethnic and sectional differences reflecting urban-rural strains indicative of the future of American politics disrupted the Democrats. Republican divisions were along the more familiar progressive and conservative lines. The antimonopoly theme that had aroused rural radicals in the post–Civil War years was reflected in Congress by their heirs in the Republican party. While most Americans were seeking to "keep cool with Coolidge," a minority of Republicans in Congress fought to have their party concern itself with the agricultural heartland of the nation, proving themselves a continual thorn in the side of their party's leaders.

With the convening of a special session of the Senate on March 4, 1925, immediately after Calvin Coolidge was inaugurated as president in his own right, altercations within the Republican ranks flared anew. The progressive faction challenged Coolidge's appointments and committee choices. Once Charles G. Dawes was inaugurated as vice-president, Senator Albert B. Cummins, who as president pro tem of the Senate had enjoyed the perquisites of the office of vice-president, chose to return to the chairmanship of the Interstate Commerce Committee, a post previously occupied because of intraparty strife by a South Carolina Democrat, Ellison D. Smith. Cummins's return to the Interstate Commerce Committee chairmanship meant that George W. Norris was next in line to head the Judiciary Committee. Because Norris was regarded as having maintained a position of neutrality in the presidential campaign, there was little opposition to his shifting in 1926 from the chairmanship of the Agriculture and Forestry Committee to that of Judiciary. On the other hand, Senators Edwin F. Ladd and Lynn J. Frazier of North Dakota and Smith W. Brookhart of Iowa were dropped by the "regulars" from the Republican organization of the Senate in the Sixty-ninth Congress for their support of LaFollette in the 1924 campaign.[1]

Shortly after the special session of the Senate Norris was faced with a serious personnel problem. His secretary, Mabelle J. Talbert, announced her intention to resign. Losing his secretary at this time, he said, was comparable to losing a "trusted lieutenant that knew the ground and understood the nature of the opposition forces and weapons. . . ." He was deeply distressed and felt that he would break under the strain of assuming her burdens in addition to his own.[2] At this juncture his son-in-law, John P. Robertson, left his bank job in Broken Bow, Nebraska, moved to Washington, and assumed responsibilities as secretary. Norris was never again bothered with this problem. When the regular session convened in December, his son-in-law soon was functioning effectively in his new position. Though the despair over Mrs. Talbert's resignation was severe, Norris's inconvenience was minimal.

At the outset of the special session Norris complained about the efficiency of the Senate. He said that senators were on too many committees; older members served on five or six. Instead of relinquishing their positions to newer members, they retained their assignments and then proved unable to meet their responsibilities.

1 *Washington Herald,* Nov. 9, 1924 (story by Cole E. Morgan). Frazier and Brookhart, later re-elected as Republicans, were taken back into the party fold. Both Ladd and LaFollette died in June, 1925. For Norris's comments on proposed assignments in the new Congress whereby progressives whenever possible were kept off key committees, see *Congressional Record,* 69th Cong., special sess. of Senate, Mar. 9, 1925, pp. 64–67. For his shifting of committee assignments, see *ibid.,* 1st sess., July 2, 1926, p. 12885; 2nd sess., Dec. 14, 1926, p. 419.

2 George W. Norris to Walter Locke, July 12, 1925.

Rather than increase the membership of committees, Norris preferred to reduce their size, limiting the number of assignments of each senator. Moreover, senior senators with major committee assignments predominated on conference committees and exerted tremendous influence, leaving little opportunity for junior members. Though interest was elicited and Norris tried to practice what he preached, little was done to challenge "standpat" control of the Senate by either party.[3]

Something was done each time Norris introduced his lame-duck amendment. His Senate colleagues quickly approved it, but it usually was prevented by the Speaker from coming to a vote in the House. At the end of each short session of the Senate Norris complained of the reckless approval of measures leading to ill-considered legislation. The necessity to legislate practically by unanimous consent encouraged "any Senator to hold up almost any measure and in that way often to secure anything he may desire." Filibusters were encouraged and retiring members were voting on bills, though their successors had already been selected. Norris asserted bitterly that in no other country or state in the Union was such an outworn system in effect. The president and the Speaker of the House received the blame for opposing his proposed amendment, which, Norris claimed, the vast majority of American people favored.[4]

[3] *Congressional Record,* 69th Cong., special sess. of Senate, Mar. 6, 1925, pp. 12–14. Norris opposed raising the salaries of members of Congress to $10,000, "not because the work if conscientiously done, is not fully worth the increased rate of compensation, but rather because there is need at this time, for every possible economy"; see Norris to Hershel A. Soskin, Mar. 19, 1925.

[4] *Congressional Record,* 68th Cong., 2nd sess., Feb. 18, 1925, pp. 4008–11; 69th Cong., 1st sess., Feb. 1, pp. 3083–84, Feb. 15, 1926, pp. 3968–70. In the Sixty-ninth Congress the joint resolution introduced by Norris calling for a constitutional amendment to abolish the short session passed the Senate for the third time. On the first occasion there were seven Senate votes against it, on Feb. 15, 1926, only two. See also *ibid.,* 2nd sess., Mar. 3, 1927, p. 5503; 70th Cong., 1st sess., Jan. 4, 1928, pp. 952–55. In this session six senators voted against the joint resolution. It passed the Senate for the fourth successive time only to be stymied again by the House leadership. The *Saturday Evening Post,* Feb. 13, 1926, carried an article by Norris entitled "Reform of the Senate Rules." An answer to Vice-President Dawes's call for reform in legislative procedures, it was largely a plea for his proposed amendment (reprinted in *Congressional Record,* 69th Cong., 1st sess., Feb. 15, 1926, pp. 3962–64). For further analytical comments, see Norris to Christian A. Herter, Jan. 1, 1925; to Elliot A. Adams, July 15, 1925; to Frank

Norris also called attention to other Senate practices he disliked. Cloture by a majority vote would remove the last vestige of fair and honest parliamentary consideration, allowing a handful of powerful senators to work their will or their party's without allowing the opposition to be fully heard. But more important than the question of cloture was the fundamental fact that filibusters usually occurred during the short session or in a long session where the date of adjournment had been definitely determined. If a majority of the Senate was in favor of any legislation and the date of adjournment was not determined, a filibuster could have but little effect and most likely would not be attempted. Eliminate the short session and the threat of filibuster would lose its potency, and the Senate could more effectively fulfill its function as a forum for discussing legislation.[5]

In Norris's judgment the Senate did have many fine attributes, despite criticism against it. Legislation was accomplished primarily there. The House was handicapped because of its size. Despite many able members, from necessity its authority had to be delegated to a few party leaders. The House could not truly deliberate. It did not have time to analyze pending bills properly and all too often it enacted "imperfect, half-baked legislation." Norris believed no remedy could be effected until men of courage and conviction awakened to the fact that the House of Representatives had to be reduced in membership.[6] This criticism was related to his attitude toward the Speaker, Nicholas Longworth. Norris believed the Speaker would have allowed the House to vote upon his lame-duck amendment if the president had been willing; Longworth

A. Harrison, June 28, 1926; to John Q. Sargent, Feb. 13, 1927; to A. S. Goss, Mar. 16, 1928; Norris, "The Lame Duck Amendment to the Constitution," n.d. [1929?] (draft article).

[5] Norris to Richard C. Browne, July 13, 1926; to Locke, Mar. 13, 1925, Mar. 6, 1927. Norris was fully aware that the legislative situation in a short session occasionally could work in his favor as well. The Underwood bill was eliminated in a short session, and the controversy over the armed-ship bill occurred during an earlier short session. Norris still favored its elimination. There is a long discussion of cloture and filibustering by Norris in "Reform of the Senate Rules," pp. 27, 169–73.

[6] Norris to Roscoe J. Anderson, Mar. 7, 1926; to Locke, Mar. 13, 1925; Norris, "Should Debate in the Senate Be Further Limited," *Congressional Digest,* 5, no. 11 (Nov., 1926): 306.

himself did not care one way or the other. The situation was humiliating, considering that "the one branch which is supposed to represent the common people of the country, could under a free Government, be thus controlled." It also demonstrated that a large legislative body could be manipulated more easily than a comparatively small one.[7]

Commenting on the power of the president to frustrate constructive legislation, Norris reflected, as Lord Bryce did earlier, on the question of why qualified men were disqualified from becoming president. Something seemed wrong when "those who are not qualified are the ones who can be elected" to high office. What was wrong was summed up in the word "partisanship"; it, combined with "the antiquated and worse than useless electoral college," was an insurmountable barrier in the pathway of any independent candidate for president.[8] If a person could run for president independently of all parties, then truly outstanding citizens might become candidates and political machines would be seriously threatened. The presidential primary was one method and Norris continually endorsed the concept and introduced an amendment calling for such a system. He assumed that most citizens were opposed to partisanship and political machines but were subjugated by a system that, in effect, deprived them of a meaningful voice in government. Accepting the proposition that American democracy was predicated upon the belief that people were sufficiently intelligent to control their government, Norris based his support on the primary upon it. Until a better system was suggested, he thought efforts should be made to improve it. Relieving party machinery of much of its responsibility, the primary placed it firmly upon the individual voter, who would have to inform himself more fully upon "all the questions pertaining to government." The result would be a more intelligent electorate and better government, though Norris did not envision the millennium because of it. What he did envision was

[7] Norris to Locke, Mar. 19, 1927.

[8] Norris to Locke, Feb. 6, 1928; to Franklin D. Roosevelt, Dec. 28, 1928. Norris suggested to Roosevelt a way of improving the operation of the Electoral College, though he was extremely critical of it as an operative institution in a democratic society.

a plan "by which the people would come as nearly as possible into the control of their own Government." [9]

Norris further incurred the wrath of the party leadership when he denounced secrecy in the Senate. To the question of whether executive sessions of the Senate were ever necessary, Norris replied that "no such necessity exists or ever has existed." The confirmation of public officials was a public duty; during the Coolidge years it was of greater moment than most matters of legislation. Norris insisted that the votes of a public official be a matter of public record. In the second session of the Seventieth Congress he was instrumental in loosening Senate rules pertaining to secrecy. Instead of the former two-thirds vote a simple majority henceforth could compel the transaction of executive business in the open.[10] Though this concession came late in the Coolidge administration, Norris waged greater battles challenging the qualifications of nominees to high public office. Rarely was he successful. But throughout these years the opposition of Norris and others revealed that the Republican party was almost as seriously split along progressive and conservative lines as during the administration of William Howard Taft.

The first Coolidge appointment Norris criticized was probably the most distinguished one made by the president. Arguing that "the man who has spent all his life in an atmosphere of big business, of corporations, of monopolies and trusts," will be imbued with ideas that inevitably would be reflected in his decisions, Norris opposed the nomination of Attorney General Harlan Fiske Stone, a former attorney for J. P. Morgan & Company, to a place on the Supreme Court of the United States. He said, "If we fill the bench and high executive offices with men who have the viewpoint of

[9] "An Article by Senator George W. Norris, of Nebraska, Regarding the Primary Elections," *Congressional Record,* 69th Cong., 2nd sess., Feb. 2, 1927, p. 2843; Norris statement regarding his presidential primary bill, n.d. [1922?]. Norris would have desired to go one step further and take the party label off the official ballot. The primary would narrow the candidates down to two; in the election there would be no party label on the ballot. For a discussion on this point, see Norris to Basil Manly, July 9, 1925.

[10] Norris to Hugh Russell Fraser, June 22, 1929; *Congressional Record,* 70th Cong., 2nd sess., Jan. 3, 1929, pp. 2519–20, 2522.

special interests and corporations, we will soon have put the common citizen under the yoke of monopoly, and will have put our Government in the hands of trusts and corporations." [11]

While the nominee changed, Norris's arguments against Coolidge's appointees were essentially variations on a theme. In successfully challenging Charles Beecher Warren of Michigan to succeed Harlan Fiske Stone as Attorney General, a severe blow was dealt the Coolidge administration. Actually, Norris did not play a major role in opposing Warren's nomination. Though he was rejected twice by the Senate, Norris spoke only the second time. Nevertheless, his remarks illuminated the entire controversy. [12] The crux of his opposition rested upon the fact that earlier in his career Warren "was quite active in assisting the American Sugar Trust in obtaining a complete control and domination of the sugar market and sugar production in the United States." Warren resigned as president of the Michigan Sugar Company in January, 1925, when Coolidge first considered bringing him into the government. [13] By recalling the sordid side of the American Sugar Refining Company's efforts to dominate the beet-sugar industries of the West, Norris identified Warren with monopoly and remarked that as Attorney General an organizer of trusts would have charge of the prosecution of trusts. Norris insisted that "we want a man who has a clean record of obedience of law himself, and who does not have to get behind the statute of limitations in order to have clean skirts, either." [14]

The Senate, twice rejecting the appointment of Charles B. Warren as Attorney General, for the first time since the presidency of Andrew Johnson refused a cabinet nomination. Out of this rejection came one of the great comic episodes in Senate history. On March 11, 1925, when the Senate first voted on Warren's nomination, the

[11] *Congressional Record,* 68th Cong., 2nd sess., Feb. 5, 1925, p. 3053; Norris to A. F. Buechler, Apr. 17, 1925.

[12] For a full discussion of "The Warren Case," see the article of that title by Felix A. Nigro in *Western Political Quarterly,* 11, no. 4 (Dec., 1958): 835–56. Warren was prominent in Republican party circles and had previously served as ambassador to Japan and Mexico. If considered for Secretary of State, he would have been well qualified.

[13] In Feb., 1925, the Federal Trade Commission charged the Michigan Sugar Company with a violation of the antitrust laws of the United States.

[14] *Congressional Record,* 69th Cong., special sess. of Senate, Mar. 16, 1925, pp. 268–69.

result was a tie, 40 yeas and 40 nays, despite the fact that Republicans predominated in the Senate 56 to 39. Vice-President Dawes, who would have broken the tie had he been in the chair, was called from his suite at the Willard Hotel, where he had retired for a nap. Dawes dressed hastily, ran frantically for a taxi, and arrived disheveled on the Senate floor—shortly after Democrat Lee Overman of North Carolina had changed his yea to a nay, thereby shifting the vote to 39 in favor and 41 opposed.[15]

The next day Norris read the following parody of "Sheridan's Ride" while gales of laughter rocked the Senate chamber:

> Up from the East, out into the day,
> Bringing to the Willard fresh dismay,
> The affrighted air with a shudder bore
> Like a herald in haste, to the chieftain's door,
> The terrible grumble and rumble and roar,
> Telling the battle was on once more.
> And Dawes fully fifteen blocks away.
>
> And under still those billows of war
> Thundered along the horizon's bar;
> And louder yet into the Willard rolled
> The roar of that Senate uncontrolled,
> Making the blood of the listener cold,
> As he thought of the stake in Senatorial fray,
> And Dawes fully fifteen blocks away.
>
> But there's a street from the Willard's feast
> A good broad highway leading east,
> And there, through the flush of the fading light,
> An auto as black as the steeds of night
> Was seen to pass as the eagle flight,
> As if it knew the terrible need;
> It stretched away with the utmost speed;
> Hills rose and fell, but its heart was gay,
> With Dawes now only ten blocks away.
>
> Still sprung from those swift wheels, thundering on,
> The dust like smoke from the cannon's mouth;
> On the trail of a comet sweeping faster and faster,

[15] Norris to H. J. Kennedy, Mar. 17, 1925 (printed in *Congressional Record*, 69th Cong., special sess. of Senate, Mar. 17, 1925, p. 297); to Clarence Reckmeyer, Mar. 30, 1925.

Foreboding to traitors the doom of disaster.
The heart of the auto and the heart of the master
Were beating like prisoners assaulting their walls.
Impatient to answer the Senate's fierce calls;
Every nerve of the auto was strained to full play,
With Dawes now only five blocks away.

Under its spurning wheels the road
Like an arrowy river flowed,
And the Willard sped away behind
Like an ocean flying before the wind.
And the auto, like a bark fed with furnace fire,
Swept on, with its wild shriek full of ire.
But lo! it is nearing its heart's desire;
It is snuffing the smoke of the roaring fray,
With Dawes now only two blocks away.

The first that the General saw were the groups
Of Senators, and then the retreating ones.
What was done? What to do? A glance told him both,
And striking his fists, with a terrible oath
He dashed down the aisle, 'mid a storm of hurrahs,
And the wave of retreat checked its course there because
The rights of the master compelled it to pause.
With steam and with dust, the black auto was gray,
By the flash of its light and its red fire's play,
It seemed to the whole great Senate to say,
"I have brought you Dawes all the way,
From the Willard, down to save the day."

Hurrah, Hurrah for Dawes!
Hurrah! hurrah for this high-minded man!
And when his statue is placed on high,
Under the dome of the Capitol sky,
The Great Senatorial temple of fame,
There with the glorious General's name
Be it said, in letters both bold and bright,
"Oh, Hell an' Maria, he has lost us the fight." [16]

Norris was more bitter than this parody suggested over Coolidge's
appointments: "No man has a ghost of a show in this administration

[16] *Congressional Record,* 69th Cong., special sess. of Senate, Mar. 12, 1925,
p. 150.

of being appointed unless he holds the viewpoint of Big Business." In failing to recognize other viewpoints, Coolidge could not be charged with dishonesty or insincerity. Basically, he believed that the best way to manage the railroads was to put a railroad man on the Interstate Commerce Commission. Hence, Thomas F. Woodlock resigned from the New York Stock Exchange and from the directorships of at least two railroads to accept the place. Twice refused confirmation by the Senate, Coolidge in 1925 gave him a recess appointment.[17]

"Whoever imagined," Norris asserted, ". . . that any President would select an official of a great railroad for a position on the Interstate Commerce Commission?" Earlier, before World War I, such a suggestion would have been ridiculed as "perfectly foolish and unthinkable." Now no protest arose. "Why have an Interstate Commerce Commission to regulate railroads if we are going to let the railroads run the Interstate Commerce Commission?" To Norris it would have been cheaper to abolish the commission and let the railroads regulate themsleves than continue the Coolidge pattern of appointments. Packing the commission with men whose sympathies were with the railroads and by implication, therefore, "against the people" controverted "the very intention and theory of the Act creating a Commission." [18]

Moreover, the Senate refused to reveal the vote upon Woodlock's confirmation. The rules provided that secret votes be taken in executive session, and nominations made by the president had to be considered in this way. Thus no senator could tell how he had voted without violating the rules and being liable to expulsion. Only by unanimous consent could a roll-call vote be published; in Woodlock's case it was not forthcoming. Upon an important question where public opinion was "sharply divided," the Senate had sought to resolve an aspect of it behind closed doors. Not only had the public the right to know but each senator had a right to

[17] After his resignation from the Interstate Commerce Commission in Aug., 1930, Woodlock became editor of the *Wall Street Journal.* For an interesting discussion of the political background of Woodlock's confirmation by the Senate in 1926, see I. L. Sharfman, *The Interstate Commerce Commission,* Part II (New York, 1931), pp. 461–62, note 211.

[18] Norris to Buechler, Apr. 17, 1925; to Harry M. Stager, Mar. 30, 1925; Norris, "Boring from Within," *Nation,* Sept. 16, 1925, p. 297.

explain or defend his vote. Otherwise, Norris said, the party in power, through the president, could control Senate action on appointments and be more influential in other matters.[19]

Even more disturbing was the situation on the Federal Trade Commission. In appointing William E. Humphrey, Coolidge had chosen a standpat politician whose record revealed no sympathy with small businessmen. The animating idea of the Federal Trade Commission was to prevent unfair competition and "extortion of the people." Instead of curbing corporations and restraining combinations engaged in illegal practices at the public's expense, appointments such as Humphrey's would provide "a fearless advocate of big business in all lines." The conclusion was similar to the one reached with Woodlock's appointment to the Interstate Commerce Commission. What was the use of a Federal Trade Commission if men who were meant to be regulated in effect owned the commission? Norris concluded, "Better abolish it and save the money of the people." Humphrey's appointment shifted the balance in support of big business and made the commission "the refuge for monopoly, unfair competition, and unfair business methods." Thereafter, it decided that much of its business could be transacted in secret, angering Norris, who thought secrecy contrary to "the very fundamental principles upon which our liberties rest." Operating as a secret tribunal, the Federal Trade Commission would decide matters in which the public interest was involved and millions of dollars were at stake. And the public would get no knowledge of what actually transpired.[20]

[19] Norris, "Secrecy in the Senate," *Nation*, May 5, 1926, pp. 498–99.

[20] Norris to Buechler, Apr. 17, 1925; to Gus Norberg, Mar. 31, 1925; to Locke, Feb. 13, 1926; Norris, "Boring from Within," pp. 297–98; Norris statement on Federal Trade Commission, Nov. 17, 1925. Howard H. Quint and Robert H. Ferrell, *The Talkative President* (Amherst, Mass., 1964), p. 68, call Humphrey a reactionary and note that his appointment "changed the character of the Commission from one that sought to some extent to police the business world to one that literally removed all government restraints upon it." Norris was further annoyed at the Federal Trade Commission because in spite of a Senate mandate for which he was largely responsible, it had refused to investigate the "Electric Trust." But with the new composition of the commission, he was not sure whether he cared for an investigation by men "so involved with reactionary sentiment and so partisan in their make-up, that they would not see a wrong committed by a big trust or a monopoly," even though it did appear as "huge as high Olympus!"; see Norris to Manly, July 9, 1925. The *New York American*, Jan. 16, 1925, con-

Another incident that illustrated the leaning of the Coolidge administration toward big business was the failure of the president to send the name of David J. Lewis, a member of the Tariff Commission, to the Senate after granting him a recess appointment. At the outset of the 1924 campaign the commission was investigating the sugar schedule. The family of one of the commissioners and possibly the commissioner himself owned large amounts of stock whose value was affected by the tariff. Lewis, whose term expired during the campaign, had brought this information to the public's attention. Rather than refuse Lewis reappointment and make the matter a campaign issue, Coolidge gave him a recess appointment and then refused to send his name to the Senate for confirmation after the election, substituting that of Alfred P. Dennis, a personal friend.

With David J. Lewis, "one of the fairest and best men who ever sat on the commission," removed from office, there still remained two commissioners, William S. Culbertson and Edward P. Costigan, who pursued their responsibilities without fear or favor. Coolidge replaced Culbertson by offering him a diplomatic appointment to Rumania, leaving Costigan to finish out his term surrounded by Coolidge's high-tariff appointees. Raising the same point as in the case of other commissions, Norris queried, "Why have a Tariff Commission if we are to place it in control of tariff lobbyists and others interested in and believing in the mountain-high Tariff?" It would be cheaper and more efficient to abolish the commission. The bureaucracy could be reduced and taxpayers would be saved the expense of staffing it.[21]

Commissions, Norris asserted, were established for a definite purpose in response "to an honest demand to regulate aspects of

tained an account of the Norris resolution. For a longer and more comprehensive analysis of the commission by Norris, see *Congressional Record,* 69th Cong., 1st sess., Mar. 20, 1926, pp. 5962–63, 5966, 5968. See also G. Cullom Davis, "The Transformation of the Federal Trade Commission," *Mississippi Valley Historical Review,* 49 (1962): 437–55.

[21] Norris, "Boring from Within," p. 298. Norris earlier had spoken against the appointment of Henry H. Glassie on the ground that he was financially interested in sugar companies directly affected by the tariff; see *Congressional Record,* 68th Cong., 1st sess., Apr. 11, 1924, pp. 6099–6100. The "packing" of the Tariff Commission, it should be mentioned, began and was well advanced under Warren G. Harding; see Norris to G. H. Payne, Feb. 17, 1924.

the American economy." Coolidge's appointments violated their spirit and indicated a return to the very conditions the commissions were designed to curb. Norris said they set the country back at least twenty-five years. Indirectly but effectively they repealed congressional enactments and nullified federal laws "by a process of boring from within." Though out of joint with his party and possibly with his times, since little public clamor was raised against Coolidge's appointments, Norris criticized and challenged them all.[22]

In January, 1926, Norris spoke in behalf of resolutions calling for an investigation of the Tariff Commission. He charged Coolidge with secret understandings with appointees and with using the commission for partisan purposes to build "a tariff without regard to scientific information." Norris followed a theme expressed by William Allen White: "After his election in 1924 President Coolidge felt definitely the mandate to reconstruct American Government along the lines of his own deep conviction that the business of America is business." [23] He examined the recent history of the Tariff Commission, showing this dictum being enforced with vengeance in the cases of Commissioners David J. Lewis, William S. Culbertson, and Henry H. Glassie. Lewis and Culbertson, who sought to enforce the law without regard to protectionist pressures, were replaced. But the president found nothing wrong in Glassie's participation in a sugar case, though his family owned at least $200,000 par value of stock in a sugar corporation. Thus the Tariff Commission, packed with avowed protectionists, sat not as an unbiased judge but rather as an avowed advocate of protected industries. Men like Norris, who placed justice before profits, were appalled at the way Coolidge imposed his almost mystical belief in the ordination of wealth on the Tariff Commission.[24]

[22] Norris to Buechler, Apr. 17, 1925; Norris, "Boring from Within," p. 299. This article had been turned down by two magazines whose editors thought it ran against the tide of public opinion. For an interesting selection of Norris's views on this trend and American journalism, see Norris to Oswald G. Villard, Aug. 5, 1925.

[23] William Allen White, "The Mind of Coolidge," *Collier's,* Dec. 26, 1925, p. 32.

[24] *Congressional Record,* 69th Cong., 1st sess., Jan. 16, pp. 2187–89, Jan. 23, 1926, pp. 2630–36. In Apr., 1926, legislation was enacted which provided that no part of the appropriation for the use of the Tariff Commission should be used to pay the salary of any member who participated in any investigation in which he

The law provided that commission members had to be divided equally between the parties. But this fact did not neutralize partisanship. Norris asserted that the president could always find men in the opposition party sympathetic to his views. Consequently, partisanship permeated the operation of the entire commission system. The few exceptions, men like William Kent, David J. Lewis, William S. Culbertson, and Edward P. Costigan, all of whom served on the Tariff Commission, either resigned, were removed, or were not reappointed. Norris believed that commission members, like judges, should transcend party lines and not be moved in their official actions by partisanship. Commissioners who behaved in this way despite demands, threats, and allurements to act otherwise received Norris's highest commendation whether he agreed with their views or not.[25]

Remarks in 1925 and 1926 against Coolidge's appointments constituted Norris's chief barrage against the administration. At the end of Coolidge's tenure he raised bitter objections to the selection of Roy O. West as Secretary of the Interior to replace Hubert Work, who in turn had succeeded Albert B. Fall in this sensitive post. West was an attorney for utility magnate Samuel J. Insull. As Secretary of the Interior he would automatically serve as a member of the Federal Power Commission, passing on applications for power sites and other related matters. The fact that the vote on West's nomination was secret further aroused Norris, serving as another example of the degradation of the democratic process during the presidency of Calvin Coolidge.[26]

One way to weaken the influence of business in government,

or his family had a direct pecuniary influence. Only then did Commissioner Glassie excuse himself from participating in the sugar tariff case.

[25] *Ibid.,* Mar. 11, 1926, pp. 5379–81. See also the important article by J. Richard Snyder, "Coolidge, Costigan and the Tariff Commission," *Mid-America,* 50, no. 2 (1968): 131–48.

[26] Norris statement, "Public Business Transacted in Secret" (draft), Jan. 24, 1929; Norris to George F. Hibner, Feb. 12, 1929. On June 18, 1929, by a vote of 69 to 5 the Senate changed its rules so that all of its business, including the consideration of nominations and treaties, would be transacted in open session unless it decided by a majority vote in closed session that a particular nomination or treaty should be considered in secret; see George W. Pepper, *Family Quarrels* (New York, 1931), pp. 13–14. For a discussion of West's connection with the Insull interests, see *Washington News,* Dec. 18, 1928.

Norris said, was to loosen the ties of partisanship. If people could realize that government was organized essentially "to perpetuate the happiness of the people governed" and that political parties were "only instrumentalities for the purpose of bringing about governmental results," then beneficial changes could occur. Removing the party circle on the state and local levels would be an initial step. Deciding state, county, and local matters on their own terms, uninfluenced by the way national parties viewed national issues, would be another step in eliminating extreme partisanship from the body politic.[27]

On the national level and in his own party, as long as Calvin Coolidge was president, little could be done. Norris even thought that Coolidge's vaunted views on economy were fraudulent. At one time Coolidge announced he was economizing by riding coach from Washington to Chicago, but later, Norris noted, "he went in a special train from Washington to Massachusetts to cast his vote when he might have performed the same operation by the use of a two cent postage stamp." But Coolidge was popular because the public believed that he was practicing economy by riding in a coach, "or prohibiting the use of paper cups at government drinking places," or receiving bids from wealthy people seeking to have him vacation on their estates. Indeed, few people were anything but satisfied with their president.[28]

With his continual attacks upon the Coolidge administration, its personnel, and its policies, Norris became, after the deaths of both Bryan and LaFollette in 1925, the outstanding progressive in

[27] Norris to John G. Maher, Apr. 16, 1927; to Bruce B. Johnson, Oct. 28, 1927; to Adam McMullen, Apr. 28, 1928.

[28] Norris to C. A. Sorensen, May 15, 1927. So critical was Norris of the president that in 1928 an accusation was made in Nebraska that he had called Coolidge a crook in a Senate debate. Actually, Norris was quoting from a 1924 Democratic campaign document but even that document made no such charge. An article in *Liberty Magazine,* Apr. 7, 1928, quoting from a speech by Joseph T. Robinson, implied that the Arkansas Democrat had said he would defend Coolidge against the charge of a Republican senator that he was a crook. Norris had said nothing of the kind and the intimation Robinson made was without any warrant whatever, but opponents of Norris in Nebraska carried the intimation to its logical conclusion. Norris wrote to the editor of *Liberty Magazine* seeking a correction; see Norris to Joseph T. Robinson, May 3, 1928; to the editor, *Liberty Magazine,* May 11, 1928.

American public life. LaFollette died on June 18, 1925, and Norris, after attending the funeral in Madison, could not recall anything in public affairs that had made such a deep impression on him. LaFollette's death was "the most serious loss that honest Government could sustain."

All roads into Madison, Norris said, were blocked with automobiles carrying people who felt they had lost a friend: "Men, women, and children stood for many hours in the hot, boiling sun, waiting for an opportunity to pass by the bier. The crowd formed two and two, and extended for many blocks. There were no silk hats and broadcloth suits. Men in shirtsleeves; little children barefooted; students of universities, teachers in public schools; laborers, —all classes of people excepting what might be termed the aristocracy." Equally impressive was the fact that this mighty throng of people needed no policemen to keep them in order. At the cemetery, standing at one end of the open grave and viewing Mrs. LaFollette standing between her two sons while the coffin was being lowered in the earth, Norris thought Belle Case LaFollette "beautiful in a loveliness" that he had never seen in her before. No tears moistened her eyes, nor did she reveal a single emotion as she looked upon the descending coffin except, Norris noted, "the twitching and the clutching of her fingers as she grasped the hand of one of her boys." Later that evening at Maple Bluff Farm she discussed the senator with Norris almost as calmly as if he had been alive and well.[29]

Though he had not always agreed with LaFollette, Norris was convinced of his greatness. He had imbued more hearts with hope than any other man of his day. A true progressive, "his was the voice of justice and humanity, calling God's common people to battle for righteousness." In his battles against monopoly and greed, Norris said, "never once did he compromise with sin or surrender to wrong" and "never once for the sake of personal advancement did he deviate from his chosen path in the cause of human freedom." LaFollette's greatness was more impressive because "in many of the greatest fights of his life, he knew in advance that he would fail." The struggle for human betterment, LaFollette knew, was slow; ultimate victory would come to those who profited by

[29] Norris to Harrison, June 26, 1925.

the sacrifices of their predecessors. To men like LaFollette, Norris wrote, "civilization is indebted for every step of human progress." [30]

No sooner had the Wisconsin senator died than Norris was deluged with letters requesting him to assume, or merely taking it for granted that he had assumed, the leadership of the Progressive party. But Norris did not want the leadership of any party and, indeed, had not been in favor of the third-party organization in 1924. Rather than lead a third party, Norris hoped others would join him in seeking independence of all parties by refusing to support nominees who would not make good officials. The choice would be an individual determinant and not a group or organizational decision. While he would work in unison with anyone, "regardless of his party affiliation," who advocated "the same progressive principles of Government" that he supported, Norris did not want to be associated with any political party as its leader.[31]

Norris was interested in who would succeed LaFollette in the Senate. During the three days he was in Madison, leading men of both parties from all parts of Wisconsin spoke to him in the hope that he could convince Belle Case LaFollette to fill the unexpired term of her husband. But she unhesitatingly declined, even though "it probably would have brought to her the greatest honor that up to this time had ever been conferred upon woman." Norris went to the funeral thinking that Philip would prove an able successor to his father. To his surprise he learned that Philip LaFollette was only twenty-eight years old and thus not qualified under the Constitution. The older son, Robert, Jr., became a candidate to succeed his father. Having served as his father's secretary, he was well acquainted with public questions and had been an active participant in his father's affairs. Moreover, Norris knew, Robert, Jr., was fundamentally right in his views on basic principles of government.[32]

[30] *Ibid.;* draft statement of Norris's eulogy of LaFollette, n.d. Norris spoke at the memorial service held in the Senate on June 20, 1926; see *Congressional Record,* 69th Cong., 1st sess., pp. 11651–52. For a moving account of the funeral of Robert M. LaFollette, see Belle Case and Fola LaFollette, *Robert M. LaFollette,* 2 vols. (New York, 1953), 2: 1170–74.

[31] Norris to Warren Shaw Fisher, July 2, 1925; *New York Evening World,* July 8, 1925, "Mr. Norris Does Not Wish to Lead a Party" (editorial); Norris to Thomas E. Pugh, July 10, 1925; to Edwin Koppel, July 12, 1925.

[32] Norris to Harrison, June 26, 1925; to Mrs. Robert M. LaFollette, Sept. 25, 1925.

Later, vacationing at his summer cottage, Norris corresponded with Robert M. LaFollette, Jr., and offered his encouragement. In September he wrote Mrs. LaFollette after having observed him campaign. The way "Young Bob" handled "the questions of the campaign, and the wonderful response that he received from that tremendous crowd and the ovation that they gave him" made Norris think that perhaps "there was satisfaction enough to have lived, to have fought, and to have died before victory was obtained." Norris was confident that "Young Bob" would win a wonderful victory in November and would make a record in the Senate of which his father would have been exceedingly proud.[33]

In July, 1925, a month after attending the funeral of LaFollette, Norris was in Washington at the funeral of William Jennings Bryan, who died shortly after his last battle at Dayton, Tennessee. Bryan's death, Norris thought, would help make the Democratic party more conservative. Thus both major parties were more firmly under conservative control because of the deaths of the two progressive leaders.[34] At his summer home in Wisconsin Norris prepared an article on Bryan. He observed that Bryan's chief flaw as a political leader was partisanship; it prevented him from fulfilling his great potential as a progressive force in American political life. Norris later admitted that he was never satisfied with the article because he wrote it "without having access to any literature on the subject." While he had considered himself a friend of Bryan's and had great admiration for him in many ways, Norris still believed him one of the most partisan persons he had ever met. Partisanship had forced Bryan to compromise his progressivism and had frustrated him as a political leader.[35]

Thus, entering his sixty-fourth year in July, 1925, Norris found himself the leading progressive of the nation. Unlike both Bryan and LaFollette, whatever leadership he exercised would be without the benefit of an organization in the ordinary political understanding of that term. Lacking patronage and powerful allies in Nebraska, Norris also had little support from the partisan press and no in-

[33] Norris to Robert M. LaFollette, Jr., Aug. 22, 1925; to Mrs. LaFollette, Sept. 25, 1925.
[34] Norris to the editor, *St. Louis Post-Dispatch*, July 28, 1925.
[35] Norris, "Bryan as a Political Leader," *Current History*, 22 (Sept., 1925): 859–67; Norris to J. Sheldon Toomer, Nov. 2, 1925.

fluence with either the Republican state or national committees.[36] He did have a popular following which was growing as he gained national attention. While concerned with moral and meliorative matters, during the 1920s his criticism was being channeled along economic lines, though his comments continued to range widely over the entire spectrum of the Senate's business.

Little concerned with popularity or effect, Norris paid a terrible price for the courage of his convictions in periodic fits of despair over the failure of progressive government. During the 1920s, as long-time leaders died or disappeared from the political scene, he thought that after twenty years in Congress he had been in battle too long and ought to retire or return to Nebraska for a last political fight to put the state "on a purely progressive basis" by establishing a model nonpartisan state government. But in 1924 the people with whom he desired to work insisted he remain in the Senate.[37] The governmental scene in Washington only added to his despair. His thwarting of the Underwood bill had come about because of his ability to perceive the parliamentary mistake his opponents had made. Otherwise Calvin Coolidge, his business allies, and his appointments reigned supreme and Norris faced the discouraging prospect of battling, knowing in advance that defeat was the only possible reward for his efforts. Moreover, personal friends his own age with whom he could discuss his doubts and concerns, owing to death and distance, were few and far between. Only on relatively rare occasions did he unburden himself in conversation or in long letters. These occasions, allowing him to express his innermost doubts, served as a safety valve. Throughout his arduous battles he retained his faith in people and in the democratic process. His experiences at the funeral of Robert M. LaFollette and in the campaign of his son convinced Norris anew of "the down-right, heartfelt sympathy of millions of people in the progressive movement." [38]

[36] The deficiencies of the newspaper business, primarily "the acquisition of the almighty dollar," were examined by Norris in a letter to Joseph Polcar, Dec. 19, 1926.

[37] Norris to William Kent, Dec. 4, 1925.

[38] *Ibid.;* to Locke, June 22, 1926. To the suggestion of a constituent that there was a difference between a republic and a democracy, Norris concluded, "The word 'Republic' has come to be used as a synonym for democracy and as a matter of fact the meaning which is now applied to the words Democracy and Republic is practically one and the same"; see Norris to W. H. Ault, Mar. 9, 1927.

With faith in the essential justice and righteousness of his views and with the realization that he was regarded as the outstanding progressive in the Senate, Norris now examined pending legislation. By default of the Democrats, Norris and a handful of progressive Republicans were serving as an opposition party in the U.S. Senate. This fact, combined with the knowledge that chances of success in any endeavor were slight, lead Norris to believe that he would be the chief target of administration supporters.

No Relief for the Farmer

20

When Norris looked at the American scene during the Coolidge years, he did not see the prosperity that most observers quickly noted. To him conditions were not healthy. Everybody was in debt and the future was mortgaged: "If something should happen to interfere with the wage earning capacity of the people, they would be unable to meet the installments of this indebtedness, which are coming due daily." It was an endless chain; if a crisis occurred, it could pull down the entire structure. Because the American people were so heavily in debt, there was continual danger of economic collapse. Conservative in his economic views, Norris explained, "I cannot see how we are in a healthy condition, when nobody appears to be saving for the rainy day we should all expect in the ordinary course of life." Individuals, unable to meet obligations, would suffer and government could give them little or no help. To Norris it was clear enough: instead of incurring obligations, people should strive to pay off their debts. But he admitted that such a view "does not seem to be popular at the present time." [1]

He became disheartened when he observed that with government assistance, assets garnered by some corporations stood "in bold relief by the side of the deficit in the bookkeeping of agriculture." He wondered how long the prosperity of "Big Business" could continue "when the fundamental industry of all was languishing."

[1] George W. Norris to W. R. Bendz, Nov. 18, 1926.

"Stock dividends which in reality represent over-charges made to consumers, are making one class of our people rich, while those who produce the food for all of us are getting poorer every day." Unless something were done to reverse this trend, Norris envisioned dire consequences, and in his capacity as a U.S. senator he fought to do so.[2]

His basic concern continued to be with the farmer; by 1926 he viewed the condition of agriculture as deplorable. As of 1923, he noted, 11 million workers on farms produced $12 billion in value while 9 million workers in manufacturing produced more than twice the same value. At the same time the 1924 earnings of national banks were 8⅓ percent of their capital, surplus, and undivided profits. This was true even though throughout the agricultural regions of the West banks had been failing by the hundreds and few of the others made any profit at all. In short, most sectors of the economy, except agriculture, seemed to be making money. The reasons for this deplorable situation had not changed since Norris had carefully examined the agricultural situation early in the Harding administration. Essentially, three factors were involved: the cost of distribution, the tariff, and the surplus.[3] In addition, the farmer of what Norris called "the great Middle West" suffered three further handicaps. First, because of his location the freight he had to pay on both what he sold and what he bought was "very much greater" than the eastern farmer paid. Second, the area in which he lived was not capable of as great agricultural diversification as the more-favored eastern localities. Third, the midwestern farmer produced crops of which there was a growing surplus above the needs of domestic consumption. Thus the great interior farming section, the breadbasket of the nation, was more seriously affected by the

[2] Norris to Frank A. Harrison, Dec. 28, 1926. Business failures in the Coolidge years were: 1923—18,718; 1924—20,615; 1925—21,214; 1926—21,773; 1927—23,146. On the other hand, in 1924 there were seventy-five individuals with an income of over a million dollars; in 1925 there were 207. Seemingly, the plight of the small businessman was not markedly different from that of the farmer. For figures, see *Statistical Abstract of the United States: 1928* (Washington, D.C., 1928), pp. 312, 180.

[3] Norris, "The Farmer's Situation a National Danger," an article inserted in the *Congressional Record*, 69th Cong., 1st sess., June 14, 1926, pp. 11257–58; Norris, "What Is the Matter with the Farmer," n.d. (draft article); Norris, "The Tariff and the Farmer," *Nation*, Sept. 1, 1926, pp. 192–93.

crisis situation in agriculture than any other part of the country.[4]

  While Norris's analysis was essentially the same as it had been earlier in the 1920s, his remedy, owing to the defeat of his suggested solutions, had changed. He did insist that any solution of the farm problem was subject to the criticism that it put government into business. During the Coolidge administration the solution favored by most farmers "of the great Middle West" called for an export corporation and provided a method by which this agency, created by federal authority, paid a price that would give the farmer a reasonable profit on domestic sales and then sold the surplus at whatever price it could command in the markets of the world. With the surplus out of the way, the domestic price would rise to the height of the tariff wall. A small pro rata assessment upon the portion of the product consumed at home would be sufficient to make up the loss upon the surplus sold abroad. But the larger the surplus, the larger the assessment or equalization fee. Thus the farmer would receive the benefit of the tariff to the same extent, less the equalization fee, that the manufacturer did. If the tariff on wheat were 50 cents a bushel, removing the surplus would raise the price of wheat in the domestic market by 50 cents a bushel. From the producers of this crop would be collected enough money to pay for the loss involved in dumping the surplus upon the world market.

  Norris admitted that the machinery was "somewhat intricate" and that there would be difficulties in enforcement. But, he insisted, there could be no doubt "that it would result in putting the American farmer upon an equal footing with the American manufacturer and would give him the benefit of whatever tariff was levied by law upon his product." This suggestion, incorporated into the McNary-Haugen bill, would grant "the great farming industry of the country" the benefits of tariff protection and would eventually equalize farmer and manufacturer. Norris supported his proposal as the best way of helping agriculture since the defeat of his measures by "very powerful political influences" in the Harding administration. As chairman of the Agriculture and Forestry Committee Norris con-

  [4] Norris, "What Is the Matter with the Farmer." Farmers in irrigation districts all too often found themselves unable to finance their operations. Their costs and charges doubled and often tripled and their plight was more severe than that of most midwestern farmers; see Norris to W. I. Farley, July 9, 1925.

ducted extended hearings on the McNary-Haugen bill and said he would vote for it, though he continued to believe that the measures he had introduced during the Harding administration went more effectively to the heart of the farm problem.[5]

By 1925 senators representing distressed farm states had begun to express resentment at the simple way large corporations resolved their surplus problems. A group, including Norris, asked the Federal Trade Commission for information on foreign corporations formed by American manufacturers for the purpose of dumping surplus products below domestic market prices. Despite their concern Norris realized it was useless to try to get any progressive legislation on the statute books. He understood, too, that the Coolidge administration reflected the apparent satisfaction of the majority of the American people with prevailing conditions. The farmer, despite rumblings of discontent, could expect no relief until a new president occupied the White House.[6]

In correspondence with constituents Norris hoped to demonstrate that the administration was taking a shortsighted view. In addition to his standard complaints—freight rates and distribution costs, the tariff and the surplus—he occasionally reiterated another telling point. He insisted, "It is not a kindness to a man to loan him money even though the rate is very low, in order that he may hold his product, unless there is some reasonable assurance that when he sells his product, he will be able to pay this interest and make a profit." Both Harding and Coolidge had opposed any bill seeking remedial legislation in any of these directions because all involved government participation. Norris said such action was unjustified because basic economic laws had long been violated by combinations and costs adversely affecting agriculture. "An educated farmer in a civilized country will not permanently submit"; otherwise he would become a peasant.[7]

[5] Norris, "The Farmer's Situation a National Danger," *Congressional Record*, 69th Cong., 1st sess., June 3, p. 10281, June 14, 1926, pp. 11258–59; Norris, "What Is the Matter with the Farmer"; Norris, "The Tariff and the Farmer," pp. 192–93.

[6] *New York Times*, Mar. 25, 1925; *Rochester* (N.Y.) *Herald*, Jan. 1, 1926; Norris to William Kent, Dec. 15, 1925 (Addition 4, William Kent Papers, Yale University Library).

[7] Norris to Walter Livingston, Feb. 20, 1926; to Ernest M. Pollard, Jan. 24, 1926; to John F. Cordeal, June 23, 1926. Norris fully understood that while the

In the first session of the Sixty-ninth Congress Norris spoke strongly on behalf of remedial legislation in general and the McNary-Haugen bill in particular. But he admitted that the question of agricultural relief would be a difficult one to resolve. Farm organizations were not in agreement and the Secretary of Agriculture and the president disagreed with the Senate Agriculture and Forestry Committee on the best course to follow. Compromise, therefore, was necessary; delay occurred because of the continual consultation needed to determine what could be compromised. Moreover, approval of the president would be necessary if success were to crown the efforts of those seeking remedial legislation. Most disagreement hinged on the question of the surplus and Norris doubted that all groups could be satisfied on this question. Nevertheless, in March, 1926, he said that the Agriculture and Forestry Committee would present a measure for consideration.[8]

As presented to Congress, the McNary-Haugen bill focused on the wheat surplus. But its provisions pertaining to cotton and corn caused considerable discussion. Eliminated from earlier versions, cotton and corn now were included with the proviso that no equalization fee was to be collected on either crop for a period of three years. Norris said his committee followed the judgment of southern spokesmen that cotton farmers were not ready for the fee portion of the program but were willing to accept benefits derived from the orderly handling of exports through a government corporation. Corn was not immediately included under the equalization fee because its surplus, unlike wheat's, was not usually exported. Indeed, the recent history of cotton and corn led members to conclude that it would be unnecessary to export either crop to maintain satisfactory prices.[9]

Norris admitted that while the surplus was not the only difficulty, it was a question that had to be resolved. He noted, too, that labor

---

McNary-Haugen bill attempted to resolve the difficulty of the surplus and the effect of the tariff, it in no way attacked the equally important problems of middlemen, transportation, and freight rates.

[8] *Congressional Record,* 69th Cong., 1st sess., Mar. 29, 1926, pp. 6502–5.

[9] *Ibid.,* June 2, 1926, p. 10493. For a discussion by Norris of the operation of the corn-hog cycle, related to the decision to exclude corn from the full operation of the equalization fee, see his remarks in *ibid.,* June 8, p. 10906, June 9, 1926, p. 11004.

representatives in their testimony emphatically endorsed McNary-Haugen and other measures designed to benefit the farmer, though they might tend to increase the cost of living. But his remarks were primarily devoted to a lengthy and careful analysis of efforts, including his own, to alleviate agricultural conditions since 1919 and to the opposition they had incurred, especially from Presidents Harding and Coolidge. After six years of study the Agriculture and Forestry Committee had concluded that no measure designed to bring relief to agriculture could succeed unless it dealt with the surplus. While the McNary-Haugen bill was technical, complicated, and undoubtedly far from perfect, it represented a serious and sound effort to do just that.[10]

Norris also devoted attention to the mounting concern of citizens about the condition of agriculture and the dimensions of the problem. There had sprung up all over the West, "the place where progressive ideas are born," organizations not only of farmers but of professional men, especially bankers and lawyers, and of businessmen designed to aid agriculture. Norris singled out George N. Peek and William Hirth, mentioning their efforts in drafting the McNary-Haugen measure. He related how they had organized farmers and businessmen in the Midwest and how Peek was seeking southern support as well for the measure. Norris was pleased with the prospect of "the great West and the great South, so often grappling each other by the throat," becoming united in seeking to resolve common problems and similar difficulties. He was impressed with the insight and ability of southern farm leaders who had testified before his committee.[11]

The Senate rejected the McNary-Haugen bill on June 24, 1926, by a vote of 39 to 45. Attention next focused on a marketing bill sponsored by Senator Simeon Fess of Ohio and endorsed by the president.[12] The substitute, Norris insisted, was a fraud. It did not

[10] *Ibid.*, June 8, pp. 10903–4, June 9, p. 11010, June 12, p. 11218, June 14, 1926, pp. 11241–46. See also p. 11255 for Norris's original doubts about the McNary-Haugen bill and his view that acreage limitation was "absolutely impracticable."

[11] *Ibid.*, June 14, 1926, pp. 11248–50.

[12] The Cooperative Marketing Act of 1926 established the Division of Cooperative Marketing in the Bureau of Agricultural Economics to undertake research on problems relating to farmer cooperatives and to provide advice and other ser-

meet a single contingency confronting agriculture and would spend money for more investigations and study. The agricultural situation had been "studied and restudied and examined and reexamined until the time for study and speculation and experimentation" had long since passed. The question was no longer what the farmer wanted but, rather, what the administration wished; not what would be beneficial to the farmer but whether it would be good politics for the administration. Norris commented bitterly on Coolidge's change of heart. Opposed to the McNary-Haugen bill, the president now professed friendship for the farmer by endorsing an innocuous measure that would allow bureaucrats in the Agriculture Department to prepare further studies of a subject that had been all but analyzed to death.[13]

Norris's lengthy remarks on the McNary-Haugen bill in June, 1926, marked his farewell performance as chairman of the Agriculture and Forestry Committee. Retaining membership on the committee, Norris explained, "I am not going to take any less interest in agriculture, rather I am going to take more. I have resigned from the chairmanship in order to free myself for the fighting that lies ahead." But Norris devoted little time thereafter to the ill-fated McNary-Haugen bill. He supported it but his actions and remarks were no longer central to the discussion. His analysis of the farm situation and his denunciation of Harding and Coolidge did not change. But he inevitably became less aware of current developments as they were reflected in committee hearings and reports received by Charles McNary, the new committee chairman.[14]

---

vices to aid in their development; see Murray R. Benedict, *Farm Policies of the United States* (New York, 1953), p. 198, note 74.

[13] *Congressional Record,* 69th Cong., 1st sess., June 25, 1926, pp. 12190–91. The technical aspects of the McNary-Haugen bill and its previous history are carefully explained in Norris to R. P. Hamlyn, Dec. 16, 1926.

[14] *Labor,* July 10, 1926; Norris to E. F. Vandiver, July 16, 1926. In this letter Norris candidly admitted that he now would have more time to exert his best efforts on behalf of Muscle Shoals. The story in *Labor* also pointed out that since the death of Senator LaFollette Norris was accounted the leader of the progressive forces in Washington and that his personal correspondence multiplied as a consequence. See, for example, the analysis presented by Norris in the *National Grange Monthly,* Sept., 1927, and his remarks in the *Washington Farmer,* Dec. 1, 1927. See also Norris to H. Wheurman, Jan. 26, 1927; to William C. Hunneman, Aug. 29, 1927; to J. T. Williams, Oct. 31, 1927.

A new dimension was added in 1927 when the Grange, which did not support the McNary-Haugen bill, championed a remedy of its own, the export-debenture plan. Norris, having heard the plan presented to the Agriculture and Forestry Committee when he was chairman, concluded along with a majority of the committee that it was a waste of time to give it consideration. Briefly, he explained, the export-debenture proposal provided for an export bounty. When wheat, for example, was exported, a certificate would be given to the exporter stating the amount shipped and the value of the rebate. It would be the difference between the world price and the tariff on wheat. The certificate, which was assignable, could be used as money by importers to pay tariff expenses at any American port. "The effect of this proposal would be to raise the price of wheat to the top of our tariff wall, but it would be the same as though the money were taken out of the Treasury of the United States." The income of the government from tariff duties would be reduced by the amount of certificates in circulation. Thus the rebate would be a subsidy paid to producers of wheat or any other exportable farm product. Norris felt that such a proposal could not pass Congress; if perchance it did, it would be vetoed. Moreover, instead of resolving the dilemma of the surplus, it would increase it, since every farmer would know he could obtain from the Treasury enough cash to pay him the difference between the world price on his product and the tariff. Norris doubted the efficacy of either the debenture plan or one proposed by former Assistant Secretary of Agriculture Carl Vrooman for limiting production by voluntary agreement.[15]

Indeed, by 1927 the only answer Norris could see to the farm problem was for the farmers of "the great Middle West" to unite. Only then could they help place in the White House a man sympathetic to their plight. But the administration was able to cloud

[15] Norris to Charles W. Bryan, Oct. 30, 1927. While the Grange had not supported the equalization-fee proposal, neither had it actively opposed the idea. Nevertheless, the Coolidge administration made efforts to enlist it in the fight against the McNary-Haugen bill. The export-debenture plan was formulated by Professor Charles L. Stewart of the University of Illinois; see Norris, "The Debenture Plan," n.d. (statement outlining the proposal). Controlling acreage could not be done by voluntary agreement and Norris was not convinced that it could be done by law because the vicissitudes of nature meant the same acreage could bring overproduction one year and underproduction another. See also Norris to O. M. Kile, Nov. 28, 1927.

the issue by continually rallying support for compromise measures which usually lent more money to the farmer. Norris insisted that it was not a kindness to lend farmers money, even at low interest rates, for the purpose of holding crops unless there was reason to believe that by the time the loan matured, the value of the crop would be sufficiently increased for the farmer to profit from the transaction. "With the surplus staring him in the face," no farmer could expect that profit. Indeed, of all the suggestions then presented, the only one that made sense to Norris was the McNary-Haugen bill. Its supporters were willing to stand the burden themselves and not call upon the general taxpayer to meet the loss that was bound to come when surpluses were sold abroad.[16]

Throughout the debates on the measure in both the second session of the Sixty-ninth and the first session of the Seventieth Congress, which saw it pass in each session only to be vetoed by President Coolidge, Norris said very little. The burden of battle fell to his successor as chairman of the Senate Agriculture and Forestry Committee. Norris had to admit doubts at the outset of the Seventieth Congress about the wisdom of passing the McNary-Haugen bill again and subjecting it to President Coolidge's veto. Congress now would be justified in seeking any legislation offering agricultural relief. For this reason he was willing to support the export-debenture plan, though most senators decided to try the McNary-Haugen bill again. But when faced with a second veto, he refused to support an amendment taking the equalization fee out of the plan. Substituting the export-debenture proposal in its place would not succeed because Calvin Coolidge was a strong protectionist, seeking to protect everybody but the farmer. Since the farmer could not get the benefit of the tariff, Norris believed that Congress would be justified in seeing that nobody benefited, that all were put on the same level. But he never suggested how this feat could be accomplished.[17]

[16] Norris to Bryan, Oct. 30, 1927; to Kile, Nov. 8, 1927; to William Hirth, Nov. 15, 1927. For an interesting discussion of the farm problem from the viewpoint of an eastern agriculturalist and a devoted Coolidge supporter who had little understanding of the problems of midwestern farmers, see James W. Wadsworth, Jr., to A. Eugene Bolles, Aug. 27, 1925; Wadsworth to William Pitkin, Dec. 19, 1925 (both in Box 17, Wadsworth Family Papers, Manuscript Division, Library of Congress). Wadsworth at the time was senator from New York.

[17] *Congressional Record,* 70th Cong., 1st sess., May 21, 1928, pp. 9304–5.

Unable to resolve the farm problem directly during the Coolidge years, Norris tried another approach. He made suggestions pertaining to freight rates which, like his previous efforts for agriculture relief, were doomed to failure. But he persisted and criticized the president and his party for failing to come to grips with this problem. While his remarks in the *Congressional Record* were relatively few, his correspondence pertaining to transportation was extensive. In most instances the topic was related to agriculture.[18] To be sure, he had already discussed this question during the Harding administration, but as the farm situation did not improve, his analysis became more critical and his call for government ownership more candid. By 1926, he claimed, freight rates were almost double what they had been before the war and the farmer absorbed them in everything he purchased while they were deducted from everything he sold. "This means that the farmer pays somewhere in the neighborhood of four times as much freight as he did before the War, that he pays double freight both going and coming." [19]

What made the picture totally distressing was the financial history of American railroads; Norris regarded it as a "disgrace to our civilization." "They have been the subject of barter and sale, of chicanery and trickery, of manipulation and dishonest financial junketing, for the last fifty years." The result in many instances was extravagant overcapitalization; regulation, according to Norris, failed to meet the situation properly. It had cost "many hundreds of millions of dollars and still the wrecking of railroads" continued. The difficulty usually was that "great financiers have used the railroads as an instrumentality of financial gain and have lost consideration entirely of service to the public." Norris concluded that the public was being bilked beyond both moral and legal proprieties. Those who toiled "in the fields of the Great West" and consumers everywhere were compelled to pay "in their cost of living, a charge

[18] *Ibid.*, 68th Cong., 1st sess., May 14, p. 8522, May 17, pp. 8787–88, May 16, pp. 8688, 8690, May 26, 1924, p. 9489. In the last citation Norris cited specific examples of the operation of the long- and short-haul evil. See also Norris to J. A. Guttery, Mar. 25, 1926; to W. P. Warner, May 18, 1926; to J. L. Baker, Mar. 25, Dec. 3, 1926; to J. W. Shorthill, Dec. 4, 1925; to I. D. Evans, July 2, 1926.

[19] Norris to Pollard, Jan. 24, 1926; Norris, "What Is the Matter with the Farmer."

that was neither just nor legal." The answer was government ownership. By using profits to decrease capitalization, the public eventually could benefit from reduced charges.

Examining the Canadian experience in railroads, as he had done
in hydroelectric power, Norris noted that the government-owned
transcontinental line fixed freight rates. Private railroads did not go
out of business, but they had to operate economically and efficiently
to compete. Government operation in Canada, in short, had decreased expenditures and increased revenue. Rates were reduced so
that the Canadian farmer was paying less freight than his American
counterpart on everything he shipped to eastern markets. If the
American government would follow the Canadian example, Norris
envisioned equally successful results.

Finally, it was not valid to argue that government ownership
would put the railroads into politics. They had been deeply involved
in politics throughout their history. Their political expenses were
enormous and every penny of it was paid by producers and consumers of foodstuffs. To Norris "a national corporation, capitalized
by public funds, operating a road from Coast to Coast and from
Lake to Gulf, would not only regulate rates in the entire country,
but it would be one great step in taking the railroads out of politics." [20]

Realizing, of course, that there was little chance of government
ownership, Norris sought more stringent regulation as a way of
curbing railroad malpractices. What was needed at the outset was
a complete valuation of railroad worth so that the Interstate Commerce Commission would have a sound base on which to levy rates.
In May, 1923, the National Conference on Valuation of American
Railroads was organized for this purpose; by order of the Interstate
Commerce Commission it became a party to all valuation proceedings. Norris said that completion of this task would enable the
commission to collect over $100 million in excess earnings from
carriers and would result in rate readjustments of immense value

[20] Norris, "What Is the Matter with the Farmer"; Norris, "The Tariff and the Farmer," p. 193; Norris to Edwin A. Smith, July 2, 1926, Nov. 17, 1927; to J. H. Brown, Mar. 4, 1927; to M. F. Harrington, Oct. 28, 1927; to C. B. Steward, Oct. 31, 1927. The letters present a comparative discussion of Canadian and American railroad practices.

to the public.[21] He also supported the Gooding bill, which would prevent railroads from charging more for a short haul than for a long haul, the short haul being included within the long haul. This legislation, Norris explained to an Omaha editor, would prevent a railroad from charging more for a shipment of freight from New York to Omaha than it charged from New York to San Francisco via Omaha. Critics argued that the Panama Canal had provided cheap water transportation between the Atlantic and Pacific coasts, and that on the through haul railroads had been compelled to reduce freight rates to meet this competition. They implied that railroads ought to be permitted to charge higher rates from the coast to interior points to recoup this loss. Norris argued that unless common carriers treated all customers alike, they could exercise power favoring one shipper or town while dealing a death blow to other competitors or communities. Most long-haul rates were profitable and the practice of charging more for a short haul was unjust. But a majority of the Senate was never persuaded by the logic of Norris's argument and the Gooding bill was defeated by a vote of 33 to 46 when it came to a vote in March, 1926.[22]

Thereafter, Norris futilely supported other measures to regulate railroad rates while remaining convinced that public ownership

[21] Norris to C. E. Childe, Dec. 26, 1924; *Congressional Record,* 70th Cong., 1st sess., May 7, 1928, p. 7950 (a resolution by Norris). For a discussion of the National Conference on Valuation of American Railroads, see two volumes by Donald R. Richberg, *My Hero* (New York, 1954), pp. 112–26, and *Tents of the Mighty* (Chicago, 1930), pp. 121–56 *passim.* Richberg was general counsel of the conference group and Norris soon became chairman. Norris was also interested in an experiment conducted by the Baltimore and Ohio Railroad wherein it had turned over to its employees the management of the repair shops. The experiment seemed successful and Norris sought further evidence as a demonstration of the efficiency and economy of organized labor on railroads; see Norris to Louis Crossette, Feb. 11, 1925.

[22] Norris to Ballard Dunn, Jan. 19, Feb. 11, 1926; to Fred Cary, Feb. 12, 1926; to Robert Walsh, Mar. 20, 1926; to John W. Steinhart, Mar. 20, 1926; to William Maupin, Mar. 22, 1926; *Congressional Record,* 69th Cong., 1st sess., Mar. 24, 1926, pp. 6148–49. Senator Frank Gooding of Idaho sponsored the measure to abolish the long- and short-haul practice during the Coolidge years. In the 1920s sugar shipped from San Francisco to Kearney, Nebr., was charged the same rate as from San Francisco to Omaha, plus the local rate back from Omaha to Kearney, although the sugar itself was never shipped to Omaha but was unloaded at Kearney; see Norris to Charles D. Blaine, Mar. 5, 1926; to Dunn, Mar. 7, 1926.

was the most satisfactory method of resolving the problem. But to
Donald Richberg, general counsel of the National Conference on
Valuation of American Railroads, Norris expressed concern that
the Supreme Court would accept the concept of reproduction cost
rather than the more moderate original-cost or prudent-investment
approach which a majority of the Interstate Commerce Commission
favored. Willingness to accept the reproduction-cost concept eventually would "drive the country to Government ownership as a matter of self-defense and self-protection" because an increase in railroad valuation would be followed by an increase in all other public
utilities. "Putting it all together," Norris believed, "it makes a burden that will be impossible for the people to bear." [23]

Valuation based on reproduction costs disregarded the original
investment. For rate-making purposes, Norris insisted, "the valuation should never exceed the original investment honestly and judiciously made, less depreciation." Investors in railroads, to be sure,
were entitled to a reasonable return. But if the value of the property
had increased through exorbitant profits secured through controversial but legal practices, then this fictitious value in turn could
become the real value upon which rates would be determined. Norris said that a railroad corporation, entitled as it was to the right of
eminent domain, had no "legal, moral or just right to such preferential treatment." If such pyramiding were permitted, it would be
only a question of time until the structure collapsed because civilization could not stand it.[24]

Because of their malpractices Norris believed that railroads had
forfeited to the public interest the right to regulate profits. If property values had been enhanced by the contributions and patronage
of the public, it should not be required to pay tribute upon the in-

[23] Norris to Donald R. Richberg, Dec. 1, 1926.

[24] *Ibid.* In *McArdle et al.* v. *Indianapolis Water Company* (272 U.S. 400,
1926) Justice Pierce Butler, a former railroad attorney, expounded the reproduction-cost concept with Brandeis and Stone in dissent. In the O'Fallon case, *St.
Louis and O'Fallon Railroad Co.* v. *United States* (279 U.S. 461, 1929), the
Court approved this concept as the method of determining railroad rates (Holmes,
Brandeis, and Stone dissented). Ironically, the O'Fallon case was decided in the
very year the business civilization of the 1920s collapsed. See Norris to Hunneman, July 15, 1927, for a discussion of rate-making practices. For an interesting
discussion of the general failure of railroad commissions to regulate, see Norris
to Joseph B. Eastman, Nov. 2, 1927.

creased value it had made. In determining rates, two factors had to be considered: the original investment, honestly and judiciously made, and the physical value of the property. If these two items were not the same, then the lower should be taken as a basis of value upon which income should be computed. Truly, as Claude Fuess in his biography of Interstate Commerce Commissioner Joseph B. Eastman remarked, "valuation is vexation." [25]

Eastman, like Norris, favored government ownership and operation of railroads but thought it would not be achieved in the near future. Norris agreed but felt that with continually deteriorating conditions, public sentiment could change rapidly. If the decision of the Supreme Court in the Indianapolis Waterworks case in 1926 accepting the replacement- or reproduction-cost concept were applied to railroads, Norris thought that government ownership and operation, "not necessarily of all the railroads," was inevitable.[26] If the public ever awoke to what was happening, then he looked "for a revolution of public sentiment" in favor of government ownership and operation—the best kind of rate regulation.[27]

The railroad problem came to a disastrous solution at the end of the Coolidge era when the Supreme Court in May, 1929, upheld the reproduction- or replacement-cost concept in the O'Fallon case. Donald Richberg, while allowed to file a brief on behalf of the National Conference on Valuation of American Railroads in district court, was not permitted to participate in the case which challenged the Interstate Commerce Commission's decision in favor of the original-investment concept. Richberg thought he would have

[25] Norris to Richberg, Dec. 19, 1926; Claude M. Fuess, *Joseph B. Eastman: Servant of the People* (New York, 1952), Chapter IX, "Valuation Is Vexation."

[26] See note 24 above for case citation.

[27] Norris to Eastman, Oct. 31, 1927, Jan. 21, 1928. Eastman in response to the former letter told Norris he encountered very few people who were friendly to government ownership and many who were strongly opposed to it, particularly among shippers. He remarked that "competition is one of the most prolific sources of extravagance and waste and the benefits go chiefly to the large shippers and the large cities." It also tended to stimulate the concentration of population in large centers. Eastman further informed Norris that "compared to the gross or even the net earnings of the companies regulated, the cost of public regulation is almost infinitesimal." The greatest expense involved was the cost of litigation initiated by carriers and shippers before federal and state commerce commissions. Under government operation, Eastman believed, much litigation could be avoided; see Eastman to Norris, Nov. 2, 1927.

difficulty filing an amicus curiae brief and participating in the oral argument. To insure his appearance before the Supreme Court, Norris boldly submitted a Senate resolution respectfully requesting it to permit Richberg to intervene for the purpose of making oral argument and filing a brief. Over the protest of conservative members the resolution was approved by a 46-to-31 vote.[28] The Court's decision, by adding to the aggregate valuation of railroad properties, would mean a difference in transportation rates amounting to hundreds of millions of dollars. Until government ownership and operation of at least a portion of the transportation system was achieved or until the prevailing civilization collapsed, the public was doomed to bear the burden of higher freight rates and their attendant consequences. Sorely beset American farmers and urban consumers were manacled by railroads and their allies, including the government of the United States. So influential were these interests and so entrenched were conservative Republican elements that Norris envisioned little relief for agriculture or for the American consumer "for a great many years to come." [29]

During the Coolidge years Norris had done everything possible to provide some relief for the farmer. And he had failed. Though he insisted that he would avail himself of every opportunity to promote the cause of the farmer, there were other legislative matters that concerned him during the administration of Calvin Coolidge; to these we must now turn.

[28] Richberg to Norris, Mar. 20, 1928; Norris to Richberg, Mar. 26, 1928; *Congressional Record,* 70th Cong., 1st sess., May 7, 1928, pp. 7950, 7959. In *St. Louis and O'Fallon Railroad Co.* v. *United States* the Supreme Court overruled the Interstate Commerce Commission because it did not give consideration to the cost of reproduction. In an interesting letter to Norris of May 6, 1928, Richberg indicated the line of reasoning he would pursue by suggesting that the determination of public policy was a legislative and administrative function which provided little scope for the exercise of judicial power. See also *New York Times,* May 8, 1928.

[29] *New York Times,* May 8, 1928; Norris to A. B. Zimmerman, Mar. 21, 1929.

Confronting Coolidge

21

When considering matters other than agriculture, transportation, and Muscle Shoals, Norris did not regard himself as an expert; consequently his remarks, if not his interest, were limited. But he was becoming thoroughly conversant with Judiciary Committee business, having officially assumed the post of chairman in December, 1926. Despite the diversity of his remarks a continual thread of criticism pervaded them so that Norris emerged as the chief critic of the Coolidge administration. Whenever possible he offered government ownership as a solution to persistent and perplexing problems.

Such was his answer to the difficulties of the coal industry. In 1926, after reading a speech by Norman Thomas on the question of nationalizing the coal industry, Norris wrote that coal, a natural resource "necessary for our very existence," was controlled by "coal barons" who could create scarcity and maintain high prices by closing their mines. The consumer paid the bill "and the coal baron reaps a profit on one of the necessities of life all out of reason." But if operators allowed the law of supply and demand to function, there would be coal enough for everybody at a price within the reach of all. "And yet, because Big Business is so firmly in the saddle, the people would crucify the man who dared to say that the remedy was to take over the coal mines and operate them by the Government." They were willing to tolerate the situation and let big business rule. Certainly, Norris bitterly remarked, "Calvin is

for it and he is the head of the whole concern." No one in authority
from the president on down was willing to interfere with the entrenched position of big business that had "the country by the
throat." [1]

When it came to legislation affecting one of the emerging new
industries, Norris arrived at a similar solution. Improvements in
the radio industry were constantly occurring and no one was quite
clear about its potentials and possibilities. While the rapid growth
of networks and large corporations led observers to concede that
legislation was necessary, there was danger that a strict law would
not be applicable to the industry a year or so later. Congress was
"to a great extent in the dark" and was undecided about what kind
of legislation should be passed.[2] Norris favored a permanent regulatory commission whose members would be selected for their knowledge of the industry. A bill introduced by Senator Clarence Dill
called for a board to administer the industry, while one presented
by Representative Wallace White gave regulatory powers to the
Secretary of Commerce. The Dill bill seemed the better one to
Norris and to a majority of Congress; in 1927 it established a Federal Radio Commission with authority to assign appropriate wavelengths to broadcasting stations.[3]

When constituents complained about chaotic conditions, about
numerous stations with differing wavelengths, Norris said he thought
stations owned by a particular system ought to use the same wave-
length. Interested in a fair and just solution to the complicated
problem of assigning radio frequencies, Norris admitted to confusion about what was fair and just. But of one thing about this new
industry Norris was sure. He protested the granting of privileges to
large corporations which amounted to a monopoly of the air. In
addition, he felt that a majority of the initial appointees to the
commission reflected the big-business viewpoint that permeated the
Coolidge administration. "When the appointing power is of the big
business idea; of the big business slant, how can we expect that our

[1] George W. Norris to Walter Locke, Dec. 16, 1925 (the letter was the possession of the late Walter Locke, who graciously allowed me to examine it); *Congressional Record*, 69th Cong., 1st sess., Feb. 4, 1926, pp. 3291–92.

[2] Norris to F. R. King, Dec. 13, 1926.

[3] Norris to Clarke G. Powell, Dec. 27, 1926; to C. Collins, Jan. 12, 1927. See
also Erik Barnouw, *A Tower in Babel* (New York, 1966), pp. 195–201.

laws will be administered in any way except in the interest of big business and big corporations." While these officials were not corrupt, they were not sympathetic to the hopes and aspirations of "the common, ordinary citizen." [4] He soon came to believe that "the radio business ought to be entirely owned, controlled, and operated by the Government." In particular, "educational institutions ought to have the right to use a proportionate share where information of an educational nature could be given to the people without paying tribute to some corporation interested in making money out of the radio business." Amazed at the way large corporations were monopolizing the air waves, Norris wished to curb them but felt handicapped because he was not versed in the technicalities of the subject.[5]

In areas where Norris did not propound government ownership as the answer to the failures of private enterprise, he was equally critical of proposals and policies. This was particularly true of those that came under the ken of Secretary of the Treasury Andrew Mellon. Norris protested the appointment of receivers for national banks on a partisan basis. Dishonest bank officials were bad enough, but putting a failed bank into politics to pay off political debts was a "horrid, inhuman crime." When partisan concerns were given prime consideration, chances that the bank's remaining assets would be squandered "on the political pie counter" were great. With the number of bank failures, particularly in the rural regions, continually increasing, the partisan atmosphere surrounding the appointment of receivers appalled Norris.[6]

His most extensive remarks about the fiscal policies of the Coolidge administration were in connection with the revenue bill during

[4] Norris to Mr. and Mrs. J. A. Graham, Feb. 23, 1928; to John Fuerst, Jan. 20, 1930; to Benjamin F. Bailey, May 23, 1930; to Bryan Harrison, June 25, 1930. The criticisms Norris leveled against Coolidge's appointees applied equally to those of his successor, Herbert Hoover. Barnouw, *Tower in Babel,* p. 201, notes that Herbert Hoover selected the first members of the Federal Radio Commission for the president.

[5] Norris to Joy Elmer Morgan, Mar. 24, 1931; to George Williams, Dec. 5, 1932.

[6] Norris to Frans Nelson, July 23, 1925. For detailed information on the incidence of bank failures, see *Statistical Abstract of the United States: 1933* (Washington, D.C., 1933), p. 257. In 1925, for example, there were 618 bank failures; in 1926 there were 976.

the Sixty-ninth Congress. Norris called for tax reduction that would reverse "the Mellon plan" and give greater benefits to "the little fellows." He hoped Congress would provide for publicity of tax returns, making the whole return available to the public. But his hopes were doomed when the House quickly passed "a millionaires bill," practically all of whose reductions were on the incomes of the very wealthy.[7] Andrew Mellon would get a larger personal reduction than the aggregate of taxpayers in the state of Nebraska. The reduction in inheritance taxes contained in the House bill disappointed Norris; he devoted long and bitter remarks to it in the Senate. But the provision repealing the partial publicity of income tax returns disturbed him more. In short, the revenue bill as it passed the House of Representatives, by reducing taxes on the wealthy, by lowering inheritance taxes, and by repealing provisions for publicity of tax returns, violated all the precepts he had valiantly and with some success fought for in the past. At the outset of the Senate debate Norris admitted to a deeper interest in the measure "than in any other thing that has been pending before the Congress at this session." [8]

In the Senate Norris said repeal of the inheritance tax would mean that people would have to make up in one way or another this loss of income. Turning the inheritance tax over to the states was no answer because the constitutions of some, like Florida, stated that neither an income tax nor an inheritance tax could be levied; millionaires would thus be induced to locate within their borders. He also objected to exempting insurance companies organized on a nonmutual basis from taxation. Grant them an exemption and soon practically all business would demand exemptions.[9]

Another provision that Norris attacked provided that a man who

[7] *Baltimore Sun,* Dec. 15, 1925; draft statement by Norris, Dec. 19, 1925.

[8] Draft statement by Norris, Dec. 19, 1925; *Congressional Record,* 69th Cong., 1st sess., Jan. 28, 1926, p. 2866.

[9] *Congressional Record,* 69th Cong., 1st sess., Jan. 28, pp. 2885, 2887, Jan. 29, 1926, p. 2952. The Senate Finance Committee in its version of the revenue bill not only repealed the inheritance tax but made the measure retroactive as well; see Norris to R. Kite, Jan. 30, 1926; to Chamber of Commerce, [Alliance, Nebr.], Feb. 10, 1926.

had an income of $500,000 or more should pay the same tax as one who had an income of only $100,000. If war-incurred debts were paid off by levying a high rate upon large incomes, Norris noted, "we shall be getting a large proportion of it from those who made their money out of the war itself." Unless this was done "now or soon," those who had made money in this way would escape forever. The proposal to tax a man with a $1-million income the same as a man who earned $100,000 could not be justified. Why, Norris queried, grant such a favor to those who could pay it "without the blinking of an eye unless they happen to be pretty stingy and even unpatriotic?" "Why grant it to them when the taxpayers of the country are bending down in toil under a $20,000,000,000 debt, upon which we have to pay interest amounting to almost a billion dollars a year?" [10] An amendment proposed by Norris increased the tax on incomes over $100,000 by progressive steps, adding 1 percent until it reached $1 million, where a tax of 30 percent, "10 percent lower than the present law," would be assessed. It was defeated, 29 yeas to 54 nays. Indeed, he observed, every amendment to increase the rates on incomes over $100,000 was rejected in the Senate with overwhelming Democratic support.[11]

Norris introduced another amendment making income tax returns public documents, subject to examination under the same conditions as any other public document. It was the same amendment he had introduced to the 1924 Revenue Act, which had passed the Senate by a 48-to-27 vote. Norris said that publicity increased revenue, discouraged evasions, and promoted honesty while secrecy discriminated against the honest man. It was only after the passage of the 1924 act with Norris's publicity provision that the public, through disclosures presented by Senator James Couzens, received information about the dimensions of wealth in the United

[10] *Congressional Record,* 69th Cong., 1st sess., Feb. 2, 1926, pp. 3159–61. Concluding his remarks on this day, Norris inserted in the *Record* the number of persons from 1916 through 1924 who had incomes exceeding $100,000 a year; see p. 3163, Feb. 3, pp. 3208–10, Feb. 4, 1926, pp. 3270–71. Norris charged (p. 3270) that Democrats in the Senate were involved in a coalition with Republicans to reduce the tax burden on the very wealthy.

[11] *Ibid.,* Feb. 3, pp. 3219, 3221, Feb. 4, 1926, p. 3266. For a brief overall discussion of the 1926 shift in tax burdens, see Sidney Ratner, *American Taxation* (New York, 1942), pp. 425–28.

States. So revealing were some of the disclosures that Norris charged that "the wealth of the country has attempted to discredit the law making income-tax returns public." So did the Treasury Department under Andrew Mellon. But, Norris insisted, "the patriotic taxpayers and citizens of our country have a right to know that everybody is being treated on the same level; that every taxpayer has the same right . . . that all public business shall be transacted according to law." [12]

The amendment this time was overwhelmingly defeated. So, too, was an amendment Norris introduced at the behest of employees of the Internal Revenue Bureau giving any employee of the bureau the right to protest to members of Congress. The amendment was prepared by employees who sought to protest suspicious tax returns without subjecting themselves to criminal prosecution. The same fate befell another Norris amendment calling for taxes on gifts, bequests, devises, or inheritances, all of which existed in the 1924 Revenue Act. He claimed that this amendment would produce about $10 million in additional revenue. A portion of it was salvaged in conference committee and enacted into law.[13]

To Norris the tax bill was a millionaire's bill, granting enormous exemptions to the very wealthy. It saved millions of dollars for the

[12] *Congressional Record*, 69th Cong., 1st sess., Feb. 8, 1926, pp. 3484, 3489, 3491–95, 3504, 3511. The vote on the Norris amendment was 49 nays to 32 yeas. The clause in the 1924 law provided for publicity not of returns but merely of tax payments. Norris had fought this substitution inserted by the conference committee. See the story by Paul Y. Anderson in the *St. Louis Post-Dispatch*, Nov. 27, 1925, wherein Norris announced that he would have his original amendment ready to present if the subject was reopened. In the next Congress Norris again introduced an amendment making all income tax returns public records. This time, with the complexion of the Senate more evenly balanced between the two parties, the amendment passed by a vote of 27 to 19 with forty-eight senators not voting. It was included in the final bill. The Democrats were not as cooperative with the administration forces as in the passage of the 1926 revenue law; see *Congressional Record*, 70th Cong., 1st sess., May 18, 1928, pp. 9059, 9082; Lawrence D. Tyson to East Tennessee National Bank, May 19, 1928 (Lawrence D. Tyson Papers, Southern Collection, University of North Carolina). Tyson opposed the Norris amendment. See also Ratner, *American Taxation*, pp. 431–32.

[13] *Congressional Record*, 69th Cong., 1st sess., Feb. 12, 1926, pp. 3872–73, 3831–33. See Ratner, *American Taxation*, pp. 428–29, for the inclusion of an estate tax in the final version of the revenue bill. An estate tax used as its basis the entire estate; an inheritance tax affected each heir's portion. They were the same only when an estate was not divided, something that very seldom happened.

rich while taxing it out of the poor. Perhaps what distressed Norris most was that provisions he protested were approved by President Coolidge and Secretary Mellon. Sadly he observed, "The wonderful power and influence of the Administration can hardly be overestimated." The average tax reduction in the bill as it passed the Senate was $48,000 for each person with an income of $100,000 and more. For those with lesser incomes it was $49.[14] Disturbing, too, was the knowledge that Calvin Coolidge regarded the inheritance tax, which Norris had helped establish during the Wilson years, as a step toward socialism. To Norris it was one of the least burdensome and most just taxes, inexpensive to collect while doing little harm to its recipient who "never so much as crooked a finger" to make the money being taxed. In the Senate Norris waged a bitter fight to reinsert it but so "wonderful and influential" was the combination "headed by the President and supported by millionaires everywhere" that his amendment was easily defeated. While a modest tax on estates was salvaged in the final bill, a provision for retroactively refunding all inheritance taxes collected under the 1924 schedule in excess of the 1927 rates was also included.[15]

An area where economy could be practiced was in the operation of the Post Office Department. Here, too, Norris confronted the Coolidge administration and found little to praise in its policies. When Coolidge in 1925 vetoed a postal employee pay-raise bill, Norris, who voted for the bill, sarcastically warned his colleagues of the dangers and pitfalls of following their conscientious convictions: ". . . the best thing to do is to swallow the dose that our leaders tell us is good for us, look as happy as we can, and in due time will come our great reward." Despite his encouragement to break ranks, the Senate sustained the president's veto by one vote. Coolidge, exerting great pressure to have it upheld, argued that "if the veto is not sustained it means the break-up of the Party." [16]

[14] *Congressional Record,* 69th Cong., 1st sess., Feb. 10, p. 3697, Feb. 12, 1926, p. 3896; Norris to Charles F. Dodge, Jan. 24, 1926; to W. H. Dressler, Feb. 7, 1926; to M. L. Wilcox, Feb. 8, 1926. An article by David Lawrence in the *Jersey City Journal,* Jan. 29, 1926, observed that the Democratic party was as eager for tax reduction as were the Coolidge Republicans.

[15] *Congressional Record,* 69th Cong., special sess. of Senate, Mar. 18, 1925; 1st sess., Feb. 10, pp. 3666–69, 3673, 3700, Feb. 12, 1926, pp. 3845, 3847–51; Norris to John M. Leyda, Jan. 27, 1926; Ratner, *American Taxation,* pp. 428–29.

[16] *Congressional Record,* 68th Cong., 2nd sess., Jan. 5, 1925, pp. 1225–26;

Shortly thereafter, when the administration proposed to increase postal rates, Norris said more information was needed. Raising parcel post rates and reducing second-class rates, as the measure proposed, seemed unfair. Business would benefit; postal income would not. Increasing parcel post rates would cripple the system and hurt both businessmen and customers, usually farmers and residents of smaller towns. More information was needed, but the administration cleverly tied increased postal rates to an increase in salaries; Norris, besides pleading for delay, proposed to separate the two facets of the bill. In both instances he was unsuccessful.[17] If the Post Office was to pay its own way as the administration desired, then, Norris believed, efficiency would be sacrificed in the form of services affecting farm areas, such as rural free delivery. Increasing rates would be detrimental to the already overburdened rural regions. He also objected to railroad companies seeking to increase rates for carrying the mail because he felt that "they have made more money than they ever made before in their history" and because such applications would make it even more difficult to reduce postal rates. In short, while economy was difficult to practice in the Post Office Department, the policies pursued by the Coolidge administration followed the overall pattern of aiding big business and established wealth at the expense of small businessmen and ordinary citizens.[18]

In only one area of senatorial business was Norris essentially a novice during the Coolidge years. While a member of the Judiciary

---

Norris to C. H. Kent, Feb. 17, 1925; Calvin Coolidge to Irvine L. Lenroot, Dec. 24, 1924, Jan. 3, 1925 (Box 2, Irvine L. Lenroot Papers, Manuscript Division, Library of Congress).

[17] *Congressional Record,* 68th Cong., 2nd sess., Jan. 29, pp. 2632–34, Jan. 30, 1925, pp. 2694–95; Norris to Kent, Feb. 17, 1925. The postal rate bill passed the Senate and eventually was enacted. Norris said it was a face-saving measure designed to aid "Administration Senators" who changed their vote to sustain Coolidge's veto of a postal employee pay-raise bill. For evidence that small businessmen were facing additional difficulties because of this measure, see Norris to Carpenter Paper Company, May 6, 1925; to K. V. Kidder, Dec. 28, 1925.

[18] *Congressional Record,* 69th Cong., 2nd sess., Feb. 14, 1927, p. 3671; Norris to Paul Cook, Dec. 4, 1926; to F. R. Robinson, Feb. 1, 1927; to Fred Hovey, July 2, 1930. Norris was also unwilling to practice economy in another area. He could not agree to establishing a statute of limitations on a soldier's proven claim to a war-derived injury; see *Congressional Record,* 69th Cong., 1st sess., June 28, 1926, p. 12081.

Committee he never had ample time to devote to its affairs because of his primary responsibility as chairman of the Agricultural and Forestry Committee. Having resigned that position in 1925, he was able to devote himself more conscientiously to matters before the Judiciary Committee. A good portion of its business, having to do with judicial appointments, never came before the Senate in the form of proposed legislation. While hearings were held to consider judicial appointees, they were not as extensive as those Norris had previously conducted. But they could help determine the quality of justice in the United States for decades to come.

Norris had begun to recall with increasing satisfaction his earlier judicial career. Now, however, he saw how judges were selected. Often politicians handed out judgeships as a reward for partisan action; often great corporations selected men who were then appointed to the bench. In the dispensation of justice men of wealth and political influence were favored. The aphorism "You cannot convict a hundred million dollars" contained an essential truth. This knowledge almost caused Norris to modify his belief about appointing judges for life and took away much of the respect he had held for the federal judiciary. The problem was not easy to solve. Judicial procedures were as old as the government and had their roots in the common law of England. "The Country," he said, "is in a judicial rut and it is extremely difficult to get it out." Justice was too expensive. Too many delays and too many expenses gave privileges to wealth that were denied to poverty. The effect, while unintended, was "to undermine the very theory of our system of jurisprudence, which proclaims equal justice to rich and poor alike." [19]

Early in his tenure as chairman of the Judiciary Committee Norris proposed abolishing all U.S. courts except the Supreme Court, conferring their jurisdiction upon state courts but providing for appeal from state supreme courts to the U.S. Supreme Court. This proposal would eliminate the dual system of jurisprudence; there was no reason "why a civilized country like ours should have

[19] Norris to I. D. Evans, May 18, 1925; to H. M. Crist, June 26, 1926; to M. F. Harrington, July 16, 1929; to William Howard Taft, Mar. 21, 1929. In the letter to Taft Norris commented on the activity being shown by railroads and other large corporations in behalf of candidates for different circuit judgeships.

all the overhead of carrying on and maintaining two systems of jurisprudence."

A trial in a federal court was always much more expensive because the parties and their witnesses often had to travel hundreds of miles. If the case were put over or delayed, it meant an expense that to the poor man was "an absolute denial of justice." Whatever historic reasons had existed for the creation of the dual court system were no longer valid. Americans retained it on the theory that the protection of property demanded it. But, Norris noted, when a human life was at stake, the state courts had jurisdiction. Abolishing federal courts below the Supreme Court necessarily would increase the need for more state judges; Norris said, "This would come about in the natural course of events." Litigation would be less expensive, overhead costs would be reduced, and serious delays would be less frequent. Norris also called for the simplification of court procedures. "There is no reason," he insisted, "why an indictment should not be stated in plain English so the ordinary person can understand it, instead of using a long list of legal technicalities that might have been necessary in the Middle Ages." Pleadings should be stated in simple, everyday language. Judicial reform was necessary; as chairman of the Judiciary Committee of the U.S. Senate, Norris continually called for it.[20]

His relations with Chief Justice William Howard Taft and Attorney General John G. Sargent were formal and polite. Taft expressed distaste for Norris as chairman of the Judiciary Committee. Alpheus Thomas Mason in *William Howard Taft: Chief Justice* wrote that "it was a sad day in 1926 when, on Cummins' death, Norris became chairman of the committee." But Norris never criticized the chief justice. The two men met occasionally and Norris discussed with both Taft and Sargent his proposal to place some federal jurisdiction with the state courts.[21] Norris knew that long agitation

[20] Norris to Crist, June 26, 1926; to John L. Benbow, Dec. 19, 1926; to Thomas S. Rice, Apr. 22, 1927; to Alben W. Barkley, Apr. 23, 1928; to Lewis S. Gannett, Apr. 28, 1928; to Carl Wheaton, May 6, 1928. In the Seventieth Congress Norris introduced a bill to take away jurisdiction of federal courts in cases involving diversity of citizenship; see *Congressional Record,* 70th Cong., 1st sess., May 8, 1928, p. 8080.

[21] Taft to Norris, Dec. 15, 1926, Apr. 16, 1927; Norris to Taft, Apr. 16, 1927, Mar. 18, 1929; Alpheus Thomas Mason, *William Howard Taft: Chief Justice* (New York, 1965), p. 96 and *passim;* Norris to John G. Sargent, Apr. 14, 1927.

was necessary. The legal profession, concerned with precedents and accepting principles with admiration and respect, would be slow to advocate reform. The law had a tendency to make one conservative and suspicious of change. Nevertheless, Norris found many judges and lawyers who agreed that something should be done and he announced his intention of calling for a federal commission to recommend improvements in criminal law and procedures in federal courts.[22]

The Fall-Sinclair trial in 1927 emanating from the Teapot Dome scandal aroused Norris's interest in reform of criminal procedures. The trial resulted in the discharge of the jury after weeks in the courtroom. The judge discharged the jury, Norris said, because Harry Sinclair, one of the defendants, had employed detectives to shadow the jury. The judge implied that the defendants "and these detectives were guilty of contempt of court" while the primary defendant, Harry Sinclair, only spent part of his time in court. He went to New York and elsewhere in pursuit of business or pleasure and in so doing violated "one of the first principles of criminal law." In another case Sinclair was prosecuted for contempt of Congress, found guilty, and sentenced to jail, but he was still free on appeal. Norris wrote, "I presume many of us will die of old age before it is finally disposed of by the Supreme Court." There were "too many technicalities, too many delays, too many discussions on technical points" that had nothing to do with the merits of the case. In sum,

Norris said that he thought Taft was in "entire sympathy" with the idea of court reform; see Norris to Carl E. Herring, May 13, 1927. In his correspondence Norris admitted to having "a great deal of respect and admiration for Justice Holmes." Such comments were rare; see Norris to G. Jay Clark, Jan. 2, 1928.

[22] Norris to Rice, May 13, Nov. 14, 1927; to Clark, Jan. 2, 1928; to James C. Kinsler, Feb. 10, 1928; to Lester E. Hoppe, Mar. 23, 1928. *Brooklyn Daily Eagle*, Nov. 7, 1927, carried a story by Rice on Norris's proposal. As the session got under way, Norris found that the Judiciary Committee was not receptive to many of his proposals. Some were bowdlerized; others were jettisoned; very few were accepted; see Norris to Clarence Venner, Mar. 27, 1928; to Newton D. Baker, Mar. 29, 1928; Norris, "Criminal Procedure in Our Courts," June 24, 1928 (draft article); Norris, "Reform in Our Judicial Procedure," *Brooklyn Daily Eagle*, Mar. 8, 1929. Norris introduced a bill calling for a U.S. court of administrative justice which would simplify and consolidate procedures and courts and bring about expedition and efficiency in the settlement of claims against the United States; see *Congressional Record*, 70th Cong., 2nd sess., Jan. 3, 1929, pp. 1030–32.

the situation was "a deplorable mess," demonstrating that court procedures had not kept up "with the advancing civilization of the age." [23]

In the matter of judicial appointments, frequently either the president or the Attorney General inquired what Norris's position would be if certain men were appointed. In each instance he frankly expressed his views, having first tried to satisfy himself of the fitness of the appointee. At the end of the Coolidge administration he had not found an appointee from Nebraska "personally objectionable." Since the president had the appointing power and the right to select his own advisers on appointments, Norris never felt piqued or angered if Coolidge did not consult him or if the president appointed a qualified person whose behavior violated his personal feelings. Judges and prosecuting attorneys, Norris always said, should be appointed without regard to politics and personal feelings. He always voted for confirmation if he believed the candidates were competent and would make good officials.[24] On almost his last day in office President Coolidge sent a number of judicial nominations to the Senate. Norris thought this action unjustifiable because there was no time to examine the qualifications of the appointees. Despite pressure from colleagues and from the White House, he refused to permit the nominations to go through. He was criticized for his action, one senator stating that Norris had succeeded in "getting even" with Coolidge. But Norris insisted he was acting "solely from a sense of duty," and several senators privately told him they agreed with him.[25]

Confronting Coolidge was a disagreeable task. Continually criticizing and fighting policies and programs of his party discouraged Norris. More disheartening was the inescapable conclusion that the Coolidge administration continually ignored "the chaos, the misery, and the suffering that so many millions of people are enduring, without their even having been guilty of any wrong." It ignored these people while pursuing goals that benefited an already established and prospering elite whose status was based primarily on material well-being. Pursued to its logical conclusion, the result

23 Norris to Kinsler, Feb. 10, 1928; to Crist, May 1, 1928.
24 Norris to G. P. North, Mar. 20, 1929; to Williams, Mar. 22, 1929.
25 Norris to Andrew M. Morrissey, Mar. 25, 1929.

could only be "agony and disaster." "I feel," Norris wrote at the end of the Coolidge administration, "an utter helplessness—that there is no hope left for civilization and humanity." His reflections on social issues in no way convinced Norris that these observations needed modifying.[26]

[26] Norris to Locke, Jan. 3, 1929.

Social Trends

22

U.S. senators are supposed to be able to speak authoritatively on issues affecting the American people. And all do just that. Actually, each senator is an authority in the fields reflected in his committee assignments. What he knows about other prominent issues is usually learned by listening to discussion on the Senate floor, by reading his correspondence and newspapers, by conversations with colleagues, friends, and government officials. But it is only on matters coming within the scope of his major committee assignments that a senator can truly speak as an expert. The senator who spends much time on the floor listening to discussion and asking searching questions is rare, but he is bound to be better informed than most of his colleagues. George W. Norris was such a senator. When he discussed matters outside his fields of competence, he was informed if not well versed on the subject.

On the "noble experiment" of prohibition every senator was continually called upon to express his opinions. Every senator had to consider his constituency carefully lest he needlessly antagonize different groups. For Norris the matter was relatively simple. He had voted to submit the resolution which became the Eighteenth Amendment to the states and he would later vote against its repeal. He believed in prohibition and this belief accurately reflected the sentiments of his rural constituency. He favored prohibition before it became a national issue; in Nebraska he had supported it by local option before state prohibition was enacted. While Norris rarely discussed it on the Senate floor, believing that other issues demanded his immediate attention, throughout the decade of the 1920s he had considerable correspondence on the subject. He realized that there were many who permitted enthusiasm to warp their judgment. He was of the opinion that the Eighteenth Amendment gave Congress the right to prohibit the manufacture, transportation, and sale of intoxicating beverages. But the Volstead Act in defining intoxicating beverages included items, beer and wine for example, usually admitted to be nonintoxicating. Norris was not in favor of the legal definition and was surprised when the Supreme Court in 1920 sustained the Volstead Act. Thereafter he was convinced that the movement to repeal the Eighteenth Amendment would not amount to anything.[1]

Though he was concerned at the vast amount of money expended in enforcing prohibition, at the outset he presumed it necessary to curb bootlegging. Suspicions were aroused in 1924 when a Senate investigation of the Internal Revenue Bureau, including the prohibition unit, prompted Secretary Mellon to write a letter denouncing it; President Coolidge sent a special message to Congress condemning it. These actions led Norris to believe that the investigation would yield "some wonderful disclosures" because he now was aware that federal enforcement in many instances was "a mockery and a sham." The investigation of Attorney General Daugherty's conduct convinced him that still greater neglect of duty could have been disclosed.[2]

One way of improving the situation would be to select enforcement officers entirely upon merit, since opportunities for fraud and financial gain were greater than in almost any other governmental activity. "The placing of these officers on the political pie counter," Norris wrote, "will result in all kinds of corruption and will mean that the law will not be honestly enforced." Prohibition would become a

[1] George W. Norris to R. D. Austin, Dec. 29, 1921; to Mrs. C. E. Garner, Apr. 2, 1924; to Hattie L. Storks, June 1, 1926; to A. L. Green, June 10, 1931. By 1931 Norris was arguing that the vendors of wine and beer always joined those interested in the sale of distilled liquor, reaching the conclusion that the only way to get prohibition "was to make a clean sweep of it"; see Norris to F. B. Fasola, Jan. 28, 1931.

[2] Norris to Austin, Dec. 29, 1921; to D. Helphand, May 13, 1922; to Emma N. Bradstock, Sept. 6, 1924; to Wayne B. Wheeler, Feb. 20, 1925.

mockery encouraging an alliance between bootleggers and bosses based on pay-offs and ignoring of violations. Political machines would be supported by profits from the bootlegging business; actions such as that of Republican Senator John W. Harreld, demanding the right to name enforcement officers for Oklahoma to help build a machine to insure his re-election, would become commonplace. Norris admitted that Omaha was wide open, that there were "practically no attempts made whatever to arrest anybody for violation of the law." He quickly concluded that the Coolidge administration was satisfied with the way things were done. While he was uncertain that the situation could be changed, he would gladly lend assistance to any one who would "enforce the law and do it honestly." [3]

Admitting that prohibition could become a party issue, Norris did not believe it wise to make it one. If it were the only issue, it would be all right. Since it was not, prohibition would confuse the political picture and encourage those who wished to use it as a smoke screen to support special interests. There were men opposed to prohibition whom Norris favored over others with whom he agreed on prohibition but who supported policies he actively opposed. It seemed better, therefore, if the cause of prohibition could be divorced from partisanship, especially in a national campaign. [4] But prohibition never had a chance; it had been made a partisan political issue. Norris noted that by violating the law and "under the guise of partisanship and faithful political services," enforcement agents could make "enormous contributions to the political machine out of the profits of their unlawful business." If the president would select men for their qualifications and ability, then Norris believed enforcement would be given a fair test and the necessity of retaining prohibition, for the "vast amount of good" it could engender, would become apparent. [5]

[3] Draft statement by Norris on prohibition enforcement, Aug. 22, 1925; Norris to Elmer E. Thomas, Jan. 24, June 1, 1926; to G. O. Van Meter, Dec. 3, 1926; to Lincoln C. Andrews, Dec. 10, 1926; to John H. Kelly, Dec. 28, 1926; to James C. Kinsler, July 23, 1926; to Peter Norbeck, Nov. 18, 1926; to Thomas B. McGovern, July 25, 1927.

[4] Norris to Wheeler, June 25, 1927; to Clinton N. Howard, July 12 and 18, 1928.

[5] Norris to Robert Barry, Aug. 22, 1927.

By 1928 he realized that many who were fighting to repeal the Eighteenth Amendment had initially supported it. They changed their minds because they felt the law was a farce involving an alliance of enforcement officers and bootleggers. Norris also was disturbed that prohibition leaders ignored every aspect of a candidate's career but the lone fact that he was either "wet" or "dry." They enthusiastically endorsed the Harding and Coolidge administrations but ignored the tie-in with bootleggers and winked at violations by enforcement officers.[6]

Observing no change in the matter of enforcement, Norris introduced a resolution in 1930 to learn two things: first, whether the failure of prohibition enforcement was due to the appointment of inefficient or dishonest officials, and second, whether the appointment of officials had been made on partisan political grounds. So widespread was the conviction that the law was not enforced in good faith that Norris thought there was a chance his resolution might be approved. Until there was an honest attempt at enforcement, he was not willing to talk about repeal. But the resolution gained little support.[7]

Mrs. Mabel Walker Willebrandt was in charge of the Treasury Department unit responsible for prohibition enforcement. According to Norris, she was lax in her job. On one occasion after she had secured the indictment of some wealthy violators, "they were all cleared because orders came from higher up" despite sufficient evidence to convict them. Norris also claimed that "several of the worst and biggest bootleggers had been pardoned after they were convicted." So much profit was to be made from violating the law that bootleggers often sought to influence the appointment of enforcement officers.[8]

If these officers devoted their attention to individuals making millions of dollars in operations extending over the entire country and to their contacts in official circles, the noble experiment would not have degenerated into a mockery. Since the intention of the law was to prevent the manufacture for sale of intoxicating liquor,

[6] Norris to Howard, July 12, 1928.

[7] Norris to Arthur W. Brooks, Mar. 3, 1930; to Fred Kockrow, Mar. 22, 1930; to Frank L. Williams, Apr. 26, 1930.

[8] Norris to Mrs. H. E. Lovelace, Mar. 17, 1930; to Williams, Apr. 26, 1930; to Mabel Walker Willebrandt, July 17, 1930.

Norris doubted that the home brewer or home distiller was violating its spirit. Interfering with such individuals and ignoring organized elements in the illicit liquor business made enemies for prohibition and encouraged bootlegging. It also encouraged criminal elements to engage in politics, to contribute large sums of money, and to seek favors from public officials. To the very end Norris was convinced prohibition had never had a fair trial. Throughout the administrations of Presidents Harding, Coolidge, and Hoover it had been used as "a political football," though the situation had improved under Herbert Hoover.[9]

The change in mores regarding liquor and drinking was also reflected by the acceptance in society of women smoking. Not denying that women had as much right as men to smoke, Norris wondered why women smoking in a public place before 1917 would have been regarded as trespassing upon the moral code of civilized society. What had happened? Why the shift in public attitudes toward drinking and smoking? Why the fluctuating moral code? Admitting that he was "somewhat of an old 'fogy,'" viewing these habits with "suspicion and fear," Norris placed the blame on World War I. It had helped change human nature and affected the moral fiber of individuals. It had been followed by corruption in high places which many Americans accepted without criticism. It helped explain why "the man in the street," seeking to emulate his superiors, felt inclined to take what was not his and was unconcerned about fair and honest law enforcement.

The drinking habits of young people were another indication of "the almost universal change which had overtaken civilization." Norris did not believe these habits were the result of the prohibition law; otherwise he would have favored its repeal. While he hoped the world would try to recover lost ground, basically he was pessimistic; "we are all at the present time in the dark." Moral deterioration was merely paralleling the decline of other aspects of American civilization evident since the war.[10]

Norris did make significant changes in his views shortly before

---

[9] Norris to Williams, Apr. 26, 1930; to Mrs. H. R. H. Williams, June 21, 1930; to M. F. Junge, Dec. 11, 1931.

[10] Norris to Ben H. Smith, Jan. 6, 1932; to J. M. Douglass, Jan. 17, 1933.

prohibition came to an end. In June, 1932, he declared in favor of light wines and beer. He also supported a plan for liquor sales by government dispensaries, thereby departing from the dry standard he had supported throughout his career. "No matter how much I have believed in prohibition," Norris said, "I cannot close my eyes to the fact that the country seems to be the other way and that enforcement seems to be a failure." His views were not very different from those recommended by the Wickersham commission, some of whose members were ardent prohibitionists. If modifications were not made, Norris was convinced, the Eighteenth Amendment would be repealed and the saloon and "all its evils" would return. As a practical prohibitionist he mixed his metaphors to assert that he "would rather have a half loaf than no bread." [11]

If prohibition raised confusing questions, Norris continued to reflect the views of his rural constituency. On the issue of immigration, which also raised difficult questions, he similarly reflected rural Nebraska. "The lessons of the war," Norris remarked, "have taught us that there is great danger in going too far in the way of opening our doors to immigrants." Though some German immigrants did not do their full share, on the whole "the so-called German-Americans were wonderfully loyal and showed under some very trying circumstances, a truly patriotic spirit." He understood that naturalized citizens were bound to be vitally interested in the fate of their native lands.

Immigration posed an "extremely important" and difficult question for Norris. It was difficult because he disliked the idea of keeping away "from our shores any of those people who are trying to better their condition in life," and he was not sure a fair formula could be developed to limit immigration. But above all, he candidly asserted, "self-preservation should be our first consideration."

[11] *San Diego Union,* June 30, 1932; *Washington Herald,* June 29, 1932; Norris to Mary Lee Seibert, July 8, 1932; to Willis J. Abbot, Dec. 29, 1932. Norris reviewed his position on prohibition and reiterated his belief in the necessity of modifying the Volstead Act in Senate debate on repeal of the Eighteenth Amendment. He was reluctant to repeal the amendment because he feared the return of the old saloon; see *Congressional Record,* 72nd Cong., 1st sess., July 11, pp. 15017–19, July 16, 1932, pp. 15671–72; 2nd sess., Feb. 15, 1933, pp. 4161–62, 4175–76.

"Until the world got back to some kind of a sane basis," Norris conceded he would vote for immigration restriction: "It is a hard duty to perform, but I believe it is a duty nevertheless." The fact that recent immigrants, as a rule, did not "go out into the country and work on the farms" made this duty a bit easier to perform. He doubted that it would be possible to admit only immigrants willing to settle in rural areas.[12]

Norris voted for immigration restriction because "millions of foreigners" still were not assimilated into American life. Although "immigrants ought to be Americanized," he was unwilling to use immigration laws to separate families. An American citizen should have the right to bring his spouse, children, and "aged parents" to the United States. He favored amending the immigration laws to remove the "cruel provisions" which denied this right.[13] He also favored basing quotas upon figures which would permit the largest immigration from the countries of northern Europe. Immigrants from southern Europe did not assimilate; they clung to their customs and native languages "in some of the larger cities" and did not mix with native-born Americans. But immigrants from northern Europe quickly became good citizens, associating "with other upright citizens" in communities where they settled. In short, Norris made a distinction between "old" and "new" immigrants. "Old" immigrants easily assimilated into American life; many became

[12] Norris to J. F. Lawrence, Jan. 10, 1921; to Edwin W. Nelson, May 8, 1922. In 1908 as a member of the House of Representatives Norris had investigated on behalf of a constituent the best class of immigrants for farm work. Terence V. Powderly, serving as chief of the Information Division, Commerce and Labor Department, told him that immigrants "from the north of Poland or north of Austria" would be best suited to farm work in Nebraska. "The North Poles," he specified, "are as a rule honest, faithful and loyal, and come from a farming community and are peculiarly fitted to perform farming labor." Since even in 1908 relatively few immigrants met these geographical specifications, it was easier for Norris to favor immigration restriction in the 1920s; see Norris to E. A. Holdrege, Jr., Feb. 26, 1908.

[13] Norris to Hazel Thompson, Mar. 27, 1924; to C. J. Claasen, Apr. 19, 1924; *Congressional Record*, 68th Cong., 1st sess., May 15, 1924, p. 8587. During this period Norris through continual agitation forced the State Department to permit the return of Anna Lerner, Russian-born wife of an American citizen. She had been deported as a radical and languished in ill health for more than a year in Russia, knowing neither the language nor any friends who might care for her; see the story by Laurence Todd in *Illinois Miner*, July 4, 1925.

farmers and settled in rural regions. "New" immigrants added to urban congestion and did not fit readily into the more established patterns of American life.[14]

As was the case in his analysis of prohibition, by the end of the decade Norris had modified his views, concluding that it would be very difficult, "if not entirely impractical," to base immigration policy upon the "national origins" system, which became fully operative in 1929. Norris claimed that, as Secretary of Commerce, Herbert Hoover had investigated this proposal and had said it was not a practical way to limit immigration. In his campaign for the presidency, Norris said, Hoover announced himself as favoring the repeal of the "national origins" system. If so, it was one of the very few points upon which Norris and Hoover agreed. Where in the case of prohibition his modification encompassed more lenient views, Norris wanted a base that "would bring in the lowest number of immigrants from southern European countries." [15] The fact that immigrants were usually urban dwellers and laborers rather than, as in the nineteenth century, farmers and residents of small towns disturbed Norris. Though he could sympathize with the urban dweller and laboring man, he was not acutely aware of their problems; not until the Hoover administration did he become involved with an issue affecting labor.[16] Otherwise his concern for the problems of labor and of minority groups was similar to his concern about immigration. His views reveal some of the tensions inherent in the struggle rural America was making to stay the sweep of urban mores and values during the 1920s.

In another area Norris always supported legislation favorable to

[14] Norris to Christopher Folck, Mar. 21, 1928. Norris favored excluding aliens in fixing the basis of representation. But he did not think this could be done without amending the Constitution; see Norris to A. B. Pierce, Dec. 27, 1930.

[15] Norris to Lester A. Thompson, Mar. 22, 1929; to J. F. Nelson, Apr. 10, 1929; to Howard W. Toner, Apr. 20, 1929. For a discussion of Hoover's immigration views, see Robert A. Divine, *American Immigration Policy* (New Haven, Conn., 1957), pp. 40–41. Divine notes that Hoover in his acceptance speech clearly stated his opposition to the national-origins concept. But throughout the campaign he was "strangely silent" on the matter.

[16] In 1925, when an American Federation of Labor official sought to discuss anti-injunction legislation, Norris, though sympathetic, regretted that his other involvements made it impossible to consider labor legislation; see Norris to Matthew Woll, Jan. 1, 1926.

the protection and education of the Negro. While he admitted to never carefully examining the provisions of antilynching measures, particularly the Dyer bill, because it had never come to a vote in the Senate, he was sympathetic to measures that sought to protect citizens "without regard to color, from mob violence." But basically race was not an issue for Norris. He thought Negroes in Nebraska were not discriminated against, nor did he believe they were discriminated against in Washington, D.C. In the few appointments he had at his disposal for jobs in the Capitol, he chose young men who were working their way through school. In 1928 two were white and one was black.[17]

Norris thought the Negro had made wonderful progress since emancipation. "A people who were liberated from bondage after years of servitude cannot be expected to at once reach the highest type." Education, necessarily a slow and tedious process, was imperative. "The best friend of the colored people," he said, "is one who does not try to make of them a political machine or to cause them to exercise the elective franchise through rank partisanship." In short, while Norris had little understanding of the race problem, he regarded the Negro as he regarded the white man, beset by partisanship and boss rule. If progress was to be made, individual thought and deliberative action would be necessary to break the power of these oppressive forces.[18]

In viewing social trends during the era of Republican ascendancy, Norris reflected the views of the majority of his constituency fairly well. He was a prohibitionist and he was concerned about new arrivals seemingly unable to assimilate into American life. The plight of labor and the problems of the Negro were of little concern, though he was sympathetic to the hopes and aspirations of both groups. But these tensions were of little interest to George W. Norris. Indeed, he felt prohibition could be used as a smoke screen to cover more important issues, the economy and exploitation. The farm situation, corporate control of and influence on the economic and political scene, intense partisanship—these were more basic

[17] Norris to Robert Smith, Apr. 1, 1924; to Austin S. Miller, Apr. 9, 1924; to J. B. Smith, Feb. 4, 1928.
[18] Norris to W. E. B. DuBois, May 26, 1931.

problems affecting American life. And in almost every instance his suggestions were either ignored or defeated. But in the most important battle he waged, that of Muscle Shoals, the tide began to turn at the end of the Coolidge administration.

The Turning of the Tide

23

Neither Calvin Coolidge nor George W. Norris was satisfied with the Muscle Shoals situation after the Sixty-eighth Congress expired in March, 1925, with no final action taken on the Underwood bill. Coolidge wished to lease the properties; Norris wanted the government to operate them. The battle between these two points of view was waged continuously throughout the Sixty-ninth and Seventieth Congresses and at the end of Coolidge's term of office the issue had yet to be resolved. But a momentous change had occurred. Congress enacted a public ownership bill only to have it vetoed by the president. It was only a matter of time before a president would approve of public ownership or Congress would override a presidential veto. At the end of Calvin Coolidge's tenure of office the tide had turned in favor of the public ownership position championed by George Norris.

Before the Sixty-ninth Congress convened, Norris traveled throughout Ontario and made a thorough investigation of the Canadian province's system of generating and distributing electricity. He acquired a mass of material and spent much time analyzing it in relation to the coming Muscle Shoals fight. He was not optimistic, but he made careful preparations.[1]

[1] George W. Norris to Carl D. Thompson, July 10, 1925; to Judson King, Mar. 6, 1925 (Box 2, Judson King Papers, Manuscript Division, Library of Congress). Norris at this time began corresponding with Morris L. Cooke, a distinguished engineer with an active interest in public power. He informed Cooke that

While Norris readied himself for the next round in the controversy, the five-man committee chosen by Coolidge at the end of the Sixty-eighth Congress to inquire into the best method of utilizing the Muscle Shoals properties was at work. Before Congress convened, the committee had prepared a report recommending that the properties be leased. If no satisfactory lease could be made, then the government should operate the properties. A member of the committee told Herbert Hoover that the report was in effect "a blank cartridge, merely saying: 'Mr. President, lease it if you can; and if you can't lease it, then run it.' " [2]

The president was informed that the report was not satisfactory, suggesting a continuation of the approach that had resulted in the deadlock on the Underwood bill. It might result in the bill's defeat because of the "growing opinion in Congress, even among conservative circles, that government operation is the only solution of the Muscle Shoals problem." A situation "somewhat similar to that which destroyed the Ford offer" could develop, "particularly in view of the fact that Senator Norris has been spending the summer in the Province of Ontario, Canada, making a study of government operation of water power in the provinces." Moreover, Coolidge was warned, Norris would exert every effort "to defeat any legislation he does not endorse." Rather than follow the formal channels of a committee in each house to consider leasing offers, it was suggested that Coolidge appoint a joint committee to consider bids, conduct negotiations, and report recommendations and thus neutralize Norris's opposition.[3]

Acting on this advice, Coolidge sent to Congress the report of his Muscle Shoals Inquiry Commission on December 10, 1925. In

public policy could not be decided by engineers alone. Engineers had an important role to play in carrying out policy but were not central to the political decision involved in the Muscle Shoals controversy; see Norris to Cooke, May 18, 1925 (Morris L. Cooke Papers, Franklin D. Roosevelt Library, Hyde Park, N.Y.).

[2] Russel F. Bower to Herbert Hoover, Nov. 6, 1925 (copy in Box 128:44A, Calvin Coolidge Papers, Manuscript Division, Library of Congress).

[3] Bower to Calvin Coolidge, Nov. 12, 1925 (Box 128:44A); C. H. Huston to Coolidge, Nov. 20, 1925 (Box 126:44, Coolidge Papers). Bower, Washington representative of the National Farmers' Union, represented agriculture on the inquiry committee. He was not in favor of public ownership. Claudius Huston, a Chattanooga lawyer, was an active lobbyist for private development of Muscle Shoals. He was president of the Tennessee River Improvement Association.

January, 1926, the House approved Concurrent Resolution 4, which was accepted by the Senate, creating a joint committee on Muscle Shoals to receive bids and recommend one for acceptance. The committee was organized on March 16 with Senator Charles S. Deneen as chairman and Representative W. Frank James as vice-chairman. It held hearings and gave serious consideration to two of the many bids it received: one from thirteen associated southern power companies incorporated as the Muscle Shoals Power Distributing Company and the Muscle Shoals Fertilizer Company, and the other from the American Cyanamid Company. The opportunity for Norris and members of the Senate Agriculture and Forestry Committee to scrutinize and challenge the offers was obviated. All that was left was unlimited debate on the floor of the Senate, and Norris used it to the utmost.

Norris said that the resolution was a step backward, "about as bad as the Ford proposition" except that it proposed leasing for a period of fifty instead of a hundred years.[4] To combat it, he introduced a public ownership bill patterned on the one presented in 1922. It provided for the development of the Tennessee River and its tributaries "with the object of producing the maximum amount of power, the maximum amount of navigation, and the maximum amount of flood control." In brief, a government corporation would operate the Muscle Shoals plants to produce nitrates for national defense, to experiment with the production of cheap fertilizer, and to sell surplus power to consumers, giving preference to states, counties, and municipalities. The corporation could construct transmission lines and operate all the power dams. It would pay back to the Treasury construction costs plus 4 percent interest. The Secretary of War would develop the system as a whole, constructing all necessary dams for power, storage, and flood control, while the Secretary of Agriculture would be responsible for fertilizer operations. The principle that before fertilizer could be cheaply produced, an improved method of manufacture would have to be developed, was recognized by providing "for the

---

[4] Draft statement by Norris, n.d. [Jan. 6, 1926]. To William Kent the report of the Coolidge inquiry committee, the concurrent resolution, and various administration statements demonstrated that all favored "this big policy of turkey for the insiders and turkey bone soup for the general public"; see Kent to Max Stern, Jan. 13, 1926 (Addition 4, William Kent Papers, Yale University Library).

largest experimentation along that score ever undertaken anywhere in the world." Though the Secretaries of War and Agriculture were granted specific assignments in the Norris measure, the corporation was to be managed by a board of three persons appointed by the president and confirmed by the Senate.[5] The bill was submitted to the Agriculture and Forestry Committee, where no action was taken on it during the session.

With the practical completion in 1925 of the Wilson Dam and its powerhouse, 160,000 horsepower were continually available. The energy was sold by the War Department to the Alabama Power Company, which owned the only transmission line connected with the plant. With additional construction above Muscle Shoals and interconnection with other systems, Norris claimed that over 300,000 horsepower soon would be available to increase the wealth and comfort of people in the South; and greater rewards were yet to come.[6] Privately he confessed that the prospects for public ownership were not bright. Southern business firms pressed for the leasing of Muscle Shoals. The members of the Tennessee Manufacturers Association unanimously demanded that the government keep its "hands off" Muscle Shoals and chambers of commerce throughout the South reiterated the chant. There was, Norris said, almost unanimous agreement among southern businessmen in opposition to the government doing anything with Muscle Shoals or the Tennessee River. Few voices were heard in the South championing public ownership as the cause of the common people.[7]

[5] Draft statement by Norris about S. 2147, n.d. [Jan. 5, 1926?]. The first members of the board were named in the bill: Morris L. Cooke, James D. Ross, and John R. Neal. Ross, like Cooke, was an engineer. He managed the municipal hydroelectric plant at Seattle, one of the largest municipal plants in the world. Neal, former dean of the University of Tennessee Law School, was vitally interested in the multiple-purpose development of the Tennessee River. For his role in the famed Scopes case, see Ray Ginger, *Six Days or Forever? Tennessee v. John Thomas Scopes* (Boston, 1958); see also Norris to John Randolph Neal, Nov. 13, 1926.

[6] *St. Louis Post-Dispatch,* Jan. 22, 1926.

[7] Norris to Alfred Truitt, Jan. 23, 1926. Essential agreement with Norris's views in favor of public ownership as best for the people of the South, and business opposition to this premise, were expressed by both George Fort Milton, editor of the *Chattanooga News,* and Senator Kenneth McKellar of Tennessee; see McKellar to Milton, Jan. 9, 1926; Milton to McKellar, Jan. 11, 1926 (both in George Fort Milton Papers, Manuscript Division, Library of Congress).

On the morning of February 3, 1926, Calvin Coolidge called members of the Senate Agriculture and Forestry Committee to the White House and urged a favorable report on the House resolution calling for a joint congressional committee to receive bids for the private operation of Muscle Shoals. In a statement issued later in the day, after the committee had acquiesced in the president's request, Norris criticized Coolidge for his tactics and announced that the committee would soon hold hearings on his bill providing for government operation of Muscle Shoals.[8]

On March 1, 1926, the Senate began consideration of the concurrent resolution and for the following two weeks Norris was active in opposition. He reiterated points he had made previously, stressing the deception in making farmers believe that fertilizer could be cheaply produced at Muscle Shoals. "The evidence stands uncontradicted before the world today," he said, "that the manufacture of fertilizer consumes, as it is improved, less and less power. There is not a single horsepower at Muscle Shoals that would be used in the modern method of producing fertilizer." He went further than in his previous remarks, calling for the systematic development of the Tennessee River and its tributaries. Flood control, navigation, and power were "three objects of improvement, coordinating, working with each other in perfect harmony." If these goals were attained and electricity distributed throughout the South, "there would be given the greatest exhibition of production of cheap power the civilized world has ever known." But the pending concurrent resolution would make it impossible for "the great Tennessee River system" to be developed for the benefit of the people of the region.[9]

On March 8, 1926, the Senate by a large majority approved the concurrent resolution. Thomas Heflin of Alabama was the floor

[8] *New York Times,* Feb. 4, 1926. To reinforce Coolidge's victory in getting the resolution out of committee, lobbyist Claudius H. Huston two weeks later wrote a memorandum to the president suggesting Senators Arthur Capper, Henry Keyes, and Thomas Heflin as Senate members of the joint committee. They all favored leasing. The selection of Norris or Smith, he said, would be disastrous; he urged Coolidge to "make it certain that the President of the Senate selects appropriate members" or "we will lose our fight, and Senator Norris will be the winner"; see Huston to Coolidge, Feb. 19, 1926 (Box 126:44, Coolidge Papers).

[9] *Congressional Record,* 69th Cong., 1st sess., Mar. 1, pp. 4763, 4768, Mar. 5, pp. 5072–73, Mar. 8, 1926, pp. 5212–13; Norris to Milton, Mar. 20, 1926.

leader, revealing once again that on matters pertaining to Muscle Shoals, Coolidge could count on southern Democratic support. Norris was chosen by Vice-President Dawes to be a member of the joint committee that would conduct negotiations for leasing Muscle Shoals along with Senators Heflin and Frederick Sackett. Norris declined the appointment and Dawes then appointed Charles S. Deneen of Illinois. Thus the Coolidge administration effectively bypassed Norris and the Agriculture and Forestry Committee. It created a joint committee willing to lease the properties to private interests.[10]

In April Norris made a ten-day visit to the South, where he "inspected a whole lot of waterpower propositions including Muscle Shoals." Meanwhile, on April 26, 1926, the joint committee recommended the proposal by thirteen associated power companies and submitted a bill embodying this offer. But trouble for the administration developed when Representative James in a minority report denounced the bid because it "did not guarantee and safeguard the production of nitrates and other fertilizer ingredients." [11] In the Senate Norris made a motion to refer the measure to the Agriculture and Forestry Committee. Since secret hearings had been held, Norris claimed the Senate had a right to learn the reasons "for this provision and that provision." He also protested because minority views were not made available with the majority report. Important and controversial issues were involved in the associated power company proposal, yet no expert testimony was available. "For heaven's sake, Senators," he pleaded, "in an important matter like this, after we have gone this far, after we have given the time and attention we have, let us not give it away now on a report that is made in secret and without any evidence, without any opportunity for anybody to be heard." But Norris's motion was tabled.[12]

---

[10] *Congressional Record,* 69th Cong., 1st sess., Mar. 8, p. 5219, Mar. 13, 1926, pp. 5515–16, 5518–19. The vote approving the concurrent resolution was 51 to 26.

[11] Norris to "Dear Boys," Apr. 26, 1926; *Senate Report 672,* Part 2, 69th Cong., 1st sess., Serial Set 8525, Minority Views of Mr. James. James's report was a blast at the power companies claiming that "their offer is a power proposition disguised as a fertilizer proposal."

[12] *Congressional Record,* 69th Cong., 1st sess., Apr. 30, 1926, pp. 8502–6, 8509; Norris to J. S. Hale, May 10, 1926.

So great were the differences between majority and minority views that the first session of the Sixty-ninth Congress ended with no action in either the Senate or the House. As the session waned, Norris had no desire to prompt consideration: "A delay will have a tendency to educate the people to the real condition and to a better understanding of the bill." Before it adjourned, he prepared an article for the *Locomotive Engineers' Journal* entitled "Muscle Shoals and the Home" in which he reviewed the development of Muscle Shoals. Afterward he again thanked Judson King for help rendered "in the fight to save Muscle Shoals for the people." When King started on a tour to investigate public ownership projects in the West, Norris sent him a check for $100 to help in the work he was doing.[13]

When Congress reconvened in December, 1926, it was evident that the power companies' offer could not be passed. Senator Deneen, chairman of the joint committee, was regarded as an ally of the Insull interests and the committee was divided on how to proceed. In the House an offer by the American Cyanamid Company was introduced on January 24, 1927, as the Willis-Madden bill. It directed the Secretary of War to lease Muscle Shoals to the American Cyanamid Company and the Air Nitrates Corporation, a subsidiary. It quickly took precedence in the House over the power companies' bid and further confused the situation. The best that could be achieved before the Sixty-ninth Congress adjourned, J. W. Worthington of the Tennessee River Improvement Association said, would be the acceptance of the Cyanamid offer, which required the building of Dam No. 3 and the Cove Creek Dam and development of the electrochemical industry in the Tennessee Valley.[14]

Benefiting from this confusion over competing bids, Norris claimed that "the real truth is that Muscle Shoals is a power proposition." But the fertilizer question, which he regarded as a smoke screen for interests desiring the hydroelectric potential of Muscle Shoals, was of paramount concern. Norris devoted much time to

[13] Norris to Thompson, May 17, 1926; Norris, "Muscle Shoals and the Home," June 24, 1926 (draft), *Locomotive Engineers' Journal;* Norris to Robert Dwing, Apr. 12, 1927; to King, July 24, Sept. 27, 1926 (Box 2, King Papers).

[14] J. W. Worthington to Huston, Jan. 23, 1927 (copy in the Milton Papers).

Norris in 1917

THE ONLY ADEQUATE REWARD

From the *New York World*, March 7, 1917

Senator Edwin F. Ladd, Mrs. Nels Radick, and Norris, March 3, 1922

Senators Wesley L. Jones, Morris Sheppard, and Norris in 1924

From the *New York Evening Post*, November 9, 1925

Wolfe's Commercial Photos

Senate Agriculture and Forestry Committee in 1926 (Norris is sixth from the left)

IN ANOTHER DAY OR TWO

Mr. and Mrs. John P. Robertson

From the *Washington Daily News*, May 21, 1928

OUT INTO THE OPEN AIR

From the *New York World*, October 25, 1928

From the *Washington Evening Star*, October 25, 1928

Speaking of "Game Refuges," This Old Bird Certainly Has a Good One!

From the *Omaha World-Herald*, April 4, 1930

A GREAT FIGHTER

From the *New York World*, August 14, 1930

Norris in 1930

Senators Robert M. LaFollette, Jr., and Norris in March, 1931

ANOTHER GEORGE W. TRYING TO CROSS THE DELAWARE.

Mr. and Mrs. John P. Robertson

From the *Washington Evening Star*, February 23, 1931

Good Fishing Along the Potomac!

From the *Los Angeles Record*, April 1, 1932

From the *Washington Evening Star*, September 26, 1932

President-elect Roosevelt, Norris, and others viewing Wilson Dam at Muscle Shoals in January, 1933

this issue, explaining that behind all the talk about fertilizer was the "Power Trust," anxious to get Muscle Shoals. If unable to secure it for themselves, "they would like to see it used in the production of nitrates, knowing full well that the manufacture of fertilizer from this source would be a failure and that this power would, as a matter of fact, be wasted." The first time in the session that he spoke on the Muscle Shoals situation, Norris had a portion of a huge map of the United States placed on a wall in the Senate chamber. It was over five feet square. If fully extended, Norris said, "there would not be wall space enough in the Chamber to hold the map"; it showed the properties owned by the General Electric Company, "the head of the Electric Trust in the United States." He suggested that the control of the company reached out and gripped properties "all over the civilized world, in every State in the Union, almost in every community in every State." Norris delineated on the map every one of the thirteen bidders in the associated power companies' offer to lease Muscle Shoals. These corporations were indicated in orange; all were traced to the General Electric Company. Then he revealed how utility companies scattered throughout the nation were ultimately controlled by corporations centered in New York City; many were also interconnected with other utilities owned by either the Mellon or the Insull interests. All of these connections were traced on the map.[15]

Then, with less than a week left to the session, Norris introduced a joint resolution providing for the completion of Dam No. 2 and other properties at Muscle Shoals. The purpose was to use these properties to experiment with a view toward cheapening the cost of fertilizer.[16] The Sixty-ninth Congress adjourned on March 3, 1927, with no action on Muscle Shoals. The matter was held in

[15] Norris to Truitt, Feb. 13, 1927; *Congressional Record,* 69th Cong., 2nd sess., Feb. 25, pp. 4752–53, Feb. 28, 1927, p. 4995.

[16] *Congressional Record,* 69th Cong., 2nd sess., Feb. 26, 1927, pp. 4890–91. Norris could not present this resolution any earlier because the Deneen bill reported from the joint committee was on the calendar and not considered till late in the session. The Senate by "a good margin" agreed to recommit the bill to the Agriculture and Forestry Committee. This move in effect meant its death and senators understood that. Once this matter was disposed of, Norris was free to submit his resolution; it died in committee at the end of the session; see Norris to Kirkman O'Neal, Mar. 6, 1927; to Allen J. Roulhac, Mar. 6, 1927; to Edward A. Fisher, Mar. 6, 1927.

abeyance until the convening of the Seventieth Congress in December, 1927. The stage was now set for a dramatic fight in which a public ownership bill introduced by Norris would gain a great victory.

As soon as Congress adjourned, Norris drafted a long article which he titled "Muscle Shoals: The Lost Opportunity." He sent it to George Fort Milton, editor of *The New South,* who printed it in the July issue as "Politics and Muscle Shoals." Senator Gerald P. Nye inserted it in the *Congressional Record* so that offprints could be cheaply made and wide distribution achieved. Norris discussed the "many possibilities of usefulness and pleasure" inherent in electricity, insisting that "if stock manipulation can be eliminated and if financial legerdemain and unconscionable profits can be removed, it is the cheapest source of power and light known to man." He mentioned the benefits that occurred from linking hydroelectric systems and he carefully reviewed the Muscle Shoals situation, stressing opportunities that would accrue to the South from the multiple-purpose development of the Tennessee River. Using the public ownership experience of Los Angeles and the province of Ontario as a yardstick, he revealed in dollars and cents what cheap electricity meant to housewives in various cities by comparing monthly utility bills. He also noted what cheap power could do for farmers and farm life, making clear, however, that Muscle Shoals was impractical for the commercial production of fertilizer. But the government could conduct experiments with the idea of developing a system that would lower the cost of fertilizer, the results to be available free of charge to the American people.[17]

Before returning to Washington after his summer vacation, Norris visited a Dupont-owned nitrate plant at Charleston, West Virginia. The trip reinforced his view that the only practical means of manufacturing fertilizer was by the synthetic ammonia process rather than by the cyanamid process requiring water power. "The plant at Charleston practically demonstrates to a mathematical certainty that the dam at Muscle Shoals should be used entirely for power purposes, and that if the Government wants to help the farmer by providing cheap fertilizer, the profit derived from the sale of power at Muscle Shoals should be used for the purpose of

---

[17] *Congressional Record,* 70th Cong., 1st sess., Dec. 19, 1927, pp. 801–3.

constructing plants in different sections of the country that would extract nitrogen from the air by the synthetic ammonia process." For about $12 million several synthetic ammonia plants could be built to extract from the air about 40,000 tons of nitrogen annually, the capacity of Nitrate Plant No. 2 at Muscle Shoals. Yet to operate Plant No. 2 would require almost all the electricity generated at the Wilson Dam, while $12 million could be realized quickly from the sale of electricity if the plant were publicly owned. To use power generated at Muscle Shoals for the manufacture of fertilizer was characterized by Norris as "criminal," comparable to a farmer using a sickle to cut a crop of wheat.[18]

Norris spent the weeks before Congress convened preparing for the renewal of the controversy. He was particularly critical of leaders of the American Farm Bureau Federation and editors of southern farm journals who favored leasing Muscle Shoals in the hope of securing cheap fertilizer. Equally discouraging were the many southern senators and representatives opposed to public ownership and the multiple-purpose development of the Tennessee River. Behind all of these people Norris saw "the same combination." He said, "The delay that has come about in the Muscle Shoals proposition is chargeable entirely and completely to these same people, to this same combination, to this same monopoly, to this same trust." [19]

The first session of the Seventieth Congress convened on December 5, 1927. On December 15 Norris introduced a joint resolution for government operation, "providing for the completion of Dam No. 2 and the steam plant at nitrate plant No. 2 in the vicinity of Muscle Shoals for the manufacture and distribution of fertilizer, and for other purposes." It was the same measure he had presented at the end of the previous Congress and it now assumed a commanding position among the Muscle Shoals measures introduced in the Senate. But the measure (S. J. Res. 46) was a compromise. It

[18] *Washington Post,* Nov. 6, 1927; Norris to Joseph Hyde Pratt, Nov. 11, 1927.

[19] Norris to C. A. Cobb, Nov. 18, 1927; to Roulhac, Nov. 23, 1927. Cobb was editor of the *Southern Ruralist* and favored leasing Muscle Shoals; Roulhac was mayor of Sheffield, Ala., and favored public operation. For insight into the lobbying activities of Chester Gray, Washington representative of the American Farm Bureau Federation, for leasing Muscle Shoals, see Norris to James W. Marton, Jan. 10, 1928.

said nothing about developing the Tennessee River and its tributaries, little about transmission lines and making cheap electricity available throughout the South. It focused on the fertilizer question, calling upon the Secretary of War to sell the current generated at Wilson Dam on a preference basis. The proceeds would be used to build plants at Muscle Shoals and elsewhere "on a sufficiently large scale to bring about improvement and economy in fertilizer, the object being to eventually cheapen the product to the farmers of the United States." [20]

On February 1, 1928, Norris's proposal was reported favorably by the Agriculture and Forestry Committee to the Senate, and he delivered a long speech extending over several days on its behalf. But before launching into a discussion of the merits of his measure, Norris examined the offer of the American Cyanamid Company, incorporated in the Willis-Madden bill, and the role of representatives of the American Farm Bureau Federation in supporting it. Several weeks later he again discussed his measure, reviewing its provisions and the legislative history of Muscle Shoals and noting that present conditions there were most unsatisfactory. Electricity was being sold on a short-term basis, pending congressional action determining the permanent policy of the government. Moreover, there was only one customer for the electricity generated at Wilson Dam; the Alabama Power Company had the lone transmission line connecting with the generating system at Muscle Shoals. To place the Secretary of War on a fair business basis in selling electricity generated at Muscle Shoals at reasonable prices, Norris's measure gave him authority to construct, or to have constructed by others, "transmission lines that will connect Muscle Shoals with other possible bidders for the current generated."

Norris admitted that his resolution did not provide for multiple-purpose development. It was not what he wanted; it was not what he thought the country ought to have. But it was the best that he thought could be achieved at the time. What he most desired was what he had called for in previous bills: development of the Tennessee River and its tributaries as a complete unit, building power and storage dams to get the maximum amount of electricity, naviga-

[20] Norris to Joseph H. Nathan, Dec. 1, 1927; to J. F. Houchins, Jan. 12, 1928.

tion, and flood control for the minimum amount of money. To help achieve these benefits, Norris said that a dam at Cove Creek, 250 miles from Muscle Shoals, would be necessary.[21]

Throughout these remarks Norris displayed an intimate knowledge of the various methods used to extract nitrogen from the air (the arc process, the cyanamid process, and the synthetic process). Not only did he describe chemical processes, but he had production and cost figures available to reinforce the points he wished to make. He discussed components and commented on qualities of the fertilizers produced by the different methods. There was nothing sacred about any of them; the goal was to secure an effective and cheap fertilizer. By every standard, Norris concluded, fertilizer could be produced more effectively and cheaply by coal than by electricity. Commercial operation of the nitrate plant at Muscle Shoals was not practicable unless the government was willing to subsidize the operation.

Even more than the Ford offer, the Cyanamid Company bid would necessitate government development of the properties at Muscle Shoals. Dams, including one at Cove Creek, would have to be built, transmission lines constructed, and existing facilities expanded by the government for the Cyanamid Company. For the exclusive use of these properties the company in effect would pay the government interest, computed by an expert for Norris, of 2.6 percent per annum. Moreover, while the Cyanamid Company produced many products, it had never sold fertilizer to farmers. It sold ingredients to dealers and manufacturers who mixed them with other materials to form a commercially acceptable fertilizer. According to the executive secretary of the Federal Power Commission, the lessee with an investment of only $5,300,000 could count on an annual profit, once the plants were in full operation, in excess of $7 million. On the other hand, the capital investment on the part of the United States, if all the provisions of the Cyanamid Company bid were complied with, would total $202,404,335.09. "Do we," Norris asked, "want to go into a partnership of that kind?" While he was willing to help the American farmer secure

[21] Norris Dam is now located here. See Norris to E. B. Stahlman, Apr. 1, 1928, for a strong statement on the need for the Cove Creek Dam.

cheap fertilizer, granting the properties at Muscle Shoals to the Cyanamid Company was not the way to do it.[22]

When his resolution came to the vote, Norris told a reporter there were sufficient votes to pass it in the Senate. But action in the House was doubtful. Congressman Martin B. Madden, co-sponsor of the Cyanamid Company leasing bid, informed Calvin Coolidge that the Norris proposal would plunge the government "deeper and deeper into a hazardous commercial venture" without any estimate of what it would cost. "The power companies and fertilizer manufacturing interests," resenting the favoritism shown the American Cyanamid Company, would favor Norris's bill. Those who considered national defense and fertilizer for farmers in time of peace would favor his proposal. But Madden's argument had little chance in Congress. The impact of Norris's logic was beginning to make itself felt. Opposition of the power companies had abated considerably, and the bid of the American Cyanamid Company was patently a weak one.[23]

Debate in the Senate on the Norris proposal continued until March 13, 1928. Norris answered questions, repeated to some extent what he had said previously, and acted as floor leader for his bill. "The Government owns Muscle Shoals now, it operates it now, and the question is, Shall we turn it over to private monopoly or shall we keep it for all the people?" On March 12 he submitted an amendment "providing that farm organizations instituted for the purpose of distributing electricity among farmers and not for profit, as well as municipalities, shall have the right to get electricity from Muscle Shoals." They would have to build transmission lines and thus compete with private companies. The amendment

[22] *Congressional Record,* 70th Cong., 1st sess., Feb. 1, pp. 2309–11, Feb. 23, pp. 3433–46, Feb. 24, pp. 3515–29, Feb. 28, pp. 3690, 3692–95, Feb. 29, pp. 3755–57, 3760–61, 3766, Mar. 5, 1928, pp. 4082–83. Norris, "What to Do with Muscle Shoals," *Public Ownership,* 10, no. 2 (Feb., 1928): 24–31, presents the essence of his remarks. The article seems to have been extracted from his comments on the Senate floor. In Norris to Thompson, Feb. 5, 1928, he commented on his views for developing the Tennessee River and its tributaries.

[23] *New York Telegram,* Feb. 21, 1928; Martin B. Madden to Coolidge, Feb. 13, 1928 (Box 127:44, Coolidge Papers). The League of Women Voters endorsed Norris's bill, and Harry Slattery drafted their strong and comprehensive statement of Mar. 3, 1928 (copy in Harry Slattery Papers, Manuscripts Collections, Duke University Library).

also provided that if municipalities distributed power to corporations, the rates charged by the corporations should not be in excess of what the Federal Power Commission defined as "fair and reasonable." It was quickly approved by a voice vote on March 13, 1928. Then, after he had answered further questions and argued against crippling amendments all of which were defeated, the vote on S. J. Res. 46 was called. By a vote of 48 to 25 it carried. For the first time a public ownership measure had been approved. If the House followed suit, even though Coolidge vetoed the measure, the leasing of Muscle Shoals to private enterprise henceforth would be a virtual impossibility.[24]

Norris had won a great victory. By making himself the best-informed man in Congress on a subject he had initially wished to avoid, and after convincing himself and a majority on the Agriculture and Forestry Committee, he now had convinced a majority of his colleagues that public ownership was the only sensible way to make a war legacy a beneficent peacetime agency. To convince members of the House of Representatives, Norris testified for four hours before the Military Affairs Committee, where his comments made a deep impression. But he knew that the Coolidge administration would exert every effort to defeat the measure in the House.[25]

Almost two months passed before Norris's resolution was brought to the House floor. During this period he alternated between despair and hope. He admitted to despair when the Military Affairs Committee eliminated the preference provision. He hoped that either on the House floor or in conference the clause might be retained. He despaired that the Rules Committee might not report the bill until "it was too late to get it passed and consideration given to a conference report." But if the House passed it, Norris believed a satisfactory bill would come out of conference committee.[26]

The measure reported by the Military Affairs Committee was

---

[24] *Congressional Record*, 70th Cong., 1st sess., Mar. 5, pp. 4085–87, Mar. 6, p. 4183, Mar. 8, pp. 4324–25, Mar. 9, p. 4386, Mar. 10, pp. 4456–57, Mar. 12, p. 4543, Mar. 13, 1928, pp. 4610, 4612, 4614–15, 4630, 4633–35.

[25] See *Nation*, Mar. 28, 1928, "Norris' Power Fight" (editorial), p. 338.

[26] Norris to Roulhac, Apr. 1, 1928; to J. L. Meeks, Apr. 28, 1928; to Donald Comer, Apr. 28, 1928. On Mar. 30, 1928, the House Military Affairs Committee favorably reported the bill, and on Apr. 10, 1928, formal application for a rule for its consideration was made.

better than any previous House bill. It acknowledged the principle of government ownership and operation of Muscle Shoals but it removed the preference clause and required that Nitrate Plant No. 2 be operated. The last point was objectionable to Norris because it compelled the operation of an antiquated and inefficient plant, involving useless expenditure of both money and power. Less objectionable was the provision for a government corporation with jurisdiction and control over the electricity generated at Muscle Shoals, replacing the Secretary of War in the Senate bill. Since the only thing to be managed was Dam No. 2 and the steam plant connected with it, Norris felt that "it would be too much overhead to have a separate corporation organized to handle it." But he was not prepared to protest the point.[27]

On May 9, 1928, the House briefly considered the amended Norris resolution, called up by the Military Affairs Committee on the first of the two "Calendar Wednesdays" to which the committee was entitled. The second came on May 16 and on that day, the last opportunity for action in the session, the House approved the measure. On May 9 by a large majority the House restored the provision deleted in committee calling for a "just and fair" price for power as determined by the Federal Power Commission. After House approval on May 16 the resolution was sent to conference with Senators McNary, Norris, and Smith representing the Senate.[28]

Norris said the conferees should be able to derive a fair and workable measure if they met in a spirit of cooperation. There were some objectionable features in the House bill, but one provision, the building of Cove Creek Dam, was a significant addition. While Norris did not object to it, he feared it would increase the opposition. Thus he was prepared to yield on this point to gain concessions elsewhere, just as he was willing to yield on a government corporation replacing the Secretary of War as manager of the properties at Muscle Shoals. The Senate bill was more specific in its preference provisions. But, in all, the differences were slight,

[27] Norris to Thompson, Apr. 28, 1928.
[28] National League of Women Voters, "Muscle Shoals and the House" (statement), May 11, 1928 (copy in Slattery Papers); *Congressional Record*, 70th Cong., 1st sess., May 16, p. 8883, May 17, 1928, p. 8928. The vote in the House was 251 to 165.

and Norris was satisfied with the measure that emerged from conference.[29]

On May 22, 1928, on the Senate floor, armed with vital data to illustrate his points, stressing navigation and flood control and viewing electricity as a valuable byproduct of the operation, Norris stoutly defended the modified provisions of the final measure. He was sharply questioned by Millard Tydings about the threat to private enterprise inherent in the measure. The questioning degenerated into sarcasm; Norris responded in kind to the delight of the galleries, which burst into peals of laughter. Debate continued for four full days with Norris becoming increasingly concerned that final action would not be taken before Congress officially adjourned on May 29, 1928. Unable to secure an agreement for a vote, on May 23 Norris moved to recommit the report to conference committee. That evening the conferees met and made minor modifications in the clauses pertaining to the experimental manufacture of fertilizer at Muscle Shoals. Finally, on May 25, after more than twenty-four hours in continuous session the Senate voted 43 to 37 to accept the conference report. The House on the same day with less than an hour of debate adopted the report by a vote of 211 to 147. Now it was up to Calvin Coolidge to decide whether Muscle Shoals would begin to fulfill the promise of its possibilities in the interest of the public welfare.[30]

On May 26, 1928, both friend and foe of Muscle Shoals called at the White House and urged President Coolidge to respectively sign or veto the measure. Norris expressed hope that the president would approve the bill, calling it "the fairest and most comprehensive legislation of its kind ever enacted by Congress." Rather than injuring any state or legitimate business, he predicted it would bring untold benefits to the South, "particularly to Tennessee and

[29] Norris to Lewis S. Gannett, May 18, 1928.

[30] *Congressional Record,* 70th Cong., 1st sess., May 22, pp. 9466–72, 9475, May 23, p. 9520, May 24, p. 9692, May 25, 1928, p. 9842; National League of Women Voters, "The Senate and the House Are Agreed" (statement), May 26, 1928 (copy in Slattery Papers). See Norris to Helen Rufener, Dec. 17, 1928, for a discussion of Cove Creek Dam. On May 24 and 25 Senator Kenneth McKellar spoke bitterly against the inclusion of Cove Creek Dam in the conference report. He voted against the bill; see *Congressional Record,* 70th Cong., 1st sess., May 25, 1928, p. 9838.

Alabama," and indirect benefits to the entire nation. But whether the president acted adversely or not, Norris had won a tremendous victory. Afraid, because of the strength of the opposition, to suggest multiple-purpose development in his resolution, the approved bill included a provision for the Cove Creek Dam and a government corporation to manage the entire operation. Exhausted from his endeavors, he awaited Coolidge's action while friends commented on his honesty, consummate tact, rare judgment, resoluteness, and courage in battling through to victory against overwhelming odds.[31]

The first session of the Seventieth Congress adjourned on May 29, 1928, without Coolidge acting on the bill. By taking no action thereafter, he pocket-vetoed the bill. At first, Norris admitted, he was disappointed, believing the president should have stated his reasons in a veto message. But with a national election in the offing, Norris understood Coolidge's desire not to offend either powerful administration supporters or farmers and "progressive-thinking citizens who desire to preserve our natural resources." [32]

Immediately a constitutional question arose. Was a pocket veto applicable to bills at any but a final session of Congress? Could a measure become law without the president's signature? Norris argued that the Muscle Shoals bill, since it was neither signed by Coolidge nor returned with a veto message within ten days after Congress had adjourned, in effect was a law, though it would "require a decision of the Supreme Court to make it certain." Fortunately, a comparable case was en route to the Supreme Court. While a pocket veto at the end of a short or lame-duck session would kill a piece of legislation, its effect on a measure approved during the long session had not been constitutionally clarified. But whatever the outcome, as far as the Coolidge administration was

31 *New York Times,* May 27, 1928; *Akron News,* June 9, 1928; *Congressional Record,* 70th Cong., 1st sess., May 26, 1928, p. 10056; Cooke to Mrs. George W. Norris, May 26, 1928 (Cooke Papers); Norris to Harry Slattery, June 2, 1928 (copy in Box 60, King Papers). For adverse comment on Norris in his moment of victory, see Worthington to Chester Gray, June 2, 1928 (copy in Box 127:44, Coolidge Papers). Worthington asserted that Norris assailed the character and infamously attempted to destroy the good name of those who differed with him.
32 Draft statement by Norris, June 8, 1928.

concerned, the controversy had ended with a Norris victory and the turning of the tide.[33]

Little occurred with regard to Muscle Shoals during the remainder of the Coolidge administration. In *Current History* in the summer of 1928 Norris discussed the possibilities and advantages of the pocket-vetoed bill. In the second session of the Seventieth Congress he said that "we ought to await action by the Supreme Court on the question." The Seventieth Congress and the Coolidge administration came to an end before the Supreme Court on May 27, 1929, a year and a day after Congress had approved Norris's public ownership bill, decided that a pocket veto at the end of any session of Congress was valid. The fight would have to be made again during the administration of Coolidge's successor, Herbert Hoover.[34]

[33] Norris to O'Neal, June 12, 1928; to Thompson, Aug. 14, 1928.

[34] Norris, "Possibilities of the Completed Plant," *Current History,* 28 (Aug., 1928): 730–33; Norris to Rufener, Dec. 17, 1928; to J. G. Baker, Feb. 7, 1929; *Congressional Record,* 70th Cong., 1st sess., Jan. 5, 1929, p. 1173. There is some evidence that Coolidge, too, had had enough of Muscle Shoals. He did not wish to put the government into either the fertilizer or the power business and was opposed to building another dam at public expense, something the Cyanamid Company bid called for; see Coolidge to E. B. Almon, Nov. 21, 1928 (Box 127:44, Coolidge Papers); *New York World,* Nov. 24, 1928, "Why the President Blocked Action" (editorial). For the decision of the Supreme Court, written by Justice Edward Sanford, see *Okanogan Indians* v. *United States* (279 U.S. 655, 1929).

Primacy of Public Interest

24

The tide turned in other controversies over the proper use of resources in the latter part of the Coolidge administration in which Norris sought to establish the primacy of the public interest. But in almost all of these controversies he was not the central figure. He supported others either in Congress or in Nebraska who bore the brunt of the burden, and in the most important instance where he initiated action, he did so as a co-sponsor with Senator Thomas J. Walsh of Montana.

Despite the failure of his Tri-County bill to gain approval in the House after having passed the Senate in the Sixty-eighth Congress, Norris remained acutely interested in this proposal for building reservoirs and canals to irrigate portions of southcentral Nebraska. Because the reservoirs would also generate power, the Tri-County project aroused the opposition of private power companies and their allies in Nebraska.[1] The congressman from the district, Ashton Shallenberger, opposed seeking through legislation a direct Treasury appropriation. Instead he introduced a resolution requesting the state of Nebraska to reimburse the Treasury for

---

[1] George W. Norris to "Dear Friend," Mar. 15, 1926. At the outset, Norris noted, the Burlington Railroad favored this development. It ran through the country where the development would take place. But once the possibilities of cheap electricity became apparent, Norris claimed, the Burlington opposed the Tri-County project.

the cost of the Tri-County project. Norris thought it became a state project, provided Nebraska could retain claim to water rights on the Platte River.[2]

Norris candidly admitted that his support of the Tri-County project was predicated on the possibilities of cheap electricity for "the people of a good share of Nebraska." Besides supplying people with power at low rates, it would help pay off the cost of the project and set aside a surplus fund. Moreover, through irrigation it would allow the country to realize its agricultural potential by adding moisture to the soil. Then even hot winds could not damage crops; short crops would become a thing of the past. In his correspondence Norris continually noted the benefits that would result from the proposed project. He noted, too, the benefits that accrued from reclamation projects in other semi-arid regions.[3]

In February, 1927, a bill encompassing the aims of the Tri-County project was introduced in the Nebraska legislature. When Norris first read it, he said that there were not sufficient safeguards guaranteeing preference to municipalities, farm organizations, and other nonprofit groups. A provision was needed which would allow the state to develop electricity, build steam plants, and develop water power anywhere in Nebraska instead of within a defined area south of the Platte River. "When money is raised by bonds voted by the public, and the funds from the sale of these bonds are used in whole or in part to generate electricity," then, Norris asserted, "it is criminally wrong to permit private parties to profiteer in any way and compel the consumers of this electricity to pay for the profit that is made." When an amendment incorporating preference was accepted, Norris endorsed the measure. But the Ne-

[2] Norris to C. W. McConaughy and G. P. Kingsley, Nov. 30, 1925; to McConaughy, Jan. 1, 1926; to Kingsley, Mar. 4, 1926; to Adam McMullen, Mar. 24, 1926; Gene E. Hamaker, *Irrigation Pioneers: A History of the Tri-County Project to 1935* (Minden, Nebr., 1964), Chapters VII–X. McMullen was governor of Nebraska and Norris suggested to him the desirability of negotiating an interstate compact for dividing the waters of the Platte River for irrigation purposes; see also Norris to Charles M. Kearney, Jan. 7, 1928. Shallenberger's bill was viewed unfavorably by the Secretary of the Interior and consequently was never reported from committee.

[3] Norris to William Finnigsmier, Apr. 8, 1926; to C. L. Rodebaugh, May 6, 1926; to C. B. Steward, Feb. 21, 1927; to L. Newell, May 18, 1926; to McConaughy, Dec. 10, 1926.

braska legislature took no action. "The defeat," writes Gene E. Hamaker in his study of the Tri-County project, "was a melancholy end to the endeavors of the Tri-County leaders, but they were not disheartened." [4]

Norris continued to endorse the project, placing it within a broader context. Considering the damage done by the terrible 1927 floods, he realized that the Tri-County project could play a role in curbing floods and improving navigation on tributaries of the Mississippi River, thereby affecting the flow of that river as well. If hydroelectric power were developed, it "would put the Government to some extent in business." To this challenge Norris responded, "If we can improve the happiness and prosperity of the people by putting the Government far enough in business to bring about the proper enjoyment of the natural resources which God has given us, then I see no objection to it." [5]

He soon was insisting that the expenditure of public funds for these purposes was justified. Saving people in the lower Mississippi River basin from floods and at the same time using the water thus held back to nourish crops on soil which otherwise would be arid land justified the expense. Hydroelectric power would help pay for it. But every time Norris supported multiple-purpose development, he found "the great electric trust" standing "in the road with a bludgeon, demanding that the electric part of it be turned over to them for private manipulation and gain." Despite this opposition he suggested a survey to ascertain where dams and storage reservoirs could be located on the western tributaries of the Mississippi River. In addition, levees would have to be built. But of one thing he was certain: levees alone would never meet the situation. Properly handled, the challenge of flood control could bring untold benefits. Unrestrained and uncontrolled, it would bring further devastation and suffering.[6]

[4] Norris to McConaughy, Mar. 11, 21, 23, and 25, 1927; to F. R. Kingsley, Mar. 18, 1927; to M. B. Patty, Mar. 18, 1927; to James N. Clarke, Mar. 18 and 25, 1927; to Charles W. Bryan, Apr. 1, 1927; Hamaker, *Irrigation Pioneers,* p. 78.

[5] Norris to P. L. Johnson, Dec. 13, 1928.

[6] Norris to Gutzon Borglum, June 23, 1927; to Robert G. Simmons, Oct. 16, 1927. Levees, of course, represented the repsonse of the Army Engineers and the Coolidge administration to the Mississippi flood of 1927, America's greatest peacetime disaster until then; see Arthur DeWitt Frank, *The Development of the Fed-*

In the Seventieth Congress when flood control legislation was being considered, Norris reiterated his views, observing that the power people, seeking control of electricity for private gain and manipulation, would strive mightily to prevent the passage of multiple-purpose tributary development legislation "even though the waters continue to go down the stream from localities that need them, to localities where they become destructive of property and of life itself." They were joined in their opposition by the president and the Army Engineers, who emphasized levees and spillways as the solution.[7]

In one area during the Coolidge administration the primacy of public interest was fully recognized, and multiple-purpose development won a resounding victory. While Norris was not the chief Senate figure battling for Boulder Dam, he was an indispensable aide to Hiram Johnson, co-sponsor of the bill calling for its construction. Familiar with the proposed project, Norris predicted in March, 1927, that a Boulder Dam bill would be enacted before the end of the Coolidge administration.[8]

Meanwhile he continued the fight. In April the National Popular Government League gave a dinner for Norris. Three hundred progressives from all walks of Washington life filled the ballroom of the City Club. A group of Washington correspondents who had not paid their way at a banquet for many a year took an entire

eral *Program of Flood Control on the Mississippi River* (New York, 1930), especially Chapter IX; Norris, "Flood Control," Oct. 20, 1927 (draft article written for Herbert S. Houston, Cosmos Newspaper Syndicate).

[7] Norris to A. J. Weaver, Mar. 28, 1928; to George A. Beecher, Mar. 31, 1928; to C. R. Trant, Mar. 9, 1928; *Congressional Record*, 70th Cong., 1st sess., May 9, pp. 8184–86, May 28, 1928, pp. 5488–89. See also a draft article by Norris entitled "Flood Control," prepared for the Apr., 1928, issue of *Nebraska Municipal Review*.

[8] For a discussion of the efforts of Hiram Johnson on behalf of Boulder Dam, see Norris to Frank A. Harrison, May 10, 1926; Hiram Johnson to Norris, May 11, 1926, Jan. 13, 1927; Norris to H. F. Canon, May 11, 1926. All items discuss the legislative picture during the first session of the Sixty-ninth Congress when the Boulder Dam bill was reported from the Irrigation and Reclamation Committee. Its supporters were afraid to press for further action, believing "educational and missionary work" necessary before a favorable vote could be achieved. See also Johnson to Steering Committee of the Senate, Nov. 27, 1926 (Box 20, Wadsworth Family Papers, Manuscript Division, Library of Congress); Norris to Karl Lee, Mar. 6, 1927; *Congressional Record*, 69th Cong., 2nd sess., Feb. 23, 1927, pp. 4529–30.

table; one of their number, Charles G. Ross of the *St. Louis Post-Dispatch,* commented: "We newspaper men of Washington sometimes grow cynical. We hear so many professions and see so little performance. We find so many corrupting influences at work in the very center of government that we sometimes lose faith in democracy and ask whether, after all, the struggle is worthwhile. And then we go and have a talk with Senator George Norris of Nebraska, and we come away with our faith renewed, and ready to continue the fight." The speakers expressed their affection for Norris and proclaimed their support in the battles he was waging to establish the importance of the public interest. Norris spoke for over an hour, commenting chiefly upon the influence and methods of the "Power Trust" and using the Boulder Dam controversy as his outstanding illustration.[9]

In the Seventieth Congress Hiram Johnson introduced a new Boulder Dam bill, granting Arizona and Nevada a larger portion of the profits from the sale of power and also granting these states and California preference with regard to the use of power in their respective areas. Another important amendment, inserted at the request of Wyoming Senator John B. Kendrick, for the upper basin states, limited the amount of water allocated to California. By these concessions Johnson gained the support of most western senators. He informed Norris, "I do not need to say how much I depend upon you in the contest which is about to ensue. . . ." At the outset of the second session the chief piece of unfinished business before the Senate was the Boulder Dam bill.[10]

The 1927 Mississippi flood played a role in winning support for the project by making it clear that the people of the lower Colorado River Valley could be saved from a similar catastrophe

[9] *Labor,* Apr. 23, 1927; National Popular Government League, Bulletins 110, Apr. 27, 1927, and 111, Apr. 30, 1927. Bulletin 110 contains the remarks of the speakers honoring Norris; Bulletin 111 contains Norris's speech.

[10] Johnson to Norris, Apr. 13, Nov. 12, 1928. In his November letter Johnson wrote, "I know you are sufficient unto yourself, and that you require from those who care for you neither expressions of unstinted admiration, nor protestations of affection; but, my dear George, I cannot tell you how your courageous and patriotic stand increased my respect and added to my love for you." Harry Slattery at the time noted that southern senators and congressmen opposed to Muscle Shoals also opposed Boulder Dam; see Slattery to Hollins N. Randolph, Feb. 14, 1928 (Harry Slattery Papers, Manuscripts Collections, Duke University Library).

by the construction of Boulder Dam. Moreover, propaganda by utility companies against the proposal was being exposed by Federal Trade Commission investigators, thereby arousing sentiment for the project. In the Senate Norris tried to convince southern senators to support Boulder Dam even if the resultant crops would compete with those raised by southern farmers, because it was necessary "to save Imperial Valley from becoming a part of the Pacific Ocean." He stated that he would vote for the bill primarily because the flood control provisions would protect the Imperial Valley from inundation, though he was fearful that "the Water Power Trust" might gain control of the generation of electricity at Boulder Dam.[11]

The Senate approved the Boulder Dam bill on December 14, 1928, and the House of Representatives did so four days later. President Coolidge signed it on December 21, 1928. After its enactment Norris called it "a wonderful piece of legislation—a progressive step on the part of the Government in the development of one of the great natural resources of the country." The eight-year legislative struggle was a demonstration of the determined opposition of the "Power Trust" against the development of natural resources by the federal government. All that remained was to hope that no flood would occur before the dam was constructed. The enactment of the bill, Norris concluded, was "at once one of the most important, humane and justifiable pieces of legislation that had been put on the statute books for many years." [12]

But in his private correspondence he was less enthusiastic: "I am not at all satisfied with the Boulder Dam bill." It gave the Secretary of the Interior alternatives with regard to power which

[11] Norris to P. L. Johnson, Dec. 13, 1928; *Congressional Record,* 70th Cong., 1st sess., Dec. 14, 1928, pp. 594, 601–2. The bill was rather general in its power requirements; the Secretary of the Interior was not held to a rigid plan with regard to the operation of the power plant.

[12] *Los Angeles Examiner,* Dec. 27, 1928 (statement by Norris). The Boulder Dam bill was approved by a substantial majority (65 to 11) in the Senate. The entire Nebraska congressional delegation was for the bill, though Norris alone was singled out for editorial criticism by some Nebraska papers for encouraging agricultural competition in the Imperial Valley with hard-pressed Nebraska farmers. They also insisted that Nebraska taxpayers would have to help pay for the project. Both assumptions were false; see Norris to McConaughy, Jan. 15, 1929; to G. P. Kingsley, Jan. 27, 1929; to C. G. Perry, Feb. 12, 1929.

Norris said Hiram Johnson and others "behind the bill" had promised to remove. They were taken out of the House bill; Norris was confident that if they were not removed by the Senate, Johnson certainly would get them removed in conference committee. But rather than risk a presidential veto, the conferees decided to leave the provisions in. Norris felt that Johnson ought not to have yielded and that if President Coolidge vetoed the bill because of the power provisions, "it would be the most unpopular thing in the country that he had ever done." Congress, supported by public sentiment, would pass the bill again. "While Hoover undoubtedly agreed with Coolidge on this power proposition, yet, being anxious to avoid any possibility of losing a second term and taking the nature of the man into consideration," Norris did not doubt that the new president would sign it. But Johnson did not want to take the chance. And Norris could understand his plight; "after all," he admitted, "the main thing in Boulder Dam is flood control."

Moreover, Norris realized that "the power people" were not satisfied with the bill. Since the power facilities would be integrated with the dam, it would be impossible to let a contract for power without interfering with the operation of the dam itself. To divide the functions into separate facilities would involve the expenditure of an enormous sum of money. On the grounds of efficiency and economy Norris was confident that the project would be owned and operated by the government. And he was satisfied that the "Power Trust" felt the same way "or they would not have fought the bill as they did." [13]

Another matter that concerned Norris at the end of the Coolidge administration pertained to the naval oil reserve leases and the corrupt activities of certain businessmen. On January 9, 1928, the Senate approved a resolution introduced by Norris requesting the Public Lands and Surveys Committee, with Thomas J. Walsh of Teapot Dome fame as the ranking minority member, to investigate further the leasing of public lands, particularly the naval oil reserves in Wyoming. The committee also was charged with investigating the

[13] *Los Angeles Examiner,* Dec. 27, 1928; Norris to McConaughy, Dec. 27, 1928; to Schelle Mathews, Jan. 3, 1929; to Walt Horan, Feb. 12, 1929. Well into the Hoover administration Norris continued to have reservations about public power prospects at the dam; see Norris to William T. Chantland, Dec. 29, 1930.

activities of the Continental Trading Company of Canada in the hope of tracing U.S. bonds held by this corporation which had been implicated in the Teapot Dome scandal.[14]

The Continental Trading Company of Canada had been sponsored in its oil purchases by Harry F. Sinclair and Robert W. Stewart. Sinclair, a prominent independent oil man, had been involved in the Teapot Dome affair. Stewart was chairman of the board of directors of the Standard Oil Company of Indiana. Others who assisted were J. E. O'Neil, president of the Prairie Oil and Gas Company, and H. M. Blackmer, an associate of Stewart's in the oil business. The Continental Trading Company quickly resold the oil it had agreed to buy to the Sinclair Crude Oil Company, owned jointly by the Sinclair Consolidated Oil Corporation, the Standard Oil Company of Indiana, and the Prairie Oil and Gas Company. The sale was made at a profit of 25 cents per barrel. Moreover, by the terms of its contracts the Continental Trading Company could get its money five days before it was required to make payments to the Texas oil producer who sold to the company.

In 1923, with 25 million barrels of Texas oil yet to be delivered, the Continental Trading Company surrendered its contract to the Sinclair Crude Oil Company for $400,000 and then went out of business, at about the same time the Senate investigation of Teapot Dome was threatened. Continental Trading Company never engaged in any other activity. While in business its profit of 25 cents a barrel amounted to $3,800,000, which had been invested in U.S. government bonds; $230,000 worth had been traced to former Secretary of the Interior Albert Fall. The balance had never been accounted for; the principal purpose of Norris's resolution was to determine what had become of these bonds.

At the time of the civil suit to recover Teapot Dome for the government, efforts were made to question key figures in the Continental Trading Company. Many had fled the country. Stewart returned from South America after the trial, claiming he knew nothing about the subpoena requesting him to testify. Others were

14 *Congressional Record,* 70th Cong., 1st sess., Jan. 10, 1928, p. 1223; Norris to W. J. Monroney, Dec. 3, 1927. Paul H. Giddens, *Standard Oil Company (Indiana)* (New York, 1955), pp. 361–435, presents a comprehensive account of the activities of the Continental Trading Company and Colonel Robert W. Stewart.

in Europe; Norris supposed they would remain there for the balance of their lives. Meanwhile Canadian and American courts had branded the Continental Trading Company "a corrupt and fradulent instrumentality for the commencement of some illegitimate purpose." The connection of John D. Rockefeller, Jr., and the Rockefeller Foundation with Stewart and Standard Oil of Indiana was noted by Norris in correspondence that he inserted in the *Congressional Record* as part of his remarks.[15]

Though not involved in the investigation, Norris showed continual interest in it. After Stewart admitted that he had received some of the disputed bonds and corroborated information about profits, Norris insisted that anyone who would do what Stewart had done "must be either a crook or a fool; and everyone knows that Stewart is not a fool." While it was not clear what the promoters had sought to do, Norris had a feeling they "were engaged in a great conspiracy in which there were profits of millions." The fact that part of the money had been traced to Albert B. Fall led him to believe that bribery of public officials was involved in the conspiracy.[16]

To critics Norris asserted that all of the exposures in the 1920s "regarding the bribery and debauchery of public officials and the control of Legislatures, commissions, courts, and the Senate of the United States" had come as the result of Senate investigations. "The guilt of Doheny, Fall, Sinclair, Daugherty, Forbes, Miller, Stewart, Blackmer, O'Neil and others, where the Government had been robbed of millions and where public officials had been bribed by the expenditure of hundreds of thousands of dollars, was all

[15] *Congressional Record,* 70th Cong., 1st sess., Jan. 10, pp. 1223–25, Apr. 28, 1928, p. 7237; 2nd sess., Feb. 7, 1929, pp. 2993–95; draft statement by Norris, n.d. [Jan., 1928]. Norris said that Paul Anderson of the *St. Louis Post-Dispatch* "had more to do with resurrecting the matter and causing an additional investigation to be made than any other one person." He worked with Anderson in preparing the resolution which the Senate approved calling for further investigation of the Continental Trading Company; see Norris to the editor, *St. Louis Post-Dispatch,* Jan. 25, 1928, Jan. 9, 1929. In the latter letter Norris fully commented on the lack of interest of prominent officials in pursuing this matter after Anderson had brought it to their attention. See also J. W. Markham, *Bovard of the Post-Dispatch* (Baton Rouge, La., 1954), pp. 100–103.

[16] *Congressional Record,* 70th Cong., 1st sess., Apr. 28, 1928, pp. 7235–38; Norris to Edward Barnes, June 19, 1928.

brought to light through Senate investigations." Moreover, these investigations had resulted in the return to the government of oil lands in California and Wyoming estimated to be worth about a billion dollars. To be sure, not all the criminal prosecutions had been successful. Still, Norris said, a vast amount of good had been accomplished in establishing the primacy of the public interest.[17]

The oil industry to Norris was a corrupt monopoly. Too many people were willing to condone corruption and to accept the view that rich men could use their wealth "to buy anything in sight." Thus public officials associated with these men applauded their virtues and overlooked their sins. What, Norris queried, was the lesson of it all to the ordinary citizen?

> What does it teach the man in the street who has to toil when he sees that Doheny can get away with it, that Sinclair can get away with it, and that the men who debauch Cabinet officers do not lose their social standing but still go to the White House to public receptions . . . ? If Daugherty can remain in the Cabinet and be pushed out only by an outraged public opinion, if Doheny can buy a Cabinet officer and make millions of dollars and still be a hero in the eyes of the people; if Sinclair can get away with his Teapot Dome affair and still be a leader in high society, why shouldn't it be all right to steal a pair of shoes or a package of coffee from the corner grocery or hold up the belated traveler and take his pocketbook?

With the lenient treatment of wealthy offenders, Norris said that poor men would get the idea that courts benefited the rich and only punished the poor. While the State Department was "having hysterics over some alleged bolsheviks in Nicaragua and Mexico," the seeds that could ripen into "bolshevistic tendencies" had already been sown in the United States.[18]

---

[17] Norris to Mrs. W. D. McMichael, Apr. 28, 1928. In a proxy contest in 1929 between John D. Rockefeller, Jr., and Robert W. Stewart the latter was defeated and ousted as president of the Standard Oil Company of Indiana; see the account in Chapter XIV of Giddens, *Standard Oil Company (Indiana)*. Norris remarked on Sinclair's jail sentence wherein he was treated for "an honor rather than a crime"; see Norris to the editor, *Philadelphia Record*, Oct. 5, 1929.

[18] Norris to Frans Nelson, Feb. 13, 1927; to H. M. Crist, Nov. 12, 1927. In 1933 at the trial of Gaston Means, a figure involved in the Teapot Dome scandal, testimony revealed that Means was employed to find something detrimental to

The oil industry, like the hydroelectric power industry, was a monopoly where in many localities the price was fixed. Both industries, Norris said, were corrupt and hesitated at nothing to carry out their ends. The usual method of coping with combinations was by a system of regulation, the object of which was to maintain fair competition. Norris realized that this method had not always proved successful; in the field of public utilities he regarded public ownership as the best way to regulate them. But he was not prepared to recommend this solution in the oil industry. He did believe that if municipalities purchased and then sold gasoline themselves, they could help lower prices.[19] Norris's role differed from that of his Democratic colleague Thomas J. Walsh, who was a central figure in the oil investigations of the 1920s. Whereas Walsh stood fast as a guardian against outright theft and corruption by oil men, Norris was concerned about the subtle uses of government for the benefit of an inner circle of wealthy and corrupt figures in the industry.

Another area in which Norris sought to establish the primacy of the public interest was the American merchant marine. He was opposed to the sale of ships owned by the Shipping Board without the consent of Congress. In this way the president could not remove members to get a board that would sell all the vessels in its possession. Norris favored a government corporation owning and operating merchant ships on a business basis. But in May, 1928, he was asked to vote upon a conference report calling for a subsidy for ship owners. To be sure, the measure also called for ships to be built and operated by the Shipping Board. Thus, after the government built and operated ships through the medium of the Shipping Board, private parties would receive federal funds at very low interest rates to compete with them. If the taxpayers' money were used to build ships, then, Norris said, "we ought to build them in the name of the taxpayers and operate them in the name of the taxpayers." Awarding public funds to corporations who would profit from the transaction seemed as if the government were

Norris or any member of his family. Means hired five or more investigators to tackle the assignment but could find nothing against him; see John P. Robertson to Borglum, May 12, 1933.

[19] Norris to Ross S. Thornton, Jan. 20, 1928; to L. L. Coryell, Apr. 29, 1928.

using for illegal purposes "the money of those who toil and pay the taxes." Despite his protest the Senate by a vote of 51 to 20 approved the conference report; once again during the Coolidge administration the public interest was ignored.[20]

In one area Norris won a major victory before the Coolidge administration came to an end. As a result of Senate initiative an executive agency, the Federal Trade Commission, started a lengthy and thorough probe of public utilities providing gas and electrical service. Like every significant Norris victory, it was several years in coming. The conventional wisdom expounded by Secretary of Commerce Herbert Hoover was that states had public utility commissions with authority to regulate rates, profits, services, and finances of electrical utilities. "It would be," Hoover insisted, "a vital sacrifice of States' rights to transfer this regulation of electric utilities from the States to the Federal Government." State regulation supposedly was more efficient than federal regulation and more responsive to public demand. The federal government could be of service in disseminating knowledge of problems involved in regulation and at times could encourage cooperation between states. But, Hoover concluded, "any attempt at Federal regulation of these questions would bring acute conflict with the States and confusion in the whole industry." [21]

Norris, of course, fundamentally disagreed with this view. To him the generation and transmission of electricity involved monopoly. "If, from the nature of things, a certain commodity must be a monopoly, then it ought to be owned, controlled, and managed by Government authority." With the advent of an age of electricity, a private monopoly would be detrimental to the public interest. It was no answer to say, as Hoover did, that state commissions would regulate effectively. They could "no more contest with this gigantic octopus than a fly could interfere with the onward march of an elephant." Only when current could be supplied at a low price would "the modern home contain all the appliances necessary to do most of the work and drudgery now done by hand." Public ownership, by eliminating the legerdemain connected with stocks and

---

[20] *Congressional Record,* 70th Cong., 1st sess., Jan. 27, p. 2144, Jan. 31, p. 2237, May 16, 1928, pp. 8791–96, 8810.

[21] *Baltimore News,* Feb. 3, 1925 (concise statement by Herbert Hoover).

bonds and by other administrative economies, could cut the cost of electricity to the consumer from one-third to one-half of what was charged by private operation.[22]

Utility company propaganda, which ultimately was included in the price the consumer paid, particularly distressed Norris. Almost as disturbing was the fact that news items expressing the public ownership view rarely appeared in the press. In 1927, when Norris spoke on "Electricity in the Home" at a banquet at the Mayflower Hotel under the auspices of *Good Housekeeping* magazine, he sought to get "some of the truth scattered among the leading women of the country in regard to electricity as it can be applied and used in home life." Not a single paper quoted a word he spoke, though Norris had distributed advance copies of his remarks to the press.[23]

Late in the Sixty-ninth Congress Senator Thomas J. Walsh called for an investigation of the financing of gas and electrical services. His resolution proposed a recess investigation and probably would have passed if brought to a vote. As the Seventieth Congress prepared to convene in December, 1927, observers thought the resolution would pass, though a contest was expected on an amendment allowing the investigation to be made by the

[22] Norris to George F. Milton, Feb. 7, 1926; Norris statement on electricity, n.d. [1926]; Norris to Judson King, July 21, 1926; to John B. Easten, Mar. 30, 1927; to J. Spalding, Nov. 17, 1927. See also an article by Norris, "Electricity: The New Household Servant," *LaFollette's Magazine,* 19 (Oct., 1927): 150, 159. Morris L. Cooke argued that until effective regulation was an automatic feature, consumers stood little chance of getting their due benefits from the industry; see his article "Toward Lower Electric Rates," *Nation,* Mar. 16, 1927, pp. 285–86. Cooke insisted that regulation, as practiced at the time, did not regulate; see Cooke to Norris, Jan. 18, 1928; draft statement by Cooke, Feb., 1928 (both items in the Morris L. Cooke Papers, Franklin D. Roosevelt Library, Hyde Park, N.Y.). Cooke's confidence in regulation as a public device had disappeared by this time. He did feel that it would be impossible to "pass over night to the public ownership of capital even if the public had decided that this should be done, which of course they have not"; see Cooke to Norris, Feb. 4, 1925 (copy in Judson King Papers, Manuscript Division, Library of Congress).

[23] Norris to Walter Locke, June 23, 1926, Mar. 29, 1927. Norris's speech, "Electricity in the Home," delivered on Mar. 25, 1927, was published as "Electricity: The New Household Servant" in *LaFollette's Magazine.* In Norris to Arthur V. White, Nov. 26, 1927, he commented on "Power Trust" propaganda designed to deceive people about conditions in Ontario. White was a member of the Ontario Hydroelectric Power Commission.

Federal Trade Commission. If the inquiry were conducted by a Senate committee, administration supporters feared that both the issues and the senators directing the investigation might be projected into the 1928 presidential campaign.

Earlier, in 1925, a resolution sponsored by Norris calling for a Federal Trade Commission investigation of the expenditures of the General Electric Company "to influence or control public opinion on the question of municipal or public ownership" failed because the Attorney General insisted that commission funds could not be expended for this purpose. Now determined to get an effective investigation, Norris proposed to expand the Walsh resolution to include lobbying practices as well. Liberals anticipated that Walsh and Norris would work together on a special investigating committee; power company advocates feared the worst. Norris would have a platform to preach the virtues of public ownership by revealing how private utility companies bilked the public. The possibility of a Walsh-Norris investigation convinced conservatives in both parties that the Federal Trade Commission rather than the Senate should conduct the hearings.[24] In Senate debate Norris argued that an FTC investigation would be "null and void" as far as effectiveness was concerned, "and, of course, that is what the Electric Light Trust wants." Defeated in this effort, he expected his predictions to come true and was amazed when they did not. To the consternation of conservatives, the Federal Trade Commission launched what one historian has called "one of the most widely publicized and extensive investigations of all time." [25]

[24] *Congressional Record,* 70th Cong., 1st sess., Feb. 13, 1928, p. 2895; Editorial Research Reports, Nov. 12, 1927; Federated Press, Washington Bureau, Sheet 1, No. 2127, Nov. 28, 1927 (story by Laurence Todd) (copies of last two items in the Slattery Papers); Norris to Alex Pope, May 6, 1928. For Norris's 1925 resolution calling for a Federal Trade Commission investigation of the General Electric Company, see *New York American,* Jan. 26, 1925; *New York World,* Feb. 10, 1925. There is some indication that Walsh was not too happy about the possibility of Norris sharing the committee spotlight with him. Apparently Norris, not wishing to offend Walsh, still wanted to put his detailed knowledge to account; see Laurence Todd to Slattery, Nov. 30, 1927 (Slattery Papers); Judson Welliver, "Battle of the Billions," *Washington Herald,* Nov. 30, 1927.

[25] *Congressional Record,* 70th Cong., 1st sess., Feb. 14, pp. 2952–55, 2957, Feb. 15, 1928, pp. 3027–28, 3053. In Norris to Pope, May 6, 1928, he speculated that "the corporations being investigated thought it would be better to submit to the investigation rather than run the risk of incurring the resentment of public senti-

Soon Norris was commenting that the Federal Trade Commission investigation was "of very far reaching importance." Indeed, he sent the commission data about rates and related matters supplied by prominent public power advocates. The information coming to light was so startling that Norris felt fair-minded people would be shocked. For example, the investigation quickly revealed that the "Power Trust" was spending millions of dollars for propaganda: "for the purpose of controlling every human endeavor, for the purpose of poisoning the minds of the school children, for the purpose of bribing professors and teachers, as well as legislators and men of prominence and influence." These activities were paid for by the people who were being deceived and fooled. In short, Norris said, "we are paying for our own deception." [26]

For the remainder of the Coolidge administration Norris hammered away at the "Power Trust," thereby aiding and abetting the Federal Trade Commission investigation. He compared public versus private ownership of electric light and power throughout the United States and Canada, observing that rates in communities with municipally owned plants were more reasonable than those charged by private plants. Rates in the Canadian province of Ontario were compared with those in neighboring cities on the American side of the border to the advantage of the public ownership system in Ontario. Actual bills rendered to individuals were compared, always to the advantage of public ownership, thus presenting

---

ment if they resorted to the courts to prevent it." See also Norris to Carl D. Thompson, June 28, 1928; Ellis W. Hawley, *The New Deal and the Problem of Monopoly* (Princeton, N.J., 1966), p. 326.

[26] *Congressional Record*, 70th Cong., 1st sess., May 4, 1928, p. 7817; Norris to S. C. Van Houten, June 2, 1928; to Charles W. Hunt, Feb. 20, 1928 (copy in Cooke Papers; this letter was undoubtedly drafted by Cooke). Cooke denounced the reproduction-cost theory as a valid way of determining rates. Such rates helped the electrical industry enjoy a maximum of prosperity. Rates, he hoped, would "eventually be based on the legitimate costs as incurred by the operating company"; see Cooke statement about utility rates, n.d. [1929] (Cooke Papers). J. D. Ross argued and Norris agreed that in public plants where the investment cost was amortized, the time would come when there would be nothing but maintenance and operating costs. If the plant were a steam plant, fuel costs would have to be considered. Neither situation could ever prevail in a private company which continually added to its investment and never sought to amortize it; see Norris to Ross, Jan. 21, 1928.

"a wonderful and conclusive argument against the private electric light companies and the prices which they charge." [27]

The maze of interests involved in the "Power Trust" made it practically impossible "to run down any particular company or the ownership of any particular utility, to ascertain just who is the real owner of it." But the Federal Trade Commission investigation was presenting more information; by March of 1928 certain patterns were clear. Power people were buying municipal electric plants throughout the United States, paying exorbitant prices, and then insisting that state utility commissions would not allow them to charge high rates. Norris said that when these companies were combined, the power people would find ways of making a return on their investment. He claimed that their activities comprised "the greatest question before the American people" in the election of 1928.[28]

Hiram Johnson agreed with Norris. So did Judson King, who addressed a section of the American Political Science Association at their December meeting. He noted the development "of a systematic, nationwide, ably managed, highly financed movement" on behalf of utility companies "to capture the whole field of higher education" and make it an adjunct of their propaganda apparatus. So, too, did the Hearst papers. Norris, who a few years earlier had bitterly denounced William Randolph Hearst, now said that his papers did "wonderful work in spreading the news of the Power Trust's activities as disclosed by the investigation made by the Federal Trade Commission." But important as Norris and others deemed the matter in this election year, Hiram Johnson observed,

[27] *Congressional Record,* 70th Cong., 1st sess., Feb. 29, pp. 3757–67, Mar. 5, pp. 4082–87, Mar. 9, 1928, pp. 4401–2; 2nd sess., Jan. 26, pp. 2256–58, Jan. 28, pp. 2331–33, Mar. 2, 1929, pp. 5032, 5042; Norris to McConaughy, June 2, 1928; to Frank H. Greteman, Feb. 1, 1929; to J. W. Cooper, Feb. 4, 1929. The *Washington Herald,* Mar. 12, 1928, on its editorial page published a chart comparing rates in Ontario and American cities that Norris had inserted in the *Congressional Record.* The chart was prepared by Judson King.

[28] Norris to W. T. Burkett, Mar. 27, 1928; to Edwin J. Clapp, Mar. 28, 1928. Clapp published a series of articles summarizing testimony elicited by the Federal Trade Commission in connection with the power lobby which Norris's colleague Robert B. Howell inserted in the *Congressional Record;* see 70th Cong., 1st sess., May 28, 1928, pp. 10229–54. The Federal Trade Commission investigation and mounting indignation against the "Power Trust" aided in congressional approval of the Norris Muscle Shoals bill in this session.

"I do not believe either candidate will touch the subject because I think each hopes for the support of this sinister though powerful group." [29] Before examining Norris's efforts to bring this matter more forcefully to public attention in the 1928 campaign, and before examining his attitude toward party politics in the Coolidge years, it remains to examine his views on the foreign policies of Calvin Coolidge.

[29] Hiram Johnson to Harold Ickes, July 13, 1928 (Box 2, Harold Ickes Papers, Manuscript Division, Library of Congress); King to Felix Frankfurter, Jan. 14, 1929 (Box 65, Felix Frankfurter Papers, Manuscript Division, Library of Congress); Norris to Locke, July 13, 1928.

Isolationism

25

Busy though he was during the Coolidge era waging battles in the public interest and combating administration zeal to aid business, Norris occasionally found time to look at the world beyond the nation's shores. What he saw did not please him. Problems and forces evident on the domestic scene had a way of reappearing on the world scene. What Norris disliked or opposed in the United States he equally disliked or opposed when evident elsewhere. His sympathies went to the victims of exploitation. His voice was raised against American policies that he considered exploitative and detrimental to the best interests of the people in the country involved. In addition, sympathy toward pacifism and international cooperation without commitments predicated on military force permeated his outlook. Surprisingly for one so deeply involved in domestic affairs, Norris was concerned with American foreign policy. In one notable instance he found himself dragged into a phase of Mexican policy.

Throughout the decade there remained unresolved a series of problems emanating from America's participation in World War I. The question of war debts aroused much discussion and Norris felt that they should be neither forgiven nor reduced. Money for the Allies had been borrowed by the government at 4¼ percent interest. During the Harding administration the rate of interest on the British loan was reduced, and early in the Coolidge administration France started seeking concessions. Norris was opposed. While France refused to meet her obligations to the United States, she provided "money, men and munitions to Poland and other Nations," waged a war in North Africa, and had the largest standing army in the world. If she curtailed her military program, Norris said, France could easily meet her contractual obligations to the United States.[1]

In 1926 a proposal was made to settle the Italian debt of more than $2 billion by reducing it more than $100 million and then providing a minimum interest on the balance for sixty-two years, at which time the debt would be canceled. Norris was opposed. If the proposal were approved, American taxpayers would have to pay the bulk of the debt. Norris noted that Italy had borrowed several hundred million dollars from "Wall Street Brokers" at over 7 percent interest. Now these brokers wanted Congress to approve the Italian debt settlement and thereby strengthen their loans. The proposed solution was not honest and deserved "the condemnation of every American citizen." To further register his distaste, Norris inserted in the *Congressional Record* an article suggesting that the bankrupt Chicago, Milwaukee & St. Paul Railway Company could resolve its financial troubles if it were purchased by Benito Mussolini. He had "drag" with the American government and could secure as favorable a loan for "the St. Paul" as he had for Italy with a little more "self-sacrifice by the taxpayers of the United States." [2]

Reducing war debts was dishonest because the people who made up the difference were citizens who had purchased war bonds in the belief that the money would be lent on the same terms and at the same rate of interest at which the government borrowed the money. The settlements suggested by the various debt commissions meant that the American taxpayer eventually would pay the debts of European governments. It seemed to Norris that "in honor, they ought to pay the same rate of interest to us that we pay." In opposing all debt settlements with European nations, Norris blamed the Coolidge administration for adding to the burdens of the American taxpayer. Late in 1925 he called for an inquiry to determine the extent to which foreign governments through decorations bestowed

1 George W. Norris to H. N. Jewett, May 22, 1925.

2 Norris to E. E. Zimmerman, Jan. 21, 1926; to Robert McAdam, Jan. 23, 1926; draft statement by Norris about the Italian debt, n.d. [1926]; *Congressional Record*, 69th Cong., 1st sess., Mar. 31, 1926, pp. 6630–31. The article, written by William Hard, appeared originally in *Nation*, Mar. 3, 1926.

upon Americans helped create sentiment favorable to their financial standing. Norris was aroused by the 2,328 American names on a roster of the French Legion of Honor. "I can understand why France should wish to honor Americans who have aided her on the battlefield, but why should bankers and American newspaper editors be so honored," Norris queried, "unless France expects some favors in return?" [3]

When he turned his attention to American participation in the Permanent Court of International Justice, more commonly known as the World Court, he touched an issue that aroused more concern than war debts or foreign decorations. It involved international cooperation and helped revive issues bitterly contested during the Wilson years. In 1923 Norris expressed hesitation, stating that while the nation should try to resolve its international difficulties, "nothing proposed so far met the situation." While Norris was listed as "doubtful" by the League of Women Voters in their poll of U.S. senators' support of the World Court, he was desirous of achieving peaceful settlement of international disputes. In December, 1925, when the Senate was debating American entry into the World Court, he informed Charles Curtis, Republican floor leader, that he would vote "yes." Norris's announcement helped Curtis conclude that there were enough votes available to assure ratification. His aye vote on January 27, 1926, was predicated on a reservation providing that under no circumstances would the United States submit a controversy until approval was given by the president and two-thirds of the Senate, signifying "absolutely no danger to America or American institutions." [4]

After the vote Norris admitted that its importance had been "wonderfully overestimated." The World Court meant "little if any-

[3] *Congressional Record,* 69th Cong., 1st sess., Apr. 26, 1926, pp. 8200–8201; Norris to C. H. Hendrickson, May 3, 1926; to L. T. Youngblood, May 15, 1926; to E. A. Morse, May 17, 1926; to Carl Meares, Dec. 17, 1926; *New York Daily Mirror,* Nov. 23, 1925; Norris to Charles Edward Russell, Nov. 27, Dec. 3, 1925.

[4] Norris statement on World Court resolution, Nov. 17, 1923 (Box 19, League of Women Voters Papers, Manuscript Division, Library of Congress); Norris to Gertrude Beers, Nov. 23, 1925; *New York Herald Tribune,* Dec. 18, 1925; *Washington Herald,* Dec. 29, 1925; Norris to John W. Little, Jan. 20, 1926; to Belle Sherwin, Feb. 4, 1926 (Box 19, League of Women Voters Papers); *Congressional Record,* 69th Cong., 1st sess., Jan. 27, 1926, p. 2825. The vote was 76 to 17.

thing to our country." He would support the court provided American interests were protected by proper reservations; "that leaves it perfectly safe, and at the same time it gives our moral approval to this court, which may mean a great deal." For the remainder of the period of Republican ascendancy Norris favored any way by which the United States could lend moral support to any agreement which would encourage international peace. Although the World Court seemed to be of primary benefit to European nations who were members of the League of Nations, American participation would have a great moral effect in encouraging the resolution of international disputes by reason rather than by war. But the United States, owing to executive action, did not enter the World Court despite Senate ratification of the protocol with reservations.[5]

In examining the plight of particular peoples or nations, the exertion of moral pressure rather than force pervaded Norris's thought. He devoted many hours, for example, to a study of the "heart-breaking" Turkish-Armenian situation but did not have any solution to offer. In 1926 he still insisted that his opposition to Woodrow Wilson's recommendation that the United States assume a mandate over Armenia was valid because "it would have taken many thousands of American soldiers and would have cost many millions of dollars, and we would have been in a continual warfare." [6]

When the Senate debated the Isle of Pines Treaty, Norris started his study of it already prejudiced against ceding the island to Cuba. After examining the question, he said it would not be honorable to keep it "simply because Cuba is weak and we are strong." But he was disturbed by the argument that in ceding the Isle of Pines to Cuba, an American coaling station should not be infringed upon. If the United States had secured it without fair and adequate compensation, then "we ought yet to make amends for it, not by giving them something that was theirs all the time . . . but we ought to pay them or even to get out of our coaling station and surrender it to them." Though the coaling station matter was never fully clari-

[5] Norris to "Dear Boys," Mar. 20, 1926; to J. E. Taylor, Dec. 20, 1929; to Daniel J. Downing, Feb. 19, 1930; to W. M. Nelson, June 7, 1930; to L. R. McGaughey, Dec. 31, 1930; to J. C. Jensen, Jan. 23, 1931; to Mary F. Paul, Jan. 6, 1932; to Harley G. Moorhead, Mar. 4, 1932.
[6] Norris to C. W. McConaughy, July 7, 1926.

fied, Norris voted for the treaty when it passed the Senate on March 13, 1925.[7]

In the same spirit he advocated the immediate freedom of the Philippine Islands. The United States had no justification for keeping people in subjection. Moreover, to the consternation of many of his constituents who feared the competition of Philippine cane sugar with Nebraska beet sugar, he opposed any tariff upon products from the Philippines while under American dominion. It was "nothing short of criminal" to hold a people against their will and at the same time levy a tariff upon their products. Grant the Philippines their independence, and then tariff legislation could be applied as with any other foreign country. Norris advocated this proposition although it engendered hostility among "sugar men" in Nebraska.[8]

Despite a general interest in foreign policy Norris was never truly aroused until he considered Latin American, particularly Mexican and Nicaraguan, affairs. He was critical of the policies pursued by the State Department, and in a personal way he became directly involved. At the outset he protested the secrecy involved in negotiations with the Mexican government over title to oil lands; it was a method of diplomacy that gave rise to propaganda, "inculcating in the hearts of the citizens of different nations a feeling of hatred" which could lead to international tensions. In 1926 he called upon the Secretary of State to submit to the Senate all correspondence pertaining to American oil titles in Mexico so that citizens of both countries could secure knowledge of the dispute and the positions of their respective governments.

Norris's resolution was important because extensive press propaganda had laid "a foundation of hatred of a religious nature and of an educational nature on the part of our people against Mexico."

[7] *Congressional Record,* 68th Cong., 2nd sess., Jan. 17, p. 2017, Feb. 2, 1925, p. 2864; 69th Cong., special sess. of Senate, Mar. 13, 1925, p. 206; Norris to J. A. Austermann, Feb. 11, 1925. In 1904 the United States agreed to relinquish all claims to the island but the Senate refused to approve it then or again in 1908. The matter came up once again in the 1920s. The vote on the treaty was 63 to 14; see Robert F. Smith, *The United States and Cuba: Business and Diplomacy, 1917–1960* (New York, 1960), pp. 107–11.

[8] Norris to Adam Breede, Feb. 7, 1926; to E. F. Howe, Mar. 3, 1930; to Walter V. Hoagland, Feb. 12, 1932; to B. J. Segur, Dec. 31, 1932. See also *Congressional Record,* 72nd Cong., 1st sess., May 25, 1932, pp. 11103–4.

Charges that Mexico excluded missionaries, ministers, and Catholic educators from her schools were designed "to create dislike, mistrust, and hatred in the hearts of the American people against the Mexican Government." If this propaganda continued while secret oil negotiations were being conducted, Norris said, there was a strong chance that millionaires would "steal oil lands in Mexico without anybody knowing it, or anybody finding it out." While the Senate accepted his resolution, publication of the correspondence had little effect upon the course of the negotiations.[9]

Continually critical of the Mexican policies pursued by the Coolidge administration, Norris received national attention when the Hearst newspapers at the end of 1927 published documents revealing that with three other senators (William E. Borah, Robert M. LaFollette, Jr., and Thomas J. Heflin) he had received funds from the Mexican government. A letter from Mexican President Plutarco Calles to Arturo N. Elias, Mexico's consul general in New York, stated that Norris would receive $350,000 as his share of the $1,215,000 to be paid to the senators. Immediately a special Senate committee inquired into the validity of the documents and the charges they contained. It quickly became evident that the documents were spurious and the charges ridiculous.

Norris was little concerned. But he did take the opportunity afforded by this incident to draft an open letter to William Randolph Hearst. Realizing that newspapers might refuse to print it for fear of libel suits, Norris, who was at home ill on December 19, 1927, asked Senator Robert Howell to insert it in the *Congressional Record*. Nearly every senator was present. The news had leaked that Norris had written a scathing letter to Hearst and there was an air of excitement in the chamber as the clerk began to read.

> A fair analysis of the recent articles published in the Hearst papers showing an alleged attempt by Mexican officials to bribe United States Senators and editors of various publications, and an analysis of your testimony before the Senate Committee, leads to the inevitable conclusion that you are not only unfair and dishonest, but that you are entirely without honor.

[9] *Congressional Record*, 69th Cong., 1st sess., Mar. 1, pp. 4573–75, Mar. 6, 1926, p. 5144. See L. Ethan Ellis, *Frank B. Kellogg and American Foreign Relations, 1925–1929* (New Brunswick, N.J., 1961), pp. 34, 41, for mention of another Norris resolution.

These articles show, on the face, a constant attempt to draw conclusions not justified from the articles themselves, but to practice deception on the American people.

It is not necessary to consider any other evidence in order to reach the fair conclusion that in them you are making an attempt not only to besmirch the character of some of your own officials and journalists, but that you are trying to excite an animosity and a hatred on the part of our people against the Mexican Government, which, if your articles and alleged official documents were true, would inevitably lead to war between the two countries.[10]

In four full columns of fine print in the *Congressional Record,* Norris delineated his charges against Hearst. He noted the flimsy evidence and the "misleading and damaging" headlines that emanated from it. For the sake of his financial investments in Mexico Hearst was willing to ruin the reputation of innocent men and plunge the United States into war with a friendly neighbor. Norris concluded, "The record which you have made in this matter is sufficient to place your publications in disrepute in the minds of all honest men, and it demonstrates that the Hearst system of newspapers, spreading like a venomous web to all parts of the country, constitutes the sewer system of American journalism." After the letter was read, members of the special committee declared the four senators innocent. They agreed there was not one scintilla of evidence to justify the charge that the senators had accepted money or that any had been offered them by Mexican officials.[11]

To Norris it seemed that Hearst was trying to secure American intervention into Mexican affairs. It was a sad commentary that he was able to publish in his twenty-six newspapers these forged, false, and defamatory documents without violating some law. Certainly he was liable for damages to the persons he had slandered, but Norris, realizing such action would consume time and money,

[10] John P. Robertson to Yale B. Huffman, Dec. 20, 1927; *New York Times,* Dec. 20, 1927.

[11] *Congressional Record,* 70th Cong., 1st sess., Dec. 19, 1927, pp. 806–8. Norris's letter was printed in full in the *Washington Herald,* Dec. 20, 1927; the *Herald* was a Hearst paper. See also *New York Times,* Dec. 20, 1927; Newton D. Baker to Norris, Dec. 22, 1927 (Box 177, Newton D. Baker Papers, Manuscript Division, Library of Congress). Baker admitted taking some interest in the documents until Norris's name was disclosed.

doubted that he and his colleagues would seek legal redress. A year later, when documents purporting to show payments of $100,000 each to Senators Norris and Borah by the Soviet government for their services in seeking American recognition of Russia were released, they were quickly declared false by the same Senate committee which had examined the Mexican documents. Public indignation was tempered by the realization of most editors and concerned citizens that the charges were too ridiculous for serious consideration.[12]

If anything, because of these fraudulent charges Norris sharpened his criticism of administration interference in Mexican affairs. He insisted that neither faction in Mexico should receive any advantage or assistance from the United States, for the right of revolution was, "after all, rather a sacred right." While he did not pretend to understand all the matters involved in the Mexican Revolution, his sympathies were with the Calles government. But, he insisted, "this should not have anything to do with Governmental action on our part." It was not a matter for Americans to decide.[13]

Critical though he was of American policy toward Mexico, Norris's criticisms paled when compared to his denunciation of the Coolidge administration's decision to land Marines in Nicaragua to protect American property. Norris insisted that the regime of Adolfo Diaz "could not last twenty-four hours, if the support of the United States Government were taken away." The administration was interfering in Nicaragua, Norris learned "on the inside," primarily to make an impression upon Mexico, to teach her "that she ought not contravene the rights of American oil companies." [14] At times he wondered if anybody, "except a few chosen inside persons," knew what was going on in the State Department. As he saw it, the United States was drifting toward war and the American people had no notion why. Marines had been used to influence presidential elections, serving "as a collection agency for Wall Street or any other interest." If people invested and lost their money in Latin

12 Norris to Gilbert E. Roe, Dec. 27, 1927; to M. W. Osborn, Jan. 18, 1928; to Jeremiah P. Eddy, Jan. 29, 1928; *Washington Star,* Jan. 9, 1929; *Nashville Banner,* Jan. 27, 1929.

13 Norris to Agnes C. Watson, Mar. 22, 1929.

14 Norris to Max Henrici, Jan. 8, 1927; to Frank A. Harrison, Jan. 8, 1927.

American countries, Norris said, they had "no right to ask the Government to go to war in order to collect it." [15]

On March 24, 1927, the State Department announced that the War Department had sold 3,000 rifles, 200 machine guns, and 3 million rounds of ammunition to the Diaz government in Nicaragua. Norris denounced the sale, asserting that the United States had lost the friendship of every nation to the south of the Rio Grande. If arms could be sold without the consent of Congress, there was no reason why the action could not be repeated with "battleships to Mussolini." There was no reason why President Coolidge and Secretary Kellogg, without the consent of Congress, "could not put a Czar on the throne in Russia and sell him, on time, upon his promissory note, the cannons and the guns now belonging to our Government." Such behavior was detrimental not only to American national honor but to American business and commerce as well. The latter point Norris no doubt thought would have a greater impact than the former. [16]

It was a source of humiliation and shame to Norris to realize that Latin American suspicion of the United States was justified because of "our domineering and unfair treatment of these weaker nations." Putting a president into office in Nicaragua, backing him with American military might though he was neither duly elected nor entitled to the presidency, meant that "in truth and in fact the United States was at war with Nicaragua." The pretense that landing Marines on Nicaraguan soil was to protect American lives and property Norris labeled "pure bunk." It was to bolster the regime of Adolfo Diaz. The result was that the United States lost both friends and customers south of the Rio Grande. With a State Department that did not take the American people into its confidence, the Wilsonian aim of "open covenants openly arrived at" was once again held up to mockery. [17]

[15] Norris to Walter Locke, Jan. 23, 1927; to Joseph Pestal, Jan. 25, 1927; to Michael F. Campbell, Apr. 5, 1927; to G. C. Peckham, Jan. 23, 1928.

[16] Norris statement for newspapers, Mar. 24, 1927; *New York Times,* Mar. 25, 1927. The sale of arms to the Diaz government was made on credit and the low price of $217,718 was quoted.

[17] Draft statements by Norris, Apr. 6 and 7, 1927; Norris to Mr. and Mrs. O. D. Shaner, Feb. 14, 1928.

To further protest administration policies, Norris agreed to become honorary president of the National Citizens Committee on Relations with Latin America, an organization which sought to restore the good will and friendly relations sacrificed by the Coolidge administration's "misguided and plundering policy of dollar diplomacy." In acting the part of "a big bully" enforcing orders at the point of a bayonet, American Marines in Nicaragua were trampling "under military foot every doctrine of democracy" and blotting the nation's record "with bloody disgrace." He could not understand why "intelligent, patriotic" citizens did not protest the "unauthorized and indefensible war" being waged against Nicaragua. If Calvin Coolidge could conduct war in Nicaragua without the consent of Congress, what was to prevent him from doing it in other countries? If U.S. Marines could secure "a fair election" in Nicaragua, why could not the president send them to Ireland or Canada to insure fair elections there? Why not send them to Philadelphia or Pittsburgh, "where it is admitted they have not had an honest election for thirty years?" Few citizens seemed to care and too many senators defended every move of the administration.[18]

The agreement made by Henry L. Stimson, Calvin Coolidge's personal representative, with President Diaz and others to use American Marines to supervise a new election did not satisfy Norris; it "would not stand even in a Justice of the Peace Court in any civilized country." The fact that Marines were sent to suppress the faction headed by Augusto Sandino, who refused to abide by the Stimson arrangement, further angered Norris. The United States was lending moral and military assistance to one side in a Nicaraguan civil war. Adolfo Diaz, Norris said, "is a man whom the President has put into office. He is our puppet." Above all, he was "dumbfounded" that the American people silently submitted to the precedents being established in Nicaragua and practiced in Mexico.

[18] Norris to *St. Louis Post-Dispatch,* telegram, July 30, 1927; see the story in *ibid.,* Aug. 2, 1927; Norris to J. Nevin Sayre, Feb. 4, 1928. For material on the National Citizens Committee on Relations with Latin America, see the papers of the organization's secretary, Mercer G. Johnston, in the Manuscript Division, Library of Congress. For an overall discussion of administration policy toward Nicaragua, see Ellis, *Kellogg and American Foreign Relations,* Chapter 3, "Nicaraguan Tensions." Norris also suggested that some Marines might be withdrawn from Nicaragua and sent to Chicago "to protect the property of American citizens"; see *Congressional Record,* 70th Cong., 1st sess., Mar. 27, 1928, p. 5415.

The United States was establishing itself "as a Great Colossus" by insisting that Latin American governments follow its wishes "not only in their relationships with other nations but in their internal affairs as well." [19]

In April, 1928, Norris reiterated his criticisms of American action in Nicaragua because he felt the question had not been fully debated on the Senate floor. Not to criticize the president violated a duty every member of Congress ought to exercise, lest the United States follow the example of the "Government of Mussolini, which no Italian dare criticize." Criticism did not mean that Coolidge's motives were being impugned; it signified that dissent with his policies was being expressed. Thus Norris recommended that Congress, to stop unwarranted and unconstitutional military interference in the internal affairs of a neighboring nation and to stand against the usurpation of constitutional authority by the president, refuse to appropriate funds to continue these actions. The time had come for Congress to assert itself, "not only because we think that Nicaraguans are not being treated right but for the salvation of our country"; otherwise the constitutional system of the United States would suffer a serious setback.[20] At the end of the Coolidge administration, after an election had occurred in Nicaragua and some semblance of order had been restored, Norris was still critical. The election should have been supervised jointly with other Latin American nations, ceding to them the same right the United States had assumed for itself. And with the election over, he wanted to know why American forces still remained in Nicaragua. With Coolidge about to leave office, why was no effort made to withdraw American troops? [21]

Nicaragua and Mexico received most of Norris's attention when he examined American foreign policy during the Coolidge years. About the Far East he said very little and his remarks were general.

[19] Norris to W. G. Lewis, Mar. 27, 1928; to Frank Roth, Apr. 24, 1928.

[20] *Congressional Record,* 70th Cong., 1st sess., Apr. 23, pp. 6966–75, Apr. 25, 1928, pp. 7150–51, 7159–60, 7183.

[21] *Ibid.,* 2nd sess., Feb. 22, 1929, pp. 4045–46; Norris to John Parker, May 11, 1928. Norris also raised the question about the retention of American forces in Haiti, where "vast financial interests have been given control and many injustices have resulted from our own actions"; see Norris to John A. Singleton, Dec. 20, 1929.

But they followed the tenor of his comments about other countries. He favored national self-determination without American interference. The United States was free to exert moral pressure but nothing beyond that. He asserted that his sympathies were with the Cantonese, who would "eventually gain control of the entire Chinese nation" because they seemed to be moved by the spirit expressed in the slogan "China for the Chinese." Americans caught in the throes of the revolution had to be protected, but they ought to be removed from China as expeditiously as possible. Likewise, American extraterritorial rights ought to be renounced. China, in short, should be treated "as we would want any other nation to treat us under the same circumstances." [22]

In April of 1927, on the tenth anniversary of American entrance into World War I, Norris was the sole senatorial opponent of the war active on the political scene. He was besieged by reporters and citizens throughout the country for his comments. As he saw it, the cause of peace had not benefited and the struggle to attain a livelihood had become "harder and more difficult" for the average American citizen. Hatreds and injustices emanating from the war continued; Wilsonian idealism was not reflected in the behavior of the United States or the Allied nations. Asked if he would have voted in 1927 as he had in 1917, Norris responded, "I would." [23]

The war that was fought to make the world safe for democracy and to establish "the rights of weak peoples and small nations" had accomplished neither. Imperialism seemed to be in the saddle: there were American soldiers in China, in Haiti, in Nicaragua, and the government was seeking an excuse to put them into Mexico. Greed predominated over idealism; money was placed on a higher standard than either life or liberty. The United States did not have a single friend in the western hemisphere south of the Rio Grande.

[22] Draft statements by Norris, Apr. 6 and 7, 1927; Norris to John G. Maher, Apr. 12, 1927.

[23] Norris statement for *New York World*, Apr. 6, 1927; Norris statement for George R. Holmes, Apr., 1927. Recalling the criticism heaped upon him for his vote against entering the war, Norris now mused, "The only pay for service that is worthwhile is a satisfied conscience and, while I like to be thought well of when I make an honest attempt to do right by my fellowman, yet, I would rather be satisfied in my own heart than to have the approval of the entire world"; see Norris to E. C. Leggett, Apr. 18, 1927.

Notwithstanding this depressing portrait, Norris believed that "the heart of the American people is right," that eventually justice would prevail, and that the United States would practice "as a national policy the golden rule," doing unto other nations and peoples as "we would have them do unto us." [24]

Norris was pleased that his views were gaining acceptance by revisionist writers. He had no doubt that the American people had been duped by "the wonderful propaganda" that the war had been brought on by one government. To be sure, Germany was not blameless, but Russia and France and to a lesser extent England had combined against Germany. All were involved in an arms race which, along with mounting commercial rivalry, could not have continued "without the crash eventually taking place." "Germany was surrounded by those she knew were her enemies in commerce and in military affairs," and Norris did not see how she could be "solely to blame for the catastrophe which took place." Moreover, he claimed, many scholars and participants now agreed with him. Norris mentioned John Kenneth Turner, Harry Elmer Barnes, Frederick Bausman, judge of the supreme court of the state of Washington, and former Senator Robert L. Owen of Oklahoma. The latter had voted for American participation and had written a book laying the principal blame for the conflict on Russia and France. Some English and French "savants," acquitting Germany of war guilt, called for the deletion of this clause from the Versailles Treaty.[25]

The greatest evil emanating from the conflict, "the one that no one had fully anticipated when we went into the war," was the moral effect on individual citizens. Norris mentioned "the lowering of the morale; the increase of greed; the increase of selfishness that applies to nations and individuals alike; the tendency of those in power to suppress those who are in a minority from free speech." All of these things impaired the social order; their results were self-evident on the American scene during the administration of Calvin

[24] Norris to A. W. Stubbs, Apr. 12, 1927; to Maher, Apr. 12, 1927; to Gilbert A. Brattland, Apr. 15, 1927.

[25] Robert L. Owen, *The Russian Imperial Conspiracy, 1892–1914* (New York, 1927). For a discussion of revisionism, see Warren I. Cohen, *The American Revisionists* (Chicago, 1967). In 1927 at the time of Norris's remarks the controversy had not yet focused on American intervention.

Coolidge. But, optimistically, Norris believed the American people "will eventually see the light and understand the truth." [26]

Along with these revisionist views of World War I went a demand for disarmament and universal peace. Norris, of course, had championed these causes before the war. Now he called for decreased military expenditures as a way of curbing both the military spirit and the arms race. Norris was opposed to the United States entering a naval race because an increase in the American Navy would mean that the other nations involved in the Five-Power Treaty at Washington in 1922 would proportionately increase their fleets. Rather, the United States "should try to agree with the other civilized nations of the world to decrease armaments and to decrease standing armies." He disliked the continual fight in Congress to secure contracts for private companies to build battleships. The propaganda, made possible by those who would profit from private construction, helped to accelerate the arms race by inducing "their Representatives to vote for larger navies and increased armaments." [27]

By November, 1928, Norris discerned an effort to connect Senate approval of the Kellogg-Briand Pact with a pending bill providing for an increase in the Navy. In Norris's judgment those who were anxious for this bill were behind "the propaganda" that the treaty should not be ratified before it was approved. To be in favor of the peace pact only if the Navy were increased would lead other nations to question the good faith of the United States. Nevertheless, ad-

---

[26] Norris to A. G. Groh, Apr. 25, 1927. The people of Great Britain apparently saw the light before their American cousins. Commenting upon the 1929 victory of the Labor party, Norris said, "It is a repudiation of the unjust Treaty of Versailles. It is a repudiation of the millionaire coal kings who refused to pay the coal miners a living wage. It is a repudiation of the unjust and indefensible treatment of Russia. It is a repudiation of the militarists who are trying to use all the energies of the people to build up a huge army and navy. It is a victory in the direction of universal peace"; see Norris statement in the *Organized Farmer,* June 7, 1929, a dispatch from the Federated Press.

[27] *Congressional Record,* 68th Cong., 1st sess., Apr. 12, 1924, pp. 6213–14; Norris to H. T. Davis, Jan. 4, 1927. In this letter Norris also mentioned that he favored the National Guard over a large standing army because "it is the citizen soldiery of the country upon which we must depend." Incidentally, Norris thought Colonel William Mitchell had done much good for the country, "particularly as regards the Army," and that he deserved promotion rather than suspension at the hands of a court-martial; see Norris to Little, Jan. 20, 1926; to Mrs. H. H. Ruhge, Mar. 31, 1928; to H. Herpolsheimer, Apr. 1, 1928.

ministration forces and President-elect Hoover were in favor of the big-navy bill. To Norris it seemed that if the peace pact were ratified, "it ought to be an argument against the increase of the navy." He stated, "I fear, however, that those who agree with me on this program are in the minority." [28]

Through parliamentary maneuvering Borah succeeded in getting the Senate to consider the Kellogg-Briand Treaty before the so-called cruiser bill. Norris was pleased. If the treaty were approved, he would have a "logical and forceful argument" against the cruiser bill, though he knew there were not enough votes to defeat it. To support a treaty in favor of world peace and the outlawing of war, and then to enact a measure providing for the enlargement of the U.S. Navy, seemed to Norris a contradiction worth protesting. If the United States was willing not to resort to war as an instrument of national policy, it should be willing to favor additional limitation of naval armaments. [29]

It was in connection with this parliamentary situation that Norris became involved in a controversy with one of his constituents, Reverend A. A. DeLarme, pastor of the First Baptist Church of Omaha. DeLarme asked Norris to vote for the Kellogg-Briand Pact and went on to say, "You do not represent us at all and we (the eight hundred and forty-two members of the church) are very much ashamed of your attitude to the administration, and on many questions of public policy." Norris sent a telegram asking how he "and the eight hundred and forty-two Baptists whom you say you represent" would have him vote on the "Big Navy Bill" pending in the Senate. The minister replied that while he favored the bill, his congregation was divided on the measure. Now Norris had the opening he desired. In a long letter he castigated DeLarme for putting party above all things, including religion. Since the minister did not specifically state what had brought him into disgrace "with you and your 842 followers," Norris proceeded to delineate his stand on numerous issues, noting that he was not in accord with Republican leaders in each instance. Confessing that in his sinful

[28] Norris to Caroline M. Platt, Nov. 22, 1928; to Theodore Foxworthy, Nov. 23, 1928.

[29] Norris to F. W. Kelsey, Dec. 31, 1928; to Edward M. Novak, Jan. 3, 1929; to Mrs. Franklin P. Boomersox, Jan. 8, 1929.

way he could not comprehend the minister's viewpoint, Norris admonished him to give heed "to that Scriptual injunction that you should judge not, lest ye be judged." [30]

After voting for the Kellogg-Briand Pact, Norris spoke and then voted against the naval construction bill which easily passed the Senate in February, 1929. Failing to curb naval expenditures, Norris next criticized increasing appropriations for the armed forces, where 70 cents of every tax dollar went "to pay for the obligations of past wars or for preparation for new wars." But his opposition to militarism extended even further. Norris favored abandoning the military training of students in high schools, colleges, and universities. He condemned the ROTC because of its compulsory feature. If students were free "to either take it or omit it," Norris would have no objection. But compulsion could encourage militarism and lead overtrained and overarmed forces to seek an outlet for their destructive talents. [31]

If the profit could be taken out of war, Norris was certain that "we would have no war." "It was a cold-blooded proposition to get us into war for the sake of money," comparable to putting a dollar sign on the American flag. To resolve this situation, he was willing to support a constitutional amendment that in time of war the government "ought to conscript property the same as it does humanity." On the basic question of going to war, he favored a referendum, though he foresaw conditions "in which it might be necessary

[30] A. A. DeLarme to Norris, Jan. 8 and 14, 1929; Norris to DeLarme, Jan. 12, telegram, Jan. 25, 1929. The entire correspondence was published by Judson King as Bulletin 125 of the National Popular Government League, Jan. 31, 1929 (copy in the Harry Slattery Papers, Manuscripts Collections, Duke University Library). The correspondence came to the attention of Reinhold Niebuhr, who published an article, "Senator Norris and His Clerical Critic," in *The World Tomorrow*, 12, no. 4 (Apr., 1929): 169–70. Niebuhr used the correspondence to illustrate the point that organized religion could make "devotion to ideal values a substitute for their attainment in specific situations." He queried, "If religion does not in some sense qualify the complacency of the nation, if it does not breed a wholesome spirit of contrition not only upon the sins of individuals but upon the sins of our society, can we really expect to have society as such take religion seriously?" Incidentally, DeLarme never answered Norris's letter of Jan. 25, 1929.

[31] Norris to George W. Platner, Feb. 28, 1929; *Congressional Record*, 70th Cong., 2nd sess., Feb. 1, pp. 2618–22, Feb. 2, pp. 2673–74, Feb. 5, 1929, pp. 2840, 2854; Norris to Mrs. A. W. Kummer, Mar. 17, 1932; to C. A. Sorensen, Apr. 12, 1926; to L. R. Gignilliat, July 16, 1926; *Omaha Bee*, Dec. 13, 1925. All of Norris's efforts to amend the bill failed; the vote on the bill was 68 to 12.

to go to war before such a referendum could be brought about." [32]

Finally, with regard to the emerging all-purpose villain of the decade, Norris noted that "a man hardly dares to say anything in favor of Russia without being denounced and condemned as a bolshevik or an anarchist." When government officials pursued this course, he was "deeply grieved and shocked." Norris had talked with many people, read much, and tried to digest so many opinions that he confessed to be in a dilemma about what conditions were like in Russia. He was critical of Secretary Kellogg's effort to have circulated "propaganda which he did not dare admit came from the State Department." This action indicated to Norris the weakness of men high in official life, an area where people expected judicious and fair-minded individuals. "How dangerous it is," he wrote, "that those who have the shaping of our destiny should be moved by such illogical and unfair methods in creating a sentiment of hostility and hate against our fellow men." [33] To illustrate how diligently Secretary Kellogg and his associates in the State Department were searching for radicals, Norris, with apologies to James Whitcomb Riley, commented:

> Once't they was a Bolshevik,
>   Who wouldn't say his prayers—
> So Kellogg sent him off to bed,
>   Away up stairs,
> An' Kellogg heerd him holler, an'
>   Coolidge heerd him bawl,
> But when they turn't the kivvers
>   Down, he wasn't there at all!

[32] Norris to Forrest Revere Black, Jan. 1, 1926; to Dwight P. Griswold, May 8, 1930; to Ica Westley, June 9, 1930; to C. J. Osborn, Aug. 12, 1924; to Hazel Thompson, Mar. 27, 1924. In the letter to Mrs. Thompson Norris wrote, "Outside of civil wars, there has never been a war fought during the last one hundred years, that could not have been settled in a court of reason by applying the ordinary principles of jurisprudence and justice which prevail in any civilized court of the world."

[33] Norris to Jacob Billikopf, Feb. 13, 1927; *Congressional Record,* 69th Cong., 2nd sess., Jan. 15, 1927, p. 1691. Kellogg on Jan. 12, 1927, had testified before the Foreign Relations Committee about the activities of "Bolsheviks and communists" seeking to destroy the American government. Late in Dec., 1926, Paul Y. Anderson in the *St. Louis Post-Dispatch* picked up the suggestion of an Assistant Secretary of State that the government thought there was a close connection between Mexico City and Moscow.

They seeked him down in Mexico,
    They cussed him in the press;
They seeked him 'round the Capitol,
    An' ever'wheres, I guess;
But all they ever found of him was
    Whiskers, hair, and clout—
An' the Bolsheviks'll get you
    Ef you
        Don't
            Watch
                Out! [34]

[34] *Congressional Record,* 69th Cong., 2nd sess., Jan. 15, 1927, p. 1691.

The Patriot's Duty

26

Party politics, despite his increasing independence, interested George Norris during the Coolidge years. His interest was confined to criticizing outrageous campaign practices and in one notable instance to acting upon his criticism. Since every instance involved Republican candidates, his criticisms serve to illustrate further his placing of principle above politics. During the Harding administration he had denounced the election of Truman Newberry to the U.S. Senate from Michigan because of the excessive expenditure of campaign funds. But Newberry and his organization appeared to be a bunch of tightwads compared to the machine behind William Vare in the 1926 Pennsylvania Republican primary for U.S. senator. The less than $200,000 spent to elect Newberry paled into insignificance when compared to the sums spent for Vare. And this case was not the only one to attract Norris's attention. It was not so much the amount of money spent but, rather, the accompanying malpractices that aroused his anger and made him a constant critic of party practices. It also projected him as the leading progressive in political life.

After the death of Robert M. LaFollette colleagues in the Senate recognized Norris as the leading progressive in that body. Because the Senate was closely divided between the two parties, the progressive group was in a position to hold the balance of power. The turning of the tide on the issue of water resources indicated their growing influence. Critical though Norris and other progressives were of party policies, they always voted to keep the Senate organization Republican. Though they were willing to cooperate with Senate Democrats to achieve their goals, though they helped veto some Coolidge appointments, and though Norris urged the election of the Democratic candidate running against William Vare in Pennsylvania, Republican progressives remained within party lines while refusing to be bound by party ties.

In Norris's case this type of maneuvering gained him national attention although slight success. The great advantage he had over most of his associates was that it was impossible for the administration to reward or punish him. Norris was probably the only senator who never recommended or endorsed aspirants for office. Having little to do with the distribution of federal patronage in Nebraska, no one in the administration could confer a favor on him or withhold one. Thus in disputed election cases Norris could act with sincerity and fearlessness, disregardful of political consequences. His standing as an independent was enhanced, and there was little Calvin Coolidge and his advisers could do about it.[1]

The first disputed election that aroused Norris during the presidency of Calvin Coolidge occurred in Iowa, where Smith W. Brookhart, a militant progressive Republican, was deprived of a Senate seat in 1925. The Senate Privileges and Elections Committee declared Daniel F. Steck, a conservative Democrat, the winner. Norris said that the Ku Klux Klan and Democratic politicians exerted pressure to influence the vote for Steck and that powerful Iowa Republicans opposed Brookhart because of his insistence that Harry Daugherty should be investigated. Some of his colleagues were seeking to place "party on a much higher pedestal" than country, though the official count gave the election to Brookhart. If Iowa law provided that upon reconsideration Brookhart was still the winner, Norris felt that his colleagues had to accept this verdict "unless we want to be violators of the law." But on April 12, 1926, in a close vote in which party lines were turned topsy-turvy, the Senate voted in Steck's favor.[2] Immediately, Brookhart announced that he would

---

[1] See the interesting story on the progressive group in the Senate by John Snure in the *New York Tribune*, Nov. 13, 1927.

[2] George W. Norris to Walter Locke, Apr. 12, 1926; to John G. Maher, June 17, 1926; *Congressional Record*, 69th Cong., 1st sess., Apr. 12, 1926, pp. 7295–96,

challenge Senator Albert Cummins in the primary, thereby antagonizing the Coolidge administration, which supported Cummins. Norris favored Brookhart, contributing $50 to his campaign fund and
printing some speeches on his behalf. He was pleased when Iowa
voters "indicated their resentment" at Brookhart's treatment by
electing him over Cummins in the primary and then in November
for a full term in the Senate.[3]

By this time Norris's disillusionment with Cummins as a progressive was complete. He was not bitter; rather, he looked with
sadness upon Cummins's straying from the progressive fold. He possessed, Norris said, "an analytical mind not surpassed by any man
with whom I have ever come in contact in my public life." Cummins had entered the Senate "with one of the best and greatest repu-
tations" and for years had fought "for progressive principles of
Government," but he was susceptible to flattery and was impressed
with "the sound of his own voice." As he advanced in the Senate,
administration supporters bombarded him with both praise and
flattery and slowly but surely "enveloped him in the meshes of their
stand pat tendencies." Norris wrote, "I saw him changing gradually,
almost daily, and it is one of the sad recollections of my public life
to have seen this man, with his ability, gradually go over to the
other side." The process was an unconscious one, Cummins not
being fully aware of what had happened to him. His case was "a
sad commentary on the perplexities and the temptations that come
to one in public life who has great ability and who starts out by
trying to serve his country according to his conscientious convictions." Norris observed that men who had gone "from one side of
the political fence to the other" and then failed had no comradeship
in either camp. "Those who by their flattery and their praise" had
brought Cummins over to their side apparently had no further use
for him by 1926 "and cast him aside as they would an old shoe."

7301. The vote was 45 to 41 in favor of seating Daniel F. Steck. Republican
Senators William Butler (Massachusetts), Ovington Weller (Maryland), and
Guy Goff (West Virginia) voted to seat Steck, while Democrats Thomas Walsh
(Montana), James Reed (Missouri), and Coleman Blease (South Carolina) fa-
vored Brookhart. Butler was chairman of the Republican National Committee.
Nine Democrats and one Farmer-Laborite supported thirty-one Republicans in
voting for Brookhart.

[3] Norris to Frank J. Lund, May 20, 1926; to Maher, June 17, 1926.

Unlike LaFollette, who went to his grave "remembered by both friends and enemies, as one who remained true to his faith and who never faltered in what he believed to be his duty," Cummins, defeated in the primary, prepared to retire to private life, an old man who had outlived his usefulness and who lacked the confidence of both factions in the Republican party. He was deprived of "the only satisfaction that is worthy of consideration," that of duty performed "faithfully and true, in the light that God has given." But death cut short his plans for retirement. Cummins died shortly after his defeat.[4]

Cummins's case was a tragedy and Norris recognized it as such. In all other instances where he became involved, Norris's concern was with party more than with person, though at times the distinction was hard to make. For a party to command confidence, it had to be able to wash its "own linen, whenever it is dirty." It could not afford to condone the sale of public offices, as the Republican party was charged with doing in the South, without serious repercussions against it by the electorate. But the Senate refused to consider the charge despite Norris's call for an investigation of patronage distribution in southern states.[5]

In the case of William S. Vare, Norris was more persistent. Though defeated in his efforts, he wrought havoc in Republican ranks. In a three-cornered contest for the senatorial nomination in the spring of 1926, Vare, a congressman, head of the Republican organization in Philadelphia, and an avowed "wet," defeated incumbent Senator George Wharton Pepper and Governor Gifford Pinchot by a majority of more than 100,000 votes. Pepper had the backing of the administration and the supporters of Andrew Mellon. Gifford Pinchot, playing a lone hand as an antimachine candidate, finished a poor third. Both Pepper and Pinchot were "dry"; Vare favored repeal of the Volstead Act. Besides prohibition and party feuding some observers, including Norris, saw in this primary "the unfolding of another Newberry case." Reports estimated that be-

[4] Norris to Locke, June 12, 1926; to J. A. Lister, June 24, 1926.

[5] Norris to David R. Grace, Dec. 21, 1926; to A. F. Knotts, Dec. 28, 1926; to Henry T. Hunt, Apr. 15, 1927; to Lowell Mellett, Aug. 8, 1927. Norris did not persist in calling for an investigation of the distribution of party patronage in the South.

tween $2 and $5 million had been spent, more than in any primary to that time.[6]

In a widely noticed article, "The Patriot's Duty in Pennsylvania," Norris denounced this excessive expenditure of funds as shocking to the "national conscience" and a threat "to the fundamental principles that underlie every free government." Taxpayers throughout the land would pay in one way or another for the legislation introduced and supported by Pennsylvania's senators, while the men who contributed in the primary expected a return on their money. Since Vare's nomination was equivalent to election, Norris claimed that "the only remedy the country has is to demand of the Senate that it refuse to seat him." But if the Senate refused to seat Vare, then the governor of Pennsylvania, who would be a representative of the Mellon machine, would appoint a senator. And, Norris observed, "the Mellon machine spent more money than the Vare machine" in the primary. Thus the Senate seat would truly go to the highest bidder.

Norris called upon "the honest, patriotic citizens of Pennsylvania" to vote in the November election for the Democratic nominee, William B. Wilson, who had served as a congressman and as the first Secretary of Labor. Wilson was able, honest, patriotic, and courageous. But he was a Democrat, and Pennsylvania had not sent a Democrat to the U.S. Senate since the Civil War. If partisanship could be set aside, "the election of Mr. Wilson would not only put a good man in the Senate from Pennsylvania but it would be the most severe rebuke that could possibly be administered to the corrupt Republican machine." The only effective way for Pennsylvania Republicans to place their party "on a high moral basis" would be to vote for the Democratic nominee. Norris observed that they had ample precedent in the recent action of the Senate in selecting the Democratic candidate in the Iowa contested election upon the advice of the Republican State Committee. If Republican leaders could justify their conduct in refusing to support Brookhart, "whose nomination was honest and unquestioned," then how could they "consistently demand that Pennsylvania Republicans should over-

[6] "The 'Vare and Beer' Victory as a National Portent," *Literary Digest,* May 29, 1926, pp. 5–7. The Pennsylvania primary occurred on May 18, 1926.

look the contamination and disgraceful influences controlling the last Republican primary in Pennsylvania?" Patriotic voters in the Keystone State could perform a great public service by repudiating "the Pennsylvania political machines that are a stench in the nostrils of liberty-loving people everywhere." [7]

Written words were not enough for Norris. In the summer of 1926 he announced that he would carry the message personally to Pennsylvania voters. Immediately he was beset with requests to speak under the auspices of the Antisaloon League and the Democratic party. Norris refused both offers, realizing that to elect Wilson, he would have to win Republican votes from many who were opposed to one or both of these organizations. He also refused personal invitations of hospitality, believing that the speaker always ought to be accessible in some public place while in a city to make a speech. Norris explained, "I want to do all the good I can in this campaign, and do not want to leave any stone unturned." [8]

Possibly to divert him from this intention, the chairman of the Republican State Committee requested his presence in Nebraska in October to lend a hand campaigning. Norris refused, claiming that he was not fully informed on the various facets of the Nebraska political scene and that his schedule in Pennsylvania was already arranged. He candidly commented that advising people to vote the straight Republican ticket would be antagonistic to his personal views and contrary to his record. Since he regarded the Pennsylvania election as the most important in the nation in 1926, he had agreed to remain there until election day. If he were to leave to campaign in Nebraska, Pennsylvania Republican leaders could claim that their attack had driven him from the state. Norris did not intend to give them that satisfaction. [9]

By mid-October Norris was speaking in Pennsylvania in as many

[7] *Congressional Record*, 69th Cong., 1st sess., July 3, 1926, pp. 12899–901. The article was inserted in the *Record* by Senator Royal S. Copeland of New York. An abbreviated version appeared in *Nation*, July 14, 1926, pp. 28–29. Over 200,000 copies of the article as it appeared in the *Record* were sent to Pennsylvania voters.

[8] Norris to H. W. Tope, Aug. 29, 1926; to W. P. Boland, Oct. 14, 1926. See also the story in the *Philadelphia Record*, July 9, 1926.

[9] Norris to Harry E. Sackett, Oct. 12 and 20, 1926; to Robert Smith, Nov. 3, 1926. Norris was not enthusiastic about Adam McMullen, who was seeking re-election as governor of Nebraska; see Norris to Carl F. Marsh, Dec. 3, 1926.

as seven cities within a twenty-four-hour period. Paying his own expenses, he asked voters to reject William S. Vare. At his first meeting in Altoona he had only 300 listeners. As he proceeded, his audiences increased. They were largely Republican, and women turned out in large numbers. All listened avidly. In both rural and urban areas he lashed at the Vare and Mellon machines that controlled Pennsylvania politics. One reporter noted that "by the time Norris warms up to the attack on machine ruled Pennsylvania and on slush-fund primaries in particular, the whole house, irrespective of its bipartisan character, is with Norris, applauding and frequently cheering his onslaughts on the things 'Bill' Vare typifies in public life."

Norris put "heart and soul" into his single-handed effort to win over Pennsylvanians to their patriotic duty. At Lancaster, stretching his family history, he said, "I am here fighting at the side of the decent men of Pennsylvania, as my brother was at the side of Pennsylvanians when he gave his last breath for the Union at Gettysburg." [10] He exerted all possible effort to make Pennsylvanians realize that the defeat of Vare was a national and not a state issue, that voting against Vare would not destroy but rather would redeem the Republican party. To be sure, one man in a fortnight on the hustings could hardly undermine the traditions of a boss-ridden state like Pennsylvania. But judging by the impact Norris made, observers believed that several more speakers of fire and fervor might have accomplished the feat. Norris believed the people were ripe for regeneration. His only regret was that there might not be enough time to accomplish it.[11]

Everywhere he found concern that whatever the vote might be in the state at large, the political machines of Philadelphia and Pittsburgh would manipulate the ballots to give Vare a majority.

[10] John Henry Norris was wounded at Resaca, Ga., and died shortly thereafter from infection on May 27, 1864. He did not join the Fifty-fifth Ohio Volunteer Infantry until Jan., 1864, half a year after the battle of Gettysburg.

[11] *Philadelphia Record,* Oct. 25 and 30, 1926 (stories were filed by Frederic William Wile). See also Norris to George W. Churchill, Nov. 2, 1926; to August Miller, Nov. 3, 1926. Norris's campaign expenses were covered in part by a contribution from W. T. Rawleigh of Freeport, Ill.; see Norris to Rawleigh, Nov. 3 and 17, 1926. In all, Rawleigh contributed $750 to help Norris's campaign in Pennsylvania. Ralph G. Sucher, at the time the Washington correspondent for several midwestern newspapers, handled campaign details for Norris.

Some voters thought it useless to go to the polls. Norris assured his audiences that the U.S. Senate would be "the sole and final judge of the qualification and the election of the Senator from Pennsylvania" and that it would not be party to a fraudulent election. The attorney general of Pennsylvania assured him that every effort would be made to insure a fair and lawful election. But he admitted that "it is almost impossible for those not supported by certain organizations, especially the so-called Republican organizations in Philadelphia and Pittsburgh, to have a fair, square vote at the polls, or a fair count of the votes which are cast." [12]

Vare won the election. But he ran several hundred thousand votes behind the Republican ticket. Outside the city of Philadelphia he was defeated by a 50,000-vote majority. Norris claimed that "the returns from some of these controlled voting precincts will open the eyes of honest citizens everywhere as to the methods followed by this machine." As an example, he cited thirty-two precincts where William Wilson received only one vote each and forty-four other precincts where not a single vote was returned for him. In seventy-six Philadelphia precincts, "casting in round numbers 17,000 votes," William B. Wilson received thirty-two votes. Norris observed that "results in some parts of Philadelphia were announced in advance, even before any votes were cast." The returns did reveal that "the honest patriotic people of Pennsylvania have revolted against the Philadelphia machine and that Mr. Vare, its candidate, had been repudiated even though technically counted in by the usual machine methods in Philadelphia." But it would be impossible to prove "any concrete item of fraud" because men feared they would be injured either physically or in their businesses. So long had machines controlled elections that most Pennsylvanians had lost any expectation of having an honest election. [13]

[12] Norris to George W. Woodruff, Oct. 25, 1926; Woodruff to Norris, Oct. 30, 1926 (both in Box 260, Gifford Pinchot Papers, Manuscript Division, Library of Congress).

[13] Draft statement by Norris, Nov. 5, 1926; Norris to William A. Mitchell, Nov. 5, 1926; to J. W. Bissell, Nov. 17, 1926; to Morris L. Cooke, Nov. 10, 1926; Norris memorandum, Nov. 11, 1926; Norris to W. O. Tillotson, Nov. 16, 1926; to W. C. Goodwin, Nov. 16, 1926; to Rawleigh, Nov. 17, 1926; to Edward Keating, Aug. 22, 1927. For an indication of the impact of Norris's campaigning, see the editorial by E. E. Miller, who thought Norris "about as wrong as a man could be on some very important questions," in *Southern Agriculturist*, Dec. 1, 1926.

It was Norris's hope that a Senate investigating committee would uncover enough corruption to allow the membership to refuse Vare his seat. It appeared that Vare would be sworn in and then, as in the Newberry case, an investigation would take place. But Norris was confident that Vare would be thrown out of the Senate. Thus, before the second session of the Sixty-ninth Congress convened, he devoted much time to gathering evidence. If the illegal votes could be discounted, the result would show the election of Wilson. Norris, of course, could not state this view as fact, but he did say, "I have heard from very reliable sources to convince me that this is probably true." One reliable source was Melville E. Ferguson, executive editor of the *Philadelphia Record,* who, Norris said, deserved great praise for battling the Vare machine and fighting for honest government in Pennsylvania.[14]

In all, Norris had some reason for satisfaction. He had so aroused the conscience of the voters in a state where it was almost considered "a sin to scratch the Republican ticket" that the Democratic candidate carried fifty-five of Pennsylvania's sixty-seven counties. Public sentiment had crystallized to such an extent that the Senate seemingly could not afford to seat Vare. Moreover, since he always voted with his party to organize the Senate, Norris doubted that any effort would be made to punish him for his participation in the Pennsylvania election. The balance in the Senate was too precarious to consider the possibility.[15]

Congress convened on December 6, 1926. Norris said that the seating of Vare would mean "the domination of the Senate and the entire country by political machines, corrupt and immoral." It would make the Senate a millionaires' club, a place no poor man could aspire to unless he agreed to do the bidding of wealthy sponsors. To manifest his opposition to the administration, which seemed to gloss over the Pennsylvania election, Norris refused to attend the White House breakfast conference for congressional leaders: "Vermont maple syrup and buckwheat cakes have no charm for me if

[14] Norris to Rawleigh, Nov. 17, 1926; to "Dear Boys," Nov. 18, 1926; to James A. Brown, Nov. 23, 1926; to Melville E. Ferguson, Nov. 24, Dec. 3, 1926; to John B. Townley, Dec. 3, 1926; to Joseph P. Kane, Dec. 3, 1926.

[15] Norris to Marsh, Dec. 3, 1926; to Gutzon Borglum, Dec. 3, 1926. See also Clinton W. Gilbert's column "The Daily Mirror of Washington" in *Philadelphia Public Ledger,* Oct. 29, 1926.

the object is bridging the chasm made by the fraud and corruption" disclosed in the recent campaigns.[16]

Early in this short session Senator Walsh of Montana inserted in the *Congressional Record* a campaign speech made by Norris as he began his battle to thwart Vare's ambition to sit in the Senate. Less than two weeks later Senator Clarence Dill of Washington inserted an article on the power and duty of the Senate to act in the Vare case as well as in that of Frank L. Smith in Illinois. In both instances excessive amounts of money had been spent to acquire the nomination. It was not until the last day of the session that Norris himself took the floor to support the investigation by James A. Reed of Missouri into Vare's election. But nothing was done and the chances were great that Vare would assume his seat when the Seventieth Congress convened in December, 1927.[17]

Crowds jammed the Senate galleries on December 6, 1927. They were treated to a long discourse in which Norris requested the Senate not to seat Vare in accordance with the precedent followed in the case of Truman Newberry. In 1922 the Senate had condemned the expenditure of $195,000 in the Michigan senatorial campaign as "dangerous to the perpetuity of free government." Vare's credentials were then presented and referred to the Privileges and Elections Committee. But Vare was not permitted to claim his seat, though his name appeared on the official list of senators and he collected his salary. No action was taken and Pennsylvania throughout the Seventieth Congress and on into the Seventy-first was represented by only one senator.[18]

Though Norris spoke about the case only once in the Seventieth

---

[16] Draft statement by Norris for National Education Association, n.d. [Dec., 1926]; *Boston Daily Globe,* Dec. 8, 1926.

[17] *Congressional Record,* 69th Cong., 2nd sess., Dec. 22, 1926, pp. 917–21, Jan. 3, pp. 987–89, Mar. 3, 1927, pp. 5545–46. The text of the December speech was reprinted from the *Philadelphia Record,* Oct. 17, 1926. Senator Dill did not present any information about the article when he submitted it. The *New York Times,* Mar. 13, 1927, carried a lengthy and bitter statement by Norris on "the disgraceful spectacle of the Senate of the United States winding up the recent session of Congress in a ridiculous helplessness to function." "Lameducks," he asserted, prevented an investigation of the corruption charges.

[18] *Congressional Record,* 70th Cong., 1st sess., Dec. 6, 1927, pp. 119–22; *New York American,* Dec. 7, 1927.

Congress, to urge postponement because of Vare's illness, his interest in it remained intense. Vindication came on December 6, 1929, when a resolution he had introduced, declaring Vare not entitled to his seat, was approved. But total victory was not achieved because the Senate then approved another resolution stating that William B. Wilson was not elected and therefore not entitled to a seat. The governor of Pennsylvania was notified that a vacancy existed; six days later Joseph R. Grundy, leader of a powerful Republican faction, was occupying the seat denied to William S. Vare. There was no legal way for the Senate to prevent him from being seated. The only remedy was for Pennsylvanians at the ballot box to represent the "righteous, patriotic sentiment of the nation" and reject the governor's choice.[19]

Contemporaneous with the Vare controversy was the case of Frank L. Smith of Illinois. Though Norris devoted more attention to the former, he mentioned the Illinois controversy when commenting upon the use of money in the 1926 Republican campaigns. In Illinois, as in Pennsylvania, a Republican nomination was "practically the equivalent" of election. But here the matter was compounded because both Republican and Democratic nominees received contributions from the Insull interests. In Smith's case it was particularly aggravating, since, as chairman of the Illinois Commerce Commission, he was charged with regulating public utilities in the state.

In Illinois, as in Pennsylvania, it quickly became the patriot's duty to protest the expenditure of large sums in the primary campaign. Smith spent $400,000 of which $125,000 came from public utilities magnate Samuel Insull. The connection with Insull, a leading figure in what Norris called "the Power Trust," added an extra dimension to the election, and Norris exploited it to the utmost.

[19] *Congressional Record*, 70th Cong., 2nd sess., Feb. 26, 1929, p. 4331; 71st Cong., 2nd sess., Dec. 6, pp. 197–98, Dec. 12, 1929, pp. 535–36; Norris to S. H. Plummer, May 6, 1928; to D. B. Marti, Dec. 20, 1929. The vote on Norris's resolution denying Vare a seat was 58 to 22, but by a 66-to-15 vote the Senate declared that Wilson was not elected. For Vare's side of the controversy, see *My Forty Years in Politics* (Philadelphia, 1933), pp. 152–219. For an overall view, see Samuel J. Astorino, "The Contested Senate Election of William Scott Vare," *Pennsylvania History*, 28 (Apr., 1961): 187–201.

Putting Senate seats on the auction block, he concluded, would destroy the primary system and would mean that candidates with limited funds could no longer get a square deal in seeking public office. When enormous sums were spent, a great proportion of it inevitably found its way "into corrupt hands." The only way to stop it was for the Senate to exclude men who spent exorbitant sums of money.[20]

Norris was confident that Smith would be excluded as soon as the committee investigating the Illinois primary presented its report. Following the death of Senator William B. McKinley in December, 1926, Governor Len Small chose Senator-elect Frank L. Smith to fill the vacancy. His credentials were referred to the Privileges and Elections Committee and he was not permitted to serve. For most of the lame-duck session of the Sixty-ninth Congress Illinois was served by only one senator. By a vote of 48 to 33 the Senate agreed not to seat Smith while his credentials were being investigated. Norris was confident that the vote would be even larger when Smith sought admission at the next session.[21]

At the outset of the Seventieth Congress both Smith and Vare were denied their seats pending recommendations by the Privileges and Elections Committee. In January, 1928, Norris discussed the case of Frank L. Smith. After citing the precedent of the Newberry case, he turned his attention to the relationship of utilities magnate Samuel J. Insull to this disputed election. "It is not a question of Illinois being deprived of her two votes in the Senate"; rather, he asserted, "it is a question of Mr. Insull being deprived of his votes in the Senate." Since Insull had contributed to the campaigns of all senatorial candidates, to admit Smith in effect would be to grant Insull a voice in the Senate. Illinois was not the only state where Insull was involved in politics. Norris mentioned his activities in Maine to illustrate further that purchasing elections disfranchised the honest voter and helped destroy a "fundamental cornerstone of

[20] Draft statement by Norris for NEA, n.d. [Dec., 1926]; Norris to A. M. Ruster, Dec. 6, 1926; to F. M. Shoukwiler, Dec. 19, 1926; to J. L. Franklin, Jan. 8, 1927; Cooke to Norris, Nov. 24, 1926 (Box 48, Morris L. Cooke Papers, Franklin D. Roosevelt Library, Hyde Park, N.Y.).

[21] Norris to Gifford Pinchot, Oct. 17, 1927; to Clinton N. Howard, Oct. 17, 1927; *Congressional Record*, 69th Cong., 2nd sess., Jan. 20, 1927, p. 2014.

this democracy." On these grounds both Smith and Vare, Norris insisted, should be refused seats in the Senate.[22]

The case of Frank Smith, unlike that of William Vare, came to an abrupt end on February 9, 1928, when Smith resigned as senator-designate from Illinois. He was replaced after a special election by Otis F. Glenn. Norris had the satisfaction of knowing that he had performed his patriotic duty, rising above the pressures of partisanship to protest the excessive expenditures in the Illinois senatorial primary. Thereafter, his chief concern with party politics in the last years of the Coolidge administration focused on Nebraska, where he had not participated in the 1926 campaign.

The governor of Nebraska, Adam McMullen, did not satisfy Norris because he felt that McMullen had not always "stood for the protection of the rights of the people against combinations and monopolies." Possibly because of this dissatisfaction, Norris spoke in a 1927 interview of reforms he would promote if he were governor of Nebraska. He admitted that perhaps the logical way to accomplish this reform program, centering around the elimination of partisanship, would be to run for governor after the expiration of his Senate term in 1930. But if his political enemies continued their fight against him, he thought it might be impossible for him to quit the Senate. The patriot's duty in Nebraska, as in Iowa, Pennsylvania, Illinois, and elsewhere, was to place country above party. And Norris was never one to flinch from the call of duty.[23]

Basically, however, in the last years of the Coolidge administration Norris had no cause for complaint. He had spent the best years of his life in public service, trying, he said, "to be useful to my

[22] *Congressional Record,* 70th Cong., 1st sess., Jan. 19, 1928, pp. 1703–5. Carroll H. Woody, *The Case of Frank L. Smith* (Chicago, 1931), is a careful monograph examining the incident as a study in representative government. The author acknowledges in his preface assistance accorded him by Norris and other senators. Forrest McDonald in his sympathetic and understanding biography *Insull* (Chicago, 1962) calls Insull's campaign contribution "a major blunder" (p. 263).

[23] Norris to John F. Cordeal, Apr. 5, 1927; to E. T. McGuire, Apr. 12, 1927; to J. D. Ream, Apr. 15, 1927; to Fred B. Howard, Apr. 21, 1927; to Edgar Howard, June 23, 1927. In the letters to Fred B. Howard and Edgar Howard, Norris was very specific about his reform program. Both men were newspaper editors.

fellow man, and to increase the happiness of the ordinary individual." In pursuing this course, he had been compelled "to travel a rather lonely and discouraging road." While he was not sure that he had made a great impression, he had done his best and managed to retain a clear conscience, "the only satisfactory pay for public service." He was ready to lay down the burden and let others "take up the banner." Norris by 1927 seemingly wished to end his public career. Others, meanwhile, talked about him for president in 1928.[24]

From his modest evaluation it would have been impossible to recognize Norris's achievements as the administration of Calvin Coolidge came to an end. As the leader of the progressive wing of the Republican party, which by default of the Democrats literally served as an opposition party, he was a continual thorn in the side of the administration. His challenge of the right of Vare and Smith to Senate seats was a potent factor in their denial. Almost single-handedly he had turned the tide in the Muscle Shoals controversy so that Congress endorsed government ownership, though the administration still wished to sell the property at Muscle Shoals. His arduous battles for multiple-purpose resource development, stressing the primacy of the public interest, were beginning to gain recognition, though the plight of the farmer was still unresolved and becoming more desperate.

His advocacy of procedural reforms to make government less partisan and more efficient had gained ample support in Congress while encountering intense opposition from the administration and its supporters on Capitol Hill. In challenging Coolidge appointments, Norris had met with some success and continually embarrassed the business-minded president. And he had proved himself a bitter critic of the Coolidge-Kellogg foreign policy, particularly with regard to Nicaragua.

Versatile in his criticisms, consistent in his principles, untiring in his efforts, Norris achieved much of a negative nature during the Coolidge administration. He helped prevent things from being done rather than launching new programs and policies. But the programs and policies that interested him were attracting attention and gaining support. As a persistent progressive Norris cast his reform program in an agrarian or rural mold. Most of the procedural re-

[24] Norris to Maher, Dec. 27, 1926.

forms he championed, along with his concern for efficiency, less partisanship, and basic integrity and honesty in government, were in accord with standard progressive patterns. While multiple-purpose resource development had been suggested during the Roosevelt administration and reiterated by Senator Francis G. Newlands in the Wilson era, the concept reached its fulfillment in Norris's plea for government ownership and operation of the facilities at Muscle Shoals. By his concern for the consumer as well as the producer, leading him to call for government operation of some middleman facilities, Norris pushed his progressivism beyond most traditional patterns. As a Nebraska senator he was concerned about the plight of rural America, sympathetic to prohibition and to the desire to curb immigration. But he never carried these sympathies to the extremes that others did in the 1920s. To Norris the fundamental issues were economic more than anything else. Largely unaware of urban tensions or of patterns in politics based on these tensions, Norris still found it possible, as part of his conception of the patriot's duty, to support in the election of 1928 the Democratic candidate, Alfred E. Smith, representative of urban America.

1928

27

Norris's increasing independence in party matters came into full bloom in 1928. Rejecting Coolidge and refusing the nomination himself either as a Republican or on a third-party ticket, Norris denounced Herbert Hoover, his party's candidate, and endorsed Alfred E. Smith, the Democratic nominee. But his main efforts were not directed toward the presidential campaign. They were focused, instead, on electing progressives to the U.S. Senate. The men he endorsed were concerned about the plight of rural America, and his reasons for denouncing Hoover were predicated upon the same base. As a result of his campaigning progressivism won some victories in 1928, triumphs that assured trouble for Herbert Hoover and the Republican party.

In the spring of 1927 Norris labeled efforts to generate a third-term movement for President Coolidge "a long step toward a monarchical form of Government." He maintained that for the good of the country and the Republican party the field should be open and candidates uninfluenced by a Coolidge-oriented machine. But propaganda "by the Federal office holding gang" and business interests was so effective, Norris feared, that large segments of the American people believed "Coolidge is a little God" and wanted him to stay in the White House.[1]

Coolidge's vacation in the summer of 1927 Norris found espe-

[1] *New York Times,* Apr. 22, 1927; George W. Norris to Walter Locke, June 25, 1927.

cially revealing of his character. After advertising nationally for bids on a vacation home, a special investigator on the public payroll examined the proposed offerings, finally selecting South Dakota as a suitable site. The president of the United States, who earlier had ridden from Washington to Chicago in a smoking car to establish an economy image, went forth in June, 1927, in a special train "filled with newspaper correspondents and propagandists and all kinds of picture taking machines" to a secluded spot to spend the summer months quietly. This "economy" gesture recalled the 1926 trip the president had made in a special train to vote in Northampton, Massachusetts, when he might have done it by absentee ballot for the price of a two-cent postage stamp, if he did not care to use his franking privilege.[2]

Coolidge's Black Hills vacation represented to Norris part of an effort by the president to win the Republican nomination in 1928. It would prevent others from seeking the nomination, while the "Federal brigade" and "the special interests satisfied with the control which this great man gives to them over Governmental matters" bellowed that Coolidge was satisfactory to everybody. The cryptic statement, released at the end of Coolidge's vacation, about not choosing to run in 1928 did not convince Norris; he continued to denounce the idea of a third term.[3]

What Norris expected in a Chief Executive he outlined in an article entitled "If I Were President." Starting with a declaration that his administration would be nonpartisan, he mentioned all of the procedural reforms he had championed. As part of his legislative program he cited his views on transportation, agriculture, and taxation and ended by calling for a complete change in the nation's foreign policy. That his views attracted some attention was evident in the calls for Norris to enter the presidential race. As early as March, 1927, Edgar Howard, a prominent Nebraska Democratic congressman, said, "I shall not be surprised if his name shall be presented before the next national Republican convention." He could be

[2] Norris to Locke, May 16, June 25, 1927.

[3] Norris to Locke, June 25, 1927; Harry Slattery to Gifford Pinchot, Oct. 10, 1927 (Harry Slattery Papers, Manuscripts Collections, Duke University Library); draft statement by Norris on a third term, n.d. [1927?]; *Congressional Record,* 70th Cong., 1st sess., Feb. 7, 1928, pp. 2623–25. In his remarks Norris called for limiting the presidency to one term of six or eight years.

elected "for the reason that millions of Democrats regard Norris as a true disciple of Thomas Jefferson, and they would support him as against any special interest Democrat who might be pitted against him." [4]

Thereafter, as the 1928 election loomed into focus, Norris's name was continually mentioned. Less than a month after Howard's statement Senator Smith Brookhart of Iowa announced that Norris might be the candidate of "the radical farm bloc leaders in the Senate." While Coolidge vacationed in the Black Hills, the *New York Times* reported that the insurgency which had flowered in the third-party candidacy of Robert M. LaFollette in 1924 now centered about Norris as a probable candidate for the Republican presidential nomination. In August it was announced that petitions to place his name on the presidential preference ballot would be filed with the Nebraska secretary of state. At the same time a "Norris for President" committee was being organized.[5]

Knowing there was no possibility of winning the Republican nomination and no practical way to run as an independent, Norris was not interested in the presidency. An independent candidacy would be too expensive and probably could do no better than Robert M. LaFollette did in 1924. A party nomination would have been plausible only if presidential primaries existed in all of the states; without them it would be a hopeless fight. Under these circumstances Norris did not wish to ask citizens to organize and support him. If he could do so conscientiously, he wanted to support the Republican candidate in 1928. But he realized that it might not be possible. The root of his dilemma rested on "the proposition that this wicked, non-sensical, illogical, and I think I can say unpatriotic, spirit of party interferes with all of us when we are trying to do our duty to our consciences and our fellowmen." [6]

So concerned was Norris about the 1928 presidential candidates

[4] Norris, "If I Were President," n.d. (draft); *Columbus Daily Telegram,* Mar. 24, 1927.

[5] *Washington Herald,* Apr. 9, 1927 (story by Charles N. Wheeler); *New York Times,* July 31, 1927; *Washington Star,* Aug. 24, 1927.

[6] Norris to Edward Keating, Aug. 22, Sept. 8, 1927. In writing to C. A. Sorensen, who was active in the "Norris for president" movement in Nebraska, Norris noted how the campaign would seriously interfere with his work in the Senate; see Norris to Sorensen, Sept. 3, 1927.

that he announced in September, 1927, that he "would rather see an honest progressive, though wet, in office, than a radical dry who is reactionary in everything else." If a candidate was "sincerely in favor of law enforcement and was right on economic issues," Norris would support him regardless of "party politics, religion or views on prohibition." He did say that Governor Alfred E. Smith of New York was an honest and genuine progressive. A month later he announced, "The West will vote for Al Smith or some other progressive rather than for an 'Eastern reactionary.' " [7] There were a number of Republicans he would gladly support, including Gifford Pinchot, Senators William Borah, Hiram Johnson, and his Nebraska colleague Robert B. Howell. Although he did not specifically favor Smith over a Republican of the "Eastern reactionary" type, it was evident that his thinking was along that line. Until late in the 1928 campaign Norris never again mentioned the New York governor in discussing presidential candidates.[8]

Observers noted that a boom for Norris would strengthen the candidacy of Herbert Hoover by frustrating the drive of Frank O. Lowden to collect rural delegates. If Lowden, as some suggested, intended to release his delegates to Vice-President Charles G. Dawes, Norris's candidacy would thwart this effort as well. But progressive Republicans behind the Norris movement saw him as a western candidate nullifying the influence of "the Eastern financial and industrial interests" in the party. Norris asserted that he did not have "the slightest chance" and would make no speeches nor try to secure delegates, although he was willing to let friends work for what he conceived to be a futile effort on his behalf. Some progressives, including Borah, were willing to support him because they hoped to use his candidacy as a lever to secure concessions in the Republican platform and possibly in the choice of the presidential nominee.[9]

Norris's dilemma was aggravated by friends in Nebraska who viewed his candidacy as the only way "home people" could express their confidence and approval. Their effort coincided with that of progressive senators seeking to place his name before voters in other

[7] *Omaha World-Herald,* Sept. 10, 1927; *Washington Post,* Oct. 9, 1927.
[8] *Washington Post,* Oct. 9, 1927.
[9] *Washington Herald,* Oct. 11, 1927; *New York Times,* Oct. 13, 1927.

states, and Norris felt he could not stop one group without curbing the other. Thus the movement to nominate him started to trudge forward much against his better judgment. With interest increasing throughout the country, Norris wondered how long his resolve not to get involved could be maintained.[10]

Meanwhile Hiram Johnson reported that while Borah officially was for Norris, he was hoping that at the convention there might be a stampede for his nomination. On his part Johnson expressed high regard for Norris but insisted that he could not get "a corporal's guard" behind him in California and felt "it would be a perfectly silly thing to enter him in the primaries against Hoover." At the time Johnson was expressing these views, Norris was explaining why he could not support Frank O. Lowden or "practically all of the candidates that seem to stand any show for the Republican nomination." The jockeying and division among progressive Republicans made the task of the Hoover forces easier, since there would be no concerted progressive opposition to his candidacy.[11]

On Wednesday, January 25, 1928, in Lincoln, Nebraska, C. A. Sorensen filed petitions with the secretary of state containing the names of over 2,000 Republican voters favoring Norris's nomination. At the April primary voters would have an opportunity to choose delegates to the Republican national convention committed to his candidacy. The *New Republic,* observing this development, hoped other "progressive states of the West" would follow Nebraska's lead. Norris's record, the periodical asserted, "certainly entitled him to an enthusiastic vote of confidence on the part of every progressive who has the opportunity of casting it." By the end of March in Minneapolis voluntary campaign headquarters had been opened. Approving letters by the thousands poured in on his Washington office. In no way did Norris encourage these actions. So involved was he with legislative matters that he was not fully

[10] Norris to Oswald Garrison Villard, Oct. 17, 1927; to Locke, Oct. 17, 1927; to J. M. Maher, Oct. 17, 1927; to William Hirth, Nov. 15, 1927; to Sorensen, Jan. 2, 1928. For a critical evaluation of Norris's candidacy, see *Lincoln Star,* Oct. 21, 1927, "The Norris Threat" (editorial).

[11] Hiram Johnson to Harold L. Ickes, Nov. 5, 1927 (Box 3, Harold L. Ickes Papers, Manuscript Division, Library of Congress); Norris to Hirth, Nov. 8, 1927. Norris later recalled that Senators Borah and Brookhart were most active in trying to get him to seek the nomination; see Norris to John F. Cordeal, Jan. 6, 1929.

aware of their dimensions. But he did decide to assist Robert Howell in securing renomination to the Senate, claiming it his "patriotic duty" to inform people of Howell's progressive record. This was the line he would follow with other progressive senators seeking election in 1928.[12]

On Sunday, April 1, 1928, statements by eight U.S. senators were released for use in the Wisconsin primary, endorsing Norris as a candidate for the Republican nomination for president. Both Wisconsin senators, John J. Blaine and Robert M. LaFollette, Jr., had made active speaking campaigns on behalf of Norris delegates. Other senators submitting statements were William E. Borah, Smith W. Brookhart, Henrik Shipstead, Lynn J. Frazier, Gerald P. Nye, and Robert B. Howell. In the Wisconsin primary on April 3 and the Nebraska primary on April 12, Norris made almost a clean sweep. In Nebraska Howell easily won the Republican nomination for another term in the Senate.[13]

Meanwhile sentiment in favor of Norris's candidacy continued. At a mock convention on the campus of UCLA Norris triumphed over Hoover on the second ballot by a vote of 580 to 458. With "no chairmen, managers, treasurers, or other representatives," expressions on his behalf continued. No money had been collected to advance his interests. The Wisconsin primary had been conducted without his cooperation. Norris referred Senator Frederick Steiwer

[12] *Lincoln Herald,* Jan. 27, 1928; *New Republic,* Feb. 8, 1928, p. 306; John P. Robertson to Donald G. Hughes, Mar. 6, 1928; to Dale W. Stump, Mar. 22, 1928; Norris to J. H. Hollingshead, Mar. 28, 1928; to Cordeal, Apr. 13, 1928. On Apr. 3, 1928, Norris delivered a radio address from a station in Shenandoah, Iowa, favoring Howell's renomination, denouncing the corrupt elections in Illinois and Pennsylvania, and criticizing the Nicaraguan policy of the Coolidge administration.

[13] *Madison* (Wis.) *Capital Times,* Apr. 1, 1928. In the Nebraska presidential preference primary Norris polled 96,726 votes to 6,815 for Hoover, his closest rival. Fourteen of the nineteen Nebraska delegates and seventeen of the twenty-six Wisconsin delegates were pledged to his candidacy. Norris was delighted with Howell's victory, in part because Howell had concluded, like Norris, that Nelson B. Updike, a prominent Omaha businessman and publisher, should be prosecuted for nonpayment of taxes. Updike had opposed Howell's renomination and had brought pressure to bear because of Norris's opposition to the reappointment of the federal attorney prosecuting the case. Updike escaped paying his taxes because the statute of limitations went into effect. For details, see Norris to Don C. Van Deusen, Apr. 17, 1928; to Frank L. Williams, Apr. 24, 1928; Addison E. Sheldon, *Nebraska: The Land and the People* (Chicago, 1931), 1: 1042–43.

of Oregon to Wisconsin's senators for information about that campaign. In the Nebraska primary he spent a total of $6.00 to cover an unpaid bill for an advertisement inserted in a country newspaper by an exuberant but irresponsible advocate.[14]

When the Republican national convention met in Kansas City in June, Norris realized that while delegates would have "the pleasure of yelling themselves hoarse, made enthusiastic by the patriotic speeches of partisan representatives," they would have little voice in the decisions made there. As Herbert Hoover noted, "It was all over before the convention met—except the noise." But it was not as completely cut and dried as Norris expected and Hoover recalled.[15]

Dutifully Norris's name was placed before the convention. Dutifully the delegates listened to the recitation by Nebraska delegate Charles E. Sandall of his virtues and accomplishments. Then they proceeded to nominate Hoover on the first ballot. But so desirous was the Republican organization for party unity and so concerned was Hoover for rural Republican support that immediately after his nomination he inquired through an aide in conference with Senators Brookhart and Howell if Norris would be interested in the vice-presidency. Quickly sounding out Norris, they learned that he, emphatically, was not interested. To leave no doubt about his position, Norris wired Senator Borah, a leading Hoover supporter at the convention, that "under no circumstances would I accept nomination even if tendered." Senator Charles Curtis of Kansas agreed to accept and the convention quickly approved his nomination.[16]

[14] John B. Hurlbut to Norris, telegram, Apr. 18, 1928; Norris to Frederick Steiwer, May 4, 1928; *New York Times,* May 8, 1928.

[15] Norris to Ruth Andrus, June 11, 1928; Herbert Hoover, *Memoirs: The Cabinet and the Presidency, 1920–1933* (New York, 1952), p. 195.

[16] *Omaha World-Herald,* June 15, 1928; Norris to William E. Borah, telegram, June 14, 1928. Hoover, of course, denied the offer to Norris and indicated his animosity toward Norris in brief, bitter, and false remarks, discussing the campaign in his *Memoirs;* see *The Cabinet and the Presidency,* pp. 197–98. Borah's most recent biographer notes that "Hoover and Borah were in daily conference during the week of June 8 preceding the convention"; then the senator went to Kansas City, where "he immediately went to work on the platform." She also observes that Borah suggested Curtis as the vice-presidential candidate "to keep the western states in line." Borah put Curtis's name in nomination and he was chosen unanimously; see Marian C. McKenna, *Borah* (Ann Arbor, Mich., 1961), pp. 253–55. Walter W. Liggett in a footnote in *The Rise of Herbert Hoover* (New

Dissatisfied with both the platform and the candidates, Norris said that the action of the Republican convention at Kansas City "will be a sad disappointment to every progressive citizen in the United States." A "direct slap" had been given the farmers of the country "with the usual promise of a glittering generality." He deplored the platform's silence on the activities of the "Water Power Trust," its disregard of the disclosures made in the investigation of the naval oil leases, its silence on Boulder Dam, Muscle Shoals, and the lame-duck constitutional amendment.[17]

Norris then criticized prominent party leaders for their roles at the convention, noting that "when the psychological moment came, it was no other person than Boss Vare, the leader of the Philadelphia political machine—the man who, on account of the disgraceful proceedings in the Pennsylvania primary, was excluded from the United States Senate—it was this same Vare who compelled the Pennsylvania delegation to go solid for Hoover." Norris queried, "Can any Republican who believes in honest Government and wants to keep his party above suspicion and reproach look upon these controlling features of the Convention without shame and disgust?" While "the rank and file of the great Republican party will be disgusted and humiliated," the "power trust," the various individuals he mentioned, "and the machine politicians everywhere will be happy and delighted." If this program was endorsed at the polls, Norris en-

York, 1932), pp. 333–34, observes that "just before the Kansas City convention Hoover was fearful over the so-called revolt of the farmers. Borah approached Senator George Norris of Nebraska . . . and asked him if he would accept the vice presidential nomination. Norris merely laughed at this fantastic proposal. Borah said the suggestion came from Hoover, who more than once had privately and violently denounced Norris as a Socialist." Alfred Lief, *Democracy's Norris* (New York, 1939), pp. 317–18, corroborates the version I present. Norris in a 1929 letter, the critical portion of which was never sent, wrote that "if the true story is ever told, the world will know that not only last year, but four years ago, I might have been the Vice-Presidential candidate if I had been willing to sacrifice what I felt to be my fundamental belief in good government"; see Norris to Cordeal, Jan. 6, 1929.

[17] In "Why the Farm Bloc," *The World Tomorrow*, 11, no. 6 (June, 1928): 255–57, Norris discussed agriculture as an issue in the campaign, though he acknowledged that "many politicians are trying to dodge the issue." He reviewed the farm situation and its disastrous consequences before discussing possible remedies. Although legislation could not fully resolve the farm problem, it could help reduce inequities borne by the farmer.

visioned special interests and notorious individuals tinged with graft and corruption reigning supreme under the protective shield of the Hoover administration.[18]

What course to pursue? Since "the real progressives of the country" could not support the Republican platform or Herbert Hoover, should he take cognizance of the demand for a third party? Norris did not want to take this course, though he realized his statements on the Republican convention could be taken as an indication of his interest in a third party. Assuming that the Democratic convention also would be controlled, Norris feared that the "great common people of the United States" were up against "a stone wall." Yet he considered the idea of a third party as a "will o' the wisp" because the fundamental issue would be neither farm relief nor prohibition, important as they were. Rather, it was "Shall the great trusts, particularly the water-power trust, control the destiny of our Republic?" Instead of waging a costly and futile third-party crusade, attention could be called to the necessity of abolishing the Electoral College as the means of providing "in any presidential campaign for the people to control their own Government." [19]

The nomination of Alfred E. Smith as the Democratic candidate in no way affected Norris's outlook. By dodging the issue of monopoly, the ensuing campaign promised to be a sham battle. The "Power Trust" could "sit back and laugh" while voters got excited about tangential issues: religion, prohibition, or the farm problem. The Democratic platform, like its Republican counterpart, was remarkable for what it avoided. Both were silent "on the sinister and deceitful activities of the Water Power Trust"; neither mentioned the Federal Trade Commission investigation and the corruption that "smelled to high heaven." In short, Norris explained, both parties lacked "the courage to take a stand in favor of the people against this monopoly—the greatest the world has ever known." Controlling both parties, monopoly could contribute equally to both

[18] Norris statement for release June 16, 1928; *Washington Post*, June 17, 1928. This statement by Norris was published in the *Campaign Book of the Democratic Party, 1928* (New York, 1928), pp. 65–67.

[19] Norris to Stephen Raushenbush, June 16, 1928; to Villard, June 19, 1928; to H. C. McNew, June 19, 1928; to Herman S. Delano, June 20, 1928; to O. Bryan Cooper, June 28, 1928; to Hugh Craig, June 29, 1928.

sides, knowing that the people would lose no matter which party was successful.[20]

In July Harry Slattery visited Norris at his summer cottage, reporting him convinced of the futility of a third party but hopeful of strengthening the group of progressives in Congress, especially in the Senate. Slattery implied that Norris would speak "and give Hoover a wallop all through the corn belt country." He was so angry about Hoover's candidacy, Slattery said, that "he is now lying about the Vice-President incident," not wishing to be associated with the Republican candidate in any way.[21]

On the evening of July 11, 1928, delegates of the Farmer-Labor party assembled in Chicago and nominated Norris for the presidency on the third ballot. The next day in Washington his secretary said that Norris had been approached to head a third-party ticket and had stated definitely that he would not accept a nomination. In a statement released at Waupaca Norris formally refused the nomination, using the occasion to denounce the Electoral College as an undemocratic device and to castigate "the Power Trust," the paramount issue upon which the dominant parties were "as silent as the grave." The only practical thing for voters to do, Norris insisted, revealing the strategy he would follow, was to elect progressives to Congress; there they could continue the "uphill and one-sided fight to retain, for the benefit of the people, the natural, God-given resources of the country." [22] Concluding that the Republican party

[20] *Labor,* June 7, 1928; Norris to Harvey Phillips, July 7, 1928; to Pinchot, July 14, Aug. 2, 1928. In these letters Norris admitted that "Smith has shown some indications that he is against this Trust." But his silence on the subject, added to the silence of the Democratic platform, did not "look right" to Norris, even though Senator Royal Copeland in an interview with Norris before he departed for his summer vacation assured him that "Smith would be right on the power proposition." In his speech of acceptance Governor Smith advocated the ownership and "control" of Muscle Shoals. But Norris felt this doctrine could have been advocated "by the Power Trust." If instead of "control" he had used the word "operation," Norris would have found his statement satisfactory; see Norris to Lewis S. Gannett, Sept. 8, 1928.

[21] Slattery to Pinchot, July 10, 1928 (Slattery Papers).

[22] *Washington Post, Washington Evening Star,* July 12, 1928; draft statement by Norris, July 12, 1928. Norris was chosen over Norman Thomas by a vote of 16 to 14. In his correspondence Norris said that consultations with a great many of those who were back of the LaFollette movement in 1924 convinced him his

was "corrupt" and no longer responsive to the hopes and aspirations of vast segments of the American people, Norris said that "for the good of the country" it ought to receive "a good threshing on the same theory that a father chastises his own child." To deserve respect from honest people, he queried, "shouldn't we clean our house and wash our dirty linen?" To do otherwise would be to place party above country; this Norris was not prepared to do. Therefore, if any candidate took a stand beyond the platform of his party, particularly on the issues of hydroelectric power and aid to agriculture, Norris was prepared to endorse him.[23]

Disillusioned though he was, Norris had no intention of quitting. Another progressive, Hiram Johnson, apparently had such thoughts and Norris sought to bolster his sagging determination. When Johnson finally decided to seek a third term in the Senate, Norris sent a statement endorsing his candidacy. He drafted similar statements on behalf of others and expressed a willingness to campaign "for all our progressive bunch"; the "bunch" included such Democrats as Burton K. Wheeler of Montana and Clarence Dill of Washington. Johnson was assured that, if requested, Norris would come to California. In short, in mid-July the only question in Norris's mind was whether he should campaign as an individual or under the auspices of a national organization created for the purpose.[24]

Though the organization never materialized, in August Norris spent a week campaigning for Robert M. LaFollette, Jr. Earlier, at a conference with Senators John J. Blaine, Henrik Shipstead, LaFollette, and progressives from Minnesota and Wisconsin, Norris announced his plan to promote the progressive cause in the coming campaign. As he prepared to leave Wisconsin, he said there would be "an unusual scratching of both Democratic and Republican tickets on President." It was a difficult and lonely role he had chosen

---

decision was correct. All mentioned the almost insurmountable financial difficulties involved in perfecting a nationwide organization; see Norris to Doremus Scudder, July 13, 1928.

[23] Norris to Z. B. Cutler, June 20, 1928; to J. L. Stewart, July 5, 1928; to Scudder, July 2, 1928.

[24] Norris to Johnson, June 13, July 12, 1928. When Senator Arthur Capper wrote Norris asking for an endorsement of his colleague Charles Curtis, who was Hoover's running mate, Norris, though admitting a high personal regard for Curtis, refused on the grounds that Curtis and Hoover were "not right" on all of the important issues; see Norris to Capper, Aug. 2, 1928.

for himself, but campaigning against William Vare in Pennsylvania in 1926 had prepared him for the vilification and abuse that would be leveled as he denounced his party and urged the election of senatorial candidates who wore "a different political tag than himself." [25]

Meanwhile in Washington Edward Keating, editor of *Labor,* and Basil Manly, a 1924 LaFollette campaign veteran, were organizing an itinerary for Norris. Wiring W. T. Rawleigh, "the world's biggest peddler," in Freeport, Illinois, Keating said that if he would put up half the money to defray Norris's trip, the railroad unions, whose weekly Keating edited, would supply the remainder. Rawleigh, also a former LaFollette supporter, agreed to finance the venture. The fact that he was supporting Hoover gave Norris some doubts about accepting his assistance, but Rawleigh insisted that Norris was free to endorse anyone he wished.[26]

Before starting his campaign, Norris learned officially from Robert Moses, secretary of state of New York, and informally from Harry Slattery that Governor Smith had suggested a conference. Expressing admiration for "some of the stands he has taken in New York," Norris refused but implied that if Smith took a satisfactory stand on the power question, his views might change. To be sure, he recognized that Smith's position was in advance of Hoover's. But it still was not satisfactory to those who believed that "natural resources should be owned by the Federal Government, or States, or municipalities, and should be used without profit to private individuals for the benefit of the people by some plan similar to the one now in such successful operation in the Province of Ontario, Canada." [27]

[25] Norris to Robert M. LaFollette, Jr., July 25, 1928; to Pinchot, Aug. 2, 1928; to Paul Y. Anderson, Sept. 8, 1928; to C. W. McConaughy, Sept. 8, 1928; to Gannett, Sept. 8, 1928. Early in September Norris was still hoping that Gifford Pinchot would campaign for progressive candidates and help subsidize a formal organization of progressives.

[26] Norris to Keating, Sept. 8, 1927; Edward Keating, *The Gentleman from Colorado* (Denver, 1964), pp. 496–97. In a long letter to W. T. Rawleigh on Sept. 27, 1928, Norris explained why he was unable to support either Hoover or Smith. After the campaign was over, Norris reconsidered his position and returned Rawleigh's check; see Norris to Rawleigh, Nov. 27, 1928.

[27] Norris to Robert Moses, Sept. 8, 1928; Harry Slattery, "From Roosevelt to Roosevelt: Forty Years in Washington" (manuscript autobiography), p. 115 (Slattery Papers).

Norris's reservations slowly gave way as Smith in his campaign addresses committed himself on major issues. At Omaha on September 18 Smith accepted the McNary-Haugen principle of farm relief and promised to find the "mechanics" to make it workable. Four days later at Denver he denounced the activities of the "Power Trust" and declared for public ownership and control of the vast water power sites. Nowhere in this address, however, did he call for government operation of Muscle Shoals. At Helena on September 24 Smith denounced Teapot Dome and fixed responsibility for it on Coolidge's official family. While Norris applauded these speeches, he did not endorse Smith. Some commentators suggested that his support would be forthcoming, since many former LaFollette men had organized into a Progressive League for Alfred E. Smith.[28]

In a statement released on October 2 in Washington, Norris announced his intention to campaign in Minnesota, North Dakota, Montana, and the state of Washington to help re-elect progressive senators. Admitting that he had praised Smith for his recent speeches, Norris said that "anybody can draw any conclusion from these comments he wants to." He would proceed as if the 1928 election involved only congressional candidates. Striving as he was to make sure that progressives returned to Congress in sufficient numbers to check the conservative coalition of the Coolidge era, it was difficult, as a *New York Times* editorial observed, "to visualize him choosing Hoover over Smith." [29]

Meanwhile, Hoover in a major address at Elizabethton, Tennessee, early in October advocated continued government ownership of Muscle Shoals, claiming that "there are local instances where the Government must enter the business field as a by-product of some great major purpose such as improvement in navigation, flood control, scientific research or national defense. . . ." Though

---

[28] Charles Michelson, "Political Undertow" (column), *New York World,* Sept. 27, 1928; *Washington Herald,* Oct. 2, 1928. Smith's speeches are available in Alfred E. Smith, *Campaign Addresses* (Washington, D.C., 1929).

[29] Draft statement by Norris for release Oct. 2, 1928; *New York Times,* Oct. 4, 1928. After the election Norris explained that "most of the speeches I made in favor of the reelection of members of the Senatorial progressive group necessarily contained arguments which logically could be construed as against the election of Mr. Hoover"; see Norris to Rawleigh, Nov. 9, 1928. Before leaving on his speaking tour, Norris wrote a letter endorsing Senator David I. Walsh, Democrat of Massachusetts, for re-election; see Norris to David K. Niles, Sept. 29, 1928.

he quickly qualified these remarks and insisted that he did not intend government operation of Muscle Shoals for anything except agricultural experimentation and national defense, Hoover's views were not very different from those of his opponent, except that Smith denounced the practices of utility companies. Hoover said nothing about this subject.[30]

Norris remained silent on the presidential campaign as he toured the northwest speaking for progressive candidates. But after Hoover's Madison Square Garden address on October 22 he could contain himself no longer. In a speech in Portland, Oregon, two days later Norris made his first definite commitment to Smith's candidacy and announced reaffirmation of it to be made in a national radio broadcast from Omaha. Hoover's speech denounced proposals, including farm relief and power control, "which, if adopted, would be a long step toward the abandonment of our American system and a surrender to the destructive operation of governmental conduct of commercial business." Norris, viewing these remarks as an all-out attack on public power, asked, "How can any progressive in the United States support him now, after his Madison Square Garden address, in which he slapped every progressive minded man and woman in America in the face? My God, I cannot conceive it." [31]

Smith, though he had not changed his views, now stood right on the power issue. On Saturday, October 27, 1928, at a meeting in Omaha Norris praised Smith's stand on water power, farm relief, and foreign policy. He predicted that Smith would keep his promise to enforce the Volstead Act and ended with a strong plea to keep

[30] *New York Times,* Oct. 9, 1928; *Washington Daily News,* Oct. 8, 1928; *Knoxville News-Sentinel,* Oct. 9, 1928. Hoover's campaign speeches appear in *The New Day* (Stanford, Calif., 1928).

[31] *New York World,* Oct. 25, 1928. Hoover, *Memoirs: The Cabinet and the Presidency,* pp. 203–5, presents an excerpt from the Madison Square Garden speech under the subheading "Some Color of Collectivism." The *Omaha World-Herald* in an editorial on Oct. 25, 1928, said that Norris's announcement was "the most sensational and momentous development" of the campaign, marking "the culmination of the progressive and agricultural revolt against Hoover and the reactionary plutocracy that has taken full control of the Republican party." Harry Slattery claimed that Norris informed him late in September that he would "come out" for Smith at the end of October in a speech at Omaha. This information, according to Slattery, was relayed with Norris's permission to Walter Lippmann of the *New York World* and through Robert Moses to Alfred E. Smith; see Slattery to Moses, Sept. 26, 1928 (Slattery Papers).

religious prejudice from influencing the choice of a candidate. As vigorously as he praised Smith, Norris denounced Hoover for his record on water power, his silence in the face of official corruption, and his inadequate proposals for farm relief. His remarks, it was thought, would influence thousands of voters throughout the corn and wheat belts, thereby brightening considerably Democratic prospects in the rural regions west of the Mississippi River. Before the campaign concluded, Norris spoke again in Nebraska, denouncing Hoover and endorsing Robert Howell and other Republican candidates. On Friday, November 2, he spoke in Minneapolis under the auspices of the Progressive League for Alfred E. Smith, focusing on the farm problem. On election eve he was in McCook to attend a barbecue and to conclude the campaign with a speech at the Temple Theater.[32]

While Norris was campaigning, Mrs. Norris spent several weeks visiting in California. Returning to McCook, she announced, "I am not following George this time. I am not going to vote for Governor Smith this time, even if he does." As a prohibitionist Mrs. Norris thought neither Smith nor Hoover truly "dry." She said she would be at home on election day. Learning of his wife's views, Norris remarked, "If she still feels that way after hearing my [Omaha] speech, it's all right with me." The *Philadelphia Record* commented editorially that "while the conflict of opinion between Senator and Mrs. Norris is typical of the campaign reactions in countless American households, its outcome is exceptional."[33]

On Saturday, November 3, 1928, Mrs. Norris said, "George has convinced me"; she would vote for Governor Alfred E. Smith. But very few progressive Republicans in Nebraska or elsewhere announced their intention of voting for Smith, John J. Blaine of Wisconsin being the only other senator to follow Norris's lead. The result was a dismal disappointment. Despite evidence of a great Democratic vote, Smith carried only a handful of counties in the states where Norris had campaigned. "It was a great victory," he remarked, "coming from a battle fought in the main on false issues. The greatest element involved in the landslide was religion. Regret

[32] *Washington Herald*, Oct. 28, 1928; *Omaha World-Herald*, Oct. 28, Nov. 1, 1928. See also Alfred E. Smith to Norris, telegram, Oct. 29, 1928.
[33] *McCook Daily Gazette*, Oct. 24, 1928; *Philadelphia Record*, Oct. 31, 1928.

and conceal it as we may, religion had more to do with the over-whelming defeat of Governor Smith than any other one thing." After religion came prohibition: "In the excitement over the arti-ficial issues of religion and prohibition, farm relief was beaten and the Power Trust given the greatest victory it had ever achieved. . . ."[34]

The immediate future was not encouraging: Muscle Shoals could not be saved; the "Power Trust" would be firmly ensconced for an-other four years; the "remaining resources still belonging to the people" probably would be lost. Notwithstanding the setback, Nor-ris said that the duty of progressives, "even in the face of defeat," was "to continue the contest in spite of the additional odds that the election has thrown in the pathway of human progress." What he did not mention was equally important and boded well for the progressive cause. Every candidate Norris endorsed in 1928 was elected. Senators Johnson, LaFollette, Howell, Shipstead, Frazier, Wheeler, and Dill would provide a powerful progressive bloc in the Hoover administration. But instead of recognizing this step forward, he spent much time reiterating why he had endorsed Smith when it was clear that Hoover would win the election.[35]

Moreover, Norris made clear that "the most abhorrent thing" he knew of was "the madness of religious prejudice and hatred." Reli-gious fanatics and bigots now believed they had won a great victory and consequently would be "bolder and more domineering" in their attempts to "frighten misinformed people in regard to the dangers of Catholic domination." The election, in short, had been decided upon a false issue which in Norris's judgment never should have been raised. While bigots were advocating religious intolerance, "the greatest monopoly that ever existed" had kept the American people from realizing "God-given possibilities for the happiness of humanity" by helping prevent Muscle Shoals from developing its full potential during the Hoover administration. Nor would serious relief for agriculture be accomplished. The outcome of the election represented a backward step. Norris considered his refusal to sup-port Herbert Hoover "intelligent citizenship" and said that only the

---

[34] *McCook Tribune,* Nov. 3, 1928; *Washington Star,* Nov. 10, 1928.

[35] *Washington Star,* Nov. 10, 1928; Norris to Rawleigh, Nov. 9, 1928. Senator David I. Walsh was also re-elected; see note 29 above.

curse of bitter partisanship prevented people from comprehending it.[36]

In remarks published in December, 1928, about the significance of the election, Norris mentioned the serious setbacks as well as the positive aspects. Although progressive principles, so far as the election of a president was concerned, had met a temporary defeat, Norris wrote, "I believe that a great majority of our people are truly progressive and at heart believe in the fundamental principles for which the progressive group have fought." He took solace in the fact that there was more independent voting, more scratching of tickets than ever before. On the legislative level this meant that "almost without exception" progressive senators were re-elected. To be sure, proponents of monopoly, imperialism, partisanship, and bigotry, along with others, had reason to rejoice in the defeat of Smith. But legislatively the 1928 election indicated that the progressive cause had been maintained and strongly endorsed by the voters. Many voters favoring Hoover also voted for senatorial candidates who would challenge almost everything Hoover endorsed. "This group," Norris said, "thus remains a nucleus for the millions of progressives throughout the country who are not content to intrust their government to machine-ridden parties and monopoly-controlled bosses." Though he did not mention it, insofar as this group, representing chiefly rural states, had an undisputed leader, that man was George W. Norris.[37]

Indicative of his attitude were his remarks upon returning to Washington. He was not worrying about action Republican leaders might take to discipline him: "There is nothing that the Republican machine can do that would cause me a moment's distress." Though endorsing Smith had cost him both friendship and support, Norris was not disturbed:

> . . . I never felt more unrepentant in my life. I have no apologies to make. There is no man on earth I want to injure or whom I would injure if I had an opportunity. I am going to defend myself

[36] Norris to Cordeal, Nov. 13, 1928; to I. D. Evans, Nov. 13, 1928; to E. A. Cook, Nov. 13, 1928; to H. M. Crane, Nov. 16, 1928; to M. K. Merns, Nov. 17, 1928; to Carl F. Marsh, Nov. 27, 1928.

[37] Norris, "Hope for Progressives," *Nation,* Dec. 19, 1928, pp. 679–80; see also Norris, "The Meaning of the Recent Election," *LaFollette's Magazine,* 20 (Dec., 1928): 180, 185.

as best I can, without caring very much what the outcome may be. I have no feeling of enmity or ill-will against anyone, but I never felt so independent in my life. I am not sorry for what I did. I am proud of it, and I have been made so, to some extent at least, by the enemies who have jumped on me and the friends who have deserted me; but the main reason for my feeling of satisfaction, or one that really counts, is that I have an absolutely clear conscience on the subject. . . .[38]

[38] *Omaha World-Herald,* Nov. 13, 1928 (Norris's remarks on returning to Washington); Norris to George Williams, Dec. 27, 1928 (the quote is from this letter). The oldest friendship that was severed was with John F. Cordeal. In a long letter to Cordeal on Jan. 6, 1929, Norris fully explained his views on the issues of the campaign. In Norris to Marsh, July 24, 1929, he further commented on his treatment by old friends and neighbors in McCook.

The Same Old Story

28

On April 16, 1929, in a special message President Hoover asked Congress "to redeem two pledges given in the last election—farm relief and limited changes in the tariff." An effective tariff upon agricultural products, the president said, would protect the farmer in the domestic market and encourage him to diversify his crops. To resolve the continuing crisis of agricultural depression, Hoover called for the creation of a federal farm board which should have as its purpose "the reorganization of the marketing system on sounder and more stable and more economic lines." [1] Legislation to achieve the president's program was introduced in Congress; George Norris, with long experience in seeking to meliorate the condition of agriculture, quickly emerged as a persistent and penetrating critic of Hoover's policies.

The president had several advantages in seeking to resolve these prickly problems. Most important, the Republican party controlled both houses of the Seventy-first Congress by large margins. In the House it held a majority of 103 seats; in the Senate there were fifty-six Republicans, thirty-nine Democrats, and one Farmer-Laborite. Though progressive Republicans chaired important Senate committees, they were unable to hold the balance of power because of the large Republican majority. Moreover, owing to his impressive election victory and his reputation as a humanitarian and as

---

[1] *Congressional Record*, 71st Cong., 1st sess., Apr. 16, 1929, pp. 42–43. The message was not delivered in person.

416

an engineer who successfully accomplished difficult jobs, Hoover had strong support. For these reasons and to avoid further tension within Republican ranks, no effort was made to discipline Norris for his defection in 1928.

During the campaign Norris had expressed doubts about Hoover's oft-quoted intention to solve the farm problem without specifically stating what his plans were. He did not believe Hoover could meet the dilemma of the surplus without an equalization fee of some sort to compensate for losses incurred by selling on the world market. Every solution proposed in the past had been rejected by the administration, yet no president until Herbert Hoover had suggested a remedy. And Norris was far from satisfied with his suggestions.[2]

Just before the Seventy-first Congress convened, the Senate Agriculture and Forestry Committee unanimously agreed to insert the so-called debenture plan in the farm bill.[3] The committee reached this conclusion after appointing a subcommittee to call on the president to ascertain his views. "The Sub-Committee reported to the whole Committee the same day they consulted with the President" and, Norris recounted, "the President said he did not know what the debenture plan was." Hoover asked the senators to discuss the matter with "some of the experts" in the Agriculture Department. Their testimony was favorable and the committee unanimously agreed to insert the debenture plan in the bill. But after the measure had been introduced, President Hoover issued a statement against the insertion. Senator McNary then called the Agriculture and Forestry

[2] George W. Norris to Peter Norbeck, Nov. 23, 1928; to W. L. Stockton, Apr. 2, 1929.

[3] "This plan was 'an arrangement whereby exporters of those agricultural products of which we produce a surplus [would] receive from the Treasury Department certificates having a face value established by Congress and intended to represent the differences in costs of production between here and abroad, such certificates being negotiable and good for their face value in the payment of import tariffs on any articles later imported.' This plan did not provide for the purchasing and storing of the surplus; it provided a bounty on agricultural imports; and its advocates called it surplus and more flexible to operate" (Theodore Saloutos and John D. Hicks, *Agricultural Discontent in the Middle West, 1900–1939* (Madison, Wis., 1951), p. 390). The plan was formulated by Professor Charles L. Stewart of the University of Illinois and found its most ardent advocates among the farm organizations in the National Grange. Norris explained its operations in a letter to E. W. Rossiter, June 19, 1929.

Committee together and "the President's opposition resulted in re-cording six votes in the Committee against the debenture amend-ment." The chairman was now directed, this time by a majority of two, to report the bill with the amendment. Norris was convinced that there was "very little hope of passing the bill through the Sen-ate with the debenture amendment in it." [4]

Nevertheless, he strongly supported the debenture plan on the Senate floor, proposing an additional amendment to guard against overproduction.[5] He noted that the debenture proposal would not give the farmer the benefit of the entire tariff "like the manufacturer gets it." It only offered him half of the existing tariff. "We are try-ing," he said, "to put the farmer under the protective-tariff um-brella. It is a leaky umbrella, it is true; half of the rain will come through; but we are trying to put him in the same class with the manufacturers." While money for the debentures would come from public funds, unlike the equalization fee of the McNary-Haugen bills, which would be paid by the farmers themselves, the process would function so long as there was sufficient money coming into the Treasury from other protected industries "to pay the farmer what he ought to have in order to be placed on an equality with other industries."

The bill called for a board of twelve experts, presided over by the Secretary of Agriculture, each receiving $12,000 a year. Ad-visory councils representing different commodities would consist of seven men per council, each member receiving $20 a day plus trav-eling expenses and a per diem allowance when their services were requested. Norris said that these councils were unnecessary. In his judgment board members, devoting full time to their tasks, could obtain information about every commodity coming under their ju-risdiction without the cumbersome and expensive apparatus of the advisory councils.[6]

---

[4] *Congressional Record,* 71st Cong., 1st sess., Apr. 29, 1929, p. 626; Norris to Walter L. Locke, Apr. 23, 1929; John P. Robertson to John N. Norton, Apr. 25, 1929. The vote was 8 to 6 in favor of retaining the debenture amendment in the bill.

[5] The National Grange, Norris said, favored his amendment to guard against overproduction.

[6] *Congressional Record,* 71st Cong., 1st sess., Apr. 26, pp. 599–602, Apr. 30, p. 694, May 10, 1929, p. 1110.

The farm bill with the debenture plan passed the Senate, but the plan was eliminated in conference committee. A conference report embodying the administration-supported House measure was approved and sent to the Senate. As a member of the conference committee Norris declined to sign the report, and in a lengthy Senate speech on June 8, 1929, he stated his reasons. The controversy revolved around the elimination of the debenture plan. Three Senate conferees retreated on the debenture matter rather than jeopardize farm legislation. But the deleted debenture amendment sought to take care of the export surplus by giving the American farmer the benefit of one-half the tariff. Without it, Norris did not have much faith that the measure would provide adequate relief. One-third of the population, "those who are engaged in the most fundamental business of all," would continue "to be borne down by the burdens of the tariff without getting the benefits of the tariff." Yet Norris voted for the bill. "Our fight," he said, "was not against farm relief, but it was to get as much farm relief in the bill as possible. Failing to get all that we fought for, we accepted it as a compromise, believing that it is better to have half a loaf than no bread." [7]

The president on June 15, 1929, signed the Agriculture Marketing Act creating a Federal Farm Board and proclaimed that "after many years of contention we have at last made a constructive start at agricultural relief with the most important measure ever passed by Congress in aid of a single industry." In evaluating the measure, Norris felt that the farmer could benefit "to some extent." The Federal Farm Board would purchase large quantities of farm produce, but it could not store it indefinitely. Norris realized that when the produce was sold, it would have to be sold on the world market, perhaps upsetting it; "and they must sell all that they have bought." While the act would facilitate orderly marketing, it did not permanently take the surplus off the domestic market. Nor did it allow the farmer to benefit from the tariff. At the outset, owing to a shortage of wheat in Canada, Farm Board operations helped prices considerably. But Norris found it sad to think that agriculture in the United States must depend for its prosperity upon crop failure in other countries. The farmer would find "that he is still selling his

---

[7] *Ibid.,* June 8, 1929, pp. 2560–61, 2563–67, 2571; Norris to Walter Howell, May 2, 1929; to M. W. Osborn, June 19, 1929; to Rossiter, June 19, 1929.

surplus product in the world market and buying the main portion of his supplies in a protective market." [8]

Norris also objected to Hoover's appointees to the Federal Farm Board. "These men have grown, and grown fat, have become millionaires, all from the money they have received from the farmers of America," while farmers "have been going down and down and down" through bankruptcy and mortgage foreclosures. He used Alexander Legge, president of the International Harvester Company and chairman of the Federal Farm Board, as his prime example. Ex-Governor Samuel McKelvie, publisher of the *Nebraska Farmer,* was the object of his bitterest comments about the wealth and social standing of some of the appointees. Yet Norris admitted that if they failed, and he suspected they would, it would be a failure emanating more from defects in the law than from anything else. The person basically responsible was President Hoover, who had failed to suggest a sensible method of reducing the surplus.[9]

Critical though Norris was of the president's program, Congress approved it with dispatch. But Hoover's second reason for calling Congress into special session—tariff revision—was not so quickly or easily resolved. The president originally desired only limited revision, chiefly of agricultural schedules. It soon became evident that Congress would not stop short of a general revision of the tariff. Once again Norris played a leading role in opposition, though he was not very hopeful about the possibility of tariff reform. Hoover and many of his supporters in the 1928 campaign had called for an increase in tariff rates; big business in general agreed. Such a situation boded no good for the agricultural sector of the economy,

[8] Norris to Rossiter, June 19, 1929; to Gifford Pinchot, Aug. 19, 1929; to William Hirth, Feb. 18, 1930. For a discussion of Canadian and American wheat prices at this time, see Norris to C. W. McConaughy, Oct. 11, 1929; Norris's remarks in the *Congressional Record,* 71st Cong., 1st sess., Oct. 18, 1929, pp. 4659-60.

[9] *Congressional Record,* 71st Cong., 1st sess., Oct. 16, 1929, pp. 4583–84, 4609–10; Norris to Henry Middendorf, Feb. 4, 1930; to Michael J. Hart, Apr. 22, 1930. Though Norris was critical of the Federal Farm Board, he was scrupulously fair and honest in evaluating charges leveled against it. At times he could even rise to its defense; see, for example, Norris to L. S. Herron, Feb. 28, 1930; *Congressional Record,* 71st Cong., 3rd sess., Feb. 9, 1931, pp. 4298–99.

and the farmer by his overwhelming endorsement of Herbert Hoover in 1928 would again be victimized.[10]

Since the "tariff game" was essentially a local matter and involved "unadulterated selfishness," Norris realized that some of his progressive colleagues would have "to go along the selfish route in order to maintain themselves in Congress." Instead of tariff protection, American industries would receive monopoly privileges. The men who stood to gain most already dominated the hearings while those opposed to the "march of monopoly" battled in vain. "Humanity," he explained, "is being forgotten and the world is worshipping at the shrine of gold. Dollars are more important than human lives. Trusts are as common as the leaves of the forest." How long the civilized world could abide these conditions in June of 1929 Norris was not prepared to say.[11]

Early in the tariff debate he again proposed the debenture plan as an amendment. With a tariff on manufactured products that forced the farmer to live in a world of protection and to sell his products on the other side of the tariff wall, Norris's amendment had the virtue of offering the farmer half the benefit of the protective tariff by taking off the market surplus products to which the debenture applied. While it met with bitter opposition from administration supporters, the Senate accepted it by a 42-to-34 vote. In Nebraska his stand was applauded. An editorial in an opposition newspaper proclaimed, ". . . Senator Norris is performing a public service. He is making the protective theory so plain that anybody can understand it and he is exposing at the same time the hypocrisy of those who demand its benefit for Pennsylvania as sound economics, and denounce as 'socialism' the extension of its benefits to Kansas and Nebraska and the Dakotas." [12]

Indeed, Norris quickly emerged as a leading figure in the Senate fight against the tariff measure. Aligned with Democrats and pro-

[10] Norris to Francis J. Beckman, Jan. 15, 1929; to John Harshfield, Feb. 1, 1929; to J. M. Kilpatrick, Apr. 2, 1929.

[11] Norris to Judson C. Welliver, June 22, 1929. The tariff measure passed the House on May 28, 1929.

[12] *Congressional Record,* 71st Cong., 1st sess., Oct. 19, 1929, pp. 4680, 4688–89, 4694; *New York Sun,* Oct. 19, 1929; *Omaha World-Herald,* June 22, 1929. The debenture amendment was deleted in the final version of the Hawley-Smoot tariff.

gressive Republicans, he helped deprive the president of his rate-making power under the flexible provision of the bill. He proposed an amendment, initially agreed upon at a September 28 meeting in the offices of Senator Borah, whereby the Tariff Commission would send its reports to Congress and to the president at the same time and that Congress then should act on their recommendations to either lower or raise rates.[13]

He also played a prominent role in censuring a colleague in the course of the tariff debate. Hiram Bingham, a member of the Senate Finance Committee, which conducted hearings on the bill, by his own admission sought the assistance of an "expert" to help him aid the industries of his home state of Connecticut. Bingham placed a paid agent of the Connecticut Manufacturers' Association on his staff to attend secret sessions of the Finance Committee while the tariff bill was under consideration. Norris quickly noted that if the supposition of Senator Bingham was correct, the tariff bill had been formulated in the interest of the states represented by the eleven majority members of the Finance Committee. A member of a great committee, framing a law for all the people, Norris said, "ought to be sufficiently broad minded to recognize the fact that he must represent more than the people of one State." [14]

As chairman of the Judiciary Committee Norris requested a subcommittee to investigate the matter. Senator Bingham, rising to a question of personal privilege in language that Norris felt was discourteous, assailed the members of the subcommittee "while not denying but rather admitting all the material facts. . . ." Then on November 1, 1929, Norris offered the following resolution (S. Res. 146):

> RESOLVED, That the action of the Senator from Connecticut, Mr. Bingham, in placing Mr. Charles L. Eyanson upon the official rolls of the Senate at the time and in the manner set forth in the report of the subcommittee of the Committee on the Judiciary . . . is contrary to good morals and senatorial ethics and tends

[13] *Omaha World-Herald,* Sept. 5, 1929; *New York World,* Sept. 29, 1929.

[14] *Congressional Record,* 71st Cong., 1st sess., Sept. 25, 1929, pp. 3951–52, 3954; *New York World,* Oct. 29, 1929. For critical comments by Norris on the arbitrary approach of the Senate Finance Committee, see *Congressional Record,* 71st Cong., 2nd sess., Feb. 7, 1930, pp. 3243–45.

to bring the Senate into dishonor and disrepute, and such conduct is hereby condemned.[15]

If the Senate did not take action, Norris felt it would be held in disrepute. If it did act to censure Bingham, the Senate "will have accomplished great good for the welfare of the country, for the practice of drafting laws, and for the honor and dignity of the United States Senate." But throughout the proceedings Bingham insisted that he had done nothing wrong. It was his business to find out what rates were best for Connecticut; by putting Mr. Eyanson on his staff to assist in drafting the tariff bill, he was doing just that. Nothing he had done was injurious to the honor and dignity of the Senate or the American public. The final resolution was modified to include a phrase that Bingham's behavior was "not the result of corrupt motives" but was, as Norris's original motion stated, "contrary to good morals and senatorial ethics and tends to bring the Senate into dishonor and disrepute." By a vote of 54 to 22 the Senate condemned Bingham's conduct.[16]

In the long tariff debate, extending over two sessions of the Seventy-first Congress, Norris found ample opportunity to discuss the bill. At times he focused on specific provisions. Occasionally he attacked the measure in a general way; for example, he offered an amendment to limit profits on imports to 25 percent. In this instance Norris prepared an analysis of consumer prices showing the percentage of cost and the percentage of profit, usually greater than 25 percent. Prompting Norris's amendment was an exhibit toted

[15] *New York World,* Oct. 29, 1929; *Congressional Record,* 71st Cong., 1st sess., Nov. 1, 1929, p. 5063.

[16] *Congressional Record,* 71st Cong., 1st sess., Nov. 4, 1929, pp. 5119–20, 5131. The *Bay City Daily Times,* Nov. 4, 1929, carried a column by David Lawrence stressing the fact that Bingham had violated no law. The whole matter revolved around the question of propriety and ethics as viewed by the senators themselves. At the time Norris's resolution was being considered by the Senate, Bingham told Raymond Clapper that he had in his possession a letter from Norris addressed to him as chairman of the Senate Patronage Committee "demanding that an old employee in the Senate post office be dismissed to make room for one of the Senator's relatives." I have been unable to find any evidence of this letter. No carbon is in the Norris Papers. Norris's secretary insists that there is no foundation to Bingham's statement and I am inclined to agree: such a request would have been totally out of character; see Raymond Clapper, *Racketeering in Washington* (Boston, 1933), p. 70; Robertson to Richard Lowitt, Jan. 9, 1967 (author's file).

onto the Senate floor of 103 articles purchased at retail in New York, "including everything from a clarinet to a dog muzzle." It prompted Senator Alben Barkley to demand of Vice-President Curtis, "By what authority have Kresge and Woolworth moved into the Senate chamber?" The exhibit, arranged by majority members of the Finance Committee, was designed to show the percentage difference between the "landed" valuation of imported merchandise and its retail sale price in the United States.

Norris dubbed the tableful of articles the "Grundy tariff-racket store" and "Mr. Grundy's 'Piggly-Wiggly store,'" after the Pennsylvania high-tariff lobbyist. Walking over to the table, he picked up several items and announced their entry cost in New York and the price charged the ultimate consumer. Profit above the landed price at New York ran in some instances from 200 to 775 percent. Consumers were gouged, imports were curtailed, and American manufacturers did not pass along enough of their tariff-inspired profits that working men could feel secure in their jobs. "While these corporations have grown rich and waxed fat from the sweat and toil of our fellowmen, they have not given labor the wages that labor has earned, and yet in the name of that labor which they have not treated fairly, they come here and ask for additional tribute." Norris made his points with biting sarcasm, using Joseph R. Grundy, soon to join him as a colleague, as the chief butt of his venom and ridicule.[17]

A specific schedule that aroused Norris, largely because it affected some of his constituents, concerned carillons, chiefly used in churches and on college campuses. To assist a church in Lincoln in securing a carillon, he introduced a special bill providing for the remittance of the 40 percent tariff duty. The Senate unanimously approved his amendment placing carillons of thirty or more bells on the free list, if they were imported for religious or educational institutions. Instead of bringing business to an American industry, this schedule, Norris argued, was a tax on religion and education. In reconciling differences on this schedule in conference committee,

[17] *Congressional Record,* 71st Cong., 1st sess., Nov. 8, pp. 5336–38, Nov. 9, 1929, p. 5376; *Racine Times,* Nov. 22, 1929. An NEA article by Rodney Dutcher discussed this incident and Laurence Todd commented on it in *Labor News,* Nov. 23, 1929. See *Congressional Record,* 71st Cong., 2nd sess., Dec. 10, 1929, p. 368, for a further example of Norris's sarcasm.

the House rate of 20 percent prevailed and was incorporated in the final version of the Hawley-Smoot tariff.[18]

The sugar schedule was another that concerned Norris and his constituents. In his remarks on the subject he spoke against the 20 percent reduction on Cuban sugar entering the United States. The consumer of this sugar received no benefit in reduced price; rather, the importer exclusively benefited from the arrangement. Both the taxpayer and the Treasury of the United States lost out. The fact that many Cuban sugar plantations were owned by wealthy Americans meant that Cuba gained little from this arrangement as well. Therefore, it seemed "a hollow mockery and a shame" to continue the 20 percent preferential on Cuban sugar.[19]

The differential in favor of Cuban sugar was bad enough. What aroused Norris more was a proposal to increase the sugar schedule. Earlier the Tariff Commission, after exhaustive hearings, concluded that sugar rates were too high. Increasing the schedule thus would impose an additional burden "upon the homes in the United States" while sugar entered free from the Philippine Islands, Puerto Rico, and Hawaii. Whatever additional tariff was placed "upon the overburdened shoulders of the American public" would benefit those who produced and manufactured beet and cane sugar in the United States and these three dependencies. A tribute was to be levied "upon the American farmer and upon the American household in order to make more profitable the production of sugar in the Philippine Islands where labor is cheap." [20] To be sure, the producer of beets in Nebraska would benefit. The increased tariff would give

[18] Norris to J. C. Seacrest, Oct. 1, 1929; to Ben F. Wyland, Oct. 9, 1929, May 29, Dec. 13, 1930, Sept. 24, 1932; Mildred Olson to Worth M. Tippy, Dec. 30, 1929; *New York World,* Jan. 27, 1930 (editorial); *Congressional Record,* 71st Cong., 2nd sess., Jan. 25, pp. 2361–69 (the debate on the carillon amendment), June 30, 1930, p. 9928 (Norris's final remarks).

[19] *Congressional Record,* 71st Cong., 1st sess., Oct. 18, 1929, pp. 4671–74.

[20] At the outset of the Senate debate Norris called for an amendment providing for Philippine independence so that the tariff bill could be considered in this light. Otherwise he thought that as long as the islands were held without the consent of the people, the Philippines "ought to have absolutely free trade with the United States. . . ." Rather than levy a tax upon Philippine products, Norris wished to grant the area its freedom first and then levy the tax. Otherwise, he insisted, "we have no honorable right, regardless of legal distinctions, to levy a tariff upon any of the products of the Philippine Islands . . ."; see *ibid.,* Oct. 9, 1929, pp. 4379–80, 4402.

him "a very small amount of the larger sum" which the American people would pay. By comparing the amount beet producers would receive with the amount other farmers would pay, Norris showed that "the amount received by beet-sugar men sinks into insignificance." Consumers everywhere would bear the burden of increased sugar rates in the form of increased everyday living expenses. Thus he voted against increasing the tariff on sugar despite the fact that he came from a state which "stands second among the States of the United States in the production of sugar. . . ." [21]

On other schedules Norris faced no such conflicts. He did not believe, for example, that there ought to be a tariff on lumber. The interests of the people of Nebraska could best be protected by putting it on the free list. As a matter of conservation it seemed the proper course to take. In this instance Norris's views were in accord with the majority of the Senate Finance Committee, which recommended free lumber. But when the schedule was discussed, leading Republican members of the committee kept silent and the "Sons of Wild Jackasses," as Senator George Moses dubbed the progressive insurgents in Congress, rose to the defense of free lumber. They were defeated in their efforts. Norris argued to no avail that "not only should we be for free lumber because it would make nearly everything in every home and on every farm cost less to our toiling masses but we would be preserving something for the children who will follow us, and who will look over the wastes of despoiled forests, and wonder why their forefathers were so shortsighted." [22]

[21] *Ibid.*, 2nd sess., Jan. 15, pp. 1632–34, Feb. 7, 1930, p. 3218; Norris to J. C. McCreary, Feb. 1, 1930; to J. Boyd Allen, May 26, 1930, Mar. 27, 1931. *Collier's,* Mar. 22, 1930 (editorial), p. 71, commended Norris for his vote against an increase of the duty on sugar, calling it "the bravest act in the Senate for many years." Norris favored a bounty to the farmer who produced beets rather than tariff protection. A bounty would save taxpayers and consumers millions of dollars more than tariff protection for the beet farmer could. Moreover, he had been presented with evidence that the importance of the sugar beet in Nebraska had been greatly exaggerated. The census of agriculture listed only 1,540 farmers who produced sugar beets; in 1919 there were 1,531 producers. The higher duties on sugar enacted in 1922 in the Fordney-McCumber tariff, which replaced the low rates in the Underwood-Simmons tariff, had the effect of adding only nine farmers to the number producing sugar beets in Nebraska. In Basil Manly to Norris, June 9, 1930, he tried to make this point.

[22] *Congressional Record,* 71st Cong., 2nd sess., Feb. 27, pp. 4405–6, Mar. 3, pp. 4632–33, Mar. 20, 1930, pp. 5680–81; Norris to R. L. Newman, Dec. 28, 1929.

Throughout the debate Norris reiterated the theme that the proposed schedules carried protection to an extreme, especially when one considered that "only about three or three and one-half percent of manufactured articles used in this country are imported." Exorbitant rates "made it possible on this side of the tariff wall to build up monopolies and trusts." Already large corporations, amply protected by prevailing tariff schedules, had built foreign factories, taking capital outside the country and depriving American workers of jobs. From the viewpoint of the farmer it was more important to reduce the rates which constituted part of his cost of living than it was to increase those on agricultural products. To remedy wrongs and to provide protection for the consumer, Norris and a small bipartisan group felt that amendments were necessary all along the line. And at times they were successful. But Norris recognized that the House, which clearly reflected the administration's wishes, would reject these amendments.[23]

Though active in opposing various rates and schedules, Norris did not believe in free trade. He claimed to be a protectionist, believing that "competition this side of the tariff wall will be continued if the right kind of a tariff is levied upon imported articles." But building "a tariff to the sky" would encourage "combinations and monopolies" and exact unfair and unjust prices from the consumer. He opposed tariffs on articles already manufactured in the United States and which were exported. He was particularly critical of the idea of an embargo, the total exclusion of any item from the United States. Exorbitant rates placed overwhelming burdens upon consumers "for the benefit of a comparatively few men or corporations who often are trying to get protection for a product which they manufacture in ways and by methods that are out of date, that are inefficient. . . ." Thus, instead of granting the American people, particularly the farmer, the benefit

Norris regarded a tariff on oil as he did one on lumber. It was a natural resource and not inexhaustible. One way to preserve natural resources was to admit competition from abroad. Oil men, of course, objected to such a view and called for an embargo rather than a tariff. An embargo or a high tariff would make it a little easier for "the larger fellows" to put the small or independent producer out of business; see Norris to A. L. Squire, Mar. 28, 1931; to George L. Keith, Dec. 11, 1931; to J. W. Radcliffe, Dec. 15, 1931.

[23] *Congressional Record,* 71st Cong., 1st sess., Oct. 21, p. 4723, Oct. 23, p. 4806, Oct. 31, 1929, p. 5028.

of the protective-tariff system, the measure would promote further inequities and hardships and bring the inevitable day of reckoning for the system itself and for the social order built upon it that much closer. Since a protective tariff was a legislative favor granted to American manufacturers and producers, it was "not only the right but the duty of Government" to revoke its favors when combinations in restraint of trade were discovered. To achieve this end, Norris proposed an amendment authorizing the president to suspend duties on all commodities controlled by monopolies.[24]

Representing a great agricultural state, Norris gave continued attention to the plight of the farmer and sought to protect his interests. In cases of conflict between divergent agricultural interests Norris usually spoke on behalf of "the man who produces wheat, corn and cattle and hogs." He consistently voted, for example, against every proposed increase in the wool schedule. His colleagues seemed to regard the schedule as a controversy between the wool producer and the wool manufacturer. His plea was, "What about the consumer?" If tariff rates were increased beyond the demands of reason and justice simply because they were farm rates, then, Norris claimed, "we will put the American farmer in the Grundy class . . . the class of those who try to get all they can. . . ."[25]

After the stock-market crash in October, 1929, men in all lines of industry claimed they were going into bankruptcy. Most of these people, it seemed to Norris, "were clamoring for a tariff on something." Indeed, the Capitol was besieged by "hundreds of men, coming on special trains," pleading for a tariff on their particular product. All claimed they were going to be ruined unless they got their tariff. At times they formed combinations to lobby more effectively; for example, Norris was concerned about an alliance of lumber and sugar men. Combinations shifted, rumors were widespread, and Norris felt that the Federal Farm Board, which officially represented agricultural interests, was "as much at sea as anyone else."

---

[24] *Ibid.,* Nov. 6, p. 5240, Nov. 8, pp. 5363, 5371, Nov. 19, 1929, p. 5780; 2nd sess., Jan. 27, pp. 2433–34, Mar. 13, p. 5150, Mar. 20, 1930, pp. 5689–90, 5692; *Baltimore News,* Mar. 21, 1930.

[25] *Congressional Record,* 71st Cong., 1st sess., Nov. 22, 1929, p. 5941; 2nd sess., Dec. 11, 1929, pp. 441–42, Mar. 21, 1930, p. 5810.

It continually changed its attitude and, so far as Norris could determine, was of little benefit to the farmer.[26]

After ten months of consideration, the Senate approved the tariff bill by a 53-to-31 vote. It went to conference committee, where Senator Reed Smoot and Congressman Willis C. Hawley led their respective delegations to iron out differences between the bills. On June 12, 1930, Norris had his final say on the revised measure. The Senate approved the conference report the following day by a two-vote margin, 44 to 42. In each instance Norris voted in the negative.[27]

However he viewed the Hawley-Smoot tariff, Norris believed it could not be defended. It represented "protection run perfectly mad."

It is conceived and written in the interest of victorious business organizations who are using their power, which they obtained by the practice, in my judgment, of many unfair and deceitful means, to put through the Congress one of the most selfish and indefensible tariff measures that has ever been considered by the American people. In my judgment, those who are behind it will see that they have used their own power to bring about their own destruction, because, after all, in the long run, assuming that all interested parties are unselfish and honest, a tariff bill which builds up a part of our people to the damage and injury of other parts of our people will bring its own ruin. Already big business itself is seeing the signs of depression and destruction which the probability of the passage of the bill brings before the entire civilized world.[28]

[26] Norris to Frank Thomas, Mar. 5, 1930. E. E. Schattschneider in *Politics, Pressure and the Tariff* (New York, 1935) carefully examines this theme as it applied to the Hawley-Smoot tariff.

[27] *Congressional Record*, 71st Cong., 2nd sess., Mar. 24, p. 6015, June 13, 1930, p. 10635. The Hawley-Smoot Tariff Act by any standard involved a prodigious amount of work. The Senate Finance Committee heard 1,232 witnesses while the House Ways and Means Committee heard 1,131. Interested parties submitted material that filled 11,000 closely printed pages. Debate ran to 2,800 pages in the *Congressional Record*. Senator Smoot, who as chairman of the Finance Committee was responsible for the measure in the Senate, lost thirty-five pounds but never missed a hearing in committee and was always present when the Senate considered the measure. See Alfred P. Dennis, *Gods and Little Fishes* (Indianapolis, 1931), pp. 213–14.

[28] *Congressional Record*, 71st Cong., 2nd sess., June 12, 1930, p. 10546.

On the last day of the session, several weeks later, Norris again lamented the failure of the administration to enact legislation of any benefit to the farmer. Even the Grange, that most conservative of farm organizations, condemned the tariff that "some people pretend was passed for the benefit of the farmer." Citing statistics to illustrate the despair affecting rural regions, Norris concluded that Hoover's program did not come to grips with the central core of the farm problem, the surplus. Every effort to deal with it through either amendments to the tariff bill or the introduction of the debenture plan had been rejected upon the assurance of the president that his Farm Board or the tariff measure would resolve the situation. Promises had not been redeemed; all attempts to bring about the promised equalization of agriculture and industry had failed dismally.[29]

The second session of the Seventy-first Congress, after so much had been promised and so little granted the farmer, provided another repetition of "The Old Old Story":

So it goes, the same old story, with the farmer as the goat;
He can only pay his taxes and the interest on his note.
O, it's fun to be a farmer and to till the dusty soil,
But the guys who farm the farmers are the ones who get the spoil.

[29] *Ibid.,* July 3, 1930, pp. 12420–22; Norris to A. F. Buechler, May 23, 1930.

The Dictates of Conscience

29

Defeated in his quest to aid agriculture, Norris next concerned himself with matters pertaining to personnel and administrative procedures. These were continuing interests that dated back to the progressive period; in both instances he emerged as a leading critic of the Hoover administration. Indeed, he was soon recognized as its most severe and effective critic.

At the outset, while the administration was seeking to establish social protocol, he wrote an open letter to Secretary of State Henry L. Stimson ridiculing the administration's anxiety about what to Norris was a petty matter:

> I most earnestly urge you to hurry up your decision on the extremely important question that has been submitted to you regarding the position at the dinner table of the sister of the Vice President of the United States. Unless this decision is expedited, very serious interference will result in many important social activities. Until it is known definitely where the Vice President's sister is going to sit, it will be impossible for many socially minded Washingtonians to properly shine in society, in accordance with their social and financial ambitions. Many social functions are awaiting breathlessly for your decision.[1]

[1] Vice-President Charles Curtis was a widower. His sister, Mrs. Edward E. Gann, agreed to serve as his official hostess, creating a question of protocol about where she should be seated at official receptions and dinners.

On behalf of "the common, ordinary citizens, who, in a very small way" contributed to the upkeep of "this great mysterious social sham which towers in importance over questions of national and international import," Norris suggested that Stimson "either decide it without delay or officially report a disagreement on your part to the President of the United States and ask him to submit it to the World Court." [2]

Norris, of course, had no interest in the social precedence of the vice-president's sister. He was one of the few social rebels who refused most official and semiofficial invitations, preferring instead visits or dinners with friends at which no consideration was given to official or social position. In a democratic government he believed that strong and rigid emphasis on social protocol encouraged extravagance and helped attract men of wealth to public service while discouraging others. An elected official could be led astray "by the bright glamor of the official social world," essentially 'a hollow mockery and a sham." [3]

During the debate on the tariff Norris, as chairman of the Senate Judiciary Committee, was asked to choose a subcommittee to investigate legislative lobbying. Both Norris and the subcommittee chairman, Thaddeus H. Caraway of Arkansas, were insistent that the Washington "social lobby" get attention. Several weeks later in a syndicated article he denounced this lobby as "one of the most influential. . . ." It permeated society in the capital and appealed to the vanities, ambitions, and weaknesses of men in Congress and occasionally their families as well. "Armed with unlimited funds,

[2] George W. Norris to Henry L. Stimson, Apr. 6, 1929. Privately, Norris thought that the Daughters of the American Revolution might render an opinion before the World Court decided the matter. "The Daughters have regulated pretty nearly everything else, but it would seem from all reports, that they have sidestepped this matter"; see Norris to Walter Locke, Apr. 23, 1929.

[3] Rodney Dutcher commented on the "Dolly Gann" affair in his column in *Madison* (Wis.) *Capital Times,* Apr. 18, 1929. See also the draft, n.d., of an interview with Norris conducted by a reporter for the *Brooklyn Daily Eagle.* In Jan., 1930, Norris, as chairman of the Senate Judiciary Committee, turned down an invitation to the White House judiciary dinner. To be sure, Norris received not the customary formal invitation but a telephone call late in the afternoon before the dinner. He informed the White House that he had a previous engagement; see *Washington Herald,* Jan. 24, 1930.

representatives of selfish interests" formed the core of the "social lobby," engaging in public business behind closed doors and thereby hampering honest and efficient government.[4] Norris then called attention to a cash refund of $15 million to the U.S. Steel Corporation, which, together with income tax "credits, abatements, and interests" of $42 million, made a grand total of $57 million in tax relief for one year. These figures were used to denounce bitterly the Treasury's method of making income tax refunds without a review by any other governmental or judicial body. Without open tax refunds openly arrived at, favoritism and even dishonesty could occur. Thus Secretary of the Treasury Andrew Mellon continued on into the Hoover administration as the chief cabinet target of critics of Republican ascendancy.[5]

Secrecy also occurred in the other branches of government and Norris found opportunity to criticize nominations that were voted upon in secret. Enemies could report his vote falsely and he would be violating a Senate rule if he revealed it. A senator's vote, Norris said, constituted a part of his record; his constituency, indeed the entire country, had a right to know what it was. To conceal it behind closed doors was not fair to the senator, his constituency, or the country. His arguments helped produce a rules change which had a significant effect when the Senate considered controversial appointments later in the Hoover administration. On June 18, 1929, the Senate decided that all of its business, including presidential

[4] *New York Daily News, Washington Sunday Star,* Oct. 6, 1929; Norris, "The Social Lobby," *Washington News,* Oct. 22, 1929.

[5] *Literary Digest,* Feb. 9, 1929, p. 13. So serious was the opposition to Andrew Mellon that President Hoover did not send his name and that of Secretary of Labor James J. Davis to the Senate for confirmation with those of the rest of his cabinet. At the same time the Senate adopted a resolution directing the Judiciary Committee to investigate whether Mellon could legally continue from the Coolidge administration and whether he was disqualified under a law barring cabinet officers from being directly or indirectly interested in commerce. Norris objected to the resolution on the constitutional ground that Mellon's possible disqualifications for office were a matter solely within the province of the House of Representatives; if it desired, it could attempt to develop evidence for impeachment. Personally, Norris was convinced that under the law Mellon was disqualified from holding his post as Secretary of the Treasury; see *New York Times,* Mar. 6, 1929; Norris to Peter O. Knight, June 22, 1929; to James M. Miller, Apr. 11, 1931.

nominations, could be considered in open executive session "unless the Senate should otherwise determine in a closed executive session and by a majority vote." [6]

Less successful was his effort to promote efficiency by expanding the civil service. He strongly supported an amendment removing from patronage "something over 100,000 appointments" as census takers.[7] More dramatic than his concern for efficiency in government were the battles waged against some of the people who wished to serve in government during the Hoover administration. At the outset Norris could "hardly believe" that the president wished to send ex-Governor Alvan T. Fuller of Massachusetts to France as ambassador, despite bitter French opposition to the appointment because of Fuller's connection with the Sacco and Vanzetti case. Norris confessed that though he had not carefully followed the case, he thought, as did Frenchmen who protested Fuller's appointment, that the two men had been convicted and put to death for their anarchistic beliefs rather than for any cause. Such a condition was so contrary "to the proper idea of human justice" that he was not surprised that many "thousands of honest-minded people" in France protested Fuller's selection as ambassador.[8]

Norris took no action on the Senate floor to block Fuller's appointment. But he played a prominent role as the Senate concluded action on a controversy he had participated in from the outset. On December 6, 1929, almost two years to the day after the claim of William Vare to a seat in the U.S. Senate had been referred to a special committee, the members were ready to vote. For a period of four days Norris recounted his experiences in Pennsylvania, analyzed the reports, reviewed the history of the case, and fought off all dilatory tactics. Finally, by a vote of 58 to 22 Norris's long battle met with success. The Senate agreed to deny William S. Vare a seat.[9] Norris's cup did not overflow, however. Protective-tariff lob-

[6] *Congressional Record,* 71st Cong., 1st sess., May 21, p. 1622, June 12, p. 2768, June 18, 1929, pp. 3042, 3051–52, 3054–55.

[7] *Ibid.,* May 24, pp. 1851–52, June 12, 1929, pp. 2768–69. Norris also continued to request that the Post Office Department be taken out of politics and placed on a business basis; see *ibid.,* 2nd sess., Dec. 11, 1929, p. 472.

[8] Norris to Gardner Jackson, Mar. 25, 1929.

[9] *Congressional Record,* 71st Cong., 1st sess., Sept. 10, pp. 3502–7, Sept. 11, 1929, pp. 3526–27; 2nd sess., Dec. 3, pp. 38, 42–44, Dec. 4, pp. 73–77, Dec. 5,

byist Joseph R. Grundy was appointed to fill the Vare vacancy. He served until the following December when former Secretary of Labor James J. Davis, chosen in a special election, assumed the seat. Norris denounced Grundy's selection as "a stench in the nostrils of all honest men" and claimed that the governor had insulted the Senate of the United States, disgraced the state of Pennsylvania, and "made an ass of himself before the entire country." [10]

In the Coolidge administration Norris chiefly criticized appointments to commissions and cabinet posts. During the Hoover years he played a prominent role in a spectacular attack on judicial appointments. But the gist of his criticism remained the same. Hoover's appointments, like those of his predecessor, were men oriented toward the business community, sympathetic with the great corporations, and in some instances, as in the case of the Radio Commission, actual representatives of the special interests to be regulated.[11]

It was in connection with the nomination of Charles Evans Hughes to be chief justice of the U.S. Supreme Court, successor to the position amply filled by William Howard Taft, that Norris's opposition gained national attention. Hughes's nomination was favorably reported to the Senate on February 10, 1930, by a 10-to-2 vote of the Judiciary Committee. Norris and John J. Blaine of Wisconsin voted against it. Norris claimed that "a high sense of duty" had compelled him to oppose the nomination. Admitting Hughes's qualifications for the post, Norris said there were "two fundamental reasons" that his appointment and confirmation would be unwise. First, having resigned from the Supreme Court in 1916 to run for president, Hughes had entered the arena of partisan political debate. After leaving the bench to enter the political world, "he ought not to be, by political power, put back again on the bench"; a precedent could be created which would lower the standards of the Su-

p. 132, Dec. 6, 1929, pp. 195, 197. For a comprehensive analysis of the case, see the article by Samuel J. Astorino, "The Contested Senate Election of William Scott Vare," *Pennsylvania History*, 28 (Apr., 1961): 187–201.

[10] *Congressional Record,* 71st Cong., 2nd sess., Dec. 12, 1929, p. 535. Norris again referred to the Vare case when discussing in the following Congress a disputed primary election in Alabama involving Thomas Heflin and John H. Bankhead in which Bankhead replaced Heflin in the Senate; see *ibid.,* 72nd Cong., 1st sess., Apr. 25, p. 8872, Apr. 27, 1932, pp. 9028–29, 9031, 9033–34.

[11] *Ibid.,* 71st Cong., 2nd sess., Feb. 20, 1930, p. 4000.

preme Court "down to the level of a political machine." To return him "to the judicial tribunal which he voluntarily left to engage in politics and the amassing of a fortune" would "encourage and stimulate" political activity on the part of other Supreme Court justices.

Second, Hughes had almost invariably represented wealthy corporations. In the previous five years he had appeared in fifty-four cases before the Supreme Court representing wealthy clients. In turn, because of his unique experience Hughes could charge almost unlimited fees. Living this kind of life, continually in contact with "wealthy clients and monopolistic corporations," Norris contended, it was reasonable to expect these influences to become part of the man and to make it difficult for Hughes "to sit in final judgment in contest between organized wealth and the ordinary citizen." "Men should not be elevated to that high tribunal who have lived this one-sided life and where the men who toil and the men who suffer have not been within the vision of the person who is to be elevated to the position of supreme and final arbitrator." Certainly he would not support a person skilled in representing the viewpoint of great corporations.[12]

Norris's objections gained Senate support, though he realized they could never succeed because of Hughes's widely acknowledged technical qualifications, probity, and respected character. Norris recognized, too, that Hughes's integrity was as good an answer as any nominee for the Supreme Court could give to the charges he had raised. But not every nominee was Charles Evans Hughes. There was a principle involved and much good could come from the debate. Thus Norris challenged Hughes's candidacy, though he understood and was satisfied that it would not succeed. What he did achieve was an awareness on the part of many citizens that the Supreme Court was more than a strict legal tribunal, that it was a policy-forming, law-making body with power greater than that exercised by duly elected representatives of the people. "If the Senate debate and public response mean anything," an editorial writer explained, "they mean that the idolatry which placed the Court above criticism has been smashed, and that hereafter the

12 *Ibid.*, Feb. 10, 1930, pp. 3372–73; *New York Sun*, Feb. 10, 1930.

President, the Senate and the public will make severer tests of candidates for that all powerful body." [13]

Debate proceeded on the Hughes nomination for a period of several days in February, 1930. As it became more intense and embittered, Norris descended from his stance of reluctant opposition. He tried to recommit the nomination to committee and said that Hughes's appointment would reinforce the assumption that the highest court of the land was controlled by elements that believed "wealth and money should rule the world." In essence, Norris concluded, "that is the question before us. I say with the greatest respect, but, as I look at it, there is nothing else involved." Despite these arguments, on February 13, 1930, by a vote of 52 to 26 the Senate approved the nomination of Charles Evans Hughes to be chief justice of the Supreme Court.[14]

The debate permeated the country; Norris in his correspondence reiterated his arguments. Expecting severe criticism, he received letters of commendation, "some from very prominent attorneys of national reputation." William Allen White, writing several days after Hughes was confirmed, most effectively summarized the significance of the controversy:

> . . . the Hughes thing was one of the things that just had to be done, but I am afraid it was done at some cost. On the whole I think it is the most effective day's work for the progressive cause that has been done in years, and I am glad that it resulted exactly as it did. Hughes is probably the best conservative that you could get, but the vote was large enough to warn the Republican conservative leaders that another man with less reputation and less real liberal record, even if in another and by gone day will be denied confirmation when he is appointed to the Supreme Court.[15]

But Republican leaders did not heed the significance of the Hughes controversy and when the next nominee, a man "with less reputation" and "less real liberal record" was presented to the Sen-

[13] *Washington News,* Feb. 14, 1930.

[14] *Congressional Record,* 71st Cong., 2nd sess., Feb. 13, pp. 3564–66, 3573, 3591, Feb. 14, 1930, p. 3645.

[15] Norris to W. C. Kelly, Feb. 26, 1930; to Charles F. Amidon, Mar. 5, 1930; to H. F. White, Mar. 12, 1930; to Joseph T. Alling, Feb. 30, 1930; to J. W. Hammond, June 13, 1931; William Allen White to Norris, Feb. 18, 1930.

ate for confirmation, he was denied appointment to the Supreme
Court. Less than two months after the confirmation of Hughes as
chief justice President Hoover sent to the Senate the name of John
J. Parker, a judge of the Fourth Circuit Court, to succeed recently
deceased Edward Terry Sanford. Opposition quickly developed
among labor and Negro leaders. They said Parker had favored the
use of injunctions and other labor-crushing techniques and was a
racist. In opposing confirmation, Norris concerned himself only
with the charge that Parker was hostile to organized labor.

Norris understood that in issuing an injunction, a judge not only
made law as expressed in the terms of the document but also had
responsibility for its enforcement, thereby assuming both legislative
and executive authority in addition to rendering judgment upon his
own acts. Injunction-made laws could send men to prison without
jury trials. Violators would be tried before the man who had made
the law they were charged with disobeying. If the courts had not
been fair to labor by indiscriminately issuing injunctions, they were
equally unfair in validating "yellow-dog" contracts. When a man
signed such a contract, he became "for the time being, the slave of
his master"; the judge in upholding it denied him "his right to freedom." Norris admitted that "Judge Parker is only an incident"; at
issue was "the preservation of human liberty."

In his extensive remarks, in which, incidentally, he rarely mentioned Parker's name, Norris revealed insight into and understanding of an aspect of the plight of labor. He believed that there ought
to be more humanity in the courts, more judges "who would have
the humanitarian viewpoint." Something more than ability and honesty was necessary. On these grounds alone Hughes and Parker were
pre-eminently qualified, but both failed, according to Norris, when
they approached the "great questions of human liberty." These men
sought a seat on "the greatest lawmaking body on earth, with power
that no one can overrule or override, whose word is final, whose
decrees are final, and from whose words and judgments there is no
appeal." Therefore, Norris insisted, "we ought to know that every
one who ascends to that holy bench should have in his heart and in
his mind the intention of looking after the liberties of his fellow
citizens, of construing every question of law on the basis of present
civilization, of discarding if necessary the old precedents of barbar-

ous days, and construing the Constitution and the laws in the light of a modern day, a present civilization." [16]

On May 7, 1930, Parker's nomination was rejected by a vote of 41 to 39. Hoover in his *Memoirs* complained that some Republican senators "ran like white mice" rather than support Parker because of fear of voter reprisal. "This failure of my party to support me," he wrote, "greatly lowered the prestige of my administration." But the man the president nominated next, Owen J. Roberts of Philadelphia, was unanimously approved by the Judiciary Committee and immediately confirmed without objection. No roll-call vote was taken. Norris called him "a high-grade man and an extremely able lawyer." Though Roberts had many corporations as clients, his work in prosecuting oil fraud cases as counsel for the government proved to Norris that he was "able, fearless and not in the least biased in favor of big business." [17]

As chairman of the Judiciary Committee, more presidential nominations (except postmasters) came to Norris's attention than to any other chairman in the Senate. He appointed subcommittees whenever necessary but most of the correspondence and objections to nominees passed through his hands. Despite opposition to two of Hoover's Supreme Court nominations, Norris remarked, "I believe

[16] *Congressional Record,* 71st Cong., 2nd sess., May 2, 1930, pp. 8182–84, 8186–87, 8189–92. The fact that Norris rarely mentioned Parker in his remarks is partially explained by the following undated note from Ray Tucker, a Washington correspondent, to Norris: "Lowell Mellett [editor of the *Washington News*] has asked me to tell you that, despite a pretty careful study and scrutiny of Judge Parker's record, he cannot find sufficient material upon which to base an 'effective attack' upon him. Parker is apparently a rather unimportant figure, etc., but there doesn't seem to be any real basis for going after him."

[17] Herbert Hoover, *Memoirs: The Cabinet and the Presidency, 1920–1933* (New York, 1952), p. 269; *Congressional Record,* 71st Cong., 2nd sess., May 20, 1930, p. 9217; *Baltimore Sun,* May 12, 1930 (Norris's comments on Owen J. Roberts). For a comprehensive discussion of the Parker nomination, see Richard L. Watson, Jr.'s excellent article "The Defeat of Judge Parker: A Study in Pressure Groups and Politics," *Mississippi Valley Historical Review,* 50 (1963): 213–34. While Norris was pleased with the appointment of Benjamin Cardozo to the Supreme Court in 1932, he felt that it was "an unwilling extraction from the 'powers that be' because they have reached a point where they fear the wrath of the people even if they do not fear the wrath of God"; see Norris to William Allen White, Mar. 4, 1932. White, on the other hand, felt that Cardozo's appointment was cause for celebration and wrote Norris an exuberant letter; see White to Norris, Feb. 19, 1932.

even my political enemies in the Senate will say that in the appointment of subcommittees I have never shown any prejudice or unfairness to the Administration." In most instances, including "some hotly contested cases," he stood by the administration. In every case, Norris asserted, "I have done the best I could to follow my conscientious convictions as to what was my duty." [18] He also pursued with some persistence earlier efforts to achieve judicial reform.

The basic judicial reform Norris favored was to abolish diversity of citizenship as a ground for removal of civil cases from state to federal courts, thereby relieving them of undue congestion. Such a law, he thought, would take out of the federal courts in 1930 between 20 and 40 percent of the contested business on their dockets. To keep the issue alive, Norris conducted a wide correspondence, stressing the economy to be gained by allowing state courts to assume responsibility in cases involving citizens of different states. He also noted the opposition of railroads, bankers, insurance companies, and corporations generally to his proposal. He was disappointed in the lack of interest evinced by the press because it indicated there would be little sentiment in Congress for his bill, though the Senate Judiciary Committee favorably reported it twice during Hoover's presidency.[19]

In 1932, surveying the various appointments of the Hoover administration, Norris concluded that it had gone further than most administrations in appointing "to high office those who have been defeated in the campaign just preceding." The Judiciary Committee had been considering such appointees at virtually every meeting and "almost always has made a favorable report" because the nominees were experienced and competent. Norris felt impelled to oppose one such appointee, nominated for attorney general of Puerto Rico, not because the candidate was unqualified but because he felt

[18] Norris to F. A. Good, May 15, 1930; to W. S. Woodworth, Feb. 5, 1931; to Charles H. Richeson, Feb. 6, 1931.

[19] Norris to Norman Thomas, May 17, 1930; to Edward Keating, May 22, 1930, Apr. 9, 1932; to William D. Mitchell, May 24, 1930; to William S. Chase, July 14, 1930; to J. E. Lawrence, Dec. 15, 1931; to Locke, Apr. 11, 1932; to Herman Oliphant, May 16, 1932; John P. Robertson to Donald Gallagher, Jan. 18, 1933. Felix Frankfurter supported Norris's position in one of the few articles examining diversity of citizenship; see Felix Frankfurter, "The Federal Courts," *New Republic*, Apr. 24, 1929, pp. 273–77.

it unwise to have men from the United States sent to govern the people of American dependencies:

> I should like to see the people of Puerto Rico become endeared in every way to the United States. We did not consult them when we took possession of their territory. They have become our wards; and the policy of sending to Puerto Rico from the United States governors and attorneys general and other officials who are unacquainted with their habits, who do not understand the psychology of the people, who do not speak their language, must drive them, as far as their affections are concerned, away from the people of the United States.[20]

The only person to whom Norris reacted with real enthusiasm during the course of the Hoover administration was his deceased colleague, Robert M. LaFollette, whose statue was unveiled in the Capitol on April 25, 1929. He did not speak on this occasion but sat through the entire proceedings. Claude Bowers recalled him "beaming and smiling broadly" when in his speech he observed that LaFollette "did not have to await the conclusion of a party caucus to determine the dictates of conscience." [21]

And, indeed, it was the dictates of conscience that led Norris to favor procedures and to oppose personnel contrary to the wishes of Republican leaders. Criticized for taking a stand contrary to that of party leaders and for not being a good Republican, Norris replied:

> I adhere to the doctrine that the best party man is the man who criticizes his party when he believes it to be wrong; that the worst party man is the one who endeavors to cover up and conceal the wrong doings of officials because they belong to his party. . . . I decline to be driven out of the party which has stood fundamentally in the past for human rights and human liberty. To some extent in the last few years its temple has been tarnished by the presence of the money changers and debauchers of public morals. I have been doing my best to drive them out. I am going to continue in that work as long as I have anything to do with the politics of my country.[22]

[20] *Congressional Record*, 72nd Cong., 1st sess., Mar. 29, 1932, pp. 7023–24.
[21] Claude Bowers, *My Life: The Memoirs of Claude Bowers* (New York, 1962), p. 211.
[22] Norris to Joy M. Hackler, Nov. 2, 1929.

Pounding Home the Message

30

As the leading critic of the Hoover administration Norris made himself a prickly thorn in the side of the president. When the progressives were in accord, he was able to exert great power in determining Senate business. When they were not, he was merely an aggravating annoyance to the administration. But at all times Norris was persistent in his devotion to the public interest. The theme of monopoly and the administration's alliance with it comprised the chief complaint that Norris made.[1]

Enforcement of prohibition was an issue in which monopoly was not a dominant theme. Yet here, too, Norris was critical of the administration. He was interested in the work of the commission chosen by the president to recommend action upon the related questions of crime and prohibition. Norris hoped it would favor overhauling judicial procedures so that "speedy justice" might be secured and undue advantage to "the man or the corporation of great wealth" eliminated. In short, he hoped to broaden the commission's mandate, and he discussed the whole matter of judicial reform, including his diversity of citizenship bill, with its chairman, George W. Wickersham. Since it was the only commission remotely concerned with law enforcement and legal procedures, Norris always

[1] Harry Slattery to Gifford Pinchot, May 25, 1929 (Harry Slattery Papers, Manuscripts Collections, Duke University Library). Slattery suggested the premise that I state. He also noted that Borah, Hoover's campaign manager in 1928, was now active in opposition to the president.

supported its appropriations. But when the Wickersham commission's contradictory and confusing report, opposing repeal of the Eighteenth Amendment while demonstrating its futility, was made available, Norris was not satisfied. He regretted that its meetings and hearings were held in executive session and was pleased that one member of the commission, a former progressive senator from Iowa, Willam S. Kenyon, agreed with him on this point.[2]

The president's habit of appointing "numerous and miscellaneous committees" reminded Norris "of a little verse" which he changed "just a little" when he recited it to his colleagues:

> Once to every man and nation
> Comes the moment to decide
> In the strife of truth with falsehood,
> For the good or evil side.

> But the case presents no problem
> To the White House engineer;
> He appoints a big commission
> To report some time next year.[3]

Instead of dilatory tactics, Norris called for action, especially when the malefactors were large corporations engaged in practices that could be construed as violations of the antitrust laws. In December, 1930, steel makers raised their prices about a dollar a ton. Norris claimed that the increase was timed to take advantage of increased expenditures for public works. U.S. Steel announced the price increase and "immediately the same day, almost the same hour, every other steel company followed suit." Such a coincidence, he insisted, ought to be noticed by the Justice Department and the courts as a violation of the antitrust laws.[4]

As the impact of the depression cut production costs, Norris expected price reductions to follow. When prices remained the same or increased, he became suspicious of possible antitrust violations. Similarly, an instance of identical bids demonstrated a combination, though Norris was distressed to learn that the Justice Department did not agree with him. The antitrust laws were founded on the

[2] *Congressional Record*, 71st Cong., 2nd sess., July 3, 1930, pp. 12377–82; 3rd sess., Jan. 26, 1931, p. 3120.

[3] *Ibid.*, Dec. 4, 1930, p. 197.

[4] *Ibid.*, pp. 175, 177.

premise that competition should be maintained. It could not be maintained if manufacturers or dealers agreed upon prices for which products should be sold. If competition were to be abandoned, Norris preferred "some governmental machinery for fixing definite prices and definite profits" to protect consumers. Until that time arrived, however, enforcement of the antitrust laws was the accepted way to promote competition and protect the consumer, though throughout the era of Republican ascendancy nothing but lip service had been given it.[5]

One notable exception existed to this generalization. Through Norris's efforts the Federal Trade Commission was engaged in a sweeping investigation of privately owned utility companies. Its findings, combined with his own, gave Norris abundant ammunition to denounce them and to call for a more sensible approach to resource development, including the utilization of the government properties at Muscle Shoals. The chief counsel of the Federal Trade Commission in charge of the investigation was Robert E. Healy. Norris responded to his inquiries and offered suggestions the commission could pursue. He presented, for example, information countering charges made by the National Electric Light Association about Ontario Hydroelectric Power Commission rates and suggested that Portland, Maine, was a community that might be examined by the Federal Trade Commission—the Insull interests were engaged in a bitter battle to gain control of newspapers there.[6]

At the same time he was presenting information to the Senate about the acquisition of newspapers by "Power people." He thought they "ought to be prohibited by law from using the funds of investors in its bonds and stocks for such purposes," since doing so struck at "the very fundamental principle of democratic government." Combined with utility company efforts to influence education and

[5] George W. Norris to J. K. Moore, Mar. 24, 1931; to B. N. Mercer, Mar. 29, 1931; to W. T. Rawleigh, May 19, 1931; to Kenneth McKellar, Dec. 18, 1931. McKellar had introduced a resolution providing for an investigation of the operation and enforcement of the antitrust laws, and Norris wrote to explain that the Judiciary Committee was "simply overwhelmed with work" and might not be able to conduct as thorough an investigation as both McKellar and he would desire.

[6] Norris to Robert E. Healy, May 7 and 15, 1929. The editor of the *Portland Evening News,* a bitter foe of the "Power Trust," was Ernest Gruening, later U.S. senator from Alaska.

to secure control of radio stations, acquisition of newspapers was "the most gigantic attempt to control the business and the homes of America that has ever been undertaken." The fact that by 1929 private utility companies controlled more wealth than the combined valuation of railroads in the United States enabled them to purchase newspapers as well as municipal power plants at exorbitant prices. Control of newspapers meant that criticism of increased rates to cover these purchases would be muted or suppressed. The revelations of the Federal Trade Commission in noting, for example, that the International Paper and Power Company had interests totaling more than $10 million in eleven newspapers in eight cities prompted Norris's extensive remarks.

There was no reason for utility companies to own newspapers. They were charged with a public duty and usually were granted a monopoly. They were given the right of eminent domain and, Norris explained, "that means that the people who give them that privilege have a right to say how far they shall go, and have a right to say that the corporations shall not make money enough in the operation of their business to buy all the newspapers in the United States." Their newspapers unremittingly fought public ownership of public utilities. Investigation had already revealed that private utility companies went "into the churches, the schools, the Boy Scouts, women's clubs, commercial organizations, and secret societies" to educate public sentiment to their viewpoint. "Half truths and complete misinformation" were their stock in trade when they discussed municipal ownership of public utilities. So great was their authority, of such magnitude was their influence, so enormous were the sums of money at their disposal that these utility companies, Norris believed, would destroy what they could not own. With the profits of extortionate rates wrung "from the toiling masses of the American people," he said, "they have subsidized the press; they have debauched the commissions that were supposed to regulate them; and from day to day they are issuing their edict as to what papers shall live and what shall not, as to what business shall prosper and what business shall fail." There was no alternative. One paid tribute to the power trust or suffered the consequences.[7]

[7] *Congressional Record,* 71st Cong., 1st sess., May 20, pp. 1526–46, May 21, 1929, pp. 1598–1602. A draft statement by Norris, Apr. 13, 1929, discusses the

On May 20, 1929, the day Norris started his lengthy analysis of power trust activities, a colleague inserted in the *Congressional Record* his article, "Politics and Your Electricity Bill," showing that public power rates were "three to five times cheaper than private power." In it he examined "the Electric Power Trust" and its lobbying activities and concluded that only government competition could break the "strangulation grip" of this monopoly. "Then, and then alone can we have real economic freedom and at the same time end the most threatening present menace to our political liberty." [8]

To Harry Slattery, a keen observer of governmental affairs, Norris's speeches and the Federal Trade Commission disclosures brought the progressive group in the Senate "back together—seemingly in a strong working agreement—and even Brookhart, Howell and Nye are holding hands with Norris." Moreover, Slattery observed, "it is said on all sides here that Norris is the strong hand in this Congress. . . ." The power disclosures, more than any other factor, were responsible for this development; "it has rocked folks more than anything that has happened in the whole power fight these many years." With Norris taking advantage of these disclosures "to pound home the old story," with "more sky rockets" promised from the Federal Trade Commission, Slattery was surprised that Hoover seemed "to be keeping hands off and letting them go ahead." [9]

Ruminating over these disclosures, Norris observed that regulation had "woefully failed" and that "the Trust is already regulating the regulator." The solution was public ownership and operation of hydroelectric utilities. Henry Ford in a recent interview had stated that the maximum development of electricity must come from a monopoly; Norris agreed. But rather than private monopoly, he

---

International Paper and Power Company. Some volumes examining testimony given in the Federal Trade Commission hearings are Carl D. Thompson, *Confessions of the Power Trust* (New York, 1932), Jack Levin, *Power Ethics* (New York, 1931), and Ernest Gruening, *The Public Pays* (New York, 1931).

[8] *Congressional Record*, 71st Cong., 1st sess., May 20, 1929, pp. 1521–23. The article originally appeared in *Plain Talk*, July, 1928. Senator Clarence C. Dill inserted it in the *Record*.

[9] Slattery to Pinchot, May 25, 1929 (Slattery Papers). Slattery soon thereafter helped Norris draft a resolution calling for an investigation of traction and power development in Chicago; see Slattery to Pinchot, July 2, 1929 (Slattery Papers); *Congressional Record*, 71st Cong., 1st sess., June 12, 1929, pp. 2722–23.

called for public operation to supply electricity at cost, not to enrich itself by the control of natural resources.[10]

The exception that proved Norris's point about the failure of regulation was New York, where Governor Franklin D. Roosevelt had appointed Frank P. Walsh, a prominent liberal lawyer, a member of a committee to investigate public utilities. Walsh's appointment indicated that Roosevelt had the courage "to take the necessary steps to bring about a fair and honest investigation." Norris continued:

> I have always had faith in Governor Roosevelt, but I have nevertheless felt that he had one more step to take before he was absolutely right. To a great extent I felt the same about Governor Smith. But I confidently believe that Governor Roosevelt has the courage, the honesty and the ability to see what is right and, if he goes into this electric proposition, he will eventually see the light as plainly as broad day, and when he does, I expect him to take the next step which will be that the natural resources of our country should be retained by governmental authority, developed by the same authority, and that the electricity should be distributed by the same authority. There is no place where individuals and private corporations should be permitted to derive profit from the transaction. . . .[11]

In Congress and in his correspondence Norris hit hard against the power trust. A widely disseminated article, "The Power Trust in the

[10] Norris to Judson King, July 13, 1929; to Oliver Cunningham, Dec. 29, 1930; to Donald Richberg, Aug. 13, 1931; to M. L. Cooke, Sept. 6, 1931. In the 1931 letters Norris called for "progressive minded men and women" to support boldly government ownership not only of generating plants but also of transmission lines. In a 1931 article Norris suggested this theme to a wider audience; see "Power," as told by Norris to Ray Tucker, *Country Home*, 55 (May, 1931): 7–9, 57–58. For Norris's comments on Henry Ford's views, see *Washington Herald*, July 9, 1929.

[11] Norris to Frank P. Walsh, July 24, 1929. Norris made the same point to Roosevelt himself when he commented on a portion of the governor's annual message. His only criticism was that Roosevelt in calling for utility regulation did not go far enough: "There is no stopping place until you have reached complete ownership and *operation* of the generation and distribution of electricity." He hoped that those who were "advocating the ownership, management and control" of the nation's natural resources by the people would be able "to point to New York as a model state instead of crossing the line into Canada"; see Norris to Roosevelt, Jan. 14, 1930.

Public Schools," was based on disclosures made by the Federal Trade Commission revealing the efforts of utility company representatives to influence public opinion by subsidizing professors and "leaders in educational lines." In it he related how power trust representatives were using funds derived from rates charged their customers to deceive them and their children. He cited the case of a college professor in Alabama paid over $600 a month by the power trust; as a director of extension work he was supposed to be interested in the industrial development of the state. In speeches before "church gatherings, farmers' organizations, Rotary clubs, Kiwanis clubs, etc." the professor always praised private power interests and condemned municipally owned electric light plants. On all levels teachers as well as textbooks preached the message of private ownership of public utilities in an effort to use the educational structure of the nation "to control public sentiment for private gain." [12] In May, 1930, in the course of his remarks Norris had two charts placed on a wall of the Senate chamber. One chart referred to industrial energy and the other to electricity generated for such domestic purposes as lighting. Black lines represented the cost in the United States, red lines the cost in Ontario. Of course, in both instances Canadian figures were lower than American rates.[13]

In another incident pertaining to hydroelectric power, Hoover had requested an overhauling of the Federal Power Commission to interlock it "with the regulating commissions of the states as a kind of extension of their powers." Congress refused, but it did agree to modify the 1920 Water Power Act to provide that the law should be administered by five full-time commissioners. Previously, three cabinet officers comprised the Federal Power Commission. Hoover appointed five commissioners and, Norris observed, "three of them, before the ink was dry upon their commissions and without any no-

[12] Norris, "The Power Trust in the Public Schools," *Nation,* Sept. 18, 1929, pp. 296–97. The article was inserted in the *Congressional Record* by Senator Gerald Nye; see 71st Cong., 1st sess., Nov. 13, 1929, pp. 5480–81.

[13] *Congressional Record,* 71st Cong., 2nd sess., May 9, 1930, pp. 8667–71 (the charts, prepared by Judson King, appear on pp. 8670–71). The bulk of Norris's lengthy remarks this day were devoted to the cost of power, chiefly to manufacturers, in numerous American cities and in Ontario. He concluded that government development resulted in lower power rates than private development. For somewhat similar suggestions pertaining to railroads in Canada and the United States, see Norris's comments in *ibid.,* 1st sess., Oct. 14, 1929, p. 4505.

tice to anybody, met and arbitrarily removed" three staff members, two of whom had zealously sought to protect the public interest; the third, the executive secretary, was equally concerned about the interests of the power companies. He quickly received a better-paying government job while "the two faithful servants were put out into the cold." As a result of the furor this incident created, one of the men was reinstated; some senators, shocked at the action of the newly approved commissioners, called for reconsideration of their approval.[14]

In the Seventy-second Congress Norris devoted his attention to holding companies, "one of the great evils connected with the power question, . . . which is something comparatively new in our industrial development." As a rule they were parasites and had little valid excuse for existence, but since they were not effectively regulated by either state or federal law, they provided one of the most important means by which the power trust was able to manipulate and conceal enormous earnings and large expenses. Citing numerous examples to illustrate his point, Norris reiterated the fact that the power trust had only one source of revenue: the sale of electricity. Thus funds for multifarious activities in politics, education, and elsewhere came from exorbitant rates charged the users of electricity. As Frederick M. Sackett, ambassador to Germany, former U.S. senator, and former president of the Louisville Lighting Company, remarked at the World Power Conference in Berlin in 1930, "I know of no other manufacturing industry where the sale price to the great mass of consumers is fifteen times the cost of production of the article sold."

With these funds, which had not been curtailed owing to the depression, power trust holding companies prospered. But the case of Samuel Insull indicated that a master of utility holding company

[14] Herbert Hoover, *Memoirs: The Cabinet and the Presidency, 1920–1933* (New York, 1952), p. 302; *Congressional Record,* 71st Cong., 3rd sess., Jan. 23, 1931, pp. 2957–61. The Senate instructed the Judiciary Committee to test in court its right to request the president to reconsider a nomination, in this instance the right of George Otis Smith to serve as a member of the Federal Power Commission; see Norris to Alex J. Grosbeck, Feb. 20, 1931. For a strong indictment of Hoover's power record as Secretary of Commerce and as president, see Amos Pinchot, "Hoover and Power," *Nation,* Aug. 5, pp. 125–28, Aug. 12, 1931, pp. 151–53.

legerdemain could overextend himself. Norris noted that while Insull, member of the board of eighty-five utility corporations, chairman of the board of fifty or sixty, and president of eleven, was pensioned "by some of the companies which he ruined," those who put their savings in his companies lost them all. In careful detail Norris examined the complex dimensions of Insull's and other holding company empires, suggesting that while stockholders purchased heavily watered securities, those who sat at the top of the holding companies enjoyed enormous profits and privileges.

He concluded with a lengthy analysis of the holding company situation in his own state of Nebraska. Here, too, the pattern was consistent. "While they are changing water into gold they are not forgetting about politicians in school districts, in legislatures, in senatorial campaigns, in presidential campaigns." The people who paid for it all were the same in Nebraska as elsewhere in the nation: "the little home owners," the laboring men and women, the consumers of electricity not serviced by municipal plants. In its determination to expand, the Nebraska Power Company, like other power trust subsidiaries, was paying exorbitant prices for municipal plants. Monopoly was its goal; a municipally owned plant that might serve as a yardstick for determining equitable rates was desired neither by the Nebraska Power Company in particular nor the power trust in general. Both were willing to spend millions of dollars to maintain their monopoly, the money collected from helpless consumers of electricity. The question Norris raised was, "When will the people take action" and condemn the practices he had been commenting upon for two days on the Senate floor? [15] His remarks

[15] *Congressional Record,* 72nd Cong., 2nd sess., July 13, pp. 15195–204, July 14, 1932, pp. 15308–33. The quote from a speech by Ambassador Frederick Sackett at the Berlin World Power Conference was not part of Norris's remarks but can be found in *Literary Digest,* July 5, 1930, p. 8. For other items wherein Norris pounded home his points on utility companies, discussed Federal Trade Commission findings, or reiterated themes developed in his speech, see Norris to S. C. Nancarrow, May 19, 1930; to Clark McAdams, Apr. 4, 1931; to J. W. Yockey, Apr. 4, 1931; draft statement by Norris, Apr. 17, 1931; Norris to Henry Feldhus, June 7, 1932; to O. A. Ralston, June 27, 1932; to Carl D. Thompson, June 27, 1932. On July 12, 1932, the day before he started his lengthy address, Norris inserted in the *Congressional Record* an analysis prepared by Louis Bartlett of comparative electric rates in California, revealing, for example, that Los Angeles consumers, where public ownership prevailed, were saving twelve to

and the publicity they received had an effect. They helped pound home the message that the Federal Trade Commission investigation had justified itself and should be allowed to continue. The picture of evasiveness, extravagance, and secrecy by some of the major holding companies, as presented by Norris, was devastating in its impact. It helped arouse public clamor against this ruthless and reckless exploitation.

The most famous antimonopoly speech Norris delivered came at the end of the Hoover administration. It was an attack upon the "spider" of corporate control by New York banks. The power trust figured only incidentally in his remarks, though the technique used in this speech had been used before in delineating the ramifications of utility company control. Pointing to an eight-foot-square chart entitled "The Spider Web of Wall Street," Norris told the Senate that it did not "come any where near" being big enough to show all the corporations under the control of the New York financial center. "Instead of 120 major corporations shown here, there would be thousands." Pointing to the eight legs of the huge black spider, each leg representing a major banking firm, Norris led his colleagues through a maze of facts and figures in painstaking fashion. The weblike maze of black lines on the chart connected the eight banks with 120 major corporations by means of interlocking directorates. Each line signified that the bank and the corporation had at least one director in common, and it also meant that these great banks could control "practically any corporation of any size in the United States." Seven "Morgan banks," for example, held 2,242 director-ships in various corporations. Most important to Norris was the fact that these banking houses, particularly the House of Morgan, had come "into a position of absolute dominance in the power business." The point he wished to make was pounded home with a four-line doggerel by Senator Marvel M. Logan of Kentucky:

> Old Noah's fleas had other fleas
> Upon their backs to bite 'em
> And those small fleas had smaller fleas,
> And so on, ad infinitum.

fifteen times more in bills for electric service than people in San Francisco, ser-viced by Pacific Gas & Electric Company; see pp. 15062–68.

These data, Norris said, clearly demonstrated "that the control of all business in the United States is drifting rapidly toward corporations," increasingly directed according to the wishes of men who controlled the "money strings" in Wall Street. In an analysis that would have appealed to a populist audience of the 1890s, though it was less emotional and more factually detailed than most populist orations, Norris hammered at the ramifications and implications of Wall Street banker control.[16]

Throughout the Hoover administration Norris not only pounded home his points in opposition to the power trust in particular and monopoly in general, but he also managed to implicate the president as one who favored monopoly and was unsympathetic to reform. Thanks to the Federal Trade Commission investigation, he had helped create a climate of opinion that was critical of utility holding companies and large corporations. Norris still understood that while the American public was antimonopoly in its views, it was not in favor of public ownership of public utilities. A splendid summary statement of his position, as herein analyzed, was presented in August, 1929, when he spoke at the unveiling of a statue of Abraham Lincoln in Freeport, Illinois. Following the example of Lincoln, Norris hoped that the great problems confronting the nation would be resolved by and for the people. He asked, "What doth it profit if we strike the chains of slavery from the black man and permit monopoly to forge the same chains upon millions of our own race?" [17]

[16] *Congressional Record*, 72nd Cong., 2nd sess., Feb. 23, 1933, pp. 4769–80. Norris began his remarks on Feb. 22, though they were published in their entirety on Feb. 23. His speech on Feb. 22 analyzed the dissolution of the National Electric Light Association and the organization of the Edison Electric Institute as the chief exponent of "Power Trust" views. He also commended the Federal Trade Commission and called for appropriation of adequate funds to allow it to continue its investigations despite presidential opposition. Several days later in a final plea at the end of the Hoover administration for adequate funds for the commission, Norris reiterated many of the points he had made in "The Spider Web of Wall Street" speech; see *ibid.*, Feb. 28, 1933, pp. 5240–42. For an earlier account of Norris using a similar technique, producing a map of the United States "covered completely by a spider web of lines representing the connection of the multitude of power companies with each other by interlocking directorates," see Arthur Sears Henning, "Power Trust Perils Nation, Norris Warns," *Chicago Tribune*, Mar. 1, 1933.

[17] *Congressional Record*, 71st Cong., 1st sess., Sept. 9, 1929, pp. 3418–21

What disturbed Norris was the fact that most citizens seemingly were not concerned about the activities of monopoly and wealth "in their gigantic attempt to control all the avenues of human activities." Though the tendency of the times was toward combination and centralized control, he was distressed when public officials remained silent at the unscrupulous activities of some corporations. Through his efforts the public pulse began to respond. But he was concerned that the day of reckoning might come too soon and bring in its wake "much suffering, some injustice, and an aroused public feeling that will cause the pendulum to swing too far." [18] Norris's championing of specific projects, particularly Muscle Shoals, now must be examined as the positive side of the message he was pounding home.

(text of the Freeport speech, delivered on Aug. 27, 1929). Norris discussed a wide variety of themes besides monopoly: abolition of the Electoral College, elimination of injunctions in labor disputes, a progressive inheritance tax, taking the profit out of war, and others. For favorable comment on Norris's Freeport speech, see editorial comment in *Milwaukee Journal* and *Illinois State Register,* Aug. 28, 1929.

[18] Norris to C. C. Flansburg, Oct. 18, 1929.

The President and the Power Trust

31

Norris supported several projects aside from the tremendous battle waged over Muscle Shoals with the Hoover administration. In no instance did his views prevail, but the closeness of the contests indicated that the tide had turned, that with the deepening impact of the depression and forthcoming elections, either the minds of key incumbents would change or new personnel would replace them. Sufficient votes would then be available to make some of Norris's dreams come true.

The Boulder Dam Act was being perverted, Norris said, by Hoover's Secretary of the Interior, who as administrative officer of the project had decided that the preference clause in the law might be modified. Under Ray Lyman Wilbur's interpretation power generated at the dam could be sold "to private parties or private corporations without giving any of it to municipalities" or other public bodies. Norris insisted that this interpretation was a violation of the preference clause and could give the power trust every kilowatt of electricity generated by the expenditure of public money at Boulder Dam. Preference, he said, was never meant to apply to private corporations. If that had been the intention of Congress, it would have accepted Senator David Reed's proposal that these "great works" not be constructed if private enterprise would build them. The overwhelming defeat of Reed's amendment convinced Norris that preference for public and not private bodies was clearly the intent of Congress in approving the Boulder Dam bill. Thus Secretary Wilbur's interpretation in effect nullified an act of Congress and allocated to the power trust electricity generated at Boulder Dam by public funds. Despite Norris's protest the Secretary's interpretation prevailed and public power advocates suffered a setback.[1]

In battling for proper tributary development, Norris achieved no outstanding success, but his views were becoming more widely accepted. In June, 1930, for example, when the Senate was considering a river and harbor bill, Norris noted how flood control, navigation, irrigation, and power all dovetailed, harmonized, and helped in the proper development of a river with minimum expenditure. Central to his approach was the construction of storage dams wherever nature had provided natural reservoirs. As far as Norris knew, he was the first man in Congress to suggest that floodwaters be controlled in this way. At the end of 1930 he thought his views were supported by "many of the best experts in the country."[2]

In an address at Minden, Nebraska, in January, 1930, Norris reiterated his views on tributary control to a large audience that included many old friends. All understood that lack of water was the chief difficulty preventing agricultural fulfillment. And all agreed that Nebraska needed more moisture than was received from rainfall. Yet available water was flowing down the Platte, the Missouri, and other tributaries that could fertilize lands "in order to give us the thing that this country wants—moisture—not water rustling by us on its way to destroy human life and property."

Further north in Nebraska, where some farmers had ample water, experience under the Reclamation Act had shown that the burden on those who had to pay for irrigation ditches was too great. The farmer in northwest Nebraska, who was required to pay all the costs of the Pathfinder Dam, the ditches, and the diversion dam, actually was paying a debt while everyone else in the valley down to the mouth of the Mississippi River benefited because the dam was hold-

[1] *Congressional Record,* 71st Cong., 2nd sess., Jan. 28, pp. 2499–2500, Feb. 1, pp. 2839–40, Mar. 5, 1930, p. 4806. Judson King explained the critical situation to Felix Frankfurter, hoping that Frankfurter would tear Wilbur's interpretation "into bits as law"; see King to Frankfurter, Jan. 31, 1930 (Box 65, Felix Frankfurter Papers, Manuscript Division, Library of Congress).

[2] *Congressional Record,* 71st Cong., 2nd sess., June 20, 1930, pp. 11295–96; George W. Norris to C. H. Swanson, Nov. 12, 1930; to F. R. Kingsley, Mar. 5, 1930.

ing back floodwaters. Only multiple-purpose development and the generation of electricity as a byproduct of these functions would lower the burden on the hard-pressed farmer and provide untold blessings for its users. In projects where electricity was generated, Norris thought the Reclamation Bureau ought to build transmission lines to nearby farms, communities, and municipalities. To be sure, the cost of the transmission lines would be charged to the farmers, "but the additional return which they would get would give to the farmers the amount" which went as profit to the utility company "with no investment on their part except the transmission lines." [3]

The proposal emanating from Nebraska that chiefly concerned Norris, as it did during the Coolidge years, was the Tri-County project. Private power companies voiced increased opposition and the fight became another dimension of his battle against the power trust. The situation was becoming confused because people in the area were not able to reach agreement. Some supported Norris's view of multiple-purpose development and envisioned the project as part of a vast network of tributary control throughout the Mississippi Valley. Others saw it as a specific project concerned only with irrigation and divorced from hydroelectric power. Then in 1931 a plan was presented to integrate Tri-County with another proposed project and thereby provide for comprehensive development of the Platte River. Norris now found himself caught in a cross fire. Because he wanted to help people in the North Platte valley resolve their problems, he was criticized for disregarding the people in the Republican River valley. Residents of Grand Island, located on the Platte River below these proposed projects, claimed they would be left high and dry because of diversion of water for irrigation purposes.

If the federal government was to prevent damage from floodwaters by building dams on tributaries of the Mississippi River, the more comprehensive the plan and the more unified the sentiment

[3] *Hastings Daily Tribune, San Francisco Call-Bulletin,* Jan. 4, 1930; Norris to Kingsley, Feb. 7, 1930; *Congressional Record,* 71st Cong., 3rd sess., Feb. 26, 1931, pp. 6087–88. Robert Howell later inserted the Minden speech in the *Congressional Record;* see 71st Cong., 3rd sess., Feb. 16, 1931, pp. 5015–17. The Senate approved an amendment by Norris with regard to the North Platte project. See also Norris to Elwood Mead, Nov. 27, 1929, Dec. 29, Jan. 31, 1931; to Charles M. Kearney, Mar. 21, 1931; to R. O. Chambers, Feb. 4, 1931.

supporting it, the better the chances of success. While irrigation was of primary concern to his constituents, Norris knew that flood control and navigation, particularly as they affected the larger tributaries of the Mississippi River, were the primary points upon which to base claims for government assistance. He never lost sight of the national ramifications of these proposals and always insisted that power production would lower the cost and further benefit the people in the vicinity of the projects. Though he did not expect to live to see the day when a plan was developed and in full operation, Norris said he would be satisfied if he could help commit the government to it.[4]

During the Hoover administration the St. Lawrence Waterway again came briefly to Norris's attention. Frank P. Walsh, a member of the New York Power Authority, hoped to conclude an arrangement between the province of Ontario and the state of New York for plants to facilitate power development in the international section of the St. Lawrence River and to help remedy the unemployment situation in the Empire State. Walsh informed Norris that private power companies objected and that the matter was stalled. In 1932, when the St. Lawrence Waterway Treaty between the United States and Canada was signed, he predicted another prolonged battle between the "Power Trust" and the people. Governor Franklin D. Roosevelt was on the side of the people while President Hoover, Norris said, represented the power trust.[5]

Muscle Shoals, however, was the most important power proposition that Norris concerned himself with during the Hoover administration. A mighty battle was waged, and Norris suffered defeat at the hands of the president, the last he would experience in this controversy. It began on May 28, 1929, when Norris introduced S. J. Res. 49, "To provide for the national defense by the creation

[4] Norris to Frank H. Wheeler, Feb. 8, 1931; to Frank L. Williams, Feb. 8, 1930; to W. V. Hoagland, Sept. 18, 1931; to Kingsley, Sept. 18, 1931; to A. F. Buechler, Oct. 27, 1931, May 3, 1932; to C. A. Sorensen, Oct. 28, 1931. Gene E. Hamaker, *Irrigation Pioneers: A History of the Tri-County Project to 1935* (Minden, Nebr., 1964), entitles one of his chapters discussing this period "Tri-County in Eclipse." Hamaker's volume is a definitive study.

[5] Norris to F. P. Walsh, Sept. 4, 1931; *Washington Herald*, July 20, 1932. The treaty was submitted to the Senate by Hoover in Dec., 1932. It was shelved, presumably until the new administration took office.

of a corporation for the operation of the government properties at and near Muscle Shoals in the State of Alabama, and for other purposes." Essentially this was the same bill that President Coolidge had pocket-vetoed in the Seventieth Congress. The Agriculture and Forestry Committee on June 3, 1929, favorably reported the resolution. It was placed on the calendar of the Senate to be considered immediately after the tariff bill.

Since the tariff fight continued well into the second session of the Seventy-first Congress, Norris had time to prepare. He sought information on percent of gross revenues paid by private corporations as state taxes in order to "provide that there shall be paid to the State of Alabama something in lieu of taxes if the Government operates Dam No. 2 at Muscle Shoals and sells electricity to counties, municipalities and private corporations." In this way he thought the objection that government pays no taxes would be obviated. The single difference in this Muscle Shoals resolution from the previous one provided "for the payment to the State of Alabama of five percent of the gross sales of electricity at Muscle Shoals; and to the State of Tennessee, five percent of the gross sales of electricity developed at Cove Creek Dam." [6]

In correspondence Norris emphasized the importance of Cove Creek Dam on the Clinch River in Tennessee and its role "primarily as a flood control proposition; secondly as an assistance to navigation; and third as a power proposition." Tributary development on the Tennessee River, owing to mounting sentiment in favor of government operation of the Muscle Shoals properties, had a greater chance of realization than anywhere else in the nation. Norris stressed the concept because he was confident that Congress would approve his Muscle Shoals proposal. Of course, he was aware that President Hoover was not favorably disposed. But if it were re-enacted by a large majority and there were strong sentiment in the country behind it, there was a chance, albeit a slight one, that Hoover would approve it. [7]

On April 1, 1930, the Senate began consideration of S. J. Res.

[6] Norris to M. L. Cooke, May 10, 1929; draft statement by Norris about S. J. Res. 49, May 29, 1929.

[7] Norris to James G. Baker, May 11, 1929; to Russell E. Simpson, May 31, 1929; to Carl D. Thompson, Aug. 8, 1929; to Alfred Truitt, Nov. 4, 1929.

49. Norris spoke the following day; for the rest of the brief debate, covering a period of three days, he played a significant role. Introducing his remarks, he said, "Mr. President, Muscle Shoals is an old friend; at least it is an old acquaintance of all of us, whether friendly or otherwise." Once again he analyzed the question of fertilizer and why it could be produced more cheaply by processes not using hydroelectric power. He examined the power potentially available and discussed previous offers for the properties. On the second day he analyzed the proposal to build Cove Creek Dam, stressing its multiple purposes of flood control, navigation, and power. His views on tributary development were voiced along with those favoring public ownership "of the facilities for the development, the distribution and the sale of electrical energy" with preference to nonprofit public groups, including farm organizations, for the purchase of power. Norris also candidly recognized that "the President is not in sympathy with some of the things that we have put in this joint resolution." Not wishing to give Hoover "any additional peg upon which he could hang a veto message," he was fearful that amendments might do just that. On April 4, 1930, the Senate approved the measure by a 45-to-23 vote and sent it to the House of Representatives, where it was referred to the Military Affairs Committee.[8]

Norris hoped that the House would approve it quickly. In the previous Congress it had approved a similar measure by a large majority. Yet when presented with practically the identical bill, Norris wrote, "the three or four leaders who represent the Adminis-

[8] *Congressional Record*, 71st Cong., 2nd sess., Apr. 2, pp. 6357–77, Apr. 3, pp. 6399–6439, Apr. 4, 1930, pp. 6503, 6507, 6511. Senator Kenneth McKellar of Tennessee, assuaged by the provision calling for payment to the states in place of taxes, enthusiastically endorsed this measure. In his remarks Norris was particularly critical of the lobbying activities of Chester Gray, Washington representative of the American Farm Bureau Federation. Norris said Gray, who supported the Cyanamid Company's bid for Muscle Shoals at the sacrifice of performing his duties for agriculture, had testified to a falsehood regarding Muscle Shoals before the Senate Agriculture and Forestry Committee and then later, without anyone's consent, had the transcript altered in a material way before it was printed. Norris wanted to have Gray indicted for perjury but he discovered that at the time he testified, Gray was not under oath. Gray, Norris declared, had conferences with power interests and was seeking to promote their purposes and not the farmers' in the Muscle Shoals controversy. See also Norris's comments in *ibid.*, Apr. 16, pp. 7153–58, 7161, Apr. 17, 1930, p. 7180.

tration succeed in having the Committee report out a bill which sets aside and cancels every provision of the Senate resolution." This was done, a member of the Military Affairs Committee confidentially told Norris, to please President Hoover. The president did not want the Senate bill and this was one way of opposing it. But Norris did not believe that the president would veto his bill if the House approved it. Thus the conference committee designed to iron out differences between House and Senate versions became of critical importance.[9]

Meanwhile mayors of communities in the vicinity of Muscle Shoals wrote their congressmen complaining that 400,000 people in the area were suffering through no fault of their own. Every line of endeavor was curtailed because capital had declined to consider enterprises owing to uncertainty about government action. While espousing no particular proposal, the mayors urged Congress to "make every effort to secure final legislation on Muscle Shoals." [10] The House responded by approving at the end of May a measure that provided for leasing the government properties at Muscle Shoals. The matter then went into conference where a deadlock quickly became evident. President Hoover declined to intercede but said he would sign any compromise that emerged. To reach some agreement, the Senate conferees, McNary, Norris, and E. D. Smith, proposed that the nitrate plants be leased under the terms of the House proposal and that the power properties be administered under the Senate proposal. The House conferees refused to accept this agreement, leading Norris to conclude that they were trying to get the power for private enterprise and cared nothing about fertilizer,

[9] Norris to F. A. Good, May 15, 1930; *Congressional Record,* 71st Cong., 2nd sess., May 9, 1930, p. 8666. Senator Hugo Black at the time inserted into the *Record* an editorial by George Fort Milton of the *Chattanooga News* in which Milton argued that Hoover's 1928 campaign promises at Elizabethton, Tenn., and clarifying interviews indicated that Hoover would support government ownership at Muscle Shoals and government construction of the Cove Creek Dam. Milton felt that the president, if faced with no other alternative, would have to approve the Norris bill; see *Congressional Record,* 71st Cong., 2nd sess., Apr. 10, 1930, p. 6829.

[10] W. S. East to W. Frank James, Apr. 24, 1930 (Box 60, Judson King Papers, Manuscript Division, Library of Congress). East was mayor of Florence, Ala., while James was a Michigan congressman whose views were in accord with Norris's. He was chairman of the House Military Affairs Committee.

using it only as a subterfuge to get agricultural support for their proposal. When Congress adjourned on July 3, 1930, the matter was held over for the third session of the Seventy-first Congress, convening the following December.[11]

Before the third or short session convened, Senate progressives threw down the gauntlet to the president and called for the acceptance of the Norris bill or the certainty of an extra session of Congress. Administration leaders feared an extra session because they thought it would help split the Republican party and insure a Democratic victory in 1932. On December 12, 1930, shortly after the lame-duck session of the Seventy-first Congress convened, Norris released a statement supporting his public ownership proposal. He also explained the differences between the Senate and House measures before the conference committee. The House conferees argued for the leasing of the properties to manufacture fertilizer and to use the power for other purposes, thereby "making fertilizer in reality a by-product." To compromise these differences, the Senate conferees submitted a proposal for leasing the nitrate properties. The president was granted authority to lease them within a period of one year provided the plants engaged exclusively in the production and manufacture of fertilizer and fertilizer ingredients. The federal government, which would maintain operation of the power facilities at Muscle Shoals, would sell electricity to the lessee at rates similar to those charged "any State, county or municipality purchasing power from said corporation." Norris observed, "If those who are contending for a lease of the nitrate properties are honest and acting in good faith, and if they really want to use the power generated at the Government dam for the manufacture of fertilizer, for the benefit of the American farmer, then this proposition gives them the opportunity." [12]

[11] *Congressional Record*, 71st Cong., 2nd sess., June 16, 1930, pp. 10852–53; *Washington Herald*, June 14, 1930; Norris to B. H. Livesay, June 30, 1930. That Hoover favored the House proposal became clearly evident in the summer of 1930 when the president wrote a letter endorsing its chief author, B. Carroll Reece, a Tennessee Republican, and claiming, "The fact is that the House plan will secure developments of this great resource more effectively and more greatly in the interests of Tennessee than would the Senate plan"; see *New York Times*, July 27, 1930.

[12] *Omaha Bee*, Nov. 15, 1930; *Washington Herald*, Nov. 25, 1930 (stories by Fraser Edwards); draft statement by Norris about S. J. Res. 49, Dec. 12, 1930.

This compromise, of course, was designed to prevent private power interests from capturing the energy output of Muscle Shoals. With the defeat in the 1930 election of the sponsor of the leasing proposal, B. Carroll Reece, who, incidentally, lost despite endorsement by the president, the House conferees were in a mood to resolve differences with their Senate brethren on the conference committee. Each side now made concessions, though the Senate group was determined that the essence of Norris's proposals remain in the final measure. The most difficult problem, as it turned out, related to the distribution of power by the government. House conferees wanted power sold at the switchboard of the generating plant; Senate members insisted that the government have the right to build transmission lines with funds received from the sale of power and fertilizer. Norris was adamant on this point, preferring to let the bill die in committee rather than make concessions. But the House conferees capitulated. Thus the bill that emerged was much closer to what Norris and his Senate conferees desired than to what Reece and the Hoover administration wanted.[13]

On February 18, 1931, agreement was reached. The measure was approved by the House on February 20 and by the Senate three days later. It contained the provisions of Norris's resolution for the construction of Cove Creek Dam, public transmission lines, and government operation of power facilities and retained the House proposal for leasing the fertilizer plants. Before the Senate voted on February 23, 1931, Hiram Johnson congratulated Norris upon his "marvelous accomplishment," claiming that "the race is not always to the swift, nor the battle to the strong." Norris's pertinacity, industry, ability, and righteousness had prevailed. No matter what the ultimate fate of the bill, Johnson said, "this is the day of the achieve-

---

If the property were not leased within the stipulated one-year period, the government corporation responsible for power production would then engage in experimental production of fertilizer. See also Norris to King, Sept. 6, 1931.

[13] Norris to Allen J. Roulhac, Dec. 27, 1930; to Thompson, Dec. 29, 1930; Charles L. McNary to John H. McNary, Dec. 26, 1930 (Charles L. McNary Papers, Manuscript Division, Library of Congress); King to Cooke, Jan. 8, 1931 (Morris L. Cooke Papers (088-B), Franklin D. Roosevelt Library, Hyde Park, N.Y.); *Washington Star*, Dec. 28, 1930; *Congressional Record*, 71st Cong., 3rd sess., Jan. 27, pp. 3291–92, 3294–95, Jan. 28, pp. 3383, 3387–90, Feb. 17, 1931, pp. 5171–74. Charles McNary was chairman of the conference committee.

ment of the Senator from Nebraska. This is his hour of triumph." [14]

On February 28 President Hoover issued a statement: ". . . to be against Senator Norris' bill appears to be a cause for denunciation as being in league with the power companies." He had to decide whether it was desirable to change "federal policies from regulation of utilities to their ownership and operation" and, "in general, to consider the commonplace, unromantic facts which test the merits and demerits of this proposition as a business." As an engineer Hoover felt himself qualified to supervise such an analysis. Once it was completed, he would render his decision. Norris ridiculed Hoover's position: "The great engineer is seeking advice on an 'engineering project' from those who are not engineers, and when those who are not engineers tell the engineer what to do with 'an engineering project' the engineer will know whether to sign or veto the bill." The president's statement reminded Norris of a country judge who, at the conclusion of a lawsuit, "said he would take it under advisement for three days at which time he would render judgment for the plaintiff." [15]

On the last day of the session, March 3, 1931, Hoover in a blistering veto message rendered judgment for the plaintiff "after analyzing and riddling" Norris's resolution "from a business point of view." [16]

> This bill would launch the Federal Government upon a policy of ownership and operation of power utilities upon a basis of competition instead of by the proper government function of regulation for the protection of all the people. I hesitate to contemplate the future of our institutions, of our government, and of our country if the preoccupation of its officials is to be no longer the promotion of justice and equal opportunity but is to be devoted to barter in the markets. This is not liberalism, it is degeneration.

The president suggested that Alabama and Tennessee create a commission "to lease the plants at Muscle Shoals in the interest of

---

[14] *Congressional Record,* 71st Cong., 3rd sess., Feb. 20, pp. 5570–71, Feb. 23, 1931, pp. 5713, 5716. The House vote was 216 yeas, 153 nays; the vote in the Senate was 55 yeas, 28 nays.

[15] *Ibid.,* Mar. 2, 1931, pp. 6605–6 (both Hoover's statement and Norris's comment).

[16] Ray Lyman Wilbur and Arthur Mastick Hyde, eds., *The Hoover Policies* (New York, 1937), p. 317.

the local community and agriculture generally." If this were done, "it would get a war relic out of politics into the realm of public service." [17]

Refuting the message almost point by point, Norris said that "our President has not been fair." It was not a question of putting the government into the "power business"; it was there already. Government had not gone into Muscle Shoals as a power proposition. National defense was the primary purpose for its initial involvement, just as navigation and flood control were basic reasons for the government's continued interest in Muscle Shoals. Nor was it a question of government operation. Rather, Norris insisted, "it is a question of whether the Government should keep its own property." He concluded that "our President—perfectly conscientious in his belief, I think—is with the Power Trust." As a result multiple-purpose development of the Tennessee River would have to wait. Utility companies, already deep in politics on all levels, would continue "taking their toll from the poor people of the land, taxing every home, taxing every factory, taxing every citizen, and doing it out of property which belongs to the people, the streams which flow down hill, which God intended should be a blessing to the people rather than to the power interests." [18]

The veto message, Senator Hugo Black of Alabama announced, was the first blast of the 1932 campaign. The *Literary Digest* headlined its discussion "Muscle Shoals to Plague the 1932 Campaign." Hoover, understanding this situation, encouraged the states of Alabama and Tennessee to create a commission to perfect a plan for operating Muscle Shoals along lines suggested in his veto message. Norris, also realizing the political implications, denounced any plan for putting Muscle Shoals into the hands of private interests and feared that the president, using the forthcoming commission report, might try to sell or lease the properties without the consent of Congress.[19]

In November, 1931, the Muscle Shoals Inquiry Commission

[17] *Congressional Record*, 71st Cong., 3rd sess., Mar. 3, 1931, pp. 7046–48.

[18] *Ibid.*, pp. 7084–89, 7098. By a vote of 49 to 34 the Senate was unable to override the president's veto of S. J. Res. 49. See also Norris to Baker, Apr. 13, 1931.

[19] *Literary Digest*, Mar. 14, 1931, p. 7; *Labor*, Sept. 29, 1931; Norris to Marshall McNeill, Sept. 19, 1931; to Baker, Sept. 26, 1931.

recommended private operation for the manufacture of fertilizer. Hoover, explaining that the commission's conclusions were unanimous, promised to submit them to Congress "at an appropriate time." Norris said of the commission report that "under the cloak of relief to the farmer, the Power Trust wolf is safely and securely disguised" for granting to large corporations "the wonderful possibility of surplus power at Muscle Shoals." He was determined to reintroduce his bill once the new session convened, claiming that it would gain votes "because the other side had not been successful in presenting anything that was in any way a good solution." But Norris knew that if his measure was approved by Congress, the president would veto it and that ultimate victory could not come until a man of different outlook occupied the White House.[20]

As the first session of the Seventy-second Congress got under way, Norris admitted to being tired of the fight which had been going on "for the last ten or twelve years." But he had no thought of surrendering on Muscle Shoals. Great strides had been made, and Norris said that a public ownership bill possibly might be enacted over a presidential veto. However, leasing legislation was introduced and lengthily debated by the House Military Affairs Committee, while Norris's bill (S. J. Res. 15) was not reported out of the Senate Agriculture and Forestry Committee until March 14, 1932. It was placed too late on the calendar for passage at this session, postponing the Muscle Shoals problem until after the presidential election. Norris was not disappointed; he would rather be delayed "and then get it right" than succeed and have Hoover appoint the first members of the government corporation to operate Muscle Shoals. This plan, he realized, depended upon the Democratic party not nominating a candidate sympathetic to the power trust.[21]

[20] *Washington Herald*, Nov. 20, 1931; Muscle Shoals Inquiry Commission, *Muscle Shoals: A Plan for the Use of the United States Properties on the Tennessee River* . . . (Washington, D.C., 1931), pp. 13–14, 17–20; Norris to Roulhac, Nov. 17, 1931; "Interview of Mrs. Harris Baldwin and Miss Gwen Geach with Senator Norris," Nov. 11, 1931 (Box 40, League of Women Voters Papers, Manuscript Division, Library of Congress).

[21] Norris to M. V. Walker, Dec. 19, 1931; to Percy E. Quin, Jan. 5, 1932; to Josephus Daniels, Mar. 17, 1932. See also editorials in *Philadelphia Record*, Mar. 11, 1932; *Waterbury* (Conn.) *Republican*, Mar. 15, 1932. Both editorials supported Norris's position and favored government operation of the facilities at Muscle Shoals.

Too many Democrats in Congress seemed to be in accord with it. After the death of Percy Quin in February, 1932, the House Military Affairs Committee, responsible for Muscle Shoals measures, came under the influence of Democrats who disagreed with Quin's public ownership views. In the Senate Agriculture and Forestry Committee John H. Bankhead insisted on holding hearings, although the other members were willing to report Norris's resolution without them. As a result of Bankhead's tactics it was not possible to get the bill onto the floor. Thus in the first session of the Seventy-second Congress the Democratic allies of the Hoover administration were responsible for the failure to enact a public ownership bill, while the House, controlled by the Democrats, approved a leasing measure. Unless the Democrats chose a winning candidate firmly committed to public ownership, Norris envisioned continuing conflict over the disposition of Muscle Shoals. Its fate, in short, depended upon the outcome of the 1932 presidential election. In August, 1932, Norris wrote of his public ownership bill that "if Roosevelt is elected it will undoubtedly be passed as soon as he is inaugurated and will no doubt be signed by him." [22]

Thus the president and the power trust throughout the era of Republican ascendancy were allies. To be sure, the trust had powerful friends in both houses of Congress among both parties. But always a handful of progressives, led by Norris and favoring government ownership and operation of the facilities at Muscle Shoals, were on hand to challenge leasing proposals and to convince their congressional colleagues of the righteousness of their views. Because of their opposition, after more than a decade of controversy no disposition had been made of the Muscle Shoals properties. Two public

[22] Norris to Daniels, Mar. 17, 1932; to Roulhac, Apr. 28, 1932; John P. Robertson to William D. Jardine, July 9, 1932; Norris to William J. Levering, Aug. 20, 1932. In a speech at the Cosmos Club, June 25, 1932, Harry Slattery paid tribute to Norris's efforts and remarked that, aside from Senator Hugo Black, southern representatives usually favored "giving away a great birthright for a mess of pottage, and that the Muscle Shoals development is going to mean more to the economic development of the South than the cotton fields, the lumber resources, the plantations, or the other great resources of the South." Slattery, a native of Greenville, S.C., was being honored for his quarter century of public service in the field of conservation. He could have added a handful of names to join Hugo Black's as exceptions to his generalization; see *Congressional Record,* 72nd Cong., 1st sess., July 15, 1932, p. 15459.

ownership measures had passed Congress only to meet with presidential vetoes. Throughout the controversy Norris had played the leading role as the chief proponent of public ownership and as the chief antagonist of the power trust. In 1924 he had been handily re-elected to a third term in the Senate; in 1930 his enemies made an overwhelming effort to prevent him from returning for a fourth term. It is this campaign which must now be examined.

"Conservatism Hits Bottom"

32

In April, 1929, the *American Mercury* published an anonymous article by a Washington correspondent lambasting "The Progressives of the Senate." Excepting only Norris and Thomas J. Walsh, they were labeled "a sorry bunch of weaklings and time servers." With the exception of Norris, they all played the political game and voted "right" when party leaders insisted. But Norris was "all that he is said to be," namely, "a fighter of great principle, courage and tenacity." The mystery was how a man as intelligent, honest, and uncompromising as Norris got elected to the Senate. In 1930 all of Norris's attributes came into play as his opponents made a strenuous effort to defeat him.[1]

When this article appeared, its author observed that Norris was telling his friends that he was through, that he would not seek re-election, that the fight was futile and unavailing. As late as September, 1929, Norris was still saying that he did not intend to be a candidate. Yet in September he also claimed that if he desired, he could secure renomination and re-election. A month later Norris announced his candidacy for re-election in what one reporter called "a remarkable human document outlining his political philosophy."[2]

---

[1] "The Progressives of the Senate," *American Mercury,* 16, no. 64 (Apr., 1929): 385, 390–91.

[2] George W. Norris to Harvey Newbranch, Aug. 8, Sept. 21, 1929; to Frank A. Harrison, Sept. 5, 1928; to Val J. Peter, Sept. 12, 1929; *Washington Herald,*

Early in October an intimate friend visited Washington and reported that "our only struggle is to keep Norris from running as an independent." He found Norris "in better spirits than I have ever seen him." What had caused Norris to seek re-election had nothing to do with inner torment and travail. Mounting antagonism toward the Hoover administration was responsible. First, a bitter political foe, former Governor Samuel R. McKelvie, a member of the Federal Farm Board, entered the Nebraska senatorial primary as the administration's candidate. Then, shortly after McKelvie's decision, James Francis Burke, counsel for the Republican National Committee and a presidential adviser, made a speech at a New York dinner in which he denounced Norris and other Republican progressives as "pygmies and obstructionists." Burke followed other speakers who had demanded "a house-cleaning of Progressives in the Senate." [3]

Announcing his decision on October 29, 1929, Norris admitted that he had originally intended to retire at the end of his term. But recent political events had destroyed those hopes. Nebraska, he said, "is to be singled out in the coming Senatorial primary campaign as one of the chief battlegrounds for the control of the United States Senate." The state Republican organization would be strongly supported by "the Old Guard stand-pat machine." The appointment of Otto H. Kahn, a New York financier, as treasurer of the Republican Senatorial Campaign Committee, Norris said, could only mean that McKelvie's campaign would be endowed with all the support administration forces could muster. Rising to this challenge, Norris retorted, "I would rather be right than be regular." He pleaded guilty to the charge of party irregularity and realized that his fight would not be an easy one—"with practically no newspaper support, with no means of publicity, and with the main newspapers of the State engaged in a campaign of misrepresentation." But, he

Oct. 30, 1929 (story by Fraser Edwards). Newbranch was the able editor of the *Omaha World-Herald,* a Democratic newspaper always opposed to Norris. In the August letter Norris reminisced about the 1924 campaign and related the story about the telegram Paul Anderson intercepted in which Norris stated he would not run for re-election. Though the story appears in the Norris literature, I have been able to find no evidence about its validity and present in Chapter 15 findings to the contrary.

[3] Harrison to C. A. Sorensen, Oct. 8, 1929 (C. A. Sorensen Papers, Nebraska State Historical Society); *Washington Herald,* Oct. 30, 1929.

explained, "I would much rather be defeated than to be deceived." On January 4, 1930, in McCook during the Christmas recess he filed for renomination for U.S. senator on the Republican ticket.[4]

With the primaries scheduled for August, Norris could not seriously concern himself with campaigning until Congress adjourned in July. In the interim, however, the political situation began to arouse interest. Once Norris announced his intentions, former Governor Samuel McKelvie claimed he was not interested in the nomination and General John J. Pershing refused to consider requests that he enter the race. Interest centered chiefly on Governor Arthur J. Weaver, Lieutenant Governor George A. Williams, State Treasurer Willis M. Stebbins, and Dr. Jennie Callfas, active in the cause of prohibition, as Norris's opponents in the primary. Early in the campaign a Nebraska correspondent assured William Allen White that German voters or those of German descent would support Norris, but that "Republican bosses" were depending on women to defeat him in the primary because he had supported a "wet" and a Catholic in 1928 and was not a "regular" Republican. A campaign stressing the temperance, morality, and fearlessness of Norris, White was informed, could probably obviate this appeal to women voters.[5]

But Norris said that "the real objectors" were the representatives of the power trust; they would not fight under their own names but would provide funds to anyone opposing his candidacy. This fact explained the candidacy of Dr. Jennie Callfas, head of the Anti-saloon League in Nebraska. With his support of prohibition, Norris

---

[4] *Washington Herald,* Oct. 30, 1929; Norris to Walter Locke, Nov. 6, 1929; to William Allen White, Nov. 7, Dec. 21, 1929; *Washington Star,* Jan. 5, 1930. See also *Baltimore Sun,* Oct. 13, 1929, "Norris of Nebraska" (editorial). The *Omaha World-Herald* published editorials favorable to Norris and his candidacy at this time, and the *Omaha Bee-News,* a Hearst paper, had been active "in exposing the intrigues and inside workings of the Power Trust." With the further exception of a few daily newspapers, most papers were against Norris. He realized that the *Omaha World-Herald* would support the Democratic candidate in the November election; see Norris to White, Dec. 21, 1929. White's paper, the *Emporia Daily Gazette,* published several editorials on Norris's behalf; see, for example, those of Nov. 2, 1929, and Jan. 25, 1930.

[5] J. P. Baldwin to White, Jan. 13, 1930 (White sent a copy of this letter to Norris); *Grand Island Independent,* Apr. 4, 1930. Arthur Weaver soon decided to seek another term as governor and State Treasurer Stebbins remained as the only serious Republican candidate to oppose Norris.

was convinced that any fight made against him on this score had to come "from some unknown and unexplained reason other than prohibition." Opposition on religious grounds he expected, but, like the power question, he realized that it would never "sail under its true name." Thus, with little newspaper support, Norris understood that the primary would be one in which he would have to rely upon "loyal friends scattered over the State" who supported "the principles of Government" which he had long advocated.[6]

A further dimension existed in this campaign. While the Republican organization in Nebraska had not always aided Norris, never did it actively try to defeat him. Now Norris heard ugly rumors that the Republican National Committee was raising $100,000 to be used against him and that two men, claiming to represent "large Eastern interests," were in Omaha surveying the political situation by interviewing leading bankers and corporation officials. Moreover, canvasses were under way by early June to determine who would be the strongest Republican to oppose him; then all but this candidate would withdraw. On the Democratic side, Norris learned, funds would be used to get numerous candidates on all levels into the race to keep Democrats from crossing party lines and voting for him in the Republican primary.[7]

C. A. Sorensen, the only state official openly supporting Norris, reported, after traveling throughout Nebraska in May and June, that he did not think the senator had anything to fear. "The head of the W.C.T.U. is one of his strongest supporters, and scores of the leading ministers are for him." All Norris had to do was tour the state and let the voters see him. To insure a Norris victory, Sorensen made arrangements for a four-page broadside containing statements from prominent people who wanted Norris returned to the Senate. Meanwhile at the end of June Norris "was very much surprised"

[6] Norris to Francis P. Matthews, Feb. 18, 1930; to Fred A. Marsh, Mar. 15, 1930; to Leslie G. Hurd, Apr. 8, 1930. Dr. Jennie Callfas was a former Democratic National Committeewoman from Nebraska. She supported Hoover in 1928 and left her party. In the 1930 primary campaign, after some hesitation, she decided to seek the Democratic senatorial nomination and thereby not challenge Norris.

[7] Norris to Robert Smith, May 22, June 2, 1930; to A. O. Abbott, Jr., June 4, 1930.

when former Senator Gilbert M. Hitchcock entered the race. Hitchcock, the best vote-getter available to the Democrats, would prevent large numbers of Democrats from crossing party lines and supporting him in the primary.[8]

Hitchcock was not the last candidate to announce before the period for filing ended on July 3, 1930. On July 1 at about 12:30 A.M. at a party in Broken Bow a young friend of Norris's noticed that a man named Paul Johnson, who had "some connection with the power people," was called out of the room by the manager of the local Skaggs Safeway grocery store, whose name was George W. Norris. The two men talked again the next day and early on the morning of July 3 the senator's young friend learned "that this Norris had filed for United States Senator on the Republican ticket." When asked what his idea was, "Grocer" Norris replied, "I think I might be elected and can you blame me." [9]

The filing of Grocer Norris was mailed from Broken Bow on July 2. It did not reach the office of Secretary of State Frank Marsh until July 5. The period for filing ended on July 3. Because the envelope had been postmarked at Broken Bow within the prescribed time, Secretary Marsh accepted it. But Attorney General C. A. Sorensen, a devoted Norris supporter, ruled that all filings not actually received by the secretary of state on or before July 3, 1930, were invalid. Therefore, according to Sorensen's ruling, which was upheld two weeks later by Nebraska Chief Justice John Goss, Grocer Norris's filing was invalid.[10]

[8] Sorensen to Harrison, June 20, 1930; to Judson King, June 30, 1930; King to Sorensen, July 1, 1930 (all items in Sorensen Papers); King to "Friends of Senator Norris," July 2, 1930 (Morris L. Cooke Papers, Franklin D. Roosevelt Library, Hyde Park, N.Y.); Norris to John G. Maher, June 21, 1930; to John J. Keegan, June 30, 1930. Senators William Borah, Hiram Johnson, Robert M. La-Follette, Jr., Bronson Cutting, and Robert Howell, Bishop Francis J. McConnell, William Allen White, Gifford Pinchot, numerous Washington correspondents, and others gladly promised King statements.

[9] Yale B. Huffman to John P. Robertson, July 3, 1930.

[10] Smith to Robert B. Howell, July 5, 1930 (copy in Norris Papers); *Omaha Bee-News,* July 6, 1930. Robert Smith, clerk of the district court of Douglas County in Omaha, filed a formal protest, but Secretary of State Frank Marsh, a "standpatter," announced on July 15, 1930, that he would rule in favor of Grocer Norris. A legal battle seemed imminent, but Attorney General Sorensen's insistence that "a document is filed with an officer when it is placed in his custody and deposited by him in the place where his papers and records are usually kept"

News of the filing of Grocer Norris attracted national attention, aroused popular indignation, and brought on a Senate investigation. Norris called the scheme "one of the most dastardly tricks yet undertaken by any man or set of men who lay any claim to respectability," recognizing at once that his namesake was merely a pawn of "Republican standpat machine politicians." He also recognized that unless Sorensen's ruling was upheld, his renomination in the Republican primary would be "a physical impossibility." He therefore made plans to withdraw from the contest and to petition for nomination in the general election as an independent candidate for senator. It is to be doubted that Norris took these plans seriously. Those supporting his namesake would hardly reveal themselves or spend the money necessary to prosecute an appeal through the courts, while the public reaction could be beneficial to his candidacy. Indeed, reports reached Washington that he would not have "a great deal of trouble in winning." [11]

As soon as Congress adjourned, Norris's secretary returned to Nebraska to set up campaign headquarters in Lincoln. The senator remained in Washington for most of July to participate in the special session. While there would be no lack of finances on the part of those seeking his defeat, Norris had to rely on the generosity of faithful friends and followers. Cornelia Bryce Pinchot was the most

prevailed. An effort to play the same trick on Sorensen failed when an Omaha man with the same name developed "cold feet" at the last minute and refused to file; see *Labor,* July 15, 1930; Norris to J. C. McGowan, July 16, 1930. On July 18, 1930, Chief Justice Goss ruled that the filing of George W. Norris of Broken Bow was void.

[11] Norris to Smith, July 10 and 11, 1930; to Robertson, July 12, 1930; John J. Carson to Morris L. Cooke, July 10, 1930 (Cooke Papers). Norris sent Robertson a letter of withdrawal in the event his namesake's name was not removed from the primary ballot. Shortly after filing, George W. Norris of Broken Bow, Nebr., disappeared and took his family with him. Grocer Norris previously had been in business in Kearney: in 1927 a petition of bankruptcy had been filed in his name there; see Thomas E. Pugh to Sorensen, July 17, 1930 (Sorensen Papers). The Aug., 1930, issue of *Plain Talk* carried an article, "Norris, of Nebraska," by a Washington correspondent. Both the editor of the magazine and the author of the article endorsed Norris in his campaign for re-election. But the issue was in press before the Grocer Norris incident attracted national attention; see *Congressional Record,* 71st Cong., special sess. of the Senate, July 19, 1930, pp. 315–17. The editorial, "Norris of Nebraska," *New York World,* July 19, 1930, did discuss the incident. Norris carefully reviewed the history of the campaign in a lengthy letter to Bruce Bliven, editor of *New Republic,* July 15, 1930.

generous. She sent a check on July 3, 1930, before the Grocer Norris story broke, for $2,000. Norris returned it with the suggestion that a smaller check would meet all of his expenses.[12]

Thereafter his campaign began to increase in tempo. Senators William E. Borah and Hiram Johnson were asked to speak in Nebraska while en route to their homes. Since the essence of the attack against Norris focused on his support of Alfred E. Smith in 1928, it was imperative that Borah, who had served as Hoover's campaign manager, appear in the state on his behalf. Norris meanwhile planned to be in Lincoln on Saturday, July 26, to make his opening speech over the radio. Since he was charged "with not doing anything, with not having any influence, with not being a good Republican," Norris considered reviewing his record in Congress.[13]

He arrived in Nebraska on July 26. In Omaha he briefly commented on the failure of the Federal Farm Board to aid agriculture. Then that evening before the Nebraska Epworth League Assembly in Lincoln, speaking on "Prohibition and Its Enforcement," he officially opened his campaign for renomination. The statewide radio address planned for that afternoon never materialized. Norris now doubted that it would be wise for him to attempt a speaking campaign because of the intense summer heat and hot winds, though he planned to keep his commitments for the first week at least. He did not think it wise to ask senators and others who wished to aid in his campaign to come to Nebraska until cool weather set in and audiences could be assured. Unless the weather changed, Norris was convinced that a speaking campaign, besides debilitating him, would not attract people.[14]

[12] Robertson to King, July 11, 1930; Norris to Cornelia Bryce Pinchot, July 5, 1930. Robertson sought former Governor Adam McMullen as head of the campaign organization and noted that many Republicans were concerned lest Norris leave the ticket and thereby jeopardize the chances of other Republican candidates; see Robertson to Norris, July 14, 1930.

[13] Mildred Olsen to Adam McMullen, July 18, 1930; Norris to Robertson, July 19, 1930. For an example of the criticism that Norris was not serving his Nebraska constituency, see E. P. Stephenson to J. V. Johnson, July 26, 1930 (copy in Norris Papers). Stephenson was active in the campaign of State Treasurer Willis Stebbins. While Borah did not appear in the primary campaign, he sent a statement endorsing Norris which was widely disseminated.

[14] *New York Times,* July 27, 1930; Norris to McMullen, July 27, 1930; to Robert M. LaFollette, Jr., July 27, 1930.

In this campaign, as in every one he had waged, Norris accepted no invitations to stay at the home of friends, staying instead at a hotel and making himself accessible to all who wished to see him. Though Adam McMullen, ex-governor of Nebraska, was his official campaign manager, its actual direction was handled by his secretary John P. Robertson, who operated from a room in the Lindell Hotel in Lincoln. At the end of July he wrote a Washington newspaperman, "I cannot believe there is any chance of Senator Norris being defeated." But he was not exuding confidence. In a bitter campaign with unscrupulous opponents, some of whom were endeavoring to inflame the religious issue, anything could happen. In Washington Judson King was raising funds. Contributions came from throughout the nation and at the end of July he sent Robertson a check for $1,000.[15]

Owing to the excessively hot weather, Norris used radio to get his message to as large an audience as possible. He spoke at local stations in Lincoln, Clay Center, and Shenandoah, Iowa, in the week before the primary. Denouncing the Grocer Norris episode, he reiterated his record as a friend of the farmer and proclaimed his support of prohibition. He also unsuccessfully challenged State Treasurer Willis Stebbins to debate the issues in an effort to expose his leading opponent's vague generalities and claims. On Monday, August 11, 1930, Norris concluded his campaign with a speech in the afternoon at Holdrege in his old congressional district and one that evening before friends and neighbors in the Temple Theater in McCook. But Norris had not campaigned alone. Senator Robert B. Howell had spoken in the eastern end of the state while Norris, as was his custom, spoke in the rural regions and did not concentrate upon the more populous eastern towns.

An alleged Ku Klux Klan political slate, labeled "Nebraska Good Government League," had endorsed Willis Stebbins because of Norris's support of Smith in 1928. Surveying the situation from

[15] Robertson to Mrs. Huffman, July 28, 1930; to W. D. Jamieson, July 31, 1930; King to Robertson, July 31, 1930. Before the primary Bishop Frederick Leete of the Nebraska-Iowa area of the Methodist Episcopal Church sent a letter endorsing State Treasurer Stebbins to 408 Methodist ministers who were members of the Nebraska conference. Earlier the bishop had sent a letter endorsing Norris. No reason for the switch was given nor was Norris's name mentioned in the letter endorsing Stebbins; see *Nebraska State Journal,* Aug. 1, 1930.

Lincoln, John Robertson claimed that "the Klan is split right down the middle, in as much as many Klansmen are very enthusiastically supporting the Senator." More of a problem than Klansmen were clergymen. The Methodist bishop of Iowa and Nebraska, Frederick D. Leete, had endorsed Stebbins, and Robertson found opposition among Lutheran ministers as well. Combined with the lack of newspaper support and the extremely hot weather, Robertson had much to worry about. Still he was pleased with the crowds Norris attracted. In Broken Bow, a town of about 3,000 inhabitants, for example, at an open-air meeting Norris spoke to approximately 5,000 people. On August 2, 1930, Robertson confided to Judson King, "I cannot believe there is any possibility of him being defeated." [16]

The primary was the liveliest in the history of Nebraska. It attracted national attention. In the August 6, 1930, issue of the *New Republic* Judson King reviewed the shabby and sordid campaign from ex-Governor McKelvie's interest through the Grocer Norris incident. King made much of power trust hostility to Norris, mentioning prominent utility company agents active in opposition to his candidacy with ample funds at their disposal. He said that his office, where he had been collecting material for a Norris broadside, had been broken into twice and only items pertaining to it had been removed. But after surveying the situation, the *New York Times* speculated that both Norris and Hitchcock would triumph in their respective primaries.[17]

For a little more than two weeks, since July 26, 1930, Norris had brought his message to the people of Nebraska, asking for renomination solely upon his record and pledging to continue the same course. Shirtsleeves rolled above his elbows, positive and vigorous in his presentation, aroused at the concerted efforts and unscrupulous methods directed against him, Norris at sixty-nine years of age

---

[16] *Nebraska State Journal*, Aug. 4, 1930; Robertson to C. W. McConaughy, Aug. 5, 1930; to King, Aug. 2 and 5, 1930; to Luke Wilson, June 2, 1931. Only five newspapers with any sizable circulation supported Norris: *Lincoln Herald*, a weekly, *Omaha Bee-News, Grand Island Independent, Norfolk Press,* and *Hastings Daily Tribune.* The *McCook Daily Gazette* on Aug. 8, 1930, came out against Norris because he favored multiple-purpose tributary control and not just local flood control relief as editor H. D. Strunk desired.

[17] Judson King, "The Fight against Norris," *New Republic*, Aug. 6, 1930, pp. 332–34; *New York Times*, Aug. 10, 1930.

was in fighting trim. In all, slightly less than $3,000 was spent on his primary campaign. Senator Bronson Cutting contributed $1,000 and Mrs. Gifford Pinchot an equal amount; Judson King gave $500 and Norris gave his own check for $200. The remainder was in small amounts of $1 to $25 each.[18]

On Tuesday, August 12, 1930, the voters of Nebraska went to the polls. Norris handily won renomination, defeating his nearest opponent, State Treasurer Stebbins, by more than 30,000 votes, 108,471 to 74,486. Gilbert M. Hitchcock easily won the Democratic nomination. Republican regulars immediately claimed that Stebbins would have been nominated but for a wholesale influx of Democratic voters into the Republican primary. Undoubtedly, thousands of Democrats did vote for Norris, but the *Lincoln Star* insisted that "it does not appear from cold inspection of the figures in the Senatorial race that the result would have been different had they stayed at home." Stebbins defeated Norris in only eleven of Nebraska's ninety-three counties; of these, only one, Lancaster, gave him a handsome majority. Norris carried his home county, Red Willow, 1,489 to 289, while Stebbins won his home county, Dawson, 1,689 to 1,556.[19]

In Washington on the day of the Nebraska primary Senator Simeon Fess, the new chairman of the Republican National Committee, emerged from a conference with the president and said that in his opinion the committee should support Norris if he won renomination. This statement was brought to the attention of the president and subsequently Senator Fess modified it, claiming it a matter for the Republican Senatorial Campaign Committee to decide. But Senator James E. Watson of Indiana, an administration stalwart, declared himself opposed to "any covert action" against Norris.[20]

Norris left McCook the morning after the election to fill several speaking engagements and to visit his grandchildren in California. In Lincoln John Robertson immediately began preparations for the

[18] *Omaha Bee-News,* Aug. 10, 1930; *Lincoln Star,* Aug. 14, 1930. Norris personally paid his filing fee of $50 and his traveling expenses.

[19] *Lincoln Star,* Aug. 15, 1930; *Grand Island Independent,* Sept. 12, 1930, "Analyzing the Official Figures" (editorial); Addison E. Sheldon, *Nebraska: The Land and the People* (Chicago, 1931), 1: 1067.

[20] *Washington Post,* Aug. 14, 1930.

general election. By mid-September Norris was back in McCook after an "immensely" enjoyable visit to California. He spoke at various meetings but was not anxious to campaign seriously, informing two of his sisters that it was "going to be a very disagreeable campaign." The fact that Gilbert M. Hitchcock, his Democratic opponent, owned the largest newspaper in Nebraska, the *Omaha World-Herald,* which was already copying editorials from "stand pat Republican papers," only added to his woes. But, basically, Norris believed he was going to win.[21]

Early in July for two days and again in late September for four days a Select Committee on Senatorial Campaign Expenditures, headed by Gerald P. Nye of North Dakota, appeared in Nebraska to investigate the tactics employed against Norris in the primary. Nothing sensational was unearthed, and Norris did not involve himself with the work of the committee, though he did attend some of its hearings. Preparing for his campaign, Norris devised a strategy which consisted of utilizing the findings of the committee, emphasizing his record, and criticizing Hitchcock's views on public issues. When a third candidate, Mrs. Beatrice Fenton Craig, challenged him to a joint debate, Norris replied that if Senator Hitchcock desired to debate with him, he would be glad to do so, but he was too busy to waste valuable time "in advertising his understudy." At the last moment she had entered the senatorial race as a candidate by petition.[22]

On September 24, 1930, Nebraska's three candidates for the U.S. Senate spoke before the annual banquet in Lincoln of the Nebraska League of Women Voters. Norris then returned to McCook for several more days of quiet planning before meeting a speaking engagement at Pawnee City. His staff consisted of Mildred Olsen, who handled his correspondence and attended to details in

[21] Olsen to C. A. Filmer, Aug. 19, 1930; Robertson to Harry Slattery, Aug. 13, 1930; Norris to Clara N. Rakestraw, Sept. 17, 1930; to Emma Norris Bradstock, Sept. 17, 1930. Former Governor Adam McMullen announced that he, too, thought Norris would win handily on Nov. 4, 1930. McMullen gave Norris's battles for the relief of agriculture as the chief reason for his support of the senator; see *Omaha Bee-News,* Sept. 18, 1930.

[22] *Omaha Bee-News,* Sept. 23, 1930; Norris to C. B. Turner, Sept. 20, 1930; to Beatrice Fenton Craig, Sept. 25, 1930.

McCook, and John P. Robertson, who managed the campaign from a room in the Cornhusker Hotel in Lincoln. Robertson felt confident, though he expected "a real fight." Officially he cooperated with the Republican State Committee, which, rather than split the party asunder, did not dump Norris. He considered the possibility of a wide distribution of the Nye committee hearings because much of it "never saw the light of day in the Nebraska papers." [23]

On Monday, October 13, 1930, at a meeting in Fremont Norris began his campaign in earnest with "one real speech a day from there on out to the finish, with perhaps several afternoon speeches sandwiched in." Robertson, further contemplating the dimensions of the fight against Norris, confessed that he now thought the situation critical. The opposition had been making considerable headway, "moving heaven and earth to organize the State for Hitchcock." The Democratic organization and the "stand pat element in the Republican party" were sending workers everywhere, advertising heavily, and securing the support of Republican newspapers. With Hitchcock vowing he would not assist in repealing the Eighteenth Amendment or weakening the Volstead law, Robertson thought the church organizations and the "drys" would "flop either way." Moreover, prominent Knights of Columbus were working "like beavers" among Catholic voters to swing them to Hitchcock, while advertising in hostile rural newspapers emphasized Norris's sympathy for labor at the expense of the farmer. No opportunity was overlooked and nothing comparable was being done by the Republican State Committee for Norris and the other Republican candidates. It claimed difficulty in raising funds, inferring that this was the case because Norris was on the ticket. But when Robertson expressed willingness to open separate headquarters, the committee would have none of it, realizing that if Norris did not win, no Republican would. Robertson, hoping the situation would "iron itself out," relied on Norris's ability as a campaigner to stem the tide.[24]

Norris set the tone of his campaign at the outset when he de-

[23] *Omaha World-Herald,* Sept. 25, 1930; *McCook Daily Gazette,* Sept. 26, 1930; Olsen to B. F. Galloway, Oct. 1, 1930; Robertson to Edward P. Costigan, Oct. 4, 1930; to Edward Keating, Oct. 4, 1930.
[24] Robertson to Keating, Oct. 9, 1930.

clared, "My political doctrine is that a public official such as a United States Senator never ought to perform an official action, never ought to cast an official vote which his conscience tells him is wrong; that he ought to be willing to listen to advice and to reason, but in the end he must be the exclusive judge of his own vote." Any U.S. senator who behaved differently was not worthy of holding the office. Speaking day in and day out, sometimes by himself, somtimes sharing the platform with Arthur J. Weaver and C. A. Sorensen, seeking re-election as governor and attorney general respectively, Norris reviewed his record, compared it with that of Hitchcock when both were in the Senate, talked of the tariff and its inability to aid agriculture, discussed multi-purpose tributary development, and denounced his opponents. The radio, which he had used extensively in the primary, he now used rarely, preferring to appear before as many voters as possible.[25]

Meanwhile Robertson helped open a Norris-for-Senator Club in Lincoln with aid from the American Federation of Labor in Nebraska. He secured permission from Nebraska Farm Bureau officials to use their names on its official stationery. And he was endeavoring to do the same with the president of the Farmers Union. Though the Republican State Committee provided no funds for advertising or speaking schedules, Robertson contacted William E. Borah and William Allen White; the Idaho senator agreed to make at least two speeches in the state. Robert M. LaFollette, Jr., made three speeches for Norris. The Hearst paper, the *Omaha Bee-News,* was the only major newspaper to endorse Norris. Robertson hoped that the Norris-for-Senator Club would disseminate campaign literature and make up for the deficiency of the state committee in this matter. Though the opposition was unrelenting "in not leaving a stone unturned," by mid-October he began to feel more confident. But as Judson King observed, "It is a desperate contest. The Hooverites and the power trust are fighting Norris to the death." [26]

[25] Campaign literature and drafts of speeches are to be found in the Norris Papers. Lack of funds probably was the basic reason radio was not used. Norris also preferred to speak extemporaneously and felt limited by the time requirements of broadcasting.

[26] Robertson to W. C. Roberts, Oct. 15, 1930; to Carl F. Marsh, Oct. 18 and 21, 1930; to LaFollette, Oct. 23, 1930; King to "Norris Broadside Contributors

Robertson thought that King exaggerated in emphasizing the power problem. As he viewed it, the fight against Norris centered on his "irregularity." In his speeches Norris met this charge head on, reviewing his record and contrasting it continually with that of Hitchcock. Meanwhile the Nye committee unearthed the fact that Willis Stebbins, state treasurer and Norris's chief rival in the primary, had financed with his own funds the project to place Grocer Norris on the Republican primary ballot. While more sensational findings were revealed later, this news undoubtedly won sympathy and votes for Norris in the closing days of the campaign. On the Sunday before election Robertson confidently predicted that Norris would win "by a nice majority." The *Omaha Bee-News,* after surveying the state, declared that Norris "was rapidly gaining in strength as election day approached." [27]

On Tuesday, November 3, 1930, Nebraska voters went to the polls and re-elected Norris for a fourth term in the U.S. Senate over Gilbert M. Hitchcock by the handsome margin of 247,118 to 172,795. The overall election, however, was a Democratic victory. C. A. Sorensen was the only Republican seeking a statewide office to be re-elected. Charles W. Bryan defeated Arthur J. Weaver for the governorship, and two additional Democratic congressmen were elected, giving the party control of four of Nebraska's six congressional districts. Norris carried every congressional district but the second, which included Omaha. He carried every county but three, and in thirty counties he had more than a two-to-one majority. His re-election, he claimed, was more than a personal triumph; it was

and Others," Oct. 21, 1930 (copy in Cooke Papers). In the *Lincoln Star,* Oct. 20, 1930, appeared a story in which C. B. Steward, secretary of the Nebraska Farm Bureau Federation, endorsed Norris: "Mr. Steward declared labor legislation for which Norris had fought was as important to agriculture as a prosperous working class was necessary to furnish a good agricultural market." William Allen White sent a statement endorsing Norris but was unable to visit the state. The *Grand Island Independent* and the *Hastings Daily Tribune* supported Norris, but they did not have as large a circulation as the *Omaha Bee-News.*

[27] Robertson to King, Oct. 24, 1930; to Emerson R. Purcell, Nov. 2, 1930; *Lincoln Star,* Oct. 23, 1930; *Omaha Bee-News,* Nov. 3, 1930. The Nye committee also learned that Walter Head, Chicago and Omaha bank executive and chairman of the board of the Nebraska Power Company, had contributed $4,000 to finance a straw vote to ascertain the strength of possible primary opponents for Norris; see *New York Times,* Oct. 23, 1930.

"a great victory for political progress and independence as against monopoly and machine politics." [28]

Shortly after the election Norris wrote to William Green, president of the American Federation of Labor, expressing gratitude for the support given him by organized working men in the cities of Nebraska. Norris had contributed $1,000 of his own money to the Republican State Committee while Robertson contributed $956, of which $870 was received from outside Nebraska. These funds, combined with a $708 balance from the primary, constituted the money with which Robertson directed the campaign. The support of farmer and labor groups played a significant role in bringing Norris's views to the attention of the voters.[29]

After the election the Senate investigating committee continued probing the primary. Norris said that his namesake from Broken Bow had violated a state statute in accepting funds for filing and that Willis Stebbins, for making a false return by not listing the money he had given Grocer Norris, had violated the law and should be prosecuted. Legal action against all parties involved "would go farther than anything else to have our laws obeyed and respected." Noting the election results, Norris said that members of the Repub-

[28] Norris victory statement, Nov., 1930. For the election results, see Sheldon, *Nebraska,* 1: 1073. Douglas County and Omaha went heavily for Hitchcock. Hitchcock said he had become "a candidate less by reason of a desire to reenter public life than for the purpose of strengthening the Democratic ticket and for the purpose of maintaining the integrity of the Democratic party in Nebraska"; see *Omaha World-Herald,* Nov. 6, 1930. Robertson had predicted that of the three top Republican candidates seeking statewide approval, Sorensen would be the top vote-getter, Norris's majority would be by about 73,000 votes, and Weaver "would have the battle of his life to be reelected"; see Robertson to Sorensen, Nov. 17, 1930; Sorensen to Robertson, Dec. 27, 1930 (both in Sorensen Papers). For a moving account of the reception and banquet given the senator and his wife by their friends in McCook before they returned to Washington after the election, see *McCook Tribune,* Nov. 14, 1930.

[29] Norris to William Green, Nov. 8, 1930; *Lincoln Star,* Nov. 15, 1930; *Grand Island Independent,* Nov. 23, 1930. Of the $870 raised out of state for Norris, $500 was from W. T. Rawleigh of Freeport, Ill., and $250 had been raised by Judson King. King filed a statement of his expenditures before the Select Committee on Senatorial Campaign Expenditures. He said that 200,000 copies of the Norris broadside had been printed. Throughout the entire campaign he had collected $3,658.17 from prominent people outside Nebraska. Some of this money he sent to Nebraska; most of it went to pay expenses incurred in printing the broadside; see King to Gerald P. Nye, Dec. 16, 1930. The Railroad Brotherhoods as well as the A. F. of L. supported Norris.

lican State Committee should be replaced with more progressive men.[30]

Stebbins's statement on October 23, 1930, about supporting Norris's namesake deflated the charge that the Republican National Committee and the power trust were behind the plot to unseat Norris. But Norris doubted Stebbins. In an excoriating speech in the Senate on December 20, 1930, he revealed further findings of the committee. The most sensational was that the executive director of the Republican National Committee, Robert H. Lucas, secretly had contributed $4,000 to bring about his defeat. Lucas's contribution was used to circulate scurrilous literature, some of which violated the law when sent through the mails. One item that especially provoked Norris contained the charge that he had supported Smith in 1928 for money. "When the Republican Party will permit a man like this man Lucas to do the things he has done under cover, under disguise, under false name, it throws out the intimation to every common citizen that it does not pay to be honest." Unless the party proved itself capable of washing its own dirty linen, it could not maintain the respect of the people. If speaking out and criticizing made him a bad Republican, Norris proclaimed, "I shall live and die as such." Public office was not so sweet that it had to be retained at a sacrifice of conscientious objections.[31]

His majority of almost 75,000 votes convinced Norris that public behavior, guided by conscientious convictions, as far as Nebraska was concerned, had been vindicated. To gain this vindication, he had campaigned harder than in any of his previous senatorial races. In no earlier campaign had he ever actively participated in the primary. Ironically, too, in no previous campaign did his manager work so well with the state organization, though Norris was being subverted by prominent Republicans all the way up to the national

[30] Norris to Sorensen, Nov. 25, 1930; to Charles A. Sandall, Nov. 25, 1930; to F. A. Good, Nov. 28, 1930.

[31] *Congressional Record*, 71st Cong., 3rd sess., Dec. 20, 1930, pp. 1257–59. Some of the literature used against Norris was printed in Washington by a company that published what was "generally regarded as the official Klan publication." Lucas paid for this literature; see Norris to "Dear Boys," Dec. 27, 1930; to McMullen, Dec. 27, 1930; "The Norris-Lucas Earthquake," *Literary Digest,* Jan. 3, 1931, pp. 5–6. For an overall examination by Norris of the campaign against him, see Norris to George L. Keith, Jan. 21, 1931.

committee. Indeed, Norris said, Hoover had countenanced the attacks against him financed by Robert H. Lucas. Though this charge was vigorously denied, it was soon revealed that Samuel R. McKelvie, member of the Federal Farm Board, ex-governor of Nebraska, and a personal friend of the president, had secretly contributed $10,000 to defeat Norris. The *New Republic* noted, "This conspiracy to drive Senator Norris out of the Senate was not concocted because he is a bad Republican, but because he is so much better than the majority. He holds the strange and almost unique belief that the Republican party ought to be devoted to the best interests of the American people, not to those of a little group of greedy capitalists." [32]

Worrying that the fracas was attracting too much attention and that demands for the resignation of Robert Lucas were being repeated with growing frequency, the president decided to dissociate himself from the controversy. Word went out to Republican leaders that too much was being made of the issue. It was to be treated as a personal dispute and not as a party matter. Republican leaders were admonished not to discuss it. But unfortunately for Herbert Hoover further revelations again brought the party's efforts to defeat Norris to national attention.[33]

In January the manager of the western headquarters of the Republican Senatorial Campaign Committee, Victor Seymour, was charged with perjury in an indictment returned by a federal grand jury, as was Grocer Norris. Seymour, an experienced Nebraska politician and a strong supporter of Samuel R. McKelvie, had told the committee headed by Senator Nye in the summer of 1930 that

[32] Norris to E. E. Cone, Dec. 30, 1930; to A. F. Buechler, Dec. 27, 1930; *New York Times,* Dec. 25, 1930; *Lincoln Star,* Dec. 23, 1930; "Who Tried to Knife Norris—and Why?" *New Republic,* Dec. 31 1930, p. 179. Lucas in a series of statements at this time denounced Norris, defended his position, and exonerated the president of any wrongdoing. Yet he could not be accused of lacking the proper Christmas spirit. On Dec. 23, 1930, Norris received a card bearing the greeting "Bright and Happy Christmas," signed by Robert H. Lucas; see *Washington News,* Dec. 23, 1930. The Hearst papers strongly supported Norris as these revelations became known; see Hearst statement, "A Political Chameleon Is Exactly What Senator Norris Is Not," *Washington Herald,* Dec. 31, 1930. So, too, did the *St. Louis Post-Dispatch.* Daniel Fitzpatrick ran several critical cartoons portraying these developments; see, for example, those that appeared on Dec. 23 and 27, 1930.

[33] *New York Sun,* Dec. 31, 1930.

he had not taken an active interest in the campaign and had no knowledge of Grocer Norris's filing until he read about it in the newspapers. Later the committee learned from a secretary employed in Seymour's Lincoln office that a statement released by Grocer Norris at the time of his filing was typed there.[34]

Norris thought that all of the Nebraska participants in the plot ought to be arrested under state laws: his namesake from Broken Bow, State Treasurer Stebbins, Omaha banker and Republican State Committee Treasurer Walter Head, and "little Sammy" McKelvie. Dishonorable methods used by men of high standing in the community disturbed Norris more than if the same tactics had been employed by men "who had not purported in the past to be leaders not only in the political world but also in the moral and Christian world." These men, besides being hypocrites, had violated the law; Norris wanted them punished for engaging in a fight which had been "founded upon injustice and falsehood from the very beginning." [35]

In February, 1931, the Select Committee on Senatorial Campaign Expenditures submitted its official report on the 1930 Nebraska campaign. It was now learned that at least four George Norrises existed in Nebraska but only the Broken Bow grocer had the same middle name as the senator. The underground campaign against Norris was examined in detail, replete with names of individuals and organizations and sums of money donated and expended. Violations of federal statutes were suggested. Details that had not received much attention previously, such as the fact that Republican National Committeeman Charles A. McCloud, a York banker, had secretly contributed over $1,000 to help defeat Norris, now came to the fore. While the committee did not conclude that a conspiracy existed, it was impressed by the fact that the agents involved were in frequent communication and used similar techniques in concealing their expenditures as well as their identities.[36]

[34] *Omaha World-Herald,* Jan. 23, 1931.

[35] Norris to Sorensen, Mar. 24 and 27, 1931; Norris memorandum, May 9, 1931. Norris always felt that the impulse for the fight made against him came from men high in official life, close to and possibly including the president. See also *Congressional Record,* 72nd Cong., 1st sess., July 13, 1932, pp. 15328–29.

[36] *Congressional Record,* 71st Cong., 3rd sess., Feb. 28, 1931, pp. 6451–57. The report covers pp. 6451–53; the remaining pages were devoted to a summary

As a result of evidence unearthed by the Nye committee, after several years of legal maneuvering Victor Seymour and Grocer Norris served brief sentences and paid small fines for perjury. Seymour was convicted in 1934, fined $100, and imprisoned for six months in a federal penitentiary. Grocer Norris's case took longer. It went to the U.S. Supreme Court, which unanimously affirmed in 1937 his conviction by a federal district court. Thus, nearly seven years after he had perjured himself before the Select Committee on Senatorial Campaign Expenditures, Grocer Norris served three months in jail and paid a $100 fine. No record is available of what these proceedings cost the government.[37]

A year after the primary election Charles A. Beard reviewed the "frantic attempts to defeat Senator Norris in the summer of 1930." To Beard the sordid spectacle of the Nebraska primary revealed "the intellectual bankruptcy of conservatism in the United States." Ineptness in action, crudity in negotiation, lack of eloquence in the presence of a crisis—all of these traits revealed how low American conservatism had sunk from the strong, rational, practical appeal it had presented in the orations of Daniel Webster, Joseph H. Choate, and John C. Spooner. Conservatism had reached such a pass, Beard said, "that its spokesmen in the forum must resort to a grocery in Broken Bow for relief, aid and comfort." In short, the 1930 Nebraska senatorial campaign proclaimed, following the title of Beard's article, that "Conservatism Hits Bottom." [38]

---

of the evidence developed in the hearings of the committee. The report was signed by Senators Gerald P. Nye, Porter H. Dale, C. C. Dill, and Robert F. Wagner.

[37] See *United States* v. *Norris* (300 U.S. 564, 1937). Justice Owen J. Roberts delivered the opinion of the Court on Mar. 29, 1937. For Norris's comments on the conviction of Victor Seymour, see Norris to Richard L. Metcalfe, June 7, 1935; to Hugh R. Brown, Dec. 18, 1935. Seymour's case went to a federal court of appeals which affirmed the district court decision.

[38] *New Republic,* Aug. 19, 1931, pp. 7–11.

Depression: Part I

33

Returning to Washington for the lame-duck session of the Seventy-first Congress after his election victory, Norris fought his last losing battle over Muscle Shoals. Though he won two great legislative victories, to be discussed in a following chapter, the remaining years of the Hoover administration were a time in which the impact of the depression made itself felt throughout the land. Norris, like every member of Congress, concerned himself with the economic dimensions of this crisis, particularly as it affected his rural constituency.

Following the stock-market crash in October, 1929, farm prices in Nebraska dramatically collapsed. In 1929 farm income was greater than in any years since the end of World War I. At the end of 1932 farm prices were the lowest in Nebraska history. Comparing December farm prices for 1929 and 1932, the figures were: corn, $.67 and $.13; wheat, $1.00 and $.27; beef cattle, $10.50 and $4.10; hogs, $8.20 and $2.30. Similar figures could be posted for other farm products. Moreover, while farm prices plummeted, the prices farmers had to pay declined less rapidly. Depression in agriculture affected all other activities in Nebraska: the number of manufacturing establishments declined from 1,483 in 1929 to 992 in 1933; wage earners dropped from 27,933 to 19,483; total wages went from $36,648,000 to $18,872,000. Other congressmen, of course, could report comparable figures for their states. A noticeable grimness settled over Congress as determined members returned to cope with the crisis situation.[1]

Norris demanded legislative action on measures favored by progressives in the Senate, lest appropriation bills be stalled. His remarks indicated that the progressive group in the Senate, if not yet holding the balance of power, would do so once the Seventy-second Congress convened. In that body, it was already clear, Norris would wield great power. Norris realized that despite administration efforts to defeat him, it feared a split in the party that would insure a Democratic victory in 1932 as a previous one had in 1912. Even in this short session some party leaders thought that parts of the Norris program, Muscle Shoals and the lame-duck amendment, should be permitted to come to a vote. Congress acted only on Muscle Shoals during the short session, and that measure, as already related, was resoundingly vetoed by President Hoover.[2]

Once the session got under way, Norris showed increasing concern about the impact of the Great Depression. He made much of the elaborate "coming out party" in December, 1930, at the Mayflower Hotel in Washington for the daughter of utility magnate H. L. Doherty, while its garage was used "for the unemployed, who congregated there nightly to sleep on the hard cement floor." He was outraged when in February, 1931, the president contended that public funds might be expended to buy seed, fertilizer, and food for animals but none could be spent for starving people. Letters pour-

[1] Figures delineating the Nebraska situation were found in James C. Olson, *History of Nebraska,* 2nd ed. (Lincoln, Nebr., 1966), pp. 289–92. On a more general level Norris noted that in 1929 the income of 504 Americans was practically equal to the total value of the combined wheat and cotton crops for the year 1930. Or, the net income in 1929 of 504 individuals was equal to the gross income in 1930 of approximately 2,335,000 wheat and cotton farmers. Unless the trend indicated by these figures was checked, disaster would follow; see George W. Norris to H. W. Neuman, May 10, 1931; John P. Robertson to F. B. Shacklett, Apr. 15, 1932. Early in 1933 C. A. Sorensen wrote to Norris, "The situation in Nebraska is desperate and pathetic. I sympathize with the farmers in their resistance to foreclosures, but unless there is a drastic change in conditions within the next nine months, all the efforts of the farmers to save themselves will be futile. In all my life I have seen nothing like we now have." See also the editorial "Down in the Basement," *Lincoln Star,* Oct. 15, 1930, surveying the abundant farm production of Nebraska and the low prices farmers received.

[2] *Washington Herald,* Nov. 22 and 24, 1930 (stories by Fraser Edwards); *New York Times,* Nov. 20, 1930 (story by Arthur Krock).

ing into his Senate office described "in common, ordinary language" the suffering experienced by the people. The tragedy of the situation was poignantly epitomized by a California clergyman who sent Norris a poem entitled "Begging for Bread." It pointed to the dilemma of profits and plenty on the one hand and wanton waste and human suffering on the other. It criticized the president for "urging the half poor, already well bled / To save our prosperity / Begging for bread!" [3]

Norris could not comprehend the proposition that human suffering must not be relieved by the appropriation of federal funds. Local situations "as a general rule" were cared for by the local communities but, he asserted, "it must be conceded that we are confronted at this time with a condition of distress and human suffering that is almost nation-wide." How anyone could close his mind and heart "to the appeal coming from all over the country for relief from human suffering" while at the same time granting "relief to animals" was more than he could "understand or comprehend." The president had to be held responsible for this deplorable situation; the Senate, Norris explained, should either make an appropriation for human food or provide nothing for animal feed and seed. [4]

Equally distressing was the way some Red Cross officials distributed donated food in payment for labor. An instance occurred in Polk County, Arkansas, where food from Nebraska was shipped. To receive it, recipients had to work under the supervision of a Red Cross official. To Norris this incident was one of many disappointments he received in observing the activities of this organization. Its action in refusing funds appropriated by Congress "was going way beyond reason"; it was, in effect, "being used as a tool of the President because he was in disagreement with Congress about the appropriation of public money for the purpose of carrying on relief work." [5]

[3] Norris to J. E. Maxwell, Dec. 29, 1930; *Congressional Record*, 71st Cong., 3rd sess., Feb. 10, 1931, pp. 4445–46. Earlier, just before the stock-market crash, Norris had complained about the high cost of medical and dental services because he believed that every person, "regardless of his financial ability to pay, ought to secure the best possible medical aid and dental services"; see Norris to Ray Lyman Wilbur, Sept. 25, 1929.

[4] *Congressional Record*, 71st Cong., 3rd sess., Jan. 14, 1931, pp. 2140–41.

[5] Norris to S. A. Carrington, Mar. 24, 1931. The situation in Polk County,

Even more distressing was the fact that the Federal Farm Board
was in no way resolving agricultural problems. By March of 1931
it had purchased more than 200 million bushels of wheat. Since
the price in America quickly rose above the world price, the administration claimed that it was aiding agriculture. But, Norris
noted, it "did not tell the farmers that they had this wheat and
that eventually they would have to sell it." In mid-March such an
announcement was made; Norris said that "disaster may come when
they dump what they already own on the market." On cotton and
wheat alone the Farm Board stood to lose over $100 million. Thus,
when the new Congress convened in December, he introduced a resolution calling for a complete investigation of the Federal Farm
Board.[6]

Though the farmer was experiencing deflation, Norris did not see
inflation or cheap money as the answer. What was needed was not
the ability to borrow money but, rather, the ability to pay off obligations already incurred. Certainly the Hawley-Smoot tariff was of
no help to the farmer; it merely added to his costs and helped close
whatever remained of a foreign market for his surplus. With the
failure of the Federal Farm Board to provide adequate remedies,
the agricultural situation was bleak indeed.[7]

Furthermore, deflation for the farmer brought no benefits to the
consumer in the form of lower prices. He still was charged "the same
old price," indicating to Norris that the law of supply and demand
was "in some way perverted." While the farmer received less than
the cost of production for his produce, the consumer paid a price
which was "really prohibitive." The producer was not getting

Ark., was delineated in R. B. Harmon to H. H. Meyer, Feb. 26, 1931. The letter
was published in a Mar., 1931, issue of the *Chappell Register,* a weekly Nebraska
newspaper (clipping in the Norris Papers). In Kentucky, Norris later learned, the
Red Cross did not extend any relief to striking miners. When a miner applied to
the Red Cross for food for his family, he was given a card which informed him
that a job was available at the company he was striking; see *Congressional Record,*
72nd Cong., 1st sess., Jan. 4, 1932, p. 1192.

[6] Norris statement on the Federal Farm Board, Mar. 23, 1931; Norris to Frank
B. Storz, May 20, 1931; to S. K. Warrick, Dec. 11, 1931; to P. P. Cedar, Mar.
29, 1932; to W. A. Fellers, May 12, 1933; *Congressional Record,* 72nd Cong.,
1st sess., Dec. 9, 1931, p. 218. The situation with regard to corn, Norris felt, was
not as serious as that of wheat; see Norris to Mark W. Woods, Sept. 25, 1931.

[7] Norris to I. J. McGinty, May 13, 1931.

enough and the consumer was paying too much; both suffered severely as economic conditions declined disastrously. The administration which had promised much did little. By the fall of 1931 Norris believed that the mystique surrounding President Hoover had been broken. The scales had fallen from people's eyes; they were discovering that he was "an ordinary man, made up of human flesh and blood like the rest of us." [8]

Under these circumstances Norris said that action ought to be taken to extend the time on farm loans, interest, and capital payments. Foreclosure would be justifiable only when the borrower made no attempt to pay the mortgage. He also wanted wheat stored by the Federal Farm Board to be processed and used for feeding the hungry. Though objections immediately arose, it was evident to Norris by December, 1931, that several million people would have to be fed and that the unemployed needed jobs rather than charity. Whatever was done was going to cost money, "millions of dollars, more money than we can possibly pay out of taxes." To meet the emergency, Norris saw no escape from the issuance of federal bonds because the federal government would have to add to what was being done by charitable organizations and municipalities. [9]

Early in 1932 Norris traveled to Harrisburg, Pennsylvania, to champion the cause of the farmer at the formal opening of the sixteenth annual state farm show. He declared that if the farmer had been granted relief after World War I, there would have been no depression, and he concluded with a plea for higher income and inheritance taxes. Returning to Washington, he was concerned about his resolution for an investigation of the Federal Farm Board. Though there was opposition, Norris hoped the investigation would soon get under way. In this hope he was doomed to disappointment even though the Senate on April 11, 1932, approved his original resolution. [10]

[8] Norris to Arthur M. Hyde, May 26, 1931; to R. M. Watson, Sept. 18, 1931.
[9] Norris to D. P. Hogan, Dec. 4 and 12, 1931; to C. R. Christiansen, Dec. 12, 1931; to Albert M. Bell, June 25, 1932; to Clark M. Jacoby, July 1, 1932; to Alfred Saeger, Dec. 12, 1931; to H. G. Keeney, Dec. 12, 1931; *Congressional Record,* 72nd Cong., 1st sess., Jan. 4, 1932, p. 1192.
[10] *Harrisburg* (Pa.) *Evening News, Harrisburg* (Pa.) *Patriot,* Jan. 19, 1932; *Congressional Record,* 72nd Cong., 1st sess., Feb. 1, 1932, p. 2998; Norris to

Concerned about economy, Norris felt it unwise to curtail all agricultural appropriations. But more important than appropriations was a growing interest in an agricultural allotment plan that would curtail production rather than grope with the dilemma of the surplus. When the Senate in June, 1932, considered an allotment proposal, Norris admitted that "until recently" he had never seriously studied this plan; he now considered it "unworkable" and possibly unconstitutional. What he sought was to safeguard the export-debenture proposal and the equalization fee. Both were included in a bill amending the Agricultural Marketing Act so that the Federal Farm Board could have the option of choosing either plan. Adding the allotment plan would make it difficult to enact the bill and impossible to repass it over a certain presidential veto. But whether or not the allotment plan was in the bill, Norris announced his intention of voting for it.[11]

For more than ten years Norris had fought to help distressed farmers. Every significant bill which he and others had brought forth was defeated, "mainly because of the influence of big business and politicians, commencing with the President and running clear through to the bottom." The administration did not realize that "we could not remain permanently prosperous so long as agriculture, the fundamental industry of all and the one industry upon which in the end all prosperity is based, remained in a languishing condition." Now with the evident failure of the Federal Farm Board, Hoover's solution to the agricultural depression, the entire country was sharing in the depression which for years had rested almost entirely upon the shoulders of the American farmer. The condition Norris and other farm spokesmen had so often prophesied had come to pass: the artificial prosperity that existed while the farmer was in distress had collapsed and men and women in all walks of life were experiencing the impact of "this terrible depression." [12]

In response to a colleague's request for support of a bill to liqui-

---

R. A. Collier, Jan. 28, 1932; to E. J. Haynes, Mar. 10, 1932; to John Swanson, Apr. 14, 1932. Though Norris's original resolution calling for a Senate investigation was approved, the Senate Agriculture and Forestry Committee never conducted one.

[11] *Congressional Record*, 72nd Cong., 1st sess., Mar. 7, pp. 5382–83, June 14, pp. 12897–98, June 15, 1932, pp. 12989–90.

[12] Norris to F. E. Edgerton, May 4, 1932; to J. P. O'Furey, May 11, 1932.

date and refinance agricultural indebtedness, Norris replied that the resulting inflation would be ruinous, "beyond what it was at its highest peak during the crazy days during and after the War." Moreover, the mortgagee and not the farmer would receive the money. Most important, the bill would be vetoed by the president and friends of the farmer would be placed in the difficult situation of trying to defend a weak measure. To be sure, something had to be done quickly to make it easier for the man in debt to meet his obligations. Financial legislation to make the dollar cheaper was necessary. Paying off a mortgage with wheat worth less than half of what it was when the money was borrowed was an impossibility. The value of the dollar had changed; "in common justice," Norris insisted, the farmer "ought to be enabled to pay his mortgage with the same kind of dollar that he received when he borrowed it." Though he doubted that this matter would be tackled during the Hoover administration, Norris did not think prosperity could be restored until it had been resolved. So desperate was the situation that he was willing to consider any remedy that might bring relief, including the domestic allotment plan.[13]

Meanwhile Norris learned that in January, 1933, a Federal Land Bank official in Nebraska had tried to hold a sheriff's sale at the courthouse in Clay Center. Nearly a thousand farmers congregated there. After the sheriff recognized the first bidder, things began to happen. A crowd gathered around him and someone called for a rope. He was told to withdraw his bid or he would decorate a tree in the courthouse yard. He called off his bid, and no further action was taken on the proposed sale. To Norris this incident was indicative of a serious condition for which a remedy had to be found immediately. Legislation limiting foreclosures would help, but he doubted that Congress could agree on what kind of legislation should be enacted. Until relief was achieved, more people would take the law into their own hands.[14]

[13] Norris to C. B. Steward, July 9, 1932; to Mrs. Louis J. Trubl, Feb. 8, 1933; to A. J. Van Ackeren, Jan. 19, 1933; to E. C. Finlay, Dec. 2, 1932; to Roland M. Hill, Dec. 21, 1932; to John F. Cordeal, Dec. 27, 1932; to A. D. Zollars, Dec. 21, 1932; to Frank D. Eager, Feb. 17, 1933.

[14] Norris to Zollars, Dec. 21, 1932; to O. A. Abbott, Jr., Jan. 7, 1933; Robertson to John T. Wood, Jan. 27, 1933. John L. Shover, *Cornbelt Rebellion* (Urbana, Ill., 1965), presents fascinating material on the farm situation in Nebraska, though

Lending money to farmers was not the answer. Norris never was sympathetic to this approach, and by the end of the Hoover administration he had not changed his mind. Neither would moratoriums resolve the farmer's problems, unless they provided for either the cancellation of a part of the debt or a reduction of the rate of interest. Thus by 1933 Norris was convinced that if any relief were to be provided for the farmer, it would have to include a modest inflation of the currency. He was willing to consider remedies he had reservations about but, basically, what was most imperative was a new approach by the executive branch of the government.[15]

While Norris devoted most of his energies to agriculture, he could not ignore "the unemployment question," believing that it vied with farm relief in its need for an immediate solution. At the end of 1930 he observed jobless men by the hundreds walking the streets. What should government do about the unemployed in Washington and elsewhere? Norris's response was, "I would rather have the Government build highways and give men jobs than to take the same amount of money and give it as charity to people who are without jobs." Rather than grant them a dole, he would give them jobs. Rather than allow people to starve, the government should issue bonds. Jobs for the needy would allow them to provide for themselves and still maintain the essence of dignity and integrity that was being sapped by humiliating unemployment and depleting relief checks. The hungry, besides being fed, would leave something of permanent value in the form of improved public works. It was imperative, Norris said, "to keep the manhood and the womanhood of America upon a high standard, by not compelling the men and women of our country to become subjects of charity for food and clothing."[16]

---

his study of the Farmers' Holiday Association is devoted primarily to Iowa. Conditions in Nebraska are focused upon more clearly in his article, "The Farm Holiday Movement in Nebraska," *Nebraska History,* 43 (Mar., 1962): 53–78.

[15] *Congressional Record,* 72nd Cong., 2nd sess., Feb. 9, 1933, pp. 3701–2.

[16] Norris to H. G. Dorr, Dec. 26, 1930; to Henry J. Thorpe, Dec. 27, 1930; to George A. Baker, Dec. 5, 1931; to C. M. Nelson, Dec. 19, 1931; to W. E. Barkley, Jan. 5, 1932; *Lincoln Star,* Nov. 9, 1931; *Congressional Record,* 72nd Cong., 1st sess., Jan. 15, 1932, p. 2008. Norris introduced a bill calling for the issuance of up to $3 billion in bonds for highway construction. A tax on large incomes and inheritances would help pay for the bonds. Norris thought the plan "would come nearer settling the unemployment question than any other proposi-

The most important thing, then, was to provide jobs for the unemployed. If that were not achieved, the unemployed would have to be supported from charity. Since local authorities had exhausted virtually all of their resources, Norris felt the federal government should step in. If while caring for the unemployed, the government could benefit the nation materially as well, then so much the better. Though Norris suggested highways as the type of construction for the unemployed to engage in, he was not wedded to them as the only solution. As long as a project provided employment along broad geographical lines, he would be satisfied. Aware that such a program would probably incur a presidential veto, Norris still hoped that Hoover might broaden his views and fight the depression like a major military operation with comprehensive tactics designed to achieve predetermined objectives.[17]

But if faced with a choice between charity and nothing, Norris insisted that "we can not refuse to give relief simply because it may have a bad effect upon the recipients, and for fear that if continued indefinitely it would make mendicants and tramps of them." Congress was not seeking to cure "an ordinary evil or daily occurrence"; human beings were "suffering and dying" for want of food while storehouses were bursting "with an oversupply of things the starving people need." People were suffering because of no illegal or wrongful acts of their own; most were women and children whose breadwinners had lost their jobs. It was no longer a question, as the depression deepened and the government refused to issue bonds for a massive public works program, of people seeking alms. It had become a question of life. Rules and regulations useful in healthy and normal times, including playing politics, no longer applied.[18]

At the end of the Hoover administration the nation was in worse straits than in time of war. To combat the situation, Norris said, war measures were going to be necessary. Laboring men needed work, not dole. Federal bonds to provide funds for jobs for the unemployed offered the best answer. If the government refused this alter-

tion" suggested. The letter to C. M. Nelson explaining his bill was published in *Better Roads*, 2 (Jan., 1932).

[17] *Congressional Record*, 72nd Cong., 1st sess., June 18, 1932, pp. 13351–52.

[18] *Ibid.*, Feb. 15, p. 3929, Feb. 16, 1932, p. 4051; Norris to Finlay, Dec. 2, 1932. For Norris's comments on the sad plight of the unemployed in Chicago, see *Congressional Record*, 72nd Cong., 1st sess., June 22, 1932, pp. 13709–10.

native, Norris was convinced that it would have to provide charity as municipalities and local agencies exhausted their abilities. The depression had to be fought on a national level by the federal government. Municipalities, states, and charitable organizations had gone "the extreme limit." There was little more they could do. There seemed to be little the Hoover administration would do. As in the case of agricultural relief, Norris knew that a massive attack upon unemployment would be delayed until after March 4, 1933.[19]

[19] *Congressional Record,* 72nd Cong., 1st sess., June 7, 1932, p. 12148; Norris to Zollars, Dec. 21, 1932.

Depression: Part II

34

Agricultural relief and jobs for the unemployed were Norris's primary concerns as the depression deepened. They were of little interest to Herbert Hoover, who had a much more elaborate program for coping with the crisis. His proposals received careful legislative scrutiny and here, too, Norris quickly emerged as a leading critic. The president deemed banks and corporations worthy of primary attention if the economy were to be revived. Norris saw the situation differently because of his agrarian suspicion of large banks and big business. But both Hoover and Norris agreed in December, 1931, that continuing bank failures indicated that the situation had not yet stabilized. Stock prices and real estate continued to decline as deflation traveled its downward path. Banks in McCook and nearby Nebraska towns where Norris knew most of the employees failed. He was surprised that with so many bank failures, there were so few excited crowds and so little critical comment.[1]

Norris listened as President Hoover outlined his home-building plans over the radio. Hoover, he said, was acting on the theory "that what we ought to do to cure all kinds of ills is to make it possible to borrow more money . . . to make it possible to buy automobiles on time and for girls to buy fur coats on the installment plan." While most financiers agreed that the country could be kept prosperous if there was ample opportunity to borrow money, Norris felt

[1] George W. Norris to Carl Marsh, Dec. 3, 1931; to Chester Lowe, Dec. 5, 1931.

that one of the reasons the nation was enveloped in depression was that everyone was borrowing money. If Hoover and Secretary Mellon had stated throughout the twenties that people should not go into debt for anything except necessities, installment buying and excessive borrowing might have been curbed and the day of reckoning less severe. Instead of lending more money, he would provide jobs "so that the people in homes might be able to pay the mortgages already upon the homes." Rather than build homes, he wished to help people who were losing their homes because they had lost their jobs. Hoover's proposal, as Norris viewed it, was neither financially sound nor seriously able to remedy the depression crisis.[2]

If Norris was dubious about the president's housing proposals, he was incredulous about the Reconstruction Finance Corporation. He remarked, "I have been called a socialist, a bolshevik, a communist, and a lot of other terms of a similar nature, but in the wildest flights of my imagination I never thought of such a thing as putting the Government into business as far as this bill would put it in." Providing a government corporation with $2 billion worth of federal bonds to aid big business and "international bankers," people who were "to a great extent responsible" for the depression crisis, did not seem a sensible way to approach the situation. There was no valid reason for Congress to grant federal funds to men who would not employ an additional person, who would not feed an additional child, and who would not clothe anyone, at least until after they had stabilized their own positions, weakened in part "through gambling in the stock markets of the country." There was no valid reason for Congress to make good the losses of security speculators any more than the losses of manufacturers or farmers. Nevertheless, the creation of the Reconstruction Finance Corporation, though a mistake to Norris, was approved by a large majority in the Senate.[3]

[2] Norris to Lowe, Dec. 5, 1931; to F. R. Kingsley, July 20, 1932. Hoover's home loan building plan called for a government corporation which would lend money to banks and building and loan associations to aid home owners and builders. Norris considered it a mere gesture because from the outset loans were confined to building and loan associations and not to individuals; see Norris to A. Barnett, Dec. 29, 1931; to C. D. Larimore, Jan. 9, 1933; to C. A. Johnson, Jan. 13, 1933; *Congressional Record,* 72nd Cong., 1st sess., July 16, 1932, p. 15633.

[3] *Congressional Record,* 72nd Cong., 1st sess., Jan. 11, pp. 1703–4, Jan. 15, 1932, p. 2007; Norris to H. H. Brown, July 19, 1932; to William Dutton, Jr.,

In July, 1932, he introduced a resolution directing the Reconstruction Finance Corporation to present the Senate with a complete and detailed list of all the loans it had made. Previously the Senate had voted down a similar proposal, but Norris believed that publicity was necessary. Concealing knowledge of how tax money was being used by a public corporation was no way to instill confidence either in the banking structure or in the public, who had a right to know what had been done with a $2-billion appropriation. Failing in his effort, Norris inserted into the *Congressional Record* a critical article by John T. Flynn delineating some of the loans made to banks.[4]

The trouble with the Reconstruction Finance Corporation was that it commenced relief at the wrong end. Rather than beginning at the top and paying the "big fellow," Norris wished it to start with farmers and laboring men, giving them purchasing power they did not possess. To be sure, the law as amended in July, 1932, provided for lending money to farmers and stockmen, but Norris soon learned that their requests were not given the attention that went to those of banks, insurance companies, or railroads. He was pleased that Governor Franklin Roosevelt of New York agreed with his contention that the problem had been tackled at the wrong end. A change in administrative officials, he was convinced, would satisfactorily resolve this situation.[5]

Rather than continue to lend money, Norris thought that larger salaries, those of government officials up to and including the president of the United States, ought to be reduced. In this way the cost of living, which had not decreased in proportion to the general

May 30, 1932; to J. P. O'Furey, May 11, 1932. The vote in the Senate was 63 to 8 for the creation of the Reconstruction Finance Corporation.

[4] *Congressional Record*, 72nd Cong., 1st sess., July 8, pp. 14850–51, July 11, 1932, pp. 14983–85; 2nd sess., Dec. 22, 1932, pp. 871–76; John P. Robertson to Louis O'Shaughnessy, July 15, 1932; to Harold W. Stoke, July 21, 1932. The article by John T. Flynn, "Inside the R.F.C.: An Adventure in Secrecy," appeared originally in *Harper's Magazine,* 166 (Jan., 1933): 161–69. Flynn noted that the bulk of the money went to leading bank and railroad corporations. When the Dawes bank in Chicago received an $80-million RFC loan, Charles G. Dawes released information about it. No action was taken on Norris's resolution, though the secrecy provision was later modified by Congress.

[5] Norris to Brown, July 19, 1932; to R. E. McDonnell, Dec. 5, 1932; to J. M. Hanson, Dec. 21, 1932; to George C. Eisenhart, Dec. 31, 1932.

slump, might be lowered. Bread was still selling at the same price when the farmer received 25 cents for wheat as it did when he received $2.00 to $2.50 a bushel. Nor had the cost of building materials declined. Wages, which should have been reduced last, usually were cut first. The approach of the Hoover administration, pleading with industry to keep men at work while discharging large groups of government employees, Norris found ridiculous. Economy could easily be practiced throughout the governmental structure, but reducing the number of employees in the lower-paid group only added to human misery while not aiding the situation in any significant way.[6]

Norris also disagreed with Hoover in his treatment of veterans. When the president vetoed a bill in May, 1930, calling for increased pensions to Spanish-American War veterans, the Senate was considering a measure to grant millions of dollars to corporations to carry the mails "without any reason or any consideration as to the cost of the service." Thus ship owners were lent federal funds to construct or purchase vessels from the government "for a song." Then they received a generous subsidy to carry the mails. Hundreds of millions of dollars went to corporations in the form of subsidies, but when it came to veterans, the president at once became economical: "Let them first prove they are paupers before they can get any of this money." Wealthy taxpayers in 1929 were remitted $160 million in taxes, but to receive public funds, veterans would have to prove that they were paupers and that they had behaved as "Sunday-school boys." The approach suggested by Hoover's veto message was "unbecoming a great nation." Norris's views prevailed; Congress overrode the veto.[7]

Immediately thereafter the question of a bonus and increased pensions for veterans of World War I again arose. Norris, in favor of aiding these veterans, commented, "How liberal is the President and the Congress, how liberal is Mr. Mellon, the watchdog of the Treasury, when we can do something by taking money out of the

[6] Norris to R. B. Weller, Jan. 2, 1932; to Mrs. W. T. Stevenson, Feb. 8, 1932; to W. L. Brayton, Apr. 6, 1932; *Lincoln Star*, Nov. 9, 1931.

[7] *Congressional Record*, 71st Cong., 2nd sess., June 2, 1930, pp. 9871–72, 9876. The Senate vote in overriding the veto was 61 to 18. For Hoover's version of this measure, see his *Memoirs: The Cabinet and the Presidency, 1920–1933* (New York, 1952), p. 286.

Treasury for the benefit of the rich men. But how penurious some of our people are when we propose to distribute a little money to the veterans of our late war." Penury prevailed in February, 1931, when the president vetoed a measure lending veterans 50 percent of their bonus certificates. Hoover favored loans if they were limited "to the men who were unemployed and destitute." Congress included all veterans. Norris, unhappy about aspects of the bill, voted for it and Congress repassed it over Hoover's veto, an action the president said helped deepen the depression.[8]

A year later Norris sided with the president and voted against a proposal to cash the $2,400,000 worth of outstanding adjusted compensation or bonus certificates. But his reasoning was different from Hoover's. Rather than a bonus, Norris called for "an employment measure on a country wide scale, with billions behind it" so that veterans and all the unemployed might have jobs. With veterans in the galleries, Norris made an impassioned plea for jobs rather than a bonus. He called for a massive public works program to help keep the economy functioning. A bonus would not put men to work, nor would it affect all the unemployed.

When bonus marchers poured into Washington, Norris, who initially opposed their coming, said, "I am reaching the conclusion now that the coming of this vast army is going to accomplish a world of good." Critics observed that they were "orderly and sober and industrious" men, asking for a right to live under "the flag for which they fought." Norris said that they preferred jobs to charity, wanting "to earn their own money and thus start the wheels of prosperity to turning." Only if Congress did not do something for the unemployed would he support a bonus payment bill. But when Congress adjourned on July 16, 1932, no bonus legislation had been enacted by the Senate, and Norris was not in Washington when bonus marchers were evicted at the end of the month.[9]

[8] *Congressional Record,* 71st Cong., 2nd sess., July 3, 1930, pp. 12400–402; 3rd sess., Feb. 19, 1931, p. 5385; Hoover, *The Cabinet and the Presidency,* pp. 286–87; Norris to Frank W. Eagleston, Apr. 14, 1932. In Jan., 1931, a resolution introduced by Norris providing for a codification of all laws affecting veterans was approved; see Robertson to the editor, *Omaha Bee-News,* Sept. 19, 1931. Norris later introduced a bill lowering the rate of interest on monies borrowed on compensation certificates; see Robertson to Percy Hocking, July 15, 1932.

[9] *Congressional Record,* 72nd Cong., 1st sess., June 17, 1932, pp. 13254–56; *Washington Herald,* June 18, 1932.

The Seventy-second Congress also had to consider appropriations, allowing Norris another opportunity to express his views on ways and means of dealing with the depression crisis. Fixed costs and numerous appropriations involved expenses that Norris was reluctant to tinker with; many were in support of agencies charged with protecting "the ordinary citizen against the encroachments of monopolies and trusts." During the Coolidge administration he would have been willing to abolish some of these agencies. But now, owing to the thorough utility investigation conducted by the Federal Trade Commission, Norris staunchly defended them.

To the cry of "balance the budget" he countered that it had not been heard when $2 billion was appropriated for big business through the Reconstruction Finance Corporation. Nor would it be echoed when military appropriations were discussed. Only when agriculture and aid to the unemployed were considered was the cry loudly chanted. Norris was not adverse to balancing the budget. But in a period of grave emergency, rather than cripple some of the necessary functions of government, he "would rather issue bonds than to abolish some of the things which I believe are necessary if we are to protect our people from the inroads of monopolies, corporations, and trusts." "If," Norris asserted, "we had made agriculture and labor prosperous, we would have restored the buying power of millions of our people who now are unable to buy even the necessaries of life." [10]

He was more critical in the discussion of military appropriations. Though he found no fault with senators who believed in enlarging the Navy, Norris said that he would rather feed people than build battleships. Similarly, he would rather give jobs to the unemployed than help make the employment of soldiers necessary to protect people and property. He would rather discontinue the National Guard, summer training camps, and the ROTC program than the public schools, a distant possibility in some localities. Discussing these appropriations, Norris bitterly ridiculed statements in an official Army training manual proclaiming that government ownership was ruin-

[10] *Congressional Record,* 72nd Cong., 1st sess., Mar. 17, 1932, pp. 6313–14. For some areas of government where Norris thought costs could be cut, particularly for social or entertainment expenses in the State Department, see *ibid.,* Mar. 22, 1932, pp. 6638–39, 6641.

ous and ought to be avoided; that initiative, referendum, recall, and the election of judges were dangerous experiments; that special legislation was "socialistic and communistic" and "wholly repugnant to the American character." Internationalism was defined as "an impractical and destructive idealism" propagated by foreign agitators and echoed by the "intellectuals." [11] Further economies could be made by cutting appropriations in the Post Office Department: not by reducing salaries or discharging clerks but by cracking down on subsidies granted to large corporations for carrying the mail, particularly the "Shipping Trust" and favored airlines.

His most bitter remarks were reserved for the indiscriminate 10 percent salary cuts that were included in all appropriation bills. With about 2,500 employees earning $1,500 or less, a 10 percent salary cut meant the deprivation of some necessities, whereas a similar cut in a $10,000 salary merely deprived its recipient of some luxuries. Norris wished to exempt all salaries of $1,500 or less and to provide for graduated cuts on all others. But his efforts were unsuccessful.[12]

Reorganization was another method of reducing federal expenditures. Norris favored the idea. Consolidating the War and Navy departments was something that ought to be done as a step toward greater efficiency. So, too, Norris favored combining the Agriculture Department with the Interior Department. The Reclamation Bureau in the Interior Department and irrigation projects had to do with agriculture, but the Agriculture Department had nothing to do with them. The Commerce and Labor departments, Norris said, could be either eliminated or combined at least until prosperity returned and Congress could re-examine the matter.[13]

To meet responsibilities imposed by the depression crisis, Norris thought expenses would have to be drastically reduced or taxes sub-

[11] *Ibid.*, May 2, p. 9366, June 9, 1932, pp. 12415–19, 12421, 12459–60; Norris to H. J. Paul, Jan. 5, 1932; to Nels P. Johnson, Jan. 23, 1933; to Mrs. C. A. Laughlin, Feb. 9, 1933.

[12] *Congressional Record*, 72nd Cong., 1st sess., May 4, pp. 9550–51, June 2, p. 11807, June 3, pp. 11899–900, June 4, 1932, pp. 11960–61, 11980; 2nd sess., Jan. 30, p. 2877, Feb. 1, 1933, pp. 3083–85; Norris to F. E. Shutt, Apr. 16, 1932; Robertson to M. J. Murphy, June 11, 1932; Norris to H. J. Heltman, Dec. 29, 1932.

[13] *Congressional Record*, 72nd Cong., 2nd sess., Feb. 7, 1933, pp. 3541–43.

stantially increased. But his efforts at securing equitable reductions were unsuccessful and his attempts to increase taxation also failed. The so-called tax-reduction bill in the Seventy-first Congress was "absolutely indefensible," but the coalition, "under the leadership of the President himself," was "absolutely invincible." Democrats, fearing popular wrath, supported the administration and left a small group of progressives in continuous opposition.

Norris advocated lowering taxes on small incomes and progressively increasing the rate as income increased. Partially successful in securing a progressive inheritance tax, he was defeated in an attempt to keep it at a meaningful rate. Furthermore, corporations secured liberal exemptions, thus making necessary greater taxation on individuals who could not as easily afford to pay. Returning taxes in the form of reductions only added to the burdens of others while doing little to revive or restore the economy. He preferred to use available income to meet the needs of suffering citizens rather than reduce or refund taxes for privileged people who were doing little to alleviate conditions.[14] If he had had his way, no taxes would be levied on automobiles, deeds of conveyance, bank checks, telephone calls, telegrams, cables, or theater or other amusement tickets, except for high-priced tickets or automobiles. But the Hoover administration opposed his views and Congress usually complied with the president's wishes, placing the burden of increased taxation on "the ordinary person and the poorer class." The administration's reward, he said, would be in the form of "increased burdens, increased unemployment and increased failure." [15]

The proper technique in taxation consisted of tapping sources where funds could be collected with as little hardship as possible, namely, from the man who had a surplus. Yet compared to rates

[14] Norris to F. D. Wead, Feb. 13, 1933; to A. E. Archer, Feb. 5, 1930; to J. M. Easterling, Dec. 21, 1929; *Congressional Record,* 71st Cong., 2nd sess., Dec. 13, pp. 599–601, 603, 605, Dec. 14, 1929, pp. 660–61; *Lincoln Star,* Nov. 9, 1931.

[15] Norris to F. H. Brandes, Dec. 29, 1931; to G. W. O'Malley, Dec. 29, 1931; to R. A. Collier, Jan. 28, 1932; to F. C. Luchsinger, Feb. 2, 1932; to S. R. Florence, May 12, 1932; to J. R. O'Neal, May 12, 1932; to W. N. Youngclaus, May 14, 1932; to J. C. Miller, May 16, 1932; to Perry J. Rushlan, Mar. 4, 1932; to Shutt, Apr. 16, 1932; to John B. Potts, May 10, 1932. See *Congressional Record,* 72nd Cong., 1st sess., May 16, 1932, pp. 10272–73, for Norris's remarks on the tax on checks. The vote on this proposal was a tie (39 to 39).

imposed by British law on all income levels, Americans, despite taunts that some in Congress were seeking to "soak the rich," paid lower rates. Taxing state securities and official salaries would be perfectly legal, provided the levies were no different from those upon other securities and salaries. But as Norris reiterated throughout the debate on the tax bill, ". . . I concede to begin with that my idea does not prevail." Thus, while many editorial writers complained that the tax bill would "soak the rich," he said that it would "sock" the poor, particularly the long-suffering farmer. In too many instances wealth and business were being taxed lightly, while farmers would have to bear the major burden of the tax on gasoline and automobiles. A tax on creameries, for example, would fall almost exclusively on the rural elements of the population.[16]

Norris was particularly disturbed about what in effect would be a tax on municipally owned hydroelectric plants. They were not operated for profit and therefore should be granted the same nontax status of a properly organized cooperative. Taxing municipal plants, he argued, would be taxing a division of a state. But to avoid the question of constitutionality, the amendment taxed electricity consumed by customers of these municipal plants, thereby jeopardizing municipal plants while leaving private utility corporations free from additional taxation. To the argument that if the company were taxed, it would pass the tax along to the consumer, Norris replied that an amendment offered by his Nebraska colleague Robert Howell would not allow this to happen for at least a year. Howell's amendment called for a 3 percent tax on electrical energy generated by privately owned plants to be paid by the producer of the current. Moreover, Norris said, the great electric power companies had not felt the impact of the depression and could be taxed without undue hardship. Their income in 1930 was greater than ever before. In 1931 it was about the same or perhaps a little greater than in 1930.

[16] *Congressional Record,* 72nd Cong., 1st sess., May 14, pp. 10189–94, May 17, 1932, pp. 10397–98; Norris to Marsh, May 28, 1932; to C. A. Kingsbury, May 24, 1932. Norris told Marsh that Hoover favored a sales tax and had asked newspaper editors to advocate support for the idea. See also Norris to Dutton, May 30, 1932; to George L. Chandler, Dec. 29, 1932. Norris also waged a losing battle to secure further exemptions and to clarify others for farmers' cooperatives; see *Congressional Record,* 72nd Cong., 1st sess., May 30, pp. 11550–56, June 6, 1932, pp. 12062–64.

To raise rates, most utilities had to go through the troublesome and expensive formality of requesting permission before the
Interstate Commerce Commission. But power companies were
spared this formality and users of electricity were burdened with
another "indefensible" and unjust tax in the final and approved
measure.[17]

To provide some relief for agriculture, Norris sought to attach
the export-debenture proposal as an amendment to the tax bill. For
the third time he explained how the debenture plan sought to give
farmers the benefit of the protective tariff.[18] He reviewed once again
the depressing dimensions of the farm problem and denounced the
intransigent views of President Hoover on agriculture and taxation.
He observed that big business and big finance were aided by the
administration in avoiding their proportionate share of increased
taxes. With appalling conditions prevailing throughout the nation,
such selfish behavior verged on madness and revealed the intellectual bankruptcy of American political leadership and its business
allies. The administration juggernaut would be capsized "by the
force of its own power." Ruin and destruction would follow if the
pleas of suffering people were continually ignored. But Norris could
only talk. Republican floor leader James E. Watson of Indiana
predicted that his amendment would be defeated. As debate proceeded, Watson began to waver and reported that while fourteen
Republicans had strayed from the administration camp, only eleven
Democrats entered it. In the end the president himself got on the
telephone; the Norris amendment to include the export-debenture
measure in the revenue bill was defeated in the Senate 46 to 33.[19]

Disappointed with the revenue measure signed by the president
in June of 1932, Norris thereafter had relatively little to say about
additional aspects of the Hoover approach to the depression crisis.

[17] *Congressional Record*, 72nd Cong., 1st sess., May 31, 1932, pp. 11606,
11611–12. Norris was speaking from memory and did not have profit statistics
available at his desk. In conference committee the tax on consumers replaced
Howell's amendment, which the Senate had adopted by a large majority; see
Norris to J. F. Hawkins, Dec. 31, 1932; Robertson to Murphy, June 11, 1932.

[18] Norris had previously introduced the plan as an amendment to the tariff
bill and to the Agricultural Marketing Act.

[19] *Congressional Record*, 72nd Cong., 1st sess., May 24, 1932, pp. 10981–88,
11006–8; Theodore G. Joslin, *Hoover, off the Record* (Garden City, N.Y., 1934),
pp. 232–33.

The administration, ignoring mass misery, continually aided those most able to endure the vicissitudes of the times and who, in Norris's view, bore some responsibility for the desperate situation the nation was in. But the situation was not totally bleak. Disappointed with the Hoover approach to the depression crisis, defeated at every turn in offering alternative suggestions, ignored by an administration which detested his views though they were gaining increasing recognition, Norris still won several outstanding victories that merited him national recognition in the last two years of the Hoover administration.

Persistence Pays Off

35

In 1928 a Philadelphia newspaper characterized George Norris as "a Republican who is almost never Republican; always wanting to retire and always being reelected; refusing to be a leader yet always having leadership thrust upon him; politically omnipotent in his State, yet never a boss, never maintaining a machine, never using patronage; a pacifist by nature yet always fighting. . . ." Following his re-election in 1930, the positive points in this paradoxical analysis came into clear focus. Norris, undisputed leader of the small band of progressives in the Senate, sought to marshal whatever power and influence they had for positive political action. When the Seventy-second Congress convened in December, 1931, twelve progressive Republican senators held the balance of power between thirty-six Republicans, forty-seven Democrats, and one Farmer-Laborite. So antagonistic were the progressives in the Republican party that it proved impossible to form a majority to elect a president pro tem. Senator George Moses of New Hampshire, the choice of the regulars and the previous president, continued to serve in the post. Thus there was a chance that when the progressives applied their political leverage, they might secure significant legislation.[1]

Before returning to Washington after the 1930 election, Norris said that congressional fights would be more frequent and more bitter. He thought his position was one to be dreaded; yet at the same

[1] *Philadelphia Public Ledger,* Apr. 22, 1928 (story by Robert B. Smith).

time he expressed a yearning to return to the Senate floor. There was much to be done. If progressive members of the Senate worked together, something, possibly, could be accomplished. Felix Frankfurter observed at the time that Norris "has shown what can be accomplished when knowlege and pertinacity are wedded." Insisting that "knowledge is power—even in the Senate," Frankfurter thought that conditions were ripe "for a new creative era in politics" if only the progressive senators specialized "so that on each of the major subjects there will be some rallying center." Norris, of course, had long operated on this premise, boring from within the Republican party and cooperating whenever possible with progressive Democrats.[2]

Progressivism won notable victories in November, 1930. In addition to Norris, Thomas J. Walsh and William E. Borah were re-elected and in Colorado Edward P. Costigan was elected to the Senate. Gifford Pinchot, Franklin D. Roosevelt, Floyd B. Olson, and Julius L. Meier were elected or returned to the governorships of Pennsylvania, New York, Minnesota, and Oregon respectively. All were recognized foes of the "Power Trust" and of Hoover's policies. Moreover, staunch friends of the administration, B. Carroll Reece and Ruth Hanna McCormick in the House, were defeated. To dramatize the growing strength of progressives and to suggest remedies for persisting problems afflicting American life, Norris proposed a conference to be held in Washington after the lame-duck session of the Seventy-first Congress. Progressives both in and out of Congress could discuss and then outline a program of constructive legislation for the next Congress to consider.

The conference was called by five senators—Norris, Edward P. Costigan of Colorado, Bronson M. Cutting of New Mexico, Robert M. LaFollette, Jr., of Wisconsin, and Burton K. Wheeler of Montana. It was nonpartisan and would take up six subjects: unemployment, industrial stabilization, public utilities, agriculture, the tariff, and a return to representative government. At the Carlton Hotel at 10 A.M. on March 11, 1931, it was called to order by Norris. He expressed the belief that programs for relieving distress and placing

[2] Press clipping, United Press, McCook, Nebr., Oct. 23, 1931 (copy in Norris Papers); Felix Frankfurter to Edward P. Costigan, Feb. 24, 1931 (Edward P. Costigan Papers, University of Colorado Library).

government "on a higher and more efficient plane of operation" would emanate from these proceedings. He made clear that the conference had no intention of organizing a political party and denounced Senator James E. Watson of Indiana for implying that such was the primary purpose.[3]

On the second day the conference was again called to order by Norris. In the afternoon he delivered a major address extemporaneously, explaining that he had thrown his prepared remarks in the wastebasket after listening on the previous day "to some of the finest arguments and most beautiful addresses I have ever heard." Admitting that there was "quite a difference of opinion among progressives" about who would hold the balance of power in the next Congress, he conceded that the way was not clear for the enactment of liberal legislation. The "engineer" was still in the White House. Until a progressive was elected president, a significant program could not be enacted. As Norris explained, "What we do need in order to bring prosperity and happiness to the common individual is another Roosevelt in the White House."

He also explained why he did not think a third party feasible. Besides the impediment of the Electoral College, a third party would require an immense amount of money and a great deal of time, neither of which progressives possessed in any abundance. Instead Norris preferred to abolish the Electoral College, feeling that "we are helpless to get a President who will respond to the will of the progressive-minded people until we get rid of the electoral college." In the final portion of his remarks Norris compared utility rates in Ontario cities with comparable cities in the United States and commented on recent power trust activities.[4]

Prominent progressives from all walks of American life either spoke at or sent messages to this two-day conference. Those present attended sessions and served on different committees. In addition, as Norris observed at the opening of the second day, there were a

[3] George W. Norris to Chester Lowe, Mar. 7, 1931; *Proceedings of a Conference of Progressives* (n.p., n.d.), pp. 5–11.

[4] *Proceedings of a Conference of Progressives*, pp. 126–35. Jim Farley later informed Ray Tucker, a prominent Washington correspondent, that Norris's remarks endorsing Roosevelt was one of the turning points in his preconvention campaign for FDR's nomination; see Tucker to Richard Lowitt, Feb. 21, 1957 (author's file).

"large number of students, college professors and young men who are enlisting in the cause of progress and humanity." While the final evening's session was canceled because too many people had to depart to attend to their own pressing affairs, Norris pronounced the conference a success and was pleased with its results.[5]

Through this conference congressional progressives in effect made their bid for power, proclaiming to the country that they were seeking solutions to vexatious political and economic problems. They were also proclaiming their opposition to administration policies and informing Democratic leaders that they expected a presidential candidate who could command progressive support. With Congress out of session, the progressives had the Washington limelight to themselves and Norris, acknowledged leader of the gathering, captured the attention of the press. With the momentum generated by these proceedings, Norris hoped to gain a lever to secure some progressive victories in the next Congress. Moreover, he had dramatically suggested that another Roosevelt in the White House would be attractive to most progressives, thereby boosting New York Governor Franklin D. Roosevelt as a presidential candidate.[6]

After the conference Norris sought funds for a widespread mailing of its proceedings, not only to those who requested a copy "but also to other people whom we know to be students of governmental affairs and who are honestly trying to improve conditions, not only with regard to the Government, but as to humanity generally." Dispersing the proceedings was deemed imperative because Norris sensed a lag in progressive interest throughout the country. When attention was called to injustice, people responded. But they were "not active in pushing anything." Moreover, progressives were few and the burdens were great. Those active in the cause were soon deluged. Initially, Norris had not intended to play a prominent part in the progressive conference. But he finally agreed, with the promise that he would not be responsible for any of the details. The re-

[5] *Proceedings of a Conference of Progressives,* pp. 156–57, 163–64. The official attendance, based on the number of registrants, was 174. When the Public Utilities Committee presented its report, Norris felt it ought to have stated directly that public utilities should be owned and operated by public authority; see Norris to Donald Richberg, Oct. 14, 1931.

[6] See, for example, "The Progressives' Bid for Power," *Literary Digest,* Mar. 28, 1931, pp. 7–8.

sult, of course, found him deluged with requests to speak throughout the country. Though his heart was in the work, he did not feel he could accept one offer and refuse others. So he declined them all and sought to husband his energies for forthcoming Senate battles.[7]

Norris dissipated some of these energies when in May, 1931, he learned that a postelection editorial in the *Fremont Tribune* had won a Pulitzer Prize. The editorial, "The Gentleman from Nebraska," argued that the voters sent Norris to Washington because he was the burr Nebraska delighted in placing under "the eastern saddle." "He is the reprisal for all the jokes of vaudevillists, the caricatures of cartoonists and the jibes of humorists that have come out of the east in the last quarter of a century." In short, Norris was the political joke that Nebraska afforded itself as a means of irritating and annoying the eastern establishment in the nation's capital, which persisted in regarding the state as provincial and its people as backward. Nebraska, the editorial claimed, was not interested in those progressive reforms Norris championed. It simply delighted every time he succeeded in "pestering his prey" and antagonizing powerful fixtures on the American scene. His antics let all know "there is a Nebraska, and Nebraska does not care how he does it." [8]

If Charles S. Ryckman, the author of the editorial, was telling the truth, then the people of Nebraska had been duped four times into sending an unworthy senator to Washington. They were ignorant, insincere, and unconcerned whether their public servants were able or patriotic. Such an analysis, Norris asserted, did damage to the integrity and the intelligence of the citizens of Nebraska. Moreover, the editorial merely rehashed campaign arguments. The falsehoods it presented had been repudiated at the polls and few people believed it. Yet Ryckman won a Pulitzer Prize. The people who paid homage to Ryckman, Norris claimed, were not doing so because he

[7] Norris to W. T. Rawleigh, Mar. 28, 1931; to John P. Davis, Apr. 2, 1931; to William T. Clarke, Apr. 17, 1931; to Jerome Davis, Mar. 27, 1931; to Seymour Stedman, Apr. 11, 1931. The conference was first scheduled for the Hotel La-Fayette and then shifted to the Carlton Hotel. Senator Cutting contributed over $1,600 toward the costs of the conference. William T. Rawleigh and Cornelia Bryce Pinchot were the leading contributors who helped defray the cost of printing and mailing the proceedings; Rawleigh contributed $1,000, Mrs. Pinchot, $500. Norris, who was responsible for the financial aspects of the conference, contributed $111.62 to balance the account.

[8] *Fremont Tribune,* Nov. 7, 1930.

had displayed any literary merit. In continuing the "tirade of false-hood and abuse," Ryckman was lending credence to the charges of those dissatisfied with the 1930 election results that the people "were a set of common ignoramuses, who did not know what they were doing, who had no patriotic feeling, and who were moved in their duty as citizens by a spirit of revenge and animosity." [9]

Norris's view received some support. Claude Bowers suggested that the Pulitzer Prize Committee was biased and called the Ryckman editorial "a lying, scurrilous article" that was "crude, stupid, and largely composed of misrepresentations and falsehoods." The *Lin-coln Star* ran a lengthy editorial citing Norris's distinguished career and insisting that in continually electing him, the people of Ne-braska needed no defense. The author, James E. Lawrence, for-merly unenthusiastic about Norris, was beginning to emerge as his most ardent defender among the newspapermen of Nebraska, the vast majority of whom were hostile to him and the views he ex-pressed.[10]

If Ryckman's editorial was designed to annoy and irritate Norris, it succeeded. But it was a tempest in a teapot. It did little to divert the impetus generated by the progressive conference. When the Sev-enty-second Congress convened in December, 1931, Norris was rested and ready; he focused his attention on procedural reform designed to make the processes of government more efficient and responsive to the popular will.

Throughout the entire era of Republican ascendancy Norris had inveighed against the Electoral College as "absolutely useless," an

[9] Norris to Clarence Reckmeyer, May 10, 1931; to Claude G. Bowers, May 21, 1931. Norris was quick to note that individuals and newspapers usually asso-ciated with the power trust were first to praise the virtues of the editorial; see Norris to S. E. Smith, June 22, 1931; John P. Robertson to Reckmeyer, June 29, 1931.

[10] Bowers to Norris, May 9, 1931; *Washington Times*, Dec. 17, 1931 (article on Norris by Bowers); *Lincoln Star*, May 10, 1931, "The Gentleman from Ne-braska" (editorial); Walter Locke to Norris, June 30, 1928. For Norris's views on Nebraska newspapers at this time, see Norris to Locke, May 3, 1929; to Ar-thur G. Wray, May 10, 1931; to William Allen White, Dec. 8, 1929; *Omaha World-Herald*, Jan. 2, 1930 (story by Walter E. Christenson); Robertson to L. E. Waddick, Apr. 22, 1933. Norris believed that a good progressive daily newspaper could make a model state of Nebraska. Philanthropists could benefit society by endowing such a paper more than by building hospitals, libraries, monuments, or other fine buildings; see Norris to Locke, May 3, 1929.

anachronism from the early years of the republic which hindered voters in freely expressing their choice for president. Besides being inefficient, it was also expensive and a deterrent to free government. An amendment to the Constitution could remedy this situation but Norris noted no great enthusiasm for one. Instead he tried to encourage states that had not done so to eliminate the names of presidential electors from the official ballot and merely allow the candidates' names to appear with the understanding that the electors chosen by the governor would respect the voters' choice for president. If this were done, an effective campaign for an independent candidate for president could become "a comparatively easy thing." Abolishing or modifying the Electoral College would accomplish far more than a third party. It would encourage independent candidates who could influence delegates to national nominating conventions more easily than the voting populace could.[11]

Norris recognized that less populous states benefited from the Electoral College. Their senators were included in their electoral representation, maintaining prestige and influence that would disappear if the Electoral College were eliminated. Norris did not believe in totaling all the votes cast for president throughout the nation and then giving the candidate with the highest number the certificate of election. Such an approach would have a tendency to produce fraud. If the states were regarded as units, fraud would not be a factor outside the state where the illegal votes were cast. Each state would retain its electoral vote without the instrumentality of presidential electors, the electoral vote being divided in proportion to the number of actual votes cast for certified candidates. Such an approach would not eliminate the power of political machines at national conventions, but it would make it possible for an independent candidate to run for president of the United States.[12]

Though Norris discussed the Electoral College in the last years of the Hoover administration, he realized that there was not enough support for its abolition to make the introduction of a resolution meaningful. There was a chance that another of his resolutions, fixing the commencement of the terms of president, vice-president, and

[11] Norris to Stella Haverstraw, Apr. 16, 1928; to Franklin D. Roosevelt, Dec. 8, 1928; to Joseph Huber, Jan. 2, 1931; to Morris Portnoy, Mar. 29, 1933.
    [12] Norris to I. D. Evans, Apr. 6, 1931.

members of Congress, could succeed. Rather than jeopardize its chances, he decided to postpone action on an amendment abolishing the Electoral College until a decision was reached on the lame-duck resolution.[13]

In the Seventy-first Congress, convening shortly after Hoover's inauguration, Norris again introduced his lame-duck resolution and for the fifth time it passed the Senate.[14] The resolution proposed to amend the Constitution by fixing the beginning of the terms of president and vice-president at noon on January 15. The terms of members of Congress would begin at noon on January 2 following their election the preceding November, thereby eliminating lame-duck sessions and the thirteen-month delay until a newly elected member could serve. Yet ten months after it was certified and delivered to the House, the Speaker had not referred the resolution to any committee for action. In April, 1930, Norris called upon the vice-president to appoint a committee to investigate and report to the Senate what action, if any, it might take. Speaker Longworth, of course, was in no way intimidated by Norris's remarks and neither was the president.[15]

[13] At the outset of the New Deal Norris introduced a resolution abolishing the Electoral College but maintaining the system of electoral votes, which would be proportionally divided according to the votes candidates received in each state; see *Lincoln Star,* Mar. 29, 1933, "Norris Scores Again" (editorial); Robertson to J. W. Kuhn, Apr. 5, 1933.

[14] It passed the Senate the first time on Feb. 13, 1923. On Feb. 22, 1923, it received a favorable report from the House committee and was placed on the House calendar. No action was taken by the House, and it died on Mar. 4, 1923, because of the adjournment of Congress. It passed the Senate the second time on Mar. 14, 1924; on Apr. 15, 1924, it was favorably reported by the House committee. It remained on the calendar of the House, without any action being taken, from Apr. 15, 1924, until the expiration of the Sixty-eighth Congress on Mar. 4, 1925. It again passed the Senate, in the Sixty-ninth Congress, on Feb. 15, 1926. It was again favorably reported by the House committee on Feb. 24, 1926, and remained on the House calendar, without any action, from then until the expiration of the Sixty-ninth Congress on Mar. 4, 1927. In the Seventieth Congress the resolution passed the Senate on Jan. 4, 1928, was referred to the House Judiciary Committee, from which it received a favorable report, and on Mar. 9, 1928, the House acted. While it received a large majority of those voting, it failed to receive the two-thirds majority required by the Constitution.

[15] *Congressional Record,* 71st Cong., 1st sess., June 5, pp. 2388–89, 2395–96, June 7, 1929, pp. 2490–93; 2nd sess., Apr. 21, 1930, pp. 7310–16. The vote in the Senate was 64 to 9. Incidentally, the resolution provided that in case of failure to elect a president and vice-president at a general election, the president

In a public statement in November Norris held Nicholas Longworth, Speaker of the House, responsible for the failure of that body to pass the Senate-adopted resolution which was then pigeonholed in a House committee. Meanwhile a substitute measure, camouflaged to look like the Senate's version, was placed on the House calendar. "If Longworth and his crew had been acting squarely," Norris asserted, "my bill would have been sent to committee in its regular order a year or more ago." Now that "so many of the old machine crowd were beaten for reelection," Norris thought that House members, a majority of whom were reportedly sympathetic, might conclude that discretion was the better part of valor and allow his resolution to go through over the opposition of "a few leaders standing in the way." [16]

Finally, in the last session of the Seventy-first Congress the House took action. Speaker Longworth in a gesture of acquiescence accepted Norris's resolution with a vitiating amendment which put a time limit of four months on the session; his action guaranteed filibusters and other dilatory tactics. Longworth's amendment was adopted by the House on February 24, 1931. House Republicans in conference committee refused to budge from their support of it, reaffirming Norris's views that powerful political interests, including the president, did not want the lame-duck session of Congress abolished. The obstinacy of the two Republican House members made it certain that no final action would be taken. Not discouraged by this development, Norris was confident that his resolution would receive favorable consideration in the next Congress.[17]

---

would be chosen by the newly elected House and the vice-president by the new Senate. The proposed amendment was recommended by the American Bar Association in 1921; see also Norris to Hiram Johnson, Mar. 24, 1931.

[16] *Lincoln Star,* Nov. 16, 1930; Norris to Nicholas Murray Butler, Nov. 22, 1930. Norris realized that party leaders, faced with the virtual certainty that the amendment would pass in the newly elected Congress, might allow it to go through in the present session so that the Republican administration could take credit for it. The principal Democratic leaders in the House, including floor leader John N. Garner, favored it; see the cogent analysis by Theodore Joslin in the *Boston Evening Transcript,* Nov. 30, 1930.

[17] *Cleveland Plain Dealer,* Feb. 26, 1931, "The Vitiating Amendment" (editorial); Norris to Josephus Daniels, Feb. 7, 1931; to Henry C. Richmond, Mar. 3, 1931. The House conferees were Charles Gifford (Massachusetts) and Arthur Free (California) for the majority and Lamar Jeffers (Alabama) for the minority. The Senate conferees were Thomas J. Walsh, Borah, and Norris.

In the Seventy-second Congress the Democrats for the first time since 1917 organized the House and elected John Nance Garner of Texas as Speaker, thereby destroying the presidential alliance with the House against the Senate which had been operative since Harding's tenure of office. Early in the session Norris introduced his resolution for the sixth time. This time he was assured of House support and on January 6, 1932, it was quickly approved in the Senate by a vote of 63 to 7.[18] The House also approved the resolution, adding an amendment which provided that at least one branch of the legislature of each state must be elected after its submission. Thus the amendment would become an issue in state campaigns and voters could express opinions on it. Norris opposed the House amendment because he did not deem it advisable to couple the question with the state and local issues involved in the election of a legislature. Since the House version differed from the Senate resolution, the matter went into conference and the vice-president appointed the same conferees as in the past session: Thomas J. Walsh, William Borah, and Norris.[19]

The measure that emerged from conference committee did not differ substantially from Norris's original resolution and he readily accepted it. In Section 1, the crux of the amendment, the date for the convening of Congress was changed from January 2 to 3; inauguration day was shifted from January 15 to 20. The other changes were of a similar nature. The heart of the House amendment, which Norris disliked, was not included, though a portion, providing that to be operative, the amendment must be ratified within seven years by three-fourths of the state legislatures, was approved. Two-thirds of all senators present and voting having responded in the affirmative, the constitutional requirement pertaining to amendments was fulfilled. Since the House had approved the report the previous day by the necessary two-thirds majority, the action of the Senate meant that ten years of effort had resulted in a great victory for efficient government. And it was achieved solely through the tenacity and persuasiveness of George W. Norris. Dur-

---

[18] *Congressional Record,* 72nd Cong., 2nd sess., Jan. 6, 1932, pp. 1372–73, 1378–79, 1384; Norris to John Nance Garner, Jan. 5, 1932.

[19] *Congressional Record,* 72nd Cong., 1st sess., Feb. 17, 1932, pp. 4117–18. The House on Feb. 16, 1932, approved the lame-duck resolution by the substantial majority of 336 to 56.

ing the Senate vote he beamed upon his colleagues and once laughed aloud. His task was finished, though the state legislatures had yet to act.[20]

On March 4, 1932, Virginia became the first state to ratify. By mid-April nine other states had followed her lead; Norris was convinced that by the end of the following winter it would be approved by the necessary number of states. In January, 1933, the amendment was ratified, Missouri being the thirty-sixth state to approve it. No state legislature to which it had been submitted failed to approve it. Thus, after October 15, 1933, the date on which the amendment became operative, each regular session of Congress would begin on January 3 with no fixed adjournment date, and each new president would be inaugurated on January 20. It represented the first fundamental modernization of the federal government since 1913, when the Seventeenth Amendment, providing for direct election of U.S. senators, was adopted.[21]

Norris hailed the outcome with a statement explaining why the amendment was necessary. Its enactment, he said, "is a great step toward placing the control of our government in the hands of the chosen representatives of the American people." He also congratulated the newspapers owned by William Randolph Hearst for "the magnificent fight they had made in behalf of the 'Lame Duck' Amendment." The following day, January 24, 1933, Norris's colleagues paid him tribute: "Your dreams," said Hiram Johnson, reiterating what he had said in 1924, "mean that humanity may benefit, people may prosper, and human beings may be a bit happier." [22]

At the time Congress was approving his lame-duck amendment, Norris was in the midst of another battle to limit the use of injunctions in labor disputes. His interest in this problem, while not as old

[20] *Ibid.*, Mar. 2, 1932, pp. 5084–86; Robertson to John Leonard, Mar. 2, 1932. On Mar. 1, 1932, the Senate passed and sent to the House Norris's bill restricting the use of labor injunctions.

[21] Norris to Roosevelt, Mar. 14, 1932; Robertson to George N. Hartmann, June 8, 1932; *Washington Star*, Jan. 23, 1933.

[22] *Washington Star*, Jan. 23, 1933; *New York Evening Journal*, Jan. 24, 1933; draft statement by Norris on lame-duck amendment, Jan. 20, 1933; *Congressional Record*, 72nd Cong., 2nd sess., Jan. 24, 1933, p. 2380. The *Eagle Beacon* of Weeping Water, Nebr., on Feb. 23, 1933, reprinted an editorial, "Statesman vs. Political Hack," from the *St. Louis Post-Dispatch* applauding Norris's achievement.

as his desire to eliminate the lame-duck session, emanated from his service as chairman of the Senate Judiciary Committee. As a progressive senator from a rural state, Norris always had been sympathetic to the plight of working men, though his focus centered on the farmer. Campaigning in 1926 against Vare, he was moved by a tombstone epitaph in a Pennsylvania mining community:

> For 40 years beneath the sod, with pick and spade
> I did my task, the coal king's slave, but now,
> Thank God, I'm free at last.

Once he examined the excessive and arbitrary use of injunctions, his interest in fair play and his hostility to groups using legal instruments for their own special purposes led him to advocate legislation curbing the excessive use of injunctions in labor disputes. Basically interested in equal justice under the law, Norris quickly emerged as a friend and champion of labor.

The anti-injunction bill was reported by a subcommittee of the Judiciary Committee. Its members, Thomas J. Walsh, John J. Blaine, and Norris, who served as chairman, were aided by a group of experts who prepared memorandums, offered suggestions, and rewrote portions of the various drafts.[23] At the 1929 convention of the American Federation of Labor, held in Toronto, after an extended debate the convention endorsed the bill with only one negative vote. Throughout the drafting period Norris conducted an extensive correspondence with members of the group of experts. Donald Richberg, one of their number, said that their purpose was "to aid in drafting a law with due regard to all interests involved." [24]

[23] Francis P. Sayre and Felix Frankfurter were at Harvard; Herman Oliphant was at Columbia and would soon transfer to Johns Hopkins. Edwin E. Witte was chief of the Wisconsin Legislative Reference Library and a former student of John R. Commons. Donald Richberg was an outstanding lawyer, active on behalf of the Railroad Brotherhoods and in progressive causes, though he insisted he was acting in this instance in the public's and not in labor's interest; see Richberg to Norris, Feb. 11, 1930.

[24] Norris to Herman Oliphant, Nov. 26, 1929; to T. J. Walsh, Dec. 2, 1929; Richberg to Norris, Feb. 11, 1930. The Norris bill was sent to the A. F. of L. for revision, reversing the process of drafting by the federation and revision by the Senate that heretofore had prevailed. William Green quickly recognized the bill as regulatory rather than revolutionary with respect to the principles on which injunctions usually were granted in equity cases. For his views, see *New York Times,* Aug. 14, 1929. Green was attending a meeting of the A. F. of L. Executive Council at the time.

Heavily involved in legislative battles, Norris did not have time to examine carefully suggestions made by this group. He filed them, awaiting a time when he could consider the matter thoroughly. When the subcommittee finally held hearings, all who wished to testify were heard without limit. But the majority of the Senate Judiciary Committee in the Seventy-first Congress was opposed. Thus in December, 1930, the anti-injunction bill was placed on the Senate calendar with an adverse report, indicating that a majority of the committee favored its indefinite postponement. Though there was little chance for Senate action, Norris initially hoped to bring it to a vote. But by February, 1931, he realized that this was impossible and announced his intention to press the matter at the beginning of the next Congress.[25]

"One of the very serious obstacles in the way of congressional action on the injunction matter," Norris said, was the attitude of Andrew Furuseth, venerable head of the International Seamen's Union. Norris, who regarded Furuseth with a feeling verging upon reverence, nevertheless realized that his views on this question were a serious handicap. Opponents could rally beneath his banner, taking advantage of a division in labor's ranks to defeat an anti-injunction bill. Furuseth, a self-taught merchant seaman, believed that the Thirteenth Amendment could serve as an instrument to curb the indiscriminate use of injunctions. He also contended that legal criteria regarding actions of individuals were coextensive with those pertaining to actions by men in concert, not comprehending that difficulties with the labor injunction arose from complicated practical situations and complicated legal doctrines. He offered simple formulas to a complex legal problem. His views were incorporated into a bill sponsored in the Senate by Henrik Shipstead of Minnesota.[26]

[25] Norris to Richberg, Mar. 6, 1930; to Alfred P. Thom, Apr. 22, 1930; Robertson to Joseph F. Stier, May 27, 1930; Norris to Roger Baldwin, Dec. 15, 1930; to J. L. McCorison, Jr., Feb. 7, 1931.

[26] Norris to Felix Frankfurter, Mar. 27, 1931; Frankfurter to Henrik Shipstead, Mar. 23, 1931; Richberg to Norris, June 18, 1928; Frankfurter to Norris, June 21, 1928 (last two letters are in Box 29, Felix Frankfurter Papers, Manuscript Division, Library of Congress). Both June letters discuss Furuseth's proposed bill and its misunderstanding of the term "property." Frankfurter felt Furuseth's proposal was "either mischievous or futile" and possibly invalid. For a biography of Andrew Furuseth, see Hyman G. Weintraub, *Andrew Furuseth, Emancipator of the Seaman* (Berkeley, Calif., 1959). See also the

With action on his bill stalled, Norris hoped that in the Seventy-second Congress it could be enacted. He was so concerned about it that he advised Theodore Dreiser, who was calling for a Senate investigation of the deprivation of civil liberties in Harlan County, Kentucky, that a committee other than Judiciary should handle the matter. While he was relatively certain that the lame-duck amendment would be approved because of Democratic control of the House, the fate of the anti-injunction measure was not clear. Even if approved by Congress, it faced the possibility of a presidential veto. But Norris was not one to be deterred. After being considered in committee for more than three years, late in January, 1932, the bill emerged with a favorable report, in part because public sentiment had begun to shift in its favor. When Congress convened in December, 1931, the National Civic Federation, the American Federation of Labor, and the American Civil Liberties Union all agreed that an anti-injunction bill was necessary and that the Norris measure was the best available. Several states, including New York under Governor Franklin Roosevelt, had enacted anti-injunction legislation. The advisers to the subcommittee, Edwin Witte, Francis Sayre, Felix Frankfurter, Herman Oliphant, and Donald Richberg, in various ways were making their views in favor of the Norris bill known to an influential if not large audience.[27]

In February, 1932, the measure came before the Senate. In a lengthy speech Norris explained that its purpose was to assist courts in interpreting the proposed law. Section 2 declared the public policy of the United States:

> Whereas under prevailing economic conditions, developed with the aid of governmental authority for owners of property to organize in the corporate and other forms of ownership association, the individual unorganized worker is commonly helpless to exercise actual liberty of contract and to protect his freedom of

comprehensive chapter, "The Anti-Injunction Movement," in Irving Bernstein, *The Lean Years: A History of the American Worker* (Boston, 1960).

[27] Norris to Theodore Dreiser, Oct. 29, 1931; to Baldwin, Dec. 12, 1931; to Andrew Furuseth, Jan. 9, 1932; *Congressional Record,* 72nd Cong., 1st sess., Feb. 4, 1932, pp. 3370–71. Norris asked Furuseth to support his bill as the only one that could secure a favorable report and eventual enactment. "A division of our forces," he explained, "will necessarily make the road harder to travel and put the final result in some doubt."

labor, and thereby to obtain acceptable terms and conditions of employment, wherefore, though he should be free to decline to associate with his fellows, it is necessary that he have full freedom of association, self-organization, and designation of representatives of his own choosing, to negotiate the terms and conditions of his employments, and that he shall be free from the interference, restraint, or coercion of employers of labor, or their agents in the designation of such representatives or in self-organization or in other concerned activities for the purpose of collective bargaining or other mutual aid or protection; therefore the following definitions of, and limitations upon, the jurisdiction and authority of the courts of the United States are hereby enacted.[28]

Section 1 stated that "no court of the United States . . . shall have jurisdiction to issue any restraining order or temporary or permanent injunction in a case involving or growing out of a labor dispute, except in strict conformity with the provisions of this act, nor shall any such restraining order or temporary or permanent injunction be issued contrary to the public policy declared in this act."

This section was really a preamble to the public policy declared in the second section. The measure was not an attack upon the principle of the injunction procedure; rather, it aimed to prevent abuse of the principle. It was intended to be protective and preservative, to restore justice and equality in the administration of the injunction writ. It did this by declaring to be public policy the right of labor to organize and bargain collectively, by curtailing the use of "yellow-dog contracts," and by insisting upon jury trials in all contempt-of-court cases.[29] Calling yellow-dog contracts contrary to

[28] This section put the stamp of government approval on the right of working men to organize for collective bargaining. New Deal legislation would guarantee the right of collective bargaining.

[29] A yellow-dog contract was a written contract of employment, signed by an employee as a condition of obtaining employment, in which he agreed not to join a union or, if he was a union member, to dissociate himself from it. Further, the employee agreed not to quit without giving sufficient notice to his employer to enable him to hire someone to take his place. The employee in many instances agreed in advance to accept such conditions of labor as the employer might from time to time decide upon. Provisions varied, but they all had the same effect in taking away from the worker the right to have anything to say about any conditions of his employment. "In other words," Norris said, "he surrenders his actual liberty of contract and to a great extent enters into voluntary servitude." Such a contract, he believed, was contrary to public policy under the common law. If

public policy and therefore unenforceable in any federal court, Norris said:

> By the abolition of these unconscionable contracts, this bill sets on the hilltop a beacon of human liberty. It gives to those who toil, to those who are poor, to those who, by the sweat of their faces, contribute to the happiness of humble homes—the enjoyment of that freedom and that liberty which is necessary in every free country for all of its citizens and not by any one class of its people. It gives liberty to the down trodden and the poor and, in this respect, puts them on an equality with those who live in luxury and plenty.

In his remarks Norris insisted that the power to make a law and the power to enforce it should be separate: judicial power should be separate from legislative and administrative power. Heretofore, injunctions did away with these fundamental principles and put in the hands of a judge the rights to make a law, to enforce it, to try those who allegedly violated the law thus made, and to inflict, at his "own sweet will," whatever punishment he deemed appropriate. Summary methods depriving people of their "day in court" were thus held to be "due process of law" and could only lead to the common knowledge and belief that, in Blackstone's words, "there can be no public liberty."

Norris's bill would prevent federal courts from issuing indiscriminate injunctions applying "only to the poor, to laboring men in labor disputes." Judge-made law would become an impossibility because of the provision for trial by jury in cases of violation of restraining orders. It also prohibited the issuing of injunctions which restrained employees from assembling peacefully to promote their interests. Virtually unknown in 1890, by 1930 seldom did a controversy of any importance between management and labor occur without the issuing of one or more injunctions. The bill further provided for a hearing with the right to cross-examine witnesses before an injunction could be issued. The court had to be satisfied that unlawful

---

sustained, no labor organizations could exist. A yellow-dog contract was signed under "duress or coercion" because the employee in most instances had no alternative if he wished to support himself and family. Since the courts enforced these contracts and issued injunctions predicated on their legality, congressional action was now necessary to outlaw what the common law already deemed a violation of public policy.

acts had been or would be committed, that irreparable injury would occur, and that the complainant had no adequate remedy at law. Moreover, the court had to find "that the public officers charged with the duty to protect complainant's property" were unable or unwilling to provide protection. In analyzing several injunctions, Norris stressed the great importance of an "untarnished judiciary," lest "a perfect law" be nullified "by an unfair and biased judge."

Norris also noted that the bill applied equally "to organizations of labor and to organizations of capital." It protected no one, employer or employee, from punishment for the commission of unlawful acts "either as against property or as against persons." In the past injunctions, which in effect made something a crime that was not a crime before, had discriminated against laboring men not financially able to make proper defenses, especially when confronted with corporations having unlimited means and attorneys of great ability. They had been faced with unsympathetic and hostile judges, and they usually accepted the court's dictum before the case reached the stage of a trial. Besides forbidding the issuance of injunctions without a full hearing and then granting persons charged with contempt the right to trial by jury under another judge, Norris asserted, his bill would place "upon a higher plane all of our courts" and eventually establish "faith in and respect for all our judiciary tribunals." [30]

On March 1, 1932, by a vote of 75 to 5 Norris's bill passed the Senate. Five New England Republicans constituted the opposition to a measure on which, until 1932, Norris had been unable to secure a favorable report, though he chaired the Judiciary Committee which considered it. Norris had won a second great victory. Delighted with the Senate vote, Norris continued about his business "of shaking intrenched power and making Government more directly responsive to the public will and the public good." No doubt he also realized that yet to be achieved was the major item in the trinity of legislative accomplishments he most desired: government

[30] *Congressional Record,* 72nd Cong., 1st sess., Feb. 23, 1932, pp. 4502–10. On Feb. 17, 1932, Norris succeeded in having his anti-injunction bill made the unfinished business of the Senate for 2 P.M. Tuesday, Feb. 23. It was ordered by unanimous consent that the bill would remain unfinished business until disposed of; see Robertson to Fred Carey, Feb. 17, 1932; to John G. Maher, Feb. 17, 1932.

operation of the Muscle Shoals facilities for the benefit of the American people.[31]

On March 8, 1932, under the guidance of Fiorello H. LaGuardia the House approved a slightly different version of the anti-injunction measure. On March 9 Norris requested unanimous consent for the Senate to consider the House bill and that it be amended by striking out all after the enacting clause and inserting instead the Senate bill. Rather than send the House bill to the Senate Judiciary Committee for a report, Norris made his proposal to insert in lieu of the House bill the Senate-approved measure. If approved, he intended to move that the Senate insist on its amendment and ask for a conference with the House.

The House started with the same bill as the Senate, LaGuardia having received the copy he introduced from Norris. The situation arose because the House had ignored the Senate bill and passed its own. Thus, if legislation was not to be delayed once again, one chamber would have to submit to the other. Feeling that there was no humiliation involved, Norris proposed a solution to the dilemma. If his unanimous-consent request was not accepted, according to Senate rules one day would have to elapse before it could again be subject to a similar motion. But the Senate unanimously approved it and the chair chose Norris, John J. Blaine, and Thomas J. Walsh to represent the Senate on the conference committee.[32]

On March 18, 1932, the Senate approved the conference committee report without a roll-call vote. The changes in the measure were minor. Most of the differing clauses in the House bill were eliminated. On the previous day the House had approved the measure and on March 23, 1932, the president signed the anti-injunction bill into law. Refraining from comment, the president made public a letter from Attorney General James D. Mitchell question-

[31] Robertson to Leonard, Mar. 2, 1932. The quote is from the *Raleigh* (N.C.) *News and Observer,* Mar. 4, 1932, "That Man Norris" (editorial). See also a congratulatory letter from Frankfurter to Norris, Mar. 9, 1932.

[32] *Congressional Record,* 72nd Cong., 1st sess., Mar. 9, 1932, pp. 5549–51; F. H. LaGuardia to Norris, Mar. 9, 1932. The vote in favor of the House bill was 326 to 14. LaGuardia, apologizing to Norris for the House's failure to consider the Senate bill, explained the parliamentary tangle that led the House to pass its own measure.

ing the clarity of some of the sections and suggesting that other parts might be unconstitutional. He did recommend that it be signed. In blasting Mitchell's letter, Norris said that taken in connection with the president's policy of elevating judges who had become famous "for their inhuman and unjust injunctions," it disclosed the true feelings of both Herbert Hoover and the Attorney General. Gratification that the anti-injunction bill had become law was intermingled with apprehension that the unusual manner of its approval might lead to attacks upon it in the courts.[33]

Actually Hoover had little choice but to sign the bill. It had passed both houses of Congress with such large majorities that it could have been repassed over his veto. Administration stalwarts on the Judiciary Committee, Charles S. Deneen and Frederick H. Gillett, had not returned to the Seventy-second Congress and the Democratic membership had increased. In this way another staunch opponent of the measure, Frederick Steiwer, had been removed from the committee. Accepting the realities of the situation, the administration made the necessary concessions; the 1932 *Campaign Book of the Republican Party* listed among Hoover's victories for labor, "Approval in the face of forceful opposition of the Bill outlawing the yellow-dog contract and providing relief from the use of injunction in labor disputes."

Thanks to Norris's efforts, citizens interested in sound public policies had some grounds for rejoicing in the sad and depressing period before the 1932 campaign got under way. The progressive conference, the lame-duck amendment, the anti-injunction law—all proved anew, as Felix Frankfurter said in another connection, "that self-less devotion to country, unflinching persistence in good causes and statesmanlike capacity to make effective general ideas for the public welfare eventually have their triumph." Frankfurter believed that the whole country was Norris's debtor, though he realized that the senator was more absorbed "in the triumph of the right" than in seeing the success within a fortnight of two great causes he had espoused. Patience, taking little heed of time, had accomplished its

[33] *Congressional Record*, 72nd Cong., 1st sess., Mar. 18, 1932, pp. 6452–55; Norris statement on anti-injunction bill, Mar. 24, 1932; *Washington Post, Washington News*, Mar. 24, 1932. Norris believed the administration had sought to weaken the bill by getting Donald Richberg to suggest some compromising changes; see Norris to Richberg, Sept. 17, 1932.

purpose. Public policies that he had long favored were now realized, but Norris was not a senator who rested upon well-earned laurels. Times were disastrously bad and much work remained to be done.[34]

[34] Frankfurter to Norris, Jan. 24, 1933 (Box 29, Frankfurter Papers).

The World at Home

36

The world beyond the boundaries of the United States was something George W. Norris was too busy to examine carefully during the Hoover administration. When he did so, it was usually to comment adversely, relating it to domestic difficulties. The center of his attention was the United States, burdened and beset with difficulties in a depression period. His committee assignments, his political and legislative concerns, and the mounting burden of work taxed his resources and energies so that Hoover's foreign policies hardly attracted his attention. In this respect Norris was no different from most of his colleagues, except, of course, members of the Foreign Relations Committee. Aside from blaming some of the nation's difficulties upon the European economic collapse, they registered little interest in world affairs.

In one respect Norris's position on international relations was unique. A decade after World War I he was the only senator who had opposed American entrance into the conflict still active in public life. As increasing numbers of Americans came to doubt the value of that venture, Norris assumed something of the wisdom of a sage and the infallibility of an oracle. In the eyes of an increasing number of disillusioned idealists and progressives Norris was assuming the mantle of an elder statesman. He had fought with Theodore Roosevelt and Robert M. LaFollette; in opposing World War I he had suggested what would follow in the 1920s; and he was still battling against powerful interests and overwhelming odds, managing by dint of persistence and ability to strike powerful blows on behalf of oppressed and overwhelmed Americans. Thus, when Norris commented on world affairs during the depression years, despite the fact that he was not an authority on the subject, his views received respectful attention.

Though he disagreed with Herbert Hoover on almost everything else, they did agree that the Great Depression was basically of European derivation. To Norris the trouble stemmed from the nation's participation in the war: "If we had stayed out of that mess, we would not be in this one." Hoover felt that the depression was rooted in European economic deficiencies that had beset the nation during his administration. It could have been overcome; indeed, Hoover believed it was being overcome by his policies and programs, despite opposition from Democrats and political opportunists like Norris and other disloyal Republicans in Congress.[1]

By 1930 Norris believed that many provisions of the Versailles Treaty had been recognized as "uncivilized and contrary to the truth." Unfortunately, it had taken many years "for this fact to percolate throughout the world." The Young plan and the Dawes plan, formulated early in the 1920s, were makeshifts brought about "mostly by international bankers to enforce as much of the Versailles Treaty as they thought the world, and particularly Germany, could stand." While the depression was merely "a natural result of the world-wide war," other themes, domestic in origin, particularly the gradual and continual accumulation of property in the hands of a comparative few, were "accentuated and greatly increased" after the war. Deflation following the conflict adversely affected purchasing power and income and accelerated tendencies toward concentration. But "the great fundamental reason for it all" was America's participation in the war. If the United States had stayed out, Norris said in 1932, "I can see how easy it would have been to balance the budget at this time and to have provided sufficient funds to meet all our financial obligations." He did not claim that the depression could have been avoided, but its impact would have been less severe and the American people "would have been relieved of the

---

[1] George W. Norris to Perry L. Hole, Mar. 22, 1932 (the quote).

payment of the billions of dollars which is chargeable one hundred percent to the war." [2]

In a 1931 Memorial Day address Norris warned that civilization could not survive another conflict and decried the international competition in armaments. While he held that nations should be able to settle their differences before a court, Norris made it clear that he did not advocate entry into the League of Nations; he thought the league might be a breeder of wars. Rather, he urged taking the profit out of war as a means of curbing concentration in the economy and of reducing tensions that could lead to conflict.[3]

On April 6, 1932, the fifteenth anniversary of America's entrance into the conflict, Norris said that while he undoubtedly had made many mistakes in his almost thirty years in Congress, voting against the declaration of war with Germany was not one of them. Through the efforts and sacrifices of the United States, the Allies were supposed to have achieved victory. But, Norris insisted, "there was no victory." Unborn generations would have to "toil and suffer and sweat to pay for our participation in that catastrophe." The unemployed, the hungry, the cold, the victims of the depression—all were paying now for the folly of America's participation in that most ruinous and most destructive of wars.[4]

Rarely did Norris view world developments outside this national context. Even in these instances his remarks often hammered home a point or reflected views he had been reiterating within an American matrix. Interviewed in 1929 on the meaning of the Labor party triumph in the British election, Norris expressed satisfaction that reaction in world politics and economics had received a setback: "It is a repudiation of the unjust Treaty of Versailles. It is a repudiation of the millionaire coal kings who refused to pay to coal miners a living wage. It is a repudiation of the unjust and indefensi-

[2] Norris to C. G. Binderup, Dec. 29, 1931; to Carl Marsh, May 28, 1932; to Charles E. Olson, July 19, 1932.

[3] *Maywood* (Nebr.) *Eagle Reporter,* June (?), 1931.

[4] Draft statement by Norris, Apr. 6, 1932. On this same day on the Senate floor Norris protested the huge Army Day parade and the proposal to allow school children and government employees time off to view it. He called attention to a grimmer unseen parade of over 6 million unemployed who would not be on hand to rejoice as soldiers paraded down Pennsylvania Avenue to celebrate America's entrance into World War I; see *Congressional Record,* 72nd Cong., 1st sess., Apr. 6, 1932, p. 7564.

ble treatment of Russia. It is a repudiation of the militarists who are trying to use all the energies of the people to build up a huge army and navy. It is a victory in the direction of universal peace." [5]

Later, when Andrew Mellon was appointed ambassador to Great Britain, Norris criticized the appointment. Hoover said that he needed "the greatest mind and the greatest statesman that he could find anywhere to fill that place"; Norris observed that Will Rogers would have to look well to his laurels because the president was challenging him as a humorist.[6] Of more vital interest was the 1930 London Naval Conference to re-examine tonnage limitations on naval vessels. Norris hoped that much good would result from it, though he thought the prospects of success "very discouraging." Since Hoover's instructions to the delegates were not made public, popular sentiment had no way of mobilizing itself. Moreover, specialists and experts often were representatives of those "who care more for the dollar than they do for the human life." They wanted war and "big armies and big navies" because of the financial profits involved. Pretentious statements that seemed fair to the public often were vitiated by secret instructions to conference delegates. Thus he was disturbed when the president directed Secretary of State Henry L. Stimson to withhold from the Foreign Relations Committee correspondence, documents, and other material that might have aided the Senate in evaluating the treaty.[7]

Despite these views Norris decided to vote for ratification. But he criticized Secretary Stimson for trying to deceive the Senate in explaining why he was not presenting all available information. The Secretary sent a letter quoting George Washington on why secret negotiations were often necessary. Norris said that Stimson did not give Washington his due. The quote was from a letter in which the first president explained why he would not release information to the House of Representatives: "all the papers affecting the negotiation" had already been placed "before the Senate when the treaty itself

[5] *Organized Farmer,* June 7, 1929. Norris was interviewed by a member of the Federated Press.

[6] *Congressional Record,* 72nd Cong., 1st sess., Feb. 10, 1932, p. 3678. Mellon's appointment was approved by a voice vote.

[7] Norris to Venice Edmondson, Mar. 13, 1930; to Mrs. C. E. Messenger, Apr. 1, 1930; to J. P. Hobson, Apr. 10, 1930; to J. E. Carlin, June 4, 1930; to W. J. Atkinson, June 16, 1930.

was communicated for their consideration and advice." These quotations were not included in the portion of the Washington letter Stimson cited among his reasons for not disclosing information to the Senate.[8]

The president, supporting his Secretary of State, declined to present any documents to the Senate. Norris then suggested a reservation: the Senate would ratify the treaty provided there were no secret agreements about any section of it. Without such a reservation the Senate "would be justified in refusing ratification of the treaty." A majority of his colleagues agreed; on July 21, 1930, by a vote of 58 to 9 the Senate consented to the treaty with the Norris reservation.[9]

Though the London Naval Conference accomplished little, it tended to stabilize the arms race temporarily by reinforcing the ratio concept of construction among the major naval powers. On these grounds Norris supported it. The following year, when French Premier Pierre Laval visited the United States, Norris interpreted his trip as an effort "to have France and the United States enter into a compact both offensive and defensive for the alleged purpose of keeping the peace of the world." But disarmament was the truer road to peace. Thus Norris supported American participation in the World Disarmament Conference at Geneva in February, 1932, calling for a delegation that would take the initiative in proposing measures.[10]

While Norris had no reservations about disarmament, he had some hesitation about the United States joining the World Court. Reservations were necessary before the United States could associate itself in the World Court with European nations, most of whom were relentless in their "hatred of the American Government" because it would not forgive their debts. While the World Court might be a good thing for Europe, Norris explained:

[8] *Congressional Record,* 71st Cong., special sess. of the Senate, July 9, 1930, pp. 51, 54; Norris to Horace A. Davis, July 16, 1930.

[9] *Congressional Record,* 71st Cong., special sess. of the Senate, July 21, 1930, p. 362. For a comprehensive discussion of the London Naval Conference, see Robert H. Ferrell, *American Diplomacy in the Great Depression: Hoover-Stimson Foreign Policy, 1929–1933* (New Haven, Conn., 1957), Chapter 6.

[10] *Omaha Bee,* Oct. 24, 1931; Norris to Alfred Lief, Dec. 30, 1931.

. . . when I realize the selfishness of European nations in getting us into the struggle, taking the lives of our boys and our money to make it possible for them to win a victory, I am again strengthened in my original viewpoint that we should never have gone into the war—that we should have stayed out entirely. And when I realize, also, that while our European allies took all the spoils of victory to themselves and were unwilling even to pay back to us the money we had loaned to make that victory possible, I am further convinced that they had only one use for us and that was to have us, at the sacrifice of human life and treasury, make it possible for their selfish chestnuts to be pulled out of the international fire.[11]

When he looked at the Far East, Norris saw Japan as a nation which had disregarded its pledge to help maintain the territorial integrity of China by invading Manchuria. Great Britain and France, by not joining Secretary Stimson "in making protest and taking peaceful action against Japan," did not live up to their agreements. Japan could have been thwarted in her invasion of Manchuria, Norris speculated, "if all the signatory powers signing the Nine-Power Pact had, for instance, followed the American Government and all of them had, by concerted action, withdrawn official connection and communication with Japan. . . ." By invading China in 1931, Japan was inflicting destruction, starvation, and death upon hordes of defenseless people "without regard for justice and honor." And the civilized world, except for the United States, did not protest her actions. Japan's renunciation of treaty obligations caused him to question the use of an agreement with "an outlaw nation" that would not keep its word. It was Japan and the European powers, none of whom by 1932 had criticized the former's actions in China, who were asking the United States to join the World Court. Thus Norris's suspicions of international cooperation were intensified by Far Eastern developments during the Hoover administration.[12]

What most historians have regarded as a statesmanlike action by

[11] *Lincoln Star,* Nov. 9, 1931; Norris to Harley G. Moorhead, May 4, 1932 (quote); to Mrs. Otto Wiese, Apr. 5, 1932; to Mary F. Paul, Jan. 6, 1932.
[12] Norris to Moorhead, Mar. 4, 1932; to Mrs. Wiese, Apr. 5, 1932.

the president, the moratorium on war debts, Norris saw as a piece of unmitigated stupidity. If the president had said, "We will give this extension on condition that you stop using your funds in armaments, in the building of navies, and the equipment of armies," then Norris could have been more sympathetic with the moratorium proposition. If these nations had ceased or stringently curtailed their military expenditures, they might have been able to meet their obligations to the United States. If they had made even an effort, Norris would have been more amenable to the moratorium concept. The American people "in toil and sweat" for more than a decade had been working "to pay the interest on the money that our Government borrowed in order to make these loans." To make matters worse in the midst of the depression crisis, "instead of using this money to make public improvements that would give jobs to hundreds and millions of men and women," the American government, thanks to Hoover's action, was asking "our debtors in Europe not to pay us anything."

In his Senate remarks and in his correspondence Norris continually mentioned the suffering of the American people and the administration's lack of interest in their plight. Granting a moratorium when one was never requested and at a time when the American government "was running behind daily" seemed to Norris the height of folly. Indeed, a moratorium for farmers would have been more beneficial than one for European creditors. The farmer had not sinned. His present plight was not exclusively his own fault. "All we ask," he said, "is that he be treated as well as the European nation that is in the condition it is now because of its own extravagance, because of its own useless and wicked expenditures in preparation for another great war." [13]

The moratorium, Norris was convinced, would do no good. It would not help Germany "one cent," though it might allow some

---

[13] *Congressional Record*, 72nd Cong., 1st sess., Dec. 22, 1931, pp. 1104–5, 1120–22; Norris to John G. Maher, Jan. 6, 1932; to Bruce Bliven, Mar. 24, 1931; to Alex M. Geist, Dec. 31, 1931. In an interesting correspondence with Henry A. Wallace, Wallace argued that the moratorium was necessary to encourage trade and increased purchases of American goods; see Norris to Wallace, Jan. 21, 1932; Wallace to Norris, Jan. 23, 1932. These letters have been published; see Richard Lowitt, ed., "Progressive Farm Leaders and Hoover's Moratorium," *Mid-America*, 50 (July, 1968): 236–39.

nations to spend a little more money "on battle ships and armaments." It would cancel the debt England and France owed the United States on the condition that they cancel an equal amount of what Germany owed them. "At first blush," Norris said, "this seems like a fifty-fifty proposition, but it requires only a moment's thought to realize that in such a case neither England nor France sacrifices a single dollar." Moreover, the resolution, by containing a clause which in effect stated that "it was not the intention of Congress to give any more moratoriums or to forgive any more of the debts," only further offended European nations. He explained that "when we loaned money to these countries, we really lost their friendship": "Uncle Sam does not have a friend among the European nations." [14]

In connection with the moratorium proposal Hoover for the first time as president communicated with Norris by sending him a long telegram, which, incidentally, went to all members of Congress. Norris was disturbed that the president sought to bind members before he formally submitted the proposal to Congress. "What will any consideration of this kind mean if all the Members are pledged in advance?" Norris queried at the end of June, 1931. He had an intimation of the answer when, shortly after Congress convened, Secretary Stimson stated that a majority approved the proposal. At the end of December he had a formal answer when the Senate approved the moratorium with only eleven senators joining Norris in opposition. The American people, as he saw it, were paying the European war debt and indirectly encouraging the arms race. [15]

The moratorium resolved little for the United States or its European beneficiaries. "It was," Norris said, "a false alarm," losing the

[14] Norris to Maher, Jan. 6, 1932; to Jerome Malone, June 23, 1931; to Val J. Peter, June 26, 1931. Norris suspected that Ambassador Mellon in London suggested the moratorium idea to President Hoover, who then made it his own; see Norris to John A. Simpson, June 30, 1931. But Hoover said, "Mr. Mellon objected that it was Europe's mess, and that we should not involve the United States"; see his *Memoirs: The Great Depression, 1929–1941* (New York, 1952), pp. 68–69.

[15] Norris to Simpson, June 30, 1931; to George W. Young, Dec. 17, 1931; to G. N. Parmenter, Dec. 29, 1931; to J. M. Alexander, Dec. 31, 1931; to Olson, June 19, 1932; to Ralph O. Canaday, Dec. 17, 1931. The vote in the Senate approving the moratorium was 69 yeas, 12 nays; see *Congressional Record,* 72nd Cong., 1st sess., Dec. 22, 1931, p. 1126.

U.S. Treasury $250 million of indebtedness which would have been received "without any doubt whatever and without even any protest" if President Hoover had not initiated the moratorium. No nation had asked for it; one had made its annual payment, which was returned after Congress approved the joint resolution calling for the moratorium. Some senators implied that they would have joined Norris in opposition had it not been for the approving telegrams they sent in response to Hoover's. If anyone benefited from the moratorium, Noris said, it was the "international bankers" who were able "to use this money to pay private debts instead." [16]

Throughout the final year of the Hoover administration Norris remained adamant in opposition to reducing war debts any further. The $11 million originally lent the Allies had been borrowed from the American people under patriotic circumstances and social pressures that compelled many to sacrifice greatly to purchase Liberty Bonds. While the amount due the United States had been reduced by about one-half and in some instances even more, Allied nations, through their representatives, had signed agreements to pay the reduced amounts. Norris had opposed these settlements, arguing that the forgiven indebtedness had been transferred from European to American taxpayers. Among other reasons Hoover's moratorium was a terrible mistake because it had led by January, 1933, to a request for further postponement. To Norris this was a disguise for cancellation. Indeed, the United States "stood a pretty fair show of losing most, if not all, of this money." But this factor did not change his ideas about cancellation. If European nations did not pay, Norris said, "I would note the indebtedness on the very sky of civilization so that future generations might read that these nations had borrowed money to carry on a war for their own benefit and neglected or refused to pay it." [17]

Norris effectively and succinctly summarized his foreign policy views late in 1932 after the presidential election: ". . . if we ever get out of our present difficulties, I do not believe anyone who has gone through it, will ever again consent that we mix up in European

[16] Norris to S. R. Florence, May 12, 1932; to William Dutton, Jr., May 30, 1932; to C. G. Wilcox, July 19, 1932; to H. H. Brown, July 19, 1932.

[17] Norris to John H. Buss, Jan. 23, 1933; to L. H. Whitehead, Jan. 7, 1933; to Harley Nettleton, Dec. 18, 1934.

affairs, send an army over there and lend them money to help carry on a war. If we had stayed out of that war, we should not be afflicted with the troubles which confront us now." [18]

[18] Norris to Mary Lowe, Dec. 27, 1932.

Fruits of Righteousness

37

A visitor during the Hoover administration would have found Norris occupying three rooms on the top floor of the Senate Office Building. His private office was a rather small room with couch, desk, several chairs, and bookcase atop which was a bust of Washington and a picture of Abraham Lincoln. Leaning back in his chair, cocking his feet on the desk, and puffing gently at an ever-present cigar, Norris gave the impression of a man without pretense or vanity who was at ease with himself and his fellow man. He smiled frequently and was easy to talk to. His hair, parted on one side and brushed back, was silver gray, but his eyebrows were quite dark and his eyes were deep-set. He used to wear a moustache, but he had been clean-shaven since his re-election in 1924. His face with its high forehead and pronounced jaw was strong and frank but gentle and friendly. There was a slight, indefinable droop to his eyelids, the relic of a hunting accident in his early years in Beaver City. When he chatted with his visitor, he usually tilted his head back a little. The droop to his lids made his blue and kindly eyes appear somewhat sad and helped present the overall impression of a slightly weary, humane, and essentially humble person.

Though he celebrated his seventieth birthday in July of 1931, his sturdy body carried no excess weight. Of medium height, five feet ten and a half inches, he generally wore a dark suit, low white collar, and a black string bow tie. An old-style gold watch chain crossed his modest midriff. A homespun man, Norris usually talked in a soft conversational tone whether speaking to a visitor in his office or addressing his colleagues on the Senate floor. In both places reason and logic rather than oratorical techniques were his primary weapons. His eloquence was in his earnestness rather than his rhetoric. Quiet and serious in his manner, Norris's abilities came not from his use of rhetoric or desire to please an audience but rather from the thoroughness of his knowledge and preparation. Rarely did he deal in generalities, and his speech was always simple and straightforward. At times, as he contemplated the depths of the depression with its human suffering and the refusal of the Hoover administration to cope fully with the crisis, he would get discouraged and become despondent. His defiant look of pride would pass into a pathetic look of pain. He would snap out of this mood by jotting down a satirical limerick or a biting jingle and reciting it on the Senate floor. At all times, however, there was an air of gentle sadness in his face in repose.

During the depression years he rarely found time to indulge his limited social habits. He enjoyed the theater but seldom went. He enjoyed watching baseball games but had to be content with listening to radio reports of them. Driving his automobile was an occasional diversion. Most evenings he spent at home studying. Long hours perusing material relevant to his work in the Senate helped make Norris one of the better-informed men in Washington. He usually read with a pencil handy, annotating and underlining passages or phrases that seemed important. When his eyes got tired, Mrs. Norris would read to him. His principal friends, Senators Borah, Johnson, Brookhart, and LaFollette, he saw at the Capitol, usually at luncheon in a little side room off the Senate restaurant where a big round table was reserved for those senators referred to as progressives. But his principles did not interfere with his personal friendships. Both Reed Smoot and Charles Curtis, staunch supporters of the Old Guard and the Hoover administration, were personally friendly and politically hostile. Unlike many prominent men, Norris could enjoy a good story as well as tell one.

Though his views appealed to a minority of his colleagues, he had the respect of all. More concerned with his convictions than with his following, Norris still was one of the most likable of senators. Courteous and candid, he never hid behind the prevalent "Now don't quote me" approach when questioned by newsmen. And he always readily admitted that he could be wrong. Considered a sincere, hard-working, intellectually honest legislator despite his insurgency, Norris was highly regarded in the Senate. All recognized him as the ablest parliamentarian in that chamber. Accepted as one of the best politicians in Congress, Norris consciously used politics as a means, not as an end.

Having deep respect for his own convictions, he had equal respect for those of others, including men with whom he basically disagreed. He would attempt to change a colleague's opinion by argument, but only rarely did he indulge in abuse or other vilifying tactics. At times he was harsh and bitter in his remarks and critics claimed that he was narrow and fanatical in his judgments. At times his wit was barbed with acridity, but he fundamentally accepted the premise that his opponents were honorable men who, out of convictions honestly held, reached conclusions different from his. As Edmund Wilson noted in 1931, "There is no virulence in his sarcasm. . . ."[1] He was as devoid of rancor as he was of arrogance. Lacking a political power base, it was largely through strength of character, unflinching courage, and flawless integrity applied in years of struggle that he gained the legislative triumphs achieved during the bleak Hoover years. Norris was a senator who made his way with honesty and independence. And he was gaining recognition primarily because of his fearless independence. Having no patronage to distribute, it was impossible for a president to reward or punish him in any ordinary way. Very few senators were honest in the way Norris was or as independent, free from pretense, or disregardful of personal political consequences as he. People respected and trusted him for the enemies he had made. Many came to see him. R. L. Duffus explained in 1930, "Sooner or later almost every one in the country who speaks or pretends to speak for the under dog drifts into Norris' office."[2]

Strong as his views were, Norris was still willing to compromise. "When I can't get what I want I take what I can get, provided the

[1] Edmund Wilson, "A Senator and an Engineer," *New Republic,* May 27, 1931, p. 36.

[2] R. L. Duffus, "A Senator without a Political Formula: Norris of Nebraska, Taking No Orders from the Republican Party, Says He Only Tries to Be Square," *New York Times Magazine,* Dec. 28, 1930, p. 7.

required concessions don't outweigh the gains. But compromises," he explained, "should be arrived at honestly, in sincere effort to do what is best, and not be used as mere devices in playing the game of practical politics." Political parties and processes were necessary instrumentalities of government. It was when they ceased to be instruments and became "ends unto themselves or mechanisms of indirection and abuse" that Norris objected and raised his voice in denunciation of partisanship.[3] Once he had made up his mind, it was difficult to move him. But Norris was never dogmatic. Frequently he would punctuate his more positive assertions with the expression "Maybe I am wrong."

In Washington he lived with his wife, Ella, and his books in a small apartment in a big apartment house that changed with each session of Congress during the Hoover years. His daughters were now married. While he was vitally interested in them and their families, he realized, of course, that his primary responsibility to them had now ended. Late spring and summer, when Congress was not in session, was a period of relaxation, far from the madding crowd, where Norris could renew his strength and visit with friends and family before assuming his political role once again in the fall. At the cabin on Rainbow Lake near Waupaca, Wisconsin, the close-knit, rugged frame Norris had developed as a farm boy was maintained by swimming, tramping through the forest, and chopping and sawing wood. Here with family and friends he would sing songs to the moon as it shone on the lake. Here he would reread the story of his beloved Cyrano de Bergerac, that dauntless poet and hero who defied oppressive overlords, derided fools, denounced rascals, and fought them all uncompromisingly to the death. Here he would enjoy more fully than in Washington his favorite comic strip characters: Andy Gump, Skeezix, and Winnie Winkle. And it was more than a chuckle or two that he found on the comics page: "Andy Gump, fool that he is, sometimes says some pretty shrewd things." [4] Here, too, though no longer an avid baseball fan, he would follow the standings of the teams. In the general news

[3] A. H. Ulm, "An Insurgent among the Insurgents," *New York Times Magazine*, Nov. 6, 1927, p. 13.

[4] Walter E. Christenson, "Norris Likes Andy Gump," *Omaha World-Herald*, Jan. 2, 1930.

section Norris was a bit impatient with sensationalism; murder stories and sexy articles and pictures were demoralizing. He read newspapers carefully though, bypassing only the society page with a shrug. At his summer cottage, which had neither doorbell nor telephone, Norris remarked, "It is certainly a relief to get away from the paved streets, tall buildings, and busy people, each one bent on doing something and doing it now." But as the twenties came to a close, he devoted more time to legislative matters and spent hours dictating to his stenographer.[5]

In late September, once the warm weather had abated, George and Ellie Norris usually returned to their home in McCook for several months prior to the convening of Congress early in December. The house was rented while they were not in residence; in 1931 the entire building was remodeled. At the end of October the job was completed. The house, redone in Spanish stucco style, was one of the most attractive in McCook. A reporter observed Norris, in striped overalls and white shirt with the collar turned under, painting a fence at the rear of the house and responding to the greeting of two school girls taking the alley shortcut to their homes. The same homey touch was noted the following year by another reporter accompanying the congressional delegation attending the funeral of Representative Percy Quin in Natchez. In Memphis between trains on the return trip to Washington, he followed Norris to a coffee counter and mounted a stool beside him. Over breakfast Norris discussed anything reporters wanted to talk about. With breakfast and interviews over and still an hour to train time, Norris eagerly accepted the reporter's offer of a brief tour of Memphis.[6]

Norris was not bothered with illness during the late 1920s. He avoided excessive heat to prevent repetition of the collapse he had experienced during the Harding administration. But in 1927 he had sciatica for the first time and complained, "While I think I have

[5] George W. Norris to Fred A. Goodrich, July 28, 1925; to Walter Locke, May 16, 1927; *Nebraska State Journal,* July 21, 1929. Unlike most senators, Norris secured his license plates in the District of Columbia, not in his home state. Until 1931 he drove a Willys-Knight, thereafter a Buick.

[6] Norris to Clara Rakestraw, June 1, 1931; to Chester Lowe, Dec. 5, 1931; *McCook Daily Gazette,* Oct. 24, 1931; *McCook Republican,* Dec. 15, 1931. The counter interview appeared in the *Memphis Press-Scimitar,* Feb. 8, 1932; Eldon F. Roark, Jr., was the reporter.

been pretty sick several times, I have never really known what it was to suffer before." The pain was so severe that he was unable to appear at his office for a period of several weeks. But X rays and extensive examinations of his right leg at the Naval Hospital revealed nothing wrong. After he spent some time resting, the pain abated and then disappeared. That he was in sound health was revealed dramatically two years later when late one afternoon, walking from the Capitol to the Senate Office Building, Norris was struck by an automobile as he started across the street. He received abrasions of the left leg and a sprained wrist and was knocked to the street. He arose almost at once, hailed a taxicab, and proceeded to his home. He said that his injuries were painful but not serious. The next day he was back at work in the Senate, indicating, besides good fortune, basically good health.[7]

Financially, Norris was better off at the end of the twenties than ever before. Not that he was wealthy or earning a large income. But he was able to live within his $10,000 annual salary and to save some money as well, though he readily admitted that senators with families might have difficulty. Those who circulated in Washington society certainly could not live on their incomes alone. Yet he was opposed to increasing senatorial salaries, exclaiming, "We ought to be willing even to sacrifice something for the good of the country." If senators practiced the right kind of economy, "they could get thru." Norris, for example, usually rode the streetcar and wondered why colleagues who habitually took taxis did not realize that they could save considerable money in this one particular "and perhaps in a great many other similar ways." [8]

Concern with financial affairs had eased considerably because after the war Norris started selling some of the land he owned, a process largely completed by the end of the twenties. He was so absorbed in senatorial matters that he neglected private affairs.

[7] Norris to C. A. Sorensen, Jan. 2, 1928; *New York Times,* Nov. 8, 1929. See Norris to "Dear Boys," Jan. 27, 1929, for a further comment on his basic good health.

[8] Norris to Locke, Mar. 4, 1925. See Norris to C. B. Gray, May 24, Nov. 6, 1919, for comments about Norris's difficulties in living on his senatorial salary. In the latter letter Norris explained why he would not be able to subscribe to the stock of a proposed hotel in McCook as liberally as he previously had done for the Masonic Temple Building.

Tenants and creditors tended to take advantage of this fact with the result that he "always seemed to get the worst of it." Money from his properties in Red Willow and Furnas counties was invested in government bonds; he did the same with funds saved from his salary. In the mid-twenties, when these bonds were selling above par, Norris ceased his purchases, not wanting to pay a premium. Buying for investment rather than speculation, he sought other securities such as school district, county, and municipal bonds because, though the income was small, his attention would not be demanded.[9]

At the onset of the depression most of Norris's investments were being handled by his son-in-law Harvey Nelson and Harvey's father, Frans. In any instance where he held a loan on a man's house, Norris wanted the Nelsons "to be just as lenient with him as possible." "I believe I ought even to be willing to sustain some loss in the right kind of a case—I don't want to get any man's home." The Nelsons worked in the Los Angeles area, while in McCook John F. Cordeal and John E. Kelley looked after personal details for Norris. Cordeal prepared his tax returns and Kelley looked after his house, including the renting of it. By 1929 Carl Marsh had assumed both of these responsibilities. The friendship with Cordeal cooled considerably when he took deep offense at Norris's support of Alfred E. Smith in 1928. Kelley also did not approve of Norris's stand. In addition, he found looking after the Norris home a troublesome and time-consuming chore. Some of the tenants had been destructive; at one time three families were living in it. In 1928 Norris was paying more for repairs than he received in rent and probably then decided to remodel the house.[10]

[9] Norris to W. G. Springer, Dec. 17, 1925; to Goodrich, Dec. 30, 1925; to John F. Cordeal, Jan. 5, Mar. 12, 1926; to Frans Nelson, Aug. 25, Dec. 14, 1927. Nelson was the father-in-law of Norris's middle daughter, Marian. He was active in real estate in the Los Angeles area and made sound suggestions about investment possibilities which in many instances Norris accepted; see Norris to Nelson, Feb. 4, 1930. Carl Marsh performed a similar service for Norris in the McCook area; see, for example, Norris to Marsh, Oct. 26, 1927, May 3, 1932.

[10] Norris to Harvey F. Nelson, Feb. 10, Apr. 24, 1933; to Marsh, Apr. 8, July 13 and 24, 1929; to John E. Kelley, Nov. 20, 1928. In 1930 Norris contacted an architect-nephew in Cleveland and asked him to prepare plans for "a one story house of the Spanish type" with a flat roof that could be insulated to be comfortable in the hot weather; see Norris to Lowe, Nov. 29, 1930. For

Carl Marsh, on the other hand, was devoted to Norris and was prompt and efficient in tending to the calls made upon his time and energies. He looked after the Norris home and handled all of Norris's complaints or requests. Norris also occasionally asked Marsh, who was actively engaged in the real estate and insurance business, about investment possibilities in southwest Nebraska. After so many years of concern about his affairs in McCook, thanks to the efforts of Carl Marsh Norris was freed from worry about this segment of his estate.[11]

Like millions of other citizens during the depression years, Norris complained about his high insurance premiums. Particularly objectionable was the practice of some companies of raising rates for older policy holders who because of their age could not purchase other insurance. In addition, he was disturbed when banks in Furnas and Red Willow counties failed and friends found themselves without jobs, bankrupt, or actually experiencing physical want. In June, 1932, McCook celebrated the fiftieth anniversary of its founding and Norris learned that possibly half the firms in the community were on the verge of failure. He did what he could to help and was deeply distressed at the plight of his friends and neighbors.[12]

By the end of the 1920s Norris was distinguished enough to receive letters from people who wished to reminisce about the old days in Ohio, at Valparaiso, or in Nebraska. Such letters always elicited a prompt response. He looked back on his youth with nostalgia and affection. Occasionally when returning to Washington, he would drive through or even stay overnight in the vicinity of "the old Mt. Carmel location." His memory was acute; his letters recounted precise details about events that occurred in some instances a half

an accounting of family heirlooms destroyed by tenants in the original home, see Ellie Norris to Robertson, May 3, 1931.

[11] Norris to Marsh, Oct. 26, 1927, Dec. 3, 1931, May 28, 1932.

[12] Norris to Arthur Folsom, June 11, 1930; to J. G. Ray, Jan. 20, 1931; Marsh to Norris, Nov. 25, 1931, May 24, 1932. Norris had seven paid-up or almost paid-up policies that were either lost or stolen. For a discussion of this matter, see Norris to Mutual Life Insurance Company of New York, Jan. 20, 1934; to Cordeal, June 25, 1934. In 1930 McCook had a population of 6,688. Its population had increased 160 percent from 1900 to 1930, but the value of land in the Republican River valley decreased nearly 50 percent from 1919 to 1934, from roughly $52 an acre in 1919 to $28 in 1934; see *Water Resources of Nebraska: Preliminary Report by Nebraska State Planning Board* (Lincoln, 1936), pp. 538, 553.

century or more earlier. Overwhelmed with work in the Senate, Norris liked to relax by dictating a response to a letter recalling his youth. In comparing the past with the present, he often found the past better, not in terms of material values but because life seemed more wholesome and youngsters seemed to have more fun than in the depression era.[13]

An old friend, George Williams of Cambridge, Nebraska, sent Norris a box of fine cigars each year as a Christmas present. In 1932 Norris responded, "I am so used to smoking stogies, clay and corn cob pipes that I am just a little afraid of the effect that good cigars may have upon my system. If they make me sick, I intend to sue you for damages. If they kill me, I will haunt you in your dreams." [14] While he smoked continually, Norris never imbibed alcoholic beverages. This was a personal matter and he never cast judgment on people with different personal views, including members of his own family. Mrs. Norris, for example, was a long-time member of the Congregational church in McCook; Norris never joined any church. Indeed, it was only after the election of 1928, when he supported Alfred E. Smith and aroused the antagonism of some of his Protestant, dry, Republican friends, that Norris gave the matter of religion serious attention and tried to formalize his views.

He concluded that religion and politics were one and the same. Politics was the science of government; political parties were instruments, albeit imperfect ones, to bring about good government. "In its truest sense," he observed, government "is only a method to bring to humanity the greatest amount of happiness and is founded, after all, upon the love of man for man." Religion was essentially the same thing. It was predicated on love of humanity rather than love of self. It was not "a means to save one's soul from a future punishment to the neglect of fellow beings." While Norris did not believe in life after death, he explained that "if we mount to Heaven," it would be on the grounds of love of mankind.

Man was the measure. To be charitable, one must respect the opinion of others, however widely they might disagree. About his be-

[13] For a sampling of reminiscent letters, see Norris to John Drury, June 21, 1927; to Ruth Andrus, June 11, 1928; to W. S. Norviel, Mar. 23, 1928; to E. F. Warner, Jan. 29, 1928; to R. D. McFadden, Oct. 1, 1925; to George L. Keith, Jan. 21, 1931.

[14] Norris to George Williams, Dec. 24, 1932.

lief in a supreme being Norris wrote, "I can conceive of no God except a just God, and I cannot understand how a just God, knowing the frailties and the weaknesses of human nature, can punish his imperfect creatures for wrongs which come about on account of the very weaknesses which He had Himself planted in the minds and hearts of all of us. I agree most heartily with the lowly Nazarene when he said: 'The Kingdom of God is within you.'"

Recognizing that he possessed as many human frailties and weaknesses as the next man, Norris also realized that he had to pursue his duty as he saw it. Despite this dedication Norris knew that he could not drastically alter prevailing conditions. He understood the necessity of dealing with men as they were, striving for the best attainable government that imperfect mankind was capable of sustaining in a democracy where the good, the bad, and the indifferent somehow had to work together. What was most important was the knowledge that he had done his best and pursued the truth as he saw it. As he exclaimed, "While I am here I am still going to continue." [15]

Judgment, as in more orthodox theology, would be reserved for the hereafter. For Norris history would judge the man:

> Somehow I cannot get away from the idea—I do not wish to get away from it—that the reward of men who have spent their lives as I have will come in increased happiness to those who will live in the future. I cannot help but believe that the worthy man progresses and that in time, long after I shall have passed away, the little that I and others like me have done will bring forth fruits of righteousness which will, in some degree at least, alleviate the suffering of humanity.[16]

Honesty of purpose and purity of motive had become a passion and not a pretense with Norris in both private conduct and political behavior. In both areas he sought to alleviate human suffering. Increasingly, people recognized his concern and held him in high regard. At the end of the Hoover administration guests at a dinner in

---

[15] Norris to Cordeal, Jan. 6, 1929. In this letter Norris indulged in a lengthy explanation of his religious views because Cordeal, a friend of long standing, fundamentally disagreed with Norris's support of Al Smith in 1928. See also Norris to J. C. Kinsler, Dec. 29, 1931.

[16] Norris to Keith, Jan. 21, 1931.

Justice Louis D. Brandeis's apartment were talking about political
personages. They unanimously agreed that Norris was the outstanding figure in political life in the United States at that time. Moreover, they went beyond this statement to express not only admiration but love for him because of his continual championship of all
that they considered right, just, decent, and honorable. Perhaps, too,
the guests had in mind Norris's role in the 1932 presidential campaign wherein he sought to bring forth the fruits of righteousness.[17]

[17] Huston Thompson to Norris, Feb. 23, 1933 (an account of the Brandeis
dinner).

Dreams Come True

38

While it was clear that Norris would not support Hoover in 1932, he assumed that the president would be renominated and feared that "the moneyed interests led by the power trust" would support a Democrat like Owen D. Young. Thus the electorate would have no real choice on "the all important issue of power." Asked in December, 1930, to name a Democrat who might appeal to western Progressives and Republicans, Norris named Franklin D. Roosevelt. He again spoke of Roosevelt in refusing a request from John Dewey, chairman of the League for Independent Political Action, that he lead a third party in the 1932 campaign. Agreeing with Dewey on the need for desirable legislation, Norris did not see a third party as the way to secure it. If the Electoral College were abolished and voters were directly responsible for the election of a president, it would be easier and less expensive than nominating "a candidate for the presidency independent of either one of the great political parties." [1]

In February, 1931, reiterating previously leveled criticisms, Norris listed eleven reasons for his opposition to the renomination of President Hoover. The following month at the conference of progressives he said that the "country needs another Roosevelt." There-

[1] George W. Norris to John Dewey, Dec. 27, 1930; to A. Cantarella, Feb. 7, 1931; *Washington News,* Dec. 27, 1930. See also Karel Denis Bicha, "Liberalism Frustrated: The League for Independent Political Action, 1928–1933," *Mid-America,* 48 (Jan., 1966): 19–28.

after in 1931 Norris continued to boost Roosevelt whenever discussing the up-coming presidential campaign. Though Hoover would be renominated, it would not be because "the rank and file" wanted him. If the power trust succeeded in securing the nomination of a Democrat whose views were no different from Hoover's, "and that means taxation, power, and the general handling of big business," the chief issue again might be prohibition. Hoover could conceivably win a second term as president. If such a situation developed, Norris admitted that he would then support a third-party candidate whose campaign would "make such a showing that [it] would startle the country, and shake it to its very foundation." [2]

While Norris was expressing doubts about the Democrats, his secretary observed that despite an effort "to shelve Governor Roosevelt," he had "a terrific following." His optimism was predicated upon private revelations by Republican "wheel horses" that they were going to be beaten badly in 1932. Norris rarely reflected this optimism, though he did concede in November, 1931, that "any man progressively inclined can beat Mr. Hoover in the west." But as the campaign year of 1932 got under way, his position became more positive. If the Democrats took advantage of the situation, they easily could elect the next president of the United States. While he was more outspoken now in his belief that Hoover would be defeated handily by a progressive Democrat, he no longer puffed Franklin Roosevelt as a candidate. [3]

[2] Norris statement, Feb. 3, 1931; Norris to Dana W. Hovey, Jan. 15, 1931; *Lincoln Star,* June 19, 1931. On the impossibility of progressives capturing control of the next Republican national convention, see Norris to Edward V. Jeffries, Mar. 23, 1931; to Jonathan Bourne, June 4, 1931. See also Norris to Jerry A. Mathews, May 10, 1931; to A. L. Green, June 23, 1931; to F. M. Richard, June 29, 1931. If someone like Gifford Pinchot, then governor of Pennsylvania, decided to challenge Hoover for the nomination, Norris admitted that he probably would help to the best of his ability; see Norris to J. M. O'Hara, June 6, 1931; to Joseph I. France, Sept. 6, 1931.

[3] John P. Robertson to N. Dwight Ford, Oct. 1, 1931; *Lincoln Star,* Nov. 9, 1931; Norris to Henry J. Thorpe, Jan. 6, 1932; to J. P. Evans, Jan. 14, 1932. Norris was pleased to observe that Hoover was being attacked in two volumes that appeared in 1931. *The Washington Merry-Go-Round* had been co-authored, he learned, by Robert Allen, who had been fired as Washington representative of the *Christian Science Monitor* because of it. He also read *The Strange Career of Mr. Hoover* by John Hamill before an injunction was issued restraining publication of the book. The claim to sustain the injunction, Norris noted, was not that anything the author had said was false but, rather, that he had stolen his

Norris insisted that he was not an aspirant for the presidency, though there was talk that pressure would be sufficiently strong to induce him to contest Hoover's renomination. To suggestions that the party had more to fear from enemies within than without, Norris responded that if all Republicans dissatisfied with President Hoover were driven from the fold, there would not be enough left "to make the necessary pallbearers for the corpse." In January, 1932, he mentioned Governor Gifford Pinchot as the possible head of a third party and asserted that Senators Hiram Johnson or William E. Borah would also be acceptable in this role. These remarks, delivered at Harrisburg, Pennsylvania, indicated Norris's basic concern about the forthcoming election: that Hoover would be renominated while a progressive Democratic candidate was still in doubt, leaving a third party as the only meaningful alternative.[4]

Norris thought it a mistake for progressive Republicans to believe they could defeat Hoover's renomination. Even if it were possible, they would not have sufficient delegate strength to name a satisfactory candidate. Moreover, he claimed on the basis of "absolutely reliable information, much of it of a confidential nature," that the Democratic machine was "turning heaven and earth to defeat Roosevelt as the Democratic nominee." If Roosevelt were nominated, Norris was convinced he would be elected, though in February he wrote that Roosevelt "would not be my first choice, if I were picking the President," and then suggested "any one of the progressives in our [Senate] group" as a better alternative. He also conceded the impossibility of electing an independent candidate, leaving one to conclude that Franklin Roosevelt was the only progressive alternative to Herbert Hoover. The *Kansas City Star* speculated that Norris would probably desert his party "if President

information from another man who had hired him to research records throughout the world for a book he was preparing; see Norris to "Dear Boys," Jan. 2, 1932.

[4] Robertson to Sam Miller, Mar. 19, 1931; *Washington Herald,* Dec. 30 (story by Louis Siebold), Dec. 31, 1931 (story by Edward L. Roddan); Norris to Kenneth Harlan, Mar. 29, 1932; *Philadelphia Record,* Jan. 30, 1932, "Keystone Farmers: Hard to Fool!" (editorial). At this time a friend informed Frank P. Walsh that Norris told him that "there would be a third party this fall unless Roosevelt is nominated but he seriously doubted whether he would be"; see Ewing Y. Mitchell to Walsh, Jan. 18, 1932 (Frank P. Walsh Papers, New York Public Library).

Hoover is opposed for reelection by Governor Franklin D. Roosevelt of New York." [5]

In April he was caught off balance by two developments which suggested his entrance into the presidential race. Early in the month in the Wisconsin Republican presidential preference primary Norris, whose name was the only one on the ballot, received 139,514 of a total of 148,051 votes; 6,588 voters wrote in the name of Herbert Hoover. At the end of the month Senator Huey Long fired a blast at his party's leadership by proposing that the Democrats nominate Norris for president. To clarify his position, Norris announced early in May that he would support Franklin Roosevelt if the Democratic party nominated him and that under any circumstances he would not back President Hoover. [6]

While it was evident that Norris favored Roosevelt, he had not expected to make his views official until after the nominations were made. His announcement came immediately after the Louisiana delegation gave its support to Roosevelt. Huey Long claimed that Norris had influenced his decision to endorse the New York governor and that in return for Louisiana's backing he wished to be the first to announce that Norris would support Roosevelt. In Atlanta on May 5, 1932, Long had declared that the Louisiana delegation was for Roosevelt and that Norris was also. When questioned in Washington later the same day, Norris confirmed Long's statement. [7]

Once he had announced for Roosevelt, Norris was besieged to explain his position. The New York governor came "much closer to representing the idea of standing for the people as against monop-

[5] Norris to Arthur G. Wray, Feb. 4, 1932; *Kansas City Star,* Mar. 16, 1931. That Norris was working behind the scenes for Roosevelt is indicated in a Mar. 5, 1932, memorandum in the Walsh Papers calling for the organization of the Roosevelt League for Progressive Democracy. In this document Norris was reported as saying that until after the convention the officers and members of the Executive and National committees should be Democrats, thereby avoiding the charge that Republicans were attempting to influence the Democratic nomination.

[6] *New York Times,* Apr. 7, 1932; *New Orleans Times-Picayune,* May 1, 1932; *Philadelphia Record,* May 6, 1932; *Wisconsin Blue Book: 1933* (Madison, Wis., 1933), p. 530.

[7] *Philadelphia Record,* May 6, 1932; Huey P. Long, *Every Man a King* (Chicago, 1964), pp. 302–3. Yet Norris still had reservations about his endorsement of Roosevelt at this time. A month later he was hedging on his endorsement of Roosevelt prior to the Democratic convention; see Norris to Robert Lowenthal, June 8, 1932.

oly than any other man" who had a chance of receiving the Democratic nomination. Therefore, progressive-minded citizens had little choice. To avoid divisions among themselves, Norris hoped they would support Roosevelt rather than back a third-party candidate like Norman Thomas, whose election was an "absolute impossibility."[8]

Yet Norris, never having met the New York governor, still had some doubts. Senator Royal Copeland of New York had told him that Roosevelt was not stable in his views and was subject to the influence of friends. But Judson King assured him that on the power issue Roosevelt would stand firm. King asked Morris L. Cooke and Frank P. Walsh, aides to Governor Roosevelt on hydroelectric power matters, to write Norris "about the real Roosevelt." Cooke responded with a review of Roosevelt's record and a statement that "in power matters he had never taken an attitude which left me questioning or done a thing with which I disagreed."[9]

Once the Democratic convention nominated Roosevelt, Norris endorsed its choice. Hesitation and doubts disappeared; the fundamental principle in the campaign, he announced on July 2, 1932, would be "the contest between organized monopoly on the one side and the common people on the other." Franklin D. Roosevelt stood for the welfare of the common people. Besides endorsing him, Norris announced that he would speak in his behalf. Norris was the first of the progressive Republicans to endorse the New York governor.[10]

In announcing for Roosevelt, Norris did not discuss his decision with any other progressives. To be sure, he had tried to prevent them from following Hoover's leadership. But when the first session of the Seventy-second Congress adjourned on July 16, only Senators Hiram Johnson and Gerald P. Nye seemed interested in supporting Roosevelt. Norris hoped that all progressive senators would get into the fight because he could not comprehend, "when we look at

[8] Norris to Norman Hapgood, May 10, 1932; to John Haynes Holmes, May 10, 1932.

[9] Judson King to Walsh and Morris L. Cooke, June 22, 1932 (Box 88A); Cooke to Norris, June 23, 1932 (Box 90, Morris L. Cooke Papers, Franklin D. Roosevelt Library, Hyde Park, N.Y.).

[10] *Cleveland Plain Dealer,* July 2, 1932; *New York Times,* July 3, 1932; *Washington News,* July 6, 1932; *Congressional Record,* 72nd Cong., 1st sess., July 7, 1932, p. 14738; Norris to W. O. Christopher, July 11, 1932; to H. W. Renquist, July 20, 1932.

the record of Hoover and see the terrible landmarks along his path since he had been President and before . . . how anyone can hesitate to take a man even in the dark in preference to him." [11]

Once Congress adjourned, Norris went to his Wisconsin cottage to prepare for the coming campaign and to survey the tumultuous political scene. The American people definitely would have a choice in November between Hoover and Roosevelt. On issues that concerned Norris, Roosevelt was sound and sympathetic. Thus he was convinced there ought to be a nationwide movement "to bring the Progressive vote of the country to Roosevelt where it naturally and logically belongs." The organization ought to be staffed and directed "by Republicans of the Progressive wing," and, indeed, such a group was in the process of formation. Norris wrote to Basil Manly, who had been active in the 1924 LaFollette campaign, suggesting prominent progressive Republicans who might become active in the organization. Incidentally, the organization would handle Norris's speaking engagements.[12]

In addition to preparing for the presidential campaign, Norris considered requests to endorse candidates for both state and local offices. Without hesitation he backed both John J. Blaine, seeking another term in the U.S. Senate, and Philip LaFollette, seeking nomination as governor, in the Wisconsin primary campaign. He also endorsed Fiorello H. LaGuardia of New York in his bid for re-election to the House. But Norris was not anxious to endorse candidates in Nebraska. Since he was openly supporting Roosevelt, he could not speak under the auspices of the Republican organization. Nor could he speak at Democratic meetings to advocate the election of the entire party slate. Therefore, it seemed best in Nebraska and elsewhere that he speak only in favor of Roosevelt and under the auspices of a progressive organization.

Since Nebraska Republicans on all levels were supporting Hoover, tensions between Norris and his party, already severely strained, became even more critical. Observers claimed that Norris and his Senate colleague Robert B. Howell were drifting apart because of their disagreement on presidential candidates. Progressive Republicans supporting Hoover, Norris said, were placing partisanship

[11] Norris to William Hirth, July 19, 1932.
[12] Norris to Chester Hart, Aug. 20, 1932; to Basil Manly, Sept. 1, 1932.

above country. But refusing to follow was enough to gain condemnation as "irregular" and "bolsheviki." If Nebraskans were to be led astray by party spirit and place men in office who did not represent their real sentiments, then Norris was convinced that they, and like-minded voters elsewhere, would never achieve equality before the law.[13]

Concerned about the possible effects of intense partisanship, Norris prepared an article, published in September in *Liberty Magazine,* entitled "Why I Am a Better Republican Than President Hoover." In it he explained, "I am a Republican legally because my constituents, whose word is final, have elected me on the Republican ticket." Aside from technicalities, Norris insisted that he was a better Republican than either Coolidge or Hoover "if fidelity to fundamental principles and basic ideals counts for more than staunch adherence to the shibboleth of regularity." Parrots in politics and yes-men in business were destroying independent thought and action and were unable to resolve the problems besetting the nation. By placing party above country, they had bartered "the forgotten rights of the common man for public office." The worst sin a public official could commit, Norris said, was to "remain dumb" when it was his "conscientious duty" to speak. If speaking out against Hoover's policies, which he considered wrong on almost every vital issue, made him a bad Republican, then, he exclaimed, "I glory in being a bad Republican." Indeed, he concluded, "I am the kind of Republican who

[13] Norris to Edward Keating, Aug. 22, 1932; to Homer L. Kyle, Sept. 10, 1932; to Fiorello H. LaGuardia, Sept. 24, 1932; *Lincoln Journal and Star,* July 24, 1932 (story by Ruby A. Black indicating that Norris and Howell were supposedly drifting apart). In September in a letter to a friend Norris explained why he would not speak on behalf of Representative Robert G. Simmons in his campaign for re-election. Simmons, Norris felt, was unable to free himself from dominance by the political machine; see Norris to Charles M. Kearney, Sept. 14, 1932. Earlier Norris had encouraged a young "Norris Republican," Kenneth S. Wherry of Pawnee City, who was entering the primary race for governor. Wherry had claimed that he looked upon the state of Nebraska as a great corporation to be administered in an efficient and nonpartisan way. Norris responded with a long letter: "If we would look upon a state as a great corporation, with the Governor as the President, the Legislature as the Board of Directors, and the people of the State as stockholders, we would at once, I think, lay the foundation for a campaign that would, if successful, revolutionize present partisan considerations"; see Norris to Wherry, Dec. 12, 1931. Wherry, a state senator at the time, was defeated in his campaign for the gubernatorial nomination. He succeeded Norris in the U.S. Senate in 1943.

believes in exposing wrong and evil wherever they fester. I prefer to wash my own dirty linen. If we desire the respect of the people, that is what we must do. Unless we proceed from this principle we forfeit the confidence and respect of honest men and women." [14]

The article received wide attention. It was reprinted as a campaign document by the National Progressive League for Roosevelt. It provoked critical comments from many Republican voters, some of whom suggested that he join the Democratic party. Norris claimed the right to decide this matter for himself. Merely because he opposed things other Republicans favored was not sufficient reason. Otherwise, he suggested as an example, all Republicans would have to agree with the policies and actions of Albert Fall and Harry Daugherty in the Harding administration.[15]

Returning to McCook after a summer spent at his Wisconsin cottage, Norris commented late in September on Roosevelt's discussion of hydroelectric power in his campaign address at Portland, Oregon. The New York governor stood "for the use of this necessity at rates that will put electricity into every home and factory without paying tribute to the power trust. . . ." On a fundamental issue that affected every American citizen, Roosevelt had spoken strongly. Though not satisfied with his idea of giving corporations the first opportunity to build transmission lines, Norris said that, if elected, Roosevelt would sign the Muscle Shoals bill and claimed that his power position was "the most advanced, the most logical, and the most progressive that had ever been taken by any candidate for President at any time." [16]

A week later, returning from what Frank Freidel has called "The

---

[14] Norris, "Why I Am a Better Republican Than President Hoover," *Liberty Magazine,* Sept. 24, 1932, pp. 13–16.

[15] Norris to Russell A. Robinson, Nov. 12, 1929.

[16] *Lincoln Star,* Sept. 23, 1932. For a discussion of Roosevelt's Portland speech, see Frank Freidel, *Franklin D. Roosevelt: The Triumph* (Boston, 1956), pp. 352–53. Judson King meanwhile prepared a pamphlet, published by the National Popular Government League, on the power records of Hoover and Roosevelt which in careful analysis merely re-echoed Norris's sentiments. That Roosevelt regarded himself as something of a disciple of Norris on power matters was suggested by Roosevelt in a letter to Mrs. LaRue Brown, Feb. 17, 1930, printed in Elliott Roosevelt, ed., *F.D.R.: His Personal Letters, 1928–1945,* 1 (New York, 1950): 107. In Norris to King, Oct. 6, 1932, he commented fully on Roosevelt's power views.

Big Trip to the Coast," Roosevelt's train stopped at McCook and the governor and the senator, who had met for the first time, emerged. Speaking to a crowd of more than 20,000 people at the Red Willow County fairgrounds, Norris said, "What this country needs is another Roosevelt. And here he is," he continued, turning toward Roosevelt, "the governor of New York, the next President of the United States."

Twilight had fallen as both men stood in the dust of a racetrack beside an auto, facing the crowd that filled the grandstand and spilled out over several acres. Responding to Norris's remarks, Roosevelt, his arm sweeping toward the white-haired Nebraskan, asserted, "Our cause is common, I welcome your support. I honor myself in honoring you." Roosevelt went on in a remarkable tribute to Norris:

> We should remember that the ultimate analysis of history asks the answer to questions which are not concerned so much with what you and I, in these modern days, call ballyhoo, or headlines, as they are with much simpler fundamentals.
>
> History asks "Did the man have integrity?"
>
> "Did the man have unselfishness?"
>
> "Did the man have courage?"
>
> "Did the man have consistency?"
>
> And if the individual under the scrutiny of the historic microscope measured up to an affirmative answer to these questions, then history has set him down as great indeed in the pages of all the years to come.
>
> There are few statesmen in America today who so definitely and clearly measure up to an affirmative answer to the four questions as does the senior Senator from Nebraska, George W. Norris. In his rare case, history has already written the verdict.
>
> Not you alone in Nebraska, but we in every part of the nation, give full recognition to his integrity, to his unselfishness, to his courage, and to his consistency. He stands forth—whether we agree with him on all the little details or not—he stands forth as the very perfect, gentle knight of American progressive ideals.
>
> I am hoping that at this moment thousands of boys and girls— thousands of first voters—are listening to my words, for I should

like them to give some thought and some study to the very remarkable public service of the man in whose home town I now
stand.

I should like them to read of the able and heroic fight on behalf
of the average citizen which he has made during his long and
honorable career. I should like them to know that sometimes he
has made this fight with his party, and sometimes—as now—
against the leader of his party.

I should like them to know that always he has been thinking of
the rights and welfare of the average citizen, of the farmer, the
laborer, the small business man—yes, and of the rights and welfare of those who have been born to or have acquired greater
wealth.

But especially it has been an unselfish fight, and directed to the
fact that it is the little fellow who has the fewest friends in high
places, and that too often it is the little fellow who has been forgotten by his government.[17]

After Roosevelt's visit it was announced that Norris would campaign for him under the auspices of the National Progressive League
beginning in mid-October. Tentatively he was scheduled to start
speaking in Pittsburgh and then to head west, concluding in Los
Angeles on election eve. Though Norris intended to endorse progressive senatorial candidates at some of his meetings, his prime
object was to help elect Roosevelt. To further that end, he assumed
the chairmanship, an honorary position, of the National Committee
of the National Progressive League.[18]

For the next two weeks Norris was "completely covered up." He

[17] *Lincoln Star,* Sept. 29 and 30, 1932 (particularly the stories by Walter T.
Brown and James E. Lawrence). McCook was a city with about 7,000 residents.
People came from distances as great as 100 miles to attend the meeting. Roosevelt
was in McCook for two and a half hours and at 8:30 P.M. his train left for
Omaha. Norris had boarded the train at Benkelman, Nebr., fifty miles west of
McCook, and conferred with the candidate and his advisers for an hour until the
train arrived at McCook.

[18] Norris to Robert M. LaFollette, Jr., Sept. 30, Oct. 1, 1932; to David K.
Niles, Sept. 30, 1932. Norris informed Homer T. Bone, seeking to replace Wesley
Jones in the Senate from the state of Washington, that he would be unable to
endorse him because his opponent was not "one of the outstanding stand patters."
Therefore, though he agreed entirely with Bone on the issue of public power, his
campaigning in Washington would be entirely on behalf of Franklin D. Roosevelt;
see Norris to Bone, Oct. 1, 1932.

did not read his mail except for items handed him by his assistant. He spent most of his time drafting speeches. Since he would be repeating portions of his remarks in various speeches, he was concerned that very few of them, preferably only the first, be broadcast. He wanted a minimum of arrangements, though he expected the assistance of local committees. He also expected to spend much time on trains, reducing the need to plan for hotels, automobiles, and the like. He said he would not be embarrassed by traveling alone. Norris wanted to play an important role because he had no doubt that Franklin Roosevelt's election would mean a victory for Muscle Shoals.[19]

On Monday, October 17, 1932, in Philadelphia Norris began his active campaign on behalf of Franklin Roosevelt. His secretary John P. Robertson came from Washington to hear him with some apprehension. He regarded the City of Brotherly Love as one of the most boss-ridden and conservative in the country. There was a steady downpour all day and he went through a drenching rain to the Opera House, where Norris was to speak. Robertson's apprehension disappeared when he found the auditorium filled to capacity, and he was delighted with the ovation Norris received after holding "his audience spellbound for two hours until he had to leave to catch the train for Cleveland." [20]

In Philadelphia Norris denounced Hoover as the embodiment of partisanship in American political life. In Cleveland he excoriated the labor record of the president, particularly the offer of a federal judgeship to Donald Richberg if he would denounce the anti-injunction bill, a measure Richberg had helped to formulate. At Saginaw on October 19 Norris intended to reply to the claims of Senator Arthur Vandenberg that a Democratic victory would mean a slash in tariffs on farm products and "ruin for the farmer." That evening he was scheduled to speak at a rally in Belding, Michigan, but illness prevented him from fulfilling both of these commitments.

[19] Norris to A. F. Buechler, Oct. 10, 1932; to Manly, Sept. 26, 1932; to King, Oct. 6, 1932. In Denver, for example, Senator Costigan was ready to look after Norris during his stay in that city; see Edward P. Costigan to Norris, Oct. 13, 1932 (Edward P. Costigan Papers, University of Colorado Library). Ralph Sucher and Yale B. Huffman traveled with Norris and handled whatever arrangements were necessary for him.

[20] Robertson to W. F. Haycock, Oct. 24, 1932.

Late in the afternoon on the next day Norris addressed a crowd in the dance hall of an amusement park at Mackinaw Dells, Illinois. Here he assailed Hoover "as a Jonah in the ship of state." On October 21 in Minneapolis at a meeting chaired by Senator Henrik Shipstead, he called for limited currency inflation and heavy inheritance and income taxes as necessary emergency measures.[21]

On Saturday, October 22, at Des Moines, Iowa, Norris lambasted the Hoover administration for failing to keep its pledges to the American farmer. He was introduced by Henry A. Wallace to an enthusiastic audience at the Des Moines Coliseum. He then went on to Springfield, Illinois, to resume campaigning the following Monday. But he had to enter St. John's Hospital in Springfield because of a severe cold complicated by a throat infection. Governor Philip LaFollette of Wisconsin spoke in his place that evening and Norris's engagements for the rest of the week were canceled. On October 28 he left the hospital and proceeded to Chicago for a train to Seattle to resume campaigning.[22] In brief stopovers at Fargo and Butte Norris lashed out at the tariff, and in a major address at Seattle he reviewed the power records of the candidates, denouncing Hoover's and endorsing Roosevelt's. On November 1, the following day, he was in Portland for an address on agriculture; on November 3 at the Dreamland Auditorium in San Francisco he again lambasted Hoover on the issue of partisanship, denouncing blind party loyalty. Earlier, at a luncheon meeting in Oakland, he said that with Senator Hiram Johnson coming out for Roosevelt, California was now safely in the New York governor's column.

Norris concluded his efforts on behalf of Roosevelt's candidacy in Los Angeles. On Saturday, November 5, at 6 P.M. he was interviewed over a local radio station. He responded to questions by

[21] Donald Richberg to Norris, Sept. 27, 1932 (material used in Norris's Cleveland speech); *Detroit Evening Times,* Oct. 19, 1932. A speech was read for Norris in Saginaw by Representative Michael J. Hart, at whose farm he was supposed to speak. On Oct. 19, 1932, Republican Senators Robert M. LaFollette, Jr., of Wisconsin and Bronson Cutting of New Mexico endorsed Franklin D. Roosevelt for president.

[22] *Des Moines Register,* Oct. 23, 1932. Governor Philip LaFollette of Wisconsin again spoke in Norris's place on Oct. 25 in Kansas City, while Senator Bronson Cutting replaced him in Denver on Oct. 26. Addresses scheduled for Salt Lake City, Laramie, and Boise were dropped. The *New York Times* covered most of Norris's speeches on this campaign trip.

denouncing Herbert Hoover's record. He criticized Mark Requa as the man "selected by Hoover to look after his interests in California." Norris examined Requa's connections with E. L. Doheny, Harry F. Sinclair, and the Elk Hills and Teapot Dome naval oil reserves, claiming that Requa, director of the Oil Division of the U.S. Fuel Administration, had recommended that the Elk Hills reserves be leased to private oil companies. Later that evening in the Philharmonic Auditorium Norris delivered his last address of the campaign on public utilities and the power trust, again excoriating Hoover and extolling Roosevelt.[23]

Gratified with the landslide triumph of Franklin Roosevelt, Norris, en route to McCook, stopped in Denver on November 10, 1932, for a visit with his colleague and vice-chairman of the National Progressive League, Senator Edward P. Costigan. He commented on the forthcoming lame-duck session, predicting that it would be the last ever held. Arriving home happy but exhausted, Norris spent the next two weeks indoors, endeavoring to shake off the effects of the cold which had hospitalized him during the campaign. To complete his recovery, he decided to return to Washington by a southern route, hoping that a leisurely trip in a milder climate would prove beneficial.[24]

Norris received numerous assurances that his efforts had played a role in Roosevelt's impressive victory. James A. Farley expressed his gratitude and Hiram Johnson said that he had made "a tremendous contribution" to Roosevelt's success. Frank P. Walsh of the National Progressive League said that his speaking tour was "a magnificent success." Every state Norris visited, where there was "an honest count," went strongly for Roosevelt. Moreover, Walsh remarked, "there can be no doubt that the active part you played, standing alone at the outset of the campaign, brought the other Pro-

[23] *San Francisco Examiner,* Nov. 6, 1932. Requa after the election wrote Norris, claiming that his statement about Requa's record was "entirely erroneous." He presumed that Norris would wish to correct it once he had the facts in hand, which he then presented. Three months later in a lengthy letter Norris responded, claiming that the information upon which he based his remarks "was practically correct, although there are one or two unimportant errors." Norris denied that he had in any material respect misrepresented the record of Mark Requa; see Requa to Norris, Dec. 31, 1932; Norris to Requa, Mar. 29, 1932.

[24] *Rocky Mountain News,* Nov. 11, 1932; Robertson to R. W. Wilson, Nov. 17, 1932.

gressives into the field." In short, Roosevelt supporters were aware that Norris's campaigning played a role in his victory. On his part Norris made it clear that he did not seek or want a cabinet position. He expressed some concern about the sweeping nature of the Democratic victory, asserting, "History shows that this often brings recklessness and abuse in its wake." [25]

It was not until the end of the year that Norris, finally able to devote himself to his correspondence and his congressional chores, carefully analyzed the recent election. Many votes were cast for Roosevelt as a protest against Hoover, though the great majority believed in him. While Norris did not agree with Roosevelt in everything he advocated and, indeed, did not know his attitude on many topics, he insisted, as he had done during the campaign, that Roosevelt would consider all issues "honestly and sympathetically." The zeal and unselfishness with which Republican progressives had supported Roosevelt Norris thought was quite remarkable. As far as he knew, none sought personal gain or advancement; none were interested in a cabinet seat. For a progressive Republican senator to accept such a post would reflect upon his motives; more important, it would reduce progressive representation in the Senate, where they were "lamentably few in number." Their role could best be fulfilled, Norris asserted, by helping the new president meet and solve problems. Norris did not mean that they were uninterested in presidential appointments. They were. They wanted progressives appointed to both cabinet and commission posts, recognizing that the task facing the new president was a staggering one. While Norris doubted that Roosevelt could resolve most of the problems besetting the American people, he wanted to help him try in a manner different from that followed by Herbert Hoover. [26]

But there was still the lame-duck session. Roosevelt's inaugura-

[25] James A. Farley to Norris, Nov. 16, 1932; Hiram W. Johnson to Norris, Nov. 11, 1932; Walsh to Norris, Nov. 12, 1932; *Lincoln Star*, Nov. 18, 1932. Norris early in 1933 suggested that "high political sources" had made it clear that he could go into the cabinet if he desired; see Norris to Grant O. Harrington, Feb. 17, 1933. Floyd B. Olson also thanked Norris for the brief endorsement he had made of his candidacy when Norris spoke in Minneapolis. Olson was elected governor of Minnesota; see Olson to Norris, Nov. 14, 1932.

[26] Norris to Bertrand V. Tibbels, Dec. 27, 1932; *Omaha World-Herald, Washington Star*, Nov. 29, 1932. Indicative of his new status was the fact that Norris sent Tibbels's letter to the president-elect with the request that he read it.

tion was almost ten weeks away and much could happen in a depression-ridden land in that time. To aid in coordinating progressive sentiment throughout the nation, Norris sought to organize Senate progressives for the purpose of propounding new ideas to aid the incoming administration. He called a meeting for this purpose in January, 1933, and the group chose Bronson Cutting of New Mexico as chairman and Burton K. Wheeler of Montana and Robert M. LaFollette, Jr., of Wisconsin as its other officers. On behalf of the Republican Senate progressives Norris presented a plan for a national organization headquartered in Washington, remarking that the group envisioned a junction with their Democratic counterparts "which in its extreme form would involve formation of a third party." It would promote liberal legislation and provide the fullest measure of cooperation between progressives both in and out of Congress. It would encourage candidates, regardless of party affiliation and work, to keep progressive objectives before the country through statements, pamphlets, speeches, and conferences. In this way "a thorough-going progressive program" might be prepared which Congress could then perfect and enact into law.[27]

To keep abreast of new and stimulating ideas, Norris attended a meeting at which Howard Scott, the leading exponent of technocracy, expounded his views to a gathering of about twenty-five senators and representatives. Technocracy was the then unformulated concept of a more rational structuring of the American industrial order through the widespread use of available resources and technicians. While Norris found the presentation "very interesting," he added that he was not in agreement with "the remedies offered by Scott." The *Washington Post* reported that Norris and others had questioned Scott closely and "picked most of his statements to pieces." [28]

In Congress Norris and his progressive colleagues patiently awaited March 4, 1933, and the inauguration of Franklin Roosevelt. Critical of Hoover's policies, they attacked them on the Senate

[27] Harold L. Ickes to Norris, Jan. 23, 1933; Norris to Ickes, Feb. 10, 1933; *Washington News,* Jan. 30, 1933; *New York Times, Denver Post,* Feb. 26, 1933. House members were consulted but were not asked to commit themselves at this time.

[28] *Washington Post,* Feb. 2, 1932. For a discussion of technocracy, see Harry Elsner, Jr., *The Technocrats: Prophets of Automation* (Syracuse, N.Y., 1967).

floor, knowing that the days of the Hoover administration were numbered and that their views would soon receive a sympathetic hearing. One of the things Norris desired was a modest inflation of the currency. The per capita circulation of money, he noted, had reached its highest point, $56.62, in December, 1920. By July of 1932 it was down to $43.85. Yet he would not support a proposal to provide $75 of currency per capita on the grounds that it was too great an increase; it might be impossible to stop inflation if any "danger signal" developed.[29]

How, then, could relief from the depression by financial legislation be achieved? Three methods were suggested: issuing larger amounts of paper money upon the gold reserve; free and unlimited coinage of silver, a proposal presented as an amendment to a bill in January, 1933; changing the gold content of the dollar. Unless some remedy was accepted, Norris argued, disaster was bound to come. While he would not accept free silver under ordinary circumstances and preferred one of the other remedies suggested, Norris argued that "we are perhaps somewhat in the position of a drowning man grasping at a straw." Though not clear about how the free-silver amendment would work, he knew that it could cheapen the dollar and make it easier for debtors to meet their obligations. So desperate had the situation become, particularly for farmers, that Norris, never sympathetic to the notion in the past, now endorsed free silver: "I would rather preserve our civilization and our country and adopt a remedy which under normal conditions I would not accept than to turn it aside and adopt none." Recognizing that the amendment would be defeated, he felt that discussion of an international agreement on free silver was valuable because the incoming president was pledged to call an international conference to cope with the economic crisis.[30]

Instead of seeking relief through financial legislation, Congress sought to aid banks by expanding Federal Reserve credit and then coping with the drastic increase in the number of bank failures

[29] *Congressional Record,* 72nd Cong., 1st sess., July 7, 1932, pp. 14767–68.

[30] *Ibid.,* 2nd sess., Jan. 24, 1933, pp. 2386–89; Norris to John H. Grossman, Jan. 7, 1933. Lessening the amount of gold in the dollar was another practical way to cheapen the dollar. The only difficulty Norris envisioned would be "a mad rush for gold" before the law could be enacted; see Norris to Walter Burch, Mar. 2, 1933.

through the nation. Norris agreed. "The prosperity of our banks and the prosperity of our country go hand in hand," he had proclaimed earlier to members of the Nebraska Bankers Association. Dishonest or unscrupulous bankers could wreak more damage than dishonest or unscrupulous businessmen. New York bankers, selling foreign bonds on a commission basis and encouraging country bankers to purchase them, were draining needed funds out of areas where they could help distressed citizens. In asking for an extension of the moratorium agreement, bankers were seeking to "postpone the debts due from foreign governments to our government, in order that their foreign investments in Europe may be paid with money that ought to be used in payment of the interest due the Government of the United States." [31]

At Hoover's request Congress considered a revision of the bankruptcy laws. The House quickly responded. But by February 20, 1933, the Senate had not acted and the President sent a second message urging prompt action. Norris, long interested in such legislation, claimed that more expert information ought to be secured. As chairman of the Judiciary Committee, to which the matter was referred, he doubted that it could receive the attention it deserved before March 4 when Congress had to adjourn. At the same time he understood the urgency of the situation, recognizing that legislation pertaining to receivership and corporate reorganization ought to be enacted. But he wanted the Senate to know that "if there are evils or jokers that afterwards are shown up in this proposed law . . . that at least the Senate had the truth told them through the Judiciary Committee so that the responsibility for anything wrong cannot be shouldered upon that committee." Therefore, rather than delay proceedings any further, the committee reported the House measure with a provision added to benefit farmers directly.[32]

On the Senate floor Norris successfully added an amendment to

[31] *Hastings Daily Tribune,* June 3, 1931; Norris to George H. Gutru, Dec. 17, 1931.

[32] *Congressional Record,* 72nd Cong., 2nd sess., Feb. 24, 1933, pp. 4886–89. In earlier correspondence Norris explained that President-elect Roosevelt was very much in favor of revamping the laws on receivership as they applied to railroads. If attempted in the lame-duck session, Norris knew that it would encounter "some very strong objections." Thus, after he stated his views, the measure was reported out of committee; see Norris to William Ritchie, Jr., Feb. 17, 1933.

the bankruptcy bill which put "the real principles that were involved in the so-called anti-injunction bill in force on a railroad that has gone into the hands of a receiver." He also supported the suggestion that the Interstate Commerce Commission ought to have an office devoted entirely to reorganizing or refinancing railroads in financial difficulties. Owing to the lateness of the session, Norris hoped that this proposal would be taken under advisement by the Interstate Commerce Committee and reported back in the next Congress. But despite his strictures the bill, including his amendment, was enacted into law before the end of the Hoover administration.[33]

In an exciting incident near the end of the session the Senate dismissed its veteran sergeant-at-arms, David S. Barry. He was accused of publishing an article "libelling and slandering" the Senate. Without mentioning names, Barry had said that it was "pretty well known" who in Congress would sell their votes. By a unanimous vote the Judiciary Committee recommended dismissal; after debating for three and a half hours, by a vote of 53 to 17 the Senate agreed. Norris, who introduced the resolution calling for Barry's dismissal, said, "In defense of its honor and integrity the Senate can do no less than to remove such an unworthy employee." Senator Otis Glenn of Illinois defended Barry and irked Norris, who exchanged sharp words with him. Twice George Moses, president pro tem of the Senate, had to call for order, so tense was the situation between them.[34]

---

[33] *Congressional Record,* 72nd Cong., 2nd sess., Feb. 27, 1933, pp. 5120–21, 5131. The amendment was accepted by voice vote without a roll call. Felix Frankfurter, for one, was delighted with the success of Norris's amendment and agreed with his high estimation of Joseph B. Eastman; see Frankfurter to Norris, Mar. 1, 1933. Norris's amendment was accepted in the final version of the bill approved by Congress and signed into law by Hoover on Mar. 3, 1933; see *New York World-Telegram,* Mar. 4, 1933; A. F. Whitney to Richberg, Mar. 7, 1933 (Box I, Donald Richberg Papers, Manuscript Division, Library of Congress). Whitney, chairman of the Railway Labor Executives Association, was "sure that the railroad boys throughout the country" would sing Norris's praises.

[34] *Washington Herald,* Feb. 8, 1933; *Lincoln Star,* Feb. 11, 1933. The account in the *Star* presented portions of the debate. Barry, a Republican, received $8,000 a year as sergeant-at-arms. He was due to lose his post as soon as the Democrats took over the Senate with the convening of the Seventy-third Congress. His article, entitled "Over the Hill to Demagoguery," appeared in *New Outlook,* 161 (Feb., 1933): 40–43. The first sentence of the article contained the controversial statement.

Because of his support of Roosevelt, which, incidentally, accounted for some of the Old Guard Republican hostility, rumors indicated that Norris would be permitted to retain the chairmanship of the Judiciary Committee. But shortly after the election Norris wrote Joseph T. Robinson, Democratic leader in the Senate, that he did not expect to retain the chairmanship and that it would be embarrassing if consideration were given these rumors. Privately he admitted that a number of Democratic senators, including his designated successor, Henry F. Ashurst, had let him understand that they would be willing for him to continue as chairman. Norris was pleased but did not change his mind.[35]

That a new day was dawning, that Norris's long battles in the public interest would soon receive a sympathetic hearing at 1600 Pennsylvania Avenue, was evident in his relations with the president-elect. Early in the session Roosevelt invited him to New York to dine and to spend the evening; "I want to talk over many things with you." Roosevelt also told Norris that he planned to visit Muscle Shoals and "see what the whole Tennessee River project looks like." He wrote, "I am particularly anxious to have you accompany me on this trip." Norris accepted the invitation to visit Roosevelt in New York, though he thought it might be difficult "to get away to go to Muscle Shoals." [36] On January 1, 1933, Roosevelt announced that he had invited Norris, the senators from Alabama and Tennessee, and a handful of public power people to accompany him on his inspection of Muscle Shoals on January 21, 1933. On Friday, January 20, Norris left Washington as a member of the party making the trip.[37]

At Sheffield, Alabama, after visiting Muscle Shoals with Roosevelt, Norris announced that he would reintroduce his bill for government operation of the power and nitrate projects in the up-coming special session of Congress. The fight would be renewed, he said,

[35] Norris to Joseph T. Robinson, Nov. 16, 1932; to Elwood Riggs, Mar. 1, 1933.

[36] Franklin D. Roosevelt to Norris, Dec. 14, 1932; Norris to Roosevelt, Dec. 23, 1932; Roosevelt, ed., *F.D.R.: His Personal Letters, 1928–1945,* 1: 309. In a footnote Elliott Roosevelt observes that the subject of a cabinet post for Harold Ickes was discussed at the New York meeting.

[37] *Washington Post, Washington Herald,* Jan. 2, 1933; Marvin McIntyre to Norris, Dec. 30, 1932. McIntyre asked Norris to join Roosevelt's party in Washington for the trip to Muscle Shoals.

"with all the energy and talent at my command. . . ." Earlier in the day at a disused railroad station at Decatur, Alabama, about an hour's ride out of Muscle Shoals, Roosevelt spoke briefly to about 15,000 people: "With the help of Congress we are going to put Muscle Shoals and the Tennessee River Valley back on the map." Later at Florence and again at Sheffield before Norris left the party, Roosevelt reiterated: "The development here is national and is going to be treated from a national point of view. It is going to be my purpose to put Muscle Shoals on the map." [38]

The most dramatic incident occurred at Muscle Shoals when Roosevelt sent for Norris, who had been riding in another automobile, so that they might be photographed together. The president-elect remarked, as he and Norris stood watching thousands of gallons of water pouring unused through the spillways of the Wilson Dam, "This should be a happy day for you, George." Tears welled in Norris's eyes as he responded, "It is, Mr. President. I see my dreams come true." [39]

The long ordeal was almost over.[40] The persistence of a progressive had revealed once again what a skillful, dedicated legislator could achieve. In the midst of the greatest economic crisis to befall the American people, with a second Roosevelt about to enter the White House, the future was full of possibilities for furthering the progressive cause. A hostile Congress had been tamed, powerful interests had been subdued, antagonistic presidents had retired or

[38] *New York Times, Washington Post,* Jan. 22, 1933. In Washington upon his return Norris expressed confidence that the incoming president would sign a bill into law in 1933. He promised to introduce a government operation bill on the first day of the special session; see *Washington News,* Jan. 23, 1933. Norris and several other officials remained another day in Alabama seeking further first-hand information.

[39] The Associated Press version of the dialogue between Roosevelt and Norris varies slightly; see *Lincoln Star,* Jan. 22, 1933, or *Washington Herald,* Jan. 23, 1933. I am following the account of James A. Hagerty in the *New York Times,* Jan. 22, 1933.

[40] Claude Bowers in a column appearing in the *Washington Times,* Jan. 25, 1933, announced that Norris's fight was won. So did Marshall McNeil in a long story in the *Washington News,* Feb. 3, 1933. Harry Slattery, who talked to Norris on his return from Alabama, reported that he felt "very sanguine" that his Muscle Shoals measure would be promptly enacted; see Slattery to Gifford Pinchot, Jan. 27, 1933 (Harry Slattery Papers, Manuscripts Collections, Duke University Library).

had been defeated. In all of these endeavors Norris had played an important role. The dawn of a new day was now at hand. Legislation calling for the greatest development of its sort in the entire world was about to be realized for the benefit of public rather than private interests. Not content to rest on his laurels, Norris was ready to rise to the challenges and promises of a New Deal for the American people.

Bibliographical Essay

The bulk of the material utilized in the preparation of this volume comes from two basic sources: the voluminous collection of George W. Norris Papers in the Manuscript Division of the Library of Congress and the equally voluminous *Congressional Record* plus assorted Senate documents from the Sixty-third through the Seventy-second Congresses. Despite the fact that the Norris Papers comprise a collection of over 1,000 boxes, the files are very sketchy for the period from 1913 through 1925. Thereafter they are virtually complete. Thus material from other manuscript collections proved particularly helpful for this period and in adding to an understanding of various facets of Norris's career.

An explanation is perhaps necessary as to why I did not mention box and tray numbers when citing the Norris Papers. Two factors influenced my decision. Full citation of tray and box number would have added immeasurably to the already copious footnote material. But, more important, eventually the staff of the Manuscript Division will reshelve and fully process the Norris Papers so that the present box and tray numbers will be meaningless. The collection, shelved in already antiquated large red boxes, was placed in these boxes as they came from Norris's office files. Little effort has yet been made to prune duplicate material and extraneous items, such as campaign posters, from the collection. The earlier portion of the collection, which my wife and I helped to process for the Library of Congress, is shelved in the more convenient and smaller blue, grey, or other color boxes that are currently used to store manuscript collections. Readers who are interested in the specific location of a citation in the Norris Papers can write to me and I will try to oblige. My notes contain the tray and box number of every item appearing in the footnotes.

The single most valuable collection, aside from the Norris Papers, was one I discovered through the good fortune of teaching summer school at Duke University. The Harry Slattery Papers in the Duke University Library provided much information on conservation politics and numerous insights into Norris himself. Slattery, serving as Gifford Pinchot's observer and confidential aide in Washington, was continually writing his mentor the latest gossip about politics and personalities on Capitol Hill and in the White House. Since he knew Norris and saw him with some frequency, his letters contain significant information. Yet he rarely corresponded with Norris himself, so there is little in the Norris Papers indicating that Slattery had the senator's confidence. Other secondary figures whose papers yielded valuable information were C. A. Sorensen, William Kent, Morris L. Cooke, and Judson King. Their papers are located in the Nebraska State Historical Society, the Yale University Library, the Franklin D. Roosevelt Library, and the Library of Congress respectively.

The papers of fellow senators and other prominent public figures rarely yielded important information about Norris. Their correspondence was mostly of an official or perfunctory nature. Occasionally, however, they would comment about Norris or the political or parliamentary situation as it affected him, and, of course, this information was of great value to me. Among the collections examined in this category are the papers of Gifford Pinchot, Theodore Roosevelt, William Howard Taft, Woodrow Wilson, Calvin Coolidge, Henry Cabot Lodge (Massachusetts Historical Society), Amos Pinchot, Irvine Lenroot, Charles Evans Hughes, Benjamin H. Bristow (Kansas State Historical Society), Gilbert M. Hitchcock, John Sharp Williams, Harold Ickes, William Jennings Bryan, Charles L. McNary, Franklin D. Roosevelt (Franklin D. Roosevelt Library), Frank L. Greene, Newton D. Baker, James W. Wadsworth, Lawrence D. Tyson (Southern Collection, University of North Carolina Library), George Fort Milton, Felix Frankfurter, Edward P.

Costigan (University of Colorado Library), and Donald Richberg. Unless otherwise noted, all of these collections are located in the Manuscript Division of the Library of Congress.

A few further collections also yielded incidental information: the papers of R. E. Moore, Frank P. Walsh, Benjamin C. Marsh, Mercer G. Johnston, and the League of Women Voters. The first are in the Nebraska Historical Society, the second in the New York Public Library, and the others in the Manuscript Division of the Library of Congress.

I was denied access to the Herbert Hoover Papers when they were housed in the Hoover Library at Stanford, and my manuscript was well advanced when they were made available at West Branch, Iowa. Thus I chose to rely on published material for my information on the views of the Hoover administration. Fortunately there is an abundance of primary printed material available. Volumes 2 and 3 of Hoover's *Memoirs, The Cabinet and the Presidency, 1920–1933* (New York, 1952) and *The Great Depression, 1929–1941* (New York, 1952), along with Ray Lyman Wilbur and Arthur Mastick Hyde, eds., *The Hoover Policies* (New York, 1937), and William S. Myers and Walter H. Newton, *The Hoover Administration: A Documented Narrative* (New York, 1936), provide a fund of official information about the thirty-first president. Hoover's 1928 campaign speeches appear in *The New Day* (Stanford, Calif., 1928) and Theodore G. Joslin, *Hoover, off the Record* (Garden City, N.Y., 1934), examines his administration from the viewpoint of a press secretary. To gain further insights into the policies of the Hoover administration, particularly in areas that concerned Norris, I read extensively in the Henry L. Stimson Diaries at Yale University. My effort yielded little that I did not already know from my perusal of the above published items.

Newspapers provided another source of important information about Norris and his career. I was aided greatly in my research in this area by the fact that Norris's staff maintained extensive scrapbooks of newspaper clippings. Furthermore, at times constituents and other correspondents of Norris would include press clippings in their letters. Items culled from these sources made my research in New York, Washington, and Nebraska newspapers much easier than I envisioned at the outset and they helped provide me with national press coverage of my subject.

Periodical articles also provided another source of primary information. Numerous articles by Norris, appearing in a wide range of periodicals, are cited in the footnotes. In many instances these articles were reprinted in the *Congressional Record*. Most of the time they comprised a reworking of his remarks on the Senate floor; occasionally an article represented an extension of a letter or the use of a speech. While Norris's monetary return from these articles was minimal, the mileage he received in getting his views before a larger audience was great. The *Nation* and the *New Republic* printed many of his articles. Others appeared in journals ranging from the *Saturday Evening Post* and *Collier's* to *Country Home, The World Tomorrow,* and *LaFollette's Magazine,* from prominent journals with a national audience to obscure periodicals with a minute readership, some of which are not listed in the *Readers Guide to Periodical Literature.* Articles about Norris and issues that involved him are also cited in the footnotes. At times some of these articles, like some by Norris, appeared in newspapers, usually a Sunday supplement. Finally, a word should be said about the great value of the *Literary Digest* as a source of information about press opinion and the general political situation in and out of Congress throughout the 1920s. Though cited infrequently, I found it an invaluable guide to many of the issues and situations involving Norris on the national scene.

To round out my understanding of the Nebraska scene during the two decades examined in this study, I relied upon James C. Olson's excellent survey *History of Nebraska* (Lincoln, 1955) and the older volume by Addison E. Sheldon, *Nebraska: The Land and the People* (Chicago, 1931), vol. 1. Gene E. Hamaker's *Irrigation Pioneers: A History of the Tri-County Project to 1935* (Minden, Nebr., 1964) provided a guide into the background of this notable accomplishment. Originally a Ph.D. dissertation at the University of Nebraska, it was published for the Central Nebraska Public Power and Irrigation District. Another dissertation, this one unpublished, that proved helpful was Verne S. Sweedlum's "A History of the Evolution of Agriculture in Nebraska, 1870–1930" (University of

Nebraska, 1940), as did Adahbelle Snodgrass's unpublished M.A. thesis, "The Congressional Election of 1918" (University of Nebraska, 1944). Patricia C. Mulvey's unpublished M.A. thesis, "The Republican Party in Nebraska" (University of Nebraska, 1934), was also of help. John L. Shover's article "The Farm Holiday Movement in Nebraska," *Nebraska History,* 43 (Mar., 1962): 53–78, examines an important aspect of the farm situation in the state during the Hoover years.

For the chapters covering the Wilson years, the works by Arthur Link provided a basic overall outline for the period through Apr., 1917. Volumes 2 through 5 of his Wilson biography (Princeton, N.J., 1956–1965) examine the period from Mar., 1913, through Apr., 1917, as does his *Woodrow Wilson and the Progressive Era* (New York, 1954). F. W. Taussig's *The Tariff History of the United States* (New York, 1931) aided my understanding of rate schedules from the Underwood-Simmons through the Hawley-Smoot Tariff Acts. Alpheus T. Mason's *Brandeis: A Free Man's Life* (New York, 1946) and *The Fall of a Railroad Empire* (Syracuse, N.Y., 1947), which he co-authored with Henry Lee Staples, provided a guide to the fight over Brandeis's appointment to the Supreme Court and his subsequent career and to the complicated affairs of the New York, New Haven and Hartford Railroad Company. Both the Brandeis appointment and the railroad's affairs actively concerned Norris during his first Senate term. For the Hetch Hetchy controversy, Norris's autobiography, *Fighting Liberal* (New York, 1945), Robert Underwood Johnson, *Remembered Yesterdays* (Boston, 1923), and Roderick Nash, *Wilderness and the American Mind* (New Haven, Conn., 1967), provide background information from different perspectives. Arthur DeWitt Frank, *The Development of the Federal Program of Flood Control on the Mississippi River* (New York, 1930), aided my understanding of the opposition Norris faced to his conservation views throughout these decades.

Belle Case and Fola LaFollette's two-volume biography, *Robert M. LaFollette* (New York, 1953), was a basic book for me. In addition, Fola LaFollette allowed me to examine items in her father's papers as they pertained to Norris and his career. Another important book for me was Sidney Ratner's *American Taxation* (New York, 1942). I benefited greatly from its discussion of the

1917 legislation and its analysis of the situation in the 1920s. The essay on Norris in Edward G. Lowry, *Washington Close-Ups* (Boston and New York, 1921), provided an excellent overall picture of Norris and his views at the end of the Wilson administration, while Stanley Coben's *A. Mitchell Palmer: Politician* (New York, 1963) helped me to understand aspects of the American scene at this time. While Ralph Stone's *The Irreconcilables* (Lexington, Ky., 1970) appeared too late for use in the preparation of this volume, his analysis of Norris during the league fight does not differ markedly from mine.

John D. Hicks, *Republican Ascendancy, 1921–1923* (New York, 1960), was a handy reference tool that I often consulted as I delved into the 1920s. Frances Parkinson Keyes, *Letters from a Senator's Wife* (New York, 1924), is a delightful volume focusing on Washington society, but it also helped me to understand aspects of the Harding administration. James H. Shideler, *Farm Crisis, 1919–1923* (Berkeley and Los Angeles, 1957), was indispensable as I sought to understand agricultural problems, as was Theodore Saloutos and John D. Hicks, *Agricultural Discontent in the Middle West, 1900–1939* (Madison, Wis., 1951). My knowledge of the Muscle Shoals controversy was greatly enhanced by Judson King's *The Conservation Fight* (Washington, D.C., 1959) and Preston Hubbard's *Origins of the TVA* (Nashville, Tenn., 1961). King was a confidant of Norris in matters pertaining to Muscle Shoals. Both volumes assisted me in placing Norris's role in perspective. W. R. Plewmen, *Adam Beck and the Ontario Hydro* (Toronto, 1947), provided information about the Canadian project that greatly interested Norris, while Paul Kleinsorge's *The Boulder Canyon Project* (Stanford, Calif., 1941) did the same for this American development.

Felix A. Nigro, "The Warren Case," *Western Political Quarterly,* 11, no. 4 (Dec., 1958): 835–56, examines the Senate's rejection of Charles B. Warren as Attorney General. G. Cullom Davis, "The Transformation of the Federal Trade Commission," *Mississippi Valley Historical Review,* 49 (1962): 437–55, stresses developments during the Coolidge administration. J. Richard Snyder, "Coolidge, Costigan, and the Tariff Commission," *Mid-America,* 50, no. 2 (1968): 131–48, examines developments in this agency. Howard

H. Quint and Robert H. Ferrell in their compilation of Coolidge's
press conferences entitled *The Talkative President* (Amherst, Mass.,
1964) further illumine the president's attitude toward various commissions. George Wharton Pepper, *Family Quarrels* (New York,
1931), provided information about the controversy surrounding
Roy West's nomination as Secretary of the Interior. Donald Richberg's *Tents of the Mighty* (Chicago, 1930) was more valuable
than his autobiography, *My Hero* (New York, 1954), in providing
an understanding of railroad valuation, while Thomas Vadney's
biography, *The Wayward Liberal* (Lexington, Ky., 1971), appeared too late for me to use. Alpheus T. Mason, *William Howard
Taft: Chief Justice* (New York, 1965), indicates Taft's concern
with judicial reform, somewhat different from Norris's. In *Bovard
of the Post-Dispatch* (Baton Rouge, La., 1954) J. W. Markham
discusses the reporting of Paul Anderson from Washington in the
1920s. Anderson, the paper's chief Washington correspondent, was
friendly with Norris. For an understanding of aspects of Coolidge's
diplomacy that aroused Norris, L. Ethan Ellis, *Frank B. Kellogg
and American Foreign Relations, 1925–1929* (New Brunswick,
N.J., 1961), was helpful, while Warren I. Cohen, *The American
Revisionists* (Chicago, 1967), notes that the revisionist arguments
during the 1920s did not yet focus on American intervention. Samuel J. Astorino, "The Contested Senate Election of William Scott
Vare," *Pennsylvania History,* 28 (Apr., 1961): 187–201, provides
an overall view of this controversy, while Carroll H. Woody, *The
Case of Frank L. Smith* (Chicago, 1931), discusses another senatorial election that aroused Norris during the Coolidge years.

My understanding of the Hawley-Smoot Tariff Act was enhanced
by E. E. Schattschneider, *Politics, Pressure and the Tariff* (New
York, 1935), and by the comments on Senator Reed Smoot in Alfred P. Dennis, *Gods and Little Fishes* (Indianapolis, 1931). Richard L. Watson's excellent article "The Defeat of Judge Parker: A
Study in Pressure Groups and Politics," *Mississippi Valley Historical Review,* 50 (1963): 213–34, was indispensable in placing Norris's opposition in focus. The *Proceedings of a Conference of Progressives* (n.p., n.d.) was published in pamphlet form and widely
disseminated. It contains Norris's remarks as well as letters and
telegrams sent to him as chairman of this 1931 conference. Hyman

G. Weintraub, *Andrew Furuseth, Emancipator of the Seaman* (Berkeley, Calif., 1959), and Irving Bernstein, *The Lean Years* (Boston, 1960), gave me an understanding of the role of Furuseth and others in the anti-injunction movement as it involved Norris. Robert H. Ferrell, *American Diplomacy in the Great Depression: Hoover-Stimson Foreign Policy, 1929–1933* (New Haven, Conn., 1957), supplemented L. Ethan Ellis's volume mentioned above. Karel Denis Bicha, "Liberalism Frustrated: The League for Independent Political Action," *Mid-America,* 48 (Jan., 1966): 19–28, increased my knowledge of this organization which wanted Norris to seek the presidency as a third-party candidate, while Frank Freidel, *Franklin D. Roosevelt: The Triumph* (Boston, 1956), aided my understanding of the 1932 Democratic campaign, in which Norris played an important role. I might also note that the *Statistical Abstract of the United States,* published annually by the U.S. Government Printing Office, though infrequently cited in the footnotes, furnished convenient and succinct statistical data about the American economy during the Wilson era, the 1920s, and the early depression years.

Finally, I must say a few words about why I did not use the three already published Norris biographies to any great extent. The best of the group, Alfred Lief, *Democracy's Norris* (New York, 1939), is the only one based on manuscript material. However, I have made fuller use of the Norris Papers and in several important instances I have found Lief's account contrary to the evidence available to me. Richard L. Neuberger and Stephen B. Kahn, *Integrity: The Life of George W. Norris* (New York, 1939), is not based on a perusal of the Norris Papers and has little to offer the scholar. Norris's autobiography, *Fighting Liberal* (New York, 1945), while an important and interesting volume, was written largely from memory after his return to McCook following the 1942 campaign. Norris's files were in Washington and in his account he seemingly determined to ignore individuals and groups who had opposed programs he favored. None of these accounts make a serious effort to place Norris in a perspective reflecting broader political, social, and economic patterns.

Index

A Note on the Author

Richard Lowitt received his Ph.D. in history from Columbia University. His previous publications include two books, *A Merchant Prince of the Nineteenth Century: A Biography of William E. Dodge* (New York, 1954), and *George W. Norris: The Making of a Progressive, 1861–1912* (Syracuse, N.Y., 1963), and many articles and essays. He has been a Guggenheim Fellow and has received grants from the Social Science Research Council, the American Council of Learned Societies, the American Philosophical Society, and from the research councils of Florida State University and the University of Kentucky. In addition to these two universities, he has taught at Connecticut College and has been a visiting professor at both Yale and Brown. At present he is professor of history and associate dean of the College of Arts and Sciences at the University of Kentucky.